Lecture Notes in Computer Science   12974

Formal Methods

Subline of Lectures Notes in Computer Science

More information about this subseries at http://www.springer.com/series/7408

Lu Feng · Dana Fisman (Eds.)

Runtime Verification

21st International Conference, RV 2021
Virtual Event, October 11–14, 2021
Proceedings

 Springer

Editors
Lu Feng 🄓
University of Virginia
Charlottesville, VA, USA

Dana Fisman 🄓
Ben-Gurion University of the Negev
Be'er Sheva, Israel

ISSN 0302-9743   ISSN 1611-3349 (electronic)
Lecture Notes in Computer Science
ISBN 978-3-030-88493-2   ISBN 978-3-030-88494-9 (eBook)
https://doi.org/10.1007/978-3-030-88494-9

LNCS Sublibrary: SL2 – Programming and Software Engineering

This Springer imprint is published by the registered company Springer Nature Switzerland AG
The registered company address is: Gewerbestrasse 11, 6330 Cham, Switzerland

Preface

This volume contains the refereed proceedings of the 21st International Conference on Runtime Verification (RV 2021), virtually held during October 11–14, 2021. The RV series is a sequence of annual meetings that brings together scientists from both academia and industry interested in investigating novel lightweight formal methods to monitor, analyze, and guide the runtime behavior of software and hardware systems. Runtime verification techniques are crucial for system correctness, reliability, and robustness; they provide an additional level of rigor and effectiveness compared to conventional testing, and are generally more practical than exhaustive formal verification. Runtime verification can be used prior to deployment, for testing, verification, and debugging purposes, and after deployment for ensuring reliability, safety, and security, for providing fault containment and recovery, and for online system repair.

RV started in 2001 as an annual workshop and turned into a conference in 2010. The workshops were organized as satellite events of established forums, including the Conference on Computer-Aided Verification and ETAPS. The proceedings of RV from 2001 to 2005 were published in Electronic Notes in Theoretical Computer Science. Since 2006, the RV proceedings have been published in Springer's Lecture Notes in Computer Science. Previous RV conferences took place in Istanbul, Turkey (2012); Rennes, France (2013); Toronto, Canada (2014); Vienna, Austria (2015); Madrid, Spain (2016); Seattle, USA (2017); Limassol, Cyprus (2018); and Porto, Portugal (2019). The conferences last year and this year were planned to take place in Los Angeles, USA, but were held virtually due to COVID-19.

This year we received 40 submissions, 29 as regular contributions and 11 as short, tool, or benchmark papers. Each of these submissions went through a rigorous single-blind review process as a result of which most papers received four reviews and all papers received at least three review reports. The committee selected 18 contributions, 11 regular and 7 short/tool/benchmark papers, for presentation during the conference and inclusion in these proceedings. The evaluation and selection process involved thorough discussions among the members of the Program Committee (PC) and external reviewers through the EasyChair conference manager, before reaching a consensus on the final decisions.

The conference featured three keynote speakers:

- Patricia Bouyer-Decitre, LSV, CNRS and ENS Paris-Saclay, France
- Radu Grosu, Technische Universität Wien, Austria
- Holger Hermanns, Saarland University, Germany

The conference also included one tutorial:

- "Formal Analysis of AI-Based Autonomy: From Modeling to Runtime Assurance" by Hazem Torfah, Sebastian Junges, Daniel Fremont, and Sanjit A. Seshia.

RV 2021 is the result of the combined efforts of many individuals to whom we are deeply grateful. In particular, we thank the PC members and sub-reviewers for their accurate and timely reviewing, all authors for their submissions, and all attendees of the conference for their participation. We thank Jyotirmoy V. Deshmukh and Dejan Ničković, chairs of RV 2020, for their generous help answering our many questions, and the RV Steering Committee for their support.

August 2021   Lu Feng
                                                                        Dana Fisman

Organization

Program Committee

Houssam Abbas	Oregon State University, USA
Wolfgang Ahrendt	Chalmers University of Technology, Sweden
Domenico Bianculli	University of Luxembourg, Luxembourg
Borzoo Bonakdarpour	Michigan State University, USA
Radu Calinescu	University of York, UK
Chih-Hong Cheng	DENSO AUTOMOTIVE Deutschland GmbH, Germany
Jyotirmoy Deshmukh	University of Southern California, USA
Georgios Fainekos	Arizona State University, USA
Yliès Falcone	Université Grenoble Alpes and Inria Grenoble, France
Chuchu Fan	MIT, USA
Lu Feng (chair)	University of Virginia, USA
Thomas Ferrère	Imagination Technologies, UK
Bernd Finkbeiner	CISPA Helmholtz Center for Information Security, Germany
Dana Fisman (chair)	Ben-Gurion University, Israel
Adrian Francalanza	University of Malta, Malta
Sylvain Hallé	Université du Québec à Chicoutimi, Canada
Klaus Havelund	NASA's Jet Propulsion Laboratory, USA
Bettina Könighofer	Technical University of Graz, Austria
Morteza Lahijanian	University of Colorado, Boulder, USA
Axel Legay	UCLouvain, Belgium
Martin Leucker	University of Luebeck, Germany
Chung-Wei Lin	National Taiwan University, Taiwan
David Lo	Singapore Management University, Singapore
Leonardo Mariani	University of Milano-Bicocca, Italy
Nicolas Markey	IRISA, CNRS, Inria, and University of Rennes 1, France
Laura Nenzi	University of Trieste, Italy
Dejan Nickovic	Austrian Institute of Technology, Austria
Gordon Pace	University of Malta, Malta
Nicola Paoletti	Royal Holloway, University of London, UK
Dave Parker	University of Birmingham, UK
Doron Peled	Bar Ilan University, Israel
Violet Ka I Pun	Western Norway University of Applied Sciences, Norway
Giles Reger	University of Manchester, UK
Cesar Sanchez	IMDEA Software Institute, Spain

Gerardo Schneider   Chalmers University of Technology, Sweden
Julien Signoles   CEA LIST, France
Oleg Sokolsky   University of Pennsylvania, USA
Stefano Tonetta   Fondazione Bruno Kessler, Italy
Hazem Torfah   University of California, Berkeley, USA
Dmitriy Traytel   University of Copenhagen, Denmark

Steering Committee

Howard Barringer   University of Manchester, UK
Ezio Bartocci   Technical University of Vienna, Austria
Saddek Bensalem   Verimag and Université Grenoble Alpes, France
Yliès Falcone   Université Grenoble Alpes and Inria Grenoble, France
Klaus Havelund   NASA's Jet Propulsion Laboratory, USA
Insup Lee   University of Pennsylvania, USA
Martin Leucker   University of Lübeck, Germany
Giles Reger   University of Manchester, UK
Grigore Rosu   University of Illinois at Urbana-Champaign, USA
Oleg Sokolsky   University of Pennsylvania, USA

Best Paper Award Committee

Martin Leucker   University of Lübeck, Germany
Dave Parker   University of Birmingham, UK
Doron Peled   Bar Ilan University, Israel

Test of Time Award Internal Committee

Georgios Fainekos   Arizona State University, USA
Lu Feng   University of Virginia, USA
Bernd Finkbeiner   CISPA Helmholtz Center for Information Security,
                              Germany
Dana Fisman   Ben-Gurion University, Israel
Insup Lee   University of Pennsylvania, USA

Test of Time Award External Committee

Alan J. Hu   University of British Columbia, Canada
Marta Kwiatkowska   University of Oxford, UK
Fabio Somenzi   University of Colorado Boulder, USA

Additional Reviewers

Attard, Duncan Paul
Azzopardi, Shaun
Baranov, Eduard
Bartolo Burlo, Christian
Baumeister, Jan
Benjamin, Thibaut
Ganguly, Ritam
Imrie, Calum
Jackson, John
Kallwies, Hannes
Kharraz, Karam
Kohn, Florian
Krish, Veena

Micheli, Andrea
Momtaz, Anik
Oliveira Da Costa, Ana
Paterson, Colin
Raszyk, Martin
Requeno, Jose Ignacio
Schwenger, Maximilian
Soueidi, Chukri
Stolz, Volker
Stümpel, Annette
Wang, Yue
Xuereb, Jasmine
Zolnai-Lucas, Jeremy

Contents

Short Papers and Tool Papers

Tutorial Paper

Regular Papers

Predicate Monitoring in Distributed Cyber-Physical Systems

Anik Momtaz[1], Niraj Basnet[2], Houssam Abbas[2],
and Borzoo Bonakdarpour[1(✉)]

[1] Michigan State University, East Lansing, MI 48824, USA
borzoo@msu.edu
[2] Oregon State University, Corvallis, OR 97331, USA

Abstract. This paper solves the problem of detecting violations of predicates over *distributed* continuous-time and continuous-valued signals in cyber-physical systems (CPS). We assume a partially synchronous setting, where a clock synchronization algorithm guarantees a bound on clock drifts among all signals. We introduce a novel *retiming* method that allows reasoning about the correctness of predicates among continuous-time signals that do not share a global view of time. The resulting problem is encoded as an SMT problem and we introduce techniques to solve the SMT encoding efficiently. Leveraging simple knowledge of physical dynamics allows further runtime reductions. We fully implement our approach on two distributed CPS applications: monitoring of a network of autonomous ground vehicles, and a network of aerial vehicles. The results show that in some cases, it is even possible to monitor a distributed CPS sufficiently fast for online deployment on fleets of autonomous vehicles.

1 Introduction

As the environment we live in develops, so does our dependency on safety-critical *cyber-physical systems* (CPS), along with the need for verifying their correctness. A particularly critical class of CPS includes software applications *distributed* over networked nodes, which we will refer to as *agents*. Examples include fleets of autonomous vehicles, network of sensors in infrastructures, health-monitoring wearables, and networks of medical devices. While the literature of distributed computing is decades old, and many important problems have been solved in the context of *discrete-event systems*, we currently lack a solid understanding of distributed CPS, as they are differentiated by three characteristics. **First**, their signals are *analog*; these signals contain an uncountable infinity of events which makes existing reasoning techniques from the discrete settings inapplicable in most cases. The applications we target, such as those above, care about continuous-time behavior: for instance, it is not enough to say that a voltage does not spike at sample times. Thus, adjusting the signal sampling rate does

This work is sponsored in part by the United States NSF FMitF-1917979 and CCF-2118356 awards.

© Springer Nature Switzerland AG 2021
L. Feng and D. Fisman (Eds.): RV 2021, LNCS 12974, pp. 3–22, 2021.
https://doi.org/10.1007/978-3-030-88494-9_1

nothing to address the need for reasoning about the *analog* signals. **Second**, each agent in these CPS has a *local* clock that drifts from other agents' clocks; thus, the notion of time, taken for granted in centralized systems, must be revised, since it is unclear when exactly events are sequential and concurrent. In fact, it is not clear how continuous events in different processes obey the *happened before* relation [21], and how one can reason about the order of occurrence of continuous events. Robust controllers do not address the issues of asynchrony in time. **Third**, CPS signals obey physical laws and dynamics. Even a rough knowledge of these dynamics might be leveraged to reason about distributed signals and predict their behavior, thus increasing efficiency. In this paper, we take the first step towards rigorous, automated reasoning about distributed CPS whose *correctness* and integrity is vital to guaranteeing the safety of the environment they operate in. A popular and practical approach to reason about the health of CPS is to *monitor* them with respect to their formal specification, and detect violations. Currently, we lack techniques for monitoring CPS where analog signals are produced by distributed agents that do not share a global clock (see the related work in Sect. 7). Lack of synchrony in particular creates significant challenges, as the monitor has to reason about signal values at local times of different agents, which may lead to inconsistent monitoring verdicts. This difficulty is compounded by the fact that agents typically communicate with each other, which imposes additional constraints on event ordering.

Motivating Example. We illustrate the urgent need for monitoring distributed CPS by a critical application in automated air traffic control (AATC). The market for unmanned aerial vehicles (UAVs) is witnessing explosive growth [18]. The Federal Aviation Administration (FAA) in the United States is envisioning a federated framework, in which UAVs that collaborate in monitoring *global* air safety properties are rewarded with faster free-flight paths to their destinations [14,15]. To enable this federated framework, analog signals like UAV position and velocity must be monitored by the ATC tower software to see whether they violate *global* instantaneous safety properties, or *predicates*. These predicates are Boolean expressions defined over the simultaneous states of the different CPS agents, like mutual separation between agents, conditional speed limits, and minimal energy storage. These predicates must be evaluated on the global state, which is the state of all UAVs combined at the *same moment in time*. However, the absence of a perfect shared clock among all UAVs may result in a situation where UAV1's clock indicates $t = 5$ and UAV2's clock indicates $t = 5.2$, at the same physical 'real' moment. Equivalently, the same value on both clocks might mean different physical moments. If the central ATC monitor uses these two states to evaluate whether the predicate is violated, it might lead to false negatives (i.e., missing violations) or false positives (i.e., declaring a violation when none exists).

The UAV example has two characteristics that are present in many other distributed CPS: first, while it is generally impossible to guarantee perfect continuous-time synchrony, clock synchronization algorithms such as NTP [23] ensure that the drift among local clocks remains within some bounds. Secondly, it is often the case that the central monitor knows some bounds on the UAV dynamics, like velocity limits. In this example, the ATC tower itself would know the UAVs' speed limits. We leverage these two characteristics in developing our solution.

1.1 Our Solution and Contributions

In this paper, we propose a sound and complete solution to the problem of predicate monitoring for distributed CPS. Our contributions are as follows:

1. a Satisfiability Modulo Theory (SMT) based algorithm for centralized monitoring of distributed analog signals for predicate violations, augmented with a clock synchronization algorithm that guarantees *bounded skew* ε between all local clocks, using the classic *happened-before* relation [21];
2. a *retiming* technique that borrows the notion of retiming functions from stochastic processes;
3. a lightweight mechanism for incorporating bounds on system dynamics to reduce monitoring overhead;
4. an analysis of the sensitivity of monitoring overhead to the skew bound and the amount of communication between agents, and
5. a technique for parallelizing the monitoring algorithm to improve scalability.

We have fully implemented our techniques and report results of experiments on monitoring a network of autonomous ground vehicles (real-world experiment) and aerial vehicles (in simulation). It should be mentioned that due to using a central monitor, naturally the system is susceptible to a single point of failure. This paper is concerned in developing the proposed theory, not account for fault tolerance. We make the following observations. First, although our approach is based on SMT solving, it can be employed for online monitoring when the monitor is invoked with appropriate frequency (i.e., the monitoring overhead does not surpass the normal operation time of the system). Second, incorporating the knowledge of system dynamics is highly beneficial in reducing the overhead of monitoring. In some cases it leads to a speedup by one order of magnitude. Finally, monitoring overhead is *in*dependent of the clock skews when practical clock synchronization protocols (e.g., NTP and PTP) are applied.

2   Model of Computation

We first set some notation. The set of reals is $\mathbb{R}$, the set of non-negative reals is $\mathbb{R}_+$, and the set of positive reals is $\mathbb{R}_+^*$. The integer set $\{1, \ldots, N\}$ is abbreviated as $[N]$. *Global* time values (kept by an *imaginary* global clock) are denoted by χ, χ', χ_1, χ_2, etc., while the letters t, t', t_1, t_2, s, s', s_1, s_2, etc. denote *local* clock values specific to given agents which will always be clear from the context.

2.1 Signal Model

In this section, we introduce our signal model, i.e., our model of the output signal of an agent. Monitoring can be done regardless of the dynamics of the agents. However, as we see later, a rough knowledge of the dynamics can be helpful.

Definition 1. *An* output signal *(of some agent A) is a function* $x : [a, b] \rightarrow \mathbb{R}^d$, *which is right-continuous, left-limited, and is not Zeno. Here,* $[a, b]$ *is an interval in* $\mathbb{R}_+$*, and will be referred to as the* timeline *of the signal.* ∎

Without loss of generality, we will henceforth assume that x is one-dimensional, i.e., $d = 1$. *Right-continuity* means that at all t in its support, $\lim_{s \rightarrow t_+} x(s) = x(t)$. *Left-limitedness* means the function has a finite left-limit at every t in its support: $\lim_{s \rightarrow t_-} x(s) < \infty$. *Not being Zeno* means that x has a finite number of discontinuities in any bounded interval in its support. This ensures that the signal cannot jump infinitely often in a finite amount of time. A *discontinuity* in a signal $x(\cdot)$ can be due to a discrete event internal to agent A (like a variable updated by software), or to a message sent to or received from another agent A'.

We assume a loosely coupled system with asynchronous message passing. Specifically, the system consists of N reliable *agents* that do not fail, denoted by $\{A_1, A_2, \ldots, A_N\}$, without any shared memory or global clock. The output signal of agent A_n is denoted by x_n, for $1 \leq n \leq N$. Agents can communicate via FIFO lossless channels. The contents of a message are immaterial to our purposes. We will need to refer to some global clock which acts as a '*real*' time-keeper. However, this global clock is a theoretical object used in definitions and theorems, and is *not* available to the agents. We make two assumptions:

- *(A1) Partial synchrony.* The *local clock* (or time) of an agent A_n can be represented as an increasing function $c_n : \mathbb{R}_+ \rightarrow \mathbb{R}_+$, where $c_n(\chi)$ is the value of the local clock at global time χ. Then, for any two agents A_n and A_m, we have:
$$\forall \chi \in \mathbb{R}_+ . |c_n(\chi) - c_m(\chi)| < \varepsilon$$
  with $\varepsilon > 0$ being the maximum *clock skew*. The value ε is assumed fixed and known by the monitor in the rest of this paper. In the sequel, we make it explicit when we refer to 'local' or 'global' time.
- *(A2) Deadlock-freedom.* The agents being analyzed do not deadlock.

Assumption (A1) is met by using a clock synchronization algorithm, like NTP [23], to ensure bounded clock skew among all agents.

In the discrete-time setting, an event is a value change in an agent's variables. We now update this definition for the continuous-time setting of this paper. Specifically, in an agent A_n, an *event* is either a (i) a pair $(t, x_n(t))$, where t is the local time (i.e., returned by function c_n); (ii) a message transmission, or (iii) a message reception. There is no assumption on the messages that the agents send to each other. Messages that are sent to the monitor are timestamped by their respective local clocks. Since the agents evolve in continuous time and their output signals are defined for all local times t, a message transmission or reception always coincides with a signal value; i.e., if A_n receives a message at local time t, its signal has value $x_n(t)$ at that time. Thus, without loss of generality, every event will be represented as a (local time, value) pair $(t, x_n(t))$, often abbreviated as e_t^n (n and t will be omitted when irrelevant).

A *distributed signal* is modeled as a set of events partially ordered by Lamport's *happened-before* ($\rightsquigarrow$) relation [21], extended by our assumption (A1) on bounded clock skew among all agents. Namely, let

$$E = \{e_t^n \mid n \in [N] \land I_n \subseteq \mathbb{R}_+ \land t \in I_n\}$$

denote a set of events, where t is local time in agent A_n, and set I_n is a bounded nonempty interval. The following defines a continuous-time distributed signal under partial synchrony.

Definition 2. *A* distributed signal *on N agents is a tuple $(E, \rightsquigarrow)$, where E is a set of events obeying the restriction: for every $n \in [N]$. The relation $\rightsquigarrow$ is a relation between events such that:*

(1) In every agent A_n, all events are totally ordered, that is,

$$\forall t, t' \in I_n : (t < t') \rightarrow (e_t^n \rightsquigarrow e_{t'}^n).$$

(2) If e is a message send event in an agent and f is the corresponding receive event by another agent, then we have $e \rightsquigarrow f$.
(3) For any two events $e_t^n, e_{t'}^m \in E$, if $t + \varepsilon < t'$, then $e_t^n \rightsquigarrow e_{t'}^m$.
(4) If $e \rightsquigarrow f$ and $f \rightsquigarrow g$, then $e \rightsquigarrow g$.   ∎

Figure 1 shows an example. The classical case of complete asynchrony is recovered by setting $\varepsilon = \infty$. The restriction on I_n is necessary in the continuous-time setting and will be re-visited in the next section.

Because the agents are only synchronized to within an ε, it is not possible to actually evaluate all signals at the same moment in global time. The notion of *consistent cut* and its frontier, defined next, capture *possible* global states: that is, states that could be valid global states (see Fig. 1).

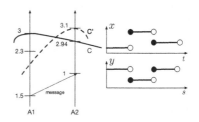

Fig. 1. Two partially synchronous continuous concurrent timelines with $\varepsilon = 0.1$, and corresponding signals x and y. (Solid dot indicates signal value at discontinuity). C is a consistent cut but C' is not.

Definition 3 (Consistent Cut). *Given a distributed signal $(E, \rightsquigarrow)$, a subset of events $C \subseteq E$ is said to form a* consistent cut *if and only if when C contains an event e, then it contains all events that happened-before e. Formally,*

$$\forall e \in E . (e \in C) \land (f \rightsquigarrow e) \Rightarrow f \in C.$$

∎

From this definition and Definition 2. (3) it follows that if $e_{t'}^m$ is in C, then C also contains every event e_t^n s.t. $t + \varepsilon < t'$.

A consistent cut C can be represented by its *frontier* front$(C) = (e_{t_1}^1, \ldots, e_{t_N}^N)$, in which each $e_{t_n}^n$ is the last event of agent A_n appearing in C. Formally:

$$\forall n \in [N] \ . \ e_{t_n}^n \in C \text{ and } t_n = \max\{t \in I_n \mid \exists e_t^n \in C\}$$

Example 1. Figure 1 shows two timelines, generated by two agents executing concurrently. Every moment in each timeline corresponds to an event e_t^n, where $n \in \{1, 2\}$. An arrow between the timelines indicates a message transmission and reception. Thus, we may see that the following hold: $e_{1.5}^1 \rightsquigarrow e_{2.3}^2$, $e_1^2 \rightsquigarrow e_{3.1}^2$, and $e_{1.5}^1 \rightsquigarrow e_1^2$. Assuming $\varepsilon = 0.1$, it comes that all events below (thus, before) the solid arc form a consistent cut C with frontier front$(C) = (e_3^1, e_{2.94}^2)$, On the other hand, all events below the dashed arc do *not* form a consistent cut since $e_{2.3}^2 \rightsquigarrow e_{3.1}^2$ and $e_{3.1}^2$ is in the set C', but $e_{2.3}^2$ is not in C'.

2.2   Signal Transmission to the Monitor

Communication between nodes necessarily involves sampling the analog signal, transmitting the samples, and reconstructing the signal at the receiving node. Our objective is to monitor the *reconstructed analog signals*. This is different from monitoring a discrete-time signal consisting of the samples – the applications we target actually care about the value of the signal between samples, and potential violations they reveal. Methods for signal transmission, including sampling and reconstruction, are standard in Communication theory. Errors due to sampling and reconstruction (say, because of bandwidth limitations) can be accounted for by strictifying the STL formula using the methods of [16]. The choice of reconstruction algorithm is application-dependent and follows from domain knowledge. In this paper's experiments, we assume that every output signal x_n is reconstructed as *piece-wise linear* between the samples. We emphasize that other reconstructions, like cubic splines, can also be used with simple modification to our algorithms at the cost of additional runtime, and that the choice of reconstruction is orthogonal to our techniques and this paper's objectives. Since we assume the agents do not deadlock, this transmission happens in *segments* of length T: at the kth transmission, agent A_n transmits $x_n|_{[(k-1)T, kT]}$, the restriction of its output signal to the interval $[(k-1)T, kT]$ as measured by its local clock. In the rest of this paper, we refer exclusively to the signal fragments received by the monitor in a given transmission.

We now re-visit the restriction placed on I_n in Definition 2, namely, that it is a non-empty bounded interval. Non-emptiness models that computation does not deadlock. That I_n is an interval expresses that no events are missed, or equivalently, that signal reconstruction is perfect at the monitor. The restriction that it be bounded models the above monitoring setup: the monitor is only ever dealing with bounded signal fragments $x_n|_{[(k-1)T, kT]}$, so

$$I_n = [(k-1)T, kT] \tag{1}$$

for every agent at the kth transmission, *measured in local time*. By the bounded skew assumption, we have:

Lemma 1. *For any two agents* $A_n, A_m,$ $|\min I_n - \min I_m| \leq \varepsilon$ *and* $|\max I_n - \max I_m| \leq \varepsilon.$ ∎

3   The Predicate Monitoring Problem

Many system requirements are often captured via predicates (e.g., invariants). A *predicate* ϕ is a global Boolean-valued function over the signal values of agents. For instance, $\phi(x_1, x_2) = (x_1 > 0) \wedge (\ln(x_2) < 3)$ is a predicate on two signals that evaluates to true when $x_1 > 0$ and $\ln(x_2) < 3$, otherwise false.

Because the agents are partially synchronized to within an ε, it is not possible to actually evaluate all signals at the same moment in global time. However, as noted above, the frontier of a consistent cut gives us a possible global state.

Definition 4 (Distributed satisfaction). *Given a distributed signal $(E, \rightsquigarrow)$ over N agents, and a predicate ϕ over the N agents, we say that $(E, \rightsquigarrow)$ satisfies ϕ iff for all consistent cuts $C \subseteq E$ with*

$$\mathsf{front}(C) = \Big((t_1, x_1(t_1)), \ldots, (t_N, x_N(t_N)) \Big)$$

we have $\phi\big(x_1(t_1), x_2(t_2), \ldots, x_N(t_N)\big) = $ true. *We write this as* $(E, \rightsquigarrow) \models \phi.$ ∎

Thus, we formally define the problem as follows.

Problem Statement

Continuous-Time Monitoring of Distributed CPS. Given a distributed signal $(E, \rightsquigarrow)$ and a predicate ϕ over N agents, determine whether $(E, \rightsquigarrow) \models \phi$.

When a distributed signal $(E, \rightsquigarrow)$ does not satisfy a predicate ϕ, we say that $(E, \rightsquigarrow)$ *violates* ϕ and write $(E, \rightsquigarrow) \not\models \phi$. In this paper, we want to detect whether there exists a consistent cut $C \subseteq E$, such that $(E, \rightsquigarrow) \not\models \phi$.

The main challenge in monitoring distributed signals is that the monitor has to reason about signals that are subject to time asynchrony. For instance, consider two signals x_1 and x_2 and the case where $x_1(2) = 5$, $x_2(3) = 1$, $\phi(x_1, x_2) = (x_1 > 4) \wedge (x_2 < 0)$, and $\epsilon = 2$ so that time points 2 and 3 form a consistent cut. In this case, since the above signal values are at local times within the possible clock skew, one has to (conservatively) consider that the predicate is violated. In the next section, we present our solution to the problem.

4   SMT-Based Monitoring Algorithm

In a nutshell, our solution has the following features:

- **Central monitor.** We assume that there is a *central* monitor that solves, at regular intervals, the monitoring problem described in Sect. 3.

- **Signal retiming.** As signals are measured using their local clocks, the monitor should somehow align them to detect possible violations of the predicate. To this end, we propose a *retiming* technique that establishes the happened-before relation in the continuous-time setting, and stretches or compacts signals to align them with each other within the ε clock skew bound.
- **SMT encoding.** We transform the monitoring decision problem into an SMT-solving problem, whose components (like input signals and the happened-before relation) are modeled as SMT entities and constraints.

4.1   Retiming Functions

Our signal model is continuous-time, that is, the signals are maps from $\mathbb{R}_+$ to $\mathbb{R}_+$. Therefore, to model the approximate re-synchronizing action of the monitor, we use a *retiming function*.

Definition 5 (Retiming functions). *A retiming function, or simply retiming, is an increasing function $\rho : \mathbb{R}_+ \to \mathbb{R}_+$. An ε-retiming is a retiming function such that: $\forall t \in \mathbb{R}_+ : |t - \rho(t)| < \varepsilon$. Given a distributed signal $(E, \rightsquigarrow)$ over N agents and any two distinct agents A_i, A_j, where $i, j \in [N]$, a retiming ρ from A_j to A_i is said to respect $\rightsquigarrow$ if we have $(e_t^i \rightsquigarrow e_{t'}^j) \Rightarrow (t < \rho(t'))$ for any two events $e_t^i, e_{t'}^j \in E$.* ∎

Figure 2 shows examples of retimings and how they relate to predicate monitoring. To detect predicate violation, we must first retime y to the t axis via a retiming map ρ. (c) shows three different retimings, including the identity. (d)–(e) show the retimed y. For the predicate $x > y$, (e)-(f) show no violations, but (d) does. The conservative monitoring answer is that the predicate is violated. An ε-retiming ρ maps $\mathbb{R}_+$ to itself, but it is easy to see that the restriction of ρ to a bounded interval I is an increasing function from I to $\rho(I)$ that respects the constraint $|t - \rho(t)| < \varepsilon$ for all $t \in I$. Thus, in what follows we restrict our attention to the action of ε-retimings on bounded intervals.

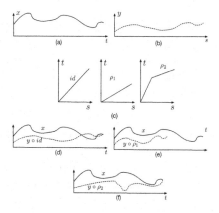

Fig. 2. Predicate violation between two signals x and y measured using partially synchronized clocks t and s.

We now state and prove the main technical result of this paper, which relates the existence of consistent cuts in distributed signals to the existence of retimings between the agents' local clocks.

Proposition 1. *Given a predicate ϕ and distributed signals $(E, \rightsquigarrow)$ over N agent, there exists a consistent cut $C \subseteq E$ that violates ϕ if and only if there* exists a finite A_1-local clock value t and $N-1$ ε-retimings $\rho_n : I_n \to I_1$ that respect $\rightsquigarrow$, $2 \le n \le N$, such that:

$$\phi\left(x_1(t), x_2 \circ \rho_2^{-1}(t), \ldots, x_N \circ \rho_N^{-1}(t)\right) = \mathsf{false} \qquad (2)$$

and such that $\rho_m^{-1} \circ \rho_n : I_n \to I_m$ is an ε-retiming for all $n \ne m$. Here, 'o' denotes the function composition operator.   ∎

Proof. ($\Leftarrow$) Suppose that such retimings exist. Define the local time values $t_1 := t$, $t_n = \rho_n^{-1}(t)$, $2 \le n \le N$, and the set $C = \{e_t^n \mid t \le t_n\}$. By the construction of C and the fact that the retimings respect $\rightsquigarrow$, it holds that if $e \in C$ and $f \rightsquigarrow e$ then $f \in C$. For every $n, m \ge 2, n \ne m$, it holds that $t_m = \rho_m^{-1}(\rho_n(t_n))$ so $|t_n - t_m| \le \varepsilon$. Thus C is a consistent cut with frontier $(e_{t_n}^n)_{n=1}^N$ that witnesses the violation of ϕ.

($\Rightarrow$) Suppose now that there exists a consistent cut C with frontier:

$$\mathsf{front}(C) = \left((t_1, x_1(t_1)), \ldots, (t_N, x_N(t_N)) \right)$$

that witnesses violation of ϕ. We need the following facts.

Fact 1. For every two events $e_{t_n}^n$ and $e_{t_m}^m$ in the frontier of a consistent cut, we have $|t_n - t_m| \le \varepsilon$. Indeed, since $e_{t_n}^n \in \mathsf{front}(C)$, we have $e_s^m \in C$ for all s s.t. $s + \varepsilon \le t_n$. Thus, $t_m \ge s$ for all such s and so $t_m \ge t_n - \varepsilon$. By symmetry of the argument, $t_n \ge t_m - \varepsilon$ holds as well.

Fact 2. Given intervals $[a, b]$ and $[c, d]$ s.t. $|a - c| \le \varepsilon$ and $|b - d| \le \varepsilon$, the map $L : [a, b] \to [c, d]$ defined by $L(t) = c + \frac{d-c}{b-a}(t - a)$ is a linear ε-retiming. This is immediate.

Suppose first that there are no message exchanges. For $2 \le n \le N$, we define the retiming $\rho_n : I_n \to I_1$ in two pieces. First, set $\rho_n(t_n) = t_1$. By preceding lemma, $|t_n - t_1| \le \varepsilon$. Write $I_1 = [a, b]$ and $I_n = [c, d]$ for notational simplicity in this proof. Call a pair of intervals that satisfies the hypothesis of Fact 2 an *admissible pair*. Then, the following pairs are clearly admissible by Lemma 1: $[a, t_1]$ and $[c, t_n]$, and $[t_1, b]$ and $[t_n, d]$. Thus, there exist two linear retimings $L_n : [a, t_1] \to [c, t_n]$ and $L_n' : [t_1, b] \to [t_n, d]$, and we can define a piece-wise ρ_n: $\rho_n(t) = L_n(t)$ on $c \le t \le t_n$ and $\rho_n(t) = L_n'(t)$ on $t_n \le t \le d$. It is easy to establish that ρ_n is an ε-retiming.

It remains to show that $\rho_n^{-1} \circ \rho_m : I_m = [f, g] \to [c, d]$ is also an ε-retiming. This too can be established in parts, first over $[f, t_m]$ then over $[t_m, g]$, using the same arguments as above and exploiting the linearity of these retimings. For instance, if we write α_n for the slope of L_n, then over $[f, t_m]$

$$\rho_n^{-1}(\rho_m(s)) = L_n^{-1}(L_m(s)) = L_n^{-1}(a + \alpha_m(s - c))$$

$$= \frac{1}{\alpha_n}[a + \alpha_m(s - c)] + f - a/\alpha_n = f + \frac{g - f}{d - c}(s - c)$$

which is a linear ε-retiming by Fact 2.

If there are message exchanges, the above argument still applies but over a more fine-grained division of the timelines I_n obtained by partitioning each timeline at message transmission times. We sketch the proof: for the admissible pair $I_1 = [a, b]$ and $I_n = [c, d]$, suppose the first message is sent from A_n to A_1 at local time $s < t_n$ and is received at local time $r < t_1$. Define $t_{(s)} := \min(s + \varepsilon, r)$. Then the pair $[a, t_{(s)}]$, $[c, s]$ is admissible. Repeat this process for all messages. We end up with a collection of admissible pairs that can be retimed to each other, as above, without violating the $\rightsquigarrow$ relation. These are concatenated to yield the desired retiming ρ_n. ∎

Thus, finding a consistent cut that violates the predicate can be achieved by finding such retimings. The proof of Proposition 1 further shows that the retimings can always be chosen as piece-wise linear (rather than any increasing function), which yields significant runtime savings in the SMT encoding in the next section.

Remark 1. An interesting consequence of Fact 2 in the proof is that it is enough to use piece-wise linear retimings. This results in the following concrete problem.

Concrete Problem Statement

Given $\varepsilon > 0$, a distributed signal $(E, \rightsquigarrow)$ over N agents, and a predicate ϕ over the N agents, find $N - 1$ ε-retiming functions $\rho_2, \ldots, \rho_N$ that satisfy the hypotheses of Prop. 1 and s.t.

$$\phi\Big(x_1(t_1), x_2(t_2), \ldots, x_N(t_N)\Big) = \mathsf{false} \tag{3}$$

4.2   SMT Formulation

We solve the monitoring problem by transforming it into an instance of *satisfiability modulo theory* (SMT). Specifically, we ask whether there exists $N - 1$ retimings, such that (3) holds; equivalently, whether there exists a consistent cut that witnesses satisfaction of $\neg\phi$.

Without loss of generality, we start with our encoding of two agents, A_1 and A_2 (shown in Fig. 1). A_1 outputs signal x supported over the bounded timeline I_1, which is discretized to $D_1 \subset I_1$ and sent to the monitor. Similarly, A_2 outputs signal y supported over the bounded timeline I_2, which is discretized to $D_2 \subset I_2$ and sent to the monitor. D_1 and D_2 are finite. Let $\delta_k > 0$ be the *sampling period* of agent A_k, so two consecutive elements of D_k differ by δ_k, $k \in \{1, 2\}$.

Consider further that A_2 transmits a message at local time t_1 and it is received by A_1 at local time t_2, and that A_1 sends a message at local time t_3 which is received by A_2 at local time t_4. The distributed signal violates the predicate iff the following SMT problem returns SAT.

SMT Entities. In our encoding, the entities are the retimings ρ_n included as *uninterpreted* functions (the solver will interpret), signals x and y, intervals

I_1 and I_2, real numbers t, s, s', t_1, t_2, t_3, and t_4. All these entities have been defined in the previous sections. The following quantities are all constants in the encoding, since they are known to the monitor: the sampling time sets D_k and sampling periods δ_k, the sampled values $\{x(t_i) \mid t_i \in D_1\}$ and $\{y(s_i) \mid s_i \in D_2\}$, and the message transmission and reception local times.

SMT Constraints. The encoding is a conjunction of the following constraints:

- *(Predicate violation)* The first constraint 'finds' local times t and s at which predicate ϕ is violated (upto ε-synchrony):

$$\exists\, t \in I_1.\, \exists s \in I_2. \tag{4a}$$

$$\left(\exists t^- \in D_1.\ t^- \leq t \leq t^- + \delta_1\right) \wedge \tag{4b}$$

$$\left(\exists s^- \in D_2\ .\ s^- \leq s \leq s^- + \delta_2\right) \wedge \tag{4c}$$

$$\left(\rho(s) = t\right) \wedge \tag{4d}$$

$$\left(\neg\phi(x(t^-), y(s^-))\right) \tag{4e}$$

Equation (4b) finds the time sample t^- such that $x(t) = x(t^-)$: this is the result of our assumption that signals are piece-wise constant. Equation(4c) does the same for y. Equation (4d) specifies that s is retimed to t: this is what guarantees that $(x(t), y(s))$ is a possible global state as per Proposition 1. Equation (4e) checks violation of the predicate at $(x(t), y(s)) = (x(t^-), y(s^-))$.
- *(Valid retiming)* Eq. (5) ensures that ρ is a valid ε-retiming from I_2 to I_1:

$$\forall s \in I_2.\ \exists t \in I_1.\ (\rho(s) = t) \wedge (|t - s| < \varepsilon) \tag{5}$$

and Eq. (6) ensures that the retiming function is increasing:

$$\forall s \in I_2.\ \forall s' \in I_2.\left(s < s' \implies \rho(s) < \rho(s')\right). \tag{6}$$

- *(Happened-before)* Eq. (7) enforces the happened-before relation for message transmissions:

$$\left(\rho(t_1) < t_2\right) \wedge \left(t_3 < \rho(t_4)\right) \tag{7}$$

- *(Inverse retiming)* When there are more than 2 agents, we must also encode the constraint that for all $n \neq m$, $\rho_m^{-1} \circ \rho_n$ is an ε-retiming. Thus, for all $n \neq m$, letting f_m be the uninterpreted function that represents the inverse of the uninterpreted ρ_m, we add

$$\forall t \in I_n \cdot\ f_m(\rho_n(t)) = t \tag{8}$$

in addition to the analogs of Eqs. (6) and (5) for $f_m \circ \rho_n$.

Other Signal Models. If output signals were piece-wise linear, say, Eq. (4e) would be modified accordingly:

$$\phi\left(x(t^-) + \frac{x(t^- + \delta_1) - x(t^-)}{\delta_1}(t - t^-),\right.$$

$$\left. y(s^-) + \frac{y(s^- + \delta_2) - y(s^-)}{\delta_2}(s - s^-)\right) = \mathsf{false} \tag{9}$$

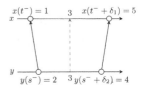

Fig. 3. Piece-wise Linear Interpolation

Our choice of signal models is limited by the SMT solver: it must be able to handle the corresponding interpolation equations, like the piece-wise linear interpolation in Eq. (9). As an example, in Fig. 3, let x and y be two signals, where the violating predicate ϕ to be monitored is $x(t) = y(s)$. Let ρ be a retiming of y on x, such that $\rho(s^-) = t^-$ and $\rho(s^- + \delta_2) = t^- + \delta_1$. It can be observed that although the discretized signal samples do not violate ϕ, due to the signals being piece-wise linear, it is easy to identify a violation at time t and s on signals x and y respectively, where $x(t) = 3$, $y(s) = 3$ and $\rho(s) = t$.

It is worth mentioning that restricting the SMT search to piece-wise linear retimings results in a significant decrease in run time, compared to the approach where the SMT is tasked with determining an interpolation. For example, for two UAVs with $\varepsilon = 1\,\mathrm{ms}$ over 5s-long signals, at segment count 5, the search for a general retiming requires 3.42 s, whereas searching for a piece-wise linear retiming requires only 1.01 s. Since, by Remark 1, there is no loss of generality in this restriction, from this point, all the reported experiments are obtained using the piece-wise linear retiming approach.

Remark 2. (i) $\rho_m^{-1} \circ \rho_n$ respects $\rightsquigarrow$ automatically so it is not necessary to encode that explicitly. (ii) Because we can restrict the SMT search to piece-wise linear retimings (see remark following proof of Proposition 1), constraint (8) can be simplified, namely, the expression for the inverse can be hard-coded. We don't show this to maintain clarity of exposition.

5   Exploiting the Knowledge of System Dynamics

Physical processes in a CPS follow the laws of physics. A runtime monitor can leverage this knowledge of the CPS dynamics to make monitoring more efficient.

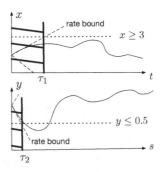

Fig. 4. Leveraging dynamics.

We explain our idea by the following example (see Fig. 4). From knowing the rate bound $|\dot{x}| \leq 1$ (shown by a dashed line), the monitor concludes that the earliest x can satisfy the atom $x \leq 3$ is τ_1. Similarly for y. Given that $\tau_1 > \tau_2$, the monitor discards, roughly speaking, the fragment $[0, \tau_2]$ from each signal and monitors the remaining pieces. Note that $x(0) = 1$ and $y(0) = 2$. Consider the predicate: $\phi = \neg(a \vee b)$, where $a := x \geq 3$ and $b := y \leq 0.5$. Let a and b be *atoms* of predicate ϕ. There are 3 Boolean assignments to atoms a and b that falsify the predicate. Let us fix one such assignment, $a = b =$ true. If the monitor knows a uniform bound on the rate of change $\dot{x}$ of x, say $\forall t.|\dot{x}(t)| \leq 1$, then it can infer that $a =$ true cannot hold before $\tau_1 = 2$ (local time). Similarly, if the monitor knows that $|\dot{y}| \leq 3$, then $b =$ true cannot hold before $\tau_2 = 0.5$ (local time). Taking into account the ε-synchrony, the monitor can limit itself to monitoring $x|_{[2,T]}$ (the restriction of x to $[2,T]$) and $y|_{[2-\varepsilon, T+\varepsilon]}$.

Now, if this yields UNSAT in the SMT instance, we select the next Boolean assignment (in terms of atoms a and b) that falsifies predicate ϕ (e.g., $a =$ false and $b =$ true), derive the useful portion of signals x and y, and repeat the same procedure until the answer to the SMT instance is affirmative or all falsifying Boolean assignments are exhausted. Of course, this requires exploring all such assignments to atoms of the predicate, but since we expect the number of atoms in realistic predicates to be relatively small, the exhaustive nature of falsifying Boolean assignments will not be a bottleneck. We generalize this idea to N agents and arbitrary predicates in Algorithm 1. We assume without loss of generality that every atom a that appears in ϕ is of the form $x_n \geq v_a$ for some n and $v_a \in \mathbb{R}$. A Boolean assignment is a map σ from atoms to {false, true}, and a violating assignment is one that makes the predicate false. Thus, given a violating assignment σ, for every atom a, $a = \sigma(a)$ iff $x_n \geq v_a$ (if $\sigma(a) =$ true) or $x_n < v_a$ (if $\sigma(a) =$ false). Obvious modification to Algorithm 1 allows the monitor to take advantage of knowing different rate bounds at different points along the signals.

Algorithm 1: Dynamics-aware monitoring.

Data: Distributed signal $(E, \leadsto)$, ε, predicate ϕ, bounds $|\dot{x}_n| \leq b_n, n \in [N]$

Result: $(E, \leadsto) \models \phi$

1   Set $t_n = \min I_n, n \in [N]$
2   **while** *not done* **do**
3   Get next violating assignment σ to the atoms of ϕ
4   **if** *there are no more violating assignments* **then**
5 | done
6   **else**
7   **for** *every atom a in ϕ* **do**
8   **if** $\sigma(a) =$ true **then**
9 | $\tau_n = \min\{\tau \mid x(t_n + \tau) \geq v_a\}, n \in [N]$
10   **else**
11 | $\tau_n = \min\{\tau \mid x(t_n + \tau) < v_a\}, n \in [N]$
12   **end**
13   Set $\tau = \max_n \tau_n$ and $m = \mathrm{argmax}_n \tau_n$
14   SMT-monitor the distributed signal E_σ made of the restrictions $x_n|_{[t_n + \tau - \varepsilon, \max I_n]}, n \neq m$ and $x_m|_{[t_m + \tau, \max I_m]}$
15   If SAT, done.
16   **end**
17 **end**

6   Case Studies and Evaluation

In this section, we evaluate our technique using two case studies on networks of autonomous ground and aerial vehicles.

6.1   Case Studies

Network of Ground Autonomous Vehicles. We collected data from two $1/10^{th}$-scale autonomous cars competing in a race around a closed track. Each car carries a LiDAR for perceiving the world, and uses Wi-Fi antennas to communicate with the central monitor. Each car is running a model predictive controller to track its racing line and RRT to adjust its path. The trajectory data is sampled at 25 Hz. In this application, the useful signal length to monitor is 1–2 s, as this is the control horizon (i.e., the controller repeatedly plans the next 1–2 s). Thus, in Eq. (1), $T = 1 - 2$ s. A reasonable range for ε is interval $[1, 5]ms$, guaranteed by ROS clock synchronization based on NTP. Unless otherwise indicated, we monitor the predicate $d(x_1, x_2) > \delta \wedge d(x_1, x_2) \leq \Delta$.

Network of UAVs. We use Fly-by-Logic [27], a path planner software for UAVs, to simulate the operation of two UAVs performing various reach-avoid missions. In a reach-avoid mission, each UAV must reach a goal within a deadline, and must avoid static obstacles as well as other UAVs. The path planner uses a temporal logic robustness optimizer to find the most robust trajectory. The trajectories are sampled at 20 Hz. In this application, the useful signal length to monitor is around 2 s, as this is the UAV's 'reaction time' (depending on current speed). Thus, in Eq. (1), $T \cong 2s$. A reasonable range for ε is again 1–5 ms, guaranteed by ROS. Unless otherwise indicated, we monitor the predicate $d(x_1, x_2) \geq \delta$.

Note that the SMT solver's effort is mostly spent on finding retiming, instead of predicate complexity. Thus, we pick simpler predicates for our experiments.

6.2   Experimental Setup

In our experiments, we choose the following parameters: (1) signal duration, (2) maximum clock skew ε, and (3) distribution of communication among agents. We measure the monitor run time. All experiments are replicated to exhibit %95 confidence interval to provide statistical significance. The experimental platform is a CentOS server with 112 Intel(R) Xeon(R) Platinum 8180 CPUs @ 3.80 GHz CPU and 754G of RAM. Our implementation invokes the SMT-solver Z3 [10] to solve the problem described in Sect. 4. Color versions of all figures are available in the digital version of the paper.

6.3   Analysis of Results

Impact of Signal Segmentation. Given a signal-to-be-monitored, we have a choice of either passing the entire signal to the monitor, or chopping it into segments and monitoring each segment separately (while accounting for ε-synchrony).

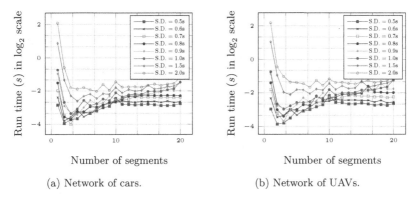

(a) Network of cars.   (b) Network of UAVs.

Fig. 5. Impact of signal segmentation on run time with varying signal duration (S.D.) and fixed $\varepsilon = 0.001$ s.

Monitoring a signal in one shot is computationally more expensive than monitoring a number of shorter segments. Figure 5 shows the results of this claim. Note that all curves are plotted in $\log_2$ scale to provide more clarity. As can be seen, for any signal duration, chopping the signal and invoking the monitor for the shorter segments reduces the run time significantly. For example, in the case of the UAV network (Fig. 5b), for a signal duration of 2 s, it takes 4.5 s to monitor the signal in one shot, but only 0.55 s if the monitor is invoked 20 times over the signal duration. We observe the same behavior in Fig. 5a. This is due to the SMT-solver having to deal with much smaller search spaces in each invocation.

Figure 6 shows the best achievable run time for different signal durations by searching over the segment count of range $[1, 25]$. For example, segment count of 4 is obtained for 1 s signal to get minimum run time of 0.17 s, while segment count of 18 is obtained for 5 s signal to get minimum run time of 0.72 s. The best run time shown is achieved by distributing the monitoring tasks across all the available cores (4) on the monitoring device. Notice that our predicate detection algorithm can be parallelized trivially, assigning one or a pool of segments to a different core.

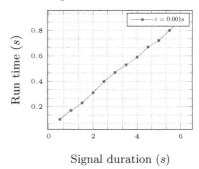

Fig. 6. Best run time (network of cars) for different signal duration.

An important consequence of segmentation is that it enables us to monitor signals in real time, as for 3 or more segments, the run time of the monitor is less than the signal duration. For this reason, in all remaining experiments, the signal-to-monitor is chopped into 20 segments and each segment is monitored separately. Cumulative run times (of monitoring all 20 segments) are reported.

Impact of Clock Skew. We now study the impact of different choices of ε on monitoring run time. We choose realistic values for ε with millisecond resolu-

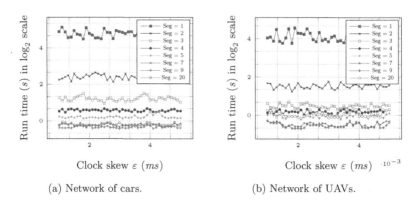

(a) Network of cars.   (b) Network of UAVs.

Fig. 7. Impact of clock skew on run time. Signal duration $= 2\,\mathrm{s}$.

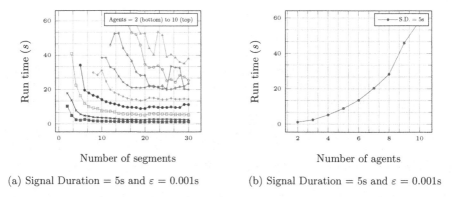

(a) Signal Duration = 5s and $\varepsilon = 0.001$s   (b) Signal Duration = 5s and $\varepsilon = 0.001$s

Fig. 8. Impact of agents on run time.

tion. Figure 7 shows the monitoring run time for a 2 s signal chopped into 1–20 segments. Both Figs. 7a and 7b show that high resolution clock synchronization results in very stable execution time for the monitor. This is a positive result, showing that for practical clock synchronization algorithms, the actual value of ε does not have an impact on the monitoring overhead.

Impact of Number of Agents. Now we observe the impact of the number of UAVs on the monitor. Figure 8a shows the effect on run time for increasing the number of agents from 2 to 10 with $\varepsilon = 1\,\mathrm{ms}$ over 5s-long signals. As each segment of a signal can be monitored independently, we improve our run time by distributing the monitoring tasks across all available cores on the monitoring device. Observe that initially the run time drastically improves as more segments are used. However, eventually the improvement becomes negligible, due to run time being dominated by non-SMT tasks, such as creating job queues, allocating jobs to cores, and so on. We refer to this run time as the *best run time*. Figure 8b shows the best run times for different number of agents with $\varepsilon = 1\,\mathrm{ms}$ over 5s-long signals.

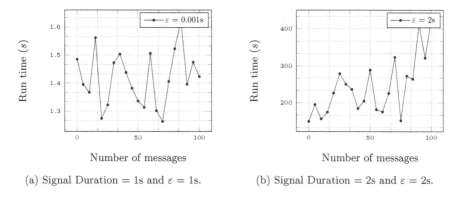

(a) Signal Duration = 1s and ε = 1s. (b) Signal Duration = 2s and ε = 2s.

Fig. 9. Impact of communication (between two agents) on run time.

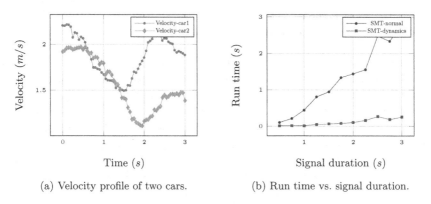

(a) Velocity profile of two cars. (b) Run time vs. signal duration.

Fig. 10. Impact of Algorithm 1 on monitoring run time. $\varepsilon = 0.001$ s.

Impact of Communication. We examine whether the number of messages exchanged between agents has a significant impact on monitor run time. Two opposing mechanisms exist: on the one hand, messages impose an order between the send and receive moments and so reduce concurrency. In the discrete-time setting this normally reduces the asynchronous monitoring complexity. On the other hand, messages result in extra constraints in the SMT encoding via Eq. 7, which could increase SMT run time.

Figure 9 shows the results. In (a) we use $\varepsilon = 1$ ms and a 1s-long signal. Run time varies with no clear trend, suggesting that neither of the above two opposing mechanisms dominates. In (b), we use $\varepsilon = 2$ s for a 2s-long signal: i.e., *all* events are concurrent. One can see the order introduced by messages are slightly increasing the runtime, instead of decreasing it. No conclusion can be drawn, and future work should study this more closely.

Impact of Knowledge of Dynamics Bounds. Here the predicate of interest is $\phi = (v_1 > 1.6) \vee (v_2 > 1.3)$, where v_i is the velocity of the ith car. The acceleration limit from system dynamics is $1\,m/s^2$. The monitor samples the received signals (Fig. 10b) at 0.25 s intervals and applies the acceleration bounds as explained in

Sect. 5 to discard irrelevant pieces of the signal. As shown in Fig. 10, applying Algorithm 1 clearly reduces the monitor run time. In general, of course, the exact run time reduction varies. For instance, while the speedup is ×10 for 3s-long signals 3 s, it is ×15 for 2s-long signals.

7   Related Work

Runtime Monitoring of CPS. Accurate time-keeping for CPS was investigated in the Roseline project [1]. Assuming perfect synchrony, [4] introduces a tool for offline monitoring of robust MTL semantics, and [12] performs online monitoring of STL [13]. The work [11] requires the full dynamical model of the system for predictive monitoring. Our work is closer to [19], which assumes worst-case a priori bounds on signal values (but without factoring dynamics). The works [29] and [2] study of how the satisfaction of a temporal property is affected by timing inaccuracies. Minimally intrusive CPS monitoring was studied in [22].

Decentralized Monitoring. Lattice-theoretic centralized and decentralized online predicate detection in distributed systems has been studied in [7,24]. Extensions of this work to include temporal operators appear in [25,26]. In [30], the authors design a method for monitoring safety properties in distributed systems using the past-time linear temporal logic. This approach, however, suffers from producing false negatives. Runtime monitoring of LTL formulas for synchronous distributed systems has been studied in [5,8,9]. Finally, fault-tolerant monitoring has been investigated in [6] for asynchronous and in [20] for synchronous networks.

Partially Synchronous Monitoring. The feasibility of monitoring partially synchronous distributed systems to detect latent bugs was first studied in [31]. This approach was generalized to the full LTL in [17]. The authors achieve this in a discrete-time/value setting by detecting the presence of latent bugs using SMT solvers. In [28], the authors propose a tool for identifying data races in distributed system traces. This approach is able to handle non-deterministic discrete event orderings. However, these approaches cannot not fully capture the continuous-time and continuous-valued behavior of CPS.

8   Conclusion

In this paper, we demonstrated a technique for online predicate detection for distributed signals that do not share a global clock. Our approach is based on causality analysis between real-valued signals, and integrates a realistic assumption on maximum clock skew among the local clocks, and rough knowledge of system dynamics, to make the problem tractable. We made several important observations by experimenting over a real network of autonomous vehicles and a simulated network of UAVs. Our approach can be effectively implemented to monitor a distributed CPS in an online fashion.

As for future work, there are many interesting research avenues. Our approach finds the first global states that violate a predicate. A crucial step in debugging distributed CPS is to find all such states. Thus, it is important to investigate data structures that can efficiently represent a set of global states of distributed continuous signals that violate a predicate. In the discrete setting, computation *slices* [24] are an example of such a data structure. One way to achieve this is by using the long-known notion of regions in timed automata [3]. Another future problem is to monitor distributed signals with respect to Signal Temporal Logic (STL) specifications.

References

1. https://sites.google.com/site/roselineproject/
2. Abbas, H., Mittelmann, H., Fainekos, G.: Formal property verification in a conformance testing framework. In: ACM-IEEE International Conference on Formal Methods and Models for System Design (MEMOCODE), October 2014
3. Alur, R., Dill, D.: A theory of timed automata. Theoret. Comput. Sci. **126**(2), 183–235 (1994)
4. Annpureddy, Y., Liu, C., Fainekos, G., Sankaranarayanan, S.: S-TaLiRo: a tool for temporal logic falsification for hybrid systems. In: Abdulla, P.A., Leino, K.R.M. (eds.) TACAS 2011. LNCS, vol. 6605, pp. 254–257. Springer, Heidelberg (2011). https://doi.org/10.1007/978-3-642-19835-9_21
5. Bauer, A., Falcone, Y.: Decentralised LTL monitoring. Form. Methods Syst. Des. **48**(1), 46–93 (2016). https://doi.org/10.1007/s10703-016-0253-8
6. Bonakdarpour, B., Fraigniaud, P., Rajsbaum, S., Rosenblueth, D.A., Travers, C.: Decentralized asynchronous crash-resilient runtime verification. In: Proceedings of the 27th International Conference on Concurrency Theory (CONCUR), pp. 16:1–16:15 (2016)
7. Chauhan, H., Garg, V.K., Natarajan, A., Mittal, N.: A distributed abstraction algorithm for online predicate detection. In: Proceedings of the 32nd IEEE Symposium on Reliable Distributed Systems (SRDS), pp. 101–110 (2013)
8. Colombo, C., Falcone, Y.: Organising LTL monitors over distributed systems with a global clock. Form. Methods Syst. Des. **49**(1), 109–158 (2016). https://doi.org/10.1007/s10703-016-0251-x
9. Danielsson, L.M., Sánchez, C.: Decentralized stream runtime verification. In: Finkbeiner, B., Mariani, L. (eds.) RV 2019. LNCS, vol. 11757, pp. 185–201. Springer, Cham (2019). https://doi.org/10.1007/978-3-030-32079-9_11
10. de Moura, L., Bjørner, N.: Z3: an efficient SMT solver. In: Ramakrishnan, C.R., Rehof, J. (eds.) TACAS 2008. LNCS, vol. 4963, pp. 337–340. Springer, Heidelberg (2008). https://doi.org/10.1007/978-3-540-78800-3_24
11. Dokhanchi, A., Hoxha, B., Fainekos, G.: On-line monitoring for temporal logic robustness. In: Bonakdarpour, B., Smolka, S.A. (eds.) RV 2014. LNCS, vol. 8734, pp. 231–246. Springer, Cham (2014). https://doi.org/10.1007/978-3-319-11164-3_19
12. Donzé, A., Ferrère, T., Maler, O.: Efficient robust monitoring for STL. In: Sharygina, N., Veith, H. (eds.) CAV 2013. LNCS, vol. 8044, pp. 264–279. Springer, Heidelberg (2013). https://doi.org/10.1007/978-3-642-39799-8_19
13. Donzé, A., Maler, O.: Robust satisfaction of temporal logic over real-valued signals. In: Chatterjee, K., Henzinger, T.A. (eds.) FORMATS 2010. LNCS, vol. 6246, pp. 92–106. Springer, Heidelberg (2010). https://doi.org/10.1007/978-3-642-15297-9_9

14. Drone Life. FAA UTM project: Decentralized UAS traffic management demonstration, September 2019. https://dronelife.com/2019/09/09/decentralized-uas-traffic-management-demonstration

15. FAA. DOT UAS initiatives, April 2019. https://www.faa.gov/uas/programs_partnerships/DOT_initiatives

16. Fainekos, G.E., Pappas, G.J.: Robust sampling for MITL specifications. In: Raskin, J.-F., Thiagarajan, P.S. (eds.) FORMATS 2007. LNCS, vol. 4763, pp. 147–162. Springer, Heidelberg (2007). https://doi.org/10.1007/978-3-540-75454-1_12

17. Ganguly, R., Momtaz, A., Bonakdarpour, B.: Distributed runtime verification under partial asynchrony. In: Proceedings of the 24nd International Conference on Principles of Distributed Systems (OPODIS), pp. 20:1–20:17 (2020)

18. Hendry-Brogan, M.: Global unmanned aerial vehicle (UAV) market report. Technical report, May 2019

19. Deshmukh, J.V., Donzé, A., Ghosh, S., Jin, X., Juniwal, G., Seshia, S.A.: Robust online monitoring of signal temporal logic. Form. Methods Syst. Des. $51(1)$, 5–30 (2017). https://doi.org/10.1007/s10703-017-0286-7

20. Kazemloo, S., Bonakdarpour, B.: Crash-resilient decentralized synchronous runtime verification. In: Proceedings of the 37th Symposium on Reliable Distributed Systems (SRDS), pp. 207–212 (2018)

21. Lamport, L.: Time, clocks, and the ordering of events in a distributed system. Commun. ACM $21(7)$, 558–565 (1978)

22. Medhat, R., Bonakdarpour, B., Kumar, D., Fischmeister, S.: Runtime monitoring of cyber-physical systems under timing and memory constraints. ACM Trans. Embed. Comput. Syst. $14(4)$, 79:1-79:29 (2015)

23. Mills, D.: Network time protocol version 4: Protocol and algorithms specification. RFC 5905, RFC Editor, June 2010

24. Mittal, N., Garg, V.K.: Techniques and applications of computation slicing. Distrib. Comput. $17(3)$, 251–277 (2005). https://doi.org/10.1007/s00446-004-0117-0

25. Mostafa, M., Bonakdarpour, B.: Decentralized runtime verification of LTL specifications in distributed systems. In: Proceedings of the 29th IEEE International Parallel and Distributed Processing Symposium (IPDPS), pp. 494–503 (2015)

26. Ogale, V.A., Garg, V.K.: Detecting temporal logic predicates on distributed computations. In: Pelc, A. (ed.) DISC 2007. LNCS, vol. 4731, pp. 420–434. Springer, Heidelberg (2007). https://doi.org/10.1007/978-3-540-75142-7_32

27. Pant, Y.V., Abbas, H., Mangharam, R.: Smooth operator: control using the smooth robustness of temporal logic. In: IEEE Conference on Control Technology and Applications (2017)

28. Pereira, J.C., Machado, N., Sousa Pinto, J.: Testing for race conditions in distributed systems via SMT solving. In: Ahrendt, W., Wehrheim, H. (eds.) TAP 2020. LNCS, vol. 12165, pp. 122–140. Springer, Cham (2020). https://doi.org/10.1007/978-3-030-50995-8_7

29. Quesel, J.-D.: Similarity, logic, and games: bridging modeling layers of hybrid systems. Ph.D. thesis, Carl Von Ossietzky Universitat Oldenburg, July 2013

30. Sen, K., Vardhan, A., Agha, G., Rosu, G.: Efficient decentralized monitoring of safety in distributed systems. In: ICSE (2004)

31. Tekken Valapil, V., Yingchareonthawornchai, S., Kulkarni, S., Torng, E., Demirbas, M.: Monitoring partially synchronous distributed systems using SMT solvers. In: Lahiri, S., Reger, G. (eds.) RV 2017. LNCS, vol. 10548, pp. 277–293. Springer, Cham (2017). https://doi.org/10.1007/978-3-319-67531-2_17

Specifying Properties over Inter-procedural, Source Code Level Behaviour of Programs

Joshua Heneage Dawes[(✉)][ID] and Domenico Bianculli[ID]

University of Luxembourg, Luxembourg, Luxembourg
{joshua.dawes,domenico.bianculli}@uni.lu

Abstract. The problem of verifying a program at runtime with respect to some formal specification has led to the development of a rich collection of specification languages. These languages often have a high level of abstraction and provide sophisticated modal operators, giving a high level of expressiveness. In particular, this makes it possible to express properties concerning the source code level behaviour of programs. However, for many languages, the correspondence between events generated at the source code level and parts of the specification in question would have to be carefully defined.

To enable expressing—using a temporal logic—properties over source code level behaviour without the need for this correspondence, previous work introduced Control-Flow Temporal Logic (CFTL), a specification language with a low level of abstraction with respect to the source code of programs. However, this work focused solely on the intra-procedural setting. In this paper, we address this limitation by introducing Inter-procedural CFTL, a language for expressing source code level, inter-procedural properties of program runs. We evaluate the new language, iCFTL, via application to a real-world case study.

Keywords: Dynamic analysis · Source code · Inter-procedural

1 Introduction

Within the context of Runtime Verification [5], many languages have been introduced in order to allow the specification of properties that executions of programs should hold. These languages include temporal logics (such as Linear Temporal Logic [24] and Metric Temporal Logic [23]), stream equations [11], rule systems [4], automata [3,10], and others [18,21].

Specification languages typically achieve a high level of expressiveness. For example, temporal logics often combine a high level of abstraction with complex modal operators such as *next*, *until*, and *eventually* (along with timed extensions of these operators). This approach has clear benefits. For example, given different correspondences between the specification and the events generated at runtime, one specification language can be used to express properties concerning multiple levels of granularity of a system (for example, properties concerning both objects and individual lines of code). An example of a tool that provides support in constructing this correspondence is JAVA-MAC [22]. However, the language then misses specific operators that would make expression of

ⓒ Springer Nature Switzerland AG 2021
L. Feng and D. Fisman (Eds.): RV 2021, LNCS 12974, pp. 23–41, 2021.
https://doi.org/10.1007/978-3-030-88494-9_2

properties over specific types of runtime events easier. As an example, we consider Metric Temporal Logic. The duration of a function call could be captured by referring to the time difference between the occurrence of the function return event, and the time the function call event. A language specialised for source code level properties could improve on this by 1) assuming a trace that contains the appropriate information and 2) introducing specific operators, such as *function call duration*.

In doing this, the expression of properties such as "the time taken by each call to the function f is no more than 0.001 times the length of the list l immediately before the call" would become more straightforward. Further, if one were to use a language specialised to the source code setting, there would be no need to define how events such as function calls and returns, or variable value changes, relate to parts of specifications.

Some approaches, such as the LARVA tool [10] (whose specification formalism is automata whose transitions trigger the execution of pieces of attached Java code), already allow properties over the source code level of programs to be expressed easily. Another example, which focuses less on the order of events, is Control-Flow Temporal Logic (CFTL) [17], which was introduced as a linear-time, temporal logic to be used specifically for expressing properties over the source code level behaviour of programs. Specifications written in CFTL do not require any additional information to have meaning with respect to a program.

CFTL has been shown to be a useful specification formalism (as seen in applications of VYPR [14, 15], the framework built for analysing programs with respect to CFTL specifications). However, only properties concerning the *intra-procedural* behaviour of programs can be expressed (because these properties were sufficient for the case studies being considered in that work). This restriction means that one cannot express properties such as "if the variable a drops below some threshold in function[1] func1, then variable flag is set to true in function func2". Given that large programs are often divided into multiple procedures, many properties that software engineers could want to express would likely involve multiple procedures, like the property mentioned above.

In this paper, we introduce an extension of CFTL that enables one to express such properties. We call this new language *inter-procedural CFTL*, or *iCFTL*. iCFTL provides the same operators as CFTL (for example, to measure the duration of a function call and to obtain the value held by a variable at a given point in time), but allows the points at runtime referred to by properties to be taken from multiple procedures. This extension of the features offered by CFTL to the inter-procedural setting allows the expression of new classes of properties, and requires us to address challenges such as 1) constructing a new kind of trace that can represent the inter-procedural behaviour of a program; 2) extending the CFTL syntax to deal with the new kind of trace; and 3) performing instrumentation in a wider scope than that required for CFTL. With these challenges addressed, we demonstrate the utility of extending CFTL's features to the inter-procedural setting via a case study involving a real-world system used by the CMS Experiment at CERN [9], in which properties that cannot be expressed in CFTL are expressed in iCFTL.

---

[1] In the rest of the paper, we use the terms *function* and *procedure* interchangeably to denote a general, callable subroutine.

$$
\begin{aligned}
Program &:= x = expr \mid func \mid Program; Program \mid \\
&\quad \text{if } expr \text{ then } (Program) \text{ else } (Program) \mid \\
&\quad \text{while } expr \text{ do } (Program) \mid \text{for } x \text{ in } iterator \text{ do } (Program) \\
expr &:= x \mid func \mid arithExpr \mid boolExpr \\
func &:= f(expr_1, \ldots, expr_n) \\
iterator &:= \text{range}(expr, expr)
\end{aligned}
\tag{1}
$$

Fig. 1. A grammar for simple imperative programs.

Structure of the Paper. In order to introduce iCFTL, the paper is structured as follows: In Sect. 2, we give background material on CFTL, since variations of much of the machinery are used by iCFTL. In Sects. 3 and 4, we introduce iCFTL by giving its syntax and semantics. In Sect. 5, we introduce an instrumentation approach based on iCFTL specifications. In Sect. 6, we acknowledge that our initial monitoring algorithm is not efficient and describe how it can be optimised based on information from instrumentation. In Sect. 7, we report on our case study. In Sect. 8, we position our contribution in the literature (alongside giving a brief discussion of the expressive power of iCFTL) and in Sect. 9 we give concluding remarks.

2   Background: Control-Flow Temporal Logic

Control-Flow Temporal Logic (CFTL) [17] is a linear-time, temporal logic used to express properties over the source code level behaviour of programs. In this section, we will introduce CFTL by first defining the structures over which its semantics is defined, and then giving examples of specifications. The structures that we will introduce are the *symbolic control-flow graph* of a program and a *dynamic run*, our version of a trace.

2.1   Symbolic Control-Flow Graphs

We introduce a graph structure that can be used to encode the state change and reachability information found in a program. For simplicity of presentation, we will assume that P is a program generated by the grammar in Fig. 1. We will also assume that each statement stmt in the program P can be associated with a unique *program point* taken from the abstract syntax tree of P. Such program points can be assigned simply by associating an integer with each node in the abstract syntax tree. We will denote the program point of a statement stmt by $\rho(\text{stmt})$. Further, for a program P we denote by $\text{Vars}(P)$ the set of program variables found in P. $\text{Vars}(P)$ can be partitioned into $\text{PVar}(P)$ (the primitive type variables) and $\text{RVar}(P)$ (the reference type variables). Note that, in the CFTL case, we do not consider concurrency and concentrate on the intra-procedural setting.

Based on these assumptions about the structure of a program, we now define the components of a symbolic control-flow graph. First, a *symbolic state* σ associated with a statement stmt is a pair $\langle \rho(\text{stmt}), m \rangle$, for a mapping m from $\text{Vars}(P)$ to *statuses* in

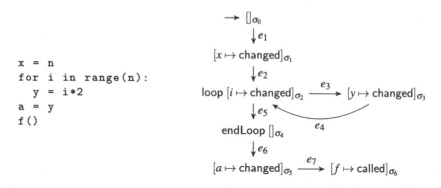

```
x = n
for i in range(n):
    y = i*2
a = y
f()
```

Fig. 2. A Python program with a for-loop with its symbolic control-flow graph.

{changed, unchanged, undefined, called}. We abuse notation and write $\sigma(x)$ to mean $m(x)$, for m the map contained in σ. The symbolic control-flow graph SCFG(P) of a program is then a directed graph with symbolic states as vertices. Formally, SCFG$(P) = \langle V, E, v_s \rangle$ where V is a set of symbolic states, $E \subset V \times V$ a set of edges, and $v_s \in V$ the *starting* symbolic state.

We say that a symbolic state σ is *final* in SCFG(P) if it has no successors, i.e., there is no edge $\langle \sigma, \sigma' \rangle \in E$ for some $\sigma' \in V$. Further, we say that a path π through SCFG(P) is a sequence of edges $e_1, e_2, \ldots, e_n$ such that each $e_i \in E$ and, for each e_i and e_{i+1}, $e_i = \langle \sigma, \sigma' \rangle$ and $e_{i+1} = \langle \sigma', \sigma'' \rangle$ (i.e., edges have to be adjacent).

We give an example of a program with its symbolic control-flow graph in Fig. 2. One could construct the symbolic control-flow graph of a program in a language allowing more complex syntax than that described in Fig. 1, provided that one can construct a scheme to translate programs to graphs.

2.2 Dynamic Runs

We now define the type of trace, which we call a *dynamic run*, over which the CFTL semantics is defined. Intuitively, a dynamic run follows a path through a symbolic control-flow graph and gives concrete timing and data values to each symbolic state encountered along the path.

More formally, a *dynamic run* of a program P is a sequence of triples $\langle t, \sigma, m \rangle$ with a timestamp $t \in \mathbb{R}_{\geq}$, a symbolic state σ, and a mapping m from program variables in Vars(P) to concrete values. Further, for each pair of consecutive triples $\langle t, \sigma, m \rangle$, $\langle t', \sigma', m' \rangle$, there is a path from σ to σ' in SCFG(P).

Each triple in a dynamic run is known as a *concrete state*. Given a concrete state $s = \langle t, \sigma, m \rangle$, we write $s(x)$ to refer to the value given to the program variable x by the map m. We denote by $t(\langle t, \sigma, m \rangle)$ the timestamp t. We call a pair $\langle \langle t, \sigma, m \rangle, \langle t', \sigma', m' \rangle \rangle$ of consecutive concrete states a *transition*, which we usually denote by tr. We denote by paths(tr) the set of paths from σ to σ' in SCFG(P). A transition tr is atomic if the only acyclic path from σ to σ' in SCFG(P) is of length 1. We define t(.) for transitions by $t(\langle \langle t, \sigma, m \rangle, \langle t', \sigma', m' \rangle \rangle) = t$, i.e., the time at which the transition started.

2.3   Examples of CFTL Specifications

With our notion of a trace introduced, we briefly describe the structure of CFTL specifications, and then give examples. CFTL specifications are always universally-quantified *at least once*, do not have existential quantifiers, and are in prenex normal form. The quantifiers use *predicates* in order to extract relevant concrete states or transitions from dynamic runs and bind them to *variables*. For example, calls(f) identifies all transitions whose second concrete state contains a symbolic state that maps f to called, and changes(x) identifies all concrete states whose symbolic states map x to changed. Further, there can be no free variables. Examples of CFTL specifications include the following:

- The property that "the next call to f after each change of the variable var should take less than 10 s" can be expressed by

$$\forall q \in \text{changes}(\text{var}) : \text{duration}(\text{next}(q, \text{calls}(f))) \in (0, 10).$$

  The predicate calls(f) captures all transitions that represent calls of the function f and next refers to the next transition (after q) in the dynamic run satisfying the predicate calls(f).
- The property "whenever the function f is called, its duration must be no more than 0.001 times the length of the list held in variable x immediately before the call" can be expressed by

$$\forall t \in \text{calls}(f) : \text{duration}(t) < \text{length}(\text{source}(t)(\text{x})) \times 0.001.$$

  source(t)(x) gives the concrete state immediately before the transition t, and then gets the value of the program variable x in that concrete state.

3   iCFTL: Inter-procedural CFTL

We now present an extension of CFTL to the inter-procedural setting. This new language is called iCFTL.

3.1   Systems of Multiple Procedures

In the intra-procedural setting, we assume that traces being checked for satisfaction of some CFTL specification are generated by single procedures. In the inter-procedural setting, we will be checking a trace generated by some *system* consisting of multiple procedures, each of which is a program obtained from the grammar in Fig. 1. This enables us to construct their symbolic control-flow graphs. We group the name and program associated with each procedure in a *system of multiple procedures*.

Definition 1. *A system of multiple procedures S is a pair $\langle \mathscr{P}, \text{prog} \rangle$ for $\mathscr{P}$ a set of names of procedures and prog a map that sends each name in $\mathscr{P}$ to a program generated by the grammar in Fig. 1.*

We will often refer to a *system of multiple procedures* simply as a *system*.

3.2 Inter-procedural Dynamic Runs

The dynamic run defined in Sect. 2.2, when considered in the scope of an entire system of multiple procedures, represents a single execution of some procedure. In order to define a language similar to CFTL, but with the ability to express properties concerning inter-procedural behaviour, we introduce a kind of trace that represents a run of a system of multiple procedures.

Our approach is to collect the dynamic runs generated by each procedure in a system, label each one with the name of the procedure that generated it, and assume that the timestamps of the concrete states in each dynamic run are synchronised[2]. We refer to a collection of dynamic runs generated by a run of a system S as an *inter-procedural dynamic run* over the system S.

Definition 2. *An inter-procedural dynamic run $\bar{\mathscr{D}}$ over the system S is a triple*

$$\langle \mathscr{P}, \{\mathscr{D}_1, \ldots, \mathscr{D}_n\}, \mathscr{L} \rangle,$$

where $\mathscr{P}$ is a set of names of procedures in the system S; $\{\mathscr{D}_i\}$ is a set of dynamic runs generated by the procedures in S; and $\mathscr{L}$ is a mapping that labels each dynamic run $\mathscr{D}_i$ with the name of the procedure in $\mathscr{P}$ that generated it.

Given a concrete state s in any dynamic run in an inter-procedural dynamic run, we denote by dynamicRun(s) the unique dynamic run to which s belongs (which exists because each s has a unique timestamp). We extend this to transitions $tr = \langle s, s' \rangle$ by dynamicRun(tr) = dynamicRun(s). We then combine dynamicRun$(.)$ with the map $\mathscr{L}$ to define a map proc by proc$(s) = \mathscr{L}(\text{dynamicRun}(s))$. Similarly for transitions $tr = \langle s, s' \rangle$, we set proc$(tr)$ = proc(s). Intuitively, proc$(.)$ gives the name of the unique procedure that had control in the system when the concrete state/transition given was attained/taking place.

To generalise our approach to multiple types of systems, we assume that there is always more to observe. While it is possible to observe everything in some cases (e.g., programs that compute a single result and terminate), for other systems it is not. For example, Web services (such as the one used in our case study described in Sect. 7) constantly receive new requests that trigger repeated executions of procedures.

3.3 Syntax of iCFTL

We give a grammar for the iCFTL syntax in Fig. 3. In the grammar, the non-terminal symbols used in rules are highlighted in blue. We also group the rules by *Quantifiers*, *Predicates*, and *Constraints*. We now describe the role of each group of rules, and give examples to illustrate how rules can be applied to construct certain specifications.

Quantifiers. The first rule to apply from the grammar to generate an iCFTL specification is ϕ. This rule can be applied repeatedly in order to generate multiple quantifiers. We will always assume specifications are in prenex normal form.

---

[2] This assumption is reasonable since either 1) everything will happen on the same machine, so the machine's clock can be used for synchronisation; or 2) if this is not the case, then protocols such as NTP can be used.

Quantifiers

$$\phi \quad \rightarrow \quad \forall q \in \Gamma_{QS} : \phi \mid \forall t \in \Gamma_{QT} : \phi \mid \phi \vee \phi \mid \neg \phi \mid \phi_S \mid \phi_T \mid true$$

Predicates

$$
\begin{array}{lcl}
\Gamma_{QS} & \rightarrow & \Gamma_S \mid \mathsf{future}(q, \Gamma_S) \mid \mathsf{future}(t, \Gamma_S) \\
\Gamma_{QT} & \rightarrow & \Gamma_T \mid \mathsf{future}_{(}q, \Gamma_T) \mid \mathsf{future}(t, \Gamma_T) \\
\Gamma_S & \rightarrow & \mathsf{changes}(x).\mathsf{during}(p) \\
\Gamma_T & \rightarrow & \mathsf{calls}(f).\mathsf{during}(p)
\end{array}
$$

Concrete State and Transition Selection

$$
\begin{array}{lcl}
S & \rightarrow & q \mid \mathsf{before}(T) \mid \mathsf{after}(T) \mid S.\mathsf{next}(\Gamma_S) \mid T.\mathsf{next}(\Gamma_S) \\
T & \rightarrow & t \mid S.\mathsf{next}(\Gamma_T) \mid T.\mathsf{next}(\Gamma_T)
\end{array}
$$

Constraints

$$
\begin{array}{lcl}
\phi_S & \rightarrow & S(x) = v \mid S(x) = S(x) \mid S(x) \in (n,m) \mid S(x) \in [n,m] \\
\phi_T & \rightarrow & \mathsf{duration}(T) \in (n,m) \mid \mathsf{duration}(T) \in [n,m] \\
& & \mid \mathsf{timeBetween}(S,S) \in (n,m) \mid \mathsf{timeBetween}(S,S) \in [n,m]
\end{array}
$$

Fig. 3. Syntax of iCFTL.

Predicates. Each quantifier requires a *predicate* in order to identify concrete states or transitions to which the variable used in the quantifier should be bound. These predicates are generated by the Γ_{QS} and Γ_{QT} rules. In these cases, there are two parts: one to select the relevant dynamic run (during) and one to select the relevant concrete state or transition from that dynamic run (see Sect. 2.3).

To give some examples, the predicate changes(x).during(p) captures concrete states generated by the procedure p in which the program variable x has just been changed. Similarly, the predicate calls(f).during(p) captures transitions representing a call of the procedure f during the procedure p. The future operators extends these predicates to identify all such concrete states or transitions in the future, rather than just the next occurrence.

Combining Quantifiers and Predicates. Quantifiers and predicates are combined to form *sequences of quantifiers*. An example is

$$\forall q \in \mathsf{changes}(x).\mathsf{during}(f) : \forall tr \in \mathsf{future}(q, \mathsf{calls}(g).\mathsf{during}(h)) : \ldots$$

This sequence of quantifiers would capture each concrete state representing a change of the program variable x (during calls of the procedure f) and, for each change, every call of the function g occurring in the future (during calls of the procedure h).

Concrete State and Transition Selection. Quantifiers allow us to select concrete states and transitions to be used in the inner-most, quantifier free part of a specification. Given these concrete states and transitions, we must be able to *navigate* the inter-procedural dynamic run in order to select others. Using the rules S and T, this can be done by 1) applying the simple operators before and after to transitions (which obtain the concrete state immediately before and immediately after the transition); or 2) using next in conjunction with one of the predicates changes(x).during(p) or calls(f).during(p) to search forwards in time. Hence, given concrete states or transitions identified by quantifiers, one can either write constraints over those directly, or use the before, after, or next operators to *navigate* the inter-procedural dynamic run.

Constraints. For an iCFTL specification φ, we denote by $\mathsf{inner}(\varphi)$ the inner-most, quantifier-free part of the specification. Once the sequence of quantifiers has been generated, one can generate $\mathsf{inner}(\varphi)$, which is intuitively the constraint to check at each combination of concrete states/transitions identified by the quantifiers. The grammar allows for disjunction and negation, but we frequently use additional Boolean connectives such as conjunction and implication.

Within the Boolean combination of constraints, each part of the specification generated by an application of either ϕ_S or ϕ_T is called an *atom*. Atoms place constraints on quantities extracted from concrete states or transitions identified using the S and T rules.

Atoms generated by rules containing only one non-terminal symbol are called *normal* and atoms generated by rules containing two non-terminal symbols are called *mixed*. Atoms are the parts of the specification that place constraints on quantities extracted from dynamic runs. We refer to the parts of specifications generated by the rules S and T as *expressions*.

Building Constraints. Suppose we have the sequence of quantifiers

$$\forall q \in \mathsf{changes}(x).\mathsf{during}(f),$$

and would like to assert that each concrete state bound to the variable q maps the program variable x to a value that is strictly less than 10. Our first step would be to take the variable q (treating it as a concrete state) and determine the value to which it maps the variable x. Since there is no *navigation* of the inter-procedural dynamic run to be performed (we are placing a constraint over a quantity measurable directly from the concrete state held by q), we can go immediately to the ϕ_S rule and generate the constraint $q(x) \in (0, 10)$ (acknowledging that there would have to be a conjunction to include the possibility of $q(x)$ being equal to 0).

Formula Trees for iCFTL. Given $\mathsf{inner}(\varphi)$ of an iCFTL specification φ, we denote by $\mathsf{tree}(\mathsf{inner}(\varphi))$ the and-or formula tree of $\mathsf{inner}(\varphi)$. This formula tree is such that leaves correspond to either normal atoms or expressions in mixed atoms. We use this mechanism when defining our monitoring procedure for iCFTL in Sect. 5.

3.4 Examples

We now give some examples of properties that can be expressed using iCFTL:

- The property "when the variable `level` drops below 10 in the method `check`, the time until the next call of `adjust` in the method `control` should be no more than 1 s" can be expressed by

$$\forall q \in \mathsf{changes}(\texttt{level}).\mathsf{during}(\texttt{check}) : q(\texttt{level}) < 10 \implies$$
$$\mathsf{timeBetween}(q, \mathsf{before}(q.\mathsf{next}(\mathsf{calls}(\texttt{adjust}).\mathsf{during}(\texttt{control})))) \in [0, 1].$$

$\bar{\mathscr{D}}, q \vdash$ changes(x).during(func) iff $\sigma(x) = $ changed and proc$(q) = $ func

$\bar{\mathscr{D}}, q \vdash$ future(s, changes(x).during(func)) iff
$$\quad\quad t(q) > t(s) \text{ and } \bar{\mathscr{D}}, q \vdash \text{changes(x).during(func)}$$

$\bar{\mathscr{D}}, tr \vdash$ calls(f).during(func) iff
$$\left(\begin{array}{l} \text{for every path } \pi \in \text{paths}(tr) \text{ there is:} \\ \quad \text{some } \langle \sigma_1, \sigma_2 \rangle \in \pi \text{ such that } \sigma_2(f) = \text{called} \end{array} \right) \text{ and } \text{proc}(tr) = \text{func}$$

$\bar{\mathscr{D}}, tr \vdash$ future(s, calls(f).during(func)) iff $t(tr) > t(s)$ and $\bar{\mathscr{D}}, tr \vdash$ calls(f).during(func)

Fig. 4. The quantifier relation $\vdash$ for the iCFTL semantics.

– The property "for each change of the variable user during an execution of the procedure login, and for each future change of the variable user during executions of the procedure getUser, the value of variable user should remain the same", taking some liberties with syntax, can be expressed by:

$$\forall q \in \text{changes(user).during(login)} :$$
$$\forall q' \in \text{future}(q, \text{changes(user).during(getUser)}) : q'(\text{user}) = q(\text{user}) \tag{2}$$

The key syntactic novelty in iCFTL is the during component of predicates, which allows one to refer to events across multiple procedures.

4 A Semantics for iCFTL

In order to align with our case study (see Sect. 7), which is a Web service whose traces must be assumed to be infinite, we define the semantics of iCFTL with respect to prefixes of infinite program traces. We take a similar approach to much existing work in the RV community: we define a semantics over prefixes of program traces [6] and give a *provisional* verdict. This semantics consists of two key steps. The first involves deriving a set of *bindings* by inspection of an inter-procedural dynamic run $\bar{\mathscr{D}}$ with respect to the quantifiers in an iCFTL specification φ. These bindings will collect together concrete states and transitions from $\bar{\mathscr{D}}$ and provide them to inner(φ). The second step involves evaluating inner(φ) with respect to each binding derived.

4.1 Finding Bindings

Given an inter-procedural dynamic run $\bar{\mathscr{D}}$ and an iCFTL specification φ, our goal is to inspect its quantifiers $\forall q_1 \in \Gamma_1 : \cdots : \forall q_n \in \Gamma_n$ in order to derive a set of maps, which we will refer to as *bindings*. These bindings will send the variable q_1 to a concrete state or transition satisfying Γ_1, the variable q_2 to a concrete state or transition satisfying Γ_2, and so on. We will then take each binding and decide on a truth value for inner(φ) based on the values given to each variable $q_1, \ldots, q_n$ by the binding.

$$\bar{\mathscr{D}} = \left\langle \begin{array}{l} \{\text{login}, \text{getUser}, \text{getUserData}\}, \{\mathscr{D}_1, \mathscr{D}_2, \mathscr{D}_3, \mathscr{D}_4\}, \\ [\mathscr{D}_1 \mapsto \text{login}, \mathscr{D}_2 \mapsto \text{getUser}, \mathscr{D}_3 \mapsto \text{getUserData}, \mathscr{D}_4 \mapsto \text{getUser}] \end{array} \right\rangle$$

$$\mathscr{D}_1 = \langle 0, [], [] \rangle, \langle 0.2, [\text{getUser} \mapsto \text{called}, \text{user} \mapsto \text{changed}], [\text{user} \mapsto 10] \rangle, \dots$$

$$\mathscr{D}_2 = \langle 0.1, [], [] \rangle, \langle 0.15, [\text{user} \mapsto \text{changed}, \dots], [\text{user} \mapsto 10] \rangle, \dots$$

$$\mathscr{D}_3 = \langle 0.3, [], [] \rangle, \langle 0.45, [\text{getUser} \mapsto \text{called}, \text{user} \mapsto \text{changed}], [\text{user} \mapsto 10] \rangle, \dots$$

$$\mathscr{D}_4 = \langle 0.35, [], [] \rangle, \langle 0.4, [\text{user} \mapsto \text{changed}, \dots], [\text{user} \mapsto 10] \rangle, \dots$$

Fig. 5. An example inter-procedural dynamic run.

We begin the construction of the set of bindings by defining the *quantifier* relation, denoted by $\vdash$, that indicates whether a given concrete state q or transition tr satisfies a predicate used in a quantifier. The definition is given in Fig. 4.

The second and final step is to recurse on the quantifiers in order to progressively construct the set of bindings, which we denote by $\text{bindings}_\varphi(\bar{\mathscr{D}}, \forall q_1 \in \Gamma_1 : \cdots : \forall q_n \in \Gamma_n)$. This is done by determining the concrete states or transitions that satisfy the predicate of the first quantifier and then, if there are multiple quantifiers, identifying the concrete states or transitions that satisfy the next predicates. The check for satisfaction at each step is based on the relation defined in Fig. 4. We highlight that, if no concrete states or transitions are identified by a predicate, a binding is generated that does not include all variables from the specification. We refer to such a binding as *partial*.

An Example. In order to illustrate the procedure for constructing bindings, we consider the iCFTL specification in Eq. 2 along with an inter-procedural dynamic run given in Fig. 5. In this inter-procedural dynamic run, there are three procedures, login, getUser, getUserData. We assume that both login and getUserData involve calls to getUser. One can see the caller-callee relationship between dynamic runs when all of the timestamps of concrete states of a callee dynamic run fall in between two timestamps of consecutive concrete states in the caller dynamic run.

Based on the inter-procedural dynamic run in Fig. 5, binding construction would go as follows: The procedure would identify concrete states that satisfy the first quantifier, and then inspect the second quantifier. For the first quantifier

$$\text{changes}(\text{user}).\text{during}(\text{login}),$$

the concrete state $\langle 0.2, [\text{getUser} \mapsto \text{called}, \text{user} \mapsto \text{changed}], [\text{user} \mapsto 10] \rangle$ would be identified. Based on this initially identified concrete state, we look for further concrete states satisfying

$$\text{future}(q, \text{changes}(\text{user}).\text{during}(\text{getUser})),$$

with respect to the concrete state $\langle 0.2, [\text{getUser} \mapsto \text{called}, \text{user} \mapsto \text{changed}], [\text{user} \mapsto 10] \rangle$ identified by the first quantifier. Hence, the concrete state $\langle 0.4, [\text{user} \mapsto \text{changed},$

...], $[user \mapsto 10]\rangle$ would be identified. Since all quantifiers have been inspected, we conclude with the set of bindings:

$$\left\{ \begin{array}{l} \left[q \mapsto \langle 0.2, [getUser \mapsto called, user \mapsto changed], [user \mapsto 10] \rangle \right], \\ \left[q \mapsto \langle 0.2, [getUser \mapsto called, user \mapsto changed], [user \mapsto 10] \rangle, \\ q' \mapsto \langle 0.4, [user \mapsto changed, \ldots], [user \mapsto 10] \rangle \right] \end{array} \right\}$$

Notice that we keep a binding that only sends q to a concrete state, and not q'. This is to capture the intuition that the binding with only q may be extended with a new value of q' given more observations from the monitored system.

4.2   Evaluation at a Binding

The next step in developing the semantics is to evaluate the constraints defined by the specification at each of the bindings in the set bindings$_\varphi(\bar{\mathscr{D}}, \forall q_1 \in \Gamma_1 : \cdots : \forall q_n \in \Gamma_n)$. For this, we introduce the $\text{eval}(\bar{\mathscr{D}}, \beta, X)$ function.

This function takes an expression from the specification, along with a binding and an inter-procedural dynamic run, and gives the unique concrete state or transition that is required by that expression. If no such concrete state or transition exists, the function returns null.

Once we have obtained the concrete state or transition referred to by an expression, we can determine the truth values of atoms, and therefore the truth values of Boolean combinations of atoms. This process is encoded in the $[.]_\beta$ function, which is defined recursively in Fig. 6. The function $[.]_\beta$ takes as input an inter-procedural dynamic run, a binding and either a Boolean combination of atoms, or a single atom, and gives a truth value from the set $\{\text{true}, \text{false}, \text{inconclusive}\}$. This set has ordering false $<$ inconclusive $<$ true with $\neg$inconclusive $=$ inconclusive.

If a single atom is given and the required concrete states and transitions are found, the truth value given is either true or false. If a single atom is given and no concrete state or transition is identified, the truth value is inconclusive. If a Boolean combination of atoms is given, the total order of the truth domain is used to determine the truth value, given the truth values of the subformulas[3].

4.3   The Semantics Function

We have now introduced the machinery for 1) extracting a set of bindings from an inter-procedural dynamic run based on a specification; and 2) determining the truth values of atoms in an iCFTL specification given a specific binding. The final step in defining the semantics for iCFTL is to combine all of these components in order to give a verdict.

While most existing work in RV concentrates on generating verdicts that are simple objects, such as true or false, taken from a truth domain, our approach differs. Instead,

---

[3] Of course, if the specification expresses a tautology or is unsatisfiable, this evaluation-by-composition approach is problematic. However, as seen in [13], satisfiability for CFTL (and therefore iCFTL) can only be decided once a sufficiently long trace has been observed, hence we do not consider it in the semantics.

$$[\bar{\mathscr{D}},\beta,\phi_1 \vee \phi_2]_\beta = [\bar{\mathscr{D}},\beta,\phi_1]_\beta \sqcup [\bar{\mathscr{D}},\beta,\phi_2]_\beta \qquad [\bar{\mathscr{D}},\beta,\neg\phi]_\beta = \neg[\bar{\mathscr{D}},\beta,\phi]_\beta$$

$$[\bar{\mathscr{D}},\beta,S(x)=n]_\beta = \begin{cases} \text{true} & \text{eval}(\bar{\mathscr{D}},\beta,S) \neq \text{null} \wedge \text{eval}(\bar{\mathscr{D}},\beta,S)(x) = n \\ \text{false} & \text{eval}(\bar{\mathscr{D}},\beta,S) \neq \text{null} \wedge \text{eval}(\bar{\mathscr{D}},\beta,S)(x) \neq n \\ \text{inconclusive} & \text{otherwise} \end{cases}$$

$$[\bar{\mathscr{D}},\beta,S_1(x)=S_2(x)]_\beta = \begin{cases} \text{true} & \begin{aligned} &\text{eval}(\bar{\mathscr{D}},\beta,S_1) \neq \text{null} \wedge \text{eval}(\bar{\mathscr{D}},\beta,S_2) \neq \text{null} \\ &\wedge\, \text{eval}(\bar{\mathscr{D}},\beta,S_1)(x) = \text{eval}(\bar{\mathscr{D}},\beta,S_2)(x) \end{aligned} \\ \text{false} & \begin{aligned} &\text{eval}(\bar{\mathscr{D}},\beta,S_1) \neq \text{null} \wedge \text{eval}(\bar{\mathscr{D}},\beta,S_2) \neq \text{null} \\ &\wedge\, \text{eval}(\bar{\mathscr{D}},\beta,S_1)(x) \neq \text{eval}(\bar{\mathscr{D}},\beta,S_2)(x) \end{aligned} \\ \text{inconclusive} & \text{otherwise} \end{cases}$$

Fig. 6. Part of the constraint function for iCFTL.

the verdict that we provide is a map from bindings extracted from the inter-procedural dynamic run to truth values. In addition, we encode in these truth values whether or not the binding associated with the truth value is partial. We do this because, if a binding is partial, we cannot be sure that it will be extended to form a complete binding given further observations from the system.

$$\text{translate}(\bar{\mathscr{D}},\beta,\varphi) = \begin{cases} \text{true} & [\bar{\mathscr{D}},\beta,\text{inner}(\varphi)]_\beta = \text{true} \wedge \beta \text{ is complete} \\ \text{false} & [\bar{\mathscr{D}},\beta,\text{inner}(\varphi)]_\beta = \text{false} \wedge \beta \text{ is complete} \\ \text{inconclusive} & [\bar{\mathscr{D}},\beta,\text{inner}(\varphi)]_\beta = \text{inconclusive} \wedge \beta \text{ is complete} \\ \text{true}_p & [\bar{\mathscr{D}},\beta,\text{inner}(\varphi)]_\beta = \text{true} \wedge \beta \text{ is partial} \\ \text{false}_p & [\bar{\mathscr{D}},\beta,\text{inner}(\varphi)]_\beta = \text{false} \wedge \beta \text{ is partial} \\ \text{inconclusive}_p & [\bar{\mathscr{D}},\beta,\text{inner}(\varphi)]_\beta = \text{inconclusive} \wedge \beta \text{ is partial} \end{cases}$$

Fig. 7. The translation function.

In order to provide this distinction, we introduce the translate function. This function, defined in Fig. 7, translates from the truth values $\{\text{true}, \text{false}, \text{inconclusive}\}$ given by the function in Fig. 6 to *complete* and *partial* versions of the same truth values:

$$\{\text{true}, \text{true}_p, \text{false}, \text{false}_p, \text{inconclusive}, \text{inconclusive}_p\}.$$

Finally, we define the semantics function $[\bar{\mathscr{D}},\varphi]_S$, which simply computes the set of bindings for a given inter-procedural dynamic run with respect to an iCFTL specification and, for each one, gives the value of the translation function:

$$[\bar{\mathscr{D}},\varphi]_S = [\beta \mapsto \text{translate}(\bar{\mathscr{D}},\beta,\varphi) : \beta \in \text{bindings}_\varphi(\bar{\mathscr{D}}, \forall q_1 \in \Gamma_1 : \cdots : \forall q_n \in \Gamma_n)].$$

Hence, for a given inter-procedural dynamic run and iCFTL specification, the *verdict* that we compute is the map given by $[\bar{\mathscr{D}},\varphi]_S$ indicating 1) the truth values given by the constraints in the specification at each binding; and 2) the type of binding for which each truth value was obtained.

5 Monitoring

We now develop an initial algorithm that processes an inter-procedural dynamic run and an iCFTL specification in order to give a verdict. The algorithm is inspired by the work on CFTL and VYPR [14, 17]. We will see that it does not scale well, and describe an instrumentation process in Sect. 6 to greatly improve the situation.

Given an inter-procedural dynamic run $\langle \mathscr{P}, \{\mathscr{D}_1, \ldots, \mathscr{D}_m\}, \mathscr{L} \rangle$, our "naive" monitoring approach for iCFTL, given in Algorithm 1, consists of iterating through the concrete states contained in all of the dynamic runs $\mathscr{D}_i$ in ascending order of timestamps. This sequence of concrete states is denoted by flattened($\bar{\mathscr{D}}$). For each concrete state curr, we see if 1) curr, or the transition leading into it, contributes to a binding and 2) curr, or the transition leading to it, contributes to the truth value of some atom. If curr or the transition leading to it contributes to the truth value of some atom, Algorithm 1 uses *formula trees* to determine the new truth value of inner(φ). We highlight that † is the *map update* operator, that is, $a \dagger [e \mapsto v]$ refers to the map that agrees with a on all elements of the domain of a, except for e which is mapped to v.

Formula Trees. The monitoring algorithm often instantiates a new formula tree tree(ϕ) (or uses an existing one) and then *updates* it with the update function. This function takes a formula tree with a concrete state or transition and replaces the relevant nodes in the formula tree accordingly.

If the concrete state/transition given is relevant to an expression, the node holding that expression is replaced by the value given to that expression by the concrete state/transition. For example, if we have the concrete state $\langle 0.1, [x \mapsto \text{changed}], [x \mapsto 1.5] \rangle$ and an expression q on a leaf of the formula tree, the latter can be replaced by 1.5 if the q is part of $q(x)$ in the specification. Alternatively, if the concrete state/transition is relevant to a normal atom, the node holding that atom is replaced with a truth value. For example, given the same concrete state and an atom $q(x) < 2$, the leaf could be replaced by true. Once this replacement has taken place, the formula tree is collapsed based on the conventional rules for propositional connectives.

Correctness. A correctness argument for Algorithm 1 involves showing that 1) the bindings generated by the algorithm and the semantics are the same; and 2) the procedure for obtaining truth values of inner(φ) in the algorithm has the same result as the semantics. It is similar to the one given in [13].

Complexity. The main loop of Algorithm 1 performs as many iterations as there are concrete states in $\bar{\mathscr{D}}$, which we will denote by $|\bar{\mathscr{D}}|$. For each of these iterations, we process the existing bindings, of which there are at most $|\bar{\mathscr{D}}|^m/m!$ [13]. Hence, the approximate complexity is $O(|\bar{\mathscr{D}}|^{m+1}/m!)$. We highlight that m is rarely greater than 2, hence the complexity can be seen as $O(|\bar{\mathscr{D}}|^{m+1})$, meaning that, even for specifications with only one quantifier, this initial monitoring algorithm scales quadratically in the length of the trace.

Algorithm 1. Monitoring for an iCFTL specification $\forall q_1 \in \Gamma_1 : \cdots : \forall q_m \in \Gamma_m : \phi$.

1: $M \leftarrow []$ ▷ empty map from bindings to formula trees
2: $\mathsf{prev} \leftarrow \langle t_1, [], [] \rangle$ ▷ to store the previous state, assuming t_1 is the first timestamp in the dynamic run
3: **for** concrete state curr $\in$ flattened($\bar{\mathcal{D}}$) **do**
4:    ▷ *Handle the cases where a new binding should be generated*
5:    ▷ *New bindings are generated if the state/transition is in Γ_1*
6:    **if** curr $\vdash \Gamma_1$ **then**
7:      $M = M \dagger ([q_1 \mapsto \mathsf{curr}] \mapsto \mathsf{update}(\mathsf{tree}(\phi), \mathsf{curr}))$
8:    **if** $(\mathsf{prev}, \mathsf{curr}) \vdash \Gamma_1$ **then**
9:      $M = M \dagger ([q_1 \mapsto \langle \mathsf{prev}, \mathsf{curr} \rangle] \mapsto \mathsf{update}(\mathsf{tree}(\phi), \langle \mathsf{prev}, \mathsf{curr} \rangle))$
10:    ▷ *Bindings are extended if the state/transition is in Γ_i for $i > 1$*
11:    **for** $(\beta = [q_1 \mapsto v_1, \ldots q_k \mapsto v_k], T)$ in M where $k < m$ **do**
12:      **if** curr $\vdash \Gamma_{k+1}$ **then**
13:        $M = M \dagger ((\beta \dagger [q_{k+1} \mapsto \mathsf{curr}]) \mapsto \mathsf{update}(T, \mathsf{curr}))$
14:      **if** $(\mathsf{prev}, \mathsf{curr}) \vdash \Gamma_{k+1}$ **then**
15:        $M = M \dagger ((\beta \dagger [q_{k+1} \mapsto \langle \mathsf{prev}, \mathsf{curr} \rangle]) \mapsto \mathsf{update}(T, \langle \mathsf{prev}, \mathsf{curr} \rangle))$
16:    **for** (β, T) in M **do**   ▷ Now update formula trees for existing bindings
17:      $T' \leftarrow \mathsf{update}(T, \mathsf{curr})$
18:    $\mathsf{prev} \leftarrow \mathsf{curr}$ ▷ Finally save the current state as the last state
19: **return** M

6 Instrumentation

The inefficiency of Algorithm 1 has two principal causes: 1) the amount of unnecessary information contained in the inter-procedural dynamic run being processed; and 2) the lookup required to decide whether a concrete state/transition contributes to a binding. To improve the situation, we traverse the symbolic control-flow graphs of the relevant procedures in order to determine which program points are relevant to a specification. This traversal is part of the process of instrumentation, whose steps are described in the following sections.

6.1 Inspection of the Quantifiers

For an iCFTL specification with quantifiers $\forall q_1 \in \Gamma_1 : \cdots : \forall q_n \in \Gamma_n$, we recursively construct maps from the variables $q_1, \ldots, q_n$ to symbolic states from the relevant symbolic control-flow graphs. As an example, suppose that we are monitoring a system $S = \langle \{f\}, \mathsf{prog} \rangle$. If a specification had the quantifier sequence $\forall q \in \mathsf{changes}(\mathtt{x}).\mathsf{during}(f)$, we would identify all symbolic states σ in the symbolic control-flow graph of the program $\mathsf{prog}(f)$ that had $\sigma(\mathtt{x}) = \mathsf{changed}$. A final step, which helps during monitoring, is the assignment of a unique integer (i.e., an index) to each map from the variables q_i to concrete states.

6.2 Inspection of the Atoms

Given the set of maps constructed from the inspection of quantifiers, we perform further traversal of the symbolic control-flow graphs of the system for each atom in $\mathsf{inner}(\varphi)$. For example, if we had the iCFTL specification

$$\forall q \in \mathsf{changes}(\mathtt{x}).\mathsf{during}(\mathtt{f}) : \mathsf{duration}(q.\mathsf{next}(\mathsf{calls}(\mathtt{g}).\mathsf{during}(\mathtt{h}))) < 1,$$

then we would traverse the symbolic control-flow graph of the procedure $\mathsf{prog}(\mathtt{h})$ in order to find symbolic states σ with $\sigma(\mathtt{g}) = \mathsf{called}$.

6.3 Filtering Dynamic Runs

After applying the procedure described in Sects. 6.1 and 6.2, we have a set of symbolic states, which we call *instrumentation points*, taken from the various symbolic control-flow graphs in the system. This set of instrumentation points is such that we can remove any concrete state from an inter-procedural dynamic run that does not correspond to one of the symbolic states in the set. More formally, if a concrete state $\langle t, \sigma, m \rangle$ appears in an inter-procedural dynamic run and σ is not in the set of instrumentation points, the concrete state can be removed from the inter-procedural dynamic run. The safety of this approach is proved in [13]. While the proof there is for CFTL, the instrumentation approaches are sufficiently similar that it applies here.

6.4 Lookup During Monitoring

An important source of inefficiency in Algorithm 1 is the requirement to find the formula trees that must be updated, given a measurement from an inter-procedural dynamic run. In order to reduce the number of formula trees that must be checked, we group formula trees by the unique integer identifying each map constructed in Sect. 6.1. For each concrete state, we can then extract its symbolic state and determine which map (if any) it belongs to (this can be performed as a pre-processing step to improve lookup speeds further). With formula trees grouped with respect to these uniquely identifying integers, we can then determine the set of formula trees that must be updated.

6.5 Implications for Complexity

These optimisations mean that 1) there can be fewer concrete states to process, since we can filter them based on relevant symbolic states; and 2) lookup of the relevant formula trees is faster. A more in-depth discussion can be found in [17] and [13].

7 Case Study

To evaluate iCFTL, we have extended the existing VYPR framework [14] to include a new library for building iCFTL specifications, along with machinery for instrumentation and monitoring. The prototype implementation is available under the Apache

2.0 license at https://doi.org/10.5281/zenodo.5195959, with development occurring at https://github.com/SNTSVV/VyPR-iCFTL.

Using this implementation, we have performed some initial experiments on a Python-based case study [12] provided by the CMS Experiment at CERN [9], where the initial work on CFTL and VYPR was performed. This case study is a Web service, therefore consisting of a server and (to simplify this initial experimental setting) a single client. The client uploads data to the server over the course of multiple HTTP requests. We note that the restriction of CFTL to the intra-procedural setting means that properties that require measurements to be taken over multiple HTTP requests certainly cannot be expressed. With iCFTL this limitation is gone, since inter-procedural also means "inter-request".

In order to demonstrate this concretely, we present an iCFTL specification that we have been able to monitor, which could not be expressed in CFTL (hence demonstrating the usefulness of taking the features offered by CFTL and extending them to the inter-procedural setting). We also present initial measurements of the overhead induced by the extended implementation of VYPR.

Specification. Our principal specification, taking liberties with syntax, is:

$$\forall c \in \mathsf{calls}(\mathtt{find\_new}).\mathsf{during}(\mathtt{app.routes.hashes}):$$
$$\mathsf{timeBetween}(\mathsf{before}(c),$$
$$\mathsf{after}(c.\mathsf{next}(\mathsf{calls}(\mathtt{get\_usage}).\mathsf{during}(\mathtt{app.routes.upload\_md}))) < 4$$

This specification expresses the property that the time between two concrete states attained at runtime in two different procedures of the system under scrutiny must be less than four seconds. The first of these concrete states is the concrete state immediately before the transition representing a call of the function $\mathtt{find\_new}$, occurring during a dynamic run generated by the $\mathtt{hashes}$ procedure (found in the module $\mathtt{app.routes}$). The second concrete state is the one immediately after the transition representing the next call of $\mathtt{get\_usage}$ that occurs during a dynamic run generated by the $\mathtt{upload\_md}$ procedure.

Overhead. In order to obtain initial measurements of the overhead induced by VYPR, we ran the same upload 100 times, with and without monitoring. When this was done with *no delay* between uploads, we obtained an overhead of approximately 3.22%. By introducing a delay between uploads, we could reduce the overhead to 1.69%. We highlight that this delay between requests allows any measurements not processed by the VYPR monitoring algorithm *during* requests to be processed between requests. A more detailed discussion of the overhead induced by VYPR is given in [13].

8   Related Work

We first discuss the relationship between iCFTL and CFTL [17]. Despite the fact that iCFTL can express properties that could not be expressed in CFTL, if we restrict the semantics of iCFTL to a single dynamic run, the newly introduced syntax does not allow any new kinds of properties to be expressed in this setting. That is, the notable extensions of the syntax (the introduction of the during(p) component to various predicates) would not be useful in the intra-procedural setting. Hence, rather than referring to iCFTL as an improvement on the expressive power of CFTL, we refer to iCFTL as an extension of the features provided by CFTL into the inter-procedural setting.

iCFTL is a departure from the conventional approach seen in (or adapted to) the RV community, which often involves an extremely expressive specification formalism with a high level of abstraction [4,21,23,24]. iCFTL does not distinguish between the symbols that are used in a specification and the events that occur during the runtime of a program. This has the disadvantage that a change to the source code requires a change to the specification, however we argue that specifications should be actively maintained as code changes. Work with a similar approach includes LARVA [10], which provides specification formalisms with a low level of abstraction, but that focus on the order of events, which is not the focus of iCFTL. Further, CARET [2,25] allows references to (untimed) function calls and returns. In contrast, iCFTL enables one to talk about time and data, alongside function calls (which are not separated into call and return events).

The monitoring approach used for iCFTL varies from many used in RV in that many approaches use automata [7,20]. Given that iCFTL specifications are universally-quantified, and must be in prenex-normal form, there is some similarity between our monitoring approach and that used for the Quantified Event Automata formalism [3]. Here, bindings are generated and a central monitor structure (an automaton) is instantiated for each binding. If one replaces these automata with our formula trees, the approaches are similar.

Our instrumentation approach applies static analysis to determine the program points from which data should be taken at runtime. We also use instrumentation to optimise lookup. There are multiple bodies of work in RV that use instrumentation to optimise the monitoring process. The most notable include CLARA [8], which applies a series of static analyses in order to decide which statements do not need to be instrumented (and in order to generate a *residual property*, which is a property that has been partially proved during static analysis), and STARVOORS [1], which attempts to prove pre- and post-conditions of specifications written in a specification formalism that combines DATEs [10] and Dynamic Logic [19].

9   Conclusion

The central contribution of this paper is our new specification language, iCFTL (Inter-procedural Control-Flow Temporal Logic). This new logic enables the expression of properties concerning the inter-procedural, source code level behaviour of programs. Such properties cannot be expressed in CFTL, which focuses on the intra-procedural setting.

Our development of iCFTL has involved introduction of an initial monitoring algorithm, along with the acknowledgement that this does not scale well for larger traces. To remedy the situation, we have made reference to our previous work on instrumentation which can be applied with almost no modification. To demonstrate the expressiveness of iCFTL, we have extended the existing VYPR framework and applied it to a case study:

a Web service used at the CMS Experiment at CERN. This case study has demonstrated that more properties can be checked, leading to enhanced analysis capability of the VYPR framework.

Key directions for future work identified so far include 1) refining our instrumentation approach and 2) translating the explanation machinery presented recently [14, 16] into the inter-procedural setting.

Acknowledgments. The research described has been carried out as part of the COSMOS, which has received funding from the European Union's Horizon 2020 Research and Innovation Programme under grant agreement No. 957254. The authors wish to thank Lionel Briand for his feedback on iCFTL, and the CMS Experiment at CERN for help with the case study.

References

1. Ahrendt, W., Pace, G.J., Schneider, G.: A unified approach for static and runtime verification: framework and applications. In: Margaria, T., Steffen, B. (eds.) ISoLA 2012, Part I. LNCS, vol. 7609, pp. 312–326. Springer, Heidelberg (2012). https://doi.org/10.1007/978-3-642-34026-0_24

2. Alur, R., Etessami, K., Madhusudan, P.: A temporal logic of nested calls and returns. In: Jensen, K., Podelski, A. (eds.) TACAS 2004. LNCS, vol. 2988, pp. 467–481. Springer, Heidelberg (2004). https://doi.org/10.1007/978-3-540-24730-2_35

3. Barringer, H., Falcone, Y., Havelund, K., Reger, G., Rydeheard, D.: Quantified event automata: towards expressive and efficient runtime monitors. In: Giannakopoulou, D., Méry, D. (eds.) FM 2012. LNCS, vol. 7436, pp. 68–84. Springer, Heidelberg (2012). https://doi.org/10.1007/978-3-642-32759-9_9

4. Barringer, H., Goldberg, A., Havelund, K., Sen, K.: Rule-based runtime verification. In: Steffen, B., Levi, G. (eds.) VMCAI 2004. LNCS, vol. 2937, pp. 44–57. Springer, Heidelberg (2004). https://doi.org/10.1007/978-3-540-24622-0_5

5. Bartocci, E., Falcone, Y., Francalanza, A., Reger, G.: Introduction to runtime verification. In: Bartocci, E., Falcone, Y. (eds.) Lectures on Runtime Verification. LNCS, vol. 10457, pp. 1–33. Springer, Cham (2018). https://doi.org/10.1007/978-3-319-75632-5_1

6. Bauer, A., Leucker, M., Schallhart, C.: Comparing LTL semantics for runtime verification. J. Log. Comput. **20**(3), 651–674 (2010)

7. Bensalem, S., Bozga, M., Krichen, M., Tripakis, S.: Testing conformance of real-time applications by automatic generation of observers. Electron. Notes Theor. Comput. Sci. **113**, 23–43 (2005)

8. Bodden, E., Lam, P., Hendren, L.: Clara: a framework for partially evaluating finite-state runtime monitors ahead of time. In: Barringer, H., et al. (eds.) RV 2010. LNCS, vol. 6418, pp. 183–197. Springer, Heidelberg (2010). https://doi.org/10.1007/978-3-642-16612-9_15

9. CERN: Compact Muon Solenoid experiment. https://home.cern/science/experiments/cms

10. Colombo, C., Pace, G.J., Schneider, G.: Dynamic event-based runtime monitoring of real-time and contextual properties. In: Cofer, D., Fantechi, A. (eds.) FMICS 2008. LNCS, vol. 5596, pp. 135–149. Springer, Heidelberg (2009). https://doi.org/10.1007/978-3-642-03240-0_13

11. D'Angelo, B., et al.: LOLA: runtime monitoring of synchronous systems. In: 12th International Symposium on Temporal Representation and Reasoning (TIME 2005), Burlington, Vermont, USA, 23–25 June 2005, pp. 166–174. IEEE Computer Society (2005). https://doi.org/10.1109/TIME.2005.26

12. Dawes, J.H.: A Python object-oriented framework for the CMS alignment and calibration data. In: Journal of Physics: Conference Series, vol. 898, p. 042059, October 2017. https://doi.org/10.1088/1742-6596/898/4/042059
13. Dawes, J.H.: Towards automated performance analysis of programs by runtime verification. Ph.D. thesis, University of Manchester (2021)
14. Dawes, J.H., Han, M., Javed, O., Reger, G., Franzoni, G., Pfeiffer, A.: Analysing the performance of Python-based web services with the VYPR framework. In: Deshmukh, J., Ničković, D. (eds.) RV 2020. LNCS, vol. 12399, pp. 67–86. Springer, Cham (2020). https://doi.org/10.1007/978-3-030-60508-7_4
15. Dawes, J.H., Han, M., Reger, G., Franzoni, G., Pfeiffer, A.: Analysis tools for the VyPR framework for Python. In: International Conference on Computing in High Energy and Nuclear Physics, Adelaide, Australia 2019 (2019)
16. Dawes, J.H., Reger, G.: Explaining violations of properties in control-flow temporal logic. In: Finkbeiner, B., Mariani, L. (eds.) RV 2019. LNCS, vol. 11757, pp. 202–220. Springer, Cham (2019). https://doi.org/10.1007/978-3-030-32079-9_12
17. Dawes, J.H., Reger, G.: Specification of temporal properties of functions for runtime verification. In: Hung, C., Papadopoulos, G.A. (eds.) Proceedings of the 34th ACM/SIGAPP Symposium on Applied Computing, SAC 2019, Limassol, Cyprus, 8–12 April 2019, pp. 2206–2214. ACM (2019). https://doi.org/10.1145/3297280.3297497
18. Dou, W., Bianculli, D., Briand, L.C.: A model-driven approach to trace checking of pattern-based temporal properties. In: 20th ACM/IEEE International Conference on Model Driven Engineering Languages and Systems, MODELS 2017, Austin, TX, USA, 17–22 September 2017, pp. 323–333. IEEE Computer Society (2017). https://doi.org/10.1109/MODELS.2017.9
19. Fischer, M.J., Ladner, R.E.: Propositional dynamic logic of regular programs. J. Comput. Syst. Sci. **18**(2), 194–211 (1979)
20. Gastin, P., Oddoux, D.: Fast LTL to Büchi automata translation. In: Berry, G., Comon, H., Finkel, A. (eds.) CAV 2001. LNCS, vol. 2102, pp. 53–65. Springer, Heidelberg (2001). https://doi.org/10.1007/3-540-44585-4_6
21. Hallé, S.: When RV meets CEP. In: Falcone, Y., Sánchez, C. (eds.) RV 2016. LNCS, vol. 10012, pp. 68–91. Springer, Cham (2016). https://doi.org/10.1007/978-3-319-46982-9_6
22. Kim, M., Viswanathan, M., Kannan, S., Lee, I., Sokolsky, O.: Java-MaC: a run-time assurance approach for Java programs. Formal Methods Syst. Des. **24**(2), 129–155 (2004)
23. Koymans, R.: Specifying real-time properties with metric temporal logic. Real Time Syst. **2**(4), 255–299 (1990)
24. Pnueli, A.: The temporal logic of programs. In: 18th Annual Symposium on Foundations of Computer Science, Providence, Rhode Island, USA, 31 October–1 November 1977, pp. 46–57. IEEE Computer Society (1977). https://doi.org/10.1109/SFCS.1977.32
25. Roşu, G., Chen, F., Ball, T.: Synthesizing monitors for safety properties: this time with calls and returns. In: Leucker, M. (ed.) RV 2008. LNCS, vol. 5289, pp. 51–68. Springer, Heidelberg (2008). https://doi.org/10.1007/978-3-540-89247-2_4

Into the Unknown: Active Monitoring of Neural Networks

Anna Lukina[1]($\boxtimes$) , Christian Schilling[2]($\boxtimes$) , and Thomas A. Henzinger[1]

[1] Institute of Science and Technology Austria, Klosterneuburg, Austria
{anna.lukina,thomas.henzinger}@ist.ac.at
[2] University of Konstanz, Konstanz, Germany
christian.schilling@uni-konstanz.de

Abstract. Neural-network classifiers achieve high accuracy when predicting the class of an input that they were trained to identify. Maintaining this accuracy in dynamic environments, where inputs frequently fall outside the fixed set of initially known classes, remains a challenge. The typical approach is to detect inputs from novel classes and retrain the classifier on an augmented dataset. However, not only the classifier but also the detection mechanism needs to adapt in order to distinguish between newly learned and yet unknown input classes. To address this challenge, we introduce an algorithmic framework for active monitoring of a neural network. A monitor wrapped in our framework operates in parallel with the neural network and interacts with a human user via a series of interpretable labeling queries for incremental adaptation. In addition, we propose an adaptive quantitative monitor to improve precision. An experimental evaluation on a diverse set of benchmarks with varying numbers of classes confirms the benefits of our active monitoring framework in dynamic scenarios.

Keywords: Monitoring · Neural networks · Novelty detection

1 Introduction

Automated classification is an essential part of numerous modern technologies and one of the most popular applications of deep neural networks [21]. Neural-network image classifiers have fast-forwarded technological development in many research areas, e.g., automated object localization as a stepping stone to successful real-world robotic applications [41]. Such applications require a high level of reliability from the neural networks.

However, when deployed in the real world, neural networks face a common problem of novel input classes appearing at prediction time, leading to possible misclassifications and system failures. For example, consider a scenario of a neural network used for labeling inputs and making decisions about the next actions for an automated system with limited human supervision: a robot assistant learning to recognize objects in a new home. Assume the neural network

L. Feng and D. Fisman (Eds.): RV 2021, LNCS 12974, pp. 42–61, 2021.
https://doi.org/10.1007/978-3-030-88494-9_3

is trained well on a dataset containing examples of a finite set of classes. However, after this robot is deployed in the real home, novel classes of objects can appear and confuse the neural network. The inherent misclassifications can stay undetected and accumulate over time, eventually reducing overall accuracy.

The likelihood of severe system damage increases with the frequency and diversity of novel input classes. Typically, this risk is addressed by detecting novel inputs, augmenting the training dataset, and retraining the classifier from scratch [29]. This procedure is not only inefficient, but also leaves the system vulnerable until such a dataset has been collected. Techniques to incrementally adapt classifiers at prediction time are beneficial for improving accuracy in real-world applications [32,34]. They, however, do not provide desired interpretability for the human. Approaches to run-time monitoring of neural networks were therefore introduced [31]. In particular, approaches based on abstractions [4,5, 15,43] proved to be effective at detecting novel input classes. In addition, they provide transparency of neural-network monitoring.

Crucially, these monitors are constructed offline and remain static at prediction time. Functionalities they are still lacking are distinguishing between "known" and "unknown" novelties and selectively adapting at prediction time.

We propose an active monitoring framework for neural networks that detects novel input classes, obtains the correct labels from a human authority, and adapts the neural network and the monitor to the novel classes, all at prediction time. The framework contains a mechanism for automatic switching between monitoring and adaptation based on run-time statistics. Adaptation consists of either learning new classes (when enough data has been collected) or retraining with more up-to-date information (when the run-time performance is unsatisfactory), where retraining is applied to the network and the monitor independently. A trained neural-network model accompanied by our framework, as an external observer and mediator between the neural network and the human, achieves improved transparency of operation through informative interaction.

Furthermore, we propose a new monitor designed for the adaptive setting. Introducing a quantitative metric at the hidden layers of the neural network, the monitor timely warns about inputs of novel classes and reports its own confidence to the authority. This allows for assessing the need of model adaptation. The quantitative metric allows for easy adaptation at prediction time to newly introduced labels and successfully maintains overall classification accuracy on inputs of known and previously novel classes combined. As such, our framework is an interactive and interpretable tool for informed decision making in neural-network based applications. We summarize the contributions of this paper below.

1. We propose an automatic framework with two modes, monitoring and adaptation, that operates in parallel with the original neural network and adapts the monitor to novel input classes at prediction time.
2. We propose a quantitative metric to measure the confidence of the novelty detection and to guide the monitor refinement. In contrast to traditional qualitative monitoring, which judges whether or not an observed input-output pair of the network is reliable, our *quantitative* monitoring approach computes a

numerical "reliability score" for each observed input-output pair. The score corresponds to the distance of values in feature space at training and prediction time.

3. We provide an experimental evaluation on a diverse set of image-classification benchmarks, demonstrating the effectiveness of the framework for achieving high monitor precision over time. Given a fixed budget of times the monitor can query the authority for a label, our monitoring approach adapts to the available classes and consumes the budget more effectively.

After reviewing the related work in the next section, we provide the background and assumptions used throughout the paper in Sect. 3. We describe our quantitative monitor and the process of adaptation in Sect. 4. We report on our experimental results in Sect. 5 and conclude in Sect. 6.

2   Related Work

Novelty Detection. Gupta and Carlone consider neural networks that estimate human poses, for which they propose a domain-specific monitoring algorithm trained on perturbed inputs [13]. Our framework is not limited to any specific domain of images. Common novelty-detection approaches [30] examine the input sample distribution [18], which is computationally heavier at run-time than our monitors. Several approaches monitor the neuron valuations and compare to a "normal" representation of those valuations per class, obtained for a training dataset: the patterns of neuron indices with highest values [36] or positive/nonpositive values [5], and a box abstraction [15,16,43]. These monitors are purely qualitative and hence not adaptive, in contrast to our metric-based monitor.

Anomaly Detection. There exist other directions for detecting more general anomalous behavior, not necessarily only novel classes. In *selective classification*, an input is rejected based on a (quantitative) confidence score, already at training time [10]. The probably best-known approach classifies based on the *softmax* score [12,14], which is shown to be limited in effect [9]. Approaches to *failure prediction* aim to identify misclassifications of *known* classes [45]. *Domain adaptation* techniques detect when the underlying data distribution changes, which is necessary for statistical methods to work reliably [33]. Notably, Royer and Lampert show that correlations in the data distribution can be exploited to increase a classifier's precision [34]; while that approach applies to arbitrary classifiers in an unsupervised setting, it cannot deal with unknown classes. Sun and Lampert study the detection of *out-of-spec situations*, when classes do not occur with the expected frequency [39]. An important aspect of domain adaptation, *transfer learning* [28,40], is challenging online [47].

Continuous/Incremental Learning. A central obstacle in incremental learning is *catastrophic forgetting*: the classifier's precision for known classes decreases over time [26]. We mitigate that obstacle by maintaining a sample of the training data and tuning the model on demand. Mensink et al. find that a simple nearest-class-mean (NCM) classifier (mapping an input to feature space and choosing the closest centroid of all known classes) is effective [27]; they also consider multiple centroids per class, as we do, but they use the Mahalanobis distance in contrast to our more lightweight distance. Guerriero et al. extend that idea to nonlinear deep models, where the focus is on efficiency to avoid constant retraining [11]; we also delay retraining (network and monitor) until precision deteriorates. Rebuffi et al. extend the NCM classifier for *class-incremental learning* with fixed memory requirements [32]. That learning approach, working in a completely supervised scenario, retrains the neural network using sample selection/herding and rehearsal. These ideas could also be integrated in our framework, but a representative sampling for our monitor is harder to obtain. Similar to the NCM approach is the proposal by Mandelbaum and Weinshall to obtain a confidence score using a k-nearest-neighbor distance based on the Euclidean distance with respect to the training dataset, for which they require to modify the training procedure [25]; we do not need access to the training procedure and we experimentally found that the Euclidean distance is not suitable for networks with different scales at different neurons.

Active Learning. Our approach is inspired by active learning. Active learning aims to maximize prediction accuracy even on unseen data by detecting the most representative novel inputs to label and incrementally retraining the neural network on a selected sample of labeled novelties [37]. In contrast, the performance of our framework is measured primarily by the run-time precision of the monitor. We therefore use the incrementally retrained neural network solely for the monitor adaptation in parallel with the original model. Our quantitative monitor also reasons about the feature space of the neural network (and not the input space).

An essential idea behind active learning is that, when selecting the training data systematically, fewer training samples are needed; this selection is usually taken at run-time by posing labeling queries to an authority [37]. Our approach follows the spirit of *selective sampling*, where data comes from a stream, from the *region of uncertainty* [7]. Das et al. follow a statistical approach to outlier detection adapting to the reactions of the authority [8].

In an *open world* setting, novel classes have to be detected on the fly and the classifier needs to be adapted accordingly. This setting is first approached in [1] using an NCM classifier and in [2] with a softmax score. More recently, Mancini et al. propose a deep architecture for learning new classes dynamically [24]. Wagstaff et al. argue that two main obstacles in this setting are the cold starts and the cost of having the classifier in the loop [42].

3   Background and Assumptions

In this paper, we deal with neural networks, which we denote by $\mathcal{N}$. For simplicity we present the concepts assuming a single feature layer ℓ of the network, but they generalize to multiple feature layers in a straightforward way. A *monitor* is a function that takes both an input and the prediction of a classifier, and then assesses whether that prediction is correct. The monitor raises a warning if it suspects that the prediction is incorrect. The assessment can be qualitative ("yes" or "no") or quantitative (expressing the confidence of the monitor). We write $\vec{x}$ for an unlabeled data point, $\mathcal{X}$ for a (possibly labeled) dataset, $y \in \mathcal{Y}$ for a class in a set of classes, and $(\vec{x}, y)$ for a labeled data point.

Observing Feature Layers: We are given a trained neural network $\mathcal{N}$ and a labeled dataset $\mathcal{X}$ with classes $\mathcal{Y}$ (which is not necessarily the dataset that $\mathcal{N}$ was trained on). When we *observe a feature layer* ℓ for some input, we obtain the corresponding neuron valuations at layer ℓ, which we regard as high-dimensional vectors. We can thus compute the set of neuron valuations $\mathcal{V}_y$ for each class $y \in \mathcal{Y}$ and each corresponding sample in $\mathcal{X}$.

Performance Metrics: As conventionally used for assessing the performance of classifiers and monitors, we compute the *precision score*. For a classifier this is the ratio of correct classifications over all predictions, while for a monitor this is the ratio of correct warnings (true positives, TP) over the total number of warnings (including false positives, FP): $\text{TP}/(\text{TP} + \text{FP})$. At run-time we can only compute the precision score based on samples that we know the ground truth for, i.e., samples reported by the monitor and subsequently labeled by an authority.

Hyperparameters: We define the *model performance threshold* $s^*_{network}$ as 95% of the precision score of the original neural-network model $\mathcal{N}$ on a test dataset (with classes known to $\mathcal{N}$), which we use for making decisions about model adaptation. The parameter $s^*_{samples}$ is the number of collected and labeled data samples of a novel class sufficient for incremental adaptation of the model to this class, which we set to $s^*_{samples} = 0.05 \cdot |\mathcal{X}|/|\mathcal{Y}|$ for an initially given dataset. The parameter $s^*_{monitor}$ is the desired precision threshold of the monitor at run-time, which we set to 0.9. The parameters $d^*(y)$ (for each class $y \in \mathcal{Y}$) are thresholds for refining the set of inputs detected by the monitor, initialized to 1.

Assumptions: In this work we make a number of assumptions. First, we assume the availability of an authority that assigns the correct label for any input that is requested. While a human can play this role in many cases, in certain applications like medical image processing such an authority does not necessarily exist. Second, in our experimental setup we assume that the authority is available in real time. We also occasionally adapt the monitor or retrain the neural network. While faster than building from scratch, this takes a non-negligible amount of time. In time-critical applications one would need to delay these interactions and adaptations accordingly. Third, neural networks require a large amount of data points in order to learn new classes. In our evaluation there is sufficient data available. Still, there are approaches that work with only few samples [3,23].

4 Approach

We design our monitoring framework to achieve high precision in detecting novel classes without depressing the learned model's run-time performance. To address this trade-off, our framework operates in stages, switching between monitoring and adaptation. This procedure is based on parallel composition of two components: a dynamically adapted copy of the original neural network and a monitor that originally knows the same classes as the network. During monitoring, inputs to the network that are reported by the monitor are submitted to an authority for assigning the correct label. From that, precision scores for both the monitor and the neural network are assessed for whether adaptation is required. During adaptation, depending on the assessment, the neural network or the monitor is incrementally adjusted, or they are retrained in order to learn an unknown class.

4.1 Quantitative Monitor

In addition to a general framework, we also propose a quantitative monitor for neural networks that fits well into the framework. In a nutshell, our quantitative monitor works as follows. At run-time, given an input $\vec{x}$ and a corresponding prediction y of the neural network, the monitor observes the feature layer ℓ and compares its valuation to a model of "typical" behavior for the class y. Next we describe the steps to initialize this monitor, i.e., to construct said behavioral model, which are also illustrated in Fig. 1. Given a labeled training dataset, we observe the neuron valuations $\mathcal{V}_y$ for each class $y \in \mathcal{Y}$ (Fig. 1(a)). We then apply a clustering algorithm to the sets $\mathcal{V}_y$ (Fig. 1(b)). In our implementation, we use a *k-means* [22] algorithm that finds a suitable k dynamically.

So far the initialization is shared with the qualitative monitor from [15], which would next compute the *box abstraction* for each cluster. A qualitative abstraction-based monitor can only determine whether a point lies inside the abstraction (here: a box) or not. Since we are interested in a quantitative monitor, we instead define a *distance function* below.

Distance Function. We set reference points for computing the distance function at the cluster centers. This way the majority of points have low distance. Below we describe the particular distance function that we found effective in our evaluation, which we also depict in Fig. 1(c) and (d). We note, however, that the idea generalizes to arbitrary metrics.

Let us fix a class $y \in \mathcal{Y}$ and a corresponding cluster B^y with center $\vec{c} = (c_1, \ldots, c_n)^{\mathrm{T}}$ of dimension n. Let $\vec{r} = (r_1, \ldots, r_n)^{\mathrm{T}}$ be the radius of the bounding box around the cluster. We define the distance of a point $\vec{p} = (p_1, \ldots, p_n)^{\mathrm{T}}$ to B^y as the maximum absolute difference to $\vec{c}$ in any projected dimension i, normalized by the radius r_i:

$$d_+(\vec{p}, B^y) = \max_i |c_i - p_i| \cdot r_i^{-1}.$$

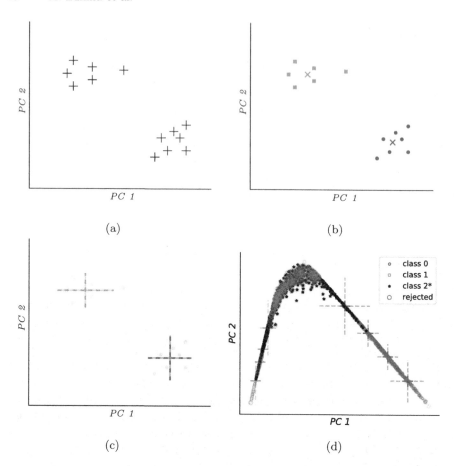

Fig. 1. Illustration of the steps for initializing the quantitative monitor on a fixed class, in a two-dimensional projection on the first two principal components PC 1 and PC 2 of the feature layer ℓ. (a) Sampling of data points. (b) Result of clustering (here: two clusters • and ▪) where $\times$ and $\times$ respectively mark the cluster centers. (c) Quantitative metric for each cluster, visualized as dashed lines. (d) Projection of an initialized quantitative monitor and its detection results for a network trained on the first two classes of the MNIST dataset.

The distance generalizes to a set $\mathcal{B}^y$ of clusters for the same class y by taking the minimum distance in the set:

$$d_+(\vec{p}, y) = \min_{B^y \in \mathcal{B}^y} d_+(\vec{p}, B^y).$$

Computing the distance is linear in the dimension (i.e., the number of neurons in the feature layer). We note that we can in principle also generalize the distance to a set of classes $\mathcal{Y}$ in order to obtain a new classifier. In this paper, for the purpose of monitoring, we just compare the distance for a fixed class to some class-specific threshold (which we explain later).

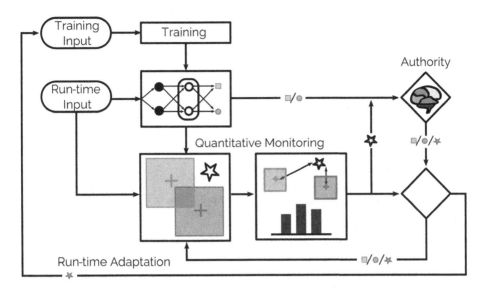

Fig. 2. High-level overview of the framework. The neural-network classifier receives an input at run-time (top left). This input is classified while the monitor watches the classification process. The authority is only queried for the correct label if the monitor reports a misclassification. That may trigger, depending on the result and the history, adaptation of the monitor or of the model.

4.2 Active Monitoring Algorithm

We now explain our active monitoring algorithm, summarized in Algorithm 1 and also illustrated in Fig. 2.

Initialization. We start with a trained neural network $\mathcal{N}$ with a feature layer ℓ and a dataset $\mathcal{X}$ with a number of classes (the "known" classes) as inputs. The first step in 2 is to initialize a monitor $\mathcal{M}$ for this network, for example as described in Sect. 4.1 for our quantitative monitor. Instead of working on the feature layer's neurons directly, we learn a transformation matrix by applying principal component analysis (PCA) [17] or Kernel PCA [35] to the neuron valuations $\mathcal{V}_y$. This transformation is not a requirement of our framework, and hence we omit it in the pseudocode; as we noticed experimentally, this step tends to further separate the valuations $\mathcal{V}_y$ and $\mathcal{V}_{y'}$ for different classes $y' \neq y$, which improves the overall monitor precision.

Monitoring Stage (Lines 4–11). At run-time, we apply our framework to a stream of inputs. For each input $\vec{x}$, we perform the following steps. We first apply the neural network to obtain both the class prediction y and the (principal components of the) neuron valuations $\vec{p}$ at the feature layer ℓ. We then query the monitor $\mathcal{M}$ about the prediction. In the case of the quantitative monitor, $\mathcal{M}$ computes the distance $d_+(\vec{p}, y)$ with respect to the predicted class y. Then $\mathcal{M}$

Algorithm 1: Active monitoring

Input: $\mathcal{N}$: trained model
$\mathcal{X}$: training data
$\mathcal{X}_{run}$: online input stream

1 **while** *True* **do**
2 | $\mathcal{M}, \mathcal{Y} \leftarrow$ **buildMonitor**$(\mathcal{N}, \mathcal{X}, \ell)$ // build monitor $\mathcal{M}$ and extract known classes $\mathcal{Y}$ from $\mathcal{X}$
3 | **while** *True* **do**
   | | // monitoring mode
4 | | $\vec{x} \leftarrow$ **get**$(\mathcal{X}_{run})$ // get next input $\vec{x}$
5 | | $y \leftarrow$ **classify**$(\mathcal{N}, \vec{x})$ // predict class of $\vec{x}$
6 | | $\vec{p} \leftarrow$ **observe**$(\mathcal{N}, \vec{x}, \ell)$ // observe output at layer ℓ
7 | | *warning*, $\vec{s} \leftarrow$ **monitor**$(\vec{p}, y, \mathcal{M})$ // monitor and compute statistics $\vec{s}$
8 | | **if** *warning* **then**
9 | | | $y^{*} \leftarrow$ **askAuthority**$(\vec{x}, y, d_{+}(\vec{p}, y))$
10 | | | $\mathcal{X} \leftarrow$ **collect**$(\vec{x}, y^{*}, \mathcal{X})$ // add labeled pair $(\vec{x}, y^{*})$ to $\mathcal{X}$
11 | | | *adapt_model* $\leftarrow$ **evaluate**$(\vec{s}, \mathcal{X}, \mathcal{Y})$
   | | | // adaptation mode
12 | | | **if** *adapt_model* **then**
13 | | | | $\mathcal{N}, \mathcal{M}, \mathcal{X} \leftarrow$ **adaptModel**$(\mathcal{N}, \mathcal{X})$ Ⓑ
14 | | | | **break**
15 | | | $\mathcal{M} \leftarrow$ **adaptMonitor**$(\vec{s}, \mathcal{M}, \mathcal{N}, \mathcal{X})$ Ⓐ
16 | | **end**
17 | **end**
18 **end**

---

compares this distance to a class-specific threshold d_{y}^{*}; initially this threshold is set to 1, but we increase this value during the course of the algorithm later.

In the simple case that $d_{+}(\vec{p}, y) \leq d_{y}^{*}$, the monitor does not raise a warning and the framework just returns the predicted class y for input $\vec{x}$ (not shown in the pseudocode). Otherwise the monitor rejects the network prediction as unknown. In this case we query the authority to provide the ground truth y^{*} for input $\vec{x}$ and add the pair $(\vec{x}, y^{*})$ to our training dataset $\mathcal{X}$. For our quantitative monitor we additional provide the authority with the distance $d_{+}(\vec{p}, y)$ as a confidence measure, while for qualitative monitors this argument is missing. The procedure **evaluate**$(\vec{s}, \mathcal{X}, \mathcal{Y})$, where $\vec{s} = \{s_{network}, s_{samples}, s_{monitor}\}$, decides between the following two scenarios, which we describe afterward.

Ⓐ The ground truth matches the prediction $(y^{*} = y)$. In this case it was not correct to raise a warning and we continue with the monitor adaptation.

Ⓑ The ground truth does not match the prediction $(y^{*} \neq y)$, possibly because y^{*} is unknown to $\mathcal{N}$. In this case it was correct to raise a warning and we continue with the model adaptation.

Monitor Adaptation (Line 15). Procedure **adaptMonitor**$(\vec{s}, \mathcal{M}, \mathcal{N}, \mathcal{X})$ for monitor adaptation in Ⓐ is triggered if a wrong warning was raised and only applies to our quantitative monitor. Recall that the reason for raising a warning is that the distance of $\vec{p}$ exceeds the threshold for class y. We do not immediately adapt the monitor every time it raises a wrong warning. Instead we keep track of the monitor's performance over time in terms of a score $s_{monitor}$ as defined in Sect. 3. We only adapt the monitor if $s_{monitor}$ drops below a user-defined threshold $s^*_{monitor}$. The adaptation performs two simple steps. First, we adapt the cluster centers to the new collected data in $\mathcal{X}$. Second, we adapt the distance threshold d^*_y as follows. Let $s_{samples}$ be the number of samples of class y that we have already collected in $\mathcal{X}$, and let $s^*_{samples}$ be a learning threshold as defined in Sect. 3. We define the new threshold d^*_y (which increases compared to the old value) as

$$d^*_y + (d_+(\vec{p}, y) - d^*_y) \cdot \frac{s^*_{samples}}{s_{samples}}.$$

Model Adaptation (Lines 12–14). In contrast to monitor adaptation, *model* adaptation in Ⓑ involves retraining the neural-network model in order to learn novel classes of inputs. Procedure **adaptModel**($\mathcal{N}$, $\mathcal{X}$) performs this adaptation only if one of the following conditions is satisfied:

Ⓑ.1 The number of collected samples labeled by the authority reaches a predefined threshold $s^*_{samples}$ (see Sect. 3).

Ⓑ.2 The precision score of the current model $s_{network}$ falls below the desired value $s^*_{network}$ (see Sect. 3).

In Ⓑ.1, using the dataset $\mathcal{X}$ replenished with the data points reported by the monitor and labeled by the authority, we identify which class (or multiple classes) should be learned, based on the collected statistics $\vec{s}$. We then employ transfer learning [28] to train a new model that recognizes this class (classes) in addition to the ones already known. Specifically, we remove the output layer and all trailing layers until the last fully connected one and then add a new output layer corresponding to the desired number of classes present in $\mathcal{X}$. From the newly compiled model we also augment the monitor. In the case of our quantitative monitor, we apply the steps from Sect. 4.1 for the new class(es) and set the corresponding distance threshold(s) to 1.

In Ⓑ.2, we rely on regular run-time measurements of the precision score for the current model. Algorithmically, this is achieved by keeping a separate (not used for retraining) test dataset after each successful transfer learning. We collect only the inputs reported by our monitor and subsequently labeled by the authority. This is in line with our main objective for the human in the loop to remain the ultimate trustee for the framework.

Remark 1. The model obtained from transfer learning on the accumulated labeled samples is not meant as a replacement for the original model provided at the initialization stage but rather as an assistant to ongoing active monitoring.

This concludes all possible cases for one iteration of the algorithm. This process is repeated for each input in the stream.

Table 1. Dataset and model description. The columns show the number of samples for training and testing, the number of classes in total and initially known to the network, the ID of the network architecture, and the full dimension (i.e., number of neurons) of the monitored layer.

Dataset	Dataset size train/test	Classes all/init	Net ID	Dimension full
MNIST	60,000/10,000	10/5	1	40
FMNIST	60,000/10,000	10/5	1	40
CIFAR10	50,000/10,000	10/5	3	256
GTSRB	39,209/12,630	43/22	2	84
EMNIST	112,800/18,800	47/24	1	40

5   Experiments

We perform two experiments. In the first experiment we compare our quantitative monitor to three other (static) monitoring strategies: a box-abstraction monitor [15], a monitor based on the softmax score [14], and a monitor that warns with uniform random rate. We evaluate these monitors on five image-classification datasets. In the second experiment we investigate the influence of different parameters on our quantitative monitor specifically.

5.1   Benchmark Datasets

We consider the following publicly available datasets, summarized in Table 1: MNIST [20], Fashion MNIST (FMNIST) [44], and Extended MNIST (EMNIST) [6] consist of 28×28 grayscale images; CIFAR10 [19] and the German Traffic Sign Recognition Benchmark (GTSRB) [38] consist of 32×32 color images.

For each of these benchmarks we trained two neural-network models: one model trained on all classes, which we refer to as the "static full" model, and one model trained on half of the classes, which we refer to as the "static half" model. We used VGG16 [46] pretrained on ImageNet for CIFAR10 and the architectures from [5] for MNIST (which we also use for FMNIST and EMNIST) and GTSRB.

5.2   Experimental Setup

We let the framework process inputs in batches of size 128. For each dataset we ran our active monitoring framework on reshuffled data five times.

We evaluate our active monitoring framework with four different monitoring strategies, each of which uses the same overall processing within the framework, e.g., the same sequence of samples in the input stream and the same policy for model adaptation. The strategy based on the softmax score rejects inputs when the score falls below 0.9. The random strategy rejects inputs with probability

$p = 5\%$ (resp. $p = 10\%$ in the EMNIST experiment). To make the comparison fair, we limit the number of available authority queries for each strategy to a budget of p (the random rejection probability) percent of the full dataset. For most of the benchmarks we used PCA and $s^*_{samples}$ as explained in Sect. 3. For CIFAR10, we used Kernel PCA and $s^*_{samples} = 0.01 \cdot |\mathcal{X}|/|\mathcal{Y}|$ instead.

We implemented our framework in Python 3.6 with Tensorflow 2.2 and scikit-learn. We ran all experiments on an i7-8550U@1.80 GHz CPU with 32 GB RAM. The source code and scripts that we used are available online[1].

Table 2. Monitor comparison. We compare four different monitoring strategies: quantitative (this paper), box abstraction, softmax score, and random warning. For each benchmark we report the interaction limit with the authority, the highest number of learned classes, and the average monitoring precision of five runs. The best results per benchmark are marked in **bold**.

Dataset	Interaction limit	Quantitative class/prec	Abstraction class/prec	Softmax class/prec	Random class/prec
MNIST	3,000	**10** **0.81 ± 0.01**	**10** 0.6 ± 0.02	**10** 0.71 ± 0.01	6 0.48 ± 0.01
FMNIST	3,000	9 **0.74 ± 0.02**	9 0.54 ± 0.02	**10** 0.7 ± 0.01	8 0.5 ± 0.01
CIFAR10	2,500	**10** **0.75 ± 0.02**	**10** 0.61 ± 0.02	**10** 0.53 ± 0.01	**10** 0.41 ± 0.01
GTSRB	1,960	37 0.67 ± 0.02	**38** 0.7 ± 0.01	34 **0.75 ± 0.03**	25 0.29 ± 0.01
EMNIST	11,280	42 **0.81 ± 0.01**	**47** 0.71 ± 0.02	**47** 0.69 ± 0.01	**47** 0.39 ± 0.01

5.3   Experimental Results

General Performance. The performance of the different monitoring strategies in terms of monitoring precision is averaged over five runs and summarized in Table 2. For all but one benchmark our monitor achieves the highest precision, and for GTSRB the precision is comparable with other monitors. Figure 3 shows the evolution of the monitor precision over time as more classes are learned. Recall that the network is dynamically retrained (using transfer learning) for new classes. Clearly, the number of new samples for this training procedure is lower than in a normal, full-fledged training. Consequently, the adapted network is less precise for these new classes (cf. Table 3) than a network trained on the full training dataset. Hence it is expected that the general trend in the monitoring precision is decreasing for all strategies.

---

[1] https://github.com/VeriXAI/Into-the-Unknown.

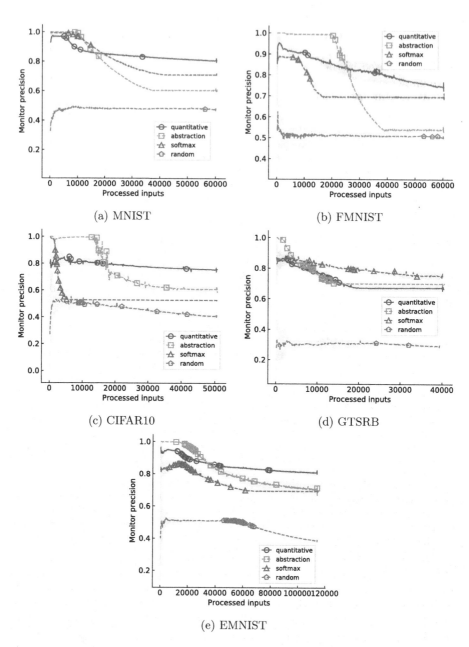

Fig. 3. Comparison of the monitor precision between four monitoring strategies, averaged over five runs and including 95%-confidence bands. The markers correspond to points in time when a model adaptation takes place.

Table 3. Model adaptation. We compare the static model trained on 50% of the classes, the static model trained on all classes, and the model obtained from our framework (using the quantitative monitor), averaged over five runs. In the static cases, the test accuracy is measured on the filtered test set (not including novelties for the 50% model). The second column shows the epochs used for the initial training resp. the retraining/transfer learning at run-time.

Dataset	Epochs init/run	Static half train/test	Static full train/test	Adaptive test
MNIST	10/10	0.99/0.99	0.99/0.99	0.97 ± 0.01
FMNIST	10/10	0.99/0.92	0.97/0.91	0.79 ± 0.05
CIFAR10	50/30	0.99/0.83	0.99/0.79	0.54 ± 0.02
GTSRB	30/30	0.99/0.95	0.99/0.88	0.87 ± 0.01
EMNIST	30/30	0.97/0.92	0.92/0.86	0.71 ± 0.04

We report the test accuracy of the neural networks in Table 3, averaged over five runs per benchmark. The accuracy is generally lower than what could be achieved by training the network with a full and balanced dataset from scratch (the "static full" model), but for some benchmarks we achieve almost the same accuracy. This shows that the framework is able to adapt to new situations.

Cost Analysis. In Fig. 4, we show the frequency of authority queries over time. Recall that there is a budget of queries (cf. Table 2). Our quantitative monitor queries the authority more frequently at the beginning but as it adapts to more novel classes the rate of requests is steadily decreasing. Thus the monitor has the fewest queries in four of the five benchmarks (except for GTSRB). The other monitors do not have an adaptation mechanism and therefore are prone to querying the authority more often. For some monitors we even observe an increase in warnings over time, in particular the monitor that uses the softmax score. As we argued above, we suspect that the network tends to be less confident for newly learned classes, which results in lower softmax scores. Learning new classes often happens at roughly the same point in time. This is because the novelties appear with uniform distribution in the input stream; hence the points in time when a fixed number per class has been seen are close to each other.

Overall the plots do not reveal a clear trend which monitor is fastest at learning new classes. There is generally a trade-off between the rate at which a warning is raised and the rate at which new classes are learned. In our scenario, raising a warning is initially correct in 50% of the cases (note that none of the monitors is in that range); taken to the extreme, a monitor that always raises a warning would be the fastest in learning new classes. On the other hand, a monitor that generally raises fewer warnings to the authority may also miss novelties and thus learn slower. However, in our experience it is more preferred to provide a low false-positive rate, i.e., warnings raised by the monitor should be genuine. In this sense the quantitative monitor works best.

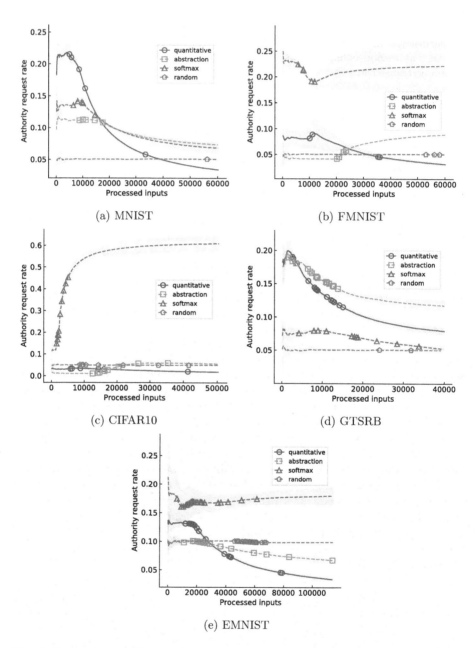

Fig. 4. Comparison of the rate of authority queries between four monitoring strategies, averaged over five runs and including 95%-confidence bands. The markers correspond to points in time when a model adaptation takes place.

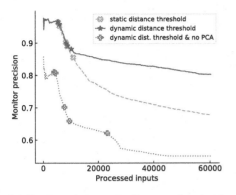
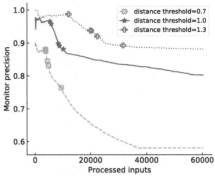

(a) Static and dynamic distance threshold.   (b) Different initial threshold values.

Fig. 5. Influence of the dynamic distance threshold $d^*(y)$ for each class y on the quantitative-monitor precision for the MNIST benchmark. The markers correspond to points in time when a model adaptation takes place. (a) Comparison between a static value and a dynamically changing value (as proposed in this paper); we also show a comparison with a run where we omit the preprocessing with PCA. (b) Influence of the initial value of the threshold.

Ablation and Sensitivity Study. All components of our framework contributed to its performance. In Fig. 3, we have illustrated how incremental retraining of the model improves the monitor precision for all monitoring strategies. In principle, other active-learning strategies can be plugged into our framework to further increase this effect. In addition, Fig. 3 demonstrates that the monitor-adaptation stage (where the monitor is incrementally adjusted without *model* adaptation), which only applies to our quantitative monitor, helps maintaining a better precision than the other monitoring strategies.

Figure 5(a) shows that dynamically changing the value of the distance threshold $d^*(y)$ (for each class y) contributes to the precision of our monitor, and so does the use of PCA for dimensionality reduction. Similarly, Fig. 5(b) shows that the starting value of the (dynamic) threshold also influences the monitor precision.

Timing Analysis. Table 4 shows a timing comparison for the individual adaptation stages of the framework, taken from the runs for the quantitative monitor strategy. (Comparing different strategies is generally difficult because they interact with the authority and adapt the model and/or the monitor in different orders and frequencies.) The time grows with the size of the dataset but on average is on the order of milliseconds per input; hence the framework can be run in real time. For CIFAR10 the time is dominated by the use of Kernel PCA.

Table 4. Average run times in seconds. For each benchmark we average (five runs) the time for retraining the neural network (when enough samples of a new class were collected), for retraining the monitor (after retraining the neural network), and for adapting the monitor (when the precision drops too much).

Dataset	Retrain network	Retrain monitor	Adapt monitor
MNIST	26 ± 1	59 ± 3	39 ± 5
FMNIST	19 ± 6	45 ± 10	59 ± 5
CIFAR10	257 ± 57	$2{,}477 \pm 282$	40 ± 3
GTSRB	228 ± 12	194 ± 24	19 ± 1
EMNIST	360 ± 191	347 ± 71	82 ± 16

6   Conclusion and Future Work

In this work, we have presented an active monitoring framework for accompanying a neural-network classifier during deployment. The framework adapts to unknown input classes via interaction with a human authority. Experiments on a diverse set of image-classification benchmarks showed that active monitoring is effective in improving accuracy over time in the setting when inputs of novel classes are frequently encountered. Moreover, we introduced a new quantitative monitor, providing the human with confidence about the reported warnings based on a distance to the predicted class in feature space. In comparison to alternative monitoring strategies, our monitor demonstrated superior performance in detection and adaptation at run-time. Our framework thus improves trustworthiness of automated decision making.

Our framework is independent of the choice of the dataset and the neural-network architecture. The only requirements for applicability of our approach are access to the output of the feature layer(s). We plan to extend our procedure toward real-world applications with particular need of active monitoring, e.g., in robotics for the trained controller to gradually adapt to the behavior of the authority. Other interesting directions are time-critical applications where the adaptation of the monitor or the neural network need to be delayed to uncritical phases, and scenarios where novel inputs occur rarely. In addition, the underlying method of our framework can serve as a suitable tool for designing an algorithmic approach to explainability of a neural network's predictions.

Acknowledgments. We thank Christoph Lampert and Alex Greengold for fruitful discussions. This research was supported in part by the Simons Institute for the Theory of Computing, the Austrian Science Fund (FWF) under grant Z211-N23 (Wittgenstein Award), and the European Union's Horizon 2020 research and innovation programme under the Marie Skłodowska-Curie grant agreement No. 754411.

References

1. Bendale, A., Boult, T.E.: Towards open world recognition. In: CVPR, pp. 1893–1902. IEEE Computer Society (2015). https://doi.org/10.1109/CVPR.2015.7298799

2. Bendale, A., Boult, T.E.: Towards open set deep networks. In: CVPR, pp. 1563–1572. IEEE Computer Society (2016). https://doi.org/10.1109/CVPR.2016.173

3. Bendre, N., Terashima-Marín, H., Najafirad, P.: Learning from few samples: a survey. CoRR abs/2007.15484 (2020). https://arxiv.org/abs/2007.15484

4. Chen, Y., Cheng, C., Yan, J., Yan, R.: Monitoring object detection abnormalities via data-label and post-algorithm abstractions. CoRR abs/2103.15456 (2021). https://arxiv.org/abs/2103.15456

5. Cheng, C., Nührenberg, G., Yasuoka, H.: Runtime monitoring neuron activation patterns. In: DATE, pp. 300–303. IEEE (2019). https://doi.org/10.23919/DATE.2019.8714971

6. Cohen, G., Afshar, S., Tapson, J., van Schaik, A.: EMNIST: extending MNIST to handwritten letters. In: IJCNN, pp. 2921–2926. IEEE (2017). https://doi.org/10.1109/IJCNN.2017.7966217

7. Cohn, D.A., Atlas, L.E., Ladner, R.E.: Improving generalization with active learning. Mach. Learn. **15**(2), 201–221 (1994). https://doi.org/10.1007/BF00993277

8. Das, S., Wong, W., Dietterich, T.G., Fern, A., Emmott, A.: Incorporating expert feedback into active anomaly discovery. In: ICDM, pp. 853–858. IEEE Computer Society (2016). https://doi.org/10.1109/ICDM.2016.0102

9. Gal, Y., Ghahramani, Z.: Dropout as a Bayesian approximation: representing model uncertainty in deep learning. In: ICML. JMLR Workshop and Conference Proceedings, vol. 48, pp. 1050–1059. JMLR.org (2016). http://proceedings.mlr.press/v48/gal16.html

10. Geifman, Y., El-Yaniv, R.: Selective classification for deep neural networks. In: NeurIPS, pp. 4878–4887 (2017). http://papers.nips.cc/paper/7073-selective-classification-for-deep-neural-networks

11. Guerriero, S., Caputo, B., Mensink, T.: DeepNCM: deep nearest class mean classifiers. In: ICLR. OpenReview.net (2018). https://openreview.net/forum?id=rkPLZ4JPM

12. Guo, C., Pleiss, G., Sun, Y., Weinberger, K.Q.: On calibration of modern neural networks. In: ICML. PMLR, vol. 70, pp. 1321–1330. PMLR (2017). http://proceedings.mlr.press/v70/guo17a.html

13. Gupta, A., Carlone, L.: Online monitoring for neural network based monocular pedestrian pose estimation. In: ITSC, pp. 1–8. IEEE (2020). https://doi.org/10.1109/ITSC45102.2020.9294609

14. Hendrycks, D., Gimpel, K.: A baseline for detecting misclassified and out-of-distribution examples in neural networks. In: ICLR. OpenReview.net (2017). https://openreview.net/forum?id=Hkg4TI9xl

15. Henzinger, T.A., Lukina, A., Schilling, C.: Outside the box: abstraction-based monitoring of neural networks. In: ECAI. Frontiers in Artificial Intelligence and Applications, vol. 325, pp. 2433–2440. IOS Press (2020). https://doi.org/10.3233/FAIA200375

16. Ibrahim, S.H., Nassar, M.: Hack the box: fooling deep learning abstraction-based monitors. CoRR abs/2107.04764 (2021). https://arxiv.org/abs/2107.04764

17. Jolliffe, I.T.: Principal Component Analysis. Springer Series in Statistics, Springer, Heidelberg (1986). https://doi.org/10.1007/978-1-4757-1904-8

18. Knorr, E.M., Ng, R.T.: A unified notion of outliers: properties and computation. In: KDD, pp. 219–222. AAAI Press (1997). http://www.aaai.org/Library/KDD/1997/kdd97-044.php
19. Krizhevsky, A.: Learning multiple layers of features from tiny images. University of Toronto, Technical report (2009)
20. LeCun, Y., Bottou, L., Bengio, Y., Haffner, P.: Gradient-based learning applied to document recognition. Proc. IEEE 86(11), 2278–2324 (1998)
21. Liu, W., Wang, Z., Liu, X., Zeng, N., Liu, Y., Alsaadi, F.E.: A survey of deep neural network architectures and their applications. Neurocomputing 234, 11–26 (2017). https://doi.org/10.1016/j.neucom.2016.12.038
22. Lloyd, S.P.: Least squares quantization in PCM. Trans. Inf. Theory 28(2), 129–136 (1982). https://doi.org/10.1109/TIT.1982.1056489
23. Lu, J., Gong, P., Ye, J., Zhang, C.: Learning from very few samples: a survey. CoRR abs/2009.02653 (2020). https://arxiv.org/abs/2009.02653
24. Mancini, M., Karaoguz, H., Ricci, E., Jensfelt, P., Caputo, B.: Knowledge is never enough: towards web aided deep open world recognition. In: ICRA, pp. 9537–9543. IEEE (2019). https://doi.org/10.1109/ICRA.2019.8793803
25. Mandelbaum, A., Weinshall, D.: Distance-based confidence score for neural network classifiers. CoRR abs/1709.09844 (2017). http://arxiv.org/abs/1709.09844
26. McCloskey, M., Cohen, N.J.: Catastrophic interference in connectionist networks: the sequential learning problem. In: Psychology of Learning and Motivation, vol. 24, pp. 109–165. Elsevier (1989). http://www.sciencedirect.com/science/article/pii/S0079742108605368
27. Mensink, T., Verbeek, J.J., Perronnin, F., Csurka, G.: Distance-based image classification: generalizing to new classes at near-zero cost. IEEE Trans. Pattern Anal. Mach. Intell. 35(11), 2624–2637 (2013). https://doi.org/10.1109/TPAMI.2013.83
28. Pan, S.J., Yang, Q.: A survey on transfer learning. IEEE Trans. Knowl. Data Eng. 22(10), 1345–1359 (2010). https://doi.org/10.1109/TKDE.2009.191
29. Parisi, G.I., Kemker, R., Part, J.L., Kanan, C., Wermter, S.: Continual lifelong learning with neural networks: A review. Neural Networks 113, 54–71 (2019). https://doi.org/10.1016/j.neunet.2019.01.012
30. Pimentel, M.A.F., Clifton, D.A., Clifton, L.A., Tarassenko, L.: A review of novelty detection. Signal Process. 99, 215–249 (2014). https://doi.org/10.1016/j.sigpro.2013.12.026
31. Rahman, Q.M., Corke, P., Dayoub, F.: Run-time monitoring of machine learning for robotic perception: a survey of emerging trends. IEEE Access 9, 20067–20075 (2021). https://doi.org/10.1109/ACCESS.2021.3055015
32. Rebuffi, S., Kolesnikov, A., Sperl, G., Lampert, C.H.: iCaRL: incremental classifier and representation learning. In: CVPR, pp. 5533–5542. IEEE Computer Society (2017). https://doi.org/10.1109/CVPR.2017.587
33. Redko, I., Morvant, E., Habrard, A., Sebban, M., Bennani, Y.: Advances in Domain Adaptation Theory. Elsevier (2019)
34. Royer, A., Lampert, C.H.: Classifier adaptation at prediction time. In: CVPR, pp. 1401–1409. IEEE Computer Society (2015). https://doi.org/10.1109/CVPR.2015.7298746
35. Schölkopf, B., Smola, A., Müller, K.-R.: Kernel principal component analysis. In: Gerstner, W., Germond, A., Hasler, M., Nicoud, J.-D. (eds.) ICANN 1997. LNCS, vol. 1327, pp. 583–588. Springer, Heidelberg (1997). https://doi.org/10.1007/BFb0020217

36. Schultheiss, A., Käding, C., Freytag, A., Denzler, J.: Finding the unknown: novelty detection with extreme value signatures of deep neural activations. In: Roth, V., Vetter, T. (eds.) GCPR 2017. LNCS, vol. 10496, pp. 226–238. Springer, Cham (2017). https://doi.org/10.1007/978-3-319-66709-6_19
37. Settles, B.: Active Learning. Synthesis Lectures on Artificial Intelligence and Machine Learning. Morgan & Claypool Publishers (2012). https://doi.org/10.2200/S00429ED1V01Y201207AIM018
38. Stallkamp, J., Schlipsing, M., Salmen, J., Igel, C.: The German traffic sign recognition benchmark: a multi-class classification competition. In: IJCNN, pp. 1453–1460. IEEE (2011). https://doi.org/10.1109/IJCNN.2011.6033395
39. Sun, R., Lampert, C.H.: KS(conf): a light-weight test if a multiclass classifier operates outside of its specifications. Int. J. Comput. Vis. **128**(4), 970–995 (2020). https://doi.org/10.1007/s11263-019-01232-x
40. Tan, C., Sun, F., Kong, T., Zhang, W., Yang, C., Liu, C.: A survey on deep transfer learning. In: Kůrková, V., Manolopoulos, Y., Hammer, B., Iliadis, L., Maglogiannis, I. (eds.) ICANN 2018. LNCS, vol. 11141, pp. 270–279. Springer, Cham (2018). https://doi.org/10.1007/978-3-030-01424-7_27
41. Tobin, J., Fong, R., Ray, A., Schneider, J., Zaremba, W., Abbeel, P.: Domain randomization for transferring deep neural networks from simulation to the real world. In: IROS, pp. 23–30. IEEE (2017). https://doi.org/10.1109/IROS.2017.8202133
42. Wagstaff, K.L., Lu, S.: Efficient active learning for new domains. In: Workshop on Real World Experiment Design and Active Learning (2020)
43. Wu, C., Falcone, Y., Bensalem, S.: Customizable reference runtime monitoring of neural networks using resolution boxes. CoRR abs/2104.14435 (2021). https://arxiv.org/abs/2104.14435
44. Xiao, H., Rasul, K., Vollgraf, R.: Fashion-MNIST: a novel image dataset for benchmarking machine learning algorithms. CoRR abs/1708.07747 (2017). http://arxiv.org/abs/1708.07747
45. Zhang, P., Wang, J., Farhadi, A., Hebert, M., Parikh, D.: Predicting failures of vision systems. In: CVPR, pp. 3566–3573. IEEE Computer Society (2014). https://doi.org/10.1109/CVPR.2014.456
46. Zhang, X., Zou, J., He, K., Sun, J.: Accelerating very deep convolutional networks for classification and detection. IEEE Trans. Pattern Anal. Mach. Intell. **38**(10), 1943–1955 (2016). https://doi.org/10.1109/TPAMI.2015.2502579
47. Zhao, P., Hoi, S.C.H.: OTL: a framework of online transfer learning. In: ICML, pp. 1231–1238. Omnipress (2010). https://icml.cc/Conferences/2010/papers/219.pdf

Monitoring with Verified Guarantees

Johann C. Dauer[1] , Bernd Finkbeiner[2] , and Sebastian Schirmer[1(✉)]

[1] German Aerospace Center (DLR), Braunschweig, Germany
{johann.dauer,sebastian.schirmer}@dlr.de
[2] Helmholtz Center for Information Security (CISPA), Saarbrücken, Germany
finkbeiner@cispa.saarland

Abstract. Runtime monitoring is generally considered a light-weight alternative to formal verification. In safety-critical systems, however, the monitor itself is a critical component. For example, if the monitor is responsible for initiating emergency protocols, as proposed in a recent aviation standard, then the safety of the entire system critically depends on guarantees of the correctness of the monitor. In this paper, we present a verification extension to the LOLA monitoring language that integrates the efficient specification of the monitor with Hoare-style annotations that guarantee the correctness of the monitor specification. We add two new operators, assume and assert, which specify assumptions of the monitor and expectations on its output, respectively. The validity of the annotations is established by an integrated SMT solver. We report on experience in applying the approach to specifications from the avionics domain, where the annotation with assumptions and assertions has lead to the discovery of safety-critical errors in the specifications. The errors range from incorrect default values in offset computations to complex algorithmic errors that result in unexpected temporal patterns.

Keywords: Formal methods · Cyber-physical systems · Runtime verification · Hoare logic

1 Introduction

Cyber-physical systems are inherently safety-critical due to their direct interaction with the physical environment – failures are unacceptable. A means of protection against failures is the integration of reliable monitoring capabilities. A *monitor* is a system component that has access to a wide range of system information, e.g., sensor readings and control decisions. When the monitor detects a failure, i.e., a violation of the behavior stated in its *specification*, it notifies the system or activates recoveries to prevent failure propagation.

The task of the monitor is critical to the safety of the system, and its correctness is therefore of utmost importance. Runtime monitoring approaches like LOLA [5,6] address this by describing the monitor in a formal specification language, and then generating a monitor implementation that is provably correct and has strong runtime guarantees, for example on memory consumption. Formal

L. Feng and D. Fisman (Eds.): RV 2021, LNCS 12974, pp. 62–80, 2021.
https://doi.org/10.1007/978-3-030-88494-9_4

monitoring languages typically feature temporal [18] and sometimes spatial [16] operators that simplify the specification of complex monitoring behaviors. However, the specification itself, the central part of runtime monitoring, is still prone to human errors during specification development. How can we check that the monitor specification itself is correct?

In this paper, we introduce a verification feature to the LOLA framework. Specifically, we extend the specification language with *assumptions* and *assertions*. The framework verifies that the assertions are guaranteed to hold if the input to the monitor satisfies the assumptions. The prime application area of LOLA is unmanned aviation. LOLA is increasingly used for the development and operation monitoring of unmanned aircraft; for example, the LOLA monitoring framework has been integrated into the DLR unmanned aircraft superAR-TIS[1] [1]. The verification extension presented in this paper is motivated by this work. In practice, system engineers report that support for specification development is necessary, e.g., sanity checks and proves of correctness. Additionally, recent developments in unmanned aviation regulations and standards indicate a similar necessity. One such development is the upcoming industry standard ASTM F3269 (Standard Practice for Methods to Safely Bound Flight Behavior of Unmanned Aircraft Systems Containing Complex Functions). ASTM F3269 introduces a certification strategy based on a Run-Time Assurance (RTA) architecture that bounds the behavior of a complex function by a safety monitor [15], similar to the well-known Simplex architecture [21]. This complex function could be a Deep Neural Network as proposed in [4]. A simplified version of the architecture[2] of ASTM F3269 is shown in Fig. 1.

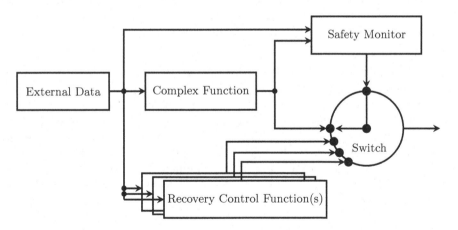

Fig. 1. Run-Time Assurance architecture proposed by ASTM F3269 to safely bound a complex function using a safety monitor.

---

[1] https://www.dlr.de/content/en/research-facilities/superartis-en.html.

[2] In its original version the data is separated into assured and unassured data and data preparation components are added.

At the core of the architecture is a safety monitor that takes the inputs and outputs of the complex function, and decides whether the complex function behaves as expected. If not, the monitor switches the control from the complex function to a matching recovery function. For instance, the flight of an unmanned aircraft could be separated into different phases: e.g., take-off, cruise flight, and landing. For each of these phases, a dedicated recovery could be defined, e.g., braking during take-off, the activation of a parachute during cruise flight, or a go-around maneuver during landing. Further, it is crucial that recoveries are only activated under certain conditions and that only one recovery is activated at a time. For instance, a parachute activation during a landing approach is considered safety-critical. The verification extension of LOLA introduced in this paper can be used to guarantee statically that such decisions are avoided within the monitor specification. Consider the simplified LOLA specification

```
input event_a, event_b, value: Bool, Bool, Float32
assume <a1> !(event_a and event_b)
output braking  : Bool := ...computation...
output parachute : Bool := ...computation...
output go_around : Bool := ...computation...
assert <a1> !(braking and parachute)
```

that declares an assumption on the system input events and asserts that braking and parachute never evaluates to *true* simultaneously.

In the following, we first give a brief introduction to the stream-based specification language LOLA, then present the verification approach, and, finally, give details on the tool implementation and our tool experience with specifications that were written based on interviews with aviation experts. Our results show that standard LOLA specifications are indeed prone to error, and that these errors can be caught with the formal verification introduced by our extension.

Related Work

Most work on the verification of monitors focuses on the correct transformation into a general programming language. For example, Copilot [17] specifications can be compiled into C code with constant time and memory requirements. Similarly, there is a translation validation toolkit for LOLA monitors implemented in Rust [6], which is based on the Viper verification tool. Translation validation of this type is orthogonal to the verification approach of this paper. Instead of verifying the correctness of a transformation, our focus is to verify the specification itself. Both activities complement each other and facilitate safer future cyber-physical systems.

Our verification approach is based on classic ideas of inductive program verification [7,11], and is closely related to the techniques used in static program verifiers like KEY [2], VeriFast [12], and Dafny [14]. In a verification approach like Dafny, we are interested in functional properties of procedures, specified as post-conditions that relate the values upon the termination of the procedure with those at the time of entry to the procedure, e.g., *ensure* $y = old(y)$. By contrast, a stream-based language like LOLA allows arbitrary access to past and future stream values. This makes it necessary to *unfold* the LOLA specification in order to properly relate the assumptions and assertions in time.

Most closely related to stream-based monitoring languages are synchronous programming languages like LUSTRE [10], ESTEREL [3], and SIGNAL [8]. For these languages, the compiler is typically used for verification – a program representing the negation of desired properties is compiled with the target program and a check for emptiness decides whether the properties are satisfied. Furthermore, a translation from past linear-time temporal logic to ESTEREL was proposed to simplify the specification of more complex temporal properties [13]. Other verification techniques also exist like SMT-based k-Induction for LUSTRE [9] or a term rewriting system on synced effects [22]. A key difference in our approach is that we do not rely on compilation. Our verification works on the level of an intermediate representation. Furthermore, synchronous programming languages are limited to past references, while the stream unfolding for the inductive correctness proof of the LOLA specification includes both past and future temporal operators. Similar to k-Induction, our approach is sound but not complete.

2   Runtime Monitoring with Lola

We now give an overview of the monitoring specification language LOLA. The verification extension is presented in the next section.

LOLA is a stream-based language that describes the translation from input streams to output streams:

$$\textbf{input } t_1 : T_1$$

$$\vdots$$

$$\textbf{input } t_m : T_m$$
$$\textbf{output } s_1 : T_{m+1} := e_1(t_1, \ldots, t_m, s_1, \ldots, s_n)$$

$$\vdots$$

$$\textbf{output } s_n : T_{m+n} := e_n(t_1, \ldots, t_m, s_1, \ldots, s_n)$$
$$\textbf{trigger } \varphi \; message$$

where input streams carry synchronous arriving data from the system under scrutiny, output streams represent calculations, and triggers generate notification *message*s at instants where their condition φ becomes *true*. Input streams $t_1, \ldots, t_m$ and output streams $s_1, \ldots, s_n$ are called *independent* and *dependent variables*, respectively. Each variable is typed: independent variables t_i are typed T_i and dependent variables s_i are typed T_{m+i}. Dependent variables are computed based on *stream expressions* $e_1, \ldots, e_n$ over dependent and independent stream variables. A stream expression is one of the following:

- an atomic stream expression c of type T if c is a constant of type T;
- an atomic stream expression s of type T if s is a stream variable of type T;
- a stream expression $ite(b, e_1, e_2)$ of type T if b is a Boolean stream expression and e_1, e_2 are stream expressions of type T. Note that ite abbreviates the control construct *if-then-else*;
- a stream expression $f(e_1, \ldots, e_k)$ of type T if $f : T_1 \times \cdots \times T_k \mapsto T$ is a k-ary operator and $e_1, \ldots, e_k$ are stream expressions of type $T_1, \ldots, T_k$;
- a stream expression $o.offset(by : i).defaults(to : d)$ of type T if o is a stream variable of type T, i is an Integer, and d is of type T.

For example, consider the LOLA specification

```
input altitude: Float32 // in m
output altitude_bound := altitude > 200.0
trigger altitude_bound "Warning: Decrease altitude!"
```

that notifies the system if the current `altitude` is above its operating limits, i.e., `200.0` m. Note that stream types are inferred, i.e., `altitude_bound` is of type `Bool`.

LOLA uses temporal operators that allow output streams to access its and others previous and future stream values. The stream

```
output alt_count := if altitude ≤ 200.0 then 0
                    else alt_count.offset(by: -1).defaults(to: 0) + 1
```

represents a count of consecutive altitude violations by accessing its own previous value, i.e., `offset(by: x)` where a negative and positive integer `x` represents past and future stream accesses, respectively. Since temporal accesses are not always guaranteed to exist, the default operator defines values which are used instead, i.e., `defaults(to: d)` where d has to be of the same type as the used stream. Here, at the first position of `alt_count` the default value zero is taken. As abbreviations for the temporal operators, `alt_count[x, d]` is used. Further, `s[x..y, d, ∘]` for `x < y` abbreviates `s[x,d] ∘ s[x+1,d] ∘ ... ∘ s[y,d]` where ∘ is a binary operator. Using `alt_count > 10` as a trigger condition is preferable if only persistent violations should be reported.

In general, LOLA is a specification language that allows to specify complex temporal properties in a precise, concise, and less error-prone way. The focus is on *what* properties should be monitored instead of *how* a monitor should be executed. Therefore, the LOLA monitor synthesis automatically infers and optimizes implementation details like evaluation order and memory management. The evaluation order [6] of LOLA streams is automatically derived by analysis of the *dependency graph* [5] of the specification. This allows to ignore the order when taking advantage of the modular structure of LOLA output streams, e.g.,:

```
output alt_avg := alt_count / (position+1)
output alt_count := if altitude ≤ 200.0 then 0
                    else alt_count.offset(by: -1).defaults(to: 0) + 1
output position := position.offset(by: -1).defaults(to: 0)
```

where `position` and `alt_count` are used before their definition. Further, the dependency graph allows to detect invalid cyclic stream dependencies, e.g., `output a := a.offset(by: 0).defaults(to: 0)`.

3 Assumptions and Assertions

In this section, we present the verification extension for the LOLA specification language. The extension allows the developer to annotate the LOLA specification with *assumptions* and *assertions* in order to verify the desired guarantees on the computed streams. As an example, consider the simplified specification in Listing 1, which is structured into stream computations in Lines 1 to 23, and assumptions and assertions from Line 26 onwards.

```
input alt : Float32 // Height above ground                              1
input x, y : Float32, Float32 // Position in local coordinate system    2
input speed : Float32 // Velocity of aircraft                           3
input landing : Bool // Indicates landing mode                          4
input lg_status : (Float32,Float32,FLoat32) // Status of landing gear   5
                                                                        6
// Complex computations                                                 7
output dst_on_runway      : Float32 := √(x² + y²)                       8
output geofence_violation : Bool     := ...                             9
output landing_gear_ready : Bool     := ...                             10
                                                                        11
// Take-off contingency                                                 12
output decelerate := alt < 1.0 ∧ speed < 10.0 ∧ dst_on_runway > 20.0    13
// In-flight contingency                                                14
output parachute := geofence_violation ∧ alt > 100.0                    15
// Landing contingency                                                  16
output gain_alt := landing ∧ alt ≥ 10.0 ∧ (speed > 10.0 ∨              17
                   !landing_gear_ready[-4..0, true, ∧])                 18
                                                                        19
// Notifications to the system                                          20
trigger decelerate "RECOVERY: Stop take-off by decelerating aircraft."  21
trigger parachute  "RECOVERY: Activate parachute."                      22
trigger gain_alt   "RECOVERY: Gain altitude for next landing attempt."  23
                                                                        24
// By concept of operations: landing is always within geofence.         25
assume <a1> ¬(landing ∧ geofence_violation)                             26
assume <a1> abs(speed) <= 80.0 // Given by data protocol                27
                                                                        28
// Only one contingency is activated at once.                           29
assert <a1> ¬( (decelerate ∧ parachute) ∨ (decelerate ∧ gain_alt)       30
             ∨ (parachute ∧ gain_alt) )                                 31
// Parachute SHALL ONLY be activated 100 m above ground.                32
assert <a2> parachute → alt > 100.0                                     33
```

Listing 1. A simplified Run-Time Assurance LOLA specification with three recovery functions for three different flight phases. Assumptions and assertions are used to show that only one recovery function is activated at once.

The computation part specifies a safety monitor within a RTA architecture that triggers recovery functions for three different flight phases. First, the take-off recovery function is triggered (Line 21) when the targeted take-off speed was not achieved on a runway up to a predefined point (Line 13). The distance between the current position and the end of the runway with local coordinates $(0,0)$ is computed in Line 8. Second, in-flight a parachute is activated (Line 22) when virtual barriers for the aircraft, i.e., a geofence, are exceeded (Line 15). For more details on a LOLA geofence specification (Line 9), we refer to [20]. Last, during landing, up to a point of no return (`alt < 10.0`), a new landing attempt is initiated (Line 23) if the aircraft's speed is too fast or its landing gear is not yet ready. To be more robust, the current and the previous value of the `landing_gear_ready` is taken into account (Lines 17–18).

With the verification extension, the specification assures that recoveries are not activated simultaneously (Lines 30–31), i.e., for instance there is no possibility that a parachute is activated during a landing approach. The first two conjunctions in Line 30 evaluate to *false* because relevant outputs use a disjoint altitude condition. The last conjunction requires an assumption. In fact, here, two assumptions are linked by the identifier $a1$ to the assertion. The assumptions specify: the known bound of received speed data (Line 27) as well as operational information (Line 26), e.g., given by the concept of operation a nominal landing is only foreseen within the predefined operational airspace. Further, a second assertion is stated in Line 33 that guarantees that *the parachute should only be activated when the aircraft is 100 m above ground*. In this case, the property can be shown assumption-free. Assertions help engineers to show that certain properties are *true*. The given assertions indicate how specification debugging and management can benefit from the extension – it avoids digging into potentially complex stream computations.

The extension and its verification approach are presented in the following. In general, the verification extension is used if a LOLA specification is annotated in the following way:

$$\textbf{assume } \langle \alpha_1 \rangle \quad \theta_1$$

$$\vdots$$

$$\textbf{assume } \langle \alpha_m \rangle \quad \theta_m$$
$$\textbf{assert } \langle \alpha_{m+1} \rangle \quad \psi_1$$

$$\vdots$$

$$\textbf{assert } \langle \alpha_{m+n} \rangle \quad \psi_n$$

where $\alpha_1, \ldots, \alpha_{m+n} \in \Gamma$ are identifiers for $\theta_1, \ldots, \theta_m, \psi_1, \ldots, \psi_n$, which are Boolean stream expressions with possibly temporal operators. For convenience, we define functions which return all θ and ψ that are linked to a given α identifier: $assume(\alpha) = \{\theta_j \mid \forall \alpha_j \in \Gamma, \alpha = \alpha_j\}$ and $assert(\alpha) = \{\psi_j \mid \forall \alpha_j \in \Gamma, \alpha = \alpha_j\}$.

The set of assertion $\psi_1, \ldots, \psi_n$ is *correct* for all input streams iff whenever an assumption is satisfied, its corresponding assertion is satisfied as well.

The verification of assertions relies on the encoding of the LOLA execution in Satisfiability Modulo Theory (SMT). We define the *smt* function that encodes a stream expression next. It can be used to encode independent and dependent variables as well as expressions of assumptions and assertions.

Definition 1 (SMT-Encoding of Stream Expressions).
Let Φ be a LOLA *specification over independent stream variables $t_1, \ldots, t_m$ and dependent stream variables $s_1, \ldots, s_n$. Further, let the natural number $N + 1$ be the length of the input streams, c be an SMT constant symbol, and $\tau_1^0, \ldots, \tau_1^N, \ldots, \tau_m^0, \ldots, \tau_m^N, \sigma_1^0, \ldots, \sigma_1^N, \ldots, \sigma_n^0, \ldots, \sigma_n^N$ be SMT variables. Then, the function smt recursively encodes a stream expression e at position j with $0 \leq j \leq N$ in the following way:*

- *Base cases:*
  - $smt(c)(j) = \mathsf{c}$
  - $smt(t_i)(j) = \tau_i^j$
  - $smt(s_i)(j) = \sigma_i^j$
- *Recursive cases:*
  - $smt(f(e_1, \ldots, e_n))(j) = \mathsf{f}(smt(e_1)(j), \ldots, smt(e_n)(j))$
  - $smt(ite(e_b, e_1, e_2))(j) = \mathsf{ite}(smt(e_b)(j), smt(e_1)(j), smt(e_2)(j))$
  - $smt(e[k, c])(j) = \begin{cases} smt(e)(j+k) & \text{if } 0 \leq j+k \leq N, \\ c & \text{otherwise} \end{cases}$

where ite *is an SMT encoding of if-then-else;* f *is an interpreted function if f is from a theory supported by the SMT solver and an uninterpreted function otherwise.*

Next, Proposition 1 shows how the correctness of asserted stream properties can be proven for finite input streams. If the set of assertions is correct, asserted stream properties are guaranteed to be valid in each step of the monitor execution. In practice, such specifications are preferable. In the following, let Φ be a LOLA specification with verification annotations. Further, we refer to the set of input streams and computed output streams as stream execution.

Proposition 1 (Assertion Verification of a Finite Stream Execution).
The set of assertions is correct for a finite stream execution with length $N + 1$ under given assumptions, if the following formula is valid:

$$\bigwedge_{i:\, 0 \leq i \leq N} \left(\bigwedge_{\alpha \in \Gamma} \left(\bigwedge_{\theta \,\in\, assume(\alpha)} smt(\theta)(i) \wedge \bigwedge_{s_k \in \Phi} \sigma_k^i = smt(e_k)(i) \rightarrow \bigwedge_{\psi \,\in\, assert(\alpha)} smt(\psi)(i) \right) \right)$$

The formula in Proposition 1 unfolds the complete stream execution and informally expresses that an assertion must hold in each stream position whenever its corresponding assumption and implementation are satisfied.

To avoid the complete unfolding and allow arbitrary stream lengths, an inductive argument is given in Proposition 2 that defines proof obligations for an annotated LOLA specification. Next, we present a template for the stream unfolding that helps to define the proof obligation at the *Beginning* (Definition 3), during *Run* (Definition 4), and at the *End* (Definition 5) of a stream execution.

Definition 2 (Template Stream Unfolding).
We define the template formula ϕ_t that states proof obligations as:

$$\bigwedge_{\alpha \in \Gamma} \left(\bigwedge_{i:\ c\_asm} \left(\bigwedge_{\theta\ \in\ assume(\alpha)} smt(\theta)(i) \right) \wedge \bigwedge_{i:\ c\_asserted} \left(\bigwedge_{\psi\ \in\ assert(\alpha)} smt(\psi)(i) \right) \right.$$

$$\left. \wedge \bigwedge_{i:\ c\_streams} \left(\bigwedge_{0<k\leq n} \sigma_k = smt(e_k)(i) \right) \rightarrow \bigwedge_{i:\ c\_assert} \left(\bigwedge_{\psi\ \in\ assert(\alpha)} smt(\psi)(i) \right) \right)$$

where c_asm, $c\_asserted$, $c\_streams$, and c_assert are template parameters for the unfolding of assumptions, previously proven assertions, output streams, and assertion, respectively.

The template formula in Definition 2 uses template parameters for the stream unfolding. For instance, the parameter assignment $c\_asm := 0 \leq i < 10$ adds assumptions at the first ten positions of the stream execution. Further, the parameter $c\_asserted$ allows to incorporate the induction hypothesis.

In the following, we will use the LOLA specification

```
assume<a1> reset[-1, f] ∨ reset[1, f]
input reset : Bool
output o1 := if reset then 0 else o1[-1, 0] + 1
output o2 := o1[-1, 0] + o1 + o1[1, 0]
assert<a1> 0 ≤ o2 and o2 ≤ 3
```

as a running example for the template stream unfolding. Here, the input *reset* represent a reset command for the output stream *o1* that counts how long no *reset* occurred. Output *o1* is used by output *o2* which aggregates over the previous, the current, and the next outcome of *o1*. As assertion, we show that *o2* is always positive and never larger than three given the assumption that in each execution step either the previous or the next *reset* is *true*. The assumption ensures that at most two consecutive *resets* are *false*. Given the *reset* sequence of input values $\langle true; false; false \rangle$ that satisfies the assumption, the resulting *o1* stream evaluates to $\langle 0; 1; 2 \rangle$. Here, at the second position of the sequence, *o2* evaluates to three. To show that the assertion also holds at the first and the last position of the sequence, out-of-bounds values must be considered.

We show how the template ϕ_t can be used at the beginning of a stream execution. Here, default values due to past stream accesses beyond the beginning of a stream need to be captured by the obligation to guarantee that the assertions hold in these cases. The combination of past out-of-bounds and future out-of-bounds default values must also be covered by the obligations in case the stream is stopped early. These scenarios are depicted for the running example in Fig. 2. The figure shows four finite stream executions with different lengths. All stream positions are colored gray, while only some positions contain a single red dot. These features indicate the unfolding of stream variables and annotations using the template ϕ_t. A gray-colored position means that the assumptions have been unfolded and a dotted position means the assertion has been unfolded. Further, arrows indicate temporal stream accesses where solid lines correspond to accesses by outputs and dashed lines correspond to accesses by annotations, i.e., assumptions and assertions. For each stream execution, only the arrows for a single position are depicted – the arrows for other positions have been omitted for the sake of clarity. For example, for $N = 0$, the accesses of output $o2$ are both out-of-bounds, i.e., the default value zero is used. While for $N = 3$, the accesses at the second position are shown where only the past access of the assumption leads to an out-of-bounds access. The figure depicts all necessary stream execution that cover all combinations of past out-of-bounds accesses, i.e., with and without future bound violations. The described unfoldings of Fig. 2 are formalized as proof obligations in Definition 3.

Definition 3 (Proof Obligations for Past Out-of-bounds Accesses).
Let $w_p = \sup(\{0\} \cup \{\ |k|\ |\ e[k,c] \in \Phi\ \text{where}\ k < 0\})$ be the most negative offset and $w_f = \sup(\{0\} \cup \{\ k\ |\ e[k,c] \in \Phi\ \text{where}\ k > 0\})$ be the greatest positive offset. The proof obligations ϕ_{Begin} for past out-of-bounds accesses are defined as the conjunction of template formulas:

$$\bigwedge_{N:\ 0 \leq N < \max(1,\ 2 \cdot (w_p + w_f))} \phi_t(c\_asm,\ c\_asserted,\ c\_streams,\ c\_assert)$$

with template parameters:
- c_asm $:= 0 \leq i \leq N,$
- $c\_asserted := false,$
- $c\_streams := 0 \leq i \leq N,$
- c_assert $:= 0 \leq i < \max(1,\ \min(N+1,\ 2 \cdot w_p)).$

Fig. 2. Four stream executions of different length $N + 1$ with the respective template unfolding are depicted. The stream executions consider all cases with past out-of-bound accesses. A gray-colored box indicates that an assumption has been unfolded at this position, while a red dotted box indicates that an assertion has been unfolded at this position. Solid and dashed arrows indicate accesses by streams and annotations, respectively. (Color figure online)

Next, the case where no out-of-bounds access occurs is considered. Hence, the obligations capture the nominal case where no default value is used. Since we have shown that past out-of-bounds accesses are valid we can use these proven assertions as assumptions. Figure 3 depicts a stream execution with a single dotted position, i.e., the position where the assertion must be proven. As can be seen, all accesses from this position are within bounds. Further, note that the accesses of the first and the last unfolded assumption, i.e., the first and the last gray-colored position, are also within bounds. The described unfolding is formalized as proof obligations in Definition 4.

Definition 4 (Proof Obligations for No Out-of-bounds Accesses).
The proof obligations ϕ_{Run} *without out-of-bounds accesses are defined as* $\phi_t(c\_asm,\ c\_asserted,\ c\_streams,\ c\_assert)$ *with template parameters:*

- $c\_asm \quad := w_p \leq i \leq N - w_f,$
- $c\_asserted := 2 \cdot w_p \leq i \leq N - 2 \cdot w_f \wedge i \neq 3 \cdot w_p,$
- $c\_streams := 2 \cdot w_p \leq i \leq N - 2 \cdot w_f,$
- $c\_assert \quad := i = 3 \cdot w_p,$

where $N = 3 \cdot (w_p + w_f).$

Last, we consider the case where only future out-of-bounds accesses occur. Hence, the respective obligations need to incorporate default values of future out-of-bounds accesses. As before, we can use the previously proven assertions as assumptions. Figure 4 depicts a stream execution with two dotted positions, i.e., positions where the assertion must be proven. The position where arrows are given represents the case where only the assumption results in a future out-of-bounds access. The last position of the stream execution represents the case in which both the assumption and the stream result in future out-of-bounds accesses. The presented unfolding is formalized as proof obligations in Definition 5.

Definition 5 (Proof Obligations for Future Out-of-bounds Accesses).
The proof obligations ϕ_{End} *for future out-of-bounds accesses are defined as the template formula* $\phi_t(c\_asm,\ c\_asserted,\ c\_streams,\ c\_assert)$ *with template parameters:*

- $c\_asm \quad := w_p \leq i \leq N,$
- $c\_asserted := 2 \cdot w_p \leq i < 3 \cdot w_p,$
- $c\_streams := 2 \cdot w_p \leq i \leq N,$
- $c\_assert \quad := 3 \cdot w_p \leq i \leq N$

where $N = 3 \cdot w_p + w_f.$

So far, we have defined proof obligations for certain positions in the stream execution with and without out-of-bounds accesses. Together, the proof obligations constitute an inductive argument for the correctness of the assertions, see Proposition 2. Here, the base case is given by Definition 3 and induction steps are given by Definitions 4 and 5. The induction steps use the induction hypothesis, i.e., valid assertions, due to the template parameter *c_asserted*.

Proposition 2 (Assertion Verification by Lola Unfolding).
The set of assertions is correct if the formula $\phi_{Begin} \wedge \phi_{Run} \wedge \phi_{End}$ *is valid.*

Proposition 2 proves the soundness of the verification approach. Soundness refers to the ability of an analyzer to prove the absence of errors—if a LOLA specification is accepted, it is guaranteed that the assertions are not violated. The converse does not hold, i.e., the presented verification approach is not complete. Completeness refers to the ability of an analyzer to prove the presence of errors—if a LOLA specification is rejected, the counter-example given should be a valid stream execution that results in an assertion violation. The following LOLA specification is rejected even though no assertion is violated:

```
input a: Int32                                                    1
assume <a1> a ≤ 10                                                2
output sum := if sum[-1, 0] ≤ 10 then 0 else sum[-1, 0] + a       3
assert < a1 > sum ≤ 100                                           4
```

Here, since the if-condition in Line 3 evaluates to *true* at the beginning of the stream execution, sum is a constant stream with value zero. Hence, the assertion in Line 4 is never violated. The verification approach rejects this specification. The reason for this is that $sum \leq 100$ is added as an *asserted* condition in ϕ_{Run}. Therefore, the SMT solver can assign a value between 91 and 100 to the earliest sum variable of the unfolding, resulting in an assertion violation of the next sum variable.

$N=6$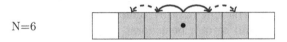

Fig. 3. A stream execution of length $N+1$ with the corresponding template unfolding is depicted. The stream execution considers the case where no out-of-bound access occurs. Gray-colored and red dotted positions represent unfolded assumptions and assertions, respectively. Solid and dashed arrows indicate accesses by streams and annotations, respectively. (Color figure online)

$N=4$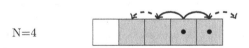

Fig. 4. A stream execution of length $N+1$ with the corresponding template unfolding is depicted. The stream execution covers all cases where future out-of-accesses occur. Gray-colored and red dotted positions represent unfolded assumptions and assertions, respectively. Solid and dashed arrows indicate accesses by streams and annotations, respectively. (Color figure online)

4   Application Experience in Avionics

In this section, we present details about the tool implementation and tool experiences on practical avionic specifications.

Tool Implementation and Usage

The tool is based on the open source LOLA framework[3] written in Rust. Specifically, it uses the LOLA frontend to parse a given specification into an intermediate representation. Based on this representation, the SMT formulas are created and evaluated with the Rust z3 crate[4]. At its current phase of the crate's development, a combined solver is implemented that internally uses either a non-incremental or an incremental solver. There is no information on the implemented tactics available, but all our requests could be solved within seconds. For functions that are not natively supported by the Rust Z3 solver, the output is arbitrarily chosen by the solver with respect to the range of the function. The tool expects a LOLA specification augmented by *assumptions* and *assertions*. The verification is done automatically and produces a counter-example stream execution, if any exists. The counter-example can then be used by the user to debug its specifications. Two different kinds of users are targeted. First, users that write the entire augmented specification. Such a user could be a systems engineer who is developing a safety monitor and wants to ensure that it contains critical properties. Second, users that augment an existing specification. Here, one reason could be that an existing monitor shall be composed with other critical components and certain behavioral properties are expected. Also, similar to software testing, the task of writing a specification and their respective assumptions and assertions could be separated between two users to ensure the independence of both.

Practical Results

To gain practical tool experience, previously written specifications based on interviews with engineers of the German Aerospace Center [19] were extended by assumptions and assertions. The previous specifications were tested using log-files and simulations – the authors considered them correct. We report several specification errors in Table 1 that were detected by the presented verification extension. In fact, the detected errors would have resulted in undetected failures. After the errors in the previous specifications were fixed, all assertions were proven correct. Note that the errors could have been found due to manual reviews. However, such reviews are tedious and error-prone, especially when temporal behaviors are involved. The detected errors in Table 1 can be grouped into three classes: *Classical Bugs*, *Operator Errors*, and *Wrong Interpretations*. Classical bugs are errors that occur when implementing an algorithm. Operator errors are LOLA specific errors, e.g., temporal accesses. Last, wrong interpretations refer to gaps between the specification and the user's design intend, e.g., violated assertions due to incomplete specifications. Next, we give one represen-

---

[3] https://rtlola.org/.
[4] https://docs.rs/z3/0.9.0/z3/.

tative example for each group. We reduced the specification to the representative fragment.

Table 1. Detected errors by the verification extension, where #o, #a, and #g represent the number of outputs, assumptions, and assertions given in the specification, respectively.

Specification	#o	#a	#g	Detected errors
gps_vel_output	14	6	6	–
gps_pos_output	19	3	10	–
imu_output	18	6	6	Wrong default value Division by zero
nav_output	25	3	5	Missing abs()
tagging	6	2	2	–
ctrl_output	25	7	8	Wrong threshold comparisons
mm_output_1	4	1	2	–
mm_output_2	17	6	9	Missing if condition Wrong default value
contingency_output	4	8	1	Observation: both contingencies could be true in case of voting, i.e., both at 50%
health_output	1	5	1	–

Example 1 (Classical Bug).
The LOLA specification in Listing 2 monitors the fuel level. A monitor shall notify the operator when one of the three different fuel levels are reached: half (Line 8), warning (Line 9), and danger (Line 10). The fuel level is computed as a percentage in Line 7. It uses the fuel level at the beginning of the flight (Line 6) as a reference for its computation. Given the documentation of the fuel sensor, it is known that `fuel` values are within $\mathbb{R}^+$ and decreasing. This is formalized in Line 4 as an assumption. As an invariant, we asserted that the starting fuel is greater or equal to `fuel` (Line 15). Further, in Lines 16 to 18, we stated that once a level is reached it should remain at this level. During our experiment, the assertion led to a counter-example that pointed to the previously used and erroneous fuel level computation:

```
output fuel_level := (start_fuel - fuel) / start_fuel
```

In short, the output computed the consumed fuel and not the remaining fuel. The computation could be easily fixed by converting consumed fuel into remaining fuel, see Line 7. Therefore, Listing 2 satisfies its assertion. Note, that offset accesses were used to assert the temporal behavior of the fuel level output stream. Further, `trigger_once` is an abbreviation which states that only the first raising edge is reported to the user.

```
// Inputs                                                              1
input fuel: Float64                                                    2
// Assumptions                                                         3
assume<a5> fuel > 0.0 and fuel < fuel[-1, fuel + 0.1]                  4
// Outputs                                                             5
output start_fuel := start_fuel[-1, fuel]                              6
output fuel_level := 1.0 - (start_fuel - fuel) / start_fuel           7
output fuel_half := fuel_level < 0.50                                  8
output fuel_warning := fuel_level < 0.25                               9
output fuel_danger := fuel_level < 0.10                               10
trigger_once fuel_half "INFO: Fuel level is half reduced"            11
trigger_once fuel_warning "WARNING: Fuel level is below 25%"         12
trigger_once fuel_danger "DANGER: Fuel level is below 10%"           13
// Assertions                                                        14
assert<a5> start_fuel >= fuel                                        15
           and (fuel_half[-1, false] -> fuel_half)                   16
           and (fuel_warning[-1, false] -> fuel_warning)             17
           and (fuel_danger[-1, false] -> fuel_danger)               18
```

Listing 2. The fixed version of the LOLA ctrl_output specification that monitors the fuel level. Three level of engagement are depicted: half, warning, and danger.

Example 2 (Operator Error).
An important monitoring property is to detect frozen values as these indicate a deteriorated sensor. Such a specification is depicted in Listing 3. Here, as an input, the acceleration in x-direction is given. The frozen value check is computed from Line 6 to Line 10. It compares previous values using LOLA's offset operator. To check this computation, we added the sanity check that asserts that no frozen value shall be detected (Line 13) when small changes in the input are present (Line 4). In the previous version, the frozen values were computed using the abbreviated offset operator:

```
output frozen_ax := ax[-5..0, 0.0, =]
```

This resulted in a counter-example that pointed to wrong default values. Although the abbreviated version is easier to read and reduces the size of the specification, it is unfortunately not suitable for this kind of property. The tool detected the unlikely situation that the first value of ax is 0.0 which would have resulted in evaluating frozen_ax to true. Although unlikely, this should be avoided as contingencies activated in such situations depend on correct results and otherwise could harm people on the ground. By unfolding the operator and adding a different default value to one of the past accesses, the error was resolved (Line 6). Listing 3 shows the fixed version which satisfies its assertion.

```
// Inputs                                                    1
input ax: Float32                                           2
// Assumptions                                              3
assume <a1> ax != ax[-1, ax + ε]                            4
// Outputs                                                  5
output frozen_ax := ax[-5, 0.1] = ax[-4, 0.0]              6
                and ax[-4, 0.0] = ax[-3, 0.0]              7
                and ax[-3, 0.0] = ax[-2, 0.0]              8
                and ax[-2, 0.0] = ax[-1, 0.0]              9
                and ax[-1, 0.0] = ax                      10
trigger frozen_ax "WARNING: x-acceleration is frozen!"    11
// Assertions                                              12
assert <a1> !frozen_ax                                    13
```

Listing 3. The LOLA imu_output specification that monitors frozen acceleration values.

Example 3 (Wrong Interpretation).
In Listing 4, two visual sensor readings are received (Lines 2–3). Both, readings argue over the same observations where `avgDist` represents the average distance to the measured obstacle, `actual` is the number of measurements, and `static` is the number of unchanged measurements. A simple rating function is introduced (Lines 5–8) that estimates the corresponding rating – the higher the better. Using these ratings, the trust in each of the sensors is computed probabilistically (Lines 9–10). When considering the integration of such a monitor as an ASTM switch condition that decides which sensor value should be forwarded, the specification should be revised. This is the case because the assertion in Line 14 produces a counter-example which indicates that both trust triggers (Lines 11–12) can be activated at the same time. A common solution for this problem is to introduce a priority between the sensors.

```
// Inputs                                                                    1
input avgDist_laser, actual_laser, static_laser: Float64                    2
input avgDist_optical, actual_optical, static_optical: Float64              3
// Outputs                                                                   4
output rating_laser :=                                                       5
    0.2 * static_laser + 0.4 * actual_laser + 0.4 * avgDist_laser          6
output rating_optical :=                                                     7
    0.2 * static_optical + 0.4 * actual_optical + 0.4 * avgDist_optical    8
output trust_laser := rating_laser / ( rating_laser + rating_optical)      9
output trust_optical := 1.0 - trust_laser                                  10
trigger trust_laser >= 0.5                                                  11
trigger trust_optical >= 0.5                                                12
// Assertions                                                               13
assert <a1> trust_laser != trust_optical                                   14
```

Listing 4. The LOLA contingency_output specification that uses an heuristic to decide which sensor is more trustworthy.

The examples show how the presented LOLA verification extension can be used to find errors in specifications. We also noticed that the annotations can serve as documentation. System assumptions are often implicitly known during development and are finally documented in natural language in separate files. Having these assumptions explicitly stated within the monitor specification potentially reduces future mistakes when reusing the specification, e.g., when composing with other monitor specifications. Listing 5 depicts such an example specification. Here, the monitor interfaces are clearly defined by the domain of input a (Line 5) and output o (Line 13). Also, *reset* is assumed to be valid at least once per second (Line 5). Further, no deeper understanding of the internal computations (Lines 7–10) is required in order to safely compose this specification with others.

```
// Inputs with frequency 5Hz                                      1
input a: Float64                                                  2
input reset: Bool                                                 3
// Assumptions                                                    4
assume <a1> 0.0 ≤ a ≤ 1.0 and reset[-4..0, false, ∨]             5
// Outputs                                                        6
output o_1 := ...                                                 7
...                                                               8
output o_n := ...                                                 9
output o := o_1 + ... + o_n                                      10
trigger o ≥ 0.5 "Warning: Output o exceeds threshold!"          11
// Assertions                                                    12
assert <a1> 0.0 ≤ o ≤ 1.0                                        13
```

Listing 5. LOLA specification annotations describe interface properties.

5   Conclusion

As both the relevance and the complexity of cyber-physical systems continues to grow, runtime monitoring is an essential ingredient of safety-critical systems. When monitors are derived from specifications it is crucial that the specifications are correct. In this paper, we have presented a verification approach for the stream-based monitoring language LOLA. With this approach, the developer can formally prove guarantees on the streams computed by the monitor, and hence ensure that the monitor does not cause dangerous situations. The verification extension is motivated by upcoming aviation regulations and standards as well as by practical feedback of engineers.

The extension has been applied to previously written LOLA specifications that were obtained based on interviews with aviation experts. In this process, we discovered and fixed several serious specification errors.

In the future, we plan to develop automatic invariant generation for LOLA specifications. Another interesting direction for future work is to exploit the results of the analysis for the optimization of the specification and the resulting monitoring code. Finally, we plan to extend the verification approach to RTLOLA, the real-time extension of LOLA.

Acknowledgement. This work was partially supported by the German Research Foundation (DFG) as part of the Collaborative Research Center Foundations of Perspicuous Software Systems (TRR 248, 389792660), by the European Research Council (ERC) Grant OSARES (No. 683300), and by the Aviation Research Programm LuFo of the German Federal Ministry for Economic Affairs and Energy as part of "Volocopter Sicherheits-Technologie zur robusten eVTOL Flugzustandsabsicherung durch formales Monitoring" (No. 20Q1963C).

References

1. Baumeister, J., Finkbeiner, B., Schirmer, S., Schwenger, M., Torens, C.: RTLola cleared for take-off: monitoring autonomous aircraft. In: Lahiri, S.K., Wang, C. (eds.) CAV 2020. LNCS, vol. 12225, pp. 28–39. Springer, Cham (2020). https://doi.org/10.1007/978-3-030-53291-8_3

2. Beckert, B., Hähnle, R., Schmitt, P.H. (eds.): Verification of Object-Oriented Software: The KeY Approach. Lecture Notes in Computer Science, vol. 4334. Springer, Heidelberg (2007). https://doi.org/10.1007/978-3-540-69061-0

3. Berry, G.: The Foundations of Esterel, pp. 425–454. MIT Press, Cambridge (2000)

4. Cluzeau, J.M., Henriquel, X., van Dijk, L., Gronskiy, A.: Concepts of design assurance for neural networks (CoDANN). Technical report, EASA European Union Aviation Safety Agency, March 2020

5. D'Angelo, B., et al.: LOLA: runtime monitoring of synchronous systems. In: 12th International Symposium on Temporal Representation and Reasoning (TIME 2005), pp. 166–174 (2005). https://doi.org/10.1109/TIME.2005.26

6. Finkbeiner, B., Oswald, S., Passing, N., Schwenger, M.: Verified rust monitors for Lola specifications. In: Deshmukh, J., Ničković, D. (eds.) RV 2020. LNCS, vol. 12399, pp. 431–450. Springer, Cham (2020). https://doi.org/10.1007/978-3-030-60508-7_24

7. Floyd, R.W.: Assigning meanings to programs. In: Colburn, T.R., Fetzer, J.H., Rankin, T.L. (eds.) Program Verification, vol. 14, pp. 65–81. Springer, Dordrecht (1993). https://doi.org/10.1007/978-94-011-1793-7_4

8. Gautier, T., Le Guernic, P., Besnard, L.: SIGNAL: a declarative language for synchronous programming of real-time systems. In: Kahn, G. (ed.) FPCA 1987. LNCS, vol. 274, pp. 257–277. Springer, Heidelberg (1987). https://doi.org/10.1007/3-540-18317-5_15

9. Hagen, G., Tinelli, C.: Scaling up the formal verification of Lustre programs with SMT-based techniques. In: 2008 Formal Methods in Computer-Aided Design, pp. 1–9 (2008). https://doi.org/10.1109/FMCAD.2008.ECP.19

10. Halbwachs, N., Caspi, P., Raymond, P., Pilaud, D.: The synchronous data flow programming language Lustre. Proc. IEEE **79**(9), 1305–1320 (1991). https://doi.org/10.1109/5.97300

11. Hoare, C.A.R.: An axiomatic basis for computer programming. Commun. ACM **12**(10), 576–580 (1969). https://doi.org/10.1145/363235.363259

12. Jacobs, B., Smans, J., Philippaerts, P., Vogels, F., Penninckx, W., Piessens, F.: VeriFast: a powerful, sound, predictable, fast verifier for C and Java. In: Bobaru, M., Havelund, K., Holzmann, G.J., Joshi, R. (eds.) NFM 2011. LNCS, vol. 6617, pp. 41–55. Springer, Heidelberg (2011). https://doi.org/10.1007/978-3-642-20398-5_4

13. Jagadeesan, L.J., Puchol, C., Von Olnhausen, J.E.: Safety property verification of Esterel programs and applications to telecommunications software. In: Wolper, P. (ed.) CAV 1995. LNCS, vol. 939, pp. 127–140. Springer, Heidelberg (1995). https://doi.org/10.1007/3-540-60045-0_45

14. Leino, K.R.M.: Dafny: an automatic program verifier for functional correctness. In: Clarke, E.M., Voronkov, A. (eds.) LPAR 2010. LNCS (LNAI), vol. 6355, pp. 348–370. Springer, Heidelberg (2010). https://doi.org/10.1007/978-3-642-17511-4_20

15. Nagarajan, P., Kannan, S.K., Torens, C., Vukas, M.E., Wilber, G.F.: ASTM F3269 - an industry standard on run time assurance for aircraft systems. https://doi.org/10.2514/6.2021-0525

16. Nenzi, L., Bortolussi, L., Ciancia, V., Loreti, M., Massink, M.: Qualitative and quantitative monitoring of spatio-temporal properties. In: Bartocci, E., Majumdar, R. (eds.) RV 2015. LNCS, vol. 9333, pp. 21–37. Springer, Cham (2015). https://doi.org/10.1007/978-3-319-23820-3_2

17. Pike, L., Goodloe, A., Morisset, R., Niller, S.: Copilot: a hard real-time runtime monitor. In: Barringer, H., et al. (eds.) RV 2010. LNCS, vol. 6418, pp. 345–359. Springer, Heidelberg (2010). https://doi.org/10.1007/978-3-642-16612-9_26

18. Reinbacher, T., Rozier, K.Y., Schumann, J.: Temporal-logic based runtime observer pairs for system health management of real-time systems. In: Ábrahám, E., Havelund, K. (eds.) TACAS 2014. LNCS, vol. 8413, pp. 357–372. Springer, Heidelberg (2014). https://doi.org/10.1007/978-3-642-54862-8_24

19. Schirmer, S.: Runtime monitoring with Lola. Master's thesis, Saarland University, December 2016

20. Schirmer, S., Torens, C., Adolf, F.: Formal monitoring of risk-based geofences. https://doi.org/10.2514/6.2018-1986. https://arc.aiaa.org/doi/abs/10.2514/6.2018-1986

21. Seto, D., Krogh, B., Sha, L., Chutinan, A.: The simplex architecture for safe online control system upgrades. In: Proceedings of the 1998 American Control Conference. ACC (IEEE Cat. No.98CH36207), vol. 6, pp. 3504–3508 (1998). https://doi.org/10.1109/ACC.1998.703255

22. Song, Y., Chin, W.-N.: A synchronous effects logic for temporal verification of pure Esterel. In: Henglein, F., Shoham, S., Vizel, Y. (eds.) VMCAI 2021. LNCS, vol. 12597, pp. 417–440. Springer, Cham (2021). https://doi.org/10.1007/978-3-030-67067-2_19

On the Specification and Monitoring of Timed Normative Systems

Shaun Azzopardi[1]($\boxtimes$)(ID), Gordon Pace[2](ID), Fernando Schapachnik[3],
and Gerardo Schneider[1](ID)

[1] University of Gothenburg, Gothenburg, Sweden
`shaun.azzopardi@gu.se, gersch@chalmers.se`
[2] University of Malta, Msida, Malta
`gordon.pace@um.edu.mt`
[3] ICC and Departamento de Computación, FCEyN, Universidad de Buenos Aires,
Buenos Aires, Argentina
`fschapachnik@dc.uba.ar`

Abstract. In this article we explore different issues and design choices that arise when considering how to fully embrace timed aspects in the formalisation of normative systems, e.g., by using deontic modalities, looking primarily through the lens of monitoring. We primarily focus on expressivity and computational aspects, discussing issues such as duration, superposition, conflicts, attempts, discharge, and complexity, while identifying semantic choices which arise and the challenges these pose for full monitoring of legal contracts.

Keywords: Deontic logic · Timed logic · Normative systems · Legal contracts · Monitoring

1 Introduction

If Alice is permitted to download a song from an online content provider, and gets a bonus that allows her to download another one, everybody would agree that now she can download up to two songs. Let's add time to the equation and consider Alice being permitted at 7am to download a song from 8am to 10am. At 9am she is granted another download permission, from 9am to 11am. At 9:30am she downloads a song. Can she download another at 10:30am? In other words, which of the two permissions did she exhaust? Is the permission involved a conditional one? How do we specify and monitor for these kind of timed normative specifications?

Reasoning about permissions and other normative modalities is the domain of *deontic logic*, while reasoning about time is usually the domain of *temporal logic* in the verification community. Verification and monitorability of temporal logics, including ones with real-time, has been extensively investigated (e.g., [9, 32, 33]).

Partially supported by UBACyT 20020130200032BA and PICT-2016 201-0112, the Swedish Research Council (*Vetenskapsrådet*) under grant Nr. 2019-04951 (*X-LEGAL: Smart Legal Contracts*), and the ERC Consolidator grant DSynMA (No. 772459).

© Springer Nature Switzerland AG 2021
L. Feng and D. Fisman (Eds.): RV 2021, LNCS 12974, pp. 81–99, 2021.
https://doi.org/10.1007/978-3-030-88494-9_5

We argue that normative concepts (e.g., *obligations, prohibitions, and permissions/rights*) are not appropriately modelled using existing monitoring logics. For example, specifying in LTL a prohibition to never download songs illegally is easy, however how can one specify that the specification may be violated but repaired by paying an appropriate fine? The naïve approach would simply use a disjunction between the two formulas, however this does not capture the difference in priority between the clauses and the different levels of violation.

Deontic logics have been proposed instead for normative reasoning. Different deontic languages have in fact been explored, with the ability to model and monitor for violations and their repair (e.g., [6,7]). Such languages involve certain normative modalities, parametrised by some state- or event-based formula, given some appropriate background theory. The difficulty and complexity of formalising untimed normative systems using deontic concepts have been studied in [43], while the justification on why LTL, CTL, and process algebra might not be sufficient to capture all the deontic notions has been presented in [18].

In this paper we want to focus on the monitorability of these logics under extensions with timed aspects. Although the different modalities that arise from adding time to deontic logic have been studied before, there are still many unanswered questions and no analysis of their monitorability. For instance, in [25] Governatori et al. analyse permissions with deadlines but do not discuss the issue of which one is discharged in case of temporal superposition nor what happens with timed permissions in the context of contracts. Superposition presents challenges for obligations too. Hashmi et al. [30] extend previous work by Governatori et al. [26] to deal with the temporal compliance of rules and present a categorisation of many types of obligations (*punctual, persistent, achievement,* etc.) based on the timing of their effect, enforcement and violation. However, some issues remain unexplored:[1] if $O[0, 10](a)$ and $O[5, 15](a)$ are two *achievement* obligations (meaning the obligation is discharged by the execution of a single action a during the period) and a is not executed in the $[0, 5)$ time interval, does it need to be performed twice during the $[5, 10]$ period?

Normative conflicts become more interesting and challenging in the presence of time. We would certainly consider $F(a)$ to be in conflict with $O(a)$ in an untimed and punctual context, but what happens with $F[0, 10](a)$ and $O[5, 15](a)$? Is this an unresolvable conflict despite the fact that compliance is possible? Should it be concluded that while there is a conflict in the $[5, 10]$ interval the contract requiring both is still valid?

In many cases it is interesting to talk about the moment a given obligation (or right) is enacted, or whenever the action or state of affairs affected by such modalities occur, and refer to them in another clauses. For instance, consider the situation in which Alice has the right to download two songs, but the second one

---

[1] In this paper we will use the notation $O[b, e](a)$ to denote the obligation to perform action a between time b and e. We use the same notation but with P to denote permission and F to denote prohibition. Note that despite the formal syntax, we are not committed to a formal semantics, since the paper is dedicated to explore the family of such semantics one can choose to adopt.

may only be downloaded between 3 and 5 days after downloading the first. Later on, an obligation to write a review on the songs is enforced, with a deadline of 30 days after having downloaded the second song. These kinds of (relative) timing constraints for deontic norms are usually not treated in the literature, as there is a need of having richer timed logics with, for example, *freeze quantifiers* [1].

In this article we continue the exploration of the different challenges that a timed deontic logic presents. Compared to previous work, we discuss the issues of timed superposition, timed deontic conflicts, discharge of deontic modalities in case of conflicts and attempting. Integrating time as a first class citizen in a logic brings not only expressivity concerns but also complexity and computability issues. In the case of a deontic logic, many other subtle issues arise, which we identify and discuss. We also discuss monitorability of deontic logics and their timed extensions, and consider the challenges to monitor synthesis.

The next section discusses different timed logics used in computer science and the trade-offs their represent in terms of expressivity and complexity, and briefly introduces deontic logic. After that, Sect. 3 digs into the different interpretation challenges presented by the inclusion of time in deontic logic. Section 4 discusses the monitorability of deontic logics and their timed extensions, and suggestions for monitor synthesis of the timed case. References to related work are made throughout the article. Section 5 concludes the paper with some final observations.

2   Background

2.1   Temporal Logics, Timed Logics and Complexity

Computer scientists have studied different *temporal* and *timed logics*, including their expressiveness, properties and decision procedures for their satisfiability, monitorability, and validity.

Temporal aspects appear in many different ways in real life, be it in computer systems or the legal domain. The simplest are probably situations related to the frequency on the occurrence of certain events, and the order between events, be it sequences, ordering or causality. *Temporal logics* have been around for a while and have been successfully used for specifying reactive and other computational systems, and also in combination with deontic logic (e.g., [24–26, 29]). In practice, as much of this work has observed before, any non-trivial normative document contains temporal aspects.

Temporal logics allow for reasoning about the ordering and causality between events, and come in different flavours, depending on whether time is discrete or continuous, whether there is a single future (linear) or it captures different possible futures (branching), whether it is possible to talk about the past or only the future, whether the logic talks about points in time or intervals, whether there is a global notion of time or only relative time, etc. Timed logics may be propositional or have quantifiers. Expressiveness and decidability are of course very much dependent on a combination of the different choices made on all the dimensions mentioned above (and others).

There is extensive work on the use of different timed logics, and we will not give details here as this is beyond the scope of this paper. That said, we will briefly describe the expressive power of three timed extensions of temporal logics namely time-bounded operators, freeze quantification, and time variables as presented by Alur and Henzinger [1], due to their relevance in what follows.

The first, and possibly least expressive, way to add timing constraints to existing temporal logics is to have *bounded temporal operators* where the classic temporal operators are enhanced with (integer) intervals. In this logic you can express properties like *"every event e_1 is followed by another event e_2 within 7 time units"*, written as $\Box(e_1 \rightarrow \Diamond_{[0,7]} e_2)$. The bounded-operator notation can only express properties relating adjacent temporal operators and cannot express non-local properties of the kind *"every event e_1 is followed by a response e_2, which is followed by another response e_3, such that the delay between e_2 and e_3 is no more than the delay between e_1 and e_2"*.

For that there is a need of a more expressive logic, one containing *freeze quantifiers*. This second variant of timed logic allows for quantification over time variables, which may be used to compare with other time variables. The non-local property given above would be expressed as follows in such a logic: $\Box \ x.(e_1 \rightarrow \Diamond \ y.(e_2 \wedge \Diamond z.(e_3 \wedge z - y \leq y - x)))$, where x and y are time variables associated with the corresponding states defined by the formula in its scope ($x.\varphi(x)$ holds at time t iff $\varphi(t)$ does).

A third, and more expressive, way to write timing constraints is by using *explicit clock variables*, based on first-order temporal logic and explicit (global) time, thus allowing to existentially and universally quantifier over clocks (see [35] for examples).

Expressivity, however, comes at the price of complexity or even undecidability. This is specially pressing when some type of tool is used or envisioned. For instance, encodings using timed automata may require one clock per variable (e.g., [16]), but the verification complexity depends on the number of clocks—and is exponential in the case of Timed Computational Tree Logic (TCTL).

Extending temporal logics with time-bounded temporal operators increases their complexity, in some cases yielding undecidability. For instance, the model checking problem for Metric Temporal Logic (MTL) is undecidable. Nevertheless, some interesting fragments of MTL, such as Metric Interval Temporal Logic (MITL) are decidable but EXPSPACE-complete [10].

For more examples and more details about expressiveness of these logics and other variants we direct the reader to [1] and the references therein.

2.2   Formalisation of Normative Systems: Deontic Logics

Deontic logic is the study of deontic modalities—mainly obligation, prohibition, and permission, meant for the modelling of legal and moral notions [22]. Initial deontic formalisms in the philosophical field (e.g., Standard Deontic Logic [23,39]) faced certain paradoxes, e.g., the inability to express what should happen to make up for an obligation being violated without introducing contradictions.

These paradoxes have remained problematic and the subject of debate [28]. However different approaches have been recently proposed to solve these problems (e.g., [16,44,45]), that have made deontic logic more useful in practice. We introduce the main concepts based on existing deontic formalisms briefly, but to keep our discussion general—we do not commit to any particular formalism for this paper.

A distinguishing feature between deontic formalisms is whether they are event/action- or propositional/state-based. One may be obliged to perform a certain action (e.g., pay a certain fee), or to reach a certain state (e.g., the state of having no pending payments to make). These approaches are dual, reaching different states typically requires performing actions (or, in a timed context, the passing of time), while actions may cause changes in state. For simplicity and without loss of generality we continue the discussion in this section by referring solely to action-based logics.

An obligation to do some action a requires a to be performed. This is often represented as $O(a)$. Similarly for permissions, $P(a)$, and prohibitions $F(a)$. These three can often be defined in terms of each other, e.g., a prohibition not to do an action is the obligation to not do it ($O(a) = F(\neg a)$), while a permission to do an action is often the lack of an obligation to do not do the action ($P(a) = \neg O(\neg a)$). Here we go beyond this and focus on the strand of work that views permission as a right to perform an action, as suggested in von Wright's seminal work [22], where permission includes an implicit obligation for the other parties to allow the permitted party to perform the action.

Variants of these modalities can also refer to a party, i.e. $O_p(a)$ where p is the name of the obliged party (e.g., [5]). Without these notational variants there may be underlying assumptions about which party or parties are associated with each action.

An important aspect of deontic formalisms is how they handle *contrary-to-duty* norms, or *reparations*. These are clauses that come into effect when there has been a violation, allowing some action/s to repair the violation, e.g., the paying of a penalty. The ability to handle these clauses is of utmost importance for practical applications of normative systems, e.g., for the monitoring of contracts or laws that use these kind of clauses routinely. We represent this, e.g., for obligations with $O_{O(\$10);O(b)}(a)$ where a 10 dollar penalty must be paid if a is not performed, and b performed after.

For more extensive and in depth material about deontic logic in general see [20] and references therein.

The combination of deontic concepts with (real-)time has been considered in an *ad hoc* manner in the literature, with different interpretations chosen without justification or contrasted with other possible ones. The effects of adding time to specific deontic operators was discussed in [25,26]. Note that those, and other similar work by Governatori et al., do not address the general more complex issue of getting a fully-fledged logic (or formal language) where many timed operators co-exist. *C-O Diagrams* [13,16,38] is a formal (visual) language (not a logic) featuring deontic concepts and timed constraints, with a timed automata semantics. The language has interesting features but does not address many of the issues discussed in this paper. No monitoring techniques has been studied for any of the above languages and logics.

3   Interpreting Timed Norms

In this section we resort to small examples to discuss different issues and design choices, that need to be taken into account when thinking about a deontic logic that is able to fully embrace all aspects of time-related expressions.[2]

State- vs. Action-Based Deontic Operators. The duality between contracts regulating events vs. regulating the state-of-affairs is also reflected in the deontic modalities themselves when taking into consideration time. On one hand, one may have pointwise modalities—for example, the obligation to perform an action at a particular point in time. Such pointwise modalities are frequently encountered when considering a system with discrete time events. For example, if the service-provider gives priority to a particular user at time point t_i, they are obliged to give priority to another user at the next time point (when an event is received) t_{i+1}. However, when one considers continuous real-time clocks, deontic modalities are typically over intervals of time. For example, an obligation with a deadline might oblige the service provider to ensure that a service is continuously available over the coming hour; or a user accessing a digital asset management system, may be prohibited from requesting the download of a file twice within a second of each other.

If we consider interval-based deontic modalities, there lies a duality with the event- vs. state-based view of the world. Does one identify the points in time when a modality starts holding and when it terminates, or does one identify the interval over which the modality holds? The most common approach one finds in the literature is the state-based approach (e.g., [26,27,29,30]), following the approach used in interval temporal logics such as Interval Temporal Logic (ITL) [41] and duration calculus [14]. This approach correlates closely with natural language clauses expressing concepts such as deadlines: *"The user is prohibited from transferring funds to a third party in the first 7 days of the creation of an account"* or *"The bank is obliged to refund a user within 15 days of a request to redeem an account."*

However, there is also work which takes the action-based approach (e.g., [17]), in which the key is to signal the start and end of a modality e.g., $\overleftarrow{O}_p(A)$ indicates the beginning of a time interval over which there is an obligation on party p to perform action A, while $\overrightarrow{O}_p(A)$ would be the end of this obligation. Such an approach corresponds to when these moments are identified in a legal text in separate ways, for instance *"The student has the right to upload a new assignment*

---

[2] It is worth noting that different interpretations of normative statements go far beyond the assignment of a formal semantics. Such differing views frequently correspond to views different parties may have of a normative text, e.g., a contract, including possibly in court.

from the first day of term" and *"If a student unregisters from a unit, he or she automatically loses the right to upload assignments.".*

The latter approach lends itself to a trace-based semantics, in which each event or time progression updates the clauses in force. However, this inherent state of active clauses makes compositional reasoning over contracts more difficult, and the former approach typically yields cleaner semantics.

A Plethora of Timed Deontic Modalities. What time should the logic refer to? Absolute time, i.e. a universal and always accessible clock that is referred to in every time-related expression, might be relatively inexpensive from a computational point of view, yet equally unrealistic from a legal perspective. Many legal expressions also require relative time, as in *"warranty period should be at least 3 month from the time of purchase"*. Is this just syntactic sugar to an expression like *"let U be the universal clock, let p be the time of purchase (according to the universal clock), and the warranty period is of w, then the purchased item is still in warranty as long as $U \leq p + w$"*? Complexity usually grows with the number of clocks, so it is in general desirable to reduce the number of clocks. This might be possible in some cases, for instance whenever what is needed is only the time-stamp associated with a given event but not how time evolves for such event (e.g., to compute duration). In some other cases, clock reusability is possible, although this kind of optimisation is usually handled under the hood by the tools.

Some use cases do require more intricate expressions of time. Consider for instance *"license can be renewed during 10 days after expiration if the expiration cause was A, or 15 days if the expiration cause was B"*, an expression where the deadline is relative to occurrences of events in the past, or *"if the item under warranty is taken to reparations, the warranty period is extended by the amount of time the item is being repaired, each time it is repaired"*, where the deadline needs to be computed. Such expressions seem to call for an algebra of time intervals, another threat to computability when real-time is involved [31].

To complicate things further, deadlines can sometimes be expressed in relation to an event still to happen (e.g., *"service should be provided until the user disconnects"*), or as a boolean expression involving many time references (e.g., *"service should be provided until the user disconnects, with a maximum of one month of service, not surpassing the calendar year"*).

Once deontic clauses have an explicit duration, the issue of possible multiple violations during that period arises. Should multiple violations trigger multiple reparations? Also, one should be able to distinguish between multiple violations vs. one violation that has a duration. Think of trespassing: if entering a facility is forbidden during the night, is trespassing twice for 1 h each the same as trespassing once for 2 h? As timed logics allow to measure the duration of an event, duration of violation should also be available as a parameter to the reparation clause. For example, an obligation to provide food and water to passengers during a flight might be redressed with a fine, possibly proportional to the duration of the flight.

Obligations with duration present challenges of their own: how should be $O[0, 10](a)$ read? If a is an event or action, should it be sustained during the $[0, 10]$ period, or it is only mandatory to do it at least once during the period? Again both cases are reasonable and may be required in different contexts, with the modalities allowing for the expression of the two. Even limiting our view to the variant to oblige the performance of the action once during the period, how should $O[0, 10](a) \oplus O[5, 15](a)$ be interpreted? Does the performance of a during the interval $[5, 10]$ satisfy both obligations, or are two occurrences required? Although the latter may appear to be more reasonable, it is worth noting that this would mean that conjunction is no longer idempotent, with $O[0, 10](a) \oplus O[0, 10](a)$ being different from $O[0, 10](a)$. Actions differ on the nature of their effects. Ensuring the door is open is idempotent, but paying or buying are not.

Part of the issue at stake in the previous example is whether modalities are *dischargeable* or *permanent*. Dischargeable modalities cease their effect once they are fulfilled, while permanent ones do not. For instance, prohibitions tend to be permanent. That is, a prohibition is still enacted (and in force) even when somebody has violated it. Furthermore, a prohibition is still in force even if a violation triggers its corresponding reparation. Note that a prohibition (and actually every modality) can be at the same time permanent and time bounded (e.g., it is forbidden to enter the pool during the night).

Dischargeable obligations are also common. Consider having ten days to fill in a report. The obligation is discharged with the execution of one instance of the action (the filling of the report), and gets violated when the deadline is met without the action happening. If the obligation were permanent (e.g., behave nicely during school time, or do what your boss asks during working hours), when the deadline is met there is no violation. In this case, violations occur within the interval when the obligation is active.

Governatori et al. [25] have characterised different types of obligations with deadlines, for instance distinguishing between *achievement* obligations (corresponding to the obligation to perform an action before the deadline), and *maintenance* obligations (corresponding to the obligation to ensure that a state holds until the deadline elapses). The variety of types of obligations with deadlines the authors present encompasses many common types of obligations even if not necessarily complete (in that not all forms of obligations over intervals are covered) already indicates the variety of choices one can adopt from when designing a real-time deontic logic with connections between our discussion above and the formalised notions in [25].

Permission and Time. In the case of an action-based logic, being permitted to do something within an interval can mean several different things, from having a continuous permission to repeat the action as many times as one wants (e.g., permission to enter the facility during daytime) to a one time permission, i.e. a dischargeable one.

In that last case it also seems to make sense to have some type of algebra of dischargeable permissions, as being granted a one day permission to download a song is not the same being granted the same permission twice. While it seems clear that meeting the deadline puts an end to every instance of the permission, what happens with the combination[3] of permissions $P[0, 10](a) \oplus P[5, 15](a)$ if at time 6 the action a is performed? When time reaches 11, is there still one permission left over? Is it always the case that the discharged permission is the oldest one? If so, why?

Another conflicting case can arise if we consider a one-time permission to use a service for half an hour. Now suppose another similar permission is granted. Can the bearer of the two half-hour permissions use the service for a full hour? In some cases there might be no difference while in others the granter of the permission may not consider them to be equivalent because a gap in between may be required (e.g., riding a horse or using a machine which might overheat).

Now consider the same example in the context of contracts, where one party can violate the other's permission to execute an action by not providing the proper synchronisation. Suppose party p has two permissions to execute synchronised action a: $P_{O(\$10)}[0, 10](a) \oplus P_{O(\$20)}[5, 15](a)$, the first having a reparation fee of \$10 and the other a fee of \$20. If at time 6 party p is not able to execute the permitted action because of lack of synchronisation by the other party, what is the fee applicable as reparation? Is it \$10, \$20 or even \$30?

Permissions with intervals, both permanent and dischargeable, present challenges to clearly define time-based conflicts. As an example, think of a permission to present a form in a government office until midnight on a specific date, yet the office is available only in working hours. Common sense states that the permission is for presenting during working hours until the midnight of the given date, and that there is no conflict involved. However, finding a formulation where this can be expressed naturally in a formal language is challenging, because of the chain of logical relations that need to be established to link the action of 'handing in the form' with the 'office being open' predicates. Furthermore, in some cases, limitations on time windows are made with the specific goal of discouraging the performance of the action (in this case the presentation of the form). If the intersection of the deadline and the working hours only left a small time frame available, should this situation be detected? This may indicate that the notion of conflict may, in some cases, be a fuzzy rather than crisp predicate.

Attempted Actions. As was mentioned before, in action-based timed deontic logics hitting a deadline without fulfilling an obligation is considered to be a violation. Think of the case of a contract, in which party A agrees to sell to party B at a discount price because party B agrees to buy at least 200 kg of goods during a one week period. During the first few days a transaction is made and B buys 100 kg at a discounted price. Then the week goes by with no other transaction being completed. The case goes to court, where A is claiming that B took advantage of the discount price without reaching the minimum agreed volume. Party B argues that she did attempt to buy several times yet on all the occasions party A's shop was either closed or out-of-stock. B even mentions one

---

[3] From this point onwards, we will use the notation $C \oplus C'$ to denote both C and C' being enacted. We avoid the use of symbols typically used for conjunction e.g., $\wedge$ or & in order to avoid implicit assumptions of idempotency of the operator.

occasion where she emailed A to arrange for a purchase and A took so long to respond that she had to get the goods from another supplier.

How should a logic handle such a case so that the attempts became observable? If buying and selling are separate actions, then that would mean parties can execute them independently, which is not the way a buy-sell agreement should be modelled. Effectively, it makes more sense to think of a synchronised buy-sell action that both parties need to agree to execute. The problem is that in most action-based logics when one party tries to synchronise on a shared action and the other party does not handshake, there is no trace of attempt in the resulting execution. Other logics, specifically those where events are timestamped, do leave a trace and the resulting execution has two events, close enough in time, and probably a third acknowledgement message, all of which can be abstracted together as a single transaction, or a high-level synchronised event.

Deontic logics usually do not allow for such a two-level interpretation: one where individual events can be seen (B trying to buy without being responded by A) and another where a successful sequence of a buy attempt and a proper response are abstracted as a single buy-sell transaction. This is common in network protocols where a 'connection' is a high-level event with an initiator and a completer. Being an initiator is a role: any of the parties can be the initiator just by sending first the proper connection initiation message. A deontic logic should probably allow for a more complicated scenario: it should let any of the parties attempt the transaction, but without a single initiation message, i.e. a buy-sell transaction can be started either with a buy or a sell attempt.

Going back to the discount-per-volume case, B's obligation of buying should be regarded as discharged because either a high-level buy-sell action took place, or a low level buy attempt was issued by B without a response from A within a proper time-frame, which may not be formal defined. Actually, whether two buy and sell messages separated by t time units are to be considered to correspond to an acknowledged request or not may be a controversial issue among the involved parties. What tools should the logic provide to ground this discussion?

Timed Conflicts. Conflicts due to time expressions are also a topic of interest. Although $F(a) \oplus O(a)$ is clearly a conflicting sentence, how should we interpret $F[0, 10](a) \oplus O[5, 15](a)$? Is this an unsatisfiable conflict? Should it be concluded that while there is a conflict during the interval $[5, 10]$—at the beginning of which $F[0, 5](a) \oplus O[0, 10](a)$ is in force?

If action a takes time to perform, does the interval specify when the action should commence, finish or all the performance time? If, for instance, we take the time of commencement, $O[5, 10](a)$ means that the action must start in the interval irrespectively of when it ends (as in *'the shipment should be sent to their the destination during the next 24 h'*), but should the time instant be the same for a prohibition as in $F[5, 10](a)$? Is there a violation if action a starts at time 3 and finishes at time 6?

We have already discussed the issue of having overlapping time intervals for obligations, permissions and prohibitions. The situation is of course even more complex in the presence of CTDs (contrary-to-duties) and CTPs (contrary-to-prohibitions) clauses. Timed CTDs and CTPs may be problematic also if their triggering is conditional to some relative notions of time, and of course in case of normal delays not necessarily due to the fault of the involved parties.

For instance, a company working regulation might state that all employees must answer company email within 24 h of receipt. If they will not be able to answer within this time-frame, they should then send a standard mail at least one hour before the 24-h deadline saying that they will not be able to answer in time and state by when an answer is to be expected. In the absence of both an answer and the canned response, the company automatically sends a message with a reprimand to the employee (after the 24 h deadline) and decreases the employee's bonus by 2 points. A concrete situation might be that Alice sends her answer exactly 23 h after having received an email but a system problem causes her answer to arrive after the 24-h deadline. The system then will produce the automatic response and will decrease her bonus balance by 2 points. A solution based on time-stamps might help here: every event should have a time-stamp and all the norms should be explicit on whether it refers to the time-stamp of attempting, sending or receiving something. This solution, however, might cause inconsistencies as certain obligations will be triggered and might need then to be recalled (similar to rollbacks in long-lived transactions). What is then the meaning of recalling such obligations? Of course we should also recall all the corresponding (eventually nested) CTDs (and similarly for CTPs).

In the above example one the main issues was caused by delays. Should we allow for reasoning only for the ideal case, or should we include a model of the delays? Which delays are acceptable and which are not (from the liability point of view)?

Other Standing Challenges. Deontic formal languages can serve many purposes such as conflict analysis, runtime verification, simulation, etc. Each of these domains of application impose its own constraints. For instance, matching real occurrence time of the events is an issue in run-time monitoring, specially for distributed events. Thus, coping with rollback-able attribution of guilt for failed deadlines (like the example given in Sect. 3) or fuzzy-matching of events [11] (i.e. being able to deal with the fuzziness of timestamps of real-life events) might become a requirement that is not really necessary for other types of applications.

Although there are purely logic-based approaches successfully dealing with time (e.g., [30,36]), most of the existing tools are automata-based (e.g., [37]), thus, if one wants to warrant tool support, one might want to use some kind of underlying timed transition system with annotations on the deontic imperatives.

From the design point of view, the choice might be between starting with timed automata, one of the most popular automata-based timed formalisms, and add the deontic information, or start with the standard deontic logic Kripke semantics and add time to it. This choice might be driven by different considerations and we do not have a formal argument in favour or against any of them.

A good example of how deontic modalities and timed constraints may be combined, somehow following the first approach mentioned above (interpreting and encoding the deontic modalities into timed automata), is the case of C-O Diagrams [16], for which a timed automata semantics was given (see [16] for a first translation and [13] for a new optimised translation for an extension of the original diagrams). The translation was implemented as UPPAAL automata and integrated into a toolchain called *Contract Verifier* [12].

4   Monitoring Norms and Timed Norms

In the previous section we introduced and reviewed different interpretations of deontic modalities that arise in a real-time context. In this section, we continue the discussion with a focus on monitoring of normative systems under these different modalities and interpretations.

4.1   Monitorability

The appropriateness of a logic for runtime verification depends, amongst other things, on its *monitorability*, that is whether for any finite execution we can eventually make a determination whether a specification is satisfied or violated [9,46]. For example, monitoring for linear temporal logic (LTL) has certain limitations, e.g., the LTL specification $\mathbf{F}a$ can only be monitored for satisfaction (if a occurs), but not for violation (without some knowledge of the underlying system). We discuss these standard notions of satisfaction- and violation-monitorability with regards to deontic logics. Although one finds literature on the monitoring of norms in specific logics (e.g., [2,21]), rather than focus on a particular logic in this section we take a more high level view.

Consider an 'obligation' to eventually do a positive action, without any time limit. Is this truly an obligation? Such an 'obligation' can essentially be postponed forever, and thus we cannot monitor for its violation. If we allow it, we can however monitor for its satisfaction (similarly to $\mathbf{F}a$ in LTL). On the other hand, the obligation not to do an action (or prohibition) without any time limit does have more meaningful normative semantics over finite traces—it is violated if the prohibited action is done.

Similar to prohibitions, permissions (here the *right* to do something) do not need to be bounded to make sense—the notion of perpetual rights is standard. However, they differ to obligations and prohibitions with regards to satisfaction and violation semantics. Permissions cannot be violated by the permitted party, but instead they can be violated by others when the permitted action requires the other party or parties to synchronise in their performance [8]. One interpretation is that the parties always, at each time step, provide the required synchronising actions, or at least at the time steps the permitted party wants to exercise the permission [3]. Essentially this is a safety property when we can monitor attempts to perform actions: just monitor for the attempt to exercise the permission and if it fails then the permission has been violated [7]. This interpretation can be relaxed to take into account that there may be real-world limitations on the performance of the action, and only enforce the obligation on the other parties at time steps where it is possible for them to provide the synchronising actions, or within a bounded time-frame, without any effect on monitorability. It is worth noting that there are different types of rights identified in the literature [34], and the interpretation of permission as the liberty of one party from other parties interfering with that first party's performance of the permitted action is but one of them.

Another pertinent issue is that when monitoring deontic specifications we are not just interested in trace violation. In deontic logic there are multiple parties to a contract, and thus we are more often also interested in which party or parties caused the violation. This kind of blame assignment may not always be possible, for example when the specification is unsatisfiable, or is difficult when the actions of a party in the past may force another party to violate the contract in the future. Another aspect is that a party may still be in compliance with a contract if they reasonably attempt to satisfy it but are prevented to do so by the environment (the real world and the other parties). For example, one may not be able to satisfy an obligation because another has not provided the synchronising action, and thus the other is at fault. Capturing and analysing this also requires the monitoring of attempts to perform an action (e.g., [7]), otherwise this kind of compliance cannot be monitored for.

We have considered the monitorability of the different kinds of atomic norms, however norms can also be composed together in different ways. Allowing unconstrained logical combinations causes certain paradoxes and dilemmas (see [28,43]), since normative modalities are not truth statements. However, deontic logics with constrained interpretations of these combinations that avoid these paradoxes also exist (e.g., [40]). Here we consider the monitorability of combinations of normative modalities with unconstrained logical operators for completeness.

Sequence and conjunction clearly both maintain monitorability given monitorability of the sub-formulas (the resulting property remains co-/safety). A clause can also have an associated reparation clause, which can be modelled using a monitor for the first clause that upon detecting a violation of the first clause triggers a monitor for the second.

Norms can also be guarded or conditioned on something happening. The monitorability of the guards depends on the allowed expressions. If the expression is a regular expression or a past-time LTL formula then monitorability is maintained. It seems unlikely that allowing unmonitorable expressions would add anything to the logic, e.g., allowing future-time LTL to guard norms would allow us to write $[\mathbf{FG}p]O(a)$ (if p is true infinitely often from this point on, then you are obliged to do a), which seems counter-intuitive—the party cannot reasonably be held to have violated a contract if the contract expects impossible things of them, such as clairvoyance.

We also consider the remaining usual logical operations: negation, and disjunction. Usually, a negated prohibition becomes a permission, a negated obligation becomes the permission not to do the action, and a negated permission becomes a prohibition. In deontic logics the disjunction can usually be moved to the event/state parameter side given appropriate background theories (e.g., $O(a) \vee O(b) = O(a \vee b)$), or involves clauses with mutually exclusive guards (e.g., $[p]O(a) \vee [!p]O(a) = [p]O(a) \oplus [!p]O(a)$). The former is more difficult in the timed case, e.g., $O_{[0,5]}(a) \vee O_{[4,10]}(b)$, but can be solved in the same way by moving timing to the event side, i.e., $O(a_{[0,5]} \vee b_{[4,10]})$. In the case of disjunction of more complex clauses, e.g., with sequence $O(a); P(b) \vee O(b); P(a)$, guards can be used to remove the disjunction, i.e., $O(a \vee b); ([a]P(b) \oplus [b]P(a))$ (assuming only one action can happen in each time step).

Other deontic logics use the notion of *defeasability*, where certain clauses may be in conflict with each other but have a priority function that resolves the conflict (e.g., if the first rule does not hold then try the second) [27]. This has a disjunctive nature that does not affect monitorability.

Then full monitorability here requires the ability to observe failed actions, and knowledge about the synchronising actions made available by the parties. Without these we are unable to talk about whether parties have fulfilled their obligations with respect to a deontic contract.

4.2   Monitor Synthesis

One approach to monitoring deontic logics could involve their translation into established runtime verification logics, however there are some features of deontic logics that do not translate well. For example, the notion of *reparations*, where a party may be obligated to perform a certain action, and failing that they are in violation of the contract, but may perform certain actions as reparations for this violation and return into compliance. The best attempt at writing $O_{O(b)}(a)$ in LTL would involve disjunction, i.e., $a \vee (\neg a \wedge \mathbf{X}(b))$. However in LTL this loses the priority implicit in the deontic logic representation. Reparations are not simply other options, but imply recognition by the performing party that they have violated a contract, an action which can have legal effect. Moreover, violation of certain clauses does not mean other obligations are not still in effect—there are different levels of violation that are not captured accurately by existing approaches to monitoring. They could perhaps be added through certain meta-level considerations, but not at the level of existing monitoring languages. Working at the level of deontic logic instead allows us to directly take into account all these considerations that are required for legal contract monitoring.

In previous work we have given operational semantics to different untimed deontic languages (e.g., [7,19]) which can easily be used for monitor synthesis. An automata construction could also be constructed, through a Kripke structure where states are associated with the sets of norm clauses that must hold when at that state. Contract automata [6,8] may be able to be re-purposed for this.

The timed case has different needs, as discussed previously. Effective and efficient monitors for relative timing constraints are especially important in the monitoring of normative systems. These often specify norms that activate at the point another norm is satisfied, or penalties that start holding at the time another norm is violated.

Looking to LTL with (real-)time as inspiration we find different approaches for monitor synthesis. Focusing on *metric temporal logic* (MTL), i.e. temporal logic with until and since modalities holding over a certain interval, we find translations to deterministic timed automata that can be re-purposed for monitoring (e.g., [42]). Another interesting approach involves reducing the problem to monitoring LTL with atoms corresponding to bounded (i.e., with bounded intervals) MTL formulas [32]. Essentially the proposed algorithm uses dynamic programming techniques to determine the value of the bounded MTL formulas by collecting events appropriately depending on the associated time they occur and the interval associated with the formula. The authors extend this work for MTL with predicates that can refer to time points, allowing for monitoring of specifications with relative timing [33]. This suggests that separately combining monitoring of timing aspects and higher-level normative aspects may also be effective.

One issue not considered in detail in previous work is that of the underlying theory. One event/state parameter may correspond to the evaluation of a more complex predicate. For example, in a state-based deontic logic we may want to specify that at the end of each month there is an obligation that the average number of transactions is below a certain number. Operationalising such specifications can involve having a layer of monitors that compute these predicates' values, which can be queried by the norm monitors. For a rich monitorable language, forms of symbolic monitor automata (e.g., DATES [15], or [4]) can be used to compute the values of these predicates.

The proposed solution for complex event predicates above may be combined with an approach inspired by that of [32] for MTL—the bounds associated with an obligation may be moved to the events: $O[x, y](a) = O(a_{[x,y]})$. Thus we may be able to re-use monitor synthesis for the untimed case by simply adding a layer that transforms timed events into appropriate timed action atoms (e.g., if $x \leq z \leq y$ then the transformation $(a, z \rightarrow a_{[x,y]}$ can be applied, where the event (a, z) denotes action a occurring at time z), which are then processed by appropriate monitors for the deontic-level specifications.

5   Conclusions

In this article we explored the different issues and design choices that arise when considering how to fully embraced timed aspects into a deontic logic, mainly from a computational point of view. To do so we ask questions beyond those addressed in prior work by others (e.g., [11, 16, 17, 25, 26, 30]). We resorted to small examples to discuss issues such as duration, superposition, conflicts, attempts, discharge, complexity and tool support among others, many of which were not covered in the literature.

In summary, we considered the state- and action-based approaches for interval-based deontic modalities, which respectively require the identification of the interval on which the modality holds, and the actions that identify the start and end of the interval. We discussed choices with regards to underlying clocks (universal or relative), and different constraints required out of modalities (that something must hold until a deadline, or within a certain interval). The latter allows for different interpretations—given two intersecting obligations, doing one event may be able to satisfy both, or not. The issue of dischargeability and permanence of norms was also discussed (a norm may no longer hold after being first satisfied, or it may continue holding). Moreover, taking into account that attempts to fulfil a norm may fail, through no fault of the actor, in a timed context requires reasoning about synchronising actions not necessarily occurring at the same time step. Finally, we discussed conflicts due to overlapping time intervals, where a contract may have satisfying traces but other traces that exercise the conflict. This can be a problem especially in the context of reparations with some relative deadline.

One thing that many of the used examples have in common is that the different interpretations proposed seem to correspond with interpretations that different stakeholders might sustain in case of conflict, even in court. One research direction is to investigate a logic using nondeterminism to correspond to possible interpretations. What such a logic would provide is not settling over an interpretation but rather coherence: one branch might flag violations for actions that commence during the prohibited interval, irrespectively of where they end, while another one might only flag violations for prohibited action that happen entirely in the interval, but no branch would mix both interpretations. Thus, legal arguments become arguments about choosing (or pruning) branches in the logic.

Finally, we have discussed and analysed what are the main issues and challenges in the monitoring of (un)timed deontic logics. To the best of our knowledge no work exists on the monitoring of such logics. This is an open research direction for researchers in the RV community to consider. Though a successful approach might first need to address all the issues discussed in this paper concerning the extension of deontic modalities with time, we believe that existing approaches for MTL can inspire monitor synthesis techniques for timed deontic logics.

References

1. Alur, R., Henzinger, T.A.: Logics and models of real time: a survey. In: de Bakker, J.W., Huizing, C., de Roever, W.P., Rozenberg, G. (eds.) REX 1991. LNCS, vol. 600, pp. 74–106. Springer, Heidelberg (1992). https://doi.org/10.1007/BFb0031988
2. Alvarez-Napagao, S., Aldewereld, H., Vázquez-Salceda, J., Dignum, F.: Normative monitoring: semantics and implementation. In: De Vos, M., Fornara, N., Pitt, J.V., Vouros, G. (eds.) COIN -2010. LNCS (LNAI), vol. 6541, pp. 321–336. Springer, Heidelberg (2011). https://doi.org/10.1007/978-3-642-21268-0_18
3. Azzopardi, S.: Extending contract automata with reparation, hypothetical and conditional clauses. Technical report, University of Malta, May 2014
4. Azzopardi, S., Colombo, C., Ebejer, J.-P., Mallia, E., Pace, G.J.: Runtime verification using VALOUR. In: RV-CuBES 2017. Kalpa Publications in Computing, vol. 3, pp. 10–18 (2017)
5. Azzopardi, S., Gatt, A., Pace, G.J.: Reasoning about partial contracts. In: JURIX 2016, pp. 23–32 (2016)

6. Azzopardi, S., Pace, G.J., Schapachnik, F.: Contract automata with reparations. In: JURIX 2014, pp. 49–54 (2014)
7. Azzopardi, S., Pace, G.J., Schapachnik, F.: On observing contracts: deontic contracts meet smart contracts. In: JURIX 2018, pp. 21–30 (2018)
8. Azzopardi, S., Pace, G.J., Schapachnik, F., Schneider, G.: Contract automata - an operational view of contracts between interactive parties. Artif. Intell. Law **24**(3), 203–243 (2016)
9. Bauer, A., Leucker, M., Schallhart, C.: Runtime verification for LTL and TLTL. ACM Trans. Softw. Eng. Methodol. **20**(4) (2011)
10. Bouyer, P., Laroussinie, F.: Model checking timed automata. In: Modeling and Verification of Real-Time Systems: Formalisms and Software Tools, pp. 111–140 (2010)
11. Cambronero, M., Llana, L., Pace, G.J.: Timed contract compliance under event timing uncertainty (2019, submitted for publication)
12. Camilleri, J.J., Haghshenas, M.R., Schneider, G.: A web-based tool for analysing normative documents in English. In: SAC-SVT 2018, pp. 1865–1872. ACM (2018)
13. Camilleri, J.J., Schneider, G.: Modelling and analysis of normative documents. Logical Algebraic Methods Program. **91**, 33–59 (2017)
14. Chaochen, Z., Hoare, C.A.R., Ravn, A.P.: A calculus of durations. Inf. Process. Lett. **40**(5), 269–276 (1991)
15. Colombo, C., Pace, G.J., Schneider, G.: Dynamic event-based runtime monitoring of real-time and contextual properties. In: Cofer, D., Fantechi, A. (eds.) FMICS 2008. LNCS, vol. 5596, pp. 135–149. Springer, Heidelberg (2009). https://doi.org/10.1007/978-3-642-03240-0_13
16. Díaz, G., Cambronero, M.-E., Martínez, E., Schneider, G.: Specification and verification of normative texts using C-O Diagrams. Trans. Softw. Eng. **40**(8), 795–817 (2014)
17. Farrell, A.D.H., Sergot, M.J., Sallé, M., Bartolini, C.: Using the event calculus for tracking the normative state of contracts. Int. J. Cooperative Inf. Syst. **14**(2–3), 99–129 (2005)
18. Fenech, S., Okika, J., Pace, G.J., Ravn, A.P., Schneider, G.: On the specification of full contracts. In: FESCA 2009. ENTCS, vol. 253(1), pp. 39–55 (2009)
19. Fenech, S., Pace, G.J., Schneider, G.: Automatic conflict detection on contracts. In: Leucker, M., Morgan, C. (eds.) ICTAC 2009. LNCS, vol. 5684, pp. 200–214. Springer, Heidelberg (2009). https://doi.org/10.1007/978-3-642-03466-4_13
20. Gabbay, D., van der Meyden, R., Horty, J., Parent, X., van der Torre, L.: The Handbook of Deontic Logic. College Publications (2013)
21. Aranda García, A., Cambronero, M.-E., Colombo, C., Llana, L., Pace, G.J.: Runtime verification of contracts with Themulus. In: de Boer, F., Cerone, A. (eds.) SEFM 2020. LNCS, vol. 12310, pp. 231–246. Springer, Cham (2020). https://doi.org/10.1007/978-3-030-58768-0_13
22. Wright, G.H.V.: Deontic logic. Mind **60**(237), 1–15 (1951)
23. Wright, G.H.V.: Deontic logic: a personal view. Ratio Juris **12**, 26–38 (1999)
24. Gorín, D., Mera, S., Schapachnik, F.: A software tool for legal drafting. In: FLACOS 2011, pp. 1–15. Elsevier (2011)
25. Governatori, G., Hulstijn, J., Riveret, R., Rotolo, A.: Characterising deadlines in temporal modal defeasible logic. In: Orgun, M.A., Thornton, J. (eds.) AI 2007. LNCS (LNAI), vol. 4830, pp. 486–496. Springer, Heidelberg (2007). https://doi.org/10.1007/978-3-540-76928-6_50

26. Governatori, G., Rotolo, A.: Justice delayed is justice denied: logics for a temporal account of reparations and legal compliance. In: Leite, J., Torroni, P., Ågotnes, T., Boella, G., van der Torre, L. (eds.) CLIMA 2011. LNCS (LNAI), vol. 6814, pp. 364–382. Springer, Heidelberg (2011). https://doi.org/10.1007/978-3-642-22359-4_25

27. Governatori, G., Rotolo, A., Sartor, G.: Temporalised normative positions in defeasible logic. In: ICAIL 2005, pp. 25–34 (2005)

28. Hansen, J.: The paradoxes of deontic logic: alive and kicking. Theoria **72**(3), 221–232 (2006)

29. Hashmi, M., Governatori, G., Wynn, M.T.: Modeling obligations with event-calculus. In: Bikakis, A., Fodor, P., Roman, D. (eds.) RuleML 2014. LNCS, vol. 8620, pp. 296–310. Springer, Cham (2014). https://doi.org/10.1007/978-3-319-09870-8_22

30. Hashmi, M., Governatori, G., Wynn, M.T.: Normative requirements for regulatory compliance: an abstract formal framework. Inf. Syst. Front. **18**(3), 429–455 (2015). https://doi.org/10.1007/s10796-015-9558-1

31. Henzinger, T.A.: It's about time: real-time logics reviewed. In: Sangiorgi, D., de Simone, R. (eds.) CONCUR 1998. LNCS, vol. 1466, pp. 439–454. Springer, Heidelberg (1998). https://doi.org/10.1007/BFb0055640

32. Ho, H.-M., Ouaknine, J., Worrell, J.: Online monitoring of metric temporal logic. In: Bonakdarpour, B., Smolka, S.A. (eds.) RV 2014. LNCS, vol. 8734, pp. 178–192. Springer, Cham (2014). https://doi.org/10.1007/978-3-319-11164-3_15

33. Ho, H.-M., Ouaknine, J., Worrell, J.: On the expressiveness and monitoring of metric temporal logic. CoRR, abs/1803.02653 (2018)

34. Kanger, S., Kanger, H.: Rights and parliamentarism. Theoria **32**(2), 85–115 (1966)

35. Konur, S.: Real-time and probabilistic temporal logics: an overview. CoRR, abs/1005.3200 (2010)

36. Lamport, L.: Specifying Systems: The TLA+ Language and Tools for Hardware and Software Engineers. Addison-Wesley Longman Publishing Co., Inc. (2002)

37. Larsen, K.G., Pettersson, P., Yi, W.: UPPAAL in a nutshell. Softw. Tools Technol. Transfer **1**(1), 134–152 (1997)

38. Martínez, E., Díaz, G., Cambronero, M.-E., Schneider, G.: A model for visual specification of E-contracts. In: IEEE SCC 2010, pp. 1–8. IEEE Computer Society (2010)

39. McNamara, P.: Deontic logic. In: Gabbay, D.M., Woods, J., (eds.) Handbook of the History of Logic, vol. 7, pp. 197–289. North-Holland Publishing (2006)

40. Meyer, J.-J., Dignum, F., Johannes, R.: The Paradoxes of Deontic Logic Revisited: A Computer Science Perspective. Technical report UU-CS-1994-38, EWI-IS: Department of Computer Science, University of Utrecht, Utrecht, September 1994

41. Moszkowski, B., Manna, Z.: Reasoning in interval temporal logic. In: Clarke, E., Kozen, D. (eds.) Logic of Programs 1983. LNCS, vol. 164, pp. 371–382. Springer, Heidelberg (1984). https://doi.org/10.1007/3-540-12896-4_374

42. Ničković, D., Piterman, N.: From MTL to deterministic timed automata. In: Chatterjee, K., Henzinger, T.A. (eds.) FORMATS 2010. LNCS, vol. 6246, pp. 152–167. Springer, Heidelberg (2010). https://doi.org/10.1007/978-3-642-15297-9_13

43. Pace, G.J., Schneider, G.: Challenges in the specification of full contracts. In: Leuschel, M., Wehrheim, H. (eds.) IFM 2009. LNCS, vol. 5423, pp. 292–306. Springer, Heidelberg (2009). https://doi.org/10.1007/978-3-642-00255-7_20

44. Prisacariu, C., Schneider, G.: A formal language for electronic contracts. In: Bonsangue, M.M., Johnsen, E.B. (eds.) FMOODS 2007. LNCS, vol. 4468, pp. 174–189. Springer, Heidelberg (2007). https://doi.org/10.1007/978-3-540-72952-5_11

45. Prisacariu, C., Schneider, G.: A dynamic deontic logic for complex contracts. J. Logic Algebraic Program. **81**(4), 458–490 (2012)
46. Stucki, S., Sánchez, C., Schneider, G., Bonakdarpour, B.: Gray-box monitoring of hyperproperties. In: ter Beek, M.H., McIver, A., Oliveira, J.N. (eds.) FM 2019. LNCS, vol. 11800, pp. 406–424. Springer, Cham (2019). https://doi.org/10.1007/978-3-030-30942-8_25

Efficient Black-Box Checking via Model Checking with Strengthened Specifications

Junya Shijubo$^{(\boxtimes)}$, Masaki Waga , and Kohei Suenaga

Graduate School of Informatics, Kyoto University, Kyoto, Japan
shijubo@fos.kuis.kyoto-u.ac.jp

Abstract. *Black-box checking (BBC)* is a testing method for cyber-physical systems (CPSs) as well as software systems. BBC consists of *active automata learning* and *model checking*; a Mealy machine is learned from the system under test (SUT), and the learned Mealy machine is verified against a specification using model checking. When the Mealy machine violates the specification, the model checker returns an input witnessing the specification violation of the Mealy machine. We use it to refine the Mealy machine or conclude that the SUT violates the specification. Otherwise, we conduct *equivalence testing* to find an input witnessing the difference between the Mealy machine and the SUT. In the BBC for CPSs, equivalence testing tends to be time-consuming due to the time for the system execution. In this paper, we enhance the BBC utilizing model checking with *strengthened specifications*. By model checking with a strengthened specification, we more chance to obtain an input witnessing the specification violation than model checking with the original specification. The refinement of the Mealy machine with such an input tends to reduce the number of equivalence testing, which improves the efficiency. We conducted experiments with an automotive benchmark. Our experiment results demonstrate the merit of our method.

Keywords: black-box checking · Cyber-physical system falsification · Specification strengthening · Automata learning

1 Introduction

Due to its safety-critical nature, the safety assurance of a cyber-physical system (CPS) is crucial. However, since a CPS is implemented as a combination of software and physical systems, traditional safety-assurance techniques for software such as testing and formal verification are hard to apply to a CPS.

Much effort has been devoted to adapt these safety-assurance methods for software to a CPS [16]. Representatives of these methods are *falsification* [13] and *formal verification* [7,17]. Given a CPS $\mathcal{M}$ and a specification φ that describes how the system should work, a falsification method tries to discover an input to $\mathcal{M}$ that violates φ to reveal a flaw of $\mathcal{M}$. In contrast, a formal verification

© Springer Nature Switzerland AG 2021
L. Feng and D. Fisman (Eds.): RV 2021, LNCS 12974, pp. 100–120, 2021.
https://doi.org/10.1007/978-3-030-88494-9_6

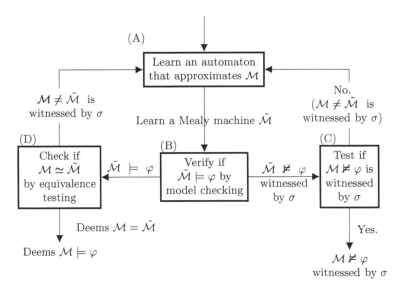

Fig. 1. The workflow of black-box checking.

method tries to guarantee the absence of bugs by mathematically proving that $\mathcal{M}$ conforms to φ.

There is a tradeoff between these two groups. Although formal verification ensures high-level safety by resorting to mathematical proofs, its cost is too heavy to be applied to a large CPS. Furthermore, it cannot be applied if the system $\mathcal{M}$ is a black box. On the contrary, falsification is cheaper than formal verification and applicable even if $\mathcal{M}$ is a black box. However, efficiently driving the counterexample search for a black box $\mathcal{M}$ is often challenging.

Black-box checking (BBC) [32], one of the falsification methods, is an approach to address this tradeoff. The main idea of BBC is to combine *active automata learning* such as L* [2], which synthesizes an automaton approximating the behavior of a black-box system, with *model checking*—one of the formal verification techniques—to search for a counterexample in an organized way.

Figure 1 shows the workflow of BBC. It first learns a Mealy machine $\tilde{\mathcal{M}}$ that approximates the behavior of the black-box system $\mathcal{M}$ under test ((A) in Fig. 1); this can be done by using the candidate-generation phase of automata learning algorithm such as L* [2]. Notice that the learned $\tilde{\mathcal{M}}$ may not be equivalent to $\mathcal{M}$. Next, BBC decides whether $\tilde{\mathcal{M}} \models \varphi$ holds by model checking ((B) in Fig. 1.) If this does not hold (i.e., $\tilde{\mathcal{M}} \not\models \varphi$), the model-checking procedure returns a counterexample input to $\tilde{\mathcal{M}}$ that drives $\tilde{\mathcal{M}}$ to a state that satisfies $\neg\varphi$. BBC then checks whether σ is a true counterexample or a spurious one by feeding σ to the original system $\mathcal{M}$ and observing its behavior ((C) in Fig. 1.) If σ is a true counterexample (i.e., σ witnesses $\mathcal{M} \not\models \varphi$), then BBC has disproved $\mathcal{M} \models \varphi$; it returns σ as a counterexample. If σ is not a counterexample to the actual system $\mathcal{M}$, then σ is a spurious counterexample that exhibits the difference between $\mathcal{M}$ and $\tilde{\mathcal{M}}$. Then, BBC uses σ as a new input to the automata-learning procedure

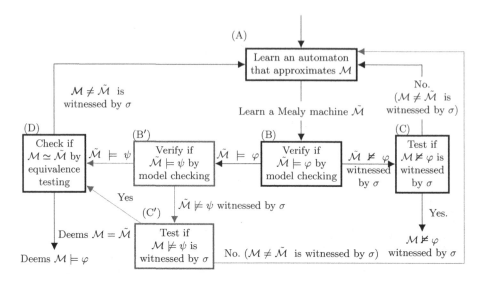

Fig. 2. The workflow of our method, where ψ is a strengthened specification of φ. The red part is the changes from the original BBC (Fig. 1). (Color figure online)

to obtain a new automaton. If $\tilde{\mathcal{M}} \models \varphi$ holds in the model-checking step in (B), BBC gives $\tilde{\mathcal{M}}$ and $\mathcal{M}$ to an equivalence-testing procedure ((D) in Fig. 1). The equivalence-testing procedure tries to find an input trace that differentiates $\mathcal{M}$ and $\tilde{\mathcal{M}}$ by generating many inputs and executing $\mathcal{M}$ and $\tilde{\mathcal{M}}$. One may use random sampling for the input generation or may use more sophisticated techniques like hill climbing and evolutionary computation. If an input σ that exhibits the difference between $\mathcal{M}$ and $\tilde{\mathcal{M}}$ is discovered, BBC uses σ as a new input to the automata learning procedure. Otherwise, BBC deems that $\tilde{\mathcal{M}}$ and $\mathcal{M}$ are equivalent and returns $\mathcal{M} \models \varphi$.

One of the practical issues in BBC for CPSs is its long execution time. In particular, the computational cost of the equivalence testing between a CPS and an automaton is high compared to that of the model checking. This is because the number of the states of a synthesized automaton to be model-checked is small, but a simulation of the system takes time; therefore, the computational cost of equivalence testing, which requires many runs of simulations, is high.

Based on the above observation, we propose a method to optimize BBC by reducing the number of equivalence tests. The basic observation is that the number of the equivalence tests conducted by an execution of BBC is the number of the transitions from (B) to (D) in Fig. 1; therefore, if we can reduce the number of such transitions, the time spent for an execution of BBC is reduced.

To this end, we adapt BBC so that the model checking of a learned automaton $\tilde{\mathcal{M}}$ is conducted against a *stronger* specification ψ than the original φ. A model checking with ψ tends to return a counterexample than it is checked against φ, which promotes transition from (B) to (C) rather than to (D).

Figure 2 shows the workflow of the proposed method; the difference from the original BBC is presented in red. If $\tilde{\mathcal{M}} \models \varphi$ is successfully verified by a model checker ((B) in Fig. 2), our procedure generates a stronger specification ψ and applies a model checker to verify $\tilde{\mathcal{M}} \models \psi$ ((B') in Fig. 2). If the verification fails with a counterexample σ, our procedure checks whether σ witnesses that the original $\mathcal{M}$ violates the strengthened specification ψ ((C') in Fig. 2). If it is not the case, σ exhibits the difference between $\mathcal{M}$ and $\tilde{\mathcal{M}}$ since σ does not drive $\mathcal{M}$ to the violation of ψ but it does for $\tilde{\mathcal{M}}$. Then, the learned automaton $\tilde{\mathcal{M}}$ is refined by using the new data σ ((A) in Fig. 2). If $\tilde{\mathcal{M}}$ is verified to conform to ψ or σ drives $\mathcal{M}$ to the violation of ψ, then our procedure conducts an equivalence test ((D) in Fig. 2).

To generate a stronger specification ψ than φ, we define syntactic rewriting rules to strengthen φ. The rules include, for example, rewriting of $p \vee q$ to $p \wedge q$, where p and q are atomic propositions, and rewriting of an STL formula $\Diamond_I \varphi$ to $\Diamond_{I'} \varphi$, where the interval I' is a subset of I. We define the strengthening relation and prove its correctness.

We implemented our method as an extension of FalCAuN [37] that implements BBC for CPSs. To check the effectiveness of our method, we evaluated our implementation using the Simulink model of an automatic transmission system [19]. The result shows that our method is up to 66% faster than the original BBC, which demonstrates the effectiveness of our method.

1.1 Related Work

Active automata learning has various applications in software engineering [18, 35], e.g., specification mining [12,31] and synthesis [25]. *Black-box checking (BBC)* [32], which is also known as *learning-based testing (LBT)*, is an application of active automata learning for system testing. BBC has been used for testing numerical software [28], distributed systems [29], and autonomous systems [23]. BBC is implemented in LBTest [30] and LearnLib [22,27].

As one of the quality assurance methods of CPSs, falsification [5,13] has been attracting attention from both academia and industry. There are several practical tools for falsification, for example, S-TaLiRo [3] and Breach [9]. See also the report [11] of the annual friendly competition on the falsification problem. There are various industrial case studies utilizing these tools for falsification. Yamaguchi et al. [38] presents a case study that uses the falsification tool Breach to find issues in automotive systems. Hoxha et al. [20] demonstrates falsification on industrial size engine model using S-TaLiRo. Cameron et al. [6] uses S-TaLiRo to search for violations of artificial pancreas controllers that automate insulin delivery to patients with type-1 diabetes.

Robustness-guided falsification [13] is a widely-used technique to solve the falsification problem with optimization, e. g., simulated annealing [24] and CMA-ES [4]. Robustness-guided falsification reduces the falsification problem to minimizing the quantitative satisfaction degree called *robustness* [10,14] of the specification φ in *signal temporal logic (STL)* [26]. Recently, BBC is also used for the falsification of CPSs [37]. In [37], an equivalence testing dedicated to CPS falsification called *robustness-guided equivalence testing* is introduced. Robustness-guided equivalence testing tries to find a witness σ of $\tilde{\mathcal{M}} \neq \mathcal{M}$ useful for the falsification problem by minimizing the robustness.

Robust linear temporal logic (rLTL) [36] is an extension of LTL with 5-valued semantics. rLTL is used to guarantee that a requirement violation due to a *small* assumptions violation is *small*. The 5-valued semantics of rLTL is based on a *weakening* of temporal operators in rLTL formulas related to our *strengthening*.

After recalling the preliminaries in Sect. 2, we introduce our enhancement of BBC via model checking with strengthened specifications in Sect. 3. We show the experimental evaluation in Sect. 4, and conclude in Sect. 5.

2   Preliminaries

For a set S, we denote its power set by $\mathcal{P}(S)$. For a set S, an infinite sequence $s = s_0, s_1, \cdots \in S^\omega$ of S, and $i, j \in \mathbb{N}, i \leq j$, we denote the subsequence $s_i, s_{i+1}, \ldots, s_j \in S^*$ by $s[i,j]$. For a set S, a finite sequence $s \in S^*$ of S, and an infinite sequence $s' \in S^\omega$ of S, we denote their concatenation by $s \cdot s'$.

2.1   Linear Temporal Logic

Linear temporal logic (LTL) [33] is a temporal logic which is commonly used to describe temporal behaviors of systems.

Definition 1 (Syntax of linear temporal logic). *For a finite set* **AP** *of atomic propositions, the syntax of* linear temporal logic *is defined as follows, where* $p \in$ **AP** *and* $i, j \in \mathbb{N} \cup \{\infty\}$ *satisfying* $i \leq j$[1].

$$\varphi, \psi ::= \top \mid p \mid \neg\varphi \mid \varphi \vee \psi \mid \varphi \, \mathcal{U}_{[i,j)} \, \psi \mid \mathcal{X}\varphi$$

We denote the set of linear temporal logic formulas by **LTL**.

In addition to the syntax in Definition 1, we use the following syntactic abbreviations of LTL formulas. Intuitively, $\Diamond\varphi$ stands for "eventually φ holds" and $\Box\varphi$ stands for "globally φ holds".

$$\bot \equiv \neg\top, \quad \varphi \wedge \psi \equiv \neg((\neg\varphi) \vee (\neg\psi)), \quad \varphi \to \psi \equiv (\neg\varphi) \vee \psi,$$
$$\Diamond_{[i,j)}\varphi \equiv \top \, \mathcal{U}_{[i,j)} \, \varphi, \quad \Box_{[i,j)}\varphi \equiv \neg(\Diamond_{[i,j)}\neg\varphi), \quad \varphi \, \mathcal{U} \, \psi \equiv \varphi \, \mathcal{U}_{[0,\infty)} \, \psi$$
$$\Diamond\varphi \equiv \Diamond_{[0,\infty)}\varphi, \quad \Box\varphi \equiv \Box_{[0,\infty)}\varphi$$

The semantics of LTL formulas is defined by the following satisfaction relation $(\pi, k) \models \varphi$. For an infinite sequence π, an index k, and an LTL formula φ, $(\pi, k) \models \varphi$ intuitively stands for "π satisfies φ at k".

---

[1] In the standard definition of LTL, the interval $\mathcal{U}_{[i,j)}$ is always $[0, \infty)$ and it is omitted. We employ the current syntax to emphasize the similarity to STL. We note that this does not change the expressive power.

Definition 2 (Semantics of linear temporal logic). *For an LTL formula* φ, *an infinite sequence* $\pi = \pi_0, \pi_1, \cdots \in (\mathcal{P}(\mathbf{AP}))^\omega$ *of subsets of atomic propositions, and* $k \in \mathbb{N}$, *we define the satisfaction relation* $(\pi, k) \models \varphi$ *as follows.*

$$(\pi, k) \models \top$$
$$(\pi, k) \models p \iff p \in \pi_k$$
$$(\pi, k) \models \neg\varphi \iff (\pi, k) \nvDash \varphi$$
$$(\pi, k) \models \varphi \vee \psi \iff (\pi, k) \models \varphi \vee (\pi, k) \models \psi$$
$$(\pi, k) \models \mathcal{X}\varphi \iff (\pi, k+1) \models \varphi$$
$$(\pi, k) \models \varphi \, \mathcal{U}_{[i,j)} \, \psi \iff \exists l \in [k+i, k+j).\, (\pi, l) \models \psi$$
$$\wedge \forall m \in \{k, k+1, \ldots, l\}.\, (\pi, m) \models \varphi$$

If we have $(\pi, 0) \models \varphi$, *we denote* $\pi \models \varphi$.

In this paper, we mainly use a subclass of LTL called *safety* LTL. Safety LTL is a subclass of LTL whose violation can be witnessed by a *finite* sequence. The existence of finite witness simplifies the application to BBC.

Definition 3 (safety LTL). *An LTL formula* φ *is* safety *if for any infinite sequence* $\pi \in (\mathcal{P}(\mathbf{AP}))^\omega$ *satisfying* $\pi \nvDash \varphi$, *there is* $i \in \mathbb{N}$ *such that for any prefix* $\pi[0, j]$ *of* π *longer than* i *(i.e.,* $j > i$*), and for any infinite sequence* $\pi' \in (\mathcal{P}(\mathbf{AP}))^\omega$, *we have* $\pi[0, j] \cdot \pi' \nvDash \varphi$

2.2 LTL Model Checking

Model checking is a technique to verify the correctness of a system model $\mathcal{M}$ against a specification φ. We utilize Mealy machines for system modeling and LTL formulas for a specification φ.

Definition 4 (Mealy machine). *For an input alphabet* Σ *and an output alphabet* Γ, *a* Mealy machine *is a 3-tuple* $\mathcal{M} = (L, l_0, \Delta)$, *where* L *is the finite set of locations,* $l_0 \in L$ *is the initial location, and* $\Delta : (L \times \Sigma) \to (L \times \Gamma)$ *is the transition function.*

For a Mealy machine $\mathcal{M} = (L, l_0, \Delta)$ over Σ and Γ, the language $\mathcal{L}(\mathcal{M}) \subseteq (\Sigma \times \Gamma)^\omega$ is defined as follows.

$$\mathcal{L}(\mathcal{M}) = \{(a_0, b_0), (a_1, b_1), \cdots \mid \exists l_1, l_2, \ldots, \forall i \in \mathbb{N}.\, \Delta(l_i, a_i) = (l_{i+1}, b_i)\}$$

For an infinite sequence $\sigma = (a_0, b_0), (a_1, b_1), \cdots \in (\Sigma \times \Gamma)^\omega$, we define $\mathbf{pr_1}(\sigma) = a_0, a_1, \cdots \in \Sigma^\omega$ and $\mathbf{pr_2}(\sigma) = b_0, b_1, \cdots \in \Gamma^\omega$. For a Mealy machine $\mathcal{M}$, the input language $\mathcal{L}_{in}(\mathcal{M}) \subseteq \Sigma^\omega$ and the output language $\mathcal{L}_{out}(\mathcal{M}) \subseteq \Gamma^\omega$ are $\mathcal{L}_{in}(\mathcal{M}) = \{\mathbf{pr_1}(\sigma) \mid \exists \sigma \in \mathcal{L}(\mathcal{M})\}$ and $\mathcal{L}_{out}(\mathcal{M}) = \{\mathbf{pr_2}(\sigma) \mid \exists \sigma \in \mathcal{L}(\mathcal{M})\}$.

In the model checking, we use a Mealy machine $\mathcal{M}$ with the output alphabet $\Gamma = \mathcal{P}(\mathbf{AP})$ to model the system, and check if all the sequences in its language $\mathcal{L}(\mathcal{M})$ satisfy the LTL formula φ. Moreover, if there is a sequence in the language $\mathcal{L}(\mathcal{M})$ and violating the LTL formula φ, the model checker returns a sequence witnessing the violation. The formal definition of model checking is as follows.

Definition 5 (LTL model checking). *Let Σ be the input alphabet and let* **AP** *be the set of the atomic propositions. Given an LTL formula φ over* **AP** *and a Mealy machine $\mathcal{M}$ over Σ and $\mathcal{P}(\mathbf{AP})$, LTL model checking decides if for any $\pi \in \mathcal{L}_{out}(\mathcal{M})$, we have $\pi \models \varphi$. If there is $\sigma \in \mathcal{L}(\mathcal{M})$ satisfying $\mathbf{pr_2}(\sigma) \not\models \varphi$, the LTL model checker returns such σ. We denote $\forall \pi \in \mathcal{L}_{out}(\mathcal{M}).\, \pi \models \varphi$ by $\mathcal{M} \models \varphi$.*

In this paper, we utilize *safety* LTL formulas in Definition 3. For any safety LTL formula φ with $\mathcal{M} \not\models \varphi$, there is a finite sequence $\sigma \in (\Sigma \times \mathcal{P}(\mathbf{AP}))^*$ such that for any $\sigma' \in (\Sigma \times \mathcal{P}(\mathbf{AP}))^\omega$ satisfying $\sigma \cdot \sigma' \in \mathcal{L}(\mathcal{M})$, we have $\mathbf{pr_2}(\sigma \cdot \sigma') \not\models \varphi$. We use such a finite sequence σ as a witness of $\mathcal{M} \not\models \varphi$. For the discussion on such a finite witness, we define the *finite* language $\mathcal{L}^{fin}(\mathcal{M})$ of a Mealy machine $\mathcal{M}$ as $\mathcal{L}^{fin}(\mathcal{M}) = \{\sigma \in (\Sigma \times \mathcal{P}(\mathbf{AP}))^* \mid \exists \sigma' \in (\Sigma \times \mathcal{P}(\mathbf{AP}))^\omega.\, \sigma \cdot \sigma' \in \mathcal{L}(\mathcal{M})\}$.

2.3 Signal Temporal Logic

Signal temporal logic (STL) [26] is a variant of LTL dedicated to representing behaviors of real-valued signals. Although the standard definition is for *continuous*-time signals, we employ *discrete*-time STL [14] since we use STL for BBC.

Definition 6 (signal). *For a finite set Y of variables, a (discrete-time) signal $\sigma \in (\mathbb{R}^Y)^\infty$ is a finite or infinite sequence of valuations $u_i : Y \to \mathbb{R}$. For a finite signal $\sigma = u_0, u_1, \ldots, u_{n-1} \in (\mathbb{R}^Y)^*$, we denote the length n of σ by $|\sigma|$.*

Definition 7 (discrete-time STL). *For a finite set Y of variables, the syntax of STL is defined as follows, where $y \in Y$, $\bowtie \in \{<,>\}$, $c \in \mathbb{R}$, and $i,j \in \mathbb{N} \cup \{\infty\}$.*

$$\varphi, \psi ::= \top \mid y \bowtie c \mid \neg \varphi \mid \varphi \vee \psi \mid \varphi\, \mathcal{U}_{[i,j)}\, \psi \mid \mathcal{X}\varphi$$

Similarly to LTL, we use the following syntactic abbreviations.

$$\bot \equiv \neg\top, \quad y \geq c \equiv \neg(y < c), \quad y \leq c \equiv \neg(y > c), \quad \varphi \wedge \psi \equiv \neg((\neg\varphi) \vee (\neg\psi)),$$
$$\varphi \to \psi \equiv (\neg\varphi) \vee \psi, \quad \Diamond_{[i,j)}\varphi \equiv \top\, \mathcal{U}_{[i,j)}\, \varphi, \quad \Box_{[i,j)}\varphi \equiv \neg(\Diamond_{[i,j)}\neg\varphi),$$
$$\varphi\, \mathcal{U}\, \psi \equiv \varphi\, \mathcal{U}_{[0,\infty)}\, \psi, \quad \Diamond\varphi \equiv \Diamond_{[0,\infty)}\varphi, \quad \Box\varphi \equiv \Box_{[0,\infty)}\varphi$$

The semantics of STL formulas is defined similarly to that of LTL formulas. While the satisfaction of an LTL formula is defined for an infinite sequence $\pi \in (\mathcal{P}(\mathbf{AP}))^\omega$ of a set of atomic propositions, the satisfaction of an STL formula is defined for an infinite signal $\sigma \in (\mathbb{R}^Y)^\infty$. Each inequality constraint in an STL formula is evaluated with the valuation u_i in the signal σ, and the satisfaction of the other formulas is defined inductively. Formally, the satisfaction relation $(\sigma, k) \models \varphi$ is inductively defined as follows, where φ is an STL formula over Y, $\sigma \in (\mathbb{R}^Y)^\omega$ is an infinite length signal over Y, and $k \in \mathbb{N}$ is an index.

$$(\sigma, k) \models \top$$
$$(\sigma, k) \models y > c \quad \Longleftrightarrow u_k(y) > c$$
$$(\sigma, k) \models y < c \quad \Longleftrightarrow u_k(y) < c$$
$$(\sigma, k) \models \neg\varphi \quad \Longleftrightarrow (\sigma, k) \not\models \varphi$$
$$(\sigma, k) \models \varphi \vee \psi \quad \Longleftrightarrow (\sigma, k) \models \varphi \vee (\sigma, k) \models \psi$$
$$(\sigma, k) \models \mathcal{X}\varphi \quad \Longleftrightarrow (\sigma, k+1) \models \varphi$$
$$(\sigma, k) \models \varphi \, \mathcal{U}_{[i,j)} \, \psi \Longleftrightarrow \exists l \in [k+i, k+j). \, (\sigma, l) \models \psi$$
$$\wedge \, \forall m \in \{k, k+1, \ldots, l\}. \, (\sigma, m) \models \varphi$$

The notion of *safety* is defined similarly to that of LTL. Moreover, model checking with an STL formula is defined similarly. The main difference is that the output alphabet Γ of the Mealy machine $\mathcal{M}$ is not $\mathcal{P}(\mathbf{AP})$ but $\mathbb{R}^Y$.

2.4   Active Automata Learning

Active automata learning is a class of algorithms to construct an automaton by a series of interactions between the *learner* and a *teacher*. In L* [2] and TTT [21] algorithms, the learner constructs the minimum DFA $\mathcal{A}_U$ over Σ recognizing the target language $U \subseteq \Sigma^*$ utilizing *membership* and *equivalence* questions to the teacher.

In a membership question, the learner asks if a word $w \in \Sigma^*$ is a member of U, i.e., $w \in U$. In an equivalence question, the learner asks if a candidate DFA $\mathcal{A}$ recognizes the target language U, i.e., $\mathcal{L}(\mathcal{A}) = U$. In the equivalence question, if we have $\mathcal{L}(\mathcal{A}) \neq U$, the teacher returns a word w' satisfying $w' \in \mathcal{L}(\mathcal{A}) \triangle U$ as a witness of $\mathcal{M} \neq \tilde{\mathcal{M}}$, where $\mathcal{L}(\mathcal{A}) \triangle U$ is the symmetric difference, i.e., $\mathcal{L}(\mathcal{A}) \triangle U = (\mathcal{L}(\mathcal{A}) \setminus U) \cup (U \setminus \mathcal{L}(\mathcal{A}))$. We note that a Mealy machine $\mathcal{M}$ can also be learned similarly. See e.g., [35].

Algorithm 1 outlines the L*-style active automata learning algorithm. In L*-style active automata learning, the learning process proceeds in two repetitive phases: candidate generation and equivalence testing. First, in the candidate generation phase (lines 3 to 5), the learner asks several membership questions to the teacher and constructs a candidate automaton. Once the automaton is constructed, the learning process proceeds to the equivalence testing phase (lines 7 to 11). The learner asks an equivalence question, and if the teacher returns a witness of inequivalence in line 10, the learning process returns to the first phase.

For any (even *black-box*) system $\mathcal{M}$, we can learn a Mealy machine $\tilde{\mathcal{M}}$ approximating the system behavior by implementing a teacher answering membership and equivalence questions. It is usually easy to answer a membership question— we can answer it by executing $\mathcal{M}$. In contrast, it is not straightforward to answer an equivalence question if the internal structure of the system $\mathcal{M}$ is unknown. When we know the size of the automaton to represent the system $\mathcal{M}$, we can utilize conformance testing with the correctness guarantee, such as W-method [8] and Wp-method [15]. However, we usually do not know the size of such an

---

Algorithm 1: L*-style active automata learning

---

   input   : A teacher T that answers membership and equivalence questions of
           target language U
   output : The minimum DFA $\mathcal{A}$ satisfying $U = \mathcal{L}(\mathcal{A})$

1 observations $\leftarrow \emptyset$
2 **while** $\top$ **do**
      // Candidate generation phase
3   **while** $\exists w.$ *we need to know if $w \in U$ to construct a candidate automaton $\mathcal{A}$*
       from observations **do**
4 | add $(w, \texttt{askMembershipQuestion}(T, w))$ to observations
5      $\mathcal{A} \leftarrow \texttt{constructCandidateAutomaton}(\text{observations})$
6

      // Equivalence testing phase
7   **if** $U = \mathcal{L}(\mathcal{A})$ *by equivalence question* **then**
8 | **return** $\mathcal{A}$
9   **else**
10 | $w \leftarrow$ a witness of $U \neq \mathcal{L}(\mathcal{A})$
11 | add $(w, \texttt{askMembershipQuestion}(T, w))$ to observations

---

automaton, and thus, we need an approximate method to test the equivalence of the system $\mathcal{M}$ under learning and the candidate automaton $\tilde{\mathcal{M}}$, e. g., by random testing and mutation testing [1]. We note that, in general, these equivalence testing methods execute the system $\mathcal{M}$ for many times, and tend to be time-consuming when the system execution is expensive.

2.5   Black-Box Checking

Black-box checking (BBC) [32] is a testing method that combines active automata learning and model checking to test if the given black-box system $\mathcal{M}$ satisfies its specification φ. Given a black-box system $\mathcal{M}$ over an input alphabet Σ and an output alphabet $\mathcal{P}(\mathbf{AP})$, and a safety LTL formula φ, BBC deems $\mathcal{M} \models \varphi$ or returns a counterexample $\sigma \in (\Sigma \times \mathcal{P}(\mathbf{AP}))^*$ such that for any $\sigma' \in (\Sigma \times \mathcal{P}(\mathbf{AP}))^\omega$ satisfying $\sigma \cdot \sigma' \in \mathcal{L}(\mathcal{M})$, we have $\mathbf{pr_2}(\sigma \cdot \sigma') \not\models \varphi$.

Figure 1 outlines the workflow of BBC. BBC combines L*-style active automata learning in Algorithm 1 and model checking. More precisely, candidate generation phase (lines 3 to 5 in Algorithm 1) corresponds to (A) in Fig. 1, equivalence testing phase of active automata learning (lines 7 to 11 in Algorithm 1) corresponds to (D) in Fig. 1, and model checking is used in (B) in Fig. 1. First, we learn a Mealy machine $\tilde{\mathcal{M}}$ approximating the behavior of the system $\mathcal{M}$ under test ((A) in Fig. 1). We learn such a Mealy machine $\tilde{\mathcal{M}}$ by the candidate generation of active automata learning (lines 3 to 5 in Algorithm 1). We note that the behavior of the learned Mealy machine $\tilde{\mathcal{M}}$ may be different from that of the system $\mathcal{M}$ under test.

Then, we check if we have $\tilde{\mathcal{M}} \models \varphi$ by model checking ((B) in Fig. 1). If $\tilde{\mathcal{M}} \not\models \varphi$ holds, the model checker returns a witness $\sigma \in (\Sigma \times \mathcal{P}(\mathbf{AP}))^*$ of

$\tilde{\mathcal{M}} \not\models \varphi$, and we feed σ to the system $\mathcal{M}$ under test to check if σ is a witness of $\mathcal{M} \not\models \varphi$ ((C) in Fig. 1). If σ witnesses $\mathcal{M} \not\models \varphi$, we conclude that $\mathcal{M} \not\models \varphi$ holds, and BBC returns σ as a counterexample. Otherwise, since we have $\sigma \in \mathcal{L}^{fin}(\tilde{\mathcal{M}})$ and $\sigma \notin \mathcal{L}^{fin}(\mathcal{M})$, σ differentiates $\tilde{\mathcal{M}}$ and $\mathcal{M}$, and we use σ to refine the learned Mealy machine $\tilde{\mathcal{M}}$.

If $\tilde{\mathcal{M}} \models \varphi$ holds in the model-checking step ((B) in Fig. 1), we test if the behavior of $\tilde{\mathcal{M}}$ and $\mathcal{M}$ are similar enough by equivalence testing of active automata learning ((D) in Fig. 1). If we find an input σ that differentiates $\mathcal{M}$ and $\tilde{\mathcal{M}}$, we use σ to refine the learned Mealy machine $\tilde{\mathcal{M}}$. Otherwise, we deem that $\tilde{\mathcal{M}}$ and $\mathcal{M}$ are equivalent, and BBC returns $\mathcal{M} \models \varphi$.

BBC for CPSs. To apply BBC to test a CPS $\mathcal{M}$, we need a finite abstraction of the real-valued input and output of $\mathcal{M}$. Following [37], we utilize input and output mappers $\mathcal{I}$ and $\mathcal{O}$ to bridge the real values for the CPS execution and the finite values for the BBC. For a CPS model $\mathcal{M}$ over X and Y, we fix the abstract input alphabet Σ and the atomic propositions **AP**, and define an input mapper $\mathcal{I} : \Sigma \to \mathbb{R}^X$ assigning one valuation of the input signal to each $a \in \Sigma$ and an output mapper $\mathcal{O} : \mathbb{R}^Y \to \mathcal{P}(\mathbf{AP})$ assigning a set of atomic propositions to each valuation of the output signal. Typically, Σ is a finite subset of $\mathbb{R}^X$ and $\mathcal{I}$ is the canonical injection, and **AP** is a set of predicates over Y and $\mathcal{O}$ assigns their satisfaction.

3   BBC Enhanced via Model Checking with Strengthened LTL Formulas

In this section, we show how we optimize BBC utilizing model checking with strengthened LTL formulas. Figure 2 shows the workflow of our enhanced BBC. The high-level strategy is to reduce the number of the equivalence testing ((D) in Fig. 2) via model checking with a strengthened LTL formula ψ ((B') and (C') in Fig. 2). Since, one equivalence test consists of many executions of the system $\mathcal{M}$ under test, equivalence testing tends to be time-consuming if each execution of $\mathcal{M}$ is expensive. In contrast, in BBC, the size of the learned Mealy machine $\tilde{\mathcal{M}}$ tends to be small, and the model checking may be relatively fast. Overall, the workflow in Fig. 2 may be more efficient than the original workflow of BBC in Fig. 1, which we experimentally confirm in Sect. 4.

3.1   Strengthening Relation of LTL Formulas

To formalize our strengthening of LTL formulas, we define the strengthening relation $\rightarrowtail \subseteq \mathbf{LTL} \times \mathbf{LTL}$ over LTL formulas. Given an LTL formula φ, we strengthen it to another LTL formula ψ satisfying $\varphi \rightarrowtail \psi$. The syntactic definition of $\rightarrowtail$ is suitable for the generation of the strengthened LTL formulas.

Definition 8 (Strengthening relation of LTL formulas). *For LTL formulas φ, ψ, $\rightarrowtail \subseteq \mathbf{LTL} \times \mathbf{LTL}$ is the minimum relation satisfying the following.*

1. For any $\mu, \nu \in \mathbf{LTL}$, we have $(\mu \vee \nu) \rightarrowtail (\mu \wedge \nu)$.
2. For any $\mu \in \mathbf{LTL}$, we have $\Diamond\mu \rightarrowtail \Box\Diamond\mu$.
3. For any $\mu \in \mathbf{LTL}$, we have $\Box\Diamond\mu \rightarrowtail \Diamond\Box\mu$.
4. For any $\mu \in \mathbf{LTL}$, we have $\Diamond\Box\mu \rightarrowtail \Box\mu$.
5. For any $\mu \in \mathbf{LTL}$ and for any indices $i, j \in \mathbb{N} \cup \{\infty\}$ satisfying $i < j$, we have $\Diamond_{[i,j)}\mu \rightarrowtail \Box_{[i,j)}\mu$.
6. For any $\mu, \nu \in \mathbf{LTL}$, we have $(\mu \, \mathcal{U} \, \nu) \rightarrowtail (\Box\mu \wedge \Box\Diamond\nu)$.
7. For any $\mu \in \mathbf{LTL}$ and for any indices $i, j, i', j' \in \mathbb{N} \cup \{\infty\}$ satisfying $[i,j) \supsetneq [i',j')$, we have $\Diamond_{[i,j)}\mu \rightarrowtail \Diamond_{[i',j')}\mu$.
8. For any $\mu, \nu \in \mathbf{LTL}$, if we have $\nu \rightarrowtail \mu$, we have $\neg\mu \rightarrowtail \neg\nu$.
9. For any $\mu, \mu', \nu \in \mathbf{LTL}$ satisfying $\mu \rightarrowtail \mu'$, we have $(\mu \vee \nu) \rightarrowtail (\mu' \vee \nu)$.
10. For any $\mu, \nu, \nu' \in \mathbf{LTL}$ satisfying $\nu \rightarrowtail \nu'$, we have $(\mu \vee \nu) \rightarrowtail (\mu \vee \nu')$.
11. For any $\mu, \nu \in \mathbf{LTL}$ satisfying $\mu \rightarrowtail \nu$, we have $\mathcal{X}\mu \rightarrowtail \mathcal{X}\nu$.
12. For any $\mu, \nu, \nu' \in \mathbf{LTL}$ satisfying $\nu \rightarrowtail \nu'$ and for any indices $i, j \in \mathbb{N} \cup \{\infty\}$ satisfying $i < j$, we have $(\mu \, \mathcal{U}_{[i,j)} \, \nu) \rightarrowtail (\mu \, \mathcal{U}_{[i,j)} \, \nu')$.
13. For any $\varphi, \mu, \psi \in \mathbf{LTL}$ satisfying $\varphi \rightarrowtail \mu$ and $\mu \rightarrowtail \psi$, we have $\varphi \rightarrowtail \psi$.

We note that for the other operators than the ones in Definition 1, $\rightarrowtail$ is defined using their definition as the syntactic abbreviation.

Example 1. For any $p \in \mathbf{AP}$, we have $\Box_{[0,2)}p \rightarrowtail \Box_{[0,10)}p$. This is because, by condition 7 of Definition 8, we have $\Diamond_{[0,10)}\neg p \rightarrowtail \Diamond_{[0,2)}\neg p$. By applying condition 8 of Definition 8, we obtain $\neg\Diamond_{[0,2)}\neg p \rightarrowtail \neg\Diamond_{[0,10)}\neg p$. By definition of the syntactic abbreviation, $\neg\Diamond_{[0,2)}\neg p \rightarrowtail \neg\Diamond_{[0,10)}\neg p$ is equivalent to $\Box_{[0,2)}p \rightarrowtail \Box_{[0,10)}p$.

We have the following correctness by induction.

Theorem 1 (Correctness of the strengthening relation). *For any LTL formulas φ and ψ satisfying $\varphi \rightarrowtail \psi$, ψ is stronger than φ, i.e., for any $\pi \in (\mathcal{P}(\mathbf{AP}))^\omega$ and $k \in \mathbb{N}$, $(\pi, k) \models \varphi$ implies $(\pi, k) \models \psi$.* $\qquad\square$

Example 2. Let $\varphi_{example} = p_1 \vee \Diamond_{[0,10)}p_2$, with $p_1, p_2 \in \mathbf{AP}$. By condition 1 of Definition 8, we have $(p_1 \vee \Diamond_{[0,10)}p_2) \rightarrowtail (p_1 \wedge \Diamond_{[0,10)}p_2)$. Therefore, $p_1 \wedge \Diamond_{[0,2)}p_2$ is one of the candidates in the strengthening of $\varphi_{example}$. By conditions 7 and 10 of Definition 8, we have $\Diamond_{[0,10)}p_2 \rightarrowtail \Diamond_{[0,5)}p_2$, and $(p_1 \vee \Diamond_{[0,10)}p_2) \rightarrowtail (p_1 \vee \Diamond_{[0,5)}p_2)$. Therefore, $p_1 \vee \Diamond_{[0,5)}p_2$ is another candidate in the strengthening of $\varphi_{example}$. We note that by condition 7 of Definition 8, we have $\Diamond_{[0,10)}p_2 \rightarrowtail \Diamond_{[i',j')}p_2$ for any $[i',j') \subsetneq [0,10)$, and in the strengthening, we have many candidates that are different only in the interval in their temporal operator. For example, $p_1 \vee \Diamond_{[0,8)}p_2$, $p_1 \vee \Diamond_{[0,3)}p_2$, and $p_1 \vee \Diamond_{[0,1)}p_2$ are the candidates in the strengthening of $\varphi_{example}$.

3.2 BBC Enhanced via Model Checking with Strengthened Formulas

We present how we enhance BBC utilizing model checking with strengthened LTL formulas. In this section, we show the high-level scheme of our enhancement and, in Sect. 3.3, we explain the design choice in our implementation. We fix the system $\mathcal{M}$ under test and the specification $\varphi \in \mathbf{LTL}$.

Algorithm 2: BBC enhanced via model checking with strengthened LTL formulas

---

    input   : System $\mathcal{M}$ under test and an LTL formula φ
    output : Returns $\top$ if BBC deems $\mathcal{M} \models \varphi$, otherwise, a witness σ of $\mathcal{M} \not\models \varphi$

1   $\Psi \leftarrow \texttt{GenCandidate}(\varphi)$ // Generate a subset Ψ of $\{\psi \in \mathbf{LTL} \mid \varphi \rightarrowtail \psi\}$
2   $\tilde{\mathcal{M}} \leftarrow \texttt{ConstructInitialMealy}(\mathcal{M})$
3   **repeat**
4   **if** $\tilde{\mathcal{M}} \not\models \varphi$ **then**
5        $\sigma \leftarrow$ a witness of $\tilde{\mathcal{M}} \not\models \varphi$
6   **if** σ *witnesses* $\mathcal{M} \not\models \varphi$ **then**
7   **return** σ
8   **else**
9   foundWitness $\leftarrow \bot$
10       $\Psi_{chosen} \leftarrow \texttt{ChooseFml}(\Psi)$
11   **forall** $\psi_i \in \Psi_{chosen}$ **do** // Try the strengthened specifications
12   **if** $\tilde{\mathcal{M}} \not\models \psi_i$ **then**
13             $\sigma \leftarrow$ a witness of $\tilde{\mathcal{M}} \not\models \psi_i$
14   **if** σ *witnesses* $\mathcal{M} \not\models \psi_i$ **then**
15   remove ψ_i from Ψ
16   **else** // σ is a witness of $\tilde{\mathcal{M}} \neq \mathcal{M}$
17   foundWitness $\leftarrow \top$
18   **break**
19   **if** foundWitness $= \bot$ **then**
20   **if** $\tilde{\mathcal{M}} \simeq \mathcal{M}$ *by equivalence testing* **then**
21   **return** $\top$
22   **else**
23                $\sigma \leftarrow$ a witness of $\tilde{\mathcal{M}} \neq \mathcal{M}$
24     $\tilde{\mathcal{M}} \leftarrow \texttt{RefineMealy}(\mathcal{M}, \sigma)$
25   **until** $\texttt{isTimeout}()$
26   **return** $\top$

Figure 2 outlines our enhanced BBC scheme. When we have $\tilde{\mathcal{M}} \models \varphi$ in (B) of Fig. 2, before conducting the equivalence testing ((D) of Fig. 2), we try to find a witness of $\mathcal{M} \neq \tilde{\mathcal{M}}$ by a model checking with an LTL formula ψ satisfying $\varphi \rightarrowtail \psi$ ((B') of Fig. 2). Since $\tilde{\mathcal{M}} \not\models \varphi$ implies $\tilde{\mathcal{M}} \not\models \psi$, by model checking, we have more chance to obtain a witness σ of $\tilde{\mathcal{M}} \not\models \psi$ than that of $\tilde{\mathcal{M}} \not\models \varphi$. When ψ is much stronger than φ, the witness σ of $\tilde{\mathcal{M}} \not\models \psi$ is also a witness of $\mathcal{M} \not\models \psi$. In such a case, σ does not differentiate $\tilde{\mathcal{M}}$ and $\mathcal{M}$, and thus, we cannot use σ to refine $\tilde{\mathcal{M}}$. Nevertheless, we claim that if the LTL formula φ is strengthened appropriately, we can often refine $\tilde{\mathcal{M}}$ by such a witness σ. Moreover, the refinement by such a witness σ tends to lead to a Mealy machine useful for falsification of φ, which is observed in our experiment result in Sect. 4.

Algorithm 2 outlines our BBC enhanced via model checking with strengthened LTL formulas. In line 1, we generate the candidates Ψ of the strengthened LTL formulas used in the model checking. After constructing the initial Mealy machine $\tilde{\mathcal{M}}$ in line 2, we conduct model checking of $\tilde{\mathcal{M}}$ with φ. When we have $\tilde{\mathcal{M}} \nvDash \varphi$ (line 4), we obtain a witness σ of $\tilde{\mathcal{M}} \nvDash \varphi$ and check if σ also witnesses $\mathcal{M} \nvDash \varphi$ by running $\mathcal{M}$ with σ as the input (line 6). When σ also witnesses $\mathcal{M} \nvDash \varphi$, we return σ as a result of BBC. Otherwise, we use σ to refine the leaned Mealy machine $\tilde{\mathcal{M}}$ (line 24).

When we have $\tilde{\mathcal{M}} \models \varphi$, we look for an input σ to refine $\tilde{\mathcal{M}}$. In the original BBC in Fig. 1, we try the equivalence testing to find such σ, In contrast, in order to reduce the number of the equivalence testing, we conduct model checking of $\tilde{\mathcal{M}}$ with some of the LTL formulas $\psi \in \Psi$ before trying the equivalence testing. The strengthened LTL formulas Ψ_{chosen} is chosen by a function `ChooseFml`. Although the stronger LTL formulas should be chosen before the weaker ones, `ChooseFml` can be an arbitrary function to choose a finite set of the strengthened specifications Ψ_{chosen} from Ψ. We note that the choice of `GenCandidate` and `ChooseFml` defines the granularity of the strengthening of φ used in the model checking, which may affect the effectiveness of our enhancement.

For each LTL formula $\psi_i \in \Psi_{chosen}$, we check if $\tilde{\mathcal{M}} \nvDash \psi_i$ holds by model checking in line 11. When $\tilde{\mathcal{M}} \nvDash \psi_i$ holds (line 12), we obtain a witness σ of $\tilde{\mathcal{M}} \nvDash \psi_i$. Then, we check if σ also witnesses $\mathcal{M} \nvDash \psi_i$ by running $\mathcal{M}$ with σ as input (line 14). When σ also witnesses $\mathcal{M} \nvDash \varphi_i$, we remove ψ_i from Ψ in line 15. Otherwise, we use σ to refine the learned Mealy machine $\tilde{\mathcal{M}}$ in line 24.

When for any $\psi_i \in \Psi_{chosen}$, we can not find σ to refine $\tilde{\mathcal{M}}$, we fallback to the normal loop of the BBC. Namely, we use equivalence testing to find a witness σ of $\mathcal{M} \neq \tilde{\mathcal{M}}$ in line 20. When equivalence testing deems $\tilde{\mathcal{M}}$ and $\mathcal{M}$ are equivalent, we return $\top$ as the result of BBC. Otherwise, equivalence testing returns a witness σ of $\tilde{\mathcal{M}} \neq \mathcal{M}$, and we use σ to refine $\tilde{\mathcal{M}}$ (line 24).

3.3 `GenCandidate` and `ChooseFml` in our implementation

Algorithm 3 shows our candidate generation algorithm `GenCandidate`. The candidates Ψ of the strengthened LTL formulas consists of Ψ_{Int} and Ψ_{noInt}[2]: Ψ_{Int} and Ψ_{noInt} are obtained by strengthening the operators with and without intervals. They are constructed by `GenIntFml` and `GenNoIntFml` (in Algorithm 4), respectively. Moreover, we remove ψ_i from Ψ_{Int} or Ψ_{noInt} when ψ_i is removed from Ψ in line 15 of Algorithm 2.

First, we use `GenNoIntFml` to construct $\Psi_{\text{noInt}} \subseteq \{\psi \in \mathbf{LTL} \mid \varphi \rightarrowtail \psi\}$ that is constructed by inductively strengthening the operators without intervals. For example, for $\varphi = (\Box_{[2,6)}p) \vee \Diamond q$, we have `GenNoIntFml`$(\varphi) = \{(\Box_{[2,6)}p) \wedge \Diamond q, (\Box_{[2,6)}p) \vee \Box q, (\Box_{[2,6)}p) \vee \Diamond \Box q, (\Box_{[2,6)}p) \vee \Box \Diamond q\}$. We note that for any LTL formula φ, `GenNoIntFml`(φ) is a finite set.

Then, we use `GenIntFml` to construct a finite set Ψ_{Int} of LTL formulas by modifying the "Eventually" and "Globally" operators with intervals in φ. We employ heuristics to take the midpoint of the lower or upper bound when shrinking the interval. For example, let $\varphi = (\Box_{[2,6)}p) \vee \Diamond q$ and the bound N of the

---

[2] More precisely, Ψ_{noInt} is a queue and its FIFO order is used in `ChooseFml` in Algorithm 5.

Algorithm 3: The candidate generation `GenCandidate` in our implementation, where $N \in \mathbb{N}$ is the bound of the time horizon

---

1 **Function** `GenCandidate`(φ):

    input : An LTL formula φ

    output : The strengthened LTL formulas Ψ used in Algorithm 2

2    $\Psi_{\text{noInt}} \leftarrow$ `GenNoIntFml`(φ) // Strengthen the operators without intervals

3    $\Psi_{\text{Int}} \leftarrow$ `GenIntFml`(φ) // Strengthen the operators with intervals

4   **return** $\Psi_{\text{noInt}} \cup \Psi_{\text{Int}}$

5 **Function** `GenIntFml`(φ):

6    $\Psi_{\text{Int}} \leftarrow \emptyset$

7   **switch** *the syntactic structure of* φ **do**

8   **case** $\varphi = \square_{[i,j)}\mu$ **do**

9            $i' \leftarrow 0;\ j' \leftarrow \infty$

10   **while** $[i,j) \subsetneq [i',j')$ **do**

11                $\Psi_{\text{Int}} \leftarrow \Psi_{\text{Int}} \cup \{\square_{[i',j')}\mu\}$

12   **if** $i > i'$ **then** $i' \leftarrow \lceil \frac{i+i'}{2} \rceil;\ j' \leftarrow N$

13   **else** $j' \leftarrow \lfloor \frac{i+j'}{2} \rfloor$

14   **case** $\varphi = \lozenge_{[i,j)}\mu$ **do**

15            $\Psi_{\text{Int}} \leftarrow$ `GenIntFml`$(\square_{[i,i+1)}\mu)$

16            $i' \leftarrow i;\ j' \leftarrow i+1$

17   **while** $[i,j) \supsetneq [i',j')$ **do**

18                $\Psi_{\text{Int}} \leftarrow \Psi_{\text{Int}} \cup \{\lozenge_{[i',j')}\mu\}$

19   **if** $i < i'$ **then** $i' \leftarrow \lfloor \frac{i+i'}{2} \rfloor$

20   **else** $j' \leftarrow \lceil \frac{i+j'}{2} \rceil$

21   **case** $\varphi = \square\mu$ **do**

22 | $\Psi_{\text{Int}} \leftarrow \{\square\mu' \mid \mu' \in$ `GenIntFml`$(\mu)\}$

23   **case** $\varphi = \mu \vee \nu$ **do**

24 | $\Psi_{\text{Int}} \leftarrow \{\mu' \vee \nu \mid \mu' \in$ `GenIntFml`$(\mu)\} \cup \{\mu \vee \nu' \mid \nu' \in$ `GenIntFml`$(\nu)\}$

25   **case** $\varphi = \mu \wedge \nu$ **do**

26 | $\Psi_{\text{Int}} \leftarrow \{\mu' \wedge \nu \mid \mu' \in$ `GenIntFml`$(\mu)\} \cup \{\mu \wedge \nu' \mid \nu' \in$ `GenIntFml`$(\nu)\}$

27   **return** Ψ_{Int}

---

time horizon be $N = 30$. We start from $[i',j') = [0,\infty)$ (in line 9 of Algorithm 3) and repeatedly update the lower bound i' to the midpoint of i and i' (line 12) to generate an LTL formula with it. Namely, we generate $(\square_{[0,\infty)}p) \vee \lozenge q$, $(\square_{[1,30)}p) \vee \lozenge q$, and $(\square_{[2,30)}p) \vee \lozenge q$. Once we have $i = i'$, we repeatedly update the upper bound j' to the midpoint of j and j' (line 13), and use $[i',j')$ for the LTL generation. Namely, we generate $(\square_{[2,18)}p) \vee \lozenge q$, $(\square_{[2,12)}p) \vee \lozenge q$, $(\square_{[2,9)}p) \vee \lozenge q$, and $(\square_{[2,7)}p) \vee \lozenge q$. By this construction, we have finer-grained strengthening when the strengthened formula is closer to the original formula while ignoring many strengthened formulas far from the original one for efficiency.

In `ChooseFml` (in Algorithm 5), we take one of the strongest LTL formulas in Ψ_{noInt} and take all the strongest LTL formulas in Ψ_{Int}. We note that the strength of LTL formulas is a strict partial order, and there may be multiple strongest specifications.

Algorithm 4: Candidate generation by strengthening the operators without intervals

---

  input : An LTL formula φ
  output : A queue Ψ_{noInt} of LTL formulas that are obtained by strengthening
       the operators without intervals in φ

1   **Function** GenNoIntFml(φ):
2    $\Psi_{\mathrm{noInt}} \leftarrow ()$ // Ψ_{noInt} is a queue of strengthened specs
3   **switch** *the form of φ* **do**
4   **case** $\varphi = \mu \vee \nu$ **do**
5   **push** $\mu \wedge \nu$ **to** Ψ_{noInt}
6   **forall** $\mu' \in$ GenNoIntFml(μ) **do**
7 | **push** $\mu' \vee \nu$ **to** Ψ_{noInt}
8   **forall** $\nu' \in$ GenNoIntFml(ν) **do**
9 | **push** $\mu \vee \nu'$ **to** Ψ_{noInt}
10   **case** $\varphi = \Diamond \mu$ **do**
11 | **return** $(\Box \mu, \Diamond \Box \mu, \Box \Diamond \mu, \Diamond \mu)$
12   **case** $\varphi = \mu \, \mathcal{U} \, \nu$ **do**
13 | **return** $(\Box \mu \wedge \Box \nu, \Box \mu \wedge \Diamond \Box \nu, \Box \mu \wedge \Box \Diamond \nu)$
14   **case** $\varphi = \mu \wedge \nu$ **do**
15   **forall** $\mu' \in$ GenNoIntFml(μ) **do**
16 | **push** $\mu' \wedge \nu$ **to** Ψ_{noInt}
17   **forall** $\nu' \in$ GenNoIntFml(ν) **do**
18 | **push** $\mu \wedge \nu'$ **to** Ψ_{noInt}
19   **case** $\varphi = \Box \mu$ **do**
20   **forall** $\mu' \in$ GenNoIntFml(μ) **do**
21 | **push** $\Box \mu'$ **to** Ψ_{noInt}
22   **return** Ψ_{noInt}

Algorithm 5: Our implementation of ChooseFml

---

  input : A set Ψ of the candidates of the strengthened LTL formulas consists
       of Ψ_{Int} and Ψ_{noInt}
  output : A set Ψ_{chosen} of LTL formulas chosen from Ψ

1   $\Psi_{chosen} \leftarrow \emptyset$
2   $\Psi'_{\mathrm{noInt}} \leftarrow \Psi_{\mathrm{noInt}}$
   // Find the first formula in Ψ_{noInt} with no stronger formulas in
    Ψ_{noInt}
3   **while** $\Psi'_{\mathrm{noInt}} \neq \emptyset$ **do**
4   **pop** ψ **from** Ψ'_{noInt}
5   **if** $\forall \psi' \in \Psi'_{\mathrm{noInt}}.\, \psi \not\succeq \psi'$ **then**
6     $\Psi_{chosen} \leftarrow \Psi_{chosen} \cup \{\psi\}$
7   **break**
8   $\Psi_{chosen} \leftarrow \Psi_{chosen} \cup \{\psi \in \Psi_{\mathrm{Int}} \mid \forall \psi' \in \Psi_{\mathrm{Int}}.\, \psi \not\succeq \psi'\}$
9   **return** Ψ_{chosen}

---

4   Experiment

We conducted experiments to evaluate the efficiency of our BBC enhanced by model checking with strengthened LTL formulas. We compared our method with a tool FalCAuN [37] for robustness-guided BBC for CPSs. We implemented a prototype tool based on FalCAuN in Java[3].

4.1   Experiment Setup

As the CPS $\mathcal{M}$ under test, we used the Simulink model of an automatic transmission system [19], one of the standard models in the falsification literature. Given a 2-dimensional signal of the throttle and the brake, the automatic transmission model $\mathcal{M}$ returns a 3-dimensional signal of the velocity v, the engine rotation ω, and the gear g. The range of the throttle and the brake are $[0, 100]$ and $[0, 325]$, respectively. The domains of v and ω are positive reals, and the domain of g is $\{1, 2, 3, 4\}$. As the specification, we used the set of the STL formulas in Table 1. The STL formulas φ_1 and φ_2 are taken from [39], and φ_3-φ_5 are our original. Since the length of the input and output signals in our experiment is less than 30, we let the bound N in Algorithm 3 be 30.

Since the input and the output of the system $\mathcal{M}$ under test are continuous, we cannot directly apply BBC for the falsification of $\mathcal{M}$. In our experiments, we use the following discretization both in time and values. For the discretization in time, we use fixed-interval sampling of every one second. For the discretization of input values, we use the following $4 (= 2 \times 2)$ values: the throttle is either 0 or 100, and the brake is either 0 or 325. For the discretization of output values, we use the coarsest atomic propositions **AP** that is a partition of the output range compatible with the inequalities in the STL formula in each benchmark. For example, since the inequality constraints in the STL formula φ_1 are $v < 100$ and $v > 75$, the atomic propositions **AP** for φ_1 is $\{v \leq 75, 75 < v < 100, 100 \leq v\}$.

Among the optimization methods supported by FalCAuN to search for a counterexample in the equivalence testing, we use a genetic algorithm. Due to the stochastic nature of a genetic algorithm, we executed each benchmark 50 times. For each execution, we measured the time and the number of the Simulink executions to falsify the STL formula. We set the timeout of each execution to 4 h. We experimented on a Google Cloud Platform c2-standard-4 instance (4 vCPUs and 15.67 GiB RAM). We used Debian 10 buster and MATLAB R2020b.

4.2   Performance Evaluation

Table 2 shows the summary of the experiment results. Execution times are shown in minutes. For each STL formula φ_i, we observe that, on average, our method falsified φ_i in a shorter time than the baseline. Moreover, on average, the number of Simulink executions of our method is smaller than that of baseline. Furthermore, the number of timeouts of our method is smaller than or equal to that

---

[3] Our implementation is publicly available in https://github.com/MasWag/FalCAuN/releases/tag/RV2021.

Table 1. List of the STL formulas in our benchmarks

	STL formula
φ_1	$\square_{[0,26]}(v < 100) \vee \square_{[28,28]}(v > 75)$
φ_2	$\square((\omega < 4770) \vee (\square_{[1,1]}(\omega > 600)))$
φ_3	$\square((g > 3) \vee (\omega < 4775) \vee \Diamond_{[0,2]}(g > 3))$
φ_4	$\square((g > 2) \vee ((g < 2) \, \mathcal{U} \, (v > 30)))$
φ_5	$\square((\Diamond_{[0,3]}(\omega < 4000)) \vee (\Diamond_{[0,3]}(v > 100)))$

Table 2. Summary of the experiment result of 50 executions for our benchmarks. The numbers T/N in each cell at "average" and "std. dev." columns are the time T [min.] to falsify the specification and the number N of Simulink executions to falsify the specification. The number N in each cell at "timeout" column is the number N of timeouts to falsify the specification. In this experiment, the timeout is 4 h. For each benchmark φ_i, we highlight the best cell in average column in terms of the following order: T/N is better than T'/N' if and only if we have $T < T'$ or we have both $T = T'$ and $N < N'$. For each benchmark, the cells of the smallest number of timeouts is highlighted.

	Our method			Baseline (FalCAuN)		
	average	std. dev.	timeout	average	std. dev.	timeout
φ_1	19.29 / 6664.7	7.16 / 1962.7	0	26.70 / 9471.0	15.19 / 5412.2	0
φ_2	54.89 / 19066.1	42.38 / 13609.3	5	78.71 / 27362.6	57.85 / 18761.1	13
φ_3	16.43 / 6068.8	18.65 / 6622.2	1	17.35 / 6306.3	25.60 / 8195.7	1
φ_4	2.53 / 957.0	1.08 / 478.6	0	7.48 / 2323.5	5.40 / 1683.2	0
φ_5	4.92 / 1785.4	2.07 / 803.5	0	5.19 / 2003.4	2.31 / 904.5	0

of the baseline. Overall, the experiment results in Table 2 suggest that model checking with strengthened STL formulas makes the BBC more efficient.

Although our method outperforms the baseline for all the STL formulas, we also observe that the amount of acceleration differs among the formulas. For φ_4, our method was about 66% faster than the baseline, and acceleration was the largest. This is because our method generates four strengthened specifications by strengthening the "Until" operator in φ_4. They guided the learning of an automaton in BBC. For φ_1 and φ_2, acceleration by our enhancement was about 27% to 30%, which is significant but not as much as the one for φ_4. This is because our method generates many strengthened specifications by changing the interval of the "Globally" operators while model checking with them guided the Mealy machine learning in the BBC. Although many specifications are generated by our specification strengthening, the falsification of the original specifications in φ_1 and φ_2 is difficult and time consuming, the overhead due to the model checking with many strengthened LTL formulas is not significant.

In contrast, for φ_3 and φ_5, our method was only about 5% faster than the baseline. For φ_3, by definition of the strengthening relation in Definition 8, falsification of most of the strengthened specifications requires the output signal to violate both $g > 3$ and $\omega < 4775$ (almost) at the same time, which is a falsification of a disjunctive specification and tends to be difficult [34]. Since falsification of most of the strengthened STL formulas is difficult, the improvement thanks to the model checking with them is limited. One of the future directions to overcome this issue is enhancing genetic algorithm-based equivalence testing, e. g., utilizing *ranking* [34]. Another direction is to strengthen the specification by modifying the thresholds to make the specification strengthening finer-grained.

For φ_5, since the original specification φ_5 is not difficult and we can falsify it relatively quickly, we cannot ignore the overhead of model checking with the strengthened specifications. For such a situation, possible future work is an improvement of the choice of the strengthened STL formulas, e. g., by performing binary search on the strengthening of specifications to reduce the number of specifications to be model-checked.

5   Conclusions and Future Work

One of the issues in BBC for CPSs is its long execution time. In particular, the execution time of the equivalence test tends to be the bottleneck because an equivalence test consists of many system executions and each execution of a CPS is time-consuming. To reduce the number of the equivalence tests, we proposed an enhancement of BBC via model checking with strengthened specifications. By model checking with an LTL formula ψ stronger than the original formula φ, we have more chance to obtain a witness of the violation, and such a witness tends to be helpful for the refinement of the learned Mealy machine $\tilde{\mathcal{M}}$. Our experiment result shows that our method accelerates BBC, and our method is up to 66 % faster than the conventional BBC.

When the complexity of the original LTL formula φ is high, e. g., containing many temporal operators, the number of the strengthened formulas tends to be huge. In such a case, our current naive choice of the LTL formulas to be model checked, i. e., GenCandidate and ChooseFml in Algorithm 2, may cause significant overhead. One of the future works is to optimize such a choice of the model-checked formulas. For example, utilizing a binary search on the strengthened formulas or rewriting multiple operators in the original formula at one time may reduce the number of the model checking execution. Another future work is to investigate other kinds of specification strengthening. One example is to change the threshold in the inequalities. Optimization of the robustness-guided equivalence testing with recent falsification techniques, e. g., [34], is also future work.

Acknowledgments. This work is partially supported by JST ACT-X Grant No. JPMJAX200U, JSPS KAKENHI Grant Number 19H04084, and JST CREST Grant Number JPMJCR2012, Japan.

References

1. Aichernig, B.K., Tappler, M.: Efficient active automata learning via mutation testing. J. Autom. Reasoning **63**(4), 1103–1134 (2018). https://doi.org/10.1007/s10817-018-9486-0

2. Angluin, D.: Learning regular sets from queries and counterexamples. Inf. Comput. **75**(2), 87–106 (1987). https://doi.org/10.1016/0890-5401(87)90052-6

3. Annpureddy, Y., Liu, C., Fainekos, G., Sankaranarayanan, S.: S-TALIRO: a tool for temporal logic falsification for hybrid systems. In: Abdulla, P.A., Leino, K.R.M. (eds.) TACAS 2011. LNCS, vol. 6605, pp. 254–257. Springer, Heidelberg (2011). https://doi.org/10.1007/978-3-642-19835-9_21

4. Auger, A., Hansen, N.: A restart CMA evolution strategy with increasing population size. In: Proceedings of the IEEE Congress on Evolutionary Computation, CEC 2005, Edinburgh, UK, 2–4 September 2005, pp. 1769–1776. IEEE (2005). https://doi.org/10.1109/CEC.2005.1554902

5. Bartocci, E., et al.: Specification-based monitoring of cyber-physical systems: a survey on theory, tools and applications. In: Bartocci, E., Falcone, Y. (eds.) Lectures on Runtime Verification. LNCS, vol. 10457, pp. 135–175. Springer, Cham (2018). https://doi.org/10.1007/978-3-319-75632-5_5

6. Cameron, F., Fainekos, G., Maahs, D.M., Sankaranarayanan, S.: Towards a verified artificial pancreas: challenges and solutions for runtime verification. In: Bartocci, E., Majumdar, R. (eds.) RV 2015. LNCS, vol. 9333, pp. 3–17. Springer, Cham (2015). https://doi.org/10.1007/978-3-319-23820-3_1

7. Casagrande, A., Piazza, C.: Model checking on hybrid automata. In: 15th Euromicro Conference on Digital System Design, DSD 2012, Cesme, Izmir, Turkey, 5–8 September 2012, pp. 493–500. IEEE Computer Society (2012). https://doi.org/10.1109/DSD.2012.87

8. Chow, T.S.: Testing software design modeled by finite-state machines. IEEE Trans. Software Eng. **4**(3), 178–187 (1978). https://doi.org/10.1109/TSE.1978.231496

9. Donzé, A.: Breach, a toolbox for verification and parameter synthesis of hybrid systems. In: Touili, T., Cook, B., Jackson, P. (eds.) CAV 2010. LNCS, vol. 6174, pp. 167–170. Springer, Heidelberg (2010). https://doi.org/10.1007/978-3-642-14295-6_17

10. Donzé, A., Maler, O.: Robust satisfaction of temporal logic over real-valued signals. In: Chatterjee, K., Henzinger, T.A. (eds.) FORMATS 2010. LNCS, vol. 6246, pp. 92–106. Springer, Heidelberg (2010). https://doi.org/10.1007/978-3-642-15297-9_9

11. Ernst, G., et al.: Arch-comp 2020 category report: falsification. In: Frehse, G., Althoff, M. (eds.) ARCH20. 7th International Workshop on Applied Verification of Continuous and Hybrid Systems (ARCH20). EPiC Series in Computing, vol. 74, pp. 140–152. EasyChair (2020). https://doi.org/10.29007/trr1, https://easychair.org/publications/paper/ps5t

12. Esparza, J., Leucker, M., Schlund, M.: Learning workflow petri nets. In: Lilius, J., Penczek, W. (eds.) PETRI NETS 2010. LNCS, vol. 6128, pp. 206–225. Springer, Heidelberg (2010). https://doi.org/10.1007/978-3-642-13675-7_13

13. Fainekos, G., Hoxha, B., Sankaranarayanan, S.: Robustness of specifications and its applications to falsification, parameter mining, and runtime monitoring with S-TaLiRo. In: Finkbeiner, B., Mariani, L. (eds.) RV 2019. LNCS, vol. 11757, pp. 27–47. Springer, Cham (2019). https://doi.org/10.1007/978-3-030-32079-9_3

14. Fainekos, G.E., Pappas, G.J.: Robustness of temporal logic specifications for continuous-time signals. Theoret. Comput. Sci. **410**(42), 4262–4291 (2009). https://doi.org/10.1016/j.tcs.2009.06.021

15. Fujiwara, S., von Bochmann, G., Khendek, F., Amalou, M., Ghedamsi, A.: Test selection based on finite state models. IEEE Trans. Software Eng. **17**(6), 591–603 (1991). https://doi.org/10.1109/32.87284

16. Hasuo, I.: Metamathematics for systems design - comprehensive transfer of formal methods techniques to cyber-physical systems. New Gener. Comput. **35**(3), 271–305 (2017). https://doi.org/10.1007/s00354-017-0023-1

17. Herber, P., Adelt, J., Liebrenz, T.: Formal verification of intelligent cyber-physical systems with the interactive theorem prover KeYmaera X. In: Götz, S., Linsbauer, L., Schaefer, I., Wortmann, A. (eds.) Proceedings of the Software Engineering 2021 Satellite Events, Braunschweig/Virtual, Germany, 22–26 February 2021. CEUR Workshop Proceedings, vol. 2814. CEUR-WS.org (2021). http://ceur-ws.org/Vol-2814/short-A3-2.pdf

18. Howar, F., Steffen, B.: Active automata learning in practice. In: Bennaceur, A., Hähnle, R., Meinke, K. (eds.) Machine Learning for Dynamic Software Analysis: Potentials and Limits. LNCS, vol. 11026, pp. 123–148. Springer, Cham (2018). https://doi.org/10.1007/978-3-319-96562-8_5

19. Hoxha, B., Abbas, H., Fainekos, G.E.: Benchmarks for temporal logic requirements for automotive systems. In: Frehse, G., Althoff, M. (eds.) 1st and 2nd International Workshop on Applied veRification for Continuous and Hybrid Systems, ARCH@CPSWeek 2014, Berlin, Germany, 14 April 2014/ARCH@CPSWeek 2015, Seattle, WA, USA, 13 April 2015. EPiC Series in Computing, vol. 34, pp. 25–30. EasyChair (2014). https://easychair.org/publications/paper/4bfq

20. Hoxha, B., Abbas, H., Fainekos, G.E.: Using S-TaLiRo on industrial size auimmlertomotive models. In: Frehse, G., Althoff, M. (eds.) 1st and 2nd International Workshop on Applied veRification for Continuous and Hybrid Systems, ARCH@CPSWeek 2014, Berlin, Germany, 14 April 2014/ARCH@CPSWeek 2015, Seattle, WA, USA, 13 April 2015. EPiC Series in Computing, vol. 34, pp. 113–119. EasyChair (2014). https://easychair.org/publications/paper/r8gZ

21. Isberner, M., Howar, F., Steffen, B.: The TTT algorithm: a redundancy-free approach to active automata learning. In: Bonakdarpour, B., Smolka, S.A. (eds.) RV 2014. LNCS, vol. 8734, pp. 307–322. Springer, Cham (2014). https://doi.org/10.1007/978-3-319-11164-3_26

22. Isberner, M., Howar, F., Steffen, B.: The open-source LearnLib. In: Kroening, D., Păsăreanu, C.S. (eds.) CAV 2015. LNCS, vol. 9206, pp. 487–495. Springer, Cham (2015). https://doi.org/10.1007/978-3-319-21690-4_32

23. Khosrowjerdi, H., Meinke, K.: Learning-based testing for autonomous systems using spatial and temporal requirements. In: Perrouin, G., Acher, M., Cordy, M., Devroey, X. (eds.) Proceedings of the 1st International Workshop on Machine Learning and Software Engineering in Symbiosis, MASES@ASE 2018, Montpellier, France, 3 September 2018, pp. 6–15. ACM (2018). https://doi.org/10.1145/3243127.3243129

24. Kirkpatrick, S., Gelatt, C.D., Vecchi, M.P.: Optimization by simulated annealing. Science **220**(4598), 671–680 (1983)

25. Lin, S.-W., Hsiung, P.-A.: Compositional synthesis of concurrent systems through causal model checking and learning. In: Jones, C., Pihlajasaari, P., Sun, J. (eds.) FM 2014. LNCS, vol. 8442, pp. 416–431. Springer, Cham (2014). https://doi.org/10.1007/978-3-319-06410-9_29

26. Maler, O., Nickovic, D.: Monitoring temporal properties of continuous signals. In: Lakhnech, Y., Yovine, S. (eds.) FORMATS/FTRTFT -2004. LNCS, vol. 3253, pp. 152–166. Springer, Heidelberg (2004). https://doi.org/10.1007/978-3-540-30206-3_12

27. Meijer, J., van de Pol, J.: Sound black-box checking in the LearnLib. Innov. Syst. Softw. Eng. **15**(3–4), 267–287 (2019). https://doi.org/10.1007/s11334-019-00342-6

28. Meinke, K., Niu, F.: A learning-based approach to unit testing of numerical software. In: Petrenko, A., Simão, A., Maldonado, J.C. (eds.) ICTSS 2010. LNCS, vol. 6435, pp. 221–235. Springer, Heidelberg (2010). https://doi.org/10.1007/978-3-642-16573-3_16

29. Meinke, K., Nycander, P.: Learning-based testing of distributed microservice architectures: correctness and fault injection. In: Bianculli, D., Calinescu, R., Rumpe, B. (eds.) SEFM 2015. LNCS, vol. 9509, pp. 3–10. Springer, Heidelberg (2015). https://doi.org/10.1007/978-3-662-49224-6_1

30. Meinke, K., Sindhu, M.A.: LBTest: a learning-based testing tool for reactive systems. In: Sixth IEEE International Conference on Software Testing, Verification and Validation, ICST 2013, Luxembourg, Luxembourg, 18–22 March 2013, pp. 447–454. IEEE Computer Society (2013). https://doi.org/10.1109/ICST.2013.62

31. Nitto, E.D., Harman, M., Heymans, P. (eds.): Proceedings of the 2015 10th Joint Meeting on Foundations of Software Engineering, ESEC/FSE 2015, Bergamo, Italy, 30 August–4 September 2015. ACM (2015). https://doi.org/10.1145/2786805

32. Peled, D.A., Vardi, M.Y., Yannakakis, M.: Black box checking. In: Wu, J., Chanson, S.T., Gao, Q. (eds.) Formal Methods for Protocol Engineering and Distributed Systems, FORTE XII/PSTV XIX 1999, IFIP TC6 WG6.1 Joint International Conference on Formal Description Techniques for Distributed Systems and Communication Protocols (FORTE XII) and Protocol Specification, Testing and Verification (PSTV XIX), Beijing, China, 5–8 October 1999. IFIP Conference Proceedings, vol. 156, pp. 225–240. Kluwer (1999)

33. Pnueli, A.: The temporal logic of programs. In: 18th Annual Symposium on Foundations of Computer Science, Providence, Rhode Island, USA, 31 October–1 November 1977, pp. 46–57. IEEE Computer Society (1977). https://doi.org/10.1109/SFCS.1977.32

34. Sato, S., Waga, M., Hasuo, I.: Constrained optimization for falsification and conjunctive synthesis. CoRR abs/2012.00319 (2020). https://arxiv.org/abs/2012.00319

35. Steffen, B., Howar, F., Merten, M.: Introduction to active automata learning from a practical perspective. In: Bernardo, M., Issarny, V. (eds.) SFM 2011. LNCS, vol. 6659, pp. 256–296. Springer, Heidelberg (2011). https://doi.org/10.1007/978-3-642-21455-4_8

36. Tabuada, P., Neider, D.: Robust linear temporal logic. In: Talbot, J., Regnier, L. (eds.) 25th EACSL Annual Conference on Computer Science Logic, CSL 2016, 29 August–1 September 2016, Marseille, France. LIPIcs, vol. 62, pp. 10:1–10:21. Schloss Dagstuhl - Leibniz-Zentrum für Informatik (2016). https://doi.org/10.4230/LIPIcs.CSL.2016.10

37. Waga, M.: Falsification of cyber-physical systems with robustness-guided blackbox checking. In: Ames, A.D., Seshia, S.A., Deshmukh, J. (eds.) HSCC 2020: 23rd ACM International Conference on Hybrid Systems: Computation and Control, Sydney, New South Wales, Australia, 21–24 April 2020, pp. 11:1–11:13. ACM (2020). https://doi.org/10.1145/3365365.3382193

38. Yamaguchi, T., Kaga, T., Donzé, A., Seshia, S.A.: Combining requirement mining, software model checking and simulation-based verification for industrial automotive systems. In: Piskac, R., Talupur, M. (eds.) 2016 Formal Methods in Computer-Aided Design, FMCAD 2016, Mountain View, CA, USA, 3–6 October 2016, pp. 201–204. IEEE (2016). https://doi.org/10.1109/FMCAD.2016.7886680

39. Zhang, Z., Ernst, G., Sedwards, S., Arcaini, P., Hasuo, I.: Two-layered falsification of hybrid systems guided by monte Carlo tree search. IEEE Trans. Comput. Aided Des. Integr. Circuits Syst. **37**(11), 2894–2905 (2018). https://doi.org/10.1109/TCAD.2018.2858463

Neural Predictive Monitoring Under Partial Observability

Francesca Cairoli[1]([✉]), Luca Bortolussi[1,2], and Nicola Paoletti[3]

[1] Department of Mathematics and Geosciences, Università di Trieste, Trieste, Italy
`francesca.cairoli@phd.units.it`
[2] Modeling and Simulation Group, Saarland University, Saarbrücken, Germany
[3] Department of Computer Science, Royal Holloway University, London, Egham, UK

Abstract. We consider the problem of predictive monitoring (PM), i.e., predicting at runtime future violations of a system from the current state. We work under the most realistic settings where only partial and noisy observations of the state are available at runtime. Such settings directly affect the accuracy and reliability of the reachability predictions, jeopardizing the safety of the system. In this work, we present a learning-based method for PM that produces accurate and reliable reachability predictions despite partial observability (PO). We build on Neural Predictive Monitoring (NPM), a PM method that uses deep neural networks for approximating hybrid systems reachability, and extend it to the PO case. We propose and compare two solutions, an *end-to-end* approach, which directly operates on the rough observations, and a *two-step* approach, which introduces an intermediate state estimation step. Both solutions rely on conformal prediction to provide 1) probabilistic guarantees in the form of prediction regions and 2) sound estimates of predictive uncertainty. We use the latter to identify unreliable (and likely erroneous) predictions and to retrain and improve the monitors on these uncertain inputs (i.e., active learning). Our method results in highly accurate reachability predictions and error detection, as well as tight prediction regions with guaranteed coverage.

1 Introduction

We focus on *predictive monitoring (PM) of cyber-physical systems (CPSs)*, that is, the problem of predicting, at runtime, if a safety violation is imminent from the current CPS state. In particular, we work under the (common) setting where the true CPS state is unknown and we only can access partial (and noisy) observations of the system.

With CPSs having become ubiquitous in safety-critical domains, from autonomous vehicles to medical devices [4], runtime safety assurance of these systems is paramount. In this context, PM has the advantage, compared to traditional monitoring [6], of detecting potential safety violations before they occur, in this way enabling preemptive countermeasures to steer the system back to safety (e.g., switching to a failsafe mode as done in the Simplex architecture [18]).

© Springer Nature Switzerland AG 2021
L. Feng and D. Fisman (Eds.): RV 2021, LNCS 12974, pp. 121–141, 2021.
https://doi.org/10.1007/978-3-030-88494-9_7

Thus, effective PM must balance between prediction accuracy, to avoid errors that can jeopardize safety, and computational efficiency, to support fast execution at runtime. Partial observability (PO) makes the problem more challenging, as it requires some form of state estimation (SE) to reconstruct the CPS state from observations: on top of its computational overhead, SE introduces estimation errors that propagate in the reachability predictions, affecting the PM reliability. Existing PM approaches either assume full state observability [8] or cannot provide correctness guarantees on the combined estimation-prediction process [13].

We present a learning-based method for predictive monitoring designed to produce efficient and highly reliable reachability predictions under noise and partial observability. We build on neural predictive monitoring (NPM) [8,9], an approach that employs neural network classifiers to predict reachability at any given state. Such an approach is both accurate, owing to the expressiveness of neural networks (which can approximate well hybrid systems reachability given sufficient training data [26]), and efficient, since the analysis at runtime boils down to a simple forward pass of the neural network.

We extend and generalize NPM to the PO setting by investigating two solution strategies: an *end-to-end* approach where the neural monitor directly operates on the raw observations (i.e., without reconstructing the state); and a *two-step* approach, where it operates on state sequences estimated from observations using a dedicated neural network model. See Fig. 1 for an overview of the approach.

Independently of the strategy chosen for handling PO, our approach offers two ways of quantifying and enhancing PM reliability. Both are based on conformal prediction [5,34], a popular framework for reliable machine learning. First, we complement the predictions of the neural monitor and state estimator with prediction regions guaranteed to cover the true (unknown) value with arbitrary probability. To our knowledge, we are the first to provide probabilistic guarantees on state estimation and reachability under PO. Second, as in NPM, we use measures of predictive uncertainty to derive optimal criteria for detecting (and rejecting) potentially erroneous predictions. These rejection criteria also enable active learning, i.e., retraining and improving the monitor on such identified uncertain predictions.

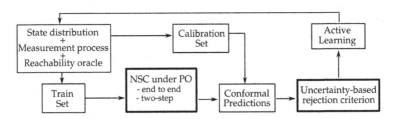

Fig. 1. Overview of the NPM framework under partial observability. The components used at runtime have a thicker border.

We evaluate our method on a benchmark of six hybrid system models. Despite PO, we obtain highly accurate reachability predictions (with accuracy above 99% for most case studies). These results are further improved by our uncertainty-based rejection criteria, which manage to preemptively identify the majority of prediction errors (with a detection rate close to 100% for most models). In particular, we find that the two-step approach tends to outperform the end-to-end one. The former indeed benefits from a neural SE model, which provides high-quality state reconstructions and is empirically superior to Kalman filters [35] and moving horizon estimation [2], two of the main SE methods. Moreover, our method produces prediction regions that are efficient (i.e., tight) yet satisfy the *a priori* guarantees. Finally, we show that active learning not just improves reachability prediction and error detection, but also increases both coverage and efficiency of the prediction regions, which implies stronger guarantees and less conservative regions.

2 Problem Statement

We consider hybrid systems (HS) with discrete time and deterministic dynamics and state space $S = V \times Q$, where $V \subseteq \mathbb{R}^n$ is the domain of the continuous variables, and Q is the set of discrete modes.

$$v_{i+1} = F_{q_i}(v_i, a_i, t_i); \quad q_{i+1} = J_{q_i}(v_i); \quad a_i = C_{q_i}(v_i); \quad y_i = \mu(v_i, q_i) + w_i, \quad (1)$$

where $v_i = v(t_i)$, $q_i = q(t_i)$, $a_i = a(t_i)$, $y_i = y(t_i)$ and $t_i = t_0 + i \cdot \Delta t$. Given a mode $q \in Q$, F_q is the mode-dependent dynamics of the continuous component, J_q is mode switches (i.e., discrete jumps), C_q is the (given) control law. Partial and noisy observations $y_i \in Y$ are produced by the observation function μ and the additive measurement noise $w_i \sim W$ (e.g., white Gaussian noise).

Predictive monitoring of such a system corresponds to deriving a function that approximates a given reachability specification $\mathsf{Reach}(U, s, H_f)$: given a state $s = (v, q)$ and a set of unsafe states U, establish whether the HS admit a trajectory starting from s that reaches U in a time H_f. The approximation is w.r.t. some given distribution of HS states, meaning that we can admit inaccurate reachability predictions if the state has zero probability. We now illustrate the PM problem under the ideal assumption that the full HS can be accessed.

Problem 1 (PM for HS under full observability). Given an HS (1) with state space S, a distribution S over S, a time bound H_f and set of unsafe states $U \subset S$, find a function $h^* : S \to \{0, 1\}$ that minimizes the probability

$$Pr_{s \sim S}\Big(h^*(s) \neq \mathbf{1}\big(\mathsf{Reach}(U, s, H_f)\big)\Big),$$

where $\mathbf{1}$ is the indicator function. A state $s \in S$ is called *positive* w.r.t a predictor $h : S \to \{0, 1\}$ if $h(s) = 1$. Otherwise, s is called *negative*.

As discussed in the next section, finding h^*, i.e., finding a function approximation with minimal error probability, can be solved as a supervised classification problem, provided that a reachability oracle is available for generating supervision data.

The problem above relies on the assumption that full knowledge about the HS state is available. However, in most practical applications, state information is partial and noisy. Under PO, we only have access to a sequence of past observations $\mathbf{y}_t = (y_{t-H_p}, \ldots, y_t)$ which are generated as per (1), that is, by applying the observation function μ and measurement noise to the *unknown* state sequence $s_{t-H_p}, \ldots, s_t$.

In the following, we consider the distribution $\mathcal{Y}$ over Y^{H_p} of the observations sequences $\mathbf{y}_t = (y_{t-H_p}, \ldots, y_t)$ induced by state $s_{t-H_p} \sim \mathcal{S}$, HS dynamics (1), and iid noise $\mathbf{w}_t = (w_{t-H_p}, \ldots, w_t) \sim \mathcal{W}^{H_p}$.

Problem 2 (PM for HS under noise and partial observability). Given the HS and reachability specification of Problem 1, find a function $g^* : Y^{H_p} \to \{0,1\}$ that minimizes

$$Pr_{\mathbf{y}_t \sim \mathcal{Y}}\Big(g^*(\mathbf{y}_t) \neq \mathbf{1}\big(\mathsf{Reach}(U, s_t, H_f)\big)\Big).$$

In other words, g^* should predict reachability values given in input only a sequence of past observations, instead of the true HS state. In particular, we require a sequence of observations for the sake of identifiability. Indeed, for general non linear systems, a single observation does not contain enough information to infer the HS state[1].

The predictor g is an approximate solution and, as such, it can commit safety-critical prediction errors. Building on [8], we endow the predictive monitor with an error detection criterion R. This criterion should be able to *preemptively* identify – and hence, reject – sequences of observations $\mathbf{y}$ where g's prediction is likely to be erroneous (in which case R evaluates to 1, 0 otherwise). R should also be optimal in that it has minimal probability of detection errors. The rationale behind R is that uncertain predictions are more likely to lead to prediction errors. Hence, rather than operating directly over observations $\mathbf{y}$, the detector R receives in input a measure of predictive uncertainty of g about $\mathbf{y}$.

Problem 3 (Uncertainty-based error detection under noise and partial observability). Given an approximate reachability predictor g for the HS and reachability specification of Problem 2, and a measure of predictive uncertainty $u_g : Y^{H_p} \to D$ over some uncertainty domain D, find an optimal error detection rule, $R_g^* : D \to \{0,1\}$, that minimizes the probability

$$Pr_{\mathbf{y}_t \sim \mathcal{Y}} \, \mathbf{1}\Big(g(\mathbf{y}_t) \neq \mathbf{1}(\mathsf{Reach}(U, s_t, H_f))\Big) \neq R_g^*(u_g(\mathbf{y_t})).$$

---

[1] Feasibility of state reconstruction is affected by the time lag and the sequence length. Our focus is to derive the best predictions for fixed lag and sequence length, not to fine-tune these to improve identifiability.

In the above problem, we consider all kinds of prediction errors, but the definition and approach could be easily adapted to focus on the detection of only e.g., false negatives (the most problematic errors from a safety-critical viewpoint).

The general goal of Problems 2 and 3 is to minimize the risk of making mistakes in predicting reachability and predicting predictions errors, respectively. We are also interested in establishing probabilistic guarantees on the expected error rate, in the form of predictions regions guaranteed to include the true reachability value with arbitrary probability.

Problem 4 (Probabilistic guarantees). Given the HS and reachability specification of Problem 2, find a function $\Gamma^\epsilon : Y^{H_p} \to 2^{\{0,1\}}$, mapping a sequence of past observations $\mathbf{y}$ into a prediction region for the corresponding reachability value, i.e., a region that satisfies, for any error probability level $\epsilon \in (0,1)$, the *validity* property below

$$Pr_{\mathbf{y}_t \sim \mathcal{Y}}\Big(\mathbf{1}\big(\mathsf{Reach}(U, s_t, H_f)\big) \in \Gamma^\epsilon(\mathbf{y}_t)\Big) \geq 1 - \epsilon.$$

Among the maps that satisfy validity, we seek the most *efficient* one, meaning the one with the smallest, i.e. less conservative, prediction regions.

3   Methods

In this section, we first describe our learning-based solution to PM under PO (Problem 2). We then provide background on conformal prediction (CP) and explain how we apply this technique to endow our reachability predictions and state estimates with probabilistic guarantees (Problem 4). Finally, we illustrate how CP can be used to derive measures of predictive uncertainty to enable error detection (Problem 3) and active learning.

3.1   Predictive Monitoring Under Noise and Partial Observability

There are two natural learning-based approaches to tackle Problem 2 (see Fig. 2):

1. an **end-to-end** solution that learns a direct mapping from the sequence of past measurements $\mathbf{y}_t$ to the reachability label $\{0,1\}$.
2. a **two-step** solution that combines steps (a) and (b) below:
   (a) learns a *state estimator* able to reconstruct the history of full states $\mathbf{s}_t = (s_{t-H_p}, \ldots, s_t)$ from the sequence of measurements $\mathbf{y}_t = (y_{t-H_p}, \ldots, y_t)$;
   (b) learns a *state classifier* mapping the sequence of states $\mathbf{s}_t$ to the reachability label $\{0,1\}$;

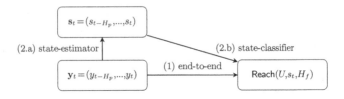

Fig. 2. Diagram of NSC under noise and partial observability.

Dataset Generation. Since we aim to solve the PM problem as one of supervised learning, the first step is generating a suitable training dataset. For this purpose, we need reachability oracles to label states s as safe (negative), if $\neg\mathsf{Reach}(U, s, H_f)$, or unsafe (positive) otherwise. Given that we consider deterministic HS dynamics, we use simulation (rather than reachability checkers like [3,7,12]) to label the states.

The reachability of the system at time t depends only on the state of the system at time t, however, one can decide to exploit more information and make a prediction based on the previous H_p states. Formally, the generated dataset under full observability can be expressed as $\mathcal{D}_{NPM} = \{(\mathbf{s}_t^i, l^i)\}_{i=1}^N$, where $\mathbf{s}_t^i = (s_{t-H_p}^i, s_{t-H_p+1}^i, \ldots, s_t^i)$ and $l^i = \mathbf{1}(\mathsf{Reach}(U, s_t^i, H_f))$. Under partial observability, we use the (known) observation function $\mu : S \to Y$ to build a dataset $\mathcal{D}_{PO-NPM}$ made of tuples $(\mathbf{y}_t, \mathbf{s}_t, l_t)$, where $\mathbf{y}_t$ is a sequence of noisy observations for $\mathbf{s}_t$, i.e., such that $\forall j \in \{t - H_p, \ldots, t\}$ $y_j = \mu(s_j) + w_j$ and $w_j \sim \mathcal{W}$. The distribution of $\mathbf{s}_t$ and $\mathbf{y}_t$ is determined by the distribution $\mathcal{S}$ of the initial state of the sequences, s_{t-H_p}.

We consider two different distributions: *independent*, where the initial states s_{t-H_p} are sampled independently, thus resulting in independent state/observation sequences; and *sequential*, where states come from temporally correlated trajectories in a sliding-window fashion. The latter is more suitable for real-world runtime applications, where observations are received in a sequential manner. On the other hand, temporal dependency violates the exchangeability property, which affects the theoretical validity guarantees of CP, as we will soon discuss.

Starting from $\mathcal{D}_{PO-NPM}$, the two alternative approaches, end-to-end and two-step, can be developed as follows.

End-to-End Solution. We train a one-dimensional convolutional neural net (CNN) that learns a direct mapping from $\mathbf{y}_t$ to l_t, i.e., we solve a simple binary classification problem. This approach ignores the sequence of states $\mathbf{s}_t$. The canonical binary cross-entropy function can be considered as loss function for the weights optimization process.

Two-Step Solution. A CNN regressor, referred to as Neural State Estimator (NSE), is trained to reconstruct the sequence of states $\hat{s}_t$ from the sequence of noisy observations $\mathbf{y}_t$. This is combined with, a CNN classifier, referred to as Neural State Classifier (NSC), trained to predict the reachability label l_t from the sequence of states s_t. The mean square error between the sequences of real states $\mathbf{s}_t$ and the reconstructed ones $\hat{s}_t$ is a suitable loss function for the NSE, whereas for the NSC we use, once again, a binary cross-entropy function.

The network resulting from the combination of the NSE and the NSC maps the sequence of noisy measurements into the safety label, exactly as required in Problem 2. However, the NSE inevitably introduces some errors in reconstructing $\mathbf{s}_t$. Such error is then propagated when the NSC is evaluated on the reconstructed state, $\hat{s}_t$, as it is generated from a distribution different from $\mathcal{S}$, affecting the overall accuracy of the combined net. To alleviate this problem, we introduce a *fine-tuning* phase in which the weights of the NSE and the weights of the NSC are updated together, minimizing the sum of the two respective loss functions. In this phase, the NSC learns to classify correctly the state reconstructed by the NSE, $\hat{s}_t$, rather than the real state $\mathbf{s}_t$, so to improve the task specific accuracy.

Neural State Estimation. The two-step approach has an important additional advantage, the NSE. In general, any traditional state estimator could have been used. Nevertheless, non-linear systems make SE extremely challenging for existing approaches. On the contrary, our NSE reaches very high reconstruction precision (as demonstrated in the result section). Furthermore, because of the fine-tuning, it is possible to calibrate the estimates to be more accurate in regions of the state-space that are safety-critical.

3.2 Conformal Prediction for Regression and Classification

In the following, we provide background on conformal prediction considering a generic prediction model. Let X be the input space, T be the target space, and define $Z = X \times T$. Let $\mathcal{Z}$ be the data-generating distribution, i.e., the distribution of the points $(x, t) \in Z$. The prediction model is represented as a function $f : X \rightarrow T$. For a generic input x, we denote with t the true target value of x and with $\hat{t}$ the prediction by f. Test inputs, whose unknown true target values we aim to predict, are denoted by x_*.

In our setting of reachability prediction, inputs are observation sequences, target values are the corresponding reachability values. The data distribution $\mathcal{Z}$ is the joint distribution of observation sequences and reachability values induced by state $s_{t-H_P} \sim \mathcal{S}$ and iid noise vector $\mathbf{w}_t \sim \mathcal{W}^{H_p}$.

Conformal Prediction associates measures of reliability to any traditional supervised learning problem. It is a very general approach that can be applied across all existing classification and regression methods [5,34]. CP produces *prediction regions with guaranteed validity*, thus satisfying the statistical guarantees illustrated in Problem 4.

Definition 1 (Prediction region). *For significance level $\epsilon \in (0,1)$ and test input x_*, the ϵ-prediction region for x_*, $\Gamma_*^\epsilon \subseteq T$, is a set of target values s.t.*

$$\Pr_{(x_*, t_*) \sim \mathcal{Z}} (t_* \in \Gamma_*^\epsilon) = 1 - \epsilon. \tag{2}$$

The idea of CP is to construct the prediction region by "inverting" a suitable hypothesis test: given a test point x_* and a tentative target value t', we *exclude* t' from the prediction region only if it is unlikely that t' is the true value for x_*. The test statistic is given by a so-called *nonconformity function (NCF)* $\delta : Z \to \mathbb{R}$, which, given a predictor f and a point $z = (x, t)$, measures the deviation between the true value t and the corresponding prediction $f(x)$. In this sense, δ can be viewed as a generalized residual function. In other words, CP builds the prediction region Γ_*^ϵ for a test point x_* by excluding all targets t' whose NCF values are unlikely to follow the NCF distribution of the true targets:

$$\Gamma_*^\epsilon = \left\{ t' \in T \mid Pr_{(x,t) \sim \mathcal{Z}} \left(\delta(x_*, t') \geq \delta(x, t) \right) > \epsilon \right\}. \tag{3}$$

The probability term in Eq. 3 is often called p-value. From a practical viewpoint, the NCF distribution $Pr_{(x,t) \sim \mathcal{Z}}(\delta(x,t))$ cannot be derived in an analytical form, and thus we use an empirical approximation derived using a sample Z_c of $\mathcal{Z}$. This approach is called *inductive CP* [24] and Z_c is referred to as *calibration set*.

Remark 1 (Assumptions and guarantees of inductive CP). Importantly, CP prediction regions have *finite-sample validity* [5], i.e., they satisfy (2) for any sample of $\mathcal{Z}$ (or reasonable size), and not just asymptotically. On the other hand, CP's theoretical guarantees hold under the *exchangeability* assumption (a "relaxed" version of iid) by which the joint probability of any sample of $\mathcal{Z}$ is invariant to permutations of the sampled points. Of the two observation distributions discussed in Sect. 2, we have that independent observations are exchangeable but sequential ones are not (due to the temporal dependency). Even though sequential data violate CP's theoretical validity, we find that the prediction regions still attain empirical coverage consistent with the nominal coverage (see results section), that is, the probabilistic guarantees still hold in practice (as also found in previous work on CP and time-series data [5]).

Validity and Efficiency. CP performance is measured via two quantities: 1) *validity* (or *coverage*), i.e. the empirical error rate observed on a test sample, which should be as close as possible to the significance level ϵ, and 2) *efficiency*, i.e. the size of the prediction regions, which should be small. CP-based prediction regions are automatically valid (under the assumptions of Remark 1), whereas the efficiency depends on the chosen nonconformity function and thus the underlying model.

CP for Classification. In classification, the target space is a discrete set of possible labels (or classes) $T = \{\ell^1, \ldots, \ell^c\}$. We represent the classification model as a function $f : X \to [0, 1]^c$ mapping inputs into a vector of class likelihoods, such that the predicted class is the one with the highest likelihood[2]. Classification

---

[2] Ties can be resolved by imposing an ordering over the classes.

is relevant for predictive monitoring as the reachability predictor of Problem 2 is indeed a binary classifier ($T = \{0, 1\}$) telling whether or not an unsafe state can be reached given a sequence of observation.

The inductive CP algorithm for classification is divided into an offline phase, executed only once, and an online phase, executed for every test point x_*. In the offline phase (steps 1–3 below), we train the classifier f and construct the calibration distribution, i.e., the empirical approximation of the NCF distribution. In the online phase (steps 4–5), we derive the prediction region for x_* using the computed classifier and distribution.

1. Draw sample Z' of $\mathcal{Z}$. Split Z' into training set Z_t and calibration set Z_c.
2. Train classifier f using Z_t. Use f to define an NCF δ.
3. Construct the calibration distribution by computing, for each $z_i \in Z_c$, the NCF score $\alpha_i = \delta(z_i)$.
4. For each label $\ell^j \in T$, compute $\alpha_*^j = \delta(x_*, \ell^j)$, i.e., the NCF score for x_* and ℓ^j, and the associated p-value p_*^j:

$$p_*^j = \frac{|\{z_i \in Z_c \mid \alpha_i > \alpha_*^j\}|}{|Z_c| + 1} + \theta \frac{|\{z_i \in Z_c \mid \alpha_i = \alpha_*^j\}| + 1}{|Z_c| + 1}, \tag{4}$$

   where $\theta \in \mathcal{U}[0, 1]$ is a tie-breaking random variable.
5. Return the prediction region $\Gamma_*^\epsilon = \{\ell^j \in T \mid p_*^j > \epsilon\}$.

In defining the NCF δ, we should aim to obtain high δ values for wrong predictions and low δ values for correct ones. Thus, a natural choice in classification is to define $\delta(x, l^j) = 1 - f(x)_j$, where $f(x)_j$ is the likelihood predicted by f for class l_j. Indeed, if l^j is the true target for x and f correctly predicts l^j, then $f(x)_j$ is high (the highest among all classes) and $\delta(x, l^j)$ is low; the opposite holds if f does not predict l^j.

CP for Regression. In regression we have a continuous target space $T \subseteq \mathbb{R}^n$. Thus, the regression case is relevant for us because our state estimator can be viewed as a regression model, where T is the state space.

The CP algorithm for regression is similar to the classification one. In particular, the offline phase of steps 1–3, i.e., training of regression model f and definition of NCF δ, is the same (with obviously a different kind of f and δ).

The online phase changes though, because T is a continuous space and thus, it is not possible to enumerate the target values and compute for each a p-value. Instead, we proceed in an equivalent manner, that is, identify the critical value $\alpha_{(\epsilon)}$ of the calibration distribution, i.e., the NCF score corresponding to a p-value of ϵ. The resulting ϵ-prediction region is given by $\Gamma_*^\epsilon = f(x_*) \pm \alpha_{(\epsilon)}$, where $\alpha_{(\epsilon)}$ is the $(1 - \epsilon)$-quantile of the calibration distribution, i.e., the $\lfloor \epsilon \cdot (|Z_c| + 1) \rfloor$-th largest calibration score[3].

---

[3] Such prediction intervals have the same width ($\alpha_{(\epsilon)}$) for all inputs. There are techniques like [30] that allow to construct intervals with input-dependent widths, which can be equivalently applied to our problem.

A natural NCF in regression, and the one used in our experiments, is the norm of the difference between the real and the predicted target value, i.e., $\delta(x) = ||t - f(x)||$.

3.3 CP-Based Quantification of Predictive Uncertainty

We illustrate how to complement reachability predictions with uncertainty-based error detection rules, which leverage measures of predictive uncertainty to pre-emptively identify the occurrence of prediction errors. Detecting errors efficiently requires a fine balance between the number of errors accurately prevented and the overall number of discarded predictions.

We use two uncertainty measures, *confidence* and *credibility*, that are extracted from the CP algorithm for classification. The method discussed below was first introduced for NPM [8], but here this is extended to the PO case.

Confidence and Credibility. Let us start by observing that, for significance levels $\epsilon_1 \geq \epsilon_2$, the corresponding prediction regions are such that $\Gamma^{\epsilon_1} \subseteq \Gamma^{\epsilon_2}$. It follows that, given an input x_*, if ϵ is lower than all its p-values, i.e. $\epsilon < \min_{j=1,\ldots,c} p_*^j$, then the region Γ_*^ϵ contains all the labels. As ϵ increases, fewer and fewer classes will have a p-value higher than ϵ. That is, the region shrinks as ϵ increases. In particular, Γ_*^ϵ is empty when $\epsilon \geq \max_{j=1,\ldots,c} p_*^j$.

The *confidence* of a point $x_* \in X$, $1 - \gamma_*$, measures how likely is our prediction for x_* compared to all other possible classifications (according to the calibration set). It is computed as one minus the smallest value of ϵ for which the conformal region is a single label, i.e. the second largest p-value γ_*:

$$1 - \gamma_* = \sup\{1 - \epsilon : |\Gamma_*^\epsilon| = 1\}.$$

The *credibility*, c_*, indicates how suitable the training data are to classify that specific example. In practice, it is the smallest ϵ for which the prediction region is empty, i.e. the highest p-value according to the calibration set, which corresponds to the p-value of the predicted class:

$$c_* = \inf\{\epsilon : |\Gamma_*^\epsilon| = 0\}.$$

Note that if $\gamma_* \leq \epsilon$, then the corresponding prediction region Γ_*^ϵ contains at most one class. If both $\gamma_* \leq \epsilon$ and $c_* > \epsilon$ hold, then the prediction region contains *exactly* one class, denoted as $\hat{\ell}_*$, i.e. the one predicted by f. In other words, the interval $[\gamma_*, c_*)$ contains all the ϵ values for which we are sure that $\Gamma_*^\epsilon = \{\hat{\ell}_*\}$. It follows that the higher $1 - \gamma_*$ and c_* are, the more reliable the prediction $\hat{\ell}_*$ is, because we have an expanded range $[\gamma_*, c_*)$ of significance values by which $\hat{\ell}_*$ is valid. Indeed, in the extreme scenario where $c_* = 1$ and $\gamma_* = 0$, then $\Gamma_*^\epsilon = \{\hat{\ell}_*\}$ for any value of ϵ. This is why, as we will soon explain, our uncertainty-based rejection criterion relies on excluding points with low values of $1 - \gamma_*$ and c_*. In binary classification problems, each point x_* has only two p-values, one for each class, which coincide with c_* (p-value of the predicted class) and γ_* (p-value of the other class).

Given a reachability predictor g, the uncertainty function u_g can be defined as the function mapping a sequence of observations $\mathbf{y}^*$ into the confidence γ^* and the credibility c^* of $g(\mathbf{y}^*)$, thus $u_g(\mathbf{y}^*) = (\gamma^*, c^*)$. In order to learn a good decision rule to identify trustworthy predictions, we solve another binary classification problem on the uncertainty values. In particular, we use a cross-validation strategy to compute values of confidence and credibility over the entire calibration set, as it is not used to train the classifier, and label each point as 0 if it is correctly classified by the predictor and as 1 if it is misclassified. We then train a Support Vector Classifier (SVC) that automatically learns to distinguish points that are misclassified from points that are correctly classified based on the values of confidence and credibility. In particular, we choose a simple linear classifier as it turns out to perform satisfactorily well, especially on strongly unbalanced datasets. Nevertheless, other kinds of classifiers can be applied as well.

To summarize, given a predictor g and a new sequence of observations $\mathbf{y}^*$, we obtain a prediction about its safety, $g(\mathbf{y}^*) = \hat{l}^*$, and a quantification of its uncertainty, $u^* = u_g(\mathbf{y}^*) = (\gamma^*, c^*)$. If we feed u^* to the rejection rule R_g we obtain a prediction about whether or not the prediction of g about $\mathbf{y}^*$ can be trusted.

3.4   Active Learning (AL)

NPM depends on two related learning problems: the reachabiliy predictor g and the rejection rule R_g. We leverage the *uncertainty-aware active learning* solution presented in [9], where the re-training points are derived by first sampling a large pool of unlabeled data, and then considering only those points where the current predictor g is still uncertain, i.e. those points which are rejected by our rejection rule R_g. A fraction of the labeled samples is added to the training set, whereas the remaining part is added to the calibration set, keeping the training/calibration ratio constant. As a matter of fact, a principled criterion to select the most informative samples would benefit both the accuracy and the efficiency of the method, as the size of the calibration set affects the runtime efficiency of the error detection rule.

The addition of such actively selected points results in a shift of the data generating distribution, that does not match anymore the distribution of the test samples. This implies that the theoretical guarantees of CP are lost. However, as we will show in the experiments, AL typically results in an empirical increase of the coverage, i.e., in even stronger probabilistic guarantees. The reason is that AL is designed to improve on poor predictions, which, as such, have prediction regions more likely to miss the true value. Improving such poor predictions thus directly cause an increased coverage (assuming that the classifier remains accurate enough on the inputs prior to AL).

4   Experimental Evaluation

We evaluate both end-to-end and two-step approaches under PO on six benchmarks of cyber-physical systems with dynamics presenting a varying degree of complexity and with a variety of observation functions. We include white Gaussian noise to introduce stochasticity in the observations.

4.1   Case Studies

- **IP:** classic two-dimensional non-linear model of an Inverted Pendulum on a cart. Given a state $s = (s_1, s_2)$, we observe a noisy measure of the energy of the system $y = s_2/2 + \cos(s_1) - 1 + w$, where $w \sim \mathcal{N}(0, 0.005)$. Unsafe region $U = \{s : |s_1| \geq \pi/6\}$. $H_p = 1$, $H_f = 5$.
- **SN:** a two-dimensional non-linear model of the Spiking Neuron action potential. Given a state $s = (s_1, s_2)$ we observe a noisy measure of s_2, $y = s_2 + w$, with $w \sim \mathcal{N}(0, 0.1)$. Unsafe region $U = \{s : s_1 \leq -68.5\}$. $H_p = 4$, $H_f = 16$.
- **CVDP:** a four-dimensional non-linear model of the Coupled Van Der Pol oscillator [15], modeling two coupled oscillators. Given a state $s = (s_1, s_2, s_3, s_4)$ we observe $y = (s_1, s_3) + w$, with $w \sim \mathcal{N}(\underline{0}, 0.01 \cdot I_2)$. Unsafe region $U = \{s : s_2 \geq 2.75 \wedge s_2 \geq 2.75\}$. $H_p = 8$, $H_f = 7$.
- **LALO:** the seven-dimensional non-linear Laub Loomis model [15] of a class of enzymatic activities. Given a state $s = (s_1, s_2, s_3, s_4, s_5, s_6, s_7)$ we observe $y = (s_1, s_2, s_3, s_5, s_6, s_7) + w$, with $w \sim \mathcal{N}(\underline{0}, 0.01 \cdot I_6)$. Unsafe region $U = \{s : s_4 \geq 4.5\}$. $H_p = 5$, $H_f = 20$.
- **TWT:** a three-dimensional non-linear model of a Triple Water Tank. Given a state $s = (s_1, s_2, s_3)$ we observe $y = s + w$, with $w \sim \mathcal{N}(\underline{0}, 0.01 \cdot I_3)$. Unsafe region $U = \{s : \vee_{i=1}^3 s_i \notin [4.5, 5.5]\}$. $H_p = 1$, $H_f = 1$.
- **HC:** the 28-dimensional linear model of an Helicopter controller. We observe only the altitude, i.e. $y = s_8 + w$, with $w \sim \mathcal{N}(0, 1)$. Unsafe region $U = \{s : s_8 < 0\}$. $H_p = 5$, $H_f = 5$.

Details about the case studies are available in the Appendix A of [11].

4.2   Experimental Settings

Implementation. The workflow can be divided in steps: (1) define the CPS models, (2) generate the synthetic datasets $\mathcal{D}_{PO-NPM}$ (both the independent and the sequential version), (3) train the NPM (either end-to-end or two-step), (4) train the CP-based error detection rules, (5) perform active learning and (6) evaluate both the initial and the active NPM on a test set. From here on, we call *initial setting* the one with no active learning involved. The technique is fully implemented in Python[4]. In particular, PyTorch [25] is used to craft, train and evaluate the desired CNN architectures. Details about the CNN architectures and the settings of the optimization algorithm are described in Appendix

---

[4] The experiments were performed on a computer with a CPU Intel x86, 24 cores and a 128 GB RAM and 15 GB of GPU Tesla V100.

D of [11]. The source code for all the experiments can be found at the following link: https://github.com/francescacairoli/Stoch_NSC.git.

Datasets. For each case study we generate both an independent and a sequential dataset.

- *Independent:* the train set consists of 50K independent sequences of states of length 32, the respective noisy measurements and the reachability labels. The calibration and test set contains respectively 8.5K and 10K samples.
- *Sequential:* for the train set, 5K states are randomly sampled. From each of these states we simulate a long trajectory. From each long trajectory we obtain 100 sub-trajectories of length 32 in a sliding window fashion. The same procedure is applied to the test and calibration set, where the number of initial states is respectively 1K and 850.

Data are scaled to the interval $[-1, 1]$ to avoid sensitivity to different scales. While the chosen datasets are not too large, our approach would work well even with smaller datasets, resulting however in lower accuracy and higher uncertainty. In these cases, our proposed uncertainty-based active learning would represent the go-to solution as is designed for situations where data collection is particularly expensive.

Computational Costs. NPM is designed to work at runtime in safety-critical applications, which translates in the need of high computational efficiency together with high reliability. The time needed to generate the dataset and to train both methods does not affect the runtime efficiency of the NPM, as it is performed only once (offline). Once trained, the time needed to analyse the reachability of the current sequence of observations is the time needed to evaluate one (or two) CNN, which is almost negligible (in the order of microseconds on GPU). On the other hand, the time needed to quantify the uncertainty depends on the size of the calibration set. This is one of the reasons that make active learning a preferable option, as it adds only the most significant points to the dataset. It is important to notice that the percentage of points rejected, meaning points with predictions estimated to be unreliable, affects considerably the runtime efficiency of the methods. Therefore, we seek a trade-off between accuracy and runtime efficiency. Training the end-to-end approach takes around 15 min. Training the two-step approach takes around 40 min: 9 for the NSE, 11 for the NSC and 20 min for the fine-tuning. Making a single prediction takes around 7×10^{-7} s in the end-to-end scenario and 9×10^{-7} s in the two-step scenario. Training the SVC takes from 0.5 to 10 s, whereas computing values of confidence and credibility for a single point takes from 0.3 to 2 ms. Actively query new data from a pool of 50K samples takes around 5 min.

Performance Measures. The measures used to quantify the overall performance of the NPM under PO (both end-to-end and two-step) are: the *accuracy* of the reachability predictor, the *error detection rate* and the *rejection rate*. We seek high accuracies and detection rates without being overly conservative, meaning keeping a rejection rate as low as possible. We also check if and when the statistical guarantees are met empirically, via values of coverage and efficiency. We analyse and compare the performances of NPM under PO on different configurations: an initial and active configuration for independent states and a temporally correlated (sequential) configuration. Additionally, we test the method for anomaly detection.

4.3   Results

Initial Setting. Table 1 compares the performances of the two approaches to PO-NPM via predictive accuracy, detection rate, i.e. the percentage of prediction errors, either false-positives (FP) or false-negatives (FN), recognized by the error detection rule, and the overall rejection over the test set. We can observe how both methods work well despite PO, i.e., they reach extremely high accuracies and high detection rate. However, the two-step approach seems to behave slightly better than the end-to-end. As a matter of fact, accuracy is almost always greater than 99% with a detection rate close to 100.00. The average rejection rate is around 11% in the end-to-end scenario, and reduces to 9% in the two-step scenario, making the latter less conservative ant thus more efficient from a computational point of view. These results come with no surprise, because, compared to the end-to-end one, the two-step approach leverages more information available in the dataset for training, that is the exact sequence of states.

Table 1. Initial results: *Acc.* is the accuracy of the PO-NPM, *Det.* the detection rate, *Rej.* the rejection rate of the error detection rule and *FN* (*FP*) is the number of detected false negative (positive) errors.

Model	End-to-end					Two-step				
	Acc.	Det.	FN	FP	Rej.	Acc.	Det.	FN	FP	Rej.
SN	97.72	94.30	79/88	136/140	11.30	97.12	95.49	53/54	222/234	19.98
IP	96.27	93.48	148/155	153/167	27.32	98.42	91.14	81/91	63/66	10.01
CVDP	99.19	100.00	30/30	51/51	5.75	99.68	100.00	17/17	15/15	3.51
TWT	98.93	95.51	18/20	67/69	7.45	98.93	96.26	52/56	51/51	10.46
LALO	98.88	99.11	66/66	45/46	7.39	99.24	100.00	52/52	24/24	6.11
HC	99.63	100.00	19/19	15/15	8.47	99.84	100.00	8/8	8/8	4.03

Benefits of Active Learning. Table 2 presents the results after one iteration of active learning. Additional data were selected from a pool of 50K points, using the error detection rule as query strategy. We observe a slight improvement in the performance, mainly reflected in higher detection rates and smaller rejection rates, with an average that reduces to 8% for the end-to-end and to 6% for the two-step.

Table 2. Active results (1 iteration): *Acc.* is the accuracy of the PO-NPM, *Det.* the detection rate, *Rej.* the rejection rate of the error detection rule and *FN* (*FP*) is the number of detected false negative (positive) errors.

Model	End-to-end					Two-step				
	Acc.	Det.	FN	FP	Rej.	Acc.	Det.	FN	FP	Rej.
SN	98.06	94.87	81/88	104/107	9.80	98.41	100.00	55/55	104/104	12.00
IP	99.47	87.91	150/166	119/140	15.44	98.75	92.86	63/69	52/56	7.72
CVDP	99.10	95.55	43/46	43/44	4.81	99.69	100.00	19/19	12/12	2.48
TWT	99.04	100.00	45/45	62/62	10.45	99.07	94.62	44/49	44/44	6.20
LALO	98.79	96.69	87/90	30/31	6.88	99.27	100.00	40/40	33/33	4.28
HC	99.86	100.00	5/5	9/9	2.35	99.79	100.00	17/17	4/4	2.73

Probabilisic Guarantees. In our experiments, we measured the efficiency as the percentage of singleton prediction regions over the test set. Table 3 compares the empirical coverage and the efficiency of the CP prediction regions in the initial and active scenario for both the end-to-end and two-step classifiers. The confidence level is set to $(1 - \epsilon) = 95\%$. Figure 6 in Appendix C of [11] shows coverage and efficiency for different significance levels (ranging from 0.01 to 0.1). CP provides theoretical guarantees on the validity, meaning empirical coverage matching the expected one of 95%, only in the initial setting. As a matter of fact, with active learning we modify the data-generating distribution of the training and calibration sets, while the test set remains the same, i.e., sampled from the original data distribution. As a result, we observe (Table 3) that both methods in the initial setting are valid. In the active scenario, even if theoretical guarantees are lost, we obtain both better coverage and higher efficiency. This means that the increased coverage is not due to a more conservative predictor but to an improved accuracy.

Table 3. Coverage and efficiency for both the approaches to PO-NPM. Initial results are compared with results after one active learning iteration. Expected coverage 95%.

Model	End-to-end				Two-step			
	Initial		Active		Initial		Active	
	Cov.	Eff.	Cov.	Eff.	Cov.	Eff.	Cov.	Eff.
SN	95.12	95.70	97.19	98.50	94.80	99.54	97.32	98.37
IP	95.30	89.31	96.60	99.62	94.85	94.92	97.28	97.88
CVDP	95.73	95.73	98.00	98.02	95.63	95.63	98.31	98.34
TWT	96.43	96.43	99.99	97.26	96.60	96.97	99.66	97.20
LALO	94.59	94.61	97.28	98.52	94.66	94.66	97.48	97.55
HC	95.03	95.03	97.65	97.65	94.97	94.97	97.69	97.69

Table 4 shows values of coverage and efficiency for the two separate steps (state estimation and reachability prediction) of the two-step approach. Recall that the efficiency in the case of regression, and thus of state estimation, is given by the volume of the prediction region. So, the smaller the volume, the more efficient the regressor. The opposite holds for classifiers, where a large value of efficiency means tight prediction regions. It is interesting to observe how active learning makes the NSC reach higher coverages at the cost of more conservative prediction regions (lower efficiency), whereas the NSE coverage is largely unaffected by active learning (except for TWT). Reduction in NSC efficiency, differently from the two-step combined approach, is likely due to an adaptation of the method to deal with and correct noisy estimates. Such behaviour suggests that the difficulty in predicting the reachability of a certain state is independent of how hard it is to reconstruct that state[5].

Table 4. Coverage and efficiency for the two steps of the two-step approach. NSC is a classifier, whereas NSE is a regressor. Initial results are compared with results after one active learning iteration. Expected coverage 95%.

Model	NSC				NSE			
	Initial		Active		Initial		Active	
	Cov.	Eff.	Cov.	Eff.	Cov.	Eff.	Cov.	Eff.
SN	94.82	99.51	97.23	90.12	94.49	1.361	95.18	1.621
IP	94.51	99.69	97.23	91.63	94.65	3.064	95.44	3.233
CVDP	95.60	95.64	98.25	98.32	95.37	0.343	96.40	0.358
TWT	96.68	96.98	98.72	95.61	95.07	0.770	100.00	1.366
LALO	94.88	98.18	98.01	80.86	95.29	0.6561	95.36	0.8582
HC	94.67	94.74	97.33	99.12	94.50	12.44	94.58	12.464

State Estimator. We compare the performances of the NSE with two traditional state estimation techniques: Unscented Kalman Filters[6] (UKF) [35] and Moving Horizon Estimation[7] (MHE) [1]. In particular, for each point in the test set we compute the relative error given by the norm of the difference between the real and reconstructed state trajectories divided by the maximum range of state values. The results, presented in full in Appendix E of [11], show how our neural network-based state estimator significantly outperforms both UKF and MHE in our case studies. Moreover, unlike the existing SE approaches, our state estimates come with a prediction region that provides probabilistic guarantees on the expected reconstruction error, as shown in Fig. 3.

---

[5] We select re-training points based on the uncertainty of the reachability predictor; if the SE performed badly on those same points, re-training would have led to a higher SE accuracy and hence, increased coverage.

[6] pykalman library: https://pykalman.github.io/.

[7] do-mpc library: https://www.do-mpc.com/en/latest/.

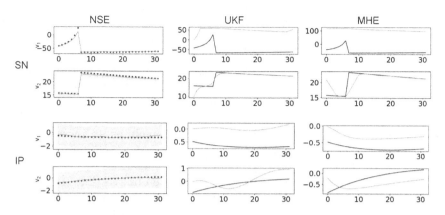

Fig. 3. Comparison of different state estimators on a state of the SN (top) and IP (bottom) model. Blue is the exact state sequence, orange is the estimated one. (Color figure online)

Sequential Data. All the results presented so far consider a dataset $\mathcal{D}_{PO-NPM}$ of observation sequences generated by independently sampled initial states. However, we are interested in applying NPM at runtime to systems that are evolving in time. States will thus have a temporal correlation, meaning that we lose the exchangeability requirement behind the theoretical validity of CP regions. Table 5 shows the performance of predictor and error detection trained and tested on sequential data. In general, accuracy and detection rates are still very high (typically above 95%), but the results are on average worse than the independent counterpart. The motivation could be two-fold: on one side, it is reasonable to assume that a recurrent neural net would perform better on sequential data, compared to CNN, on the other, the samples contained in the sequential dataset are strongly correlated and thus they may cover only poorly the state space. The table also shows values of coverage and efficiency of both the end-to-end and the two-step approach. Even if theoretical validity is lost, we still observe empirical

Table 5. Sequential results: *Acc.* is the accuracy of the PO-NPM, *Det.* the detection rate, *Rej.* the rejection rate, *Cov.* the CP coverage and *Eff.* the CP efficiency.

Model	End-to-end					Two-step				
	Acc.	Det.	Rej.	Cov.	Eff.	Acc.	Det.	Rej.	Cov	Eff.
SN	94.96	85.83	19.74	93.93	97.73	90.37	81.93	26.59	95.01	88.66
IP	94.17	91.08	31.74	95.31	84.32	91.47	98.01	30.81	95.23	90.23
CVDP	98.97	99.12	7.97	94.88	94.92	98.33	98.20	9.89	94.89	95.19
TWT	96.95	95.33	16.84	93.42	94.52	95.74	92.72	23.52	93.60	96.16
LALO	98.99	97.75	7.18	95.93	97.08	99.26	100.00	5.37	95.78	95.80
HC	99.57	100.00	3.89	94.29	94.29	99.64	97.22	3.84	94.51	94.52

coverages that match the nominal value of 95%, i.e., the probabilistic guarantees are satisfied in practice.

Anomaly Detection. The data-generating distribution at runtime is assumed to coincide with the one used to generate the datasets. However, in practice, such distribution is typically unknown and subject to runtime deviations. Thus, we are interested to observe how the sequential PO-NPM behave when an anomaly takes place. In our experiments, we model an anomaly as an increase in the variance of the measurement noise, i.e. $\mathcal{W}' = \mathcal{N}(0, 0.25 \cdot I)$. Figure 4 compares the performances with VS without anomaly on a single case study (the other case studies are shown in Appendix B of [11]). We observe that the anomaly causes a drop in accuracy and error detection rate, which comes with an increase in the number of predictions rejected because deemed to be unreliable. These preliminary results show how an increase in the NPM rejection rate could be used as a significant measure to preemptively detect runtime anomalies.

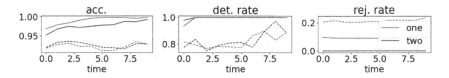

Fig. 4. Anomaly detection (TWT model). Dashed lines denotes the performances on observations with anomaly in the noise. Blue is for the two-step approach, green for the end-to-end. (Color figure online)

5   Related Work

Our approach extends and generalize neural predictive monitoring [8,9] to work under partial observability. To our knowledge, the only existing work to focus on PM and PO is [13], which combines Bayesian estimation with pre-computed reach sets to reduce the runtime overhead. While their reachability bounds are certified, no correctness guarantees can be established for the estimation step. Our work instead provides probabilistic guarantees as well as techniques for preemptive error detection. A related but substantially different problem is to verify signals with observation gaps using state estimation to fill the gaps [20,33].

In [28] a model-based approach to predictive runtime verification is presented. However, PO and computational efficiency are not taken into account. A problem very similar to ours is addressed in [19], but for a different class of systems (MDPs).

Learning-based approaches for reachability prediction of hybrid and stochastic systems include [10,14,16,26,31,36]. Of these, [36] develop, akin to our work, error detection techniques, but using neural network verification methods [17].

Such verification methods, however, do not scale well on large models and support only specific classes of neural networks. On the opposite, our uncertainty-based error detection can be applied to any ML-based predictive monitor. Learning-based PM approaches for temporal logic properties [22,29] typically learn a time-series model from past observations and then use such model to infer property satisfaction. In particular, [29] provide (like we do) guaranteed prediction intervals, but (unlike our method) they are limited to ARMA/ARIMA models. Ma et al. [22] use uncertainty quantification with Bayesian RNNs to provide confidence guarantees. However, these models are, by nature, not well-calibrated (i.e., the model uncertainty does not reflect the observed one [21]), making the resulting guarantees not theoretically valid[8].

PM is at the core of the Simplex architecture [18,32] and recent extensions thereof [23,27], where the PM component determines when to switch to the fail-safe controller to prevent imminent safety violations. In this context, our approach can be used to guarantee arbitrarily small probability of wrongly failing to switch.

6   Conclusion

We presented an extension of the Neural Predictive Monitoring [9] framework to work under the most realistic settings of noise and partially observability. We proposed two alternative solution strategies: an end-to-end solution, predicting reachability directly from raw observations, and a two-step solution, with an intermediate state estimation step. Both methods produce extremely accurate predictions, with the two-step approach performing better overall than the end-to-end version, and further providing accurate reconstructions of the true state. The online computational cost is negligible, making this method suitable for run-time applications. The method is equipped with an error detection rule to prevent reachability prediction errors, as well as with prediction regions providing probabilistic guarantees. We demonstrated that error detection can be meaningfully used for active learning, thereby improving our models on the most uncertain inputs.

As future work, we plan to extend this approach to fully stochastic models, investigating the use of deep generative models for state estimation. We will further explore the use of recurrent or attention-based architectures in place of convolutional ones to improve performance for sequential data.

References

1. Allan, D.A., Rawlings, J.B.: Moving horizon estimation. In: Raković, S.V., Levine, W.S. (eds.) Handbook of Model Predictive Control. CE, pp. 99–124. Springer, Cham (2019). https://doi.org/10.1007/978-3-319-77489-3_5

---

[8] The authors develop a solution for Bayesian RNNs calibration, but such solution in turn is not guaranteed to produce well-calibrated models.

2. Allgöwer, F., Badgwell, T.A., Qin, J.S., Rawlings, J.B., Wright, S.J.: Nonlinear predictive control and moving horizon estimation - an introductory overview. In: Frank, P.M. (ed.) Advances in Control, pp. 391–449. Springer, London (1999). https://doi.org/10.1007/978-1-4471-0853-5_19

3. Althoff, M., Grebenyuk, D.: Implementation of interval arithmetic in CORA 2016. In: Proceedings of the 3rd International Workshop on Applied Verification for Continuous and Hybrid Systems (2016)

4. Alur, R.: Principles of Cyber-Physical Systems. MIT Press, Cambridge (2015)

5. Balasubramanian, V., Ho, S.S., Vovk, V.: Conformal Prediction for Reliable Machine Learning: Theory, Adaptations and Applications. Newnes, London (2014)

6. Bartocci, E., et al.: Specification-based monitoring of cyber-physical systems: a survey on theory, tools and applications. In: Bartocci, E., Falcone, Y. (eds.) Lectures on Runtime Verification. LNCS, vol. 10457, pp. 135–175. Springer, Cham (2018). https://doi.org/10.1007/978-3-319-75632-5_5

7. Bogomolov, S., Forets, M., Frehse, G., Potomkin, K., Schilling, C.: JuliaReach: a toolbox for set-based reachability. In: Proceedings of the 22nd ACM International Conference on Hybrid Systems: Computation and Control, pp. 39–44 (2019)

8. Bortolussi, L., Cairoli, F., Paoletti, N., Smolka, S.A., Stoller, S.D.: Neural predictive monitoring. In: Finkbeiner, B., Mariani, L. (eds.) RV 2019. LNCS, vol. 11757, pp. 129–147. Springer, Cham (2019). https://doi.org/10.1007/978-3-030-32079-9_8

9. Bortolussi, L., Cairoli, F., Paoletti, N., Smolka, S.A., Stoller, S.D.: Neural predictive monitoring and a comparison of frequentist and Bayesian approaches. Int. J. Softw. Tools Technol. Transf. (2021). https://doi.org/10.1007/s10009-021-00623-1

10. Bortolussi, L., Milios, D., Sanguinetti, G.: Smoothed model checking for uncertain continuous-time Markov chains. Inf. Comput. **247**, 235–253 (2016)

11. Cairoli, F., Bortolussi, L., Paoletti, N.: Neural predictive monitoring under partial observability. In: Feng, L., Fisman, D. (eds.) RV 2021, LNCS 12974, pp. 121–141. Springer, Cham (2021)

12. Chen, X., Ábrahám, E., Sankaranarayanan, S.: Flow*: an analyzer for non-linear hybrid systems. In: Sharygina, N., Veith, H. (eds.) CAV 2013. LNCS, vol. 8044, pp. 258–263. Springer, Heidelberg (2013). https://doi.org/10.1007/978-3-642-39799-8_18

13. Chou, Y., Yoon, H., Sankaranarayanan, S.: Predictive runtime monitoring of vehicle models using Bayesian estimation and reachability analysis. In: International Conference on Intelligent Robots and Systems (IROS) (2020)

14. Djeridane, B., Lygeros, J.: Neural approximation of PDE solutions: an application to reachability computations. In: Proceedings of the 45th IEEE Conference on Decision and Control, pp. 3034–3039. IEEE (2006)

15. Ernst, G., et al.: ARCH-COMP 2020 category report: falsification. In: EPiC Series in Computing (2020)

16. Granig, W., Jakšić, S., Lewitschnig, H., Mateis, C., Ničković, D.: Weakness monitors for fail-aware systems. In: Bertrand, N., Jansen, N. (eds.) FORMATS 2020. LNCS, vol. 12288, pp. 283–299. Springer, Cham (2020). https://doi.org/10.1007/978-3-030-57628-8_17

17. Ivanov, R., Weimer, J., Alur, R., Pappas, G.J., Lee, I.: Verisig: verifying safety properties of hybrid systems with neural network controllers. In: Proceedings of the 22nd ACM International Conference on Hybrid Systems: Computation and Control, pp. 169–178 (2019)

18. Johnson, T.T., Bak, S., Caccamo, M., Sha, L.: Real-time reachability for verified simplex design. ACM Trans. Embedded Comput. Syst. (TECS) **15**(2), 1–27 (2016)

19. Junges, S., Torfah, H., Seshia, S.A.: Runtime monitors for Markov decision processes. In: Silva, A., Leino, K.R.M. (eds.) CAV 2021. LNCS, vol. 12760, pp. 553–576. Springer, Cham (2021). https://doi.org/10.1007/978-3-030-81688-9_26
20. Kalajdzic, K., Bartocci, E., Smolka, S.A., Stoller, S.D., Grosu, R.: Runtime verification with particle filtering. In: Legay, A., Bensalem, S. (eds.) RV 2013. LNCS, vol. 8174, pp. 149–166. Springer, Heidelberg (2013). https://doi.org/10.1007/978-3-642-40787-1_9
21. Kuleshov, V., Fenner, N., Ermon, S.: Accurate uncertainties for deep learning using calibrated regression. In: International Conference on Machine Learning, pp. 2796–2804. PMLR (2018)
22. Ma, M., Stankovic, J.A., Bartocci, E., Feng, L.: Predictive monitoring with logic-calibrated uncertainty for cyber-physical systems. CoRR abs/2011.00384v2 (2020)
23. Mehmood, U., Stoller, S.D., Grosu, R., Roy, S., Damare, A., Smolka, S.A.: A distributed simplex architecture for multi-agent systems. arXiv preprint arXiv:2012.10153 (2020)
24. Papadopoulos, H.: Inductive conformal prediction: theory and application to neural networks. In: Tools in Artificial Intelligence. InTech (2008)
25. Paszke, A., et al.: Automatic differentiation in Pytorch. In: NIPS-W (2017)
26. Phan, D., Paoletti, N., Zhang, T., Grosu, R., Smolka, S.A., Stoller, S.D.: Neural state classification for hybrid systems. In: Lahiri, S.K., Wang, C. (eds.) ATVA 2018. LNCS, vol. 11138, pp. 422–440. Springer, Cham (2018). https://doi.org/10.1007/978-3-030-01090-4_25
27. Phan, D.T., Grosu, R., Jansen, N., Paoletti, N., Smolka, S.A., Stoller, S.D.: Neural simplex architecture. In: Lee, R., Jha, S., Mavridou, A., Giannakopoulou, D. (eds.) NFM 2020. LNCS, vol. 12229, pp. 97–114. Springer, Cham (2020). https://doi.org/10.1007/978-3-030-55754-6_6
28. Pinisetty, S., Jéron, T., Tripakis, S., Falcone, Y., Marchand, H., Preoteasa, V.: Predictive runtime verification of timed properties. J. Syst. Softw. **132**, 353–365 (2017)
29. Qin, X., Deshmukh, J.V.: Predictive monitoring for signal temporal logic with probabilistic guarantees. In: Proceedings of the 22nd ACM International Conference on Hybrid Systems: Computation and Control, pp. 266–267. ACM (2019)
30. Romano, Y., Patterson, E., Candès, E.J.: Conformalized quantile regression. arXiv preprint arXiv:1905.03222 (2019)
31. Royo, V.R., Fridovich-Keil, D., Herbert, S., Tomlin, C.J.: Classification-based approximate reachability with guarantees applied to safe trajectory tracking. arXiv preprint arXiv:1803.03237 (2018)
32. Sha, L., et al.: Using simplicity to control complexity. IEEE Softw. **18**(4), 20–28 (2001)
33. Stoller, S.D., et al.: Runtime verification with state estimation. In: Khurshid, S., Sen, K. (eds.) RV 2011. LNCS, vol. 7186, pp. 193–207. Springer, Heidelberg (2012). https://doi.org/10.1007/978-3-642-29860-8_15
34. Vovk, V., Gammerman, A., Shafer, G.: Algorithmic Learning in a Random World. Springer, Boston (2005). https://doi.org/10.1007/b106715
35. Wan, E.A., Van Der Merwe, R.: The unscented Kalman filter for nonlinear estimation. In: Proceedings of the IEEE 2000 Adaptive Systems for Signal Processing, Communications, and Control Symposium (Cat. No. 00EX373), pp. 153–158. IEEE (2000)
36. Yel, E., et al.: Assured runtime monitoring and planning: toward verification of neural networks for safe autonomous operations. IEEE Robot. Autom. Mag. **27**(2), 102–116 (2020)

A Compositional Framework
for Quantitative Online Monitoring
over Continuous-Time Signals

Konstantinos Mamouras$^{(\boxtimes)}$, Agnishom Chattopadhyay, and Zhifu Wang

Rice University, Houston, TX 77005, USA
{mamouras,agnishom,zfwang}@rice.edu

Abstract. We investigate online monitoring algorithms over dense-time and continuous-time signals for properties written in metric temporal logic (MTL). We consider an abstract algebraic semantics based on complete lattices, which subsumes the Boolean (qualitative) semantics and the real-valued robustness (quantitative) semantics. Our semantics also extends to truth values that are partially ordered and allows the modeling of uncertainty in satisfaction. We propose a compositional approach for the construction of online monitors based on a class of infinite-state deterministic signal transducers that (1) are allowed to produce the output signal with some bounded delay relative to the input signal, and (2) do not introduce unbounded variability in the output signal. A key ingredient of our monitoring framework is a novel efficient algorithm for sliding-window aggregation over dense-time signals.

Keywords: Online monitoring · Signal temporal logic (STL) ·
Quantitative semantics · Cyber-physical systems (CPS) · Transducers

1 Introduction

Metric temporal logic (MTL) [38] and signal temporal logic (STL) [41] are extensions of linear temporal logic (LTL) that have been widely used for specifying properties over the execution traces of cyber-physical systems (CPS). These traces are commonly represented as dense-time or continuous-time signals. Both MTL and STL have been extensively used as specification formalisms in the context of *monitoring*, where a system trace of finite duration is examined to determine whether it satisfies the desired temporal specification.

Our focus here is on *online* monitoring, where the system trace is presented incrementally, i.e., in a streaming fashion. This contrasts to the setting of offline monitoring, where the system trace is available in its entirety at the beginning of the computation. We choose MTL as the specification formalism, and we consider its interpretation over signals whose domain is the set of rational numbers (dense time) or the real numbers (continuous time). Our goal is to provide a unifying semantic and algorithmic framework that encompasses (1) the traditional Boolean semantics and the associated monitoring with qualitative (i.e.,

© Springer Nature Switzerland AG 2021
L. Feng and D. Fisman (Eds.): RV 2021, LNCS 12974, pp. 142–163, 2021.
https://doi.org/10.1007/978-3-030-88494-9_8

Boolean) verdicts, and (2) the real-valued quantitative semantics for MTL (also called *robustness* semantics) and the corresponding quantitative online monitors.

There is a wealth of proposals for quantitative semantics for MTL, such as [3,23,27]. We consider here the *spatial* robustness semantics of Fainekos and Pappas [26,27]. This uses the set of the extended real numbers, denoted by $\mathbb{R}^{\pm\infty} = \mathbb{R} \cup \{-\infty, \infty\}$, as the domain of truth values. A positive number indicates truth, a negative number indicates falsity, and zero is ambiguous. Disjunction (resp., existential quantification) is interpreted as max (resp., supremum), and conjunction (resp., universal quantification) is interpreted as min (resp., infimum). Two quantitative semantic notions are considered in [27]. The first one is the *robustness degree* $\mathsf{degree}(\varphi, \mathbf{x})$ of a signal $\mathbf{x}$ w.r.t. a formula φ, which is defined in a global way using distances between signals. This is the primary semantics, as it captures the intuitive idea of the degree of satisfaction using distances. The second notion is the *robustness estimate* $\rho(\varphi, \mathbf{x})$ of a formula φ w.r.t. a trace $\mathbf{x}$, which is defined by induction on the structure of φ. As the name suggests, the robustness estimate approximates the robustness degree; it is, in fact, an under-approximation (see Theorem 13 in page 4268 of [27]). The robustness estimate of [27] has been used in prior work on online monitoring [19,20], as it is amenable to efficient evaluation. For this reason, we will be using here the robustness estimate, not the robustness degree.

The robustness semantics of [27] can be generalized to other notions of quantitative truth values, as has already been done in [18] using an algebraic semantics based on bounded distributive lattices (where "join"/sup/$\sqcup$ generalizes max and "meet"/inf/$\sqcap$ generalizes min). The algebraic framework of [18] was developed for discrete-time signals only, since the considered class of lattices supports only finitary suprema and infima. For this reason, it is not appropriate for interpreting temporal formulas over dense-time or continuous-time signals. The semantics of [18] has been generalized further in [45] by considering semirings as truth domains, again in the context of discrete-time signals.

In this paper, we consider the class of *complete lattices*, infinitary algebraic structures of the form $(V, \bigsqcup, \bigsqcap)$, where $\bigsqcup$ is an arbitrary join/supremum operation (which models disjunction, existential quantification) and $\bigsqcap$ is an arbitrary meet/infimum operation (which models conjunction, universal quantification). The class of complete lattices contains $\mathbb{B} = \{\bot, \top\}$ (the Boolean values), and the lattice $(\mathbb{R}^{\pm\infty}, \sup, \inf)$ of extended real numbers. The lattice of intervals with join given by $\bigsqcup_i [a_i, b_i] = [\sup_i a_i, \sup_i b_i]$ and meet given by $\bigsqcap_i [a_i, b_i] = [\inf_i a_i, \inf_i b_i]$ is an especially interesting example, as it can be used to model *uncertainty* in the truth value: an element $[a, b]$ indicates that the truth value lies somewhere within this interval.

Using the algebraic quantitative semantics described in the previous paragraph, we introduce a compositional framework for online monitoring over dense-time and continuous-time signals. In order to ensure compositionality, we consider monitors that are infinite-state deterministic signal transducers. A key difference from other approaches is that our monitors do not require the input and output to be perfectly synchronized, but they can compute with some delay (or negative delay). That is, it is possible that the output signal falls behind the input signal (positive delay), or that the output signal is ahead of the input signal (negative delay). We distinguish those monitors where the delay is bounded and fixed throughput the computation. More specifically, we introduce a typing judgment $f : \mathsf{delay} = d$, where $d \in \mathbb{R}$, which says that the monitor f has a fixed bounded delay d during the entire course of the computation. This concept has been explored in [47] for discrete-time signal transducers. Another key feature of our approach is that we distinguish monitors that do not introduce unbounded variability. More specifically, we use a typing judgment $\{\mathsf{ivar} = k\}f\{\mathsf{ovar} = \ell\}$ to indicate that if the monitor f receives an input signal whose variability (number of value changes per time unit) is bounded above by k, then the variability of its output signal is bounded above by ℓ. The two properties of *bounded delay* and *bounded signal variability* are essential for constructing efficient monitors.

The monitoring of temporal formulas written in MTL (with unbounded past-time and bounded future-time connectives) can be reduced to a small number of computational primitives. An important fact is that we need two distributivity laws for lattices. Using the distributivity of finite meets over arbitrary joins (resp., finite joins over arbitrary meets) we show that the monitoring of the connective $\mathsf{S}_{[a,b]}$ (resp., the dual connective $\bar{\mathsf{S}}_{[a,b]}$) can be reduced to an online aggregation over a sliding window. For every MTL formula, we construct an online monitor by composing the following basic monitors: (1) $\mathsf{map}(op)$, which applies the function op pointwise, (2) $\mathsf{aggr}(init, op)$, which performs a running aggregation, (3) $\mathsf{emit}(v, dt)$, which emits an initial signal prefix with value v and duration dt, (4) $\mathsf{ignore}(dt)$, which removes an initial prefix of duration dt from the input signal, and (5) $\mathsf{wnd}(dt, 1_{\otimes}, \otimes)$, which performs an associative aggregation $\otimes$ over a sliding window of duration dt. Monitors are composed using two *dataflow combinators*: (1) serial composition $f \gg g$, and (2) parallel composition $\mathsf{par}(f, g)$. The space efficiency of the monitors hinges on the preservation of bounded delay and bounded variability. The time efficiency relies on a novel sliding-window aggregation algorithm with $O(1)$ amortized time-per-item. The algorithm achieves this efficiency by maintaining partial aggregates of the window and reusing them as much as possible as the window slides forward.

We provide an implementation of our monitoring framework in Rust. Our experiments show that our monitors scale reasonably well and they compare favorably against the monitoring tool Reelay [52]. We chose Reelay for comparison because (1) it supports dense-time traces as input, (2) it uses a temporal semantics for specifications that is consistent with ours, and (3) it is implemented in a low-overhead compiled language (C++).

2   Algebraic Semantics with Complete Lattices

In this section, we present a quantitative semantics for MTL that uses complete lattices for the truth values. Using algebraic reasoning, we show that the temporal connectives of MTL can be rewritten into equivalent forms that suggest a simple approach for online monitoring. In particular, we show later in Proposition 4 that some distributivity laws are needed to deal with the "Since" temporal connective and its dual. Using the distributivity of finite meets over arbitrary joins (resp., finite joins over arbitrary meets) we can reduce the monitoring of $S_{[a,b]}$ (resp., its dual $\bar{S}_{[a,b]}$) to a sliding-window join (resp., meet). This suggests the class of (co)infinitely distributive complete lattices as an appropriate algebraic generalization of the Boolean and real-valued semantic domains.

A lattice is a partial order in which every two elements have a least upper bound and a greatest lower bound. We will use an equivalent algebraic definition. A *lattice* $(V, \sqcup, \sqcap)$ is a set V together with associative and commutative binary operations $\sqcup$ and $\sqcap$, called *join* and *meet* respectively, that satisfy the *absorption laws*, i.e., $x \sqcup (x \sqcap y) = x$ and $x \sqcap (x \sqcup y) = x$ for all $x, y \in V$. Define the relation $\leq$ as follows: $x \leq y$ iff $x \sqcup y = y$ for all $x, y \in A$. The relation $\leq$ is a partial order. It also holds that $x \leq y$ iff $x \sqcap y = x$. A lattice V is said to be *bounded* if there exists a *bottom* element $\bot \in V$ and a *top* element $\top \in V$ such that $\bot \sqcup x = x$ and $x \sqcap \top = x$ (equivalently, $\bot \leq x \leq \top$) for every $x \in V$. Let V be a bounded lattice. It is easy to check that $x \sqcup \top = \top$ and $x \sqcap \bot = \bot$ for every $x \in V$. A lattice V is said to be *distributive* if $x \sqcap (y \sqcup z) = (x \sqcap y) \sqcup (x \sqcap z)$ and $x \sqcup (y \sqcap z) = (x \sqcup y) \sqcap (x \sqcup z)$ for all $x, y, z \in V$.

Example 1. Consider the two-element set $\mathbb{B} = \{\top, \bot\}$ of Boolean values, where $\top$ represents truth and $\bot$ represents falsity. The set $\mathbb{B}$, together with disjunction as join and conjunction as meet, is a bounded and distributive lattice. The set $\mathbb{T} = \{\bot, ?, \top\}$ can be endowed with bounded lattice structure in a unique way so that $\bot \leq ? \leq \top$. It can be easily verified that $\mathbb{T}$ is distributive. The structure $\mathbb{T}$ is used to give a *three-valued* interpretation of formulas (? is inconclusive).

The set $\mathbb{R}$ of real numbers, together with min as meet and max as join, is a distributive lattice. However, $(\mathbb{R}, \max, \min)$ is not a bounded lattice. It is commonplace to adjoin the elements ∞ and $-\infty$ to $\mathbb{R}$ so that they serve as the top and bottom element respectively. The structure $(\mathbb{R}^{\pm\infty}, \max, \min, -\infty, \infty)$ is a bounded distributive lattice. We interpret the max-min lattice $\mathbb{R}^{\pm\infty}$ as degrees of truth, where positive means true and negative means false.

A *complete lattice* is a partially ordered set V in which all subsets have both a supremum (join) and an infimum (meet). For a subset $S \subseteq V$, the join is denoted by $\bigsqcup S$ and the meet is denoted by $\bigsqcap S$. Notice that $\bigsqcup \emptyset$ is the bottom element of V and $\bigsqcap \emptyset$ is the top element of V. We say that V is *infinitely distributive* if $x \sqcap (\bigsqcup_{i \in I} y_i) = \bigsqcup_{i \in I}(x \sqcap y_i)$ for every index set I (finite meets distribute over arbitrary joins). We say that V is *co-infinitely distributive* if $x \sqcup (\bigsqcap_{i \in I} y_i) = \bigsqcap_{i \in I}(x \sqcup y_i)$ for every index set I (finite joins distribute over arbitrary meets). We will say that V is *(co)infinitely distributive* if it is both infinitely and co-infinitely distributive. The lattices $\mathbb{B}$ and $\mathbb{R}^{\pm\infty}$ are complete and (co)infinitely distributive.

Example 2 (Uncertainty). We will consider now an example of quantitative semantics that goes beyond linear orders, and therefore it cannot be directly handled by prior monitoring frameworks based on truth values from $\mathbb{B}$ or $\mathbb{R}^{\pm\infty}$.

Suppose we want to identify a notion of quantitative truth values in situations where we interpret formulas over a signal $\mathbf{x}(t)$ that is not known with perfect

$$\rho(\varphi \vee \psi, \mathbf{x}, t) = \rho(\varphi, \mathbf{x}, t) \sqcup \rho(\psi, \mathbf{x}, t) \qquad \rho(\varphi \wedge \psi, \mathbf{x}, t) = \rho(\varphi, \mathbf{x}, t) \sqcap \rho(\psi, \mathbf{x}, t)$$

$$\rho(\mathsf{P}_I \varphi, \mathbf{x}, t) = \bigsqcup_{u \in t-I,\, u \in \mathrm{dom}(\mathbf{x})} \rho(\varphi, \mathbf{x}, u) \qquad \rho(\mathsf{H}_I \varphi, \mathbf{x}, t) = \bigsqcap_{u \in t-I,\, u \in \mathrm{dom}(\mathbf{x})} \rho(\varphi, \mathbf{x}, u)$$

$$\rho(\mathsf{F}_I \varphi, \mathbf{x}, t) = \bigsqcup_{u \in t+I,\, s \in \mathrm{dom}(\mathbf{x})} \rho(\varphi, \mathbf{x}, u) \qquad \rho(\mathsf{G}_I \varphi, \mathbf{x}, t) = \bigsqcap_{u \in t+I,\, u \in \mathrm{dom}(\mathbf{x})} \rho(\varphi, \mathbf{x}, u)$$

$$\rho(\varphi \, \mathsf{S}_I \, \psi, \mathbf{x}, t) = \bigsqcup_{u \in t-I,\, u \in \mathrm{dom}(\mathbf{x})} \left(\rho(\psi, \mathbf{x}, u) \sqcap \bigsqcap_{v \in (u,t]} \rho(\varphi, \mathbf{x}, v) \right)$$

$$\rho(\varphi \, \bar{\mathsf{S}}_I \, \psi, \mathbf{x}, t) = \bigsqcap_{u \in t-I,\, u \in \mathrm{dom}(\mathbf{x})} \left(\rho(\psi, \mathbf{x}, u) \sqcup \bigsqcup_{v \in (u,t]} \rho(\varphi, \mathbf{x}, v) \right)$$

$$\rho(\varphi \, \mathsf{U}_I \, \psi, \mathbf{x}, t) = \bigsqcup_{u \in t+I,\, u \in \mathrm{dom}(\mathbf{x})} \left(\bigsqcap_{v \in [t,u)} \rho(\varphi, \mathbf{x}, v) \sqcap \rho(\psi, \mathbf{x}, u) \right)$$

$$\rho(\varphi \, \bar{\mathsf{U}}_I \, \psi, \mathbf{x}, t) = \bigsqcap_{u \in t+I,\, u \in \mathrm{dom}(\mathbf{x})} \left(\bigsqcup_{v \in [t,u)} \rho(\varphi, \mathbf{x}, v) \sqcup \rho(\psi, \mathbf{x}, u) \right)$$

Fig. 1. Quantitative semantics for MTL based on complete lattices.

accuracy, but we can put an upper and lower bound on each sample, i.e., $a \leq \mathbf{x}(t) \leq b$. For example, suppose that we know that $99.9 \leq \mathbf{x}(0) \leq 100.1$ and we want to evaluate the atomic predicate $p = \text{``}x \geq 99\text{''}$ at time 0. The truth value can be taken to be the interval $[0.9, 1.1]$ in this case, since there is uncertainty in the distance of signal value from the threshold.

In order to model this kind of uncertainty, we consider the set $\mathcal{I}(\mathbb{R}^{\pm\infty})$ of intervals of the form $[a, b]$ with $a \leq b$ and $a, b \in \mathbb{R}^{\pm\infty}$. An interval $[a, b] \subseteq \mathbb{R}^{\pm\infty}$ can be thought of as an uncertain truth value (it can be any one of those contained in $[a, b]$). For an arbitrary family of intervals $[a_i, b_i]$ we define $\bigsqcup_i [a_i, b_i] = [\sup_i a_i, \sup_i b_i]$ and $\bigsqcap_i [a_i, b_i] = [\inf_i a_i, \inf_i b_i]$. The structure $(\mathcal{I}(\mathbb{R}^{\pm\infty}), \bigsqcup, \bigsqcap)$ is a (co)infinitely distributive complete lattice.

The lattice $\mathcal{I}(\mathbb{R}^{\pm\infty})$ is a partial order and therefore does not fit in existing monitoring frameworks that consider only linear orders (e.g., the max-min lattice $\mathbb{R}^{\pm\infty}$ of the extended reals and the associated sliding-max/min algorithms).

Let T be the **time domain**. This can be chosen to be either $\mathbb{Q}_{\geq 0}$, the set of nonnegative rational numbers, or $\mathbb{R}_{\geq 0}$, the set of nonnegative real numbers.

An A-valued *infinite signal* is a function $\mathbf{x} : T \to A$. We write $\mathsf{ISig}(A)$ to denote the set of all A-valued infinite signals. An A-valued *finite signal* is a function $\mathbf{x} : [0, t) \to A$ or $\mathbf{x} : [0, t] \to A$, where $t \in T$. We denote the set of all A-valued finite signals by $\mathsf{FSig}(A)$. We write $\mathsf{Sig}(A) = \mathsf{FSig}(A) \cup \mathsf{ISig}(A)$. The *duration* of a finite signal $\mathbf{x} : [0, t) \to A$ or $\mathbf{x} : [0, t] \to A$ is $|\mathbf{x}| = t$. The *duration* of an infinite signal $\mathbf{x} : T \to A$ is $|\mathbf{x}| = \infty$. The empty signal is $\varepsilon : \emptyset \to A$.

We will consider formulas of Metric Temporal Logic (MTL) interpreted over signals with domain T. We consider a set D of signal values, a complete lattice V whose elements represent quantitative truth values, and *unary quantitative predicates* $p : D \to V$. We write $\mathbb{1}, \mathbb{0} : D \to V$ for the predicates given by $\mathbb{1}(d) = \top$ and $\mathbb{0}(d) = \bot$ for every $d \in D$. The set $\mathsf{MTL}(D, V)$ of **temporal formulas** is built from the atomic predicates $p : D \to V$ using the Boolean connectives $\vee$ and $\wedge$, the unary temporal connectives $\mathsf{P}_I, \mathsf{H}_I, \mathsf{F}_I, \mathsf{G}_I$, and the binary temporal connectives $\mathsf{S}_I, \bar{\mathsf{S}}_I, \mathsf{U}_I, \bar{\mathsf{U}}_I$, where I is an interval of the form $[s, t]$ or $[t, \infty)$ with $s, t \in T$. For every temporal connective $X \in \{\mathsf{P}, \mathsf{H}, \mathsf{S}, \bar{\mathsf{S}}, \mathsf{F}, \mathsf{G}, \mathsf{U}, \bar{\mathsf{U}}\}$, we write X_t as an abbreviation for $X_{[t,t]}$ and X as an abbreviation for $X_{[0,\infty)}$.

$$P_{[a,\infty)}\varphi \equiv P_a P_{[0,\infty)}\varphi \qquad H_{[a,\infty)}\varphi \equiv H_a H_{[0,\infty)}\varphi \qquad \varphi\, S_{[a,\infty)}\,\psi \equiv P_a(\varphi\, S_{[0,\infty)}\,\psi) \wedge H_{[0,a)}\varphi$$

$$P_{[a,b]}\varphi \equiv P_a P_{[0,b-a]}\varphi \qquad H_{[a,b]}\varphi \equiv H_a H_{[0,b-a]}\varphi \qquad \varphi\, S_{[a,b]}\,\psi \equiv P_a(\varphi\, S_{[0,b-a]}\,\psi) \wedge H_{[0,a)}\varphi$$

$$F_{[a,b]}\varphi \equiv F_b P_{[0,b-a]}\varphi \qquad G_{[a,b]}\varphi \equiv G_b H_{[0,b-a]}\varphi \qquad \varphi\, U_{[a,b]}\,\psi \equiv G_{[0,a)}\varphi \wedge F_a(\varphi\, U_{[0,b-a]}\,\psi)$$

Fig. 2. Equivalences between temporal formulas.

We interpret the formulas in $\mathsf{MTL}(D,V)$ over traces from $\mathsf{Sig}(D)$ and at specific time points. For the *interpretation function* $\rho : \mathsf{MTL}(D,V) \times \mathsf{Sig}(D) \times T \to V$, the value $\rho(\varphi,\mathbf{x},t)$ is defined when $t \in \mathrm{dom}(\mathbf{x})$. The base case is $\rho(p,\mathbf{x},t) = p(\mathbf{x}(t))$ and the rest are shown in Fig. 1. We say that the formulas φ and ψ are *equivalent*, and we write $\varphi \equiv \psi$, if $\rho(\varphi,\mathbf{x},t) = \rho(\psi,\mathbf{x},t)$ for every $\mathbf{x} \in \mathsf{Sig}(D)$ and $t \in \mathrm{dom}(\mathbf{x})$. For every formula φ and every interval I, it holds that $P_I\varphi \equiv \mathbb{1}\,S_I\,\varphi$, $H_I\varphi \equiv \mathbb{0}\,\bar{S}_I\,\varphi$, $F_I\varphi \equiv \mathbb{1}\,U_I\,\varphi$, and $G_I\varphi \equiv \mathbb{0}\,\bar{U}_I\,\varphi$. So, the temporal connectives P_I, H_I, F_I, G_I can be defined as abbreviations in terms of $S_I, \bar{S}_I, U_I, \bar{U}_I$.

Lemma 3. Let D be a set of data items and V be a complete lattice. The identities of Fig. 2 hold for all formulas $\varphi, \psi \in \mathsf{MTL}(D,V)$.

The identities of Fig. 2 are shown using the axioms of complete lattices. The identities below can reduce the monitoring of $S_{[a,b]}/\bar{S}_{[a,b]}$ to $P_{[a,b]}/H_{[a,b]}$.

$$\varphi\, S_{[0,b]}\,\psi \equiv P_{[0,b]}\psi \wedge (\varphi\, S\,\psi) \tag{1}$$

$$\varphi\, S_{[a,b]}\,\psi \equiv P_{[a,b]}\psi \wedge (\varphi\, S_{[a,\infty)}\,\psi) \tag{2}$$

$$\varphi\, \bar{S}_{[0,b]}\,\psi \equiv H_{[0,b]}\psi \vee (\varphi\, \bar{S}\,\psi) \tag{3}$$

$$\varphi\, \bar{S}_{[a,b]}\,\psi \equiv H_{[a,b]}\psi \vee (\varphi\, \bar{S}_{[a,\infty)}\,\psi) \tag{4}$$

Earlier occurrences of this idea are found in [25] (for the Boolean semantics) and in [22] (for the real-valued quantitative semantics), where the authors consider the future-time form $\varphi\, U_{[a,b]}\,\psi \equiv F_{[a,b]}\psi \wedge (\varphi\, U_{[a,\infty)}\,\psi)$. Prior work on efficient monitoring [19] uses an algorithm based on it. Specifically, [19] uses a sliding-max algorithm [39], which can be applied to the lattice $\mathbb{R}^{\pm\infty}$ and other similar linear orders, but is not applicable to partial orders.

Proposition 4. Let D be a set and V be a complete lattice. Then, we have:

(1) If V is infinitely distributive, then the identities (1) and (2) hold.
(2) If V is co-infinitely distributive, then the identities (3) and (4) hold.

Proposition 4 suggests the class of (co)infinitely distributive complete lattices as an appropriate algebraic generalization of $\mathbb{R}^{\pm\infty}$ for efficient quantitative online monitoring, as the monitoring of $S_{[a,b]}$ and $\bar{S}_{[a,b]}$ can be reduced to sliding aggregations (for which we present an efficient algorithm later in Fig. 7).

3   Monitors

In this section, we define the class of transducers that we will use for online monitoring. We consider infinite-state deterministic signal transducers. The transducers that we use operate on representations of *piecewise constant* signals, which are alternating sequences of points and open (left-open and right-open) segments. Our transducers are allowed to have output that is not perfectly synchronized with the input, that is, the output can either fall behind or run ahead of the input. We distinguish those transducers that have a bounded and fixed delay and we use a typing judgment $\mathbf{f} : \mathsf{delay} = d$ to indicate that the transducer $\mathbf{f}$ has fixed delay d. We also distinguish those transducers that do not introduce unbounded variability into the output signal. More specifically, we use a typing judgment of the form $\{\mathsf{ivar} = k\}\mathbf{f}\{\mathsf{ovar} = \ell\}$ to indicate that if the monitor $\mathbf{f}$ receives input with variability at most k then it will produce output with variability at most ℓ.

Let A be a set. We define the set $\mathsf{Item}(A) = \{\mathsf{Pt}(a) \mid a \in A\} \cup \{\mathsf{Seg}(a, dt) \mid a \in A \text{ and } dt \in T\}$ of *data items*. A data item is either a *point* of the form $\mathsf{Pt}(a)$, where $a \in A$, or an *open segment* of the form $\mathsf{Seg}(a, dt)$, where $a \in A$ and $dt \in T$ is a time delta. When no confusion arises we write a instead of $\mathsf{Pt}(a)$, and a^{dt} instead of $\mathsf{Seg}(a, dt)$. We also consider $\mathsf{PCSig}(A) = \mathsf{Pt}(A) \cdot (\mathsf{Seg}(A, T) \cdot \mathsf{Pt}(A))^* \cdot (\{\varepsilon\} \cup \mathsf{Seg}(A, T)) \subseteq \mathsf{Item}(A)^*$, the set of alternating point-segment sequences of data items that start with a point. An element of $\mathsf{PCSig}(A)$ represents a finite piecewise constant signal. We will use the term *trace* to refer to elements of $\mathsf{Item}(A)^*$ in order to differentiate them from the signals that they represent. For a trace $\mathbf{x}$, we write $|\mathbf{x}| \in \mathbb{N}$ to denote its *length*, that is, the number of items that is contains. We write $\mathsf{dur}(\mathbf{x}) \in T$ to denote its *duration*, that is, the total amount of time that it spans. More formally, $\mathsf{dur}(\varepsilon) = 0$, $\mathsf{dur}(\mathbf{x}a) = \mathsf{dur}(\mathbf{x})$ and $\mathsf{dur}(\mathbf{x}a^{dt}) = \mathsf{dur}(\mathbf{x}) + dt$ for every $\mathbf{x} \in \mathsf{Item}(A)^*$, $a \in A$ and $dt \in T$.

We define the ***variability*** of a trace $\mathbf{x} \in \mathsf{Item}(A)^*$ as the maximum number of items that fall within any one time interval of unit duration. For example, the variability of the trace $a\,b^1\,c\,d^1$ is 3, and the variability of the trace $a\,b^{0.5}\,c\,d^{0.5}\,e\,f^{0.5}$ is 5. Intuitively, the variability is the maximum number of times that the value of the signal can change within any one unit interval.

Let A and B be sets. A ***monitor*** of type $\mathsf{M}(A, B)$ is a state machine $\mathbf{f} = (\mathsf{St}, \mathsf{init}, \mathsf{o}, \mathsf{next}, \mathsf{out})$, where St is a set of *states*, $\mathsf{init} \in \mathsf{St}$ is the *initial state*, $\mathsf{o} \in \mathsf{Item}(B)^*$ is the *initial output*, $\mathsf{next} : \mathsf{St} \times \mathsf{Item}(A) \to \mathsf{St}$ is the *transition function*, and $\mathsf{out} : \mathsf{St} \times A \to \mathsf{Item}(B)$ is the *output function*. The monitor denotes the transduction $[\![\mathbf{f}]\!] : \mathsf{Item}(A)^* \to \mathsf{Item}(B)^*$. We require additionally that a monitor respects the representation of piecewise constant signals, that is: $[\![\mathbf{f}]\!](\mathbf{x}) \in \mathsf{PCSig}(B)$ for every $\mathbf{x} \in \mathsf{PCSig}(A)$. In other words, if the input stream is an alternating sequence of points and segments, then so is the output stream.

In Fig. 3 we give several examples of simple monitors that can be used as building blocks. The monitor $\mathtt{map}(op)$ applies the function $op : A \to B$ elementwise. The monitor $\mathtt{aggr}(b, op)$ applies a running aggregation to the input trace that is specified by the initial aggregate $b \in B$ and the aggregation function $op : B \times A \to B$ (similar to the fold combinator used in functional programming). The monitor $\mathtt{emit}(v, t)$ emits a (left-closed, right-open) segment with duration $t \in T$ and value $v \in A$ upon initialization and then echoes the input trace. The monitor $\mathtt{ignore}(t)$ discards the initial (left-closed, right-open) signal segment of duration $t \in T$ and proceeds to echo the rest of the signal. The monitor

$$\begin{array}{ccc}
\mathtt{map}(op) : \mathrm{M}(A,B) & \mathtt{aggr}(b, op) : \mathrm{M}(A,B) & \mathtt{aggrV}(b, op) : \mathrm{M}(A,B) \\
\mathsf{St} = \mathtt{Unit} & \mathsf{St} = B & \mathsf{St} = B \\
\mathsf{init} = \mathtt{u} & \mathsf{init} = b & \mathsf{init} = b \\
\mathsf{o} = \varepsilon & \mathsf{o} = \varepsilon & \mathsf{o} = \varepsilon \\
\mathsf{next}(s, a) = s & \mathsf{next}(s, a) = op(s, a) & \mathsf{next}(s, a) = op(s, a) \\
\mathsf{next}(s, a^{dt}) = s & \mathsf{next}(s, a^{dt}) = op(s, a) & \mathsf{next}(s, a^{dt}) = op(s, a) \\
\mathsf{out}(s, a) = op(a) & \mathsf{out}(s, a) = op(s, a) & \mathsf{out}(s, a) = s \\
\mathsf{out}(s, a^{dt}) = op(a)^{dt} & \mathsf{out}(s, a^{dt}) = op(s, a)^{dt} & \mathsf{out}(s, a^{dt}) = op(s, a)^{dt}
\end{array}$$

$$\begin{array}{lll}
\mathtt{emit}(v, t) : \mathrm{M}(A, A) & \mathtt{ignore}(t) : \mathrm{M}(A, A) & \\
\quad \mathsf{St} = \mathtt{Unit} & \quad \mathsf{St} = T & \mathsf{out}(s, a) = \varepsilon, \text{ if } s < t \\
\quad \mathsf{init} = \mathtt{u} & \quad \mathsf{init} = 0 & \mathsf{out}(s, a) = a, \text{ if } t \le s \\
\quad \mathsf{o} = \langle v, v^t \rangle & \quad \mathsf{o} = \varepsilon & \mathsf{out}(s, a^{dt}) = \varepsilon, \text{ if } s + dt \le t \\
\mathsf{next}(s, x) = s & \mathsf{next}(s, a) = s & \mathsf{out}(s, a^{dt}) = a^{dt - (t - s)}, \text{ if } s < t < s + dt \\
\mathsf{out}(s, x) = x & \mathsf{next}(s, a^{dt}) = s + dt & \mathsf{out}(s, a^{dt}) = a^{dt}, \text{ if } t \le s
\end{array}$$

Fig. 3. Basic building blocks for constructing temporal quantitative monitors.

$\mathtt{wnd}(\Delta, 1_\otimes, \otimes)$ (described later in Fig. 6 and Fig. 7 with pseudocode) performs an aggregation, given by the associative function $\otimes : A \times A \to A$, over a sliding window of time duration Δ. The value $1_\otimes$ is a left and right identity for $\otimes$. We combine monitors using the operations

$$\frac{\mathtt{f} : \mathrm{M}(A,B) \qquad \mathtt{g} : \mathrm{M}(B,C)}{\mathtt{f} \gg \mathtt{g} : \mathrm{M}(A,B)} \qquad \frac{\mathtt{f} : \mathrm{M}(A,B) \qquad \mathtt{g} : \mathrm{M}(A,C)}{\mathtt{par}(\mathtt{f}, \mathtt{g}) : \mathrm{M}(A, B \times C)}$$

serial composition $\gg$ and *parallel composition* $\mathtt{par}$. In the serial composition $\mathtt{f} \gg \mathtt{g}$ the output signal of $\mathtt{f}$ is propagated as input signal to $\mathtt{g}$. In the parallel composition $\mathtt{par}(\mathtt{f}, \mathtt{g})$ the input signal is copied to two concurrently executing monitors $\mathtt{f}$ and $\mathtt{g}$ and their output signals are combined. Both combinators $\gg$ and $\mathtt{par}$ are given by variants of the product construction on state machines. In the case of $\mathtt{par}$ the output traces of $\mathtt{f}$ and $\mathtt{g}$ may not be synchronized (one may be ahead of the other), which requires buffering in order to properly align them. This amount of buffering is bounded when the input signal and the monitors satisfy the conditions that ensure bounded variability of their outputs. A construction similar to the one for $\mathtt{par}$ is described in [47] (in a discrete-time setting). Some of the basic monitors of Fig. 3 are similar to queries of the StreamQL language [37], which has been proposed for the processing of streaming time series.

Monitors and Delay. Let $\mathtt{f} : \mathrm{M}(A, B)$ be a monitor. We define the *delay* of the monitor $\mathtt{f}$ at $\mathtt{x} \in \mathsf{PCSig}(A)$ to be the signed time duration $\mathsf{delay}(\mathtt{f})(\mathtt{x}) = \mathsf{dur}(\mathtt{x}) - \mathsf{dur}(\mathtt{f}(\mathtt{x}))$. We say that $\mathtt{f}$ has a fixed (positive) delay d if $\mathsf{delay}(\mathtt{f})(\mathtt{x}) = \mathsf{dur}(\mathtt{x})$ when $\mathsf{dur}(\mathtt{x}) \le d$ and $\mathsf{delay}(\mathtt{f})(\mathtt{x}) = d$ when $\mathsf{dur}(\mathtt{x}) > d$. We indicate this by writing $\mathtt{f} : \mathsf{delay} = d$. Similarly, we say that $\mathtt{f}$ has a fixed (negative) delay $-d$ if $\mathsf{delay}(\mathtt{f})(\mathtt{x}) = -d$ for every $\mathtt{x}$. We indicate this by writing $\mathtt{f} : \mathsf{delay} = -d$.

$\{\mathsf{ivar} = k\}\mathtt{map}(op)\{\mathsf{ovar} = k\}$

$\{\mathsf{ivar} = k\}\mathtt{aggr}(b, op)\{\mathsf{ovar} = k\}$

$\{\mathsf{ivar} = k\}\mathtt{emit}(v, t)\{\mathsf{ovar} = k + 1\}$

$\{\mathsf{ivar} = k\}\mathtt{ignore}(t)\{\mathsf{ovar} = k\}$

$\{\mathsf{ivar} = k\}\mathtt{wnd}(\Delta, 1_{\otimes}, \otimes)\{\mathsf{ovar} = ck\}$

$$\frac{\{\mathsf{ivar} = k\}\mathtt{f}\{\mathsf{ovar} = \ell\} \quad \{\mathsf{ivar} = \ell\}\mathtt{g}\{\mathsf{ovar} = m\}}{\{\mathsf{ivar} = k\}\mathtt{f} \gg \mathtt{g}\{\mathsf{ovar} = m\}}$$

$$\frac{\{\mathsf{ivar} = k\}\mathtt{f}\{\mathsf{ovar} = \ell\} \quad \{\mathsf{ivar} = k\}\mathtt{g}\{\mathsf{ovar} = m\}}{\{\mathsf{ivar} = k\}\mathtt{par}(\mathtt{f}, \mathtt{g})\{\mathsf{ovar} = \ell + m\}}$$

Fig. 4. Typing judgments for the preservation of finite variability.

All the monitors defined in Fig. 3 have a fixed (positive or negative) delay. Moreover, the combinators $\gg$ and $\mathtt{par}$ preserve this property.

$$\mathtt{map}(op) : \mathsf{delay} = 0 \qquad \mathtt{aggr}(b, op) : \mathsf{delay} = 0 \quad \mathtt{emit}(v, t) : \mathsf{delay} = -t$$

$$\mathtt{ignore}(t) : \mathsf{delay} = t \quad \mathtt{wnd}(\Delta, 1_{\otimes}, \otimes) : \mathsf{delay} = 0$$

$$\frac{\mathtt{f} : \mathsf{delay} = s \qquad \mathtt{g} : \mathsf{delay} = t}{\mathtt{f} \gg \mathtt{g} : \mathsf{delay} = s + t} \qquad \frac{\mathtt{f} : \mathsf{delay} = s \qquad \mathtt{g} : \mathsf{delay} = t}{\mathtt{par}(\mathtt{f}, \mathtt{g}) : \mathsf{delay} = \max(s, t)}$$

This means that any monitor built from the basic ones (monitors of Fig. 3 and Fig. 7) using serial and/or parallel composition has fixed delay.

Monitors and Input/Output Variability. We are especially interested in monitors that do not introduce unbounded variability in their output. For a monitor $\mathtt{f} : \mathsf{M}(A, B)$ we write the typing judgment $\{\mathsf{ivar} = k\}\mathtt{f}\{\mathsf{ovar} = \ell\}$ to indicate that for every input trace $\mathbf{x} \in \mathsf{PCSig}(A)$ with variability at most k, the output trace $\mathtt{f}(\mathbf{x})$ of the monitor has variability at most ℓ. In other words, this says that the monitor does not introduce unbounded variability.

Lemma 5. The typing judgments of Fig. 4 hold.

None of the monitors of Fig. 3 introduces unbounded variability. Moreover, the combinators $\gg$ and $\mathtt{par}$ preserve this property. The typing judgments of Fig. 4 imply that every monitor built from the basic ones (Fig. 3) using $\gg$ and $\mathtt{par}$ preserves the bounded variability of the input signal.

Bounded Memory Footprint. Notice that $\mathtt{map}(op)$ and $\mathtt{emit}(v, t)$ are stateless, which means that they need no memory. The monitor $\mathtt{aggr}(b, op)$ needs one memory location to store the running aggregate. The monitor $\mathtt{ignore}(t)$ needs one memory location for a clock that records the amount of time that has passed since the start of the computation. The sliding-window monitor $\mathtt{wnd}(\Delta, 1_{\otimes}, \otimes)$ needs $2 \cdot \Delta \cdot Var$ memory locations, where Var is the variability of the input trace, for the buffers *bufL*, *bufR*, *bufL_agg* used by the sliding window algorithm (see Fig. 6 and Fig. 7 later). The combinator $\gg$ does not require additional memory. The combinator $\mathtt{par}$, on the other hand, needs buffers that can store pending input from either input channel. Consider the monitoring $\mathtt{par}(\mathtt{f}_1, \mathtt{f}_2)$ with

$$\mathtt{f}_1 : \mathsf{delay} = d_1 \qquad \{\mathsf{ivar} = k\}\mathtt{f}_1\{\mathsf{ovar} = \ell_1\}$$

$$\mathtt{f}_2 : \mathsf{delay} = d_2 \qquad \{\mathsf{ivar} = k\}\mathtt{f}_2\{\mathsf{ovar} = \ell_2\}.$$

If $d_2 \geq d_1$ (the second channel is behind the first channel), then we need a buffer of size $\lceil d_2 - d_1 \rceil \cdot \ell_1$ for buffering the first channel. If $d_1 \geq d_2$ (the first channel is behind the second channel), then we need a buffer of size $\lceil d_1 - d_2 \rceil \cdot \ell_2$ for buffering the second channel.

Notice that both bounded delay and bounded variability are crucial for putting a bound of the size of buffers used by **par** and **wnd**.

4 MTL Monitoring

In this section, we will see how temporal formulas are translated into monitors using the combinators of Sect. 3. Since we focus in this paper on online monitoring, we restrict attention to the **future-bounded** fragment of MTL, where the future-time temporal connectives are bounded. That is, every U_I connective is of the form $U_{[a,b]}$ for $a \leq b < \infty$ (and similarly for F_I, G_I, $\bar{U}_I$).

For an infinite input signal $\mathbf{x}$, the output of the monitor for the time instant t should be $\rho(\varphi, \mathbf{x}, t)$, but the monitor has to compute it by observing only a finite prefix of $\mathbf{x}$. In order for the output value of the monitor to agree with the standard temporal semantics over infinite traces we may need to delay an output item until some part of the future input is seen. For example, in the case of $F_1 p$ we need to wait for one time unit: the output at time t is given after the input item at time $t + 1$ is seen. In other words, the monitor for $F_1 p$ has a *delay* (the output is falling behind the input) of one time unit. Symmetrically, we can allow monitors to emit output early when the correct value is known. For example, the output value for $P_1 p$ is $\perp$ in the beginning and the value at time t is already known from time $t - 1$. So, we also allow monitors to have negative delay (the output is running ahead of the input). The function $dl : MTL \to T$ gives the amount of delay required to monitor a formula. It is defined by $dl(p) = 0$ and

$$dl(\varphi \wedge \psi) = \max(dl(\varphi), dl(\psi)) \qquad dl(\varphi\, S_{[a,b]}\, \psi) = \max(dl(\varphi), dl(\psi)) - a$$
$$dl(\varphi\, S_{[a,\infty)}\, \psi) = \max(dl(\varphi), dl(\psi)) - a \qquad dl(\varphi\, U_{[a,b]}\, \psi) = \max(dl(\varphi), dl(\psi)) + b.$$

$TL(\varphi)$ is a signal transducer. If $dl(\varphi) = 0$, the $TL(\varphi)$ is transducer where the input and output signals are perfectly synchronized. If $dl(\varphi) > 0$, then $TL(\varphi)$ emits no output for the first $dl(\varphi)$ time units and then behaves like a synchronized transducer. If $dl(\varphi) < 0$, then $TL(\varphi)$ emits a signal prefix of duration $dl(\varphi)$ upon initialization and continues to behave like synchronized transducer.

The identities of Fig. 2 suggest that MTL monitoring can be reduced to a small set of computational primitives. The primitives of Sect. 3 are sufficient to specify the monitors, as shown in Fig. 5. We write $\pi_1 : A \times B \to A$ for the left projection and $\pi_2 : A \times B \to B$ for the right projection. Observe that the temporal connectives $X_{[0,\infty)}$ are encoded with **aggr** (running aggregation), whereas the temporal connectives $X_{(0,\infty)}$ are encoded with **aggrV** (a slight variant of running aggregation). The connectives P_a and H_a are encoded using **emit**. The connective $P_{[0,a]}$ (resp., $H_{[0,a]}$) is encoded using the sliding-window monitor **wnd** of Fig. 7, where the sliding aggregation is $\sqcup$ (resp., $\sqcap$). Similarly, the connectives

$$\mathtt{TL}(p) = \mathtt{map}(p)$$

$$\mathtt{TL}(\varphi \vee \psi) = \mathtt{par}(\mathtt{TL}(\varphi), \mathtt{TL}(\psi)) \gg \mathtt{map}(\sqcup)$$

$$\mathtt{TL}(\varphi \wedge \psi) = \mathtt{par}(\mathtt{TL}(\varphi), \mathtt{TL}(\psi)) \gg \mathtt{map}(\sqcap)$$

$$\mathtt{TL}(\mathsf{P}_{[0,\infty)}\varphi) = \mathtt{TL}(\varphi) \gg \mathtt{aggr}(\bot, \sqcup) \quad \text{and} \quad \mathtt{TL}(\mathsf{H}_{[0,\infty)}\varphi) = \mathtt{TL}(\varphi) \gg \mathtt{aggr}(\top, \sqcap)$$

$$\mathtt{TL}(\mathsf{P}_{(0,\infty)}\varphi) = \mathtt{TL}(\varphi) \gg \mathtt{aggrV}(\bot, \sqcup) \quad \text{and} \quad \mathtt{TL}(\mathsf{H}_{(0,\infty)}\varphi) = \mathtt{TL}(\varphi) \gg \mathtt{aggrV}(\top, \sqcap)$$

$$\mathtt{TL}(\mathsf{P}_a\varphi) = \mathtt{TL}(\varphi) \gg \mathtt{emit}(\bot, a) \quad \text{and} \quad \mathtt{TL}(\mathsf{H}_a\varphi) = \mathtt{TL}(\varphi) \gg \mathtt{emit}(\top, a)$$

$$\mathtt{TL}(\mathsf{P}_{[a,\infty)}\varphi) = \mathtt{TL}(\mathsf{P}_a\mathsf{P}_{[0,\infty)}\varphi) \quad \text{and} \quad \mathtt{TL}(\mathsf{H}_{[a,\infty)}\varphi) = \mathtt{TL}(\mathsf{H}_a\mathsf{H}_{[0,\infty)}\varphi)$$

$$\mathtt{TL}(\mathsf{P}_{[0,b]}\varphi) = \mathtt{wnd}(b, \bot, \sqcup) \quad \text{and} \quad \mathtt{TL}(\mathsf{H}_{[0,b]}\varphi) = \mathtt{wnd}(b, \top, \sqcap)$$

$$\mathtt{TL}(\mathsf{P}_{[a,b]}\varphi) = \mathtt{TL}(\mathsf{P}_a\mathsf{P}_{[0,b-a]}\varphi) \quad \text{and} \quad \mathtt{TL}(\mathsf{H}_{[a,b]}\varphi) = \mathtt{TL}(\mathsf{H}_a\mathsf{H}_{[0,b-a]}\varphi)$$

$$\mathtt{TL}(\varphi \mathbin{\mathsf{S}} \psi) = \mathtt{par}(\mathtt{TL}(\varphi), \mathtt{TL}(\psi)) \gg \mathtt{aggr}(\bot, opS)$$

$$opS : V \times (V \times V) \to V, \text{ where } opS(s, \langle x, y \rangle) = (s \sqcap x) \sqcup y$$

$$\mathtt{TL}(\varphi \mathbin{\mathsf{S}_{[a,\infty)}} \psi) = \mathtt{TL}(\mathsf{P}_a(\varphi \mathbin{\mathsf{S}} \psi) \wedge \mathsf{H}_{[0,a)}\varphi)$$

$$\mathtt{TL}(\varphi \mathbin{\mathsf{S}_{[0,b]}} \psi) = \mathtt{TL}(\mathsf{P}_{[0,b]}\psi \wedge (\varphi \mathbin{\mathsf{S}} \psi))$$

$$\mathtt{TL}(\varphi \mathbin{\mathsf{S}_{[a,b]}} \psi) = \mathtt{TL}(\mathsf{P}_a(\varphi \mathbin{\mathsf{S}_{[0,b-a]}} \psi) \wedge \mathsf{H}_{[0,a)}\varphi)$$

$$\mathtt{TL}(\mathsf{F}_a\varphi) = \mathtt{TL}(\varphi) \gg \mathtt{ignore}(a) \quad \text{and} \quad \mathtt{TL}(\mathsf{G}_a\varphi) = \mathtt{TL}(\varphi) \gg \mathtt{ignore}(a)$$

$$\mathtt{TL}(\mathsf{F}_{[a,b]}\varphi) = \mathtt{TL}(\mathsf{F}_b\mathsf{P}_{[0,b-a]}\varphi) \quad \text{and} \quad \mathtt{TL}(\mathsf{G}_{[a,b]}\varphi) = \mathtt{TL}(\mathsf{G}_b\mathsf{H}_{[0,b-a]}\varphi)$$

$$\mathtt{TL}(\varphi \mathbin{\mathsf{U}_{[0,b]}} \psi) = \mathtt{par}(\mathtt{TL}(\varphi), \mathtt{TL}(\psi)) \gg \mathtt{wnd}(b, 1_{\otimes_\mathsf{U}}, \otimes_\mathsf{U}) \gg \mathtt{map}(\pi_2) \gg \mathtt{ignore}(b)$$

$$\mathtt{TL}(\varphi \mathbin{\mathsf{U}_{[a,b]}} \psi) = \mathtt{TL}(\mathsf{F}_a(\varphi \mathbin{\mathsf{U}_{[0,b-a]}} \psi) \wedge \mathsf{G}_{[0,a)}\varphi)$$

Fig. 5. Online monitors for bounded-future MTL formulas.

$X_{[0,a)}$, $X_{(0,a]}$, $X_{(0,a)}$ can be encoded with a sliding aggregation that is a minor variant of the algorithm of Fig. 7 (the only difference is how the leftmost and rightmost points of the window are handled). Each connective of the form $X_{\langle a,b \rangle}$ is reduced to the connectives X_a and $X_{\langle 0,b-a \rangle}$. The "since" connectives $\mathsf{S}_{[a,\infty)}$, $\mathsf{S}_{[0,b]}$, $\mathsf{S}_{[a,b]}$ are reduced to other simpler temporal connectives. The future connectives F_a and G_a are encoded using $\mathtt{ignore}$. The connective $\mathsf{F}_{[a,b]}$ is encoded using F_b and $\mathsf{P}_{[0,b-a]}$, and similarly for $\mathsf{G}_{[a,b]}$. Finally, the "until" connective $\mathsf{U}_{[a,b]}$ is reduced to $\mathsf{U}_{[0,b-a]}$, which in turn is monitored using a sliding-window aggregation that we describe below. The connectives $\mathsf{U}_{[0,b)}$, $\mathsf{U}_{(0,b]}$, $\mathsf{U}_{(0,b)}$ are handled similarly.

Let $\mathbf{x} \in \mathsf{Sig}(D)$. If $\mathsf{dur}(\mathbf{x}) \geq t + a$ then $\rho(\varphi \mathbin{\mathsf{U}_{[0,a]}} \psi, \mathbf{x}, t) = \rho(\varphi \mathbin{\mathsf{U}} \psi, \mathbf{x}|_{[t,t+a]}, 0)$, where $\mathbf{x}|_{[t,t+a]}$ is the restriction of $\mathbf{x}$ to the interval $[t, t + a]$ (also translated so that the left endpoint is at 0). So, we can implement a monitor for the connective $\mathsf{U}_{[0,a]}$ by computing U over a window of duration exactly a time units.

Proposition 6 (Aggregation for Until). Let V be a (co)infinitely distributive complete lattice. For every piecewise constant trace $\mathbf{x} \in \mathsf{PCSig}(V \times V)$ whose underlying sequence of values is $\mathsf{val}(\mathbf{x}) = (x_0, y_0)(x_1, y_1) \dots (x_n, y_n) \in (V \times V)^+$, the value $\rho(\pi_1 \mathbin{\mathsf{U}} \pi_2, \mathbf{x}, 0)$ can be written as an aggregate of the form $\pi_2((x_0, y_0) \otimes (x_1, y_1) \otimes \cdots \otimes (x_n, y_n))$.

```
// size = size(bufL) + size(bufR)
// Invariant: if size > 0 then size(bufL) > 0.
bufL ← []        // empty left buffer (items)
bufL_agg ← []         // empty left buffer (aggregates)
bufR ← [Pt(1⊗), Seg(1⊗, Δ)]    // right buffer (items)
aggR ← 1⊗        // aggregate of right buffer
agg ← 1⊗        // initial overall aggregate
dur ← Δ        // time duration of window
Reverse()        // restore the invariant
Function Reverse():
    // Called when size(bufL) = 0 and size(bufR) > 0.
    // This function restores the window invariant.
    bufL ← bufR        // move right buffer to left
    bufR ← []        // empty right buffer
    aggR ← 1⊗        // identity value
    tmp_agg ← 1⊗        // running aggregate
    bufL_agg ← []        // empty left buffer of aggregates
    for i ← size(bufL) − 1 to 0 do // calculate partial aggregates
        tmp_agg ← bufL[i].value ⊗ tmp_agg        // new aggregate
        bufL_agg ← [tmp_agg] · bufL_agg        // prepend partial aggregate
    agg ← bufL_agg[0]        // update overall aggregate
Function AddRight(x):
    // item x is either a point or a segment
    bufR ← bufR · [x]        // add new item to the right
    aggR ← aggR ⊗ x.value        // update right aggregate
    agg ← bufL_agg[0] ⊗ aggR        // update overall aggregate
    dur ← dur + x.duration        // update window duration
    // dur does not change when adding a point: Pt(a).duration = 0
Function AddLeft(x):
    tmp_agg ← x.value ⊗ bufL_agg[0]        // new partial aggregate
    bufL ← [x] · bufL        // add new item to the left
    bufL_agg ← [tmp_agg] · bufL_agg        // prepend partial aggregate
    agg ← bufL_agg[0] ⊗ aggR        // update overall aggregate
    dur ← dur + x.duration        // update window duration
Function Remove():
    // remove oldest item from window
    old ← bufL[0]        // the oldest item
    bufL ← tail(bufL)        // remove oldest item from bufL
    bufL_agg ← tail(bufL_agg)        // remove corresponding aggregate
    if size(bufL) = 0 then
        Reverse()        // restore the invariant
    else // size(bufL) > 0
        agg ← bufL_agg[0] ⊗ aggR        // update overall aggregate
    dur ← dur − old.duration        // update window duration
```

Fig. 6. Auxiliary functions for the sliding-window aggregation algorithm of Fig. 7.

Function NextP(*a*):
    AddRight(Pt(*a*))   // add new point to the right
    Emit(Pt(*agg*))   // emit an output point
    Remove()   // remove oldest item (it should be a point)

Function NextS(*a*, *dt*):
    AddRight(Seg(*a*, *dt*))   // add new segment to the right
    over ← *dur* − Δ // calculate extra duration
    while *over* > 0 **do**
        old ← *bufL*[0]   // the oldest item
        if *old* = Pt(*a'*) **then**
            Emit(Pt(*agg*))   // emit an output point
            Remove()   // remove oldest item (it should be a point)
        else if *old* = Seg(*a'*, *dt'*) **then**
            if *dt'* ≤ *over* **then**
                Emit(Seg(*agg*, *dt'*))   // emit output segment
                Remove()   // remove old segment
            else // *dt'* > *over*
                Emit(Seg(*agg*, *over*))   // emit output segment
                // modify oldest segment to reduce its duration by *over*
                bufL[0] ← Seg(*a'*, *dt'* − *over*)   // update
                dur ← *dur* − *over*   // update duration
                AddLeft(Pt(*a'*))   // add a point back to the left
        over ← *dur* − Δ // recalculate extra duration

Fig. 7. Sliding aggregation over a continuous-time signal with wnd($\Delta, 1_\otimes, \otimes$).

Proposition 6 justifies the translation of $U_{[0,b]}$ into the monitor shown in Fig. 5. Now, we will describe the data structure that performs the sliding aggregation, which is used in wnd($\Delta, 1_\otimes, \otimes$). The implementation is shown in Fig. 6 (state, initialization of monitor, auxiliary functions) and Fig. 7 (transition when a point or a segment is received). Suppose that the current window (of duration Δ) is $bufL \cdot bufR$, where $bufL = [x_1, x_2, \ldots, x_m]$ and $bufR = [x_{m+1}, \ldots, x_{m+n}]$. That is, the window is split into two buffers: $bufL$ (left buffer) contains older elements, and $bufR$ (right buffer) contains newer elements. We maintain a buffer of partial aggregates for the older elements: $bufL\_agg = [y_1, y_2, \ldots, y_m]$, where $y_i = x_i \otimes \cdots \otimes x_m$. We also maintain the aggregate $aggR = x_{m+1} \otimes \cdots \otimes x_{m+n}$ of the right buffer. So, the overall aggregate (for the entire window) is $agg = y_1 \otimes aggR$. When a new point Pt(*a*) arrives, we add it to the right buffer, we update $aggR$ and agg, and we evict the oldest point from the window. When a new open segment Seg(*a*, *dt*) arrives, we add it to the right buffer, update $aggR$, agg and the current duration of the window, and then we evict as many old items as necessary in order to bring the window back to its desired duration Δ. Whenever the left buffer becomes empty, we convert the entire right buffer into a left buffer by performing all partial aggregations from right to left. We call this a "reversal" and it requires $O(n)$ applications of $\otimes$, where n is the size of window. If the variability of the input signal is bounded by a constant,

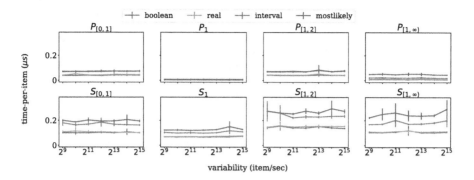

Fig. 8. Performance of our monitoring tool for various lattices of truth values.

then a reversal occurs only once every $\Theta(n)$ items. So, the algorithm needs $O(1)$ amortized time-per-item.

Theorem 7. *Let D be a set of signal values, V be a (co)infinitely distributive complete lattice, and $\varphi : \mathsf{MTL}(D, V)$ be a bounded-future formula. Assuming that the input signal has variability that is bounded by a constant, the monitor $\mathsf{TL}(\varphi) : \mathsf{M}(D, V)$ uses memory that is exponential in $|\varphi|$.*

Proof. The algorithm needs memory that is exponential in the size of φ because of the connectives of the form $X_{[a,\infty)}$ and $X_{[a,b]}$. The monitor uses buffers of size proportional to a or $b - a$ (there is a multiplicative factor corresponding to variability). Since the constants a, b are written in binary notation, we need space that is exponential in the size.

Every temporal connective is implemented in $\mathsf{TL}(\varphi)$ as a sub-algorithm that uses constant amortized time-per-item. This hinges on the algorithm of Fig. 7, which is used for $X_{[0,b]}$ where $X \in \{\mathsf{P}, \mathsf{H}, \mathsf{S}, \mathsf{U}\}$. As discussed earlier, this sliding-window algorithm needs $O(1)$ amortized time-per-item.

5   Experiments

We have implemented the monitoring framework of Sect. 4 as a library in Rust, and we have compared our implementation with the monitoring tool Reelay [52]. We chose Reelay for the comparison because it supports dense-time traces and uses a semantics for temporal formulas that is consistent with ours. Additionally, Reelay is implemented as a C++ library, which makes the comparison with our Rust library more fair because both Rust and C++ are low-overhead compiled languages. We leave as future work the comparison with other monitoring tools (such as RTAMT [48], Breach [21], and S-TaLiRo [11]).

In our Rust implementation, we represent the values from the truth domain $\mathbb{R}^{\pm\infty}$ using 64-bit floating-point numbers. In Fig. 8, we show the performance of our tool when four different truth domains are used. We consider the lattice of

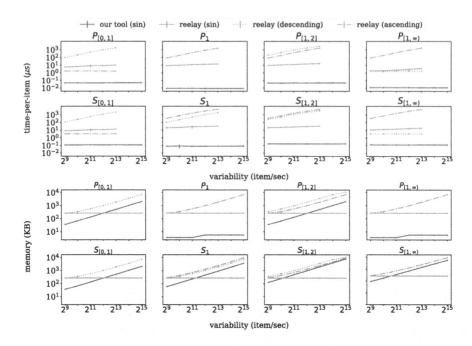

Fig. 9. Micro benchmarks w.r.t. different variability

Boolean values, the lattice $\mathbb{R}^{\pm\infty}$ of the extended real numbers, and the lattice $\mathcal{I}(\mathbb{R}^{\pm\infty})$ of intervals from Example 2. We also consider a variant of the lattice $\mathcal{I}(\mathbb{R}^{\pm\infty})$, labeled as "most-likely" in Fig. 8, which contains triples of the form $\langle a, m, b \rangle$ with $a \leq m \leq b$ with the interpretation that m is the most likely value and $[a, b]$ is the interval within which the value lies.

In Fig. 9, we show the time performance of the monitors with respect to the variability of the monitored signal (number of samples per time unit). We consider the formulas $X_{[0,1]}$, X_1, $X_{[1,2]}$, $X_{[1,\infty)}$ where $X \in \{\mathsf{P}, \mathsf{S}\}$. The time performance of our tool is independent of the specific signal being monitored, so we show the performance for only one kind of input signal (sinusoidal). The performance of Reelay, on the other hand, depends on the input signal. We therefore consider three different input signals: monotonically increasing, monotonically decreasing, and sinusoidal. It is desirable to have a monitoring algorithm which processes items at a fixed rate regardless of variability. We observe this behavior with our tool, and with Reelay in the case of sinusoidal input.

We have used the profiling tool Valgrind [51] to analyze the memory consumption of the monitors. In Fig. 9, we show the peak memory usage of the monitors as a function of the variability of the input signal. For Reelay, we report the performance for three different signals. The memory consumption of our monitor is independent of the values of the input signal (but is dependent on the sampling), so we have only reported the performance for the sinusoidal input signal. For our monitor, we see that the memory consumption for

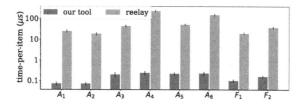

Fig. 10. Case studies from the automotive domain

$P_{[0,1]}, P_{[1,2]}, S_{[0,1]}, S_1, S_{[1,2]}, S_{[1,\infty)}$ increases linearly with variability. This is what we expect to observe because a larger signal variability leads to a larger number of elements for a window of fixed time duration, all of which need to be stored. For our monitor, the amount of memory allocated for P_1 and $P_{[1,\infty)}$ is roughly constant. This is because the corresponding monitors do not allocate buffers. In the case of Reelay, we observe an increase in memory consumption for certain input signals. We also notice that Reelay uses at least 100 KB of memory, even for signals of low variability. We believe that this can be attributed to the complex interval-map data structures that Reelay uses from the Boost libraries [28].

We also consider two benchmarks from the automotive domain suggested in [33,34]. The system traces are generated from Simulink models using simulation. One of the benchmarks involves an automatic transmission system which has two input signals (a throttle and a brake) and three output signals: the gear sequence, the engine rotation speed (in rpm, denoted ω) and the vehicle speed (denoted v). We use a sawtooth wave of frequency 0.5 Hz for the throttle and a square wave of 0.1 Hz for the brake. We run the simulation for (a simulated time of) 300 s in Simulink and export the data for monitoring with our tool. The formulas that we consider are: $A_1 = H_{[0,30]}(\omega < 4000)$, $A_2 = P_{[0,45]}(v > 70)$, $A_3 = H_{[27,57]}P_{[0,13]}(v > 65)$, $A_4 = P_{[60,100]}(v > 90) \rightarrow P_{[70,100]}(\omega > 3000)$, $A_5 = H_{[0,40]}(v < 100) \wedge H_{[0,40]}(\omega < 4000)$, $A_6 = P_{[0,40]}((v > 80) \rightarrow H_{[0,40]}(\omega > 4000))$. The second benchmark involves a fuel control system which has a throttle and outputs the fuel flow rate (denoted λ) and the air-fuel ratio (denoted φ). We use a sawtooth wave as before for the throttle. The formulas that we consider are $F_1 = H_{[0,49]}P_{[0,1]}(\lambda > 0)$, $F_2 = \neg(\neg H_{[0,1]}(\varphi < 1.0) \wedge P_{[1,3]}(\varphi > 1.0))$. The experimental results for these two benchmarks are shown in Fig. 10.

All experiments were executed on a laptop with a 2.3 GHz Intel Core i7 10610 CPU with 16 GB of memory. Each reported value for time-per-item is the mean of 20 experiment trials. The whiskers in the plots indicate the standard deviation across all trials. Each reported value for memory consumption corresponds to one measurement, since the memory measurements are consistent across trials.

6   Related Work

Metric interval temporal logic (MITL) [5] was proposed as a restriction of MTL [38] in which non-singular intervals (i.e., intervals of the form $[a, a]$) were disallowed. Maler and Nickovic [41] proposed STL as an extension of MITL with the aim of monitoring properties of continuous signals. In that paper, STL was presented as a dense future-time logic with bounded intervals along with predicates over real-valued signals. An offline monitoring algorithm was also discussed with the assumption that the interpretation of each predicate has bounded variability (i.e., changes at most a constant number of times in each interval of fixed length). In [43], the models are restricted to signals whose time domain can be covered by left-closed right-open intervals. We consider a larger class of signals by representing our time domain in the form of a sequence of alternating points and open segments.

Fainekos and Pappas [27] defined a robustness semantics which quantifies the degree to which a given signal satisfies a specification. This semantics was generalized in [18] by using bounded distributive lattices for truth domains. The present paper employs a similar semantics, where complete lattices are used to accommodate dense and continuous time. The papers [35, 45] consider two different algebraic semantics of temporal formulas using semirings, both of which only apply to the discrete-time setting. In [53], a dense-time online monitoring framework is presented with quantitative semiring-based semantics using weighted automata. In the frameworks given by [35] and [53], the semantics is based on shortest distances (i.e., standard semantics of weighted automata) as opposed to an inductive definition on formula structure like ours.

In [13, 16] some generalizations of the Boolean semantics to finite lattices are considered in the context of runtime verification. It is worth noting that the standard algorithms used for Boolean semantics can be easily adopted to a semantics using finite lattices with a small number of elements. However, this is not the case with the infinite lattices, such as $(\mathbb{R}^{\pm\infty}, \sup, \inf)$, that we consider. The problem of *parametric identification* for STL [12] (where the syntax of STL is extended with symbolic parameters) is related to the problem of monitoring when the truth values are sets of possible parameter assignments/valuations. In this setting, the truth values form a complete lattice with union as join and intersection as meet. This suggests a relationship to our algebraic framework.

Timed automata [4] are a formalism for specifying real-time properties of systems. A discussion of the past and future fragments of MITL and their connection to timed automata can be found in [43]. The notion of a temporal tester is used in [31, 42]. Temporal testers [49] are transducers which output the truth value of a temporal formula at each position. In these papers, the authors provide a compositional framework to construct testers from MITL formulas. We also consider a compositional transducer framework here, but our model of computation is more general and can support online quantitative monitoring that goes beyond temporal logic (e.g., general running and sliding-window aggregations with **aggr** and **wnd** respectively).

The line of work on SRV (Stream Runtime Verification) [32, 50] is also relevant, because SRV languages can be used to encode quantitative monitoring algorithms. The stream-based specification language RTLola [30] provides a construct for aggregation over a sliding window. In contrast to our sliding windows,

RTLola relies on the periodic partitioning and pre-aggregation along the time axis (an idea described earlier in [40]) in order to reduce the space requirements. So, the output signal can be viewed as a fixed-rate approximation of the desired sliding aggregation. This technique is therefore not suitable for implementing the temporal connectives (e.g., $P_{[0,b]}$ and $H_{[0,b]}$) of the logical formalism that we consider here. The StreamLAB tool [29], which is used for monitoring cyber-physical systems, uses RTLola as its specification language. Closely related to the aforementioned works on SRV are other formalisms and domain-specific languages for data stream processing. Quantitative regular expressions (QREs) [46] (see also [7] and [10]) have been used to express algorithms for medical monitoring [1,2]. The relationship between QREs and automata-theoretic models with registers is investigated in [6,8,9]. The synchronous languages [14,15,17] are based on Kahn's dataflow [36] and have been used for embedded controller design.

Originally, discussions involving offline monitoring, such as in [22] have only consisted of future-time connectives. This choice is made because the temporal formulas are interpreted at the beginning of the trace. In the context of online monitoring, however, different approaches have been taken towards future temporal connectives. While [20] assumes the availability of a predictor to interpret future connectives, [24] considers robustness intervals: the tightest intervals which cover the robustness of all possible extensions of the available trace prefix. The tool Reelay [52] uses only past-time temporal connectives. The tool RTAMT [48] *pastifies* a future-time formula by converting it into a past-time formula. The inductive definition of pastification is detailed in [44].

It was observed in [22] that the key ingredient for efficiently monitoring STL is an online algorithm for calculating the maximum/minimum over a sliding window. The commonly used algorithm [39] maintains a so-called monotonic wedge of values. In contrast, we use a more general algorithm, which applies to any associative aggregation (not only max/min) and does not require the domain of values to be totally ordered.

7   Conclusion

We have presented a new efficient algorithm for the online monitoring of MTL properties over dense-time and continuous-time signals. We have used an abstract algebraic semantics based on complete lattices satisfying certain infinitary distributivity laws, which can be instantiated to the widely-used Boolean (qualitative) and robustness (quantitative) semantics, as well as to other partially ordered truth values. Our monitoring framework is compositional in the sense that we construct monitors from formulas using a set of combinators on monitors. A key feature that enables compositionality and efficiency in our framework is the use of monitors that are deterministic signal transducers with associated typing judgments for ensuring that: (1) each monitor has a bounded and fixed delay, and (2) each monitor produces output of bounded variability given input of bounded variability. We have provided an implementation of our algebraic monitoring framework, and we have shown experimentally that our monitors scale reasonably well and are competitive against the tool Reelay [52].

Acknowledgments. This research was supported in part by US National Science Foundation award 2008096.

References

1. Abbas, H., Alur, R., Mamouras, K., Mangharam, R., Rodionova, A.: Real-time decision policies with predictable performance. Proc. IEEE Spec. Issue Des. Autom. Cyber-Phys. Syst. **106**(9), 1593–1615 (2018). https://doi.org/10.1109/JPROC. 2018.2853608
2. Abbas, H., Rodionova, A., Mamouras, K., Bartocci, E., Smolka, S.A., Grosu, R.: Quantitative regular expressions for arrhythmia detection. IEEE/ACM Trans. Comput. Biol. Bioinf. **16**(5), 1586–1597 (2019). https://doi.org/10.1109/TCBB. 2018.2885274
3. Akazaki, T., Hasuo, I.: Time robustness in MTL and expressivity in hybrid system falsification. In: Kroening, D., Păsăreanu, C.S. (eds.) CAV 2015. LNCS, vol. 9207, pp. 356–374. Springer, Cham (2015). https://doi.org/10.1007/978-3-319-21668-3_21
4. Alur, R., Dill, D.L.: A theory of timed automata. Theoret. Comput. Sci. **126**(2), 183–235 (1994). https://doi.org/10.1016/0304-3975(94)90010-8
5. Alur, R., Feder, T., Henzinger, T.A.: The benefits of relaxing punctuality. J. ACM **43**(1), 116–146 (1996). https://doi.org/10.1145/227595.227602
6. Alur, R., Fisman, D., Mamouras, K., Raghothaman, M., Stanford, C.: Streamable regular transductions. Theoret. Comput. Sci. **807**, 15–41 (2020). https://doi.org/10.1016/j.tcs.2019.11.018
7. Alur, R., Mamouras, K.: An introduction to the StreamQRE language. Dependable Softw. Syst. Eng. **50**, 1–24 (2017). https://doi.org/10.3233/978-1-61499-810-5-1
8. Alur, R., Mamouras, K., Stanford, C.: Automata-based stream processing. In: Leibniz International Proceedings in Informatics (LIPIcs), ICALP 2017, vol. 80, pp. 112:1–112:15. Schloss Dagstuhl-Leibniz-Zentrum fuer Informatik, Dagstuhl, Germany (2017). https://doi.org/10.4230/LIPIcs.ICALP.2017.112
9. Alur, R., Mamouras, K., Stanford, C.: Modular quantitative monitoring. Proc. ACM Progr. Lang. **3**(POPL), 50:1–50:31 (2019). https://doi.org/10.1145/3290363
10. Alur, R., Mamouras, K., Ulus, D.: Derivatives of quantitative regular expressions. In: Aceto, L., Bacci, G., Bacci, G., Ingólfsdóttir, A., Legay, A., Mardare, R. (eds.) Models, Algorithms, Logics and Tools. LNCS, vol. 10460, pp. 75–95. Springer, Cham (2017). https://doi.org/10.1007/978-3-319-63121-9_4
11. Annpureddy, Y., Liu, C., Fainekos, G., Sankaranarayanan, S.: S-TaLiRo: a tool for temporal logic falsification for hybrid systems. In: Abdulla, P.A., Leino, K.R.M. (eds.) TACAS 2011. LNCS, vol. 6605, pp. 254–257. Springer, Heidelberg (2011). https://doi.org/10.1007/978-3-642-19835-9_21
12. Bakhirkin, A., Ferrère, T., Maler, O.: Efficient parametric identification for STL. In: HSCC 2018, New York, NY, USA, pp. 177–186. ACM (2018). https://doi.org/10.1145/3178126.3178132
13. Bauer, A., Leucker, M., Schallhart, C.: Comparing LTL semantics for runtime verification. J. Log. Comput. **20**(3), 651–674 (2010). https://doi.org/10.1093/logcom/exn075

14. Benveniste, A., Le Guernic, P., Jacquemot, C.: Synchronous programming with events and relations: the SIGNAL language and its semantics. Sci. Comput. Program. **16**(2), 103–149 (1991). https://doi.org/10.1016/0167-6423(91)90001-E
15. Berry, G., Gonthier, G.: The Esterel synchronous programming language: design, semantics, implementation. Sci. Comput. Program. **19**(2), 87–152 (1992). https://doi.org/10.1016/0167-6423(92)90005-V
16. Bonakdarpour, B., Fraigniaud, P., Rajsbaum, S., Rosenblueth, D.A., Travers, C.: Decentralized asynchronous crash-resilient runtime verification. In: Desharnais, J., Jagadeesan, R. (eds.) Leibniz International Proceedings in Informatics (LIPIcs), CONCUR 2016, vol. 59, pp. 16:1–16:15. Schloss Dagstuhl-Leibniz-Zentrum fuer Informatik, Dagstuhl, Germany (2016). https://doi.org/10.4230/LIPIcs.CONCUR.2016.16
17. Caspi, P., Pilaud, D., Halbwachs, N., Plaice, J.A.: LUSTRE: a declarative language for real-time programming. In: POPL 1987, New York, NY, USA, pp. 178–188. ACM (1987). https://doi.org/10.1145/41625.41641
18. Chattopadhyay, A., Mamouras, K.: A verified online monitor for metric temporal logic with quantitative semantics. In: Deshmukh, J., Ničković, D. (eds.) RV 2020. LNCS, vol. 12399, pp. 383–403. Springer, Cham (2020). https://doi.org/10.1007/978-3-030-60508-7_21
19. Deshmukh, J.V., Donzé, A., Ghosh, S., Jin, X., Juniwal, G., Seshia, S.A.: Robust online monitoring of signal temporal logic. Formal Methods Syst. Des. **51**(1), 5–30 (2017). https://doi.org/10.1007/s10703-017-0286-7
20. Dokhanchi, A., Hoxha, B., Fainekos, G.: On-line monitoring for temporal logic robustness. In: Bonakdarpour, B., Smolka, S.A. (eds.) RV 2014. LNCS, vol. 8734, pp. 231–246. Springer, Cham (2014). https://doi.org/10.1007/978-3-319-11164-3_19
21. Donzé, A.: Breach, a toolbox for verification and parameter synthesis of hybrid systems. In: Touili, T., Cook, B., Jackson, P. (eds.) CAV 2010. LNCS, vol. 6174, pp. 167–170. Springer, Heidelberg (2010). https://doi.org/10.1007/978-3-642-14295-6_17
22. Donzé, A., Ferrère, T., Maler, O.: Efficient robust monitoring for STL. In: Sharygina, N., Veith, H. (eds.) CAV 2013. LNCS, vol. 8044, pp. 264–279. Springer, Heidelberg (2013). https://doi.org/10.1007/978-3-642-39799-8_19
23. Donzé, A., Maler, O.: Robust satisfaction of temporal logic over real-valued signals. In: Chatterjee, K., Henzinger, T.A. (eds.) FORMATS 2010. LNCS, vol. 6246, pp. 92–106. Springer, Heidelberg (2010). https://doi.org/10.1007/978-3-642-15297-9_9
24. Dreossi, T., Dang, T., Donzé, A., Kapinski, J., Jin, X., Deshmukh, J.V.: Efficient guiding strategies for testing of temporal properties of hybrid systems. In: Havelund, K., Holzmann, G., Joshi, R. (eds.) NFM 2015. LNCS, vol. 9058, pp. 127–142. Springer, Cham (2015). https://doi.org/10.1007/978-3-319-17524-9_10
25. D'Souza, D., Tabareau, N.: On timed automata with input-determined guards. In: Lakhnech, Y., Yovine, S. (eds.) FORMATS/FTRTFT -2004. LNCS, vol. 3253, pp. 68–83. Springer, Heidelberg (2004). https://doi.org/10.1007/978-3-540-30206-3_7
26. Fainekos, G.E., Pappas, G.J.: Robustness of temporal logic specifications. In: Havelund, K., Núñez, M., Roşu, G., Wolff, B. (eds.) FATES/RV -2006. LNCS, vol. 4262, pp. 178–192. Springer, Heidelberg (2006). https://doi.org/10.1007/11940197_12
27. Fainekos, G.E., Pappas, G.J.: Robustness of temporal logic specifications for continuous-time signals. Theoret. Comput. Sci. **410**(42), 4262–4291 (2009). https://doi.org/10.1016/j.tcs.2009.06.021

28. Faulhaber, J.: Boost library documentation: interval container library (2021). https://www.boost.org/doc/libs/1_76_0/libs/icl/doc/html/index.html. Accessed 20 Aug 2021

29. Faymonville, P., et al.: StreamLAB: stream-based monitoring of cyber-physical systems. In: Dillig, I., Tasiran, S. (eds.) CAV 2019. LNCS, vol. 11561, pp. 421–431. Springer, Cham (2019). https://doi.org/10.1007/978-3-030-25540-4_24

30. Faymonville, P., Finkbeiner, B., Schwenger, M., Torfah, H.: Real-time stream-based monitoring. CoRR abs/1711.03829 (2017). http://arxiv.org/abs/1711.03829

31. Ferrère, T., Maler, O., Ničković, D., Pnueli, A.: From real-time logic to timed automata. J. ACM **66**(3), 19:1–19:31 (2019). https://doi.org/10.1145/3286976

32. Gorostiaga, F., Sánchez, C.: Striver: stream runtime verification for real-time event-streams. In: Colombo, C., Leucker, M. (eds.) RV 2018. LNCS, vol. 11237, pp. 282–298. Springer, Cham (2018). https://doi.org/10.1007/978-3-030-03769-7_16

33. Hoxha, B., Abbas, H., Fainekos, G.E.: Benchmarks for temporal logic requirements for automotive systems. In: Frehse, G., Althoff, M. (eds.) ARCH@CPSWeek 2014, 2015. EPiC Series in Computing, vol. 34, pp. 25–30. EasyChair (2014). https://doi.org/10.29007/xwrs

34. Hoxha, B., Bach, H., Abbas, H., Dokhanchi, A., Kobayashi, Y., Fainekos, G.: Towards formal specification visualization for testing and monitoring of cyber-physical systems. In: International Workshop on Design and Implementation of Formal Tools and Systems. DIFTS 2014 (2014)

35. Jakšić, S., Bartocci, E., Grosu, R., Ničković, D.: An algebraic framework for runtime verification. IEEE Trans. Comput. Aided Des. Integr. Circuits Syst. **37**(11), 2233–2243 (2018). https://doi.org/10.1109/TCAD.2018.2858460

36. Kahn, G.: The semantics of a simple language for parallel programming. Inf. Process. **74**, 471–475 (1974)

37. Kong, L., Mamouras, K.: StreamQL: a query language for processing streaming time series. Proc. ACM Program. Lang. **4**(OOPSLA), 183:1–183:32 (2020). https://doi.org/10.1145/3428251

38. Koymans, R.: Specifying real-time properties with metric temporal logic. Real-Time Syst. **2**(4), 255–299 (1990). https://doi.org/10.1007/BF01995674

39. Lemire, D.: Streaming maximum-minimum filter using no more than three comparisons per element. CoRR abs/cs/0610046 (2006). http://arxiv.org/abs/cs/0610046

40. Li, J., Maier, D., Tufte, K., Papadimos, V., Tucker, P.A.: No pane, no gain: efficient evaluation of sliding-window aggregates over data streams. SIGMOD Rec. **34**(1), 39–44 (2005). https://doi.org/10.1145/1058150.1058158

41. Maler, O., Nickovic, D.: Monitoring temporal properties of continuous signals. In: Lakhnech, Y., Yovine, S. (eds.) FORMATS/FTRTFT -2004. LNCS, vol. 3253, pp. 152–166. Springer, Heidelberg (2004). https://doi.org/10.1007/978-3-540-30206-3_12

42. Maler, O., Nickovic, D., Pnueli, A.: Real time temporal logic: past, present, future. In: Pettersson, P., Yi, W. (eds.) FORMATS 2005. LNCS, vol. 3829, pp. 2–16. Springer, Heidelberg (2005). https://doi.org/10.1007/11603009_2

43. Maler, O., Nickovic, D., Pnueli, A.: From MITL to timed automata. In: Asarin, E., Bouyer, P. (eds.) FORMATS 2006. LNCS, vol. 4202, pp. 274–289. Springer, Heidelberg (2006). https://doi.org/10.1007/11867340_20

44. Maler, O., Nickovic, D., Pnueli, A.: On synthesizing controllers from bounded-response properties. In: Damm, W., Hermanns, H. (eds.) CAV 2007. LNCS, vol. 4590, pp. 95–107. Springer, Heidelberg (2007). https://doi.org/10.1007/978-3-540-73368-3_12

45. Mamouras, K., Chattopadhyay, A., Wang, Z.: Algebraic quantitative semantics for efficient online temporal monitoring. In: Groote, J.F., Larsen, K.G. (eds.) TACAS 2021. LNCS, vol. 12651, pp. 330–348. Springer, Cham (2021). https://doi.org/10.1007/978-3-030-72016-2_18

46. Mamouras, K., Raghothaman, M., Alur, R., Ives, Z.G., Khanna, S.: StreamQRE: modular specification and efficient evaluation of quantitative queries over streaming data. In: PLDI 2017, New York, NY, USA, pp. 693–708. ACM (2017). https://doi.org/10.1145/3062341.3062369

47. Mamouras, K., Wang, Z.: Online signal monitoring with bounded lag. IEEE Trans. Comput. Aided Des. Integr. Circuits Syst. (2020). https://doi.org/10.1109/TCAD.2020.3013053

48. Ničković, D., Yamaguchi, T.: RTAMT: online robustness monitors from STL. In: Hung, D.V., Sokolsky, O. (eds.) ATVA 2020. LNCS, vol. 12302, pp. 564–571. Springer, Cham (2020). https://doi.org/10.1007/978-3-030-59152-6_34

49. Pnueli, A., Zaks, A.: On the merits of temporal testers. In: Grumberg, O., Veith, H. (eds.) 25 Years of Model Checking. LNCS, vol. 5000, pp. 172–195. Springer, Heidelberg (2008). https://doi.org/10.1007/978-3-540-69850-0_11

50. Sánchez, C.: Online and offline stream runtime verification of synchronous systems. In: Colombo, C., Leucker, M. (eds.) RV 2018. LNCS, vol. 11237, pp. 138–163. Springer, Cham (2018). https://doi.org/10.1007/978-3-030-03769-7_9

51. The Valgrind Developers: Valgrind: an instrumentation framework for building dynamic analysis tools (2021). https://valgrind.org/. Accessed 20 Aug 2021

52. Ulus, D.: The Reelay monitoring tool (2020). https://doganulus.github.io/reelay/. Accessed 20 Aug 2020

53. Waga, M.: Online quantitative timed pattern matching with semiring-valued weighted automata. In: André, É., Stoelinga, M. (eds.) FORMATS 2019. LNCS, vol. 11750, pp. 3–22. Springer, Cham (2019). https://doi.org/10.1007/978-3-030-29662-9_1

Nested Monitors: Monitors as Expressions to Build Monitors

Felipe Gorostiaga[1,2,3](✉) and César Sánchez[1]

[1] IMDEA Software Institute, Madrid, Spain
{felipe.gorostiaga,cesar.sanchez}@imdea.org
[2] Universidad Politécnica de Madrid (UPM), Madrid, Spain
[3] CIFASIS, Rosario, Argentina

Abstract. Stream runtime verification (SRV) is a formalism to express monitors as relations between typed input streams (observations) and typed output streams (data verdicts). In SRV, the actual data operations are separated from the temporal dependencies, therefore generalizing monitoring algorithms for temporal logics into the computation of richer verdicts. In this paper we study a new and powerful feature, which consists of lifting the execution of monitors to functions that can be used in defining expressions of enclosing specifications. At runtime, the outer monitor invokes the inner monitor passing a list of input events, called a *slice*. We present nested monitors for synchronous streams and for real-time event streams, allowing the elegant description of many specifications of interest, while still keeping the resources bounded.

We formally describe nested monitors and slices, and illustrate the practical application in many real-life examples, including electrocardiogram analysis (QRS), quantitative Metric Temporal Logic and arbitrary robustness of Signal Temporal Logic specifications.

1 Introduction

Runtime verification (RV) is a dynamic technique for software quality assurance that consists of generating a monitor from a formal specification. At runtime, the monitor inspects traces of the execution of the system under analysis, detecting violations of the specification. Motivated by the counterparts in static verification, early RV specification languages were based on temporal logics [3,14,28], regular expressions [35], timed regular expressions [1], rules [2], or rewriting [33]. Stream runtime verification (SRV), pioneered by Lola [10], defines monitors declaratively by equations that define the dependencies between output streams of results and input streams of observations, where the types of the streams and operations can be rich types of data. Unlike logical techniques, that compute Boolean verdicts, SRV allows rich observations and verdicts.

This work was funded in part by the Madrid Regional Government under project "S2018/TCS-4339 (BLOQUES-CM)", by Spanish National Project "BOSCO (PGC2018-102210-B-100)".

© Springer Nature Switzerland AG 2021
L. Feng and D. Fisman (Eds.): RV 2021, LNCS 12974, pp. 164–183, 2021.
https://doi.org/10.1007/978-3-030-88494-9_9

Examples include counting events, specifying and computing robustness values, generating models, quantitative verdicts and calculating target spatial coordinates. See [10,11,17,23] for examples illustrating the expressivity of SRV languages. The keystone of SRV is to separate two concerns: the temporal dependencies and the data manipulated. The temporal dependencies are inspired by the algorithms to monitor temporal logics which essentially capture the order of operations in monitoring algorithms. The data manipulation describes how to perform each individual operation and each element of storage that the monitor handles.

Different temporal algorithms exist for different notions of time. Early SRV works consider streams to be synchronized sequences of data (like in LTL semantics), so data observed in different streams at the same index in their sequences are considered to have occurred at the same time. Examples of synchronous SRV formalisms include the original Lola [10] and systems like Copilot [31]. Other formalisms that can be easily described using SRV include Mission-time LTL [32] and Functional Reactive Programming (FRP) [16]. Synchronous languages, like Lustre [27], Esterel [5] and Signal [21] also define relations between input and output values but these are designed to express behaviors so they assume causality and forbid future references, while in SRV future references are allowed to describe monitors that depend on future observations.

There have been approaches to extend SRV to real-time event streams, including RTLola [19], TeSSLa [9] and Striver [23], which consider streams to be sequences of timed events. Events contain data and are time-stamped with the instant of time at which the data is produced (either observed or generated). The time stamps of a stream must be monotonically increasing, but the events at a given index in two different streams can have arbitrary time stamps. These formalisms are known as asynchronous or real-time SRV. See [22] for a expressiveness comparison between synchronous time and asynchronous SRV. The data stored and computed is modeled as data types (data theories in the jargon of SRV) whose implementation is independent of the model of time. Most system include a handful of wired data types (e.g. [9,10,18]) but others study how to transparently incorporate data-types from programming languages [6].

The first contribution of this paper is *nested specifications*: using specifications to create a new data type which can be used in enclosing specifications. In this manner one can write new functions on sequences of data as an SRV specification which is invoked dynamically. The idea to decompose monitors into sub-monitors is not new. For example, in [12] the authors automatically derive cooperating monitors from a given definition, but this technique does not add expressivity to the data type language. The main concern in [12] is decentralized and distributed execution, which has also been studied in the context of RV [4,15,20] and SRV [11]. In this paper we consider expressivity and not decentralized execution. Nested specifications are particularly useful (1) when the caller monitor can invoke nested monitors with sub-traces of the original trace, which we model using *slices*; and (2) when the slice can be processed incrementally by the nested monitor to anticipate the computation of its verdict. Nested specifications can be used both in synchronous and asynchronous SRV languages. Slices in languages like Lustre or Python allow dealing with collections of values in a convenient way, but these collections cannot refer to values of streams at different moments in time. Our slices are more similar to the notion of trace slicing in RV [8], in which slices correspond to sub-traces of a trace. We allow the definition and the early manipulation of slices that are partially known because some of their elements will only be known in the future. We show an implementation of these extensions for the formalisms Lola and Striver as reference languages of synchronous and asynchronous SRV respectively, (but the core ideas can be applied to other SRV formalisms easily). In synchronous SRV, the definition of a stream s can refer to future element of s or of other streams, with a syntactic restriction to ensure that every self-referential stream exclusively depends on previous or on future values. If all the self-referential streams in a specification depend exclusively on previous values, the specification is called *efficiently monitorable*. Specifications that only use present and past offsets, in which every stream is resolved immediately, are known as *very efficiently monitorable*. Note that efficiently monitorable specifications still allow future references as long as all self-referential streams end-up referring to past values. In efficiently monitorable specifications for every stream there is a constant upper-bound on time after which the stream will be resolved (the *latency* of the stream), a property known as *bounded lag* (as a particular case, very-efficiently monitorable specifications are 0 bounded lagged). Efficiently monitorable specifications are *trace-length independent* and can be monitored with bounded resources that can be calculated statically [10,34]. In all previous SRV efforts, if cyclic future offsets are allowed, specifications are assumed to not have bounded lag, and are only given semantics for finite traces. A second contribution of this paper is a notion of *dynamic bounded lag* in which streams can refer to other streams in the future with an offset that is not bounded a-priori but that is determined dynamically, which guarantees that the amount of resources necessary to monitor a specification is *slice-sizes* dependent. If an upper bound for the sizes of the slices can be calculated beforehand, then the specification is again trace-length independent. Since dynamic bounded specifications have semantics for future unbounded time domains, these specifications cannot be expressed in previous SRV formalisms. A third contribution of this paper is two implementations of nested monitors in HLola [24] and in HStriver [25]. We illustrate how these novel features enable specifications using several examples including QRS complex detection, quantitative semantics of the Metric Temporal Logic (MTL) and robustness of Signal Temporal Logic (STL) specifications.

The rest of the paper is structured as follows. Section 2 briefly revisits two SRV languages, Lola (for synchronous time) and Striver (for real-time asynchronous event streams). In Sect. 3 we present nested monitors and slices and in Sect. 4 we illustrate these features in action in several examples. Section 5 presents an empirical evaluation. Finally, Sect. 6 concludes.

2   Preliminaries

We briefly revisit SRV for synchronous and for real-time event streams.

Time and Streams. A *synchronous stream* is a sequence of length L of values from a data domain, where L may be a finite number or ω for infinite sequences. We refer to the value at the n-th position in a sequence z as $z(n)$. For example, the sequence $co2 = [350, 360, 289, 320, 330]$ contains samples of the level of CO2 in the air (measured in parts-per-million). In this sequence $co2(0) = 350$ and $co2(2) = 289$. A *real-time stream* is a succession of events (t, d) where d is a value from a value domain (as in synchronous streams) and t is a time-stamp. Time-stamps are elements of a *temporal domain* (for example $\mathbb{R}$, $\mathbb{Q}$ or $\mathbb{Z}$), a set whose elements are totally ordered. The interpretation of the time domain is to serve as a common clock to all the streams manipulated by a monitor (inputs and outputs). Time-stamps in every legal event stream are monotonically increasing. Given an element t in the temporal domain of an event stream r, we use $r(t)$ to refer to the value with time-stamp t in r. For example, the event-stream $tv\_status = \{(1.5, \textit{off}), (4.0, \textit{on}), (6.0, \textit{off}), (7.5, \textit{on}), (8.0, \textit{off})\}$ indicates when a television is turned *on* or *off*. The event $(4.0, \textit{on})$ in tv_status indicates that the TV is switched *on* at time 4.0. In this paper we use *stream* both for synchronous and event streams when it is clear from the context.

Data Theories. Streams are typed using multi-sorted first-order theories (which we call data theories). A type has a collection of symbols used to construct expressions, together with an interpretation of these symbols. The domain of a type is the set of values. Theories are interpreted in the sense that every function symbol f is both a constructor—used to build expressions (in the term algebra used to build expressions)—and an evaluator (that produces actual elements in the domain, which is the semantic interpretation of the function). We assume that every type D has a constructor if $\cdot$ then $\cdot$ else $\cdot$ that given a Boolean expression and two expressions of type D constructs a term of type D.

   Lola is a synchronous SRV language, whose specifications declare the relation between output sequences (verdicts) and input sequences (observations). Similarly, Striver is a real-time SRV language, whose specifications describe the relation between output event-streams and input event-streams. We describe these formalisms separately. Due to space constraints we only introduce these languages concisely. See [10,23,26] for rigorous formal descriptions of Lola and Striver.

Lola: SRV for Synchronous Streams. Given a set of (typed) stream variables, Lola *stream expressions* consists of:

(1) *offsets* $v[k, d]$ where v is a stream variable of type D, k is an integer number and d a value from D, and
(2) *function applications* $f(t_1, \ldots, t_n)$ using constructors f applied to previously defined stream expression $t_1, \ldots, t_n$ of the right types.

Note that constants are 0-ary functions symbols. A stream variable v represents a sequence of the domain of the type of v. The intended meaning of an offset expression $v[-1, d]$ is to capture the value of sequence v in the previous position (or value d if there is no such previous position, that is, at the beginning). The particular case for an offset with $k = 0$ requires no default value as the index is always guaranteed to be within the range of the sequence, in which case we use $v[now]$. A Lola specification consists of a set I of input stream variables, a set O of output stream variables, and a set of defining equations, $y_i = e_i$, one per output variable $y_i \in O$ where e_i is a stream expression of the same type as y_i that can use stream variables from I and O. The defining equations describe the relation between input and output streams. The *dependency graph* of a specification captures the dependency between streams and is built as follows: (i) there is a vertex for every variable in $I \cup O$, and (ii) there is an edge from u to v of weight k if the expression $v[k, d]$ appears in the definition of u. Cycles of negative weight represent self-references to previous values, and cycles of positive weight represent self-references to future values. Legal specifications do not contain cycles of zero weight.

Example 1. The specification "*the mean level of CO2 in the air in the last 3 instants*" can be expressed as follows where denom calculates the number of instants that are taken into account:

```
input Double co2
output Double denom = (min 2 denom[-1|0]) + 1
output Double mean  = (co2[-2|0] + co2[-1|0] + co2[now]) / denom[now]
```

In this specification $I = \{co2\}$ and $O = \{denom, mean\}$.   □

The semantics of Lola is defined in terms of valuations which consist of one sequence ρ_x for each stream variable x, all of the same length L (where L can be finite or ω). Note that $\rho_x(n)$ is the value at position n of sequence ρ_x. A valuation induces a unique evaluation of all expressions $[\![e_x]\!]$ as follows:

- For offsets:
$$[\![v[i, c]]\!](j) = \begin{cases} [\![v]\!](j+i) & \text{if } 0 \leq j+i < L \\ c & \text{otherwise} \end{cases}$$

- For functions: $[\![f(e_1, \ldots, e_k)]\!](j) = f([\![e_1]\!](j), \ldots, [\![e_k]\!](j))$

Note that f on the left hand side of the semantic definition of a function represents the syntactic representation of the function while the f on the right hand side represents the function evaluator.

We say that a valuation ρ satisfies a Lola specification φ whenever every output variable y_x satisfies its defining equation e_x, i.e. when $y_x = [\![e_x]\!]$. See [10] for a more rigorous explanation of valuations, which cannot be included here due to space constraints. Note how these semantics capture when a candidate valuation is an evaluation model, but the intention of a Lola specification is to compute the unique output sequences given input sequences. Efficient online monitoring algorithms can be generated for a specification depending on its dependency graph. If there are only negative cycles the specification can be monitored efficiently with bounded resources, and every stream will be determined in bounded time (see [10,34]), a property called bounded lag. These specifications, called *efficiently monitorable* have semantics for finite and infinite streams. If there are positive cycles, then the specification only has semantics for finite traces and resources cannot be bound statically. In this paper we give semantics for infinite traces, for a sub-class of specifications with dynamic bounded future accesses, which we call *dynamic bounded lag*.

Striver: SRV for Real-Time Event Streams. Striver adapts Lola to real-time event streams. One step offsets are modified to fetch the next or previous event in the referred stream, and can be composed to access the next of the next event, the previous of the previous event, etc. Striver specifications define, for every output stream, (1) a *ticking* expression which captures when the stream may contain an event, as well as (2) a value expression that (just like in Lola) provides a value at the ticking instants. Concretely, there are three kinds of expressions in Striver:

- *Ticking Expressions*, which indicate the times at which a stream may produce an event. Ticking expressions can be $\{c\}$ for a specific time point c, or the ticking times of another stream s, unmodified with the operator **ticksOf** s, delayed by a constant k with **shift** k s, or delayed by the value of the stream itself with **delay** s. Ticking expression can be combined using $\cup$.
- *Offset Expressions*, which are the language construct that allows referring to the time instants when a given stream x contains an event. The basic offset expression is **t**, which represents the current instant. Given an offset expression τ and a stream x, we can build new offset expressions as follows. x«τ represents the last instant at which x ticked in the past of τ. For example, the expression x«x«**t** represents the second to last event of x with respect to the current time. The expression x<~τ is similar but also considers τ as a candidate instant. Analogously, x»τ refers to the first future instant at which x contains an event (with x>~τ the variant that considers the present).
- *Value Expressions*, like in Lola, compute values. The simplest value expressions are constants to represent values in the domain of the type. Then, $x(\tau)$ provides the value of stream x at instant τ, which must be an offset expression for x. The atomic constructor **notick** is used to refrain from generating an event at a candidate ticking instant. The atomic expression **cv** allows accessing the value of an event in the ticking expression of the stream, useful when the event is shifted. Finally, values can be combined with constructor functions f of the appropriate types to compute new values.

We use x[<**t**|d] and x[~**t**|d] as syntactic sugar to refer to the most recent event in x (mimicking $x[-1, d]$ and $x[now]$ from Lola).

A Striver specification consists of one value expression V_y and one ticking expression T_y for each output stream of the appropriate type. For example, the property "*count for how long has the tv been on*" can be expressed as follows, where stream variable **tv_on** computes the result.

```
input TV_Status tv

output Int tv_on:
  ticks = ticksOf tv
  val = if tv[<t|off] == on then tv_on[<t|0] + (t - tv«t) else 0
```

The stream tv_on is computed at the times at which there is an event in tv as follows: its value is either

- 0 if the tv was previously off, or
- the previous value of tv_on plus (t−tv«t) (the difference in time from the previous time-stamp of a tv event) if the tv was previously on.

Therefore, the stream is tolerant to events that do not change the tv status. □
    The semantics of Striver are also defined denotationally. Given real-time event streams for all events, ticking expressions a can be resolved to sets of instants $[a]$, offset expressions can be resolved to instants in time (or the corresponding -out or +out value) and expressions e can be resolved to a data value $[\![e]\!]$, using the events fetched via offset expressions and the interpreted functions. Finally, a set of event-streams is an evaluation model if for every output stream variable y, the candidate event-stream ρ_y satisfies both the ticking equation and the value equation (see [23] for details):

$$\rho_y = \{(t,d) \mid t \in [\![\mathcal{T}_y]\!] \text{ and } d = [\![V_y]\!](t)\}$$

Similar definitions of dependency graph, efficient monitorability, etc. can be adapted for Striver specifications. Efficiently (trace length independent) online monitoring algorithms also exist for Striver for its efficiently monitorable fragment [23].

3   Nested Monitors and Slices

3.1   Nested Monitors and Slices in Lola

Slices. To introduce slices in Lola, we extend the syntax with the operator $x[:n]$, where x is a stream and n is an integer expression (which is not necessarily a constant). The semantics of the expression $x[:n]$ is the following:

$$[\![x[:n]]\!](j) \stackrel{\text{def}}{=} [\rho_x(j), \ldots, \rho_x(j+k)] \text{ where } k = [\![n]\!](j)$$

assuming that $k \geq 0$, otherwise the slice is the empty list []. Essentially, a slice is a consecutive sequence of n elements of x starting at the current position (where n is an integer value, for example, read from an integer input stream). Since a slice expression $x[:n]$ only refers to present and future values of x, this expression generates a dependency with a non-negative weight, which is not possible to calculate or bound statically. Therefore, we extend the dependency graph with a new kind of edge $y \rightarrow^+ x$ when the defining expression of y contains $x[:n]$. A $\rightarrow^+$ edge precludes the calculation of the *latency* of y and a bound to the memory required by the monitor. The notion of well-formedness in [10] states that *"a Lola specification is well-formed if there is no closed-walk with total weight zero in its dependency graph."* Well-formed specifications are well-defined in the sense that for every collection of input sequences there is a unique collection of output sequences, which is a soundness requirement. For infinite sequences, a specification is well-formed if every closed-walk in the dependency graph has a negative total-weight. Otherwise, it cannot be guaranteed that every expression has a unique value. Therefore, translating slice edges into a self-loop would disallow semantics for infinite traces. We adapt these definitions for slices.

Definition 1. *A Lola specification with slices is well-formed if it contains no zero-weight cycles and the sum of weights in any cycle containing slice edges is strictly positive. A well-formed Lola specification with slices is very-well-formed if no cycle contains a slice edge.*

The following lemma justifies this definition.

Lemma 1. *Let φ be a Lola specification with slices. If φ is well-formed then it is well defined for finite sequences. If φ is very-well-formed it is well defined both for finite and infinite sequences.*

The main idea of the proof is that in well-formed specifications for finite streams, and in very-well-formed specifications for infinite streams, a stream at a given instant only depends on a finite number of streams and positions.

Nested Monitors. Nested monitors allow spawning and executing monitors dynamically, collecting the result in each invocation and using it as a value in the caller monitor. This extension involves minimum changes to the language, because it mainly consists of lifting specifications to become new constructor symbols that extend data theories.

Consider the following specification, which calculates whether input numeric streams r and s will cross within the following 50 instants. We define a topmost specification as follows:

```
input Double r,s
output Bool willCross = runSpec (crossspec r[:50] s[:50])
```

The output stream `willCross` invokes the nested specification `crossspec` with the slices containing the next 50 events of `r` and `s` as input. We will usually use slices as input streams for inner specifications.

Defining an *inner* specification involves giving it a name and adding an extra clause: **return** x **when** y where x is a stream of any type and y is a Boolean stream. The type of the stream x determines the type of the value returned when the specification is invoked dynamically. Optionally, parameters can be provided when defining the inner specification. Once we have defined a specification *spec*, we can execute it using the reserved keyword *runSpec*, providing the necessary parameters and lists of values for the input streams, in the order in which they are defined in the inner specification. In our example, we define the nested specification `crossspec` as follows:

```
innerspec Bool crossspec
input Double r,s
output Bool cross = sgn(r[now] - s[now]) != sgn(r[-1|r[now]] - s[-1|s[now]])
return cross when cross
```

The output stream `cross` simply checks that the relative order of the streams r and s changes. When an inner specification with a return clause **return** x **when** y is executed, the computation will return the value of the stream x at the first time y becomes *true*, or the last value of x if y never holds in the execution. *As a consequence, if y becomes true in the middle of an execution, the monitor does not have to run until the end to compute a value and can anticipate the result.* This opens the door to evaluate the inner specification incrementally as new elements of the input slice are available, and return the outcome as soon as it is definite. We call this behavior *slice anticipation*. The maximum length of the input slice considered is determined by the minimum length of the inputs to the inner spec, which have to be finite and non-empty (as slices are), but they can have different lengths in different invocations.

The return clause in our example returns *true* as soon as a signal crossover is detected, and returns *false* if the stream `cross` never becomes *true*.

Example 2. The following specification reimplements the previous example using the type richness of the language to compute how far in the future the signals will crossover, avoiding running the inner specification for the following n instants:

```
input Double r,s
output Bool willCross = will[now] > 0
output Int will = if will[-1|0] > 1 then will[-1|] - 1 else runSpec crossspec2 r[:50] s[:50]
```

In this case, we define the output stream `willCross` as equivalent to the fact that the streams `will` cross in the future. The definition of the intermediate stream `will` works in two stages. First, if at the previous instant we knew there was going to be a crossover in $n > 1$ instants, then it returns $n - 1$. Otherwise, it invokes the inner monitor with the slices to calculate how far in the future the streams will cross (and if they will cross at all).

```
innerspec Int crossspec2

input Double r,s
output Bool cross = sgn(r[now] - s[now]) != sgn(r[-1|r[now]] - s[-1|s[now]])
output Int instantN = instantN[-1|0] + 1
output Int ret = if cross[now] then instantN[now] else 0

return ret when cross
```

The inner specification returns the current instant (on its own recollection of time) at which a crossover happens, and 0 if there is no crossover. The returned instant number at which there will be a crossover within the inner specification indicates in the outer specification how far in the future it will happen.   □

Impact of the Extensions. In Lola [10, 34] if the dependency graph of a specification contains cycles of positive weight, then the specification is *non-efficiently monitorable*, which means that some output streams may require waiting an unbounded number of instants to be resolved. The incorporation of slices introduces a new class of specifications: those in which the resources necessary for the computation of every value in the output streams can be calculated at runtime when the value is about to be computed. We call these *dynamic bounded lag* specifications. Note that efficiently monitorable specifications and very efficiently monitorable specifications are dynamic bounded lag (the value is even known statically). *Past-time specifications (which contain no cycles of positive weight) that use slices are dynamic bounded lag specifications* but are not necessarily efficiently monitorable.

We say that specifications that are not dynamic bounded lag are *unbounded resource* specifications. The following table summarizes the new classification of specifications, where we mark the new class identified:

Dependency graph	Class
Only negative edges	**Very efficiently monitorable**
Only negative cycles, no $\cdot \rightarrow^+ \cdot$ edges	**Efficiently monitorable**
Only negative cycles	**Dynamic bounded lag**
Any legal graph	**Unbounded resources**

3.2 Extensions in Striver

Using the rich expressive power of Striver we can define a stream ws that contains the events of a stream s in a window of length w as shown in the following program on the left. The output stream ws updates the list of events when an event of s is leaving the sliding window of events (i.e., when s is producing a value); and also uses the shift operator to retrieve the future values of the stream s and incorporate them to the sliding window. As a consequence, it is not necessary to extend Striver with an extra operator to implement slices as slices can be implemented by a simple translation defining a

```
output [(Time, a)] ws =
  ticks = ticksOf s U shift (-w) s
  val = let (mold, mnew) = cv
        prevls = ws [<t|[]]
        nextls = if mold == null then prevls
                 else tail prevls
        in if mnew == null then nextls
        else nextls ++ [(t+w, mnew)]
```

parametric auxiliary stream *slice* (a, b) x that returns the timestamped values of the stream x within the interval $(a, b]$ along with the last value of x before a. However, in practice *the incorporation of nested specifications and slices as libraries in the language greatly simplifies some stream definitions* when we let $x[a{:}b]$ be syntactic sugar to refer to slices.

The syntax for nested monitors in Striver is very similar to Lola. We define *inner* specifications with a name and an extra **return** clause, with the difference that the returned value may be null, if the returned stream x did not generate a value before the termination stream became *true*. Again, we run the defined inner specification using the function *runSpec*, providing the necessary parameters and lists of timestamped values for the input streams and, as in the case of Lola, we will usually use slices as input streams for inner specifications.

Example 3. Consider input numeric streams x and y, and the specification of whether the maximum value of x is lower than the minimum value of y within the following 50 time units. In the output stream separable we define two auxiliary streams xs and ys using slices and we use their values as the input streams of the inner specification maxx_lt_miny,

```
input Double x,y
output Bool separable:
  ticks = ticksOf xs U ticksOf ys
  val = runSpec
        maxx_lt_miny xs[~t|[]] ys[~t|[]]
  where xs = x[0:50] ; ys = y[0:50]
```

which is defined as follows. In the inner specification we define one auxiliary stream max_x to calculate the historical maximum of x (within the slice) and one auxiliary stream min_y to calculate the historical minimum of y.

```
innerspec Bool maxx_lt_miny          output Bool ret:
input Double x,y                       ticks = ticksOf min_y U ticksOf max_x
output Double max_x:                    val = max_x[~t|infty] < min_y[~t| infty]
  ticks = ticksOf x                  output Bool stop:
  val = max cv max_x[<t|cv]            ticks = ticksOf ret
output Double min_y:                    val = not cv
  ticks = ticksOf y
  val = min cv min_y[<t|cv]          return ret when stop
```

The output Boolean stream ret checks that the historical maximum of x stays below the minimum of the historical minimum of y. The specification returns *false* as soon as the property is violated, and *true* if it always holds.   □

4   Nested Monitors and Slices in Action

We have extended two implementations of Lola and Striver (namely HLola and HStriver[1]) with nested monitors and slices. Both HLola and HStriver were written in Haskell and compiled with the version Glasgow Haskell Compiler, version 8.6.5 (see [6, 24, 25] for implementation details). In this section we illustrate how nested monitors and slices work in practice. A more advanced use case is the implementation of Kalman filter to predict trajectories of UAV in actual flight missions, described in [37].

QRS Complex Detection. We have implemented an electrocardiagram (ECG) analysis algorithm, in particular the Pan–Tompkins algorithm for real time QRS complex detection [30] (following [36] as reference ad-hoc code). Following our specification we can monitor the signal online, with an amount of memory that can be calculated statically. The specification declares output streams that iteratively transform the input signal as determined by the algorithm using statistics to detect peaks. We show below a snippet of the specification. The full specification[2] is 44 lines (while the reference implementation in Python uses 316 lines).

```
use innerspec headismax

input Double ecg_measurement
input Int timestamp

define Double convolved = ...
define [Double] rprev50 = shift rprev50[-1| replicate 50 (-0.000001)] convolved[now]
  where shift r x = x:init r
define Bool peak_candidate = convolved[now] > 0.35
                             && headisspike rprev50[now] && headisspike convolved[:50]
  where headisspike slice = runSpec (headismax slice)
define Bool ispeak = ...
define Bool isqrs  = ...
output Bool is_qrs_peak = isqrs[now] && ispeak[now]
```

---

[1] HLola and HStriver are available at http://github.com/imdea-software.

[2] Available at https://software.imdea.org/hlola/specs.html along with examples input and output events.

The specification follows an architecture of pipes and (stateful) filters. The stream `convolved` performs a convolution over a sliding window of fifteen instants of the square of the successive input value differences. A nested monitor checks if the current value of `convolved` is greater than all its previous 50 values (stored in `rprev50`) and its following 50 values, passed in `peak_candidate`. Finally, the output stream `is_qrs_peak` indicates if there is a peak in the ECG. The inner specification that assesses if the first value of an input stream is the maximum of the whole trace is shown on the left. Due to slice anticipation, the monitor produces the values at every instant as soon as possible. The following plot shows an ECG input signal and the peaks that the monitor detects (as black dots).

```
innerspec Bool headismax

input Double vals

output Double head = head[-1|vals[now]]
output Bool   ret  = head[now] >= vals[now]
output Bool   stop = not ret[now]

return ret when stop
```

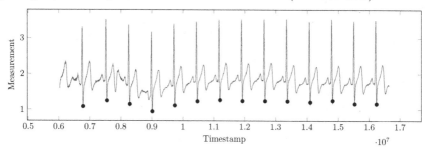

MTL and Dynamic MTL. It is well known that Lola can define MTL properties by unrolling intervals. However, the size of the resulting specification is proportional to the width of the intervals. Using the nested monitors and slices, we have written an MTL library that allows specifications of constant size regardless of interval width. With these extensions, the width of the window can be of variable lookahead and use adaptive memory, as we show in Sect. 5. Moreover, the result at every instant is computed as soon as the minimum information is available, many times without requiring the whole interval (responsiveness speed is preserved).

```
library DynMTL
use innerspec mtluntilspec

output Bool until <(Int, Expr Int) (a,eb)> <Stream Bool phi> <Stream Bool psi> =
  untilaux (a,eb) phi psi [a| until (0, eb + a) phi psi[now]]
output Bool untilaux <(Int, Expr Int) (a,eb)> <Stream Bool phi> <Stream Bool psi> =
  let winphis = phi [:eb-a] ; winpsis = psi [:eb-a]
  in runSpec (mtluntilspec winphis winpsis)
```

The parametric stream `untilaux` creates two slices of the future values of φ and ψ and runs the nested monitor `mtluntilspec` over them. The parametric stream `until` shifts the values of `untilaux` and handles the corner cases. The inner specification `mtluntilspec` is defined on the left. This specification simply returns the value of ψ whenever it becomes *true* or φ becomes *false*. If this never happens, or if it happens at the last instant, the last value of ψ is returned.

```
innerspec Bool mtluntilspec

input Bool phi, psi

output Bool stop =    psi[now] ||
              not phi[now]
return psi when stop
```

QMTL. We have defined a library for Quantitative MTL (QMTL), a more general version of MTL, which encompasses the original qualitative semantics, and provides quantitative semantics as well [7]. We first have defined a class in Haskell, shown on the left, to encapsulate the concepts of a Lattice and we have given two instances of lattices for Boolean and quantitative semantics. A Lattice consists of two operators: ⊔ and ⊓; with optional absorbing elements ⊤ and ⊥ respectively. We then define an instance for **Bool** and an instance for every numeric type as follows:

```
class Lattice x where
  sqcup      :: x -> x -> x
  sqcap      :: x -> x -> x
  opt_top    :: Maybe x
  opt_bottom :: Maybe x
```

```
instance Lattice Bool where
  sqcup      = (||)
  sqcap      = (&&)
  opt_top    = Just True
  opt_bottom = Just False
```

```
instance (Ord a, Num a) => Lattice a where
  sqcup      = max
  sqcap      = min
  opt_top    = Nothing
  opt_bottom = Nothing
```

We finally define the library for QMTL for any Lattice:

```
library QMTL
use innerspec foldspec
use innerspec foldaccumspec
output Lattice a => a eventually <(Int, Int) (x,y)> <Stream a phi> = let
  win = slidingwin (x,y) phi in
  if win == [] then opt_bottom else runSpec (foldspec sqcup opt_top win)
output Lattice a => a always <(Int, Int) (x,y)> <Stream a phi> = let
  win = slidingwin (x,y) phi in
  if win == [] then opt_top else runSpec (foldspec sqcap opt_bottom win)
output Lattice a => a since <(Int, Int) (x,y)> <Stream a phi> <Stream a psi> = let
  phis = slidingwin (x,y) phi
  psis = slidingwin (x,y) psi
  in runSpec (foldaccumspec sqcup sqcap opt_top phis psis)
output Lattice a => a since_overline <(Int, Int) (x,y)> <Stream a phi> <Stream a psi> = let
  phis = slidingwin (x,y) phi
  psis = slidingwin (x,y) psi
  in runSpec (foldaccumspec sqcap sqcup opt_bottom phis psis)
```

In this specification, `eventually` and `always` aggregate the values in the sliding window with the operators ⊔ and ⊓ respectively. If the absorbent element of the corresponding operator is found in the middle of the slice, then it is returned immediately as an optimization. This behavior is captured by the nested specification `foldspec`:

```
innerspec a foldspec <(a->a->a) op> <Maybe a mabs>
input a vals
output a ret = if instantN[now] === 1 then vals[now] else op ret [-1|] vals[now]
output Bool stop = ret[now] === abs
return ret when stop
```

Similarly, `since` and `since_overline` maintain the consecutive operation of φ along the window and combine it the current value of ψ, aggregating the results. If the value to return becomes the absorbent element mid-trace, then it is returned immediately, captured by the nested specification

```
innerspec a foldaccumspec <(a->a->a) op1> <(a->a->a) op2> <Maybe a mabs>
input a phi
input a psi
output a accum_phi = if instantN[now] === 1 then phi[now] else op2 accum_phi[-1|] phi[now]
output a ret = let val = op2 psi[now] accum_phi[now] in
  if instantN[now] === 1 then val else op1 ret[-1|] val
output Bool stop = ret[now] === abs
return ret when stop
```

The concrete types are instantiated automatically for each use of the library.

Robustl STL. We use the extensions in HStriver to define the quantitative semantics of the Signal Temporal Logic STL [13]. We show here $x\,\mathcal{U}_{[a,b]}\,y$ for which we define two slices: the slice of the events of x in $[t, t + b]$ and the slice of the events of y in $[t + a, t + b]$. Whenever an event enters or leaves any of the slices, we need to recompute the value of the stream. Since we treat the events of a stream as its change points, we use the value of the last event in the past of the slices to remember the value of the signal at the beginning of the sliding window, which we add to the slice timestamping it with t in x and $t + a$ in y. Finally, we execute the nested specification robustuntilspec with the resulting slices. This specification maintains the historical minimum of x (within the slice), compares them with each value of y, and returns the historical maximum of the results.

```
innerspec Int robustuntilspec
input Int xs, ys
output Bool never:
  ticks = {0}
  val = False
output Int xmins:
  ticks = ticksOf xs
  val = min xmins[<t|maxBound] cv
output Int theMins:
  ticks = ticksOf xmins U ticksOf ys
  val = min ys[~t|maxBound] xmins[~t|maxBound]
output Int theMaxMin:
  ticks = ticksOf theMins
  val = max theMaxMin[<t|minBound] cv
return theMaxMin when never
```

```
library RobustSTL
use innerspec robustuntilspec
define Int until <(Time, Time) (a,b)>
                  <Stream Int x>
                  <Stream Int y>:
  ticks = ticksOf xs U ticksOf ys
  val = runSpec (robustuntilspec xls yls)
  where
    xs = x[0:b]
    ys = y[a:b]
    xls = stampFst t xs[~t|(Nothing, [])]
    yls = stampFst (t+a) ys[~t|(Nothing, [])]
    stampFst _ (Nothing, r) = r
    stampFst ts (Just v, r) = (ts,v):r
```

5 Empirical Evaluation

In this section we report an empirical evaluation, executed on a MacBook Pro with a Dual Core Intel-i5 at 2.5 GHz with 8 GB of RAM running MacOS Catalina. We evaluate empirically the following hypotheses:

- (H1) An MTL specification uses constant memory throughout its execution if the data does not allow slice anticipation in the middle of an interval. This holds for both the original and the new version of the MTL library.
- (H2) The direct implementation of MTL that does not use slices consumes more memory than the implementation of MTL with slices.

- (H3) In both versions of MTL the memory consumption is affected by whether the result can be slice-anticipated. If (H2) holds, this is even more prominent in the sliceful version since memory consumption is smaller. Therefore, memory consumption is only upper-bounded by a constant and the actual (lower) memory usage cannot be fully predicted.
- (H4) For the sliceful version of MTL, a dynamic variation in the size of a slice for a trace of non-slice-anticipable data has an impact on the memory consumption.
- (H5) The memory consumption for ECG oscillates periodically within a range due to slice anticipation, as a special case of (H3).
- (H6) The concrete type instantiation in the usage of the QMTL library does not affect memory consumption.
- (H7) Unlike in Lola, the memory consumption of running a RobustSTL specification in Striver, with fixed window size and non-slice-anticipable data, depends on the event rate. With a fixed event rate, the memory consumption is constant, while with a varying event rate, the memory consumption varies accordingly.

To evaluate these hypotheses we have carried out the following experiments.

- **Experiment MTL I.** In this experiment, we run the MTL specification $\varphi \, \mathcal{U}_{(0,w)} \, \psi$ with window sizes $w = 10, 50, 100$ with data that prevents slice anticipation and we measure the memory as input is processed. We replicate the experiments for both versions of the MTL library, the naive version with unrolling and the version with slices. The results are shown in Fig. 1(a) which shows that memory consumption is constant for any window size and library implementation, validating (H1). We also observe that memory consumption for $w = 50, 100$ using the original MTL implementation (the two topmost lines in the graph) is greater, which validates (H2).
- **Experiment MTL II.** In this experiment, we run the previous MTL specification with window sizes $w = 10, 20, \ldots, 100$ over data that prevents slice anticipation in both versions of the MTL library and we measured the average memory consumption. The results are shown in Fig. 1(b). The blue bars show the memory usage for the sliceful version of MTL, and the red bars, the memory usage for the direct version that does not use slices. The figure shows that memory grows with the window size, but it does so more rapidly for the MTL version with no slices, which validates (H2).
- **Experiment MTL III.** This experiment studies the impact of slice anticipation on memory usage. We run the previous MTL specification with a window size of $w = 250$ for both versions, with data that is immediately anticipable at the beginning and at the end of the trace, and data that is not anticipable in the middle. As can be seen in Fig. 1(c) and (d), the memory consumption grows when the value is not susceptible to slice anticipation, confirming (H3). For the sliceful version of the MTL library with only non-anticipable data, reported in Fig. 1(c), the memory consumption is bounded by the worst case scenario, represented by the blue line, which fluctuates in the range $[0.95, 1]$.

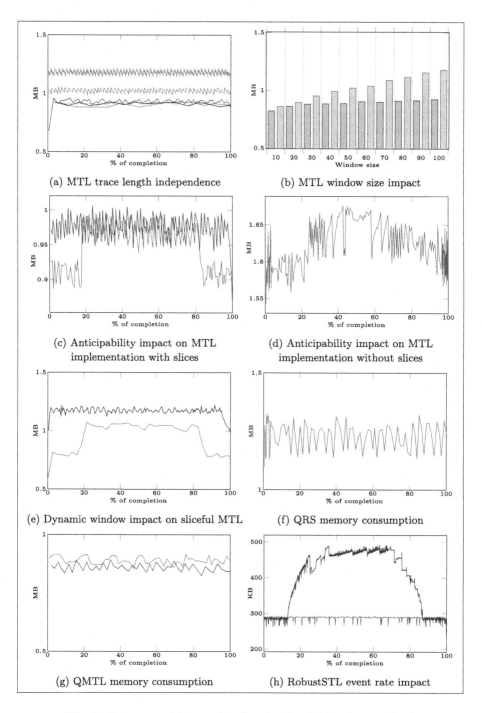

Fig. 1. Outcomes of the empirical evaluation (Color figure online)

- **Experiment MTL IV.** In this experiment we run the monitor for the MTL specification with dynamically varying window (which can only be done for the slicefull version) and non-anticipable data. We set a window size w of 5 at the beginning and at the end of the trace, and 500 in the middle. This results in an increase of the memory consumption, as shown in Fig. 1(e). We have also included a run with a constant $w = 500$ to show that it is a boundary on the memory requirement. This experiment confirms (H4).
- **Experiment ECG.** This experiment consists on the analysis of the memory consumption of the QRS complex detection for ECG. The result is shown in Fig. 1(f), which shows that the memory increases and decreases periodically (within a certain range), due to the anticipability of the data every time a peak is found. This validates (H5).
- **Experiment QMTL.** This is the last experiment using HLola, where we run the QMTL specification $\varphi \, \mathcal{S}_{(0,10)} \, \psi$ for two instances of the Lattice class: **Bool** and **Double**, with non-anticipable data as input. The result is shown in Fig. 1(g), where we see that the concrete type does not affect the memory consumption, which confirms (H6).
- **Experiment HStriver (RobustSTL).** Finally, we have executed the RobustSTL specification $\varphi \, \mathcal{U}_{(0,5)} \, \psi$ using HStriver with varying event-rate in φ and ψ. The event rate is 2 events per seconds at the beginning and at the end of the trace, but 200 events per second in the middle, which results in an increase of the memory consumption, as shown in Fig. 1(h). We also show the execution of the specification with a constant event rate of 2, which results in a constant memory consumption. This confirms (H7).

6   Conclusions

We have introduced two extensions of SRV, nested specifications and slices, both for synchronous and real-time and implemented them in HLola and HStriver. These extensions make many specifications more concise and easier to read. In turn, we have captured a new class of *dynamically bounded lag* specifications, where streams can depend unboundedly on the future but still have semantics for infinite inputs. We have used these extensions to implement a QRS complex detection algorithm, MTL, QMTL and robustness specifications for STL. The empirical evaluation shows that memory usage is predictable and, in the case of MTL, outperforms previous implementations in those cases where previous implementations existed. Future work includes evaluating quantitative STL properties for a powertrain control verification from [29], where input signals are precomputed from a MatLab simulation.

References

1. Asarin, E., Caspi, P., Maler, O.: Timed regular expressions. J. ACM **49**(2), 172–206 (2002). https://doi.org/10.1145/506147.506151
2. Barringer, H., Goldberg, A., Havelund, K., Sen, K.: Rule-based runtime verification. In: Steffen, B., Levi, G. (eds.) VMCAI 2004. LNCS, vol. 2937, pp. 44–57. Springer, Heidelberg (2004). https://doi.org/10.1007/978-3-540-24622-0_5
3. Bauer, A., Leucker, M., Schallhart, C.: Runtime verification for LTL and TLTL. ACM Trans. Softw. Eng. Methodol. **20**(4), 14 (2011). https://doi.org/10.1145/2000799.2000800
4. Bauer, A., Falcone, Y.: Decentralised LTL monitoring. In: Giannakopoulou, D., Méry, D. (eds.) FM 2012. LNCS, vol. 7436, pp. 85–100. Springer, Heidelberg (2012). https://doi.org/10.1007/978-3-642-32759-9_10
5. Berry, G.: The foundations of Esterel. In: Proof, Language, and Interaction: Essays in Honour of Robin Milner, pp. 425–454. MIT Press (2000)
6. Ceresa, M., Gorostiaga, F., Sánchez, C.: Declarative stream runtime verification (hLola). In: Oliveira, B.C.S. (ed.) APLAS 2020. LNCS, vol. 12470, pp. 25–43. Springer, Cham (2020). https://doi.org/10.1007/978-3-030-64437-6_2
7. Chattopadhyay, A., Mamouras, K.: A verified online monitor for metric temporal logic with quantitative semantics. In: Deshmukh, J., Ničković, D. (eds.) RV 2020. LNCS, vol. 12399, pp. 383–403. Springer, Cham (2020). https://doi.org/10.1007/978-3-030-60508-7_21
8. Chen, F., Roşu, G.: Parametric trace slicing and monitoring. In: Kowalewski, S., Philippou, A. (eds.) TACAS 2009. LNCS, vol. 5505, pp. 246–261. Springer, Heidelberg (2009). https://doi.org/10.1007/978-3-642-00768-2_23
9. Convent, L., Hungerecker, S., Leucker, M., Scheffel, T., Schmitz, M., Thoma, D.: TeSSLa: temporal stream-based specification language. In: Massoni, T., Mousavi, M.R. (eds.) SBMF 2018. LNCS, vol. 11254, pp. 144–162. Springer, Cham (2018). https://doi.org/10.1007/978-3-030-03044-5_10
10. D'Angelo, B.: LOLA: runtime monitoring of synchronous systems. In: Proceedings of the 12th International Symposium of Temporal Representation and Reasoning (TIME 2005), pp. 166–174. IEEE CS Press (2005). https://doi.org/10.1109/TIME.2005.26
11. Danielsson, L.M., Sánchez, C.: Decentralized stream runtime verification. In: Finkbeiner, B., Mariani, L. (eds.) RV 2019. LNCS, vol. 11757, pp. 185–201. Springer, Cham (2019). https://doi.org/10.1007/978-3-030-32079-9_11
12. Delaval, G., Girault, A., Pouzet, M.: A type system for the automatic distribution of higher-order synchronous dataflow programs. SIGPLAN Not. **43**(7), 101–110 (2008). https://doi.org/10.1145/1379023.1375672
13. Donzé, A., Ferrère, T., Maler, O.: Efficient robust monitoring for STL. In: Sharygina, N., Veith, H. (eds.) CAV 2013. LNCS, vol. 8044, pp. 264–279. Springer, Heidelberg (2013). https://doi.org/10.1007/978-3-642-39799-8_19
14. Eisner, C., Fisman, D., Havlicek, J., Lustig, Y., McIsaac, A., Van Campenhout, D.: Reasoning with temporal logic on truncated paths. In: Hunt, W.A., Somenzi, F. (eds.) CAV 2003. LNCS, vol. 2725, pp. 27–39. Springer, Heidelberg (2003). https://doi.org/10.1007/978-3-540-45069-6_3
15. El-Hokayem, A., Falcone, Y.: Monitoring decentralized specifications. In: Proceedings of the 26th ACM SIGSOFT Internaional Symposium on Software Testing and Analysis (ISSTA 2017), pp. 125–135. ACM (2017). https://doi.org/10.1145/3092703.3092723

16. Eliot, C., Hudak, P.: Functional reactive animation. In: Proceedings of ICFP 2007, pp. 163–173. ACM (1997). https://doi.org/10.1145/258948.258973

17. Faymonville, P., Finkbeiner, B., Schirmer, S., Torfah, H.: A stream-based specification language for network monitoring. In: Falcone, Y., Sánchez, C. (eds.) RV 2016. LNCS, vol. 10012, pp. 152–168. Springer, Cham (2016). https://doi.org/10.1007/978-3-319-46982-9_10

18. Faymonville, P., et al.: StreamLAB: stream-based monitoring of cyber-physical systems. In: Dillig, I., Tasiran, S. (eds.) CAV 2019. LNCS, vol. 11561, pp. 421–431. Springer, Cham (2019). https://doi.org/10.1007/978-3-030-25540-4_24

19. Faymonville, P., Finkbeiner, B., Schwenger, M., Torfah, H.: Real-time stream-based monitoring. CoRR abs/1711.03829 (2017)

20. Francalanza, A., Pérez, J.A., Sánchez, C.: Runtime verification for decentralised and distributed systems. In: Bartocci, E., Falcone, Y. (eds.) Lectures on Runtime Verification. LNCS, vol. 10457, pp. 176–210. Springer, Cham (2018). https://doi.org/10.1007/978-3-319-75632-5_6

21. Gautier, T., Le Guernic, P., Besnard, L.: SIGNAL: a declarative language for synchronous programming of real-time systems. In: Kahn, G. (ed.) FPCA 1987. LNCS, vol. 274, pp. 257–277. Springer, Heidelberg (1987). https://doi.org/10.1007/3-540-18317-5_15

22. Gorostiaga, F., Danielsson, L.M., Sánchez, C.: Unifying the time-event spectrum for stream runtime verification. In: Deshmukh, J., Ničković, D. (eds.) RV 2020. LNCS, vol. 12399, pp. 462–481. Springer, Cham (2020). https://doi.org/10.1007/978-3-030-60508-7_26

23. Gorostiaga, F., Sánchez, C.: Striver: stream runtime verification for real-time event-streams. In: Colombo, C., Leucker, M. (eds.) RV 2018. LNCS, vol. 11237, pp. 282–298. Springer, Cham (2018). https://doi.org/10.1007/978-3-030-03769-7_16

24. Gorostiaga, F., Sánchez, C.: HLola: a very functional tool for extensible stream runtime verification. In: Groote, J.F., Larsen, K.G. (eds.) TACAS 2021. LNCS, vol. 12652, pp. 349–356. Springer, Cham (2021). https://doi.org/10.1007/978-3-030-72013-1_18

25. Gorostiaga, F., Sánchez, C.: HStriver: a very functional extensible tool for the runtime verification of real-time event streams. In: FM 2021 (2021, to appear)

26. Gorostiaga, F., Sánchez, C.: Stream runtime verification of real-time event streams with the Striver language. Int. J. Softw. Tools Technol. Transfer **23**, 157–183 (2021). https://doi.org/10.1007/s10009-021-00605-3

27. Halbwachs, N., Caspi, P., Raymond, P., Pilaud, D.: The synchronous data-flow programming language LUSTRE. Proc. IEEE **79**(9), 1305–1320 (1991). https://doi.org/10.1109/5.97300

28. Havelund, K., Roşu, G.: Synthesizing monitors for safety properties. In: Katoen, J.-P., Stevens, P. (eds.) TACAS 2002. LNCS, vol. 2280, pp. 342–356. Springer, Heidelberg (2002). https://doi.org/10.1007/3-540-46002-0_24

29. Jin, X., Deshmukh, J.V., Kapinski, J., Ueda, K., Butts, K.: Powertrain control verification benchmark. In: Proceedings of the 17th International Conference on Hybrid Systems: Computation and Control (HSCC 2014), pp. 253–262. ACM (2014). https://doi.org/10.1145/2562059.2562140

30. Pan, J., Tompkins, W.J.: A real-time QRS detection algorithm. IEEE Trans. Biomed. Eng. **BME-32**(3), 230–236 (1985). https://doi.org/10.1109/TBME.1985.325532

31. Pike, L., Goodloe, A., Morisset, R., Niller, S.: Copilot: a hard real-time runtime monitor. In: Barringer, H., et al. (eds.) RV 2010. LNCS, vol. 6418, pp. 345–359. Springer, Heidelberg (2010). https://doi.org/10.1007/978-3-642-16612-9_26

32. Reinbacher, T., Rozier, K.Y., Schumann, J.: Temporal-logic based runtime observer pairs for system health management of real-time systems. In: Ábrahám, E., Havelund, K. (eds.) TACAS 2014. LNCS, vol. 8413, pp. 357–372. Springer, Heidelberg (2014). https://doi.org/10.1007/978-3-642-54862-8_24

33. Roşu, G., Havelund, K.: Rewriting-based techniques for runtime verification. Autom. Softw. Eng. **12**(2), 151–197 (2005). https://doi.org/10.1007/s10515-005-6205-y

34. Sánchez, C.: Online and offline stream runtime verification of synchronous systems. In: Colombo, C., Leucker, M. (eds.) RV 2018. LNCS, vol. 11237, pp. 138–163. Springer, Cham (2018). https://doi.org/10.1007/978-3-030-03769-7_9

35. Sen, K., Roşu, G.: Generating optimal monitors for extended regular expressions. In: Sokolsky, O., Viswanathan, M. (eds.) Electronic Notes in Theoretical Computer Science, vol. 89. Elsevier (2003)

36. Sznajder, M., Łukowska, M.: Python online and offline ECG QRS detector based on the Pan-Tomkins algorithm, July 2017. https://doi.org/10.5281/zenodo.826614

37. Zudaire, S., Gorostiaga, F., Sánchez, C., Schneider, G., Uchitel, S.: Assumption monitoring using runtime verification for UAV temporal task plan executions. In: Proceedings of IEEE International Conference on Robotics and Automation (ICRA 2021). IEEE (2021)

Diamont: Dynamic Monitoring of Uncertainty for Distributed Asynchronous Programs

Vimuth Fernando$^{(\boxtimes)}$, Keyur Joshi, Jacob Laurel, and Sasa Misailovic

University of Illinois Urbana-Champaign, Urbana, USA
{wvf2,kpjoshi2,jlaurel2,misailo}@illinois.edu

Abstract. Many application domains including graph analytics, the Internet-of-Things, precision agriculture, and media processing operate on noisy data and/or produce approximate results. These applications can distribute computation across multiple (often resource-constrained) processing units. Analyzing the reliability and accuracy of such applications is challenging, since most existing techniques operate on specific fixed error models, check for individual properties, or can only be applied to sequential programs.

We present Diamont, a system for dynamic monitoring of uncertainty properties in distributed programs. Diamont programs consist of distributed processes that communicate via asynchronous message passing. Diamont includes datatypes that dynamically monitor uncertainty in data and provides support for checking predicates over the monitored uncertainty at runtime. We also present a general methodology for verifying the soundness of the runtime system and optimizations using canonical sequentialization.

We implemented Diamont for a subset of the Go language and evaluated eight programs from precision agriculture, graph analytics, and media processing. We show that Diamont can prove important end-to-end properties on the program outputs for significantly larger inputs compared to prior work, with modest execution time overhead: 3% on average and 16.3% at maximum.

1 Introduction

Many emerging distributed applications operate on inherently noisy data or produce approximate results [41]. Emerging edge applications, including autonomous robotics and precision agriculture, routinely need to deal with noise from their sensors. Machine learning applications regularly encounter datasets that contain a high degree of noise, or other irregularity. Furthermore, the rise of highly-parallel and often heterogeneous systems have brought forth new challenges in overcoming bottlenecks in computation and communication between processing units. Many prominent systems adopted approximation in communication, e.g., MapReduce's task dropping [16], TensorFlow's precision reduction [43], or Hogwild's synchronization-eschewing stochastic gradient

© Springer Nature Switzerland AG 2021
L. Feng and D. Fisman (Eds.): RV 2021, LNCS 12974, pp. 184–206, 2021.
https://doi.org/10.1007/978-3-030-88494-9_10

descent [31]. Also, researchers explored various non-conventional architectures and networks-on-chip [7,17,30,42].

To cope with different kinds of uncertainty, researchers developed several static and run-time analyses that quantify the level of noise, reliability, or accuracy. We survey the existing techniques in Sect. 7. These existing techniques suffer from one or more of the following problems: 1) they have been developed *only for sequential* programs, 2) they are either *imprecise* (static analyses) or *lack guarantees* on result quality and soundness of monitoring code (empirical analyses), or 3) their applicability is *limited* – a single analysis is defined exclusively for a *specific* source of uncertainty (e.g., an unreliable instruction or a noisy sensor) and cannot be combined with others. Directly extending and generalizing the existing frameworks to a distributed setting can lead to subtle problems and/or run-time inefficiencies. An intriguing question is how to design a general analysis framework that will overcome these challenges, thus enabling a flexible and precise uncertainty analysis for parallel computations.

Our Work. We present Diamont, the first system for *sound, precise and efficient* runtime monitoring of uncertainty in *distributed applications*. Diamont offers a flexible runtime system for specifying and verifying uncertainty bounds in the face of *various sources of uncertainty*. Diamont supports programs consisting of distributed processes that communicate via asynchronous message-passing. Each process communicates with the others using strongly-typed communication channels through the common **send** and **receive** communication primitives. Diamont includes multiple language constructs for dynamic monitoring:

- **Dynamic types and data channels:** The developer specifies the variables that need to be dynamically monitored by annotating them using the **dynamic** type qualifier. In addition, Diamont introduces dynamic channels that use specialized communication primitives to reliably transfer the monitoring information.
- **Runtime Monitoring of Uncertainty:** Diamont maintains *uncertain intervals* for dynamically monitored variables – these map variables to a maximum error bound and a probability that the error is within the bound. Diamont propagates this uncertainty through computations. It can precisely do so even for individual array elements and unbounded loops – factors that usually reduce precision of existing analyses like Parallely [19] and DECAF [6].
- **Checkers:** Diamont's **check** statement evaluates logical predicates over the program state and the monitored uncertainty to report violations. For example, the check can verify whether the magnitude of a variable's error is less than a developer-defined threshold. Using Diamont's checks, developers can decide if further attention should be given to the results. If the uncertainty of a result is acceptable at runtime, developers can avoid costly error checking and correction mechanisms.

We implemented Diamont for a distributed fragment of the Go language, extended with the dynamic type and check statements. Diamont performs static analysis at the level of an intermediate representation (IR) extracted from the Go code. It generates instrumented Go code with dynamic monitoring implemented via a Go library.

Diamont also presents a set of optimizations to reduce the runtime overhead arising from the monitoring of uncertain intervals throughout and across processes. These optimizations include: 1) combining static analysis with dynamic monitoring 2) approximating dynamically monitored uncertainty of arrays, 3) moving check statements across processes, and 4) using compiler techniques such as constant propagation and dead-code elimination. These optimizations give Diamont a significant advantage over direct extensions of systems like Decaf [6] or AffineFloat [13] to parallel programs. However, developers who try to manually implement such run-time system optimizations that span multiple processes can easily make subtle errors.

Verified Runtime and Optimizations. We prove the soundness of the Diamont runtime and optimizations. Soundness of a Diamont program means that if the execution passes a variable uncertainty check, then the uncertainty of the variable is within the bound specified in the check statement. An optimization is sound if all check failures in a program are also guaranteed to occur in its optimized version.

Diamont's runtime system is sound for programs that satisfy the *symmetric nondeterminism* property [3] – i.e., each receive statement must have a unique matching send statement, or a set of symmetric matching send statements. Many common parallel patterns in data analytics applications [19,34] satisfy this property. We use *canonical sequentialization* [3,19], which rewrites a symmetrically nondeterministic parallel program to an equivalent sequential program. We can then prove soundness of runtime monitoring on the sequentialized program. Lastly, we show that this soundness proof also applies to the original parallel program.

Through sequentialization, Diamont can also automatically verify type safety and the absence of deadlocks of programs caused by approximations, the runtime system, or optimizations that change communication patterns.

Results. We applied Diamont on eight parallel applications. These real-world applications come from the domains of graph analytics, precision agriculture, and media processing. We modeled four sources of uncertainty: noisy communication, precision reduction (compression), noisy inputs, and timing errors.

We showed that Diamont can verify important end-to-end properties for all applications. In particular, we looked at four error probability predicates of end results, three error magnitude predicates, and one predicate on both error probability and magnitude. These properties cannot be validated by existing static techniques [10,19,26].

Our optimizations reduced the runtime overhead of Diamont with respect to the unmonitored program. Directly extending existing sequential runtime analyses to parallel settings leads to overheads between 30–80%. Our optimizations reduced the overhead to a geomean of 3% and maximum of 16.3% while satisfying strict predicates. We show that these overheads remain low and the communication of monitoring data is minimized even when the input size increases, espe-

```
1    var Q [NUMSENSORS] process; var R [NUMWORKERS] process
2    type point struct {/*@dynamic*/ temperature, humidity float64 }
3
4    func Manager { // declarations & setup skiped to preserve space
5      for i, IoTDevice := range(Q) { data[i] = receive(IoTDevice) }
6      centers = // randomly pick some nodes
7      for i, Worker := range(R) { send(Worker, data) }
8      for j:=0; j<ITERATIONS; j++ {
9        for _, Worker := range(R) { send(Worker, centers) }
10       for i, Worker := range(R) { newcenters[i] = receive(Worker) }
11       centers = AverageOverThreads(newcenters)
12     }
13     checkArr(centers, 1, 0.99, 4, 0.99)
14   }
15
16   func IoTDevice {
17     /*@dynamic*/ var temperature, humidity float64
18     tempVal, tempErr, tempConf := readTemperature()
19     humidVal, humidErr, humidConf := readHumidity()
20     temperature = track(tempVal, tempErr, tempConf)
21     humidity = track(humidVal, humidErr, humidConf)
22     send(Manager, point{temperature, humidity})
23   }
24
25   func Worker {
26     var data [NUMSENSORS] point
27     var centers, newcenters [NUMCENTERS] point
28     /*@dynamic*/ var assign [PERTHREAD] int
29     data = receive(Manager)
30     for iter:=0; iter<ITERATIONS; iter++ {
31       centers = receive(Manager)
32       newcenters = kmeansKernel(data, centers, assign)
33       send(Manager, newcenters)
34   } }
```

Fig. 1. K-means algorithm in a smart agriculture setup in the Go language

cially for applications that implement intensive communication. These results demonstrate that even in the face of both uncertainty and significant parallelism, runtime monitoring is still practical.

Contributions. The paper makes several contributions:

- **Diamont.** Diamont is a system for dynamically monitoring uncertainty properties in strongly-typed, message-passing, asynchronous programs. We show that Diamont can soundly monitor uncertainty (error probability and magnitude).
- **Optimizations for reducing overhead.** We present several optimizations that reduce the overhead of performing runtime monitoring across processes.
- **Implementation.** We implement Diamont's analysis and runtime system with optimizations for a subset of Go.
- **Evaluation.** We evaluate Diamont on 8 benchmarks. We show that Diamont can verify important correctness properties with small runtime overheads.

2   Example

We consider a scenario from precision agriculture [20]. Multiple low-power embedded systems with sensors are distributed across a field to monitor changes in the environment. Each embedded system (e.g., Raspberry Pis) can read the temperature, humidity, or other properties using their sensors. It can perform limited local processing of the readings, and periodically sends those results to a server for further (typically more expensive) analysis.

Figure 1 shows an implementation of the application in Go. The program has multiple parallel processes that communicate over typed channels using the Diamont API using matched **send** and **receive** statements (E.g., Lines 5, 22). The **Manager** process coordinates the computation.

The process group **Q** is of a set of processes running on embedded systems **IoTDevice**$_{1,...,}$NUMSENSORS that read sensor values and communicate the data to the **Manager**. Each **IoTDevice** gathers and stores datapoints using the struct **point** from Line 2. The **/*@dynamic*/** annotation indicates that the fields of **point** are of **dynamic** type. Diamont monitors the uncertainty of **dynamic** variables at runtime.

The **Manager** process first gathers sensor data (Line 5) from each **IoTDevice**. Then it performs a distributed k-means clustering analysis using the processes in the group **R**. The **Manager** picks a set of random points as the initial cluster centers (Line 6). Next, over **ITERATIONS** iterations, it updates the cluster centers (Lines 8–12).

Each **Worker** process from the group **R** processes a subset of the data points to calculate new cluster centers (Lines 30–33) for that subset. The **Manager** combines the partial results from each **Worker** and redistributes them (Line 11).

2.1   Sources of Uncertainty

Approximate Sensors. Sensors are often noisy (e.g., the AM2302-DH22 relative humidity and temperature sensor has an error range of $\pm 0.5\,°F$ for temperature and $\pm 2\%RH$ for humidity reading [24]). Each process in **Q** calculates the error of its sensors while reading the value at Lines 18 and 19. This error calculation can come from the sensor specification (e.g. [24]). Next, Lines 20 and 21 initialize **dynamic** variables using the sensor value and error.

Approximate Communication. We also consider the impact of communication over noisy channels (Line 7, 9), prevalent in situations where sensors are deployed in remote areas (E.g., [45]). Messages in such channels can be corrupted with a small probability [29]. Instead of implementing costly error correction mechanisms, a developer may choose to deal with potentially incorrect data to save resources.

An uncertainty model ψ provides parameters such as the probability of message corruption. For example, $\psi(\text{Manager}, \text{Worker}, \text{dynamic float<64>}) = 1 - 10^{-7}$ indicates that the probability of corruption of a **dynamic float<64>** type message from **Manager** to **Worker** is 10^{-7}. The specification is modeled after the ones from [5, 10, 37].

2.2   Verification

Properties. We wish to verify that the final values of `centers` are close to the true cluster centers with high probability. We encode this requirement in the `checkArr` statement in Line 13. This check specifies a maximum error magnitude and probability for each `dynamic` field in the struct. This program has features that make static verification using tools such as Parallely [19] challenging:

- The error specification of the sensors may not be known a priori. Additionally, prior static verification techniques require worst-case bounds for the number of loop iterations and the number of processes. Using worst-case estimates for these in a static analysis will invalidate many correct programs.
- Parallely treats entire arrays as single variables, and thus array analysis accumulates errors even across two different array locations. Consequently, the conservative static estimate of uncertain intervals quickly expands to unusable levels for any sufficiently large number of sensors for our example.

Workflow. Diamont combines static and dynamic analyses to verify safety and accuracy properties at *runtime*. Figure 2 shows the workflow for generating an instrumented program in Diamont. Given a Go program, Diamont 1) translates it to Diamont-IR, 2) sequentializes the program to statically verify type safety, deadlock-freeness, and the applicability of the runtime analysis, and 3) produces an instrumented version of the original Go program with an *uncertainty map* for each process. The sequentialized version of the code in Fig. 1 is in Appendix F [18].

The *uncertainty map* of a process maintains a conservative uncertain interval for each `dynamic` local variable. Uncertain intervals are stored as pairs $\langle d, r \rangle$ indicating that the maximum error of the associated variable is $\leq d$ with probability $\geq r$. The default uncertain interval is $\langle 0, 1 \rangle$ (no error with 100% confidence). Developers can use `track` statements (E.g., Line 20) to use external error specifications within Diamont. When a dynamic variable is updated, Diamont also updates the uncertain interval. Diamont's instrumentation 1) initializes the uncertain interval of the data in `IoTDevice`, 2) communicates the uncertain interval across process boundaries, 3) propagates this uncertainty through computations, and 4) checks the uncertain interval of the array at the end of the program against a developer-specified bound.

We verified this system for a setting with 128 sensors and a set of 8 workers performing the k-means computation over 10 iterations. As more and more computations containing unreliable values affect the `centers` array, the uncertain interval of individual elements widens. However, the specification is still satisfied.

Overhead. Diamont's instrumentation adds runtime overhead. To reduce overhead, Diamont applies optimizations such as constant propagation, dead code elimination, and simplification of monitoring uncertainty in arrays. To reduce overhead when transmitting arrays, Diamont transmits the maximum uncertainty among the elements of the array as the uncertainty of every element

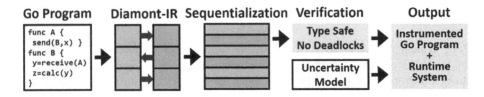

Fig. 2. Diamont workflow

of the array. This allows Diamont to only communicate one uncertain interval across processes, while maintaining high analysis precision in other parts of the program. These optimizations reduce Diamont's overhead from 42% to 3.2%. Increasing the number of sensors does not significantly increase overhead (Sect. 6.3). Even for 2–8x larger data, the overhead remains below 5%.

3   Diamont System

Diamont takes as input a Go program and an uncertainty model. Diamont first converts the program to the Diamont-IR and verifies important safety properties necessary to ensure that the runtime system will be sound. Finally, Diamont generates instrumented Go code. The full syntax and semantics of Diamont are available in Appendix A [18].

3.1   Syntax

Go Language. Diamont supports a subset of the Go Programming Language (matching the features of Diamont-IR along with external functions that do not perform communication) extended with an API for distributed communication and annotations in comments for type qualifiers.

Diamont-IR. Diamont's intermediate representation supports a strongly typed imperative language with primitives for asynchronous communication. Diamont extends the syntax of Parallely [19] with support for the additional **dynamic** type. Figure 3 defines the subset of Diamont syntax dealing with **dynamic** data. Here, d refers to reals, r to probabilities, n to positive integers, x, y to variables, and a to array variables. The full syntax includes conditionals, loops, operations on arrays, and structs.

Types. Diamont's type qualifiers explicitly split data into either **precise** (no uncertainty), **dynamic** (uncertainty monitored at runtime), or **approx** (uncertain but unmonitored). Diamont's type system ensures that uncertainties in executions do not cause errors in critical program sections and ensures that the dynamic monitoring is sound by avoiding control flow divergence. Using type inference, Diamont automatically annotates some variables as dynamic to reduce programmer burden.

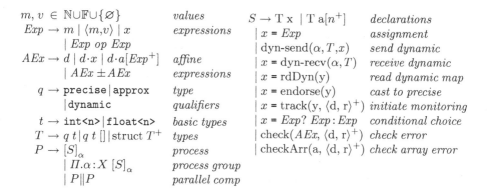

$$m, v \in \mathbb{N} \cup \mathbb{F} \cup \{\varnothing\} \quad \textit{values}$$
$$Exp \rightarrow m \mid \langle m, v \rangle \mid x \quad \textit{expressions}$$
$$\mid Exp \; op \; Exp$$
$$AEx \rightarrow d \mid d{\cdot}x \mid d{\cdot}a[Exp^{+}] \quad \textit{affine}$$
$$\mid AEx \pm AEx \quad \textit{expressions}$$
$$q \rightarrow \texttt{precise} \mid \texttt{approx} \quad \textit{type}$$
$$\mid \texttt{dynamic} \quad \textit{qualifiers}$$
$$t \rightarrow \texttt{int<n>} \mid \texttt{float<n>} \quad \textit{basic types}$$
$$T \rightarrow q\,t \mid q\,t\,[] \mid \texttt{struct } T^{+} \quad \textit{types}$$
$$P \rightarrow [S]_{\alpha} \quad \textit{process}$$
$$\mid \Pi.\alpha{:}X\,[S]_{\alpha} \quad \textit{process group}$$
$$\mid P \| P \quad \textit{parallel comp}$$

$$S \rightarrow \text{T x} \mid \text{T a}[n^{+}] \quad \textit{declarations}$$
$$\mid x = Exp \quad \textit{assignment}$$
$$\mid \text{dyn-send}(\alpha, T, x) \quad \textit{send dynamic}$$
$$\mid x = \text{dyn-recv}(\alpha, T) \quad \textit{receive dynamic}$$
$$\mid x = \text{rdDyn}(y) \quad \textit{read dynamic map}$$
$$\mid x = \text{endorse}(y) \quad \textit{cast to precise}$$
$$\mid x = \text{track}(y, \langle d, r \rangle^{+}) \quad \textit{initiate monitoring}$$
$$\mid x = Exp ? \; Exp : Exp \quad \textit{conditional choice}$$
$$\mid \text{check}(AEx, \langle d, r \rangle^{+}) \quad \textit{check error}$$
$$\mid \text{checkArr}(a, \langle d, r \rangle^{+}) \quad \textit{check array error}$$

Fig. 3. Diamont-IR syntax extensions (full language contains conditionals, loops and function calls)

Communication. Processes communicate by sending and receiving messages over typed channels. For each pair of processes, Diamont provides a set of logical sub-channels for communication, further split by message type (μ). A **send** statement asynchronously sends a value to another process using a unique process identifier. The receiving process uses the blocking **receive** statement to read the message. Diamont supports communication of **dynamic** type data through **dyn-send** and **dyn-recv** statements, which also send the monitored uncertainty using reliable channels.

Type Conversion. To explicitly convert a variable to **dynamic** type, the developer or compiler can use a **track** statement ($x = \text{track}(y, \langle d, r \rangle)$), which sets the uncertain interval to $\langle d, r \rangle$. **track** statements can be used to initiate monitoring for variables updated by external functions, or to incorporate informal specifications (e.g., from a datasheet) into Diamont. Similarly, the **endorse** statement ($x = \text{endorse}(y)$) converts an **approx** or **dynamic** variable to a **precise** variable, usually after a user-defined check (similar to EnerJ [37]). The **rdDyn** intrinsic ($\text{rdDyn}(x)$) can be used to read the monitored uncertainty of a **dynamic** variable.

Uncertainty Model (ψ). It specifies the reliability/accuracy of program components (e.g., the probability of message corruption or the probability that a sensor fails).

Specifications. Diamont exposes the following statements to check specifications of dynamically monitored variables.

- check($AEx, \langle d, r \rangle$): It checks if an affine expression AEx has a maximum error $\leq d$ with probability $\geq r$. If the specification is not satisfied, the check fails.
- checkArr($a, \langle d, r \rangle$): It checks if the dynamically monitored uncertainty for *each* element in array a satisfies the specification.

While this version of Diamont stops the execution if a check fails, it can be extended to trigger a recovery mechanism instead [1,15,22]. Aloe [22] repre-

S-ASSIGN-DYN
$$\frac{(x,\cdot,\cdot) \in D \quad \langle e,\sigma,h \rangle \Downarrow v}{d = \langle \text{calc-eps}(e,D), \text{calc-del}(e,D) \rangle}$$
$$\frac{D' = D[x \mapsto d] \quad \langle n_b, \langle 1 \rangle \rangle = \sigma(x) \quad h' = h[n_b \mapsto v]}{\langle x = e, \langle \sigma,h \rangle, \mu, D \rangle \xrightarrow{1}_\psi \langle \text{skip}, \langle \sigma,h' \rangle, \mu, D' \rangle}$$

S-DYNSEND
$$\frac{\mu[\langle \alpha,\beta,D_t \rangle] = m_d \quad \mu' = \mu[\langle \alpha,\beta,D_t \rangle \mapsto m_d {+}{+} D[y]]}{\langle [\text{dyn-send}(\beta,t,y)]_\alpha, \langle \sigma,h \rangle, \mu, D \rangle \xrightarrow{1}_\psi \langle [\text{send}(\beta,t,y)]_\alpha, \langle \sigma,h \rangle, \mu', D \rangle}$$

S-DYNRECEIVE
$$\frac{\mu[\langle \beta,\alpha,D_t \rangle] = d :: m_d \quad \mu' = \mu[\langle \beta,\alpha,D_t \rangle \mapsto m_d] \quad d_b = \langle d.\epsilon, \, d.\delta \times \psi(\beta,\alpha,t) \rangle \quad D' = D[x \mapsto d_b]}{\langle [x = \text{dyn-recv}(\beta,t)]_\alpha, \langle \sigma,h \rangle, \mu, D \rangle \xrightarrow{1}_\psi \langle [x = \text{receive}(\beta,t)]_\alpha, \langle \sigma,h \rangle, \mu', D' \rangle}$$

S-CHECK-FAIL
$$\frac{\text{calc-eps}(AEx,D) > d \ \lor \ \text{calc-del}(AEx,D) < r}{\langle \text{check}(AEx, d, r), \langle \sigma,h \rangle, \mu, D \rangle \xrightarrow{1}_\psi \langle \text{skip}, \bot, \mu, D \rangle}$$

S-CAST
$$\frac{\langle n_b', \langle 1 \rangle \rangle = \sigma(y) \quad h[n_b'] = m \quad m' = \text{cast}(T,m)}{\langle n_b, \langle 1 \rangle \rangle = \sigma(x) \quad h' = h[n_b \mapsto m']}$$
$$\frac{d = \langle \text{cast-eps}(x,y,D), \, D[y].\delta \rangle \quad D' = D[x \mapsto d]}{\langle x = (\text{dynamic } T)y, \langle \sigma,h' \rangle, \mu, D' \rangle \xrightarrow{1}_\psi \langle \text{skip}, \langle \sigma,h' \rangle, \mu, D' \rangle}$$

Fig. 4. Semantics of dynamic monitoring (selection)

sents recoverable computations with blocks of the form try {...} check (...) recover {...}. Using this construct, Diamont can recover the execution if a check fails, and calculate the effect of (possibly imperfect) checks and recovery mechanisms on uncertainty. Formalization of recovery for distributed programs, however, is out of scope of this paper.

Structs. The programmer can specify the uncertainty of each field of a struct in a track statement by using multiple $\langle d, r \rangle$ pairs. The programmer can check each field of a struct in check and checkArr statements in a similar manner.

3.2 Diamont Semantics

Semantics for precise and approx data in Diamont are the same as those from Parallely[19]. For dynamic data, the compiler adds instructions to monitor their uncertain intervals alongside the original program instructions.

References, Frames, Stacks, and Heaps. A *reference* is a pair $\langle n_b, \langle n_1, ..., n_k \rangle \rangle \in \text{Ref}$ that contains a base address $n_b \in Loc$ and dimension descriptor $\langle n_1, ..., n_k \rangle$ denoting the location and dimension of variables in the heap. A *frame* $\sigma \in E = \text{Var} \rightarrow \text{Ref}$ maps program variables to references. A *heap* $h \in H = \mathbb{N} \rightarrow \mathbb{N} \cup \mathbb{F} \cup \{\varnothing\}$ is a finite map from addresses to values (Integers, Floats or the special *empty message* $[\varnothing]$). Each process i maintains its own private environment consisting of a frame and a heap $\langle \sigma^i, h^i \rangle \in \Lambda = \{H \times E\} \cup \bot$, where $\bot$ is considered to be an error state.

Uncertainty Map. For each process, Diamont defines an *uncertainty map* (D) to attach each variable with a uncertain interval, consisting of a maximum absolute error (ϵ), and a probability/confidence (δ) that the true error is below ϵ.

Local Semantics. The small-step relation $\boxed{\langle s, \langle \sigma,h \rangle, \mu, D \rangle \xrightarrow{p}_\psi \langle s', \langle \sigma',h' \rangle, \mu', D' \rangle}$ defines a process in the program evaluating in its local frame σ, heap h,

$$\text{calc-eps}(e,D) = \begin{cases} 0 & e \text{ is a constant} \\ D[x].\epsilon & e \text{ is a variable } x \\ D[x].\epsilon + D[y].\epsilon & e \text{ is } x \pm y \\ |x| \times D[y].\epsilon + |y| \times D[x].\epsilon + D[x].\epsilon \times D[y].\epsilon & e \text{ is } x \times y \\ \infty & e \text{ is } x \div y \ \wedge \ 0 \in [y \pm D[y].\epsilon] \\ \dfrac{(|x| \times D[y].\epsilon + |y| \times D[x].\epsilon)}{(|y| \times (|y| - D[y].\epsilon))} & e \text{ is } x \div y \ \wedge \ 0 \notin [y \pm D[y].\epsilon] \end{cases}$$

$$\text{calc-del}(e,D) = \max\left(0, \left(\Sigma_{x \in \rho(e)} D[x].\delta\right) - (|\rho(e)| - 1)\right)$$

$$\text{cast-eps}(x,v,D) = \max(\max(x + D[x].\epsilon, v + D[x].\epsilon) - v, v - \min(x - D[x].\epsilon, v - D[x].\epsilon)))$$

Fig. 5. Runtime for dynamic monitoring of uncertainty

uncertainty map D, and the global channel set μ. Figure 4 presents a selection of the semantics.

- **Initialization:** Each dynamic variable is initialized by setting the maximum error ϵ to 0 and the confidence δ to 1.
- **Expressions:** The S-Assign-Dyn rule in Fig. 4 is applied when a dynamic variable is updated by assigning it an expression e. We use a big-step evaluation relation of the form $\boxed{\langle e, \sigma, h \rangle \Downarrow v}$ to compute the result of the expression. Diamont supports typical integer and floating point operations.
  For dynamic variables, in addition to the assigned variable, Diamont updates its interval using the uncertain interval arithmetic defined in Fig. 5. The calc-eps function is used to calculate an expression's maximum error. The confidence in this maximum error is then computed using calc-del ($\rho(e)$ returns the list of variables used in an expression e.) To avoid any assumptions about the independence of the uncertainties (prior approaches such as [6] restrictively assumed all the operations and probability of failures are independent) Diamont uses the conservative union bound.
- **Communication:** When sending dynamic variables of type T to another process (rule S-DynSend), Diamont uses special channels (D_T) that are assumed to be fully reliable to communicate the relevant uncertain intervals before sending the data.[1] At the receiver (rule S-DynReceive), Diamont updates the local uncertainty map. Diamont assumes the channel failure rate is independent of the message content and reduces the confidence based on the failure rate defined in the Uncertainty Model.
- **Precision Manipulation:** Diamont monitors the errors introduced to programs through *cast* statements that change the precision of values of the same general type (int or float). In the rule S-Cast, the added error is calculated using the cast-eps(x,v,D) function using the casted value v and the original variable x. Confidence remains the same.

---

[1] ++ denotes adding a element to the end of the message queue.

- **Conditionals:** For branching on `dynamic` values, Diamont supports an operator x = `cond?` $e_1 : e_2$ (conditional choice) where `cond` compares a `dynamic` value against a threshold. We check if the *entire* interval associated with the value is greater or less than the threshold. If neither case is true, we compute both expressions and the interval of x becomes the smallest closed interval that contains all possible intervals.
- **Checks:** If a check fails, the Diamont program transitions into an error state (Fig. 4 rule `S-Check-Fail`). To prevent such check failures, the user can implement error recovery mechanisms.

Global Semantics. We define a global configuration as $\langle \epsilon, \mu, \omega, P \rangle$, consisting of a global environment $\epsilon \in Env = Pid \mapsto \Lambda$, a set of typed channels $\mu \in Channel = Pid \times Pid \times Type \rightarrow Val^*$, global uncertainty map $\omega \in Pid \mapsto D$, and the program P. Small step transitions of the form $\boxed{(\epsilon, \omega, \mu, P) \xrightarrow{\alpha, r}_{\psi} (\epsilon', \omega', \mu', P')}$ define a process α taking a step and thus changing the global configuration. Inter-process communication happens using the typed channels – though processes adding to and reading from the relevant queue. Complete semantics are available in Appendix A.

3.3   Soundness of Runtime Monitoring

Diamont's runtime system works across distributed processes. We use *Canonical Sequentialization* [3] to simplify our reasoning about the soundness of the runtime system. Canonical sequentialization uses the assumption that correct programs tend to be well-structured to generate a sequential program that over-approximates the semantics of a parallel program. If such a sequentialized program can be generated, then the parallel program is deadlock-free, and local safety properties that hold for the sequentialized program also hold for the parallel program.

To be sequentializable, the parallel program must be *symmetrically nondeterministic* – each receive statement must only have a single matching send statement, or a set of symmetric matching send statements[2]. We use a set of rewrite rules of the form $\boxed{\Gamma, \mathcal{S}, P \rightsquigarrow \Gamma', \mathcal{S}', P'}$ to rewrite a parallel program P to a sequential program $\mathcal{S}'$ step by step (the rules are available in Appendix C). The *context* Γ is used as a symbolic set of messages in flight, and P' is the part of the parallel program that remains to be rewritten. The sequentialization process applies the rewrite steps until the entire program is rewritten to $\mathcal{S}'$. We extend the results from prior work [3,19] to show that rewrite rules maintain equivalent behavior between the original parallel program and the generated sequential program, i.e., they both produce the same environment and uncertainty map at the halting states of the programs.

---

[2] Many popular parallel application patterns (e.g. Map, Reduce, Scatter-Gather, Stencil) exhibit symmetric non-determinism [3,19]. Further, programs satisfying this property can be less error-prone [3].

$$\mathcal{S}=[]$$
$$P=\begin{bmatrix} \text{int } \alpha.\text{n} = 1 \text{ [r] 0;} \\ \text{send}(\beta, \text{ int, } \alpha.\text{n}); \end{bmatrix}_\alpha \quad \| \quad \begin{bmatrix} \text{int } \beta.\text{x;} \\ \beta.\text{x = receive}(\alpha, \text{ int}); \end{bmatrix}_\beta \quad \leadsto^* \quad \mathcal{S}=\begin{bmatrix} \text{int } \alpha.\text{n} = 1 \text{ [r] 0;} \\ \text{int } \beta.\text{x;} \\ \beta.\text{x = } \alpha.\text{n;} \end{bmatrix}$$
$$P=[\text{skip;}]$$

Fig. 6. Canonical sequentialization: an example of the rewriting process.

Figure 6 shows a small program with inter-process communication (P) and its canonical sequentialization ($\mathcal{S}$) generated using the rewrite rules. We show that the existence of a canonical sequentialization guarantees that uncertain intervals are not affected by the different possible interleavings of processes during execution, allowing us to generate correct monitoring code.

In contrast, consider the following program where the process α has a receive statement that receives from two other processes:

$$\begin{bmatrix} \alpha.\text{res = receive}(*); \end{bmatrix}_\alpha \quad \| \quad \begin{bmatrix} \beta.\text{out = func1();} \\ \text{send}(\alpha, \beta.\text{out}); \end{bmatrix}_\beta \quad \| \quad \begin{bmatrix} \gamma.\text{out = func2();} \\ \text{send}(\alpha, \gamma.\text{out}); \end{bmatrix}_\gamma$$

The final value of **res** depends on the runtime interleavings and it is difficult to generate monitoring code at compilation time that soundly calculates an uncertain interval combining all possible interleavings. Therefore, we limit our analysis only to programs with canonical sequentializations and prove that the runtime is sound.

We use the notation developed in Chisel [26] to state the following soundness theorem. Recall that Diamont's runtime monitors two properties for each **dynamic** variable x: (1) the maximum possible error magnitude ($D[x].\epsilon$) and (2) a probability ($D[x].\delta$) that the *precise* value of x is within $x \pm D[x].\epsilon$. The notation $\Delta(x)$ denotes the *true error* of a variable x, and $[\![\mathcal{R}^*[E]]\!](\sigma, \varphi)$ denotes the *true probability* that an environment σ sampled from the *environment distribution* φ satisfies the error comparison E.

Theorem 1 (Soundness of dynamic monitoring). *For programs not containing* **track** *and* **endorse** *statements, for all statements s, and for all x s.t. $\Theta \vdash x : dynamic\ t$, $\Theta \vdash s : \Theta'$ and $\langle s, \langle \sigma, D, \varphi \rangle \rangle \Downarrow \langle s', \langle \sigma', D', \varphi' \rangle \rangle$ $\implies [\![\mathcal{R}^*[D'[x].\epsilon \geq \Delta(x)]]\!](\sigma', \varphi') \geq D'[x].\delta$*

First, we use induction over the sequential subset of Diamont to show that, if the program s type checks, and evaluates in the global environment σ and uncertainty map D to s', resulting in the environment σ' and uncertainty map D', then, for all dynamic variables x, the *true error* of x is at most by $D'[x].\epsilon$ with probability at least $D'[x].\delta$. This indicates that we soundly over-approximate the uncertainty of x.

Next, we utilize canonical sequentialization to prove that the theorem holds for the parallel subset of the language as well. First, we extend the results from [19] to prove that if we can rewrite a parallel program P into a sequential program $\mathcal{S}$, then P and $\mathcal{S}$ have equivalent behavior. We use this fact to reason that our proof of soundness for the sequential subset of Diamont is also

$$
\begin{array}{ll}
1 \\
2 \\
3
\end{array}
\left[
\begin{array}{l}
\text{dyn-send}(\beta,\ \text{dynamic t},\ \alpha.\text{in}); \\
\alpha.\text{out} = \text{dyn-recv}(\beta,\ \text{dynamic t}); \\
\text{check}(\alpha.\text{out},\ d_{\text{check}},\ r_{\text{check}});
\end{array}
\right]_{\alpha}
\ \|\
\begin{array}{l}
4 \\
5 \\
6 \\
7
\end{array}
\left[
\begin{array}{l}
\beta.\text{dat} = \text{dyn-recv}(\alpha,\ \text{dynamic t}); \\
\text{// spec: } \langle d \geq \Delta(\text{res}), r*\mathcal{R}^*[(d_i \geq \Delta(\text{dat}))] \ \rangle \\
\beta.\text{res} = \text{fn}(\beta.\text{dat}); \\
\text{dyn-send}(\alpha,\ \text{dynamic t},\ \beta.\text{res});
\end{array}
\right]_{\beta}
$$

$$\Downarrow$$

$$
\begin{array}{ll}
8 \\
9 \\
10 \\
11 \\
12
\end{array}
\left[
\begin{array}{l}
\text{check}(\alpha.\text{in},\ d_i,\ 0); \\
\text{send}(\beta,\ \text{approx t},\ \alpha.\text{in}); \\
\alpha.\text{tmp} = \text{receive}(\beta,\ \text{approx t}); \\
\alpha.\text{out} = \text{track}(\alpha.\text{tmp},d,r*\text{rdDyn}(\alpha.\text{in}).\delta); \\
\text{check}(\alpha.\text{out},\ d_{\text{check}},\ r_{\text{check}});
\end{array}
\right]_{\alpha}
\ \|\
\begin{array}{l}
13 \\
14 \\
15 \\
16
\end{array}
\left[
\begin{array}{l}
\beta.\text{dat} = \text{receive}(\alpha,\ \text{approx t}); \\
\text{//}\langle d \geq \Delta(\text{res}), r*\mathcal{R}^*[(d_i \geq \Delta(\text{dat}))] \ \rangle \\
\beta.\text{res} = \text{fn}(\beta.\text{dat}); \\
\text{send}(\alpha,\ \text{approx t},\ \beta.\text{res});
\end{array}
\right]_{\beta}
$$

Fig. 7. Optimizations using static analysis in Diamont.

applicable to parallel programs that can be canonically sequentialized. Therefore, Theorem 1 holds and our overall analysis is sound (full proof is available in Appendix D).

Our analysis only applies to programs with **track** and **endorse** statements if developers use them in a sound manner. For **track** statements, developers must ensure that the bounds they provide are a sound over-approximation of the true uncertainty at that program point. As in prior work [37], by inserting **endorse** statements, developers certify that treating the relevant **approx** or **dynamic** value as **precise** is always safe and will not result in undesirable behavior.

4   Optimizations for Reducing Overhead

We implemented several optimizations that transform the programs to reduce the overhead of dynamic monitoring and proved them to be sound.

Communication. When communicating large **dynamic** type arrays, Diamont must also communicate the uncertain interval for each array element, resulting in a large communication overhead. One way to reduce this overhead is to calculate a single conservative approximation of the set of uncertain intervals for the array elements. For example, the maximum error of any element of an array can be soundly over-approximated by the largest maximum error among all of its elements (similarly, the smallest error confidence). The process sending the data calculates the conservative approximation while using the regular communication primitives for the data. At the end it sends the conservatively approximate uncertain interval. At the receiver, this uncertain interval is taken as the uncertain interval of *each* element in the received array and the compiler adds track statements to restart dynamic monitoring.

This optimization does not approximate the uncertain interval of the array at all program points, rather it affects only communication statements. Even with the resulting loss in precision of the analysis, Diamont still achieves better results than existing static analyses which use a single uncertain interval for arrays through the *entire* program.

Utilizing Static Analysis. We can further reduce overheads by exploiting common communication patterns. For example, the program at the top of Fig. 7 contains a remote procedure call. Process α sends an input to process β, which applies the function fn to the input and returns the value. Transferring uncertain intervals along with the data can become expensive if many such calls are made.

We use existing static analysis techniques [10, 19, 26] to analyze only the remote function call and generate function specifications (precise semantics are in Appendix A Fig. 9), even if they are unable to analyze the entire program. Consider the transformed program at the bottom of Fig. 7. Using the specification, Diamont produces the same behavior as the original program by generating code to 1) check if the specification requirements are satisfied (Line 8), 2) transfer the data as approx type (Line 9), 3) compute without dynamic monitoring, and 4) re-initialize dynamic monitoring using the error guarantees from the specification (Line 11).

This optimization can be safely used when the function performs no communication and has no other side effects. However, it may not be possible to verify some static specifications at runtime. For example: the runtime will not be able to calculate $\mathcal{R}^*[\,d_i \geq \Delta(\mathtt{dat})\,]$ for some values for d_i. Therefore, this optimization may introduce some imprecision to the dynamic monitoring.

Early Checking. For a subset of instructions we can perform static analysis to stop runtime monitoring earlier. We perform this task by *moving up* the check to the earliest possible location using a set of rewrites. This rewrite rule is one such example:

$$\begin{bmatrix} \alpha.x = \alpha.a + \alpha.b; \\ \mathtt{check(AExp, \ d, \ r)}; \end{bmatrix} \Rightarrow \begin{bmatrix} \mathtt{check(AExp[(\alpha.a+\alpha.b)/\alpha.x], \ d, \ r)}; \\ \alpha.x = \alpha.a + \alpha.b; \end{bmatrix}$$

In this rule, Diamont looks for a check immediately following an addition. Since the error magnitude of the result of the addition is the sum of the error magnitudes of the variables that are being added, we can substitute the result variable $\alpha.x$ in the check with $\alpha.a + \alpha.b$. As the calc-del function of the runtime looks for the set of variables in the specification (AExp), the error probability is calculated correctly as well. Diamont can now safely move the check before the addition.

These re-write rules closely follow the static analysis as defined and proven sound in [19] for the sequential subset of the language (Appendix D.2.2). This optimization reduces updates to the uncertainty map as monitoring can be stopped after the check is performed. However, it can only be applied when the check refers to variables from a single process. Further, the check cannot be moved up if error calculations depend on the value of variables (as in multiplication/division).

Debloating and Compiler Optimizations. Diamont further reduces overhead by using constant propagation and dead code elimination to remove unnecessary updates to the uncertainty map. In addition, Diamont eliminates either error magnitude monitoring or confidence monitoring based on the checks in

$$s^{seq} = \begin{bmatrix} \beta.\mathtt{dat} = \alpha.\mathtt{in}; \\ \beta.\mathtt{res} = \mathtt{fn}(\beta.\mathtt{dat}); \\ \alpha.\mathtt{out} = \beta.\mathtt{res}; \\ \mathtt{check}(\alpha.\mathtt{out}, d_{\mathtt{check}}, r_{\mathtt{check}}); \end{bmatrix} \quad s^{seq}_{opt} = \begin{bmatrix} \mathtt{check}(\alpha.\mathtt{in}, d_i, 0); \\ \beta.\mathtt{dat} = \alpha.\mathtt{in}; \\ \beta.\mathtt{res} = \mathtt{fn}(\beta.\mathtt{dat}); \\ \alpha.\mathtt{tmp} = \beta.\mathtt{res}; \\ \alpha.\mathtt{out} = \mathtt{track}(\alpha.\mathtt{tmp},d,r*\mathtt{rdDyn}(\alpha.\mathtt{in}).\delta); \\ \mathtt{check}(\alpha.\mathtt{out}, d_{\mathtt{check}}, r_{\mathtt{check}}); \end{bmatrix}$$

Fig. 8. Example sequentializations used in the proofs

the program. For example, if all checks require the error magnitude to be zero (reliability in [10]) Diamont will only calculate confidence at runtime.

4.1 Soundness

For each optimization we show that both the original program (s) and the optimized version (s_{opt}) produce the same behavior, i.e., if the original program fails a check, the optimized version is also guaranteed to fail. Canonical sequentialization makes such proofs easier. Formally, we define the soundness of an optimization as follows:

Definition 1 (Optimization soundness). *For a program s and its optimized version s_{opt}, $\langle s, \langle \sigma, h \rangle, \mu, D \rangle \longrightarrow^*_\psi \langle s', \bot, \_, \_\rangle \implies \langle s_{opt}, \langle \sigma, h \rangle, \mu, D \rangle \longrightarrow^*_\psi \langle s'', \bot, \_, \_\rangle$*

This definition states that if there is an execution where the original program s starting from an environment σ, heap h, uncertainty map D, and the global channel set μ evaluates to s' and enters into the error state ($\bot$), the optimized version s_{opt} starting from the same state σ, heap h, and D must also enter the error state (even if the final channel or uncertainty map states differ).

For each optimization, we show that the pairs s and s_{opt} are sound according to this definition. Consider the static analysis based optimization in Fig. 7. Proving the soundness of this optimization requires us to show that the two parallel programs produce the same result with regards to the dynamic monitoring. We can simplify this process significantly by using sequentialization. We first show that the two versions of the program can be sequentialized to s^{seq} and s^{seq}_{opt} in Fig. 8. These sequentializations produce final environments that are equivalent to the original versions as proven in Lemma 1 (Appendix C). We can now simplify the proof to reasoning over the two sequential programs s^{seq} and s^{seq}_{opt}. We can next argue over all executions resulting in a check failure in s^{seq} and show that they result in a check failure in s^{seq}_{opt} (The full proofs are in Appendix D).

5   Methodology

Implementation and Testing Setup. We parsed and translated Go programs written using a library of Diamont primitives to Diamont-IR using ANTLR. We

Table 1. Benchmarks, verified properties, and runtime monitoring overhead for Diamont. Baselines: ⋆:Decaf, †:AffineFloat

Benchmark	Pattern	Uncertainty source	Verified property	Overhead	
				Baseline	Diamont
PageRank	Scatter-Gather	Noisy Channel	checkArr(pagerank, 0, 0.9912)	30%⋆	3.63%
SSSP	Scatter-Gather	Noisy Channel	checkArr(distance, 0, 0.9925)	33%⋆	2.31%
BFS	Scatter-Gather	Noisy Channel	checkArr(visited, 0, 0.9925)	30%⋆	4.06%
SOR	Stencil	Precision Reduction	checkArr(output, 1.19×10^{-7}, 1)	60%†	3.49%
Sobel	Stencil	Precision Reduction	checkArr(output, 2.38×10^{-7}, 1)	71%†	9.71%
Matrix Mult.	Map	Precision Reduction	checkArr(product, 6.6×10^{-6}, 1)	80%†	16.27%
Kmeans-Agri	Map	Noisy Channel, Input	checkArr(centers, $\langle 1.5, 0.9948\rangle$, $\langle 2,0.9948\rangle$)	42%⋆†	3.32%
Regression	Map-Reduce	Timing Error	check(alpha, 0, 0.99)∧check(beta, 0, 0.99)	37%⋆	0.45%

used Python to sequentialize Diamont programs for checking properties such as type safety and deadlock-freedom, and then for generating instrumented Go code. We implemented distributed communication using RabbitMQ 3.8.7. We ran our experiments on a machine with a Xeon E5-1650 v4 CPU, 32 GB RAM, and Ubuntu 18.04. Each benchmark consisted of 8–10 worker processes.

Benchmarks. We implemented a set of popular parallel benchmarks from prior literature that exhibit diverse parallel patterns and verified properties that quantify uncertainty in their executions (Table 1). We looked at the following benchmarks:

- *PageRank, SSSP, BFS:* Graph benchmarks commonly used in distributed Big Data applications. PageRank is used for search result optimization [27]. Single Source Shortest Path is used to make data routing decisions. Breadth First Search is used to find connected components in graphs. From CRONO [2].
- *SOR:* A kernel for successive over-relaxation. Used to extrapolate the state of a system over time. From Chisel [26].
- *Sobel:* Sobel edge-detection filter. From AxBench [44].
- *Matrix Mult.:* Multiplies two square matrices. Each worker process computes a subset of rows of the product.
- *Kmeans-Agri:* Partitions n-dimensional input points into k clusters (Sect. 2).
- *Regression:* Performs distributed linear regression on 2-D data. Each worker performs regression on a subset of data. The master thread averages the results.

Inputs. The inputs for each benchmark used for our experiments are shown in Appendix E. For Sect. 6.3, we used larger inputs created by increasing the size of the array, the number of samples, or by using a larger input graph.

Sources of Uncertainty. *Noisy channels* occasionally corrupt data sent over them (used for PageRank, SSSP, BFS, and Kmeans-Agri). We use a corruption rate of 10^{-7}. *Precision reduction* reduces floating point precision from 64-bit to 32-bit during communication only to save bandwidth (used in SOR, Sobel, Matrix Mult.). The *input* provided to the program itself can have inherent uncertainty. For Kmeans-Agri, we assume a 50:50 mixture of two different temperature-humidity sensors with different error specifications. *Timing errors* can cause the program to use stale or incomplete values (used for Regression).

Baselines. We compare the runtime of Diamont with optimizations to a baseline which is a straightforward parallel implementation of an existing static analysis via Diamont (either Decaf [6] or AffineFloat [13] without roundoff errors).

6 Evaluation

6.1 Can We Verify Important Uncertainty Properties Using Diamont?

For each benchmark, we used Diamont to verify the properties shown in Column 3 of Table 1. Diamont successfully verified these properties on the final output of the program. Each check places an error magnitude and confidence bound on a single variable. For arrays each element must satisfy these bounds. For PageRank, SSSP, and BFS, the bounds ensure that key graph properties are calculated exactly $\geq$99% of the time per node. For SOR, Sobel and Matrix Mult., the bounds limit the maximum error of the output due precision reduction. Kmeans-Agri was discussed in the example. For Regression, the bounds ensure that the output line parameters are correct $\geq$99% of the time (high confidence is desirable for predictive models).

Parallely [19] cannot verify these properties. Diamont's dynamic analysis of arrays and unbounded loops more effectively handles irregular input structure (e.g., graphs), which had to be conservatively bounded for static analysis. This allowed us to verify stronger properties for significantly bigger inputs than previously possible for existing reliability and accuracy static analyses. We observed that, even in the presence of errors, the error magnitude of the final outputs of our programs was acceptable.

Optimizations can affect the precision of the analysis. This effect is prominent in benchmarks with irregular computations (graph benchmarks). However, in our benchmarks, we found that baseline and optimized Diamont could verify nearly the same uncertainty bounds. For example, for BFS, Diamont could verify a confidence of 0.999 when using the baseline version. For benchmarks with regular computation patterns, such as SOR and Regression, there was no significant change.

> In summary, *Diamont verifies important end-to-end uncertainty properties that cannot be verified using existing static analyses.*

6.2 What Are the Overheads Associated with Diamont?

Columns 4 and 5 of Table 1 present the overhead of the baseline and optimized Diamont benchmarks respectively. Time for I/O and setup is excluded. Overhead is calculated as the percentage increase in runtime w.r.t. an unmonitored benchmark.

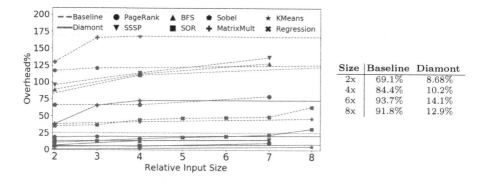

Fig. 9. Input size vs. Overhead. Table shows geomean overheads across programs.

In our benchmarks, the runtime is dominated by communication, as is common in many distributed settings. In most cases, the runtime overhead for computing the uncertain intervals is a small fraction of the total runtime. Error magnitude calculation requires more computation than error confidence (see Fig. 5). As a result, overhead for error magnitude benchmarks (SOR, Sobel, Matrix Mult.), is higher. This was especially true for the computationally intensive Matrix Mult.

Optimization Impact. The Regression benchmark used a statically verified kernel error specification to eliminate monitoring. The communication optimization contributes around 98% of savings in all other benchmarks. Debloating also provided significant speedups. For example, without debloating PageRank is 3.9x slower and Sobel is 3.3x slower (our baseline is comparable to Diamont with debloating).

Are the Overheads Justified? Approximations have led to significant savings in prior work: 1) Communication: up to 62% performance improvement in approximate NoCs [11,17], and 2) Computation: 2x speedup in loop perforation [40], 2.7x speedup in Paraprox [34], and up to 1.3x speedup from reduced precision in Precimonious [33]. As Diamont's post-optimization overhead is lower than the speedups from these approximations, it can be used in conjunction with them to provide guarantees on the quality of results while still getting speedups.

> In summary, *With optimization, overhead of Diamont analysis is at most 16.3% for our benchmarks, with a geomean of 3.04%.*

6.3   How Does Diamont Overhead Depend on the Program Inputs?

Figure 9 shows the effect of input size on Diamont overhead. The X-Axis shows the relative input size and the Y-Axis shows overhead. The dashed and solid lines show the unoptimized baseline and optimized Diamont versions respectively. Each marker indicates a different benchmark. Overall, the overhead of the optimized versions is significantly lower than the baseline versions. Most optimized versions have an overhead less than 25% for all inputs. The table in Fig. 9 shows the geomean of the overhead across all benchmarks for different relative input sizes. While baseline overhead increases to an average of 94%, optimized overhead only reaches 14%.

For Matrix Mult., computation increases faster with input size than communication ($O(n^3)$ vs. $O(n^2)$). Thus the major source of overhead becomes the computation of the monitored uncertainty, rather than communication. This benchmark illustrates that Diamont is more useful in cases where the program is communication-bound.

The unoptimized baseline also sends significantly more data (3x to 5x) compared to the optimized version. This is due to the array communication optimization. The communication overhead of the optimized version is negligible.

In summary, *as input size grows, the improvement caused by optimizations on Diamont runtime performance increases over the baseline runtime system.*

7 Related Work

Several analyses are related (in part) to Diamont's functionality, as shown in Table 2. Columns 2–4 indicate whether the analysis is static, empirical (sampling-based), or runtime based. Columns 5–6 indicate support for error confidence (reliability) and error magnitude (accuracy) analysis. Column 9 indicates if the system can support multiple sources of uncertainty. In contrast to all these analyses, Diamont is the only one flexible enough to simultaneously support *multiple* analyses and approximation sources, and in addition, extending these to *parallel* programs.

Static Analyses for Approximate Programs. Though multiple static analyses target approximate programs (e.g., [8,9,12,23,26,28,35,37]), most relevant to Diamont is Parallely [19], which retains the limitations of the underlying static analyses requiring developers to provide bounds on loop iterations, array sizes, and number of processes. In contrast, Diamont successfully combines static and dynamic analysis and works on a real language (Go), which jointly allow for verification of much larger benchmarks. Additionally, Diamont also extends sequentialization for dynamic conditions.

Dynamic Analysis and Runtime Monitoring. DECAF [6] performs dynamic reliability verification through type inference. Our work avoids DECAF's strict independence assumptions by adding reliabilities instead of multiplying (both bounds are close in practice). Ringenburg et al. [32] propose offline and online approaches to monitor the quality of programs, using methods such as dataflow techniques and comparison to the precise program. Diamont instead propagates uncertain intervals during both static and dynamic phases, allowing it to monitor uncertainty with greater precision. Maderbacher et al. [25] focus on precisely correcting bitflips with minimal checks. In contrast, Diamont monitors uncertainty from many sources in programs that can tolerate some error.

Table 2. Comparison of Related Work. ($\checkmark*$ indicate analyses that monitor confidence intervals, which is another interpretation of Diamont's uncertain intervals)

Method	Static	Empirical	Runtime	Reliability	Accuracy	Verified	Parallel	Multi-Source
Diamont	$\checkmark$	$\times$	$\checkmark$	$\checkmark$	$\checkmark$	$\checkmark$	$\checkmark$	$\checkmark$
Parallely	$\checkmark$	$\times$	$\times$	$\checkmark$	$\checkmark$	$\checkmark$	$\checkmark$	$\checkmark$
Rely	$\checkmark$	$\times$	$\times$	$\checkmark$	$\times$	$\checkmark$	$\times$	$\times$
Chisel	$\checkmark$	$\checkmark$	$\times$	$\checkmark$	$\checkmark$	$\checkmark$	$\times$	$\checkmark$
DECAF	$\checkmark$	$\times$	$\checkmark$	$\checkmark$	$\times$	$\checkmark$	$\times$	$\times$
EnerJ	$\checkmark$	$\checkmark$	$\times$	$\times$	$\times$	$\checkmark$	$\times$	$\times$
AffineFloat	$\checkmark$	$\times$	$\checkmark$	$\times$	$\checkmark$	$\checkmark$	$\times$	$\times$
PAssert	$\times$	$\checkmark$	$\checkmark$	$\checkmark*$	$\checkmark*$	$\checkmark$	$\times$	$\times$
Uncertain<T>	$\times$	$\checkmark$	$\checkmark$	$\checkmark*$	$\checkmark*$	$\times$	$\times$	$\times$

AffineFloat [13] and Ceres [14] provide dynamic analysis for numerical error. Herbgrind [38] locates possible sources of numerical error. These tools measure floating point roundoff errors, but have high overhead. Diamont focuses on analyzing error from casting and external sources e.g., sensors. Uncertain$\langle$T$\rangle$ [4] used an early form of uncertain intervals, however they use sampling to determine error. Statistical model checking tools [39] can provide statistical guarantees on program properties expressed in a temporal logic. PAssert [36] and AxProf [21] statistically verify at development time a single probabilistic assertion at the end of the program. In contrast, Diamont supports many checks at different points in the program at runtime.

8   Conclusion

The past decade brought many techniques for developing new approximations and analyzing uncertainty for specific scenarios, but much less work has been done in integrating these diverse concepts in a unifying, rigorous, and extensible framework. Diamont aims to pave the way toward that goal – it supports multiple uncertainty sources (input noise, variable-precision code, errors in communication, and unreliability in hardware), combines static analysis and dynamic monitoring, supports a significant fragment of the Go language, and operates on several emerging applications (precision agriculture, graph analytics, and media processing).

We demonstrated the benefit of our analysis and optimizations by reducing the execution overhead to 3% on average (16.3% maximum). We believe this work can serve as a starting point for sound runtime systems in domains that need to rigorously handle uncertainty, such as robotics or the Internet-of-Things.

Acknowledgements. We thank the anonymous reviewers for their useful suggestions. The research presented in this paper was supported in part by NSF Grants No. CCF-1846354, CCF-1956374, CCF-2028861, and CCF-2008883, USDA Grant No. NIFA-2024827, and a gift from Facebook.

References

1. Achour, S., Rinard, M.: Energy efficient approximate computation with Topaz. In: OOPSLA (2015)
2. Ahmad, M., Hijaz, F., Shi, Q., Khan, O.: CRONO: a benchmark suite for multithreaded graph algorithms executing on futuristic multicores. In: IISWC (2015)
3. Bakst, A., Gleissenthall, K.v., Kici, R.G., Jhala, R.: Verifying distributed programs via canonical sequentialization. In: OOPSLA (2017)
4. Bornholt, J., Mytkowicz, T., McKinley, K.S.: Uncertain <T>: a first-order type for uncertain data. In: ASPLOS (2014)
5. Boston, B., Gong, Z., Carbin, M.: Leto: verifying application-specific hardware fault tolerance with programmable execution models. In: OOPSLA (2018)
6. Boston, B., Sampson, A., Grossman, D., Ceze, L.: Probability type inference for flexible approximate programming. In: OOPSLA (2015)
7. Boyapati, R., Huang, J., Majumder, P., Yum, K.H., Kim, E.J.: APPROX-NoC: a data approximation framework for network-on-chip architectures. In: ISCA (2017)
8. Carbin, M., Kim, D., Misailovic, S., Rinard, M.: Proving acceptability properties of relaxed nondeterministic approximate programs. PLDI **47**, 169–180 (2012)
9. Carbin, M., Kim, D., Misailovic, S., Rinard, M.: Verified integrity properties for safe approximate program transformations. In: PEPM (2013)
10. Carbin, M., Misailovic, S., Rinard, M.: Verifying quantitative reliability for programs that execute on unreliable hardware. In: OOPSLA (2013)
11. Chen, Y., Louri, A.: An approximate communication framework for network-on-chips. IEEE Trans. Parallel Distrib. Syst. **31**, 1434–1446 (2020)
12. Darulova, E., Izycheva, A., Nasir, F., Ritter, F., Becker, H., Bastian, R.: Daisy-framework for analysis and optimization of numerical programs. In: TACAS (2018)
13. Darulova, E., Kuncak, V.: Trustworthy numerical computation in Scala. In: OOPSLA (2011)
14. Darulova, E., Kuncak, V.: Certifying solutions for numerical constraints. In: Qadeer, S., Tasiran, S. (eds.) RV 2012. LNCS, vol. 7687, pp. 277–291. Springer, Heidelberg (2013). https://doi.org/10.1007/978-3-642-35632-2_27
15. de Kruijf, M., Nomura, S., Sankaralingam, K.: Relax: an architectural framework for software recovery of hardware faults. ISCA **38**, 497–508 (2010)
16. Dean, J., Ghemawat, S.: MapReduce: simplified data processing on large clusters. OSDI (2004)
17. Fernando, V., Franques, A., Abadal, S., Misailovic, S., Torrellas, J.: Replica: a wireless manycore for communication-intensive and approximate data. In: ASPLOS (2019)
18. Fernando, V., Joshi, K., Laurel, J., Misailovic, S.: Appendix to Diamont (2021). https://vimuth.github.io/diamont/appendix.pdf
19. Fernando, V., Joshi, K., Misailovic, S.: Verifying safety and accuracy of approximate parallel programs via canonical sequentialization. In: OOPSLA (2019)
20. Golubovic, N., Krintz, C., Wolski, R., Sethuramasamyraja, B., Liu, B.: A scalable system for executing and scoring K-means clustering techniques and its impact on applications in agriculture. Int. J. Big Data Intell. **6**, 163–175 (2019)
21. Joshi, K., Fernando, V., Misailovic, S.: Statistical algorithmic profiling for randomized approximate programs. In: ICSE (2019)
22. Joshi, K., Fernando, V., Misailovic, S.: Aloe: verifying reliability of approximate programs in the presence of recovery mechanisms. In: CGO (2020)

23. Lahiri, S., Haran, A., He, S., Rakamaric, Z.: Automated differential program verification for approximate computing. Technical report (2015)

24. Liu, T.: Datasheet for AM2302 Sensor (2020). https://cdn-shop.adafruit.com/datasheets/Digital+humidity+and+temperature+sensor+AM2302.pdf

25. Maderbacher, B., Karl, A.F., Bloem, R.: Placement of runtime checks to counteract fault injections. In: Deshmukh, J., Ničković, D. (eds.) RV 2020. LNCS, vol. 12399, pp. 241–258. Springer, Cham (2020). https://doi.org/10.1007/978-3-030-60508-7_13

26. Misailovic, S., Carbin, M., Achour, S., Qi, Z., Rinard, M.: Chisel: reliability- and accuracy-aware optimization of approximate computational kernels. In: OOPSLA (2014)

27. Page, L., Brin, S., Motwani, R., Winograd, T.: The PageRank citation ranking: bringing order to the web. Technical report (1999)

28. Panchekha, P., Sanchez-Stern, A., Wilcox, J.R., Tatlock, Z.: Automatically improving accuracy for floating point expressions. In: PLDI (2015)

29. Paradis, L., Han, Q.: A survey of fault management in wireless sensor networks. J. Netw. Syst. Manag. **15**, 171–190 (2007). https://doi.org/10.1007/s10922-007-9062-0

30. Ranjan, A., Venkataramani, S., Fong, X., Roy, K., Raghunathan, A.: Approximate storage for energy efficient spintronic memories. In: DAC 2015 (2015)

31. Recht, B., Re, C., Wright, S., Niu, F.: HOGWILD: a lock-free approach to parallelizing stochastic gradient descent. In: Advances in Neural Information Processing Systems (2011)

32. Ringenburg, M., Sampson, A., Ackerman, I., Ceze, L., Grossman, D.: Monitoring and debugging the quality of results in approximate programs. In: ASPLOS (2015)

33. Rubio-González, C., et al.: Precimonious: tuning assistant for floating-point precision. In: SC (2013)

34. Samadi, M., Jamshidi, D.A., Lee, J., Mahlke, S.: Paraprox: pattern-based approximation for data parallel applications. In: ASPLOS (2014)

35. Sampson, A., et al.: Accept: a programmer-guided compiler framework for practical approximate computing. Technical report (2015)

36. Sampson, A., Panchekha, P., Mytkowicz, T., McKinley, K., Grossman, D., Ceze, L.: Expressing and verifying probabilistic assertions. In: PLDI (2014)

37. Sampson, A., Dietl, W., Fortuna, E., Gnanapragasam, D., Ceze, L., Grossman, D.: EnerJ: approximate data types for safe and general low-power computation. In: PLDI (2011)

38. Sanchez-Stern, A., Panchekha, P., Lerner, S., Tatlock, Z.: Finding root causes of floating point error. In: PLDI (2018)

39. Sen, K., Viswanathan, M., Agha, G.: Statistical model checking of black-box probabilistic systems. In: Alur, R., Peled, D.A. (eds.) CAV 2004. LNCS, vol. 3114, pp. 202–215. Springer, Heidelberg (2004). https://doi.org/10.1007/978-3-540-27813-9_16

40. Sidiroglou, S., Misailovic, S., Hoffmann, H., Rinard, M.: Managing performance vs. accuracy trade-offs with loop perforation. In: FSE (2011)

41. Stanley-Marbell, P., et al.: Exploiting errors for efficiency: a survey from circuits to applications. ACM Comput. Surv. J. **53**, 1–39 (2020)

42. Stevens, J.R., Ranjan, A., Raghunathan, A.: AxBA: an approximate bus architecture framework. In: ICCAD (2018)

43. TensorFlow Developers: Tensorflow (2021). https://doi.org/10.5281/zenodo.5159865. https://www.tensorflow.org

44. Yazdanbakhsh, A., Mahajan, D., Esmaeilzadeh, H., Lotfi-Kamran, P.: AxBench: a multiplatform benchmark suite for approximate computing. IEEE Design Test **34**(2), 60–68 (2017)
45. Zhuang, W., Chen, X., Tan, J., Song, A.: An empirical analysis for evaluating the link quality of robotic sensor networks. In: WCSP (2009)

Assumption-Based Runtime Verification of Infinite-State Systems

Alessandro Cimatti, Chun Tian[(✉)], and Stefano Tonetta

Fondazione Bruno Kessler, Trento, Italy
{cimatti,ctian,tonettas}@fbk.eu

Abstract. Runtime Verification (RV) basically means monitoring an execution trace of a system under scrutiny and checking if the trace satisfies or violates a specification. In Assumption-Based Runtime Verification (ABRV), runtime monitors may be synthesized from not only the specification but also a system model (either full or partial), which represents the assumptions on which the input traces are expected to follow. With assumptions the monitor can additionally check if the input traces actually follow the assumptions. Some previous research has shown that monitors under assumptions can be more precise or even predictive, while non-monitorable specifications may become monitorable under assumptions.

The question of synthesizing runtime monitors for finite-state systems and propositional or first-order temporal logics, with or without assumptions, has mostly been answered by prior work. For monitoring infinite-state systems, however, most existing approaches focus on supporting parametric or first-order specifications while they cannot be easily extended to support assumptions.

This paper presents a general solution for ABRV of infinite-state systems by a reduction of RV problems to LTL Model Checking (MC), which is further based on Satisfiability Modulo Theories and other techniques. When First-Order Quantifier Elimination (QE) is also available, the corresponding algorithm can be greatly optimized. This solution is general because in theory any LTL MC (and QE) algorithms can be used, and the supported types of infinite-state variables also depend on these underlying algorithms. In particular, the relatively expensive model checking can be minimized by a modified version of Bounded Model Checking algorithm which performs model checking incrementally on each input of the monitor.

1 Introduction

Runtime Verification (RV) [15,20] is a lightweight verification technique aiming at monitoring the execution trace of a system under scrutiny (SUS) and checking if the trace satisfies or violates a specification. The central task in RV is *monitor synthesis*, i.e. generating from the specification a *runtime monitor*, which takes a run (execution trace) from the SUS and outputs *verdicts* for each states of the

© Springer Nature Switzerland AG 2021
L. Feng and D. Fisman (Eds.): RV 2021, LNCS 12974, pp. 207–227, 2021.
https://doi.org/10.1007/978-3-030-88494-9_11

run. Although a specification[1] exists within the context of a system model, i.e. the abstraction of the system being specified, the current taxonomy for classifying RV tools [21] does not consider synthesizing runtime monitors from a system model, in addition to the specification.

Assumption-Based Runtime Verification (ABRV) [13] extends the traditional Runtime Verification (RV) [20,29] by additionally assuming an underlying system model that the input traces are expected to follow. The resulting runtime monitor checks if, under the assumptions given by the model, the SUS execution satisfies or violates the property (and additionally if the execution is compliant with the assumption). Prior research [13,24,28] has shown that, for certain combinations of models and properties, assumption-based monitors are more precise (i.e. arriving at a conclusion based on the assumption while traditional monitors would be inconclusive), or even *predictive* (i.e. arriving at a conclusion before the input trace actually says so). In particular, if the monitor would never have reached a conclusive verdict, it might do so because of the assumption. Another advantage of the assumption-based approach is the possibility of monitoring properties over partially-observable systems, capturing as the assumption the relationship between observable and internal states of the SUS.

The question of synthesizing runtime monitors for finite-state systems and propositional temporal logics, with or without assumptions, has mostly been answered by prior work [1,4,13]. In particular, for ABRV, there exist effective automata-based approaches using Binary Decision Diagrams (BDD) [7] to represent belief states, i.e., the set of automata states where the system can be according to a sequence of (partial) observations.

In the case of infinite-state systems, of which the state variables may have infinite domains (such as integer, rational and real variables), the corresponding RV problem (i.e. monitoring LTL) can be in theory resolved by evaluating the property (Boolean) propositions over the non-Boolean variables. Going from propositional to first-order temporal logic (or even further), existing work mostly put a focus on supporting things like parametric specifications [34] or specifications with first-order quantifiers [23].

This paper presents a general new approach for ABRV of infinite-state systems (the related algorithms can also be applied to finite-state systems). Instead of relying on BDDs, which is used by NuRV [14] (the previous tool implementation of ABRV), the idea is based on Satisfiability Modulo Theories (SMT) [2]. We show how to reduce RV problems directly to SMT-based LTL Model Checking (MC) problems, then solvable by model checkers like nuXmv [8]. This solution is general because in theory any LTL MC (and QE) algorithms can be used, and the supported types of infinite-state variables also depend on these underlying algorithms. For the LTL semantics over finite traces, which is also the semantics of monitoring outputs, our choice is still based on LTL_3 [1] with respect to extra

---

[1] According to [21], a *specification* is a concrete description of a *property* (a partition of traces) using a well-defined formalism (like LTL). However, this difference is not very important here, and thus we use the words "property" and "specification" interchangeably for the rest of this paper.

verdicts (out-of-model) due to RV assumptions. In comparison with other possible LTL semantics for RV purposes [3], it turns out that, with our choice, there exists a simple and elegant reduction from RV to MC problems. If, additionally, First-Order Quantifier Elimination [33] is also available (for the chosen first-order theory), the corresponding algorithm can be greatly optimized, without seeing the monotonically growing of SMT formulas during the monitoring. In this case, the algorithm keeps track of a belief state, representing all states in which the system can be according to the assumption after a sequence of observation. The RV problem is then reduced to checking, after each observation, the emptiness checking of symbolic automata with the belief states as initial conditions.

However, there are performance bottlenecks in MC- or SMT-based RV approaches, in comparison with BDD-based approaches, because both model checking and quantifier elimination are computationally heavy. To this purpose, we extend the basic RV-MC reductions with optimizations that perform (relatively cheap) incomplete checks instead of the more expensive model checking calls. One such optimization is to always check first the literal emptiness of the belief state by SMT solvers, the other is to use the incomplete plain Bounded Model Checking (BMC) [5], with improved encodings for the full class of LTL properties [12], only for detecting counterexamples (the plain use). With these significantly faster checks, the full IC3-based model checker [10] is now rarely called (at most twice in each run).

To obtain some empirical results, we have implemented our algorithms in a new version of NuRV, which is based on nuXmv and MathSAT SMT solver [11] (MathSAT provides some quantifier elimination procedures). We present an experimental evaluation of the performance of the basic monitoring algorithms and various optimizations. Results on the best optimized algorithm seem to be promising for practical applications.

Outline of the Paper. In Sect. 2 we recall some related concepts and definitions. In Sect. 3, we describe an example of ABRV with infinite-state assumptions. In Sect. 4 we give two basic RV algorithms and prove their correctness proofs. Furthermore, Sect. 4.3 discusses various optimizations of the basic algorithms. Some experimental evaluations and results are given in Sect. 5. Finally, we discuss related work in Sect. 6 and conclude the paper in Sect. 7.

2 Preliminaries

2.1 Satisfiability Modulo Theory

We work in the setting of Satisfiability Modulo Theory (SMT) [2] and LTL Modulo Theory (see, e.g., [9]). First-order formulas are built as usual by proposition logic connectives, a given set of variables V and a first-order signature Σ, and are interpreted according to a given Σ-theory $\mathcal{T}$. We assume to be given the definition of $M, s \models_{\mathcal{T}} \varphi$ where M is a Σ structure, s is a value assignment to the variables in V, and φ is a formula. Whenever M is clear from contexts we omit it and simply $s \models_{\mathcal{T}} \varphi$. With slight abuse of notations, we also use an assignment

$s = \{x_1 \mapsto v_1, \ldots, x_n \mapsto v_n\}$ to represent the corresponding formula, i.e., the conjunction $\bigwedge_i (x_i = v_i)$. We sometimes write $\phi(V)$ or $\phi(V_1, V_2)$ instead of ϕ to highlight that the free variables of formula ϕ belong to V or $V_1 \cup V_2$, respectively. Arbitrary first-order theories can be supported by our RV algorithm, as long as the underlying SMT solver and model checker support them. For illustrating purposes, we only consider $\mathcal{LRA}$, the theory of linear arithmetics with real numbers.

2.2   First-Order Quantifier Elimination

First-order quantifier elimination [33] methods, which convert formulas into $\mathcal{T}$-equivalent quantifier-free formulas, are parts of many SMT solvers (e.g., Z3, Yices and MathSAT) for checking the satisfiability of quantified formulas. Hereafter we will omit the words "first-order" and only call it "quantifier elimination" or QE. Formally speaking, if $\alpha(V_1 \cup V_2)$ is quantifier-free formula (of the theory $\mathcal{T}$) built by variables from the set $V_1 \cup V_2$, the role of quantifier elimination is to convert the first-order formula $\exists V_1. \alpha(V_1 \cup V_2)$ into an $\mathcal{T}$-equivalent formula $\beta(V_2)$, where β is quantifier-free and is built by only variables from V_2. Quantified elimination is possible only for some first-order theories. In practice, for $\mathcal{LRA}$, most SMT solvers use methods like Fourier-Motzkin [27], Ferrante-and-Rackoff [22] or Loos-and-Weispfenning [30]. Note that QE procedures do not guarentee any kind of boundedness of the resulting formulas.

2.3   Fair Transition System

Infinite-state systems (used as RV assumptions) in this paper are described as *Fair Transition Systems* (FTS) [32], denoted by $\langle V, \Theta, \rho, \mathcal{J} \rangle$, where $V = \{x_1, \ldots, x_n\}$ is a finite set of variables, Θ the *initial condition*, ρ the *transition relation*, and $\mathcal{J}$ a (finite) set of *justice conditions*. (Θ, ρ and each element of $\mathcal{J}$ are quantifier-free $\mathcal{T}$-formulas). Given an FTS $K = \langle V, \Theta, \rho, \mathcal{J} \rangle$, a *state* s of K is just a value assignment of variables in V. Any formula using variables in V can be interpreted as the set of states satisfying the formula. Θ and each $J \in \mathcal{J}$ are such formulas, while ρ is a formula about V and its *primed version* $V' = \{x'_1, \ldots, x'_n\}$ indicating the relationship between the *current* and *next* states. If s is an assignment to V, s' is the corresponding assignment to V' such that $s'(v') = s(v)$ for all $v \in V$.

The *forward image* of a set of states $\psi(V)$ on $\rho(V, V')$ is a formula

$$\mathrm{fwd}(\psi(V), \rho(V, V'))(V) \doteq (\exists V.\ \rho(V, V') \wedge \psi(V))[V/V'] \tag{1}$$

where $[V/V']$ denotes the substitution of (free) variables in V' with the corresponding one in V. The existential quantifiers in forward images can be eliminated by QE procedures.

A *fair path* $\sigma = s_0 s_1 \cdots$ of K is an infinite sequence of states such that: (1) $s_0 \models_{\mathcal{T}} \Theta(V)$; (2) for each i, $s_i \cup s'_{i+1} \models_{\mathcal{T}} \rho(V, V')$; (3) for each $J \in \mathcal{J}$ there are infinitely many i such that $s_i \models_{\mathcal{T}} J(V)$. Let $\mathcal{L}(K)$ be the set of all fair paths of K. Sometimes we write σ_i for the zero-indexed i-th element of σ, i.e. $\sigma = \sigma_0 \sigma_1 \ldots$. A *trace* is a finite or infinite sequence of value assignments of V.

2.4   Linear Temporal Logic

In this paper, we consider properties specified in first-order quantifier-free Linear Temporal Logic (LTL) [31] with both future and past operators. The set of LTL formulas can be inductively defined as follows:

$$\varphi ::= \text{true} \mid \alpha \mid \neg\varphi \mid \varphi \vee \varphi \mid \mathbf{X}\,\varphi \mid \varphi\,\mathbf{U}\,\varphi \mid \mathbf{Y}\,\varphi \mid \varphi\,\mathbf{S}\,\varphi$$

where the (quantifier-free) formula α is built by a set of variables V and a first-order signature Σ, and is interpreted according to a Σ-theory $\mathcal{T}$. The temporal operator $\mathbf{X}$ stands for *next*, $\mathbf{U}$ for *until*, $\mathbf{Y}$ for *previous*, and $\mathbf{S}$ for *since*. Other logical constants and operators like false, $\wedge$, $\rightarrow$ and $\leftrightarrow$ are used as syntactic abbreviations with their standard meanings in propositional logic. We also use the metric operators $\mathbf{X}^n$ and $\mathbf{F}^{\leq k}$ here defined as an abbreviations: $\mathbf{X}^0\varphi := \varphi$, $\mathbf{X}^{k+1}\varphi := \mathbf{X}\mathbf{X}^k\varphi$ for $k \geq 0$, and $\mathbf{F}^{\leq k}\varphi := \bigvee_{0 \leq i \leq k} \mathbf{X}^i\varphi$.

The semantics of LTL formulas over infinite traces are standard for propositional and temporal operators (see, e.g. [13] for the full definitions). For atoms the semantics is reduced to the theory-specific semantics:

$$\sigma, i \models \alpha(V, V') \quad \text{iff} \quad \sigma_i \cup \sigma'_{i+1} \models_{\mathcal{T}} \alpha(V, V')$$

Any LTL formula can be translated into an equivalent FTS such that the set of fair paths of the FTS, when projected to V, coincides with the set of infinite traces satisfying the same LTL formula. Here we use essentially the same LTL translation algorithm in [13] (Sect. 2) except that the atomic formulas are translated syntactically as Boolean variables. Note that, for any LTL formula φ and its negation $\neg\varphi$, their LTL translations (as FTS) only differ at the initial conditions (this property is indeed leveraged in all our RV algorithms to be presented in this paper).

2.5   Assumption-Based Runtime Verification

The definition of the ABRV problem and the related ABRV-LTL semantics adopted in this paper are essentially the same as in the authors' previous paper for the finite-state case [13]. There are some minor changes for the support of infinite-state systems and non-Boolean variables.

Let K be an FTS as the RV assumption on the behavior of the SUS. When the SUS is *partially observable*, the monitor has only partial information on the actual state of the SUS. For simplicity purposes we assume that the monitor receives a sequence of value assignments for a subset O of all state variables V of the FST K (see [13] for a more general setting). A trace over O, also called a trace of observations, is a finite or infinite sequence of value assignments of O.

Given a finite trace u over O, the set of fair paths *compatible* with u is defined below: (roughly speaking, each u_i is a subset of variable assignments of σ_i)

$$\mathcal{L}^K(u) \doteq \big\{ \sigma \in \mathcal{L}(K) \mid \forall i < |u|.\, \sigma_i \models_{\mathcal{T}} u_i \big\}. \tag{2}$$

The LTL semantics of φ over the finite trace u at index i, having four possible values: *conditionally true* ($\top^a$), *conditionally false* ($\perp^a$), *inconclusive* (?) and *out-of-model* ($\times$), is defined below:

$$[\![u, i \models \varphi]\!]_4^K \doteq \begin{cases} \times, & \text{if } \mathcal{L}^K(u) = \emptyset \\ \top^a, & \text{if } \mathcal{L}^K(u) \neq \emptyset \text{ and } \forall w \in \mathcal{L}^K(u). \ w, i \models \varphi \\ \perp^a, & \text{if } \mathcal{L}^K(u) \neq \emptyset \text{ and } \forall w \in \mathcal{L}^K(u). \ w, i \models \neg\varphi \\ ?, & \text{otherwise.} \end{cases} \quad (3)$$

In the finite-state ABRV, we also consider a Boolean reset signal that is used to reset the index used as reference to evaluate the property. In this paper, to simplify the presentation, we omit this additional feature (although it is implemented and supported by the tool implementation) and define the infinite-state ABRV problem as the problem of constructing a function (as *runtime monitor*) taking a finite trace u over O and returning an ABRV-LTL verdict:

$$\mathcal{M}_\varphi^K(u) \doteq [\![u, 0 \models \varphi]\!]_4^K. \quad (4)$$

3   Motivating Example

In this section, we describe a use case of ABRV with an infinite-state assumption using a simple example of a temperature controller. Consider a system that heats the water in a tank until reaching the temperature of 100. The temperature is represented by a real variable t. The internal state of the system, which may be heating or not, is represented by the Boolean variable h. The command to switch on the heating system is represented by s, while f represents a fault that switches off the system permanently. Let us define a system model K with the following formulas:

- Initial condition: $t = 0$ (the temperature is initially 0)
- Transition conditions (implicitly conjoined):
  - $t' \geq 0 \wedge t' \leq 100$ (the temperature always remains between 0 and 100)
  - $h \rightarrow ((t = 100 \wedge t' = 100) \vee (10 \leq t' - t \leq 20))$ (if the system is heating, the temperature increases by a rate between 10 and 20 or remains 100 if it already reached that temperature)
  - $\neg h \rightarrow ((t = 0 \wedge t' = 0) \vee (-20 \leq t' - t \leq -10))$ (if the system is not heating, the temperature decreases by a rate between -20 and -10 or remains 0 if it already reached that temperature)
  - $h \rightarrow (h' \leftrightarrow \neg f)$ (if the system is heating, it remains so unless there is a fault)
  - $(\neg h) \rightarrow (h' \leftrightarrow (s \wedge \neg f))$ (if the system is not heating and is not faulty, then it can be switched on with the command s)
  - $f \rightarrow f'$ (the fault is permanent)

Suppose we can only observe the temperature and the switching command, and that we want to monitor the following property: $\varphi_1 = \mathbf{G}(s \to \mathbf{F}(t = 100))$ (whenever the heating system is switched on, the temperature will eventually reach the temperature of 100). The assumption that the system behaves according to K can be exploited by the ABRV monitor to deduce things like, whenever the temperature decreases there was a fault and so the temperature will never reach the desired level. Thus the monitor can detect the violation of a property which, without assumptions, would not be monitorable.

More specifically, consider the finite trace of observations $u = \{t \mapsto 0, s \mapsto \top\}, \{t \mapsto 20, s \mapsto \bot\}, \{t \mapsto 10, s \mapsto \top\}$. Since, without considering the assumption, there is a continuation of u satisfying φ_1 and one violating φ_1, a standard RV monitor is inconclusive (the output is ?). Considering K as assumption, all fair paths of K compatible with u violate φ. Thus, $[\![u, 0 \models \varphi_1]\!]_4^K = \bot^a$.

As an additional example, consider a stronger property $\mathbf{G}(s \to \mathbf{F}^{\leq 7}(t = 100))$, i.e., whenever the heating system is switched on, the temperature will reach $100°$ within 7 steps. In this case, from the assumption on the rates of the temperature, the ABRV monitor can deduce that after a number of steps, if the temperature is still low, it will not reach $t = 100$ in time. For example, if after 4 steps, the temperature is still less than 40, even with the maximum rate, it will not reach 100 in other 3 steps. Thus, at runtime the monitor can say that the property is violated 3 steps in advance.

4   ABRV Algorithms for Infinite-State Systems

4.1   ABRV Reduced to Model Checking

We first revisit the relationship between runtime verification and model checking, as clarified in [28], to conceive a trivial solution ABRV based on calling a model checker at every observation.

Given an FTS K as the RV assumption, a set of observable variables O, an LTL formula φ as the monitoring property, and a finite trace u over O, let S_u be an FTS whose fair paths are those compatible with u (formally, an FTS such that $\mathcal{L}(S_u) = \mathcal{L}^{\mathcal{U}}(u)$, where $\mathcal{U} = \langle V, \top, \top, \emptyset \rangle$ is the FTS with an universal language). Then we have by (4),

$$\mathcal{M}_\varphi^K(u) = [\![u, i \models \varphi]\!]_4^K = \begin{cases} \times, & \text{if } K \times S_u \models \varphi \text{ and } K \times S_u \models \neg\varphi \\ \top^a, & \text{if } K \times S_u \models \varphi \text{ and } K \times S_u \not\models \neg\varphi \\ \bot^a, & \text{if } K \times S_u \not\models \varphi \text{ and } K \times S_u \models \neg\varphi \\ ?, & \text{otherwise.} \end{cases} \quad (5)$$

From this equation, we can derive a simple monitor called `monitor1`, which calls the model checker twice for each input state. It is also depicted in Fig. 1, where the output is defined as in (5).

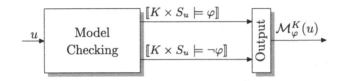

Fig. 1. ABRV reduced to MC

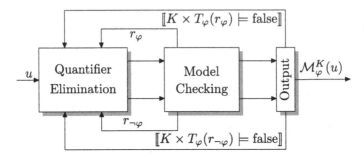

Fig. 2. ABRV reduced to MC and QE

4.2   ABRV Reduced to MC and Quantifier Elimination

In `monitor1` the entire input trace (the prefix received so far) must be encoded into a model (i.e. an FTS) S_μ, and obviously the model checker is called on increasingly bigger problems linear to the length of the trace prefix. In practice `monitor1` will be too slow after receiving even a small number of input states. The key for getting a better RV algorithm is to find a way to maintain some internal status which is updated by each input state in the trace. For automata-based RV monitors, the status is the location of monitor automata. For rewriting-based RV approaches, the status is the current form of the monitoring property after rewriting.

Recall in the finite-state ABRV algorithm [13], the BDD-based symbolic monitor keeps track of two *belief states* r_φ and $r_{\neg\varphi}$ as the possible internal locations of automata $K \times T_\varphi$ and $K \times T_{\neg\varphi}$ (K is the RV assumption, T_φ and $T_{\neg\varphi}$ are LTL translations of φ and $\neg\varphi$, resp.), reachable with fair paths compatible with the input trace. These states are updated at each input. Since previous input states are not accessible by the algorithm, and the belief states as BDDs have bounded memory consumption, the RV algorithm given in [13] is trace-length independent [17], i.e. having bounded memory consumption (with also a time complexity linear to the length of the trace prefix).

The monitor `monitor2` detailed in Algorithm 1 is very similar to the symbolic algorithm given [13]. Instead of representing formulas as BDDs, now we directly operate on raw formulas involving any type of variables. (However, in the worse case these formulas have unbounded sizes).

Table 1. Output Table of Fig. 2 and Algorithm 1

$\neg[\![K \times T_\varphi(r_\varphi) \models \text{false}]\!]$	$\neg[\![K \times T_\varphi(r_{\neg\varphi}) \models \text{false}]\!]$	$\mathcal{M}_\varphi^K(\cdot)$
$\top$	$\top$	?
$\top$	$\bot$	$\top^a$
$\bot$	$\top$	$\bot^a$
$\bot$	$\bot$	$\times$

Algorithm 1: The RV monitor for infinite-state systems

```
 1  function monitor2(K ≐ ⟨V_K, Θ_K, ρ_K, J_K⟩, φ, u)
 2  |    T_φ  ≐ ⟨V_φ, Θ_φ  , ρ_φ, J_φ⟩ := ltl_translation(φ);        // χ(φ) is in Θ_φ
 3  |    T_¬φ ≐ ⟨V_φ, Θ_¬φ, ρ_φ, J_φ⟩ := ltl_translation(¬φ);
 4  |    V := V_K ∪ V_φ;
 5  |    ⟨r_φ, r_¬φ⟩ := ⟨Θ_K ∧ Θ_φ, Θ_K ∧ Θ_¬φ⟩;
 6  |    if |u| > 0 then
 7  |    └   ⟨r_φ, r_¬φ⟩ := ⟨r_φ ∧ u_0, r_¬φ ∧ u_0⟩;
 8  |    for 1 ⩽ i < |u| do
 9  |    |    r_φ  := quantifier_elimination(V, ρ_K ∧ ρ_φ ∧ r_φ  ) ∧ u_i;
10  |    |    r_¬φ := quantifier_elimination(V, ρ_K ∧ ρ_φ ∧ r_¬φ) ∧ u_i;
11  |    b_1 := ¬model_checking(⟨V, r_φ, ρ_K ∧ ρ_φ, J_K ∪ J_φ⟩, false);
12  |    b_2 := ¬model_checking(⟨V, r_¬φ, ρ_K ∧ ρ_φ, J_K ∪ J_φ⟩, false);
13  |    if b_1 ∧ b_2 then return ? ;                           // inconclusive
14  |    else if b_1 then return ⊤^a;                           // conditionally true
15  |    else if b_2 then return ⊥^a;                           // conditionally false
16  |    else return ×;                                        // out of model
```

The inputs of the algorithm are the RV assumption K (as an FTS), the monitoring property φ and a finite input trace u. See also Fig. 2, where $K \times T_\varphi(r_\varphi)$ is an abbreviation of $\langle V, r_\varphi, \rho_K \wedge \rho_\varphi, J_K \cup J_\varphi \rangle$. At first, φ and $\neg\varphi$ are translated into two FTS T_φ and $T_{\neg\varphi}$ (line 2–3). The initial conditions of T_φ and $T_{\neg\varphi}$, namely Θ_φ and $\Theta_{\neg\varphi}$ are respectively in the form $\chi(\varphi) \wedge \xi$ and $\neg\chi(\varphi) \wedge \xi$, where $\chi(\varphi)$ restricts the paths to satisfy φ and ξ initializes the encoding of past operators.

Initially, the belief states r_φ and $r_{\neg\varphi}$ are the initial conditions of T_φ and $T_{\neg\varphi}$, composed with the initial condition of K (line 5). The first input state u_0 is directly intersected with belief states (line 7). The *forward images* of current belief states are computed and then intersected with the current input state u_i (line 9–10).

The undefined function quantifier_elimination can be any (first-order) quantifier elimination procedure (for more details, see Sect. 2.2) such that

$$\texttt{quantifier\_elimination}(V, \alpha(V \cup V')) \doteq (\exists V.\alpha(V \cup V'))[V/V'] = \beta(V) \quad (6)$$

where $[V/V']$ substitutes the prefixed formula with all variables in V' to the corresponding variables in V. All variables in V must be eliminated from $\exists V.\alpha(V, V')$. $\beta(V)$ as the outcome of quantifier elimination is quantifier-free.

The main difference with the previous BDD-based algorithm (Algorithm 1 of [13]) is the treatment of fair states. For BDD-based FTS, the set of fair states can be computed a priori (by algorithms like Emerson-Lei [19]) and intersected with the belief states whenever they are computed. However, for infinite-state FTS represented by raw formulas this is impossible. Thus r_φ and $r_{\neg\varphi}$ may have non-fair states in them. To check their (non)emptiness w.r.t. fair states, we leverage LTL model checking, by checking LTL formula false on the model $K \times T_\varphi$ (or $K \times T_{\neg\varphi}$, resp.) with r_φ (or $r_{\neg\varphi}$, resp.) as the initial condition (line 11–12). Here is the idea: if the model checking returned $\top$ saying for all fair paths in the input model the LTL property "false" holds (which is impossible), then the only possibility is that the input model actually does not have any fair path, i.e. the belief state is empty. The output of the monitor w.r.t. the model checking results (line 13–16) is summarized in Table 1.

The correctness of Algorithm 1 is given by the following theorem: (the proof is omitted due to page limits.)

Theorem 1. *The function* monitor2 *given in Algorithm 1 correctly implements the ABRV monitor* $\mathcal{M}_\varphi^K(\cdot)$.

4.3   Optimizations

In this section, we present few simple optimizations that reduce unnecessary (complete) MC calls, which are computationally expensive, or to replace them with relatively-cheap incomplete MC calls, which can only be used to detect counterexamples, e.g. the plain Bounded Model Checking (BMC). (Also note that, for infinite-state systems, the property may be violated but no lasso-shaped counterexample exists; in this case, neither BMC or the full IC3-IA algorithm can find it). The following 4 *basic* optimizations, namely *o1–o4*, are identified:

o1 If the monitor has already reached conclusive verdicts ($\top^a$ or $\bot^a$), then for the runtime verification of the next input state *at most one* MC call is need. In fact, in this case, one of the belief states r_φ or $r_{\neg\varphi}$ becomes empty, while empty belief states can only lead to empty belief states by forward image computations. Furthermore, if the monitor has reached the verdict $\times$ (out-of-model), then it will maintain the same verdict, thus in this case no more MC (and QE) calls are necessary.

o2 Before calling model checkers to detect the emptiness of a belief state (w.r.t. fairness), an SMT checking can be done first, to check if the belief state formula can be satisfied or not. If the SMT solver returns UNSAT, then it means the formula is equivalent to $\bot$, then there is no need to further call model checkers to detect its emptiness.

o3 When monitor2 is used as online monitor, the same LTL properties are sent to LTL model checkers with different models and are internally translated into equivalent FTS. The translation can be done just once as part of the RV algorithm, if the involved model checkers can be modified to take pre-translated tableaux instead of LTL properties.

o4 Some model checking algorithms such as IC3-IA are more effective in proving properties, while others such as BMC can be used in practice to find counterexamples. This optimization is to call the incomplete plain BMC (or any other MC procedure which detects counterexamples) before calling a complete model checker such as IC3-IA. Note that the BMC bound parameter max_k can be chosen arbitrarily without hurting the correctness of the entire RV algorithm: if the counterexample does exist but BMC fails to find it due to a small max_k, the next complete MC call will still find it and lead to the same monitoring output as in the algorithm without this BMC optimization.

One may think that the calls of complete model checkers (IC3_IA) are a bottleneck rendering the whole idea infeasible. In fact, given all above optimizations we can prove that IC3_IA is called at most twice for each input trace:

Theorem 2. *Assuming* BMC *always find the counterexample whenever it exists,* IC3_IA *is called at most twice in the "online" version of Algorithm 2 with all optimizations.*

Proof. Without loss of generality, we analyze how the values of b_1 and b_2 change during the verification of a typical trace:

1. Initially $b_1 = b_2 = \top$ (so that the verdict is ?). This means that both calls of check_nonemptiness (at line 13–14) return $\top$, which further means that the underlying call to model_checking (line 22) returns $\bot$, i.e. BMC is involved returning $\bot$ (counterexamples found).
2. If the monitor maintains the current verdict (?), we have $b_1 = b_2 = \top$, and two BMC calls are performed, each returning $\bot$.
3. At the moment when the monitor firstly returns $\top^a$, we have $b_1 = \top, b_2 = \bot$, i.e. the call to check_nonemptiness at line 14 returns $\bot$. There are two possibilities:
   – The belief state $r_{\neg\varphi}$ is literally $\bot$ or unsatisfiable, detected by SMT (line 20) due to [o2]. No call to IC3_IA in this case.
   – The call to model_checking (line 22) returns $\top$, which means IC3_IA is called once (after BMC fails to find a counterexample.)
4. If the monitor maintains the current verdict ($\top^a$), IC3_IA will not be called again, because it is disabled by [o1] (at line 14) when $b_2 = \bot$.
5. At the moment when the monitor firstly returns $\times$, we have $b_1 = b_2 = \bot$ (the value of b_1 changed). check_nonemptiness returns $\bot$ is line 13. Either SMT is called (line 20) when r_φ is unsatisfiable (due to [o2]), or IC3_IA is called internally by model_checking (line 22) returning $\top$.
6. From now on, no BMC nor IC3_IA is called, as they are all disabled by [o1], and the monitor maintains the verdict $\times$ (out of model).

Thus, in summary IC3_IA is called at most twice for any input trace.   □

Algorithm 2: The optimized version of Algorithm 1

---

1 **function** monitor2_optimized($K \doteq \langle V_K, \Theta_K, \rho_K, \mathcal{J}_K \rangle, \varphi, u$)

2 $\quad T_\varphi \doteq \langle V_\varphi, \Theta_\varphi, \rho_\varphi, \mathcal{J}_\varphi \rangle := \text{ltl\_translation}(\varphi);$ $\quad$ // $\chi(\varphi)$ is in Θ_φ

3 $\quad T_{\neg\varphi} \doteq \langle V_\varphi, \Theta_{\neg\varphi}, \rho_\varphi, \mathcal{J}_\varphi \rangle := \text{ltl\_translation}(\neg\varphi);$

4 $\quad V := V_K \cup V_\varphi;$

5 $\quad \langle r_\varphi, r_{\neg\varphi} \rangle := \langle \Theta_K \wedge \Theta_\varphi, \Theta_K \wedge \Theta_{\neg\varphi} \rangle;$

6 $\quad$ **if** o_1 **then** $b_1 := b_2 := \top$;

7 $\quad$ **if** o_3 **then** $F := \text{ltl\_translation}((\bigwedge_{\psi \in \mathcal{J}_K \cup \mathcal{J}_\varphi} \mathbf{GF}\,\psi) \to \text{false})$;

8 $\quad$ **if** $|u| > 0$ **then**

9 $\quad\quad \langle r_\varphi, r_{\neg\varphi} \rangle := \langle r_\varphi \wedge u_0, r_{\neg\varphi} \wedge u_0 \rangle;$

10 $\quad$ **for** $1 \leqslant i < |u|$ **do**

11 $\quad\quad r_\varphi := \text{quantifier\_elimination}(V, \rho_K \wedge \rho_\varphi \wedge r_\varphi\,) \wedge u_i;$

12 $\quad\quad r_{\neg\varphi} := \text{quantifier\_elimination}(V, \rho_K \wedge \rho_\varphi \wedge r_{\neg\varphi}) \wedge u_i;$

13 $\quad$ **if** $o_1 \to b_1$ **then** $b_1 := \text{check\_nonemptiness}(r_\varphi)$;

14 $\quad$ **if** $o_1 \to b_2$ **then** $b_2 := \text{check\_nonemptiness}(r_{\neg\varphi})$;

15 $\quad$ **if** $b_1 \wedge b_2$ **then return** ? ; $\quad$ // inconclusive

16 $\quad$ **else if** b_1 **then return** $\top^{\text{a}}$; $\quad$ // conditionally true

17 $\quad$ **else if** b_2 **then return** $\perp^{\text{a}}$; $\quad$ // conditionally false

18 $\quad$ **else return** $\times$; $\quad$ // out of model

19 **function** check_nonemptiness(r)

20 $\quad$ **if** $o_2 \wedge (\text{SMT}(r) = \textbf{unsat})$ **then return** $\perp$;

21 $\quad$ **else**

22 $\quad\quad$ **return** $\neg\text{model\_checking}(\langle V, r, \rho_K \wedge \rho_\varphi, \mathcal{J}_K \cup \mathcal{J}_\varphi \rangle, o_3 \,?\, F \,:\, \text{false})$

23 **function** model_checking(M, ψ)

24 $\quad$ **if** o_4 **then**

25 $\quad\quad$ **if** BMC(M, ψ) $= \perp$ **then return** $\perp$; $\quad$ // counterexample found

26 $\quad\quad$ **else** $\quad$ // max_k reached

27 $\quad\quad\quad$ **return** IC3_IA(M, ψ)

28 $\quad$ **else return** IC3_IA(M, ψ);

4.4 ABRV Reduced to Model Checking and Incremental BMC

Further optimizations can be done by leveraging the *incrementality* of Bounded Model Checking occurred in Algorithm 2, where the function BMC are called as incomplete preliminary steps before the full IC3_IA calls. In the following discussions we assume the audience is familiar with the internal work of BMC algorithms (otherwise see [5] and [12]).

We first define a BMC encoding of the belief states after a sequence of observations $u_0 u_1 \cdots u_n$, denoted by $\text{bs}(u_0 u_1 \cdots u_n)$. These are inductively given by

$$\text{bs}(u_0)(V) = I(V) \wedge u_0(V), \tag{7}$$

$$\text{bs}(u_0 u_1 \cdots u_{i+1})(V) = \text{fwd}\big(\text{bs}(u_0 u_1 \cdots u_i)(V), T(V, V')\big)(V) \wedge u_{i+1}(V). \tag{8}$$

The following theorem shows the relation between the belief states and a BMC encoding conjoined with the sequence of observations:

Theorem 3 (Equisatisfiability). *When $k > 1$, the following two formulas*

$$I(V_0) \wedge u_0(V_0) \wedge \bigwedge_{j=0}^{k-1} \left[T(V_j, V_{j+1}) \wedge u_{j+1}(V_{j+1}) \right], \tag{9}$$

and

$$\mathrm{bs}(u_0 u_1 \cdots u_k)(V) \tag{10}$$

are equi-satisfiable.

Now comes the second part of this idea: there is also no need to restart BMC inner loop from 0 (to the maximal bound k) after asserting a new observation. This is because, whenever the BMC inner loop stops at a value k in the previous call, all SMT formulas corresponding in steps $i < k$ are UNSAT, and they are still UNSAT after asserting anything new.[2]

In Algorithm 3 we gave the pseudo code of the optimized RV monitor based on incremental BMC. There are several undefined functions (methods) used here (to be given later in Algorithm 4 and 5):

- `init_nonemptiness` for creating a persistent SMT solver instance,
- `update_nonemptiness` for checking the nonemptiness of the belief states after a new observation,
- `reset_nonemptiness` for resetting the SMT solver, cleaning up all existing observations.

Here the code is given in object-oriented styles, with two instances of SMT solvers created by `init_nonemptiness`. Others methods operates on these instances, possibly with further arguments.

The correctness of Algorithm 3 (relative to the correctness of undefined methods) can be seen by a comparison with Algorithm 1. Now the computation of belief states from a sequence of observations is done in a new function `compute_belief_states` on the object, which holds a sequence of observations asserted by each call of `update_nonemptiness`.

In Algorithm 4 the code of `init_nonemptiness` and `reset_nonemptiness` are given. Note that, although new BMC solver instances are created from just the initial condition and transition relation for simplification purposes, the actual code also needs the translation of LTL property $\left(\bigwedge_{\psi \in \mathcal{J}_K \cup \mathcal{J}_\varphi} \mathbf{GF}\, \psi \right) \rightarrow$ false as in Algorithm 2. The unrolling of this translated formula at time i, as the ending terms of BMC encodings, will be simply presented as $[[F]]_i$ in the related code (`update_nonemptiness`). The BMC solver object has some extra member variables, whose purposes are given in the comments of `reset_nonemptiness`. Whenever SMT solving is needed, it is done on the member variable *problem*.

---

[2] In the ideal case (when BMC stopped by having found a counterexample, and the overall monitoring verdicts is conclusive), the monitor only needs to call SMT solver *once* to decide the next monitoring output.

Algorithm 3: The optimized RV monitor based on incremental BMC

---

1 **function** bmc_monitor($K \doteq \langle V_K, \Theta_K, \rho_K, \mathcal{J}_K \rangle$, φ, u, max_k, $window\_size$)

2     $T_\varphi \doteq \langle V_\varphi, \Theta_\varphi, \rho_\varphi, \mathcal{J}_\varphi \rangle :=$ ltl_translation(φ);   // $\chi(\varphi)$ is in Θ_φ

3     $T_{\neg\varphi} \doteq \langle V_\varphi, \Theta_{\neg\varphi}, \rho_\varphi, \mathcal{J}_\varphi \rangle :=$ ltl_translation($\neg\varphi$);

4     $V := V_K \cup V_\varphi$;

5     $e_1 :=$ init_nonemptiness($\Theta_K \wedge \Theta_\varphi$, $\rho_K \wedge \rho_\varphi$);

6     $e_2 :=$ init_nonemptiness($\Theta_K \wedge \Theta_{\neg\varphi}$, $\rho_K \wedge \rho_\varphi$);

7   **if** $|u| > 0$ **then**

8        $b_1 :=$ update_nonemptiness(e_1, u_0);

9        $b_2 :=$ update_nonemptiness(e_2, u_0);

10   **for** $1 \leqslant i < |u|$ **do**

11        $b_1 :=$ update_nonemptiness(e_1, u_i);

12        $b_2 :=$ update_nonemptiness(e_2, u_i);

13   **if** $b_1 \wedge b_2$ **then return** ? ;   // inconclusive

14   **else if** b_1 **then return** $\top^a$;   // conditionally true

15   **else if** b_2 **then return** $\bot^a$;   // conditionally false

16   **else return** $\times$;   // out of model

17 **function** compute_belief_states(e)

18     $r := e.I(V)$;

19   **for** $i \leftarrow 0$ **to** $e.n$ **do**

20   **if** $i = 0$ **then** $r := r \wedge e.observations[i](V)$;

21   **else**

22           $r :=$ quantifier_elimination(V, $r \wedge T(V, V')$) $\wedge e.observations[i](V)$;

23   **return** r;

The core of incremental BMC algorithm for RV, update_nonemptiness, is finally given in Algorithm 5.

5 Experimental Evaluation

The RV algorithms presented in this paper have been implemented in NuRV [14][3]. The usefulness of RV assumptions has been explored in previous papers (see, e.g., Sect. 5 of [13]), thus the focus of experimental evaluations here is mainly at the correctness and performance of ABRV algorithms for infinite-state systems. All performance results are obtained on a MacBook Pro laptop with an 8-core Intel Core i9 (2.3 GHz).

The correctness of these RV algorithms, beside the related theorems and proofs, lies also on the fact that, for each input trace (and RV assumptions) being tested, all five RV algorithms (monitor1, monitor1_optimized, monitor2, monitor2_optimized, and bmc_monitor) give the same results (except that

---

[3] The official site of NuRV is now at https://es-static.fbk.eu/tools/nurv/.

Algorithm 4: Methods for checking (non)emptiness (part 1)

```
 1  function init_nonemptiness(I, T)
 2  │   e := new BMC solver with initial formula I and transition relation T;
 3  │   reset_nonemptiness(e, I);
 4  └   return e;

 5  procedure reset_nonemptiness(e, I)
 6  │   e.problem := I(V₀);        // the initial formula unrolled at time 0
 7  │   e.observations := [];                // an array holding observations
 8  │   e.n := 0;                            // the number of observations
 9  │   e.map := {};          // a hash map from time to (unused) observations
10  │   e.k := 0;              // the number of unrolled transition relations
11  └   e.max_k := max_k;                           // a local copy of max_k
```

`monitor1` and `monitor1_optimized` only give the verdicts for the last state of the input trace). Below we mainly focus on their (relative) performance.

5.1 Tests on the Motivating Example (Sect. 3)

The actual monitoring results on the motivating example in Sect. 3 are the same with those expected. The total execution time for the offline monitoring of the two sample properties on the three-state sample trace u is about: 2.3 s (`monitor1_optimized`), 13 s (`monitor2_optimized`) and 0.9 s (`bmc_monitor`). Note that `monitor1_optimized` is faster than `monitor2_optimized` mostly because the input trace is very short and it only needs to output the verdict for the last input state. On the other hand, the BMC search bound (`max_k`) in `bmc_monitor` was set to 50, while the execution time can be shorten to 0.6 s if `max_k` were set to 30.

5.2 Tests on Dwyer's LTL Patterns

We use again Dwyer's LTL patterns [18] (55 in total[4]) as the main LTL benchmark, which comes from a wide coverage of practical specifications and has a good coverage on different kind of LTL properties. The original patterns involve six Boolean variables p, q, r, s, t, z, and to adapt them for infinite-state scenarios we have changed to use one integer variable i and one real variable x for the replacements of q and r: $q \leftrightarrow 0 \leqslant i$ and $r \leftrightarrow 0.0 \leqslant x$. Then we generated random traces where $i \in [-500, 500]$ and $x \in [-0.500, 0.500]$ are uniformly chosen, such that q and r become random in the original patterns. Furthermore, we choose a model with fairness as the RV assumptions, in which the p-transition (i.e., from $\neg p$ to p) happens at most 4 times. The purpose of this assumption is to force the monitor to arrive at × verdicts at certain moments, so that the related monitors could go through different verdicts as much as possible.

---

[4] See also https://matthewbdwyer.github.io/psp/patterns/ltl.html.

Algorithm 5: Methods for checking (non)emptiness (part 2)

---

1 **function** update_nonemptiness(e, o)
2      $e.map[e.n] = o$;   // store new observation in the map
3      $e.observations[e.n + +] = o$;   // store new observation in the list
4   **for** $(k, v) : e.map$ **do**
5   **if** $k \leqslant e.k$ **then**
6              $e.problem := e.problem \wedge v(V_i)$;
7   delete $e.map[k]$;

8      $result := ?$;
9   **while** $e.k \leqslant e.max\_k$ **and** $result = ?$ **do**
10         $i := e.k$;
11   **if** SMT$(e.problem) =$ UNSAT **then**
12             $result := \bot$;   // literally empty believe states
13   **break**
14   **if** SMT$(e.problem \wedge [[F]]_i) =$ SAT **then**
15             $result = \top$;   // counterexample found (nonempty)
16   **break**
17         $e.problem := e.problem \wedge e.T(V_i, V_{i+1})$;
18   **if** $e.map[i + 1]$ *exists* **then**
19             $e.problem := e.problem \wedge e.map[i + 1](V_{i+1})$;
20   delete $e.map[i + 1]$;
21         $e.k + +$;

22     $e.max\_k + +$;   // increase the search bound for next calls
23   **if** $e.k > window\_size$ **or** $result = ?$ **then**
24         $r :=$ compute_belief_states(e);
25   reset_nonemptiness(e, r);
26   **if** $result = \top$ **or** $result = \bot$ **then**
27   **return** $result$;
28   **else**
29   **return** $\neg$IC3_IA$(\langle V, r, e.T, \mathcal{J}_K \cup \mathcal{J}_\varphi \rangle,$ false$)$;

Figure 3 gives the relative performance of all five RV algorithms on Pattern 49 (s, t responds to p after q until r, results are similar for other patterns), a complex property for showing the performance of RV algorithms in practical. The monitors are generated under the above chosen assumptions, which is expressed as an infinite-state model. The length of input traces increases from 1 to 30. Each plot represents the average time of a monitor spent on certain length of three random traces. We found that 1) the optimizations on monitor1 and monitor2 indeed work; 2) bmc_monitor is about 10x faster than monitor2_optimized, which is again about 10x faster than monitor1_optimized. Note that these relative performance ("10x faster") between different monitors is based middle-sized traces: if the trace is too short, usually monitor1 is faster.

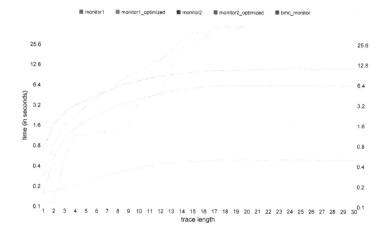

Fig. 3. Performance of five RV algorithms on Pattern 49

Figure 4 additionally shows the relative performance between `bmc_monitor` and `monitor2_optimized`. For each LTL pattern, the two monitors with the fairness assumptions take 10 random traces as input, each with 50 states. The x- and y-axes of each plot (identified by pattern ID) corresponds to the overall time spent on the two monitors. For most patterns (and also on average), `bmc_monitor` is about 10x faster than `monitor2_optimized`.

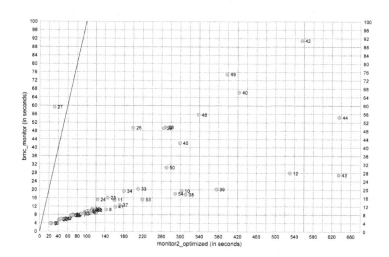

Fig. 4. Performance of `bmc_monitor` and `monitor2_optimized` on all patterns

6   Related Work

Despite the vast literature on SAT- and SMT-based symbolic model checking [6], currently there are only few works on applying SAT/SMT solvers to Runtime Verification. One of the prominent approaches in this direction is the one on Monitoring Modulo Theories (MMT) [16] for monitoring Temporal Data Logic (TDL): propositional LTL extended with first-order quantifiers and theories. MMT is implemented on top of the Z3 SMT solver. The SMT solver in MMT is mainly to deal with first-order quantifiers of TDL. In [35], SMT solvers are used to monitor partially synchronous distributed systems. In this work, SMT solvers evaluate partially observable formulas that contain non-observable variables that can have any possible value. However, in this work the SMT formula is generated in highly domain-specific ways and is directly treated as the monitoring property, without temporal extensions.

The relationship between MC and RV has been explored in previous research. The value of models (as RV assumptions) in synthesizing better monitors was first reported in [28]. Adapting existing model checkers for RV purposes is a natural idea for reducing the costs of tool development from scratch. Similar with NuRV (which is adapted from nuXmv), the DIVINE model checker was adapted to perform runtime verification [26]. We consider the predictive feature of ABRV monitors as a side effect of the assumption-based approach, but there exist dedicated work on predictive semantics of runtime monitors, e.g. [36].

Belief states have been used in planning under partial observability. See, for example, the work of in [25], from which we borrow the idea of representing them with symbolic formulas. To the best of our knowledge, our approach is the first attempt to combine them with the evaluation of temporal properties for RV.

7   Conclusion

ABRV is a recently proposed framework for RV based on the definition of some assumption on the SUS behavior, which is exploited by the runtime monitor to achieve early detection, prediction and partial observability. The framework has been extended in this paper to assumptions defined as infinite-state system, where infinite-state belief states are represented as quantifier-free first-order formulas and the emptiness checkings are reduced to SMT-based model checking. We start from a trivial reduction from RV to MC, and eventually obtained an highly optimized RV algorithm, based on Incremental BMC. The final version is hundreds of times faster than the initial one.

As observed in [35], a "major question regarding the use of SMT solvers in performing runtime monitoring is whether they are fast enough." We argue that, for some partially-observable systems, like planets explorers, where the frequency of observations is low, there is a trade-off between the required speed of the monitor and the complexity of the assumptions needed to reason on the non-observable parts. In the future, we plan to investigate such trade-off in realistic scenarios. We will also consider real-time temporal properties with timed assumptions and address the problem of generating monitor's code taking into account infinite-state assumptions.

References

1. Arafat, O., Bauer, A., Leucker, M., Schallhart, C.: Runtime verification revisited. Technical report TUM-I0518, Technische Universität München, München (2005)
2. Barrett, C., Sebastiani, R., Seshia, S.A., Tinelli, C.: Satisfiability modulo theories. In: Handbook of Satisfiability, pp. 825–885. IOS Press, January 2009. https://doi.org/10.3233/978-1-58603-929-5-825
3. Bauer, A., Leucker, M., Schallhart, C.: Comparing LTL semantics for runtime verification. J. Log. Comput. **20**(3), 651–674 (2010). https://doi.org/10.1093/logcom/exn075
4. Bauer, A., Leucker, M., Schallhart, C.: Runtime verification for LTL and TLTL. ACM Trans. Softw. Eng. Methodol. **20**(4), 14–64 (2011). https://doi.org/10.1145/2000799.2000800
5. Biere, A., Cimatti, A., Clarke Jr, E.M., Strichman, O., Zhu, Y.: Bounded model checking. In: Advances in Computers: Highly Dependable Software, pp. 117–148. Academic Press (2003)
6. Biere, A., Cimatti, A., Clarke, E., Zhu, Y.: Symbolic model checking without BDDs. In: Cleaveland, W.R. (ed.) TACAS 1999. LNCS, vol. 1579, pp. 193–207. Springer, Heidelberg (2008). https://doi.org/10.1007/3-540-49059-0_14
7. Bryant, R.E.: Binary decision diagrams. In: Clarke, E., Henzinger, T., Veith, H., Bloem, R. (eds.) Handbook of Model Checking, pp. 191–217. Springer, Cham (2018). https://doi.org/10.1007/978-3-319-10575-8_7
8. Cavada, R., et al.: The nuXmv symbolic model checker. In: Biere, A., Bloem, R. (eds.) CAV 2014. LNCS, vol. 8559, pp. 334–342. Springer, Cham (2014). https://doi.org/10.1007/978-3-319-08867-9_22
9. Cimatti, A., Griggio, A., Magnago, E., Roveri, M., Tonetta, S.: SMT-based satisfiability of first-order LTL with event freezing functions and metric operators. Inf. Comput. **272**, 104502 (2020). https://doi.org/10.1016/j.ic.2019.104502
10. Cimatti, A., Griggio, A., Mover, S., Tonetta, S.: IC3 modulo theories via implicit predicate abstraction. In: Ábrahám, E., Havelund, K. (eds.) TACAS 2014. LNCS, vol. 8413, pp. 46–61. Springer, Heidelberg (2014). https://doi.org/10.1007/978-3-642-54862-8_4
11. Cimatti, A., Griggio, A., Schaafsma, B.J., Sebastiani, R.: The MathSAT5 SMT solver. In: Piterman, N., Smolka, S.A. (eds.) TACAS 2013. LNCS, vol. 7795, pp. 93–107. Springer, Heidelberg (2013). https://doi.org/10.1007/978-3-642-36742-7_7
12. Cimatti, A., Pistore, M., Roveri, M., Sebastiani, R.: Improving the encoding of LTL model checking into SAT. In: Cortesi, A. (ed.) VMCAI 2002. LNCS, vol. 2294, pp. 196–207. Springer, Heidelberg (2002). https://doi.org/10.1007/3-540-47813-2_14
13. Cimatti, A., Tian, C., Tonetta, S.: Assumption-based runtime verification with partial observability and resets. In: Finkbeiner, B., Mariani, L. (eds.) RV 2019. LNCS, vol. 11757, pp. 165–184. Springer, Cham (2019). https://doi.org/10.1007/978-3-030-32079-9_10
14. Cimatti, A., Tian, C., Tonetta, S.: NuRV: a nuXmv extension for runtime verification. In: Finkbeiner, B., Mariani, L. (eds.) RV 2019. LNCS, vol. 11757, pp. 382–392. Springer, Cham (2019). https://doi.org/10.1007/978-3-030-32079-9_23

15. Colin, S., Mariani, L.: 18 run-time verification. In: Broy, M., Jonsson, B., Katoen, J.-P., Leucker, M., Pretschner, A. (eds.) Model-Based Testing of Reactive Systems. LNCS, vol. 3472, pp. 525–555. Springer, Heidelberg (2005). https://doi.org/10.1007/11498490_24

16. Decker, N., Leucker, M., Thoma, D.: Monitoring modulo theories. Int. J. Softw. Tools Technol. Transf. **18**(2), 205–225 (2015). https://doi.org/10.1007/s10009-015-0380-3

17. Du, X., Liu, Y., Tiu, A.: Trace-length independent runtime monitoring of quantitative policies in LTL. In: Bjørner, N., de Boer, F. (eds.) FM 2015. LNCS, vol. 9109, pp. 231–247. Springer, Cham (2015). https://doi.org/10.1007/978-3-319-19249-9_15

18. Dwyer, M.B., Avrunin, G.S., Corbett, J.C.: Patterns in property specifications for finite-state verification. In: Proceedings of the 21st International Conference on Software Engineering, pp. 411–420. ACM Press, New York (1999). https://doi.org/10.1145/302405.302672

19. Allen Emerson, E., Lei, C.-L.: Temporal reasoning under generalized fairness constraints. In: Monien, B., Vidal-Naquet, G. (eds.) STACS 1986. LNCS, vol. 210, pp. 21–36. Springer, Heidelberg (1986). https://doi.org/10.1007/3-540-16078-7_62

20. Falcone, Y., Havelund, K., Reger, G.: A tutorial on runtime verification. Eng. Dependable Softw. Syst. **34**, 141–175 (2013). https://doi.org/10.3233/978-1-61499-207-3-141

21. Falcone, Y., Krstić, S., Reger, G., Traytel, D.: A taxonomy for classifying runtime verification tools. In: Colombo, C., Leucker, M. (eds.) RV 2018. LNCS, vol. 11237, pp. 241–262. Springer, Cham (2018). https://doi.org/10.1007/978-3-030-03769-7_14

22. Ferrante, J., Rackoff, C.: A decision procedure for the first order theory of real addition with order. SIAM J. Comput. **4**(1), 69–76 (1975). https://doi.org/10.1137/0204006

23. Havelund, K., Peled, D.: Runtime verification: from propositional to first-order temporal logic. In: Colombo, C., Leucker, M. (eds.) RV 2018. LNCS, vol. 11237, pp. 90–112. Springer, Cham (2018). https://doi.org/10.1007/978-3-030-03769-7_7

24. Henzinger, T.A., Saraç, N.E.: Monitorability under assumptions. In: Deshmukh, J., Ničković, D. (eds.) RV 2020. LNCS, vol. 12399, pp. 3–18. Springer, Cham (2020). https://doi.org/10.1007/978-3-030-60508-7_1

25. Hoffmann, J., Brafman, R.I.: Contingent planning via heuristic forward search with implicit belief states. In: Biundo, S., Myers, K.L., Rajan, K. (eds.) Proceedings of the Fifteenth International Conference on Automated Planning and Scheduling (ICAPS 2005), 5–10 June 2005, Monterey, California, USA, pp. 71–80. AAAI (2005). http://www.aaai.org/Library/ICAPS/2005/icaps05-008.php

26. Kejstová, K., Ročkai, P., Barnat, J.: From model checking to runtime verification and back. In: Lahiri, S., Reger, G. (eds.) RV 2017. LNCS, vol. 10548, pp. 225–240. Springer, Cham (2017). https://doi.org/10.1007/978-3-319-67531-2_14

27. Khachiyan, L.: Fourier-Motzkin elimination method. In: Floudas, C., Pardalos, P. (eds.) Encyclopedia of Optimization, pp. 1074–1077. Springer, Boston (2009). https://doi.org/10.1007/978-0-387-74759-0_187

28. Leucker, M.: Sliding between model checking and runtime verification. In: Qadeer, S., Tasiran, S. (eds.) RV 2012. LNCS, vol. 7687, pp. 82–87. Springer, Heidelberg (2013). https://doi.org/10.1007/978-3-642-35632-2_10

29. Leucker, M., Schallhart, C.: A brief account of runtime verification. J. Log. Algebraic Program. **78**(5), 293–303 (2009). https://doi.org/10.1016/j.jlap.2008.08.004

30. Loos, R., Weispfenning, V.: Applying linear quantifier elimination. Comput. J. **36**(5), 450–462 (1993). https://dblp.org/rec/journals/cj/LoosW93
31. Manna, Z., Pnueli, A.: The Temporal Logic of Reactive and Concurrent Systems: Specification. Springer, New York (1992). https://doi.org/10.1007/978-1-4612-0931-7
32. Manna, Z., Pnueli, A.: Temporal Verification of Reactive Systems: Safety. Springer, New York (1995). https://doi.org/10.1007/978-1-4612-4222-2
33. Marcja, A., Toffalori, C.: Quantifier elimination. In: Marcja, A., Toffalori, C. (eds.) A Guide to Classical and Modern Model Theory, pp. 43–83. Springer, Dordrecht (2003). https://doi.org/10.1007/978-94-007-0812-9_2
34. Reger, G., Rydeheard, D.: From first-order temporal logic to parametric trace slicing. In: Bartocci, E., Majumdar, R. (eds.) RV 2015. LNCS, vol. 9333, pp. 216–232. Springer, Cham (2015). https://doi.org/10.1007/978-3-319-23820-3_14
35. Tekken Valapil, V., Yingchareonthawornchai, S., Kulkarni, S., Torng, E., Demirbas, M.: Monitoring partially synchronous distributed systems using SMT solvers. In: Lahiri, S., Reger, G. (eds.) RV 2017. LNCS, vol. 10548, pp. 277–293. Springer, Cham (2017). https://doi.org/10.1007/978-3-319-67531-2_17
36. Zhang, X., Leucker, M., Dong, W.: Runtime verification with predictive semantics. In: Goodloe, A.E., Person, S. (eds.) NFM 2012. LNCS, vol. 7226, pp. 418–432. Springer, Heidelberg (2012). https://doi.org/10.1007/978-3-642-28891-3_37

Short Papers and Tool Papers

Differential Monitoring

Fabian Muehlboeck$^{(\boxtimes)}$ and Thomas A. Henzinger

IST Austria, 3400 Klosterneuburg, Austria
{fabian.muehlboeck,tah}@ist.ac.at

Abstract. We argue that the time is ripe to investigate differential monitoring, in which the specification of a program's behavior is implicitly given by a second program implementing the same informal specification. Similar ideas have been proposed before, and are currently implemented in restricted form for testing and specialized run-time analyses, aspects of which we combine. We discuss the challenges of implementing differential monitoring as a general-purpose, black-box run-time monitoring framework, and present promising results of a preliminary implementation, showing low monitoring overheads for diverse programs.

Keywords: Run-time verification · Software engineering · Implicit specification

1 Introduction

Run-time verification has a major advantage on static verification: it is easier to decide whether one particular run of a program conforms to a specification than reasoning about all possible runs. While some run-time verification frameworks are based on similar techniques as static approaches [3,16], run-time verification also allows us to focus on end-to-end properties of the program, by checking the correctness of the response of a program to some input while ignoring its inner workings. Such a black-box approach is especially appealing if the program source is unavailable, or untrusted. However, for long-running and stateful programs, which transform input streams into output streams, the complete specification of the program's end-to-end behavior may itself become complicated and can amount to essentially writing the program a second time, often in a more cumbersome language that is also slower to execute.

Differential monitoring is the idea of running different versions of the same program in parallel, duplicating any external inputs and merging any outputs after checking them for equivalence. In this way, each program acts as an end-to-end specification for the other. On a system with enough idle hardware resources, this represents a natural method for improving software quality and security through redundancy and over-engineering.

Supported in part by Austrian Science Fund (FWF) grant Z211-N23 (Wittgenstein Award).

L. Feng and D. Fisman (Eds.): RV 2021, LNCS 12974, pp. 231–243, 2021.
https://doi.org/10.1007/978-3-030-88494-9_12

The underlying idea is not new—it dates back to the 1960s [8,9] under the name of n-version programming. The closest current incarnation of this concept is called n-version execution [4,11,26,41], where the system calls of the executed programs need to match (almost) exactly. Hence, the differences between the programs must be minimal and typically are variations on possible memory layouts to catch (often security-related) memory over/underflow errors, or updated versions of the original program that should largely behave the same.

In contrast, differential testing [15,24,32] exploits *true* diversity of implementations to find bugs with respect to a common specification, e.g. for compilers [42] or SQL-databases [40]. However, differential testing mainly applies to finite (and not necessarily parallel) runs in a controlled environment.

We argue that the time is ripe to explore the idea of running and monitoring truly diverse versions of the same program in parallel: the two versions could be written by independent development teams, in different languages, implementing different algorithms, against a common input-output interface. In this way, run-time monitoring can increase the trust in the correctness of programs and program updates without looking into the internals of the different implementations: if both independent implementations yield the same results, our confidence increases that the results are correct. On the other hand, if the monitor discovers a run-time discrepancy, a warning can be issued. This set-up presupposes, of course, that the duplication and monitoring can be done with little overhead. This can be the case, for example, if there are available hardware resources such as unused cores (/nodes) on a processor (cluster), or if the gain in confidence is worth the extra hardware, such as in safety-critical applications (where redundancy has long been a dominant paradigm) or in finance.

In comparison to traditional run-time monitoring, no formal specification of the program is needed in order to monitor it: on any given input, the expected outputs of one implementation are generated by the second implementation, and vice versa. The main overhead of differential monitoring comes from code comparing these outputs. Given sufficient operating system support, much of this work can be done when the program is paused anyway, such as during file operations. Preliminary benchmarks on a modified Linux kernel to monitor such file operations show very low overheads from monitoring and merging the outputs, even if the two implementations are written in different languages.

The main challenge for differential monitoring is that one implementation may overconstrain the expected behavior of the other implementation, mainly due to acceptable non-determinism and differences in timing, but also due to acceptable differences in system calls. Therefore, a differential monitor may also need a specification of how the output streams of two equivalent implementations may differ for the same input stream, and how the monitor can check and enforce such an equivalence run-time, for example, by delaying an implementation to let the other implementation catch up. The complexity of the monitor is proportional to the amount of acceptable differences in a program's behaviors. The specification and monitoring/enforcement of equivalence relations on input/output traces is an important area for future work; for now, we describe a relatively simple version of our vision, and how to extend it in the future.

The main goal of the present paper is to demonstrate that for a practical definition of behavioral equivalence—essentially, trace equality where individual inputs/outputs can be delayed by the monitor—the equivalence monitoring can be performed on real systems with a very modest overhead.

In summary, differential monitoring is a low-cost, black-box, on-line, and end-to-end run-time verification method requiring redundant hardware but no or little formal specification. These properties make it ideal for scenarios where one seeks to gain confidence in or improve the quality of continuously running software by using otherwise unused or easily obtainable hardware resources.

The rest of the paper is organized as follows:

- In Sect. 2, we review the current state of the art in related fields, and discuss how differential monitoring builds upon and extends it.
- In Sect. 3, we discuss the logical setup of differential monitoring and its main challenges.
- Finally, in Sect. 4, we present the results of preliminary experiments on differentially monitored programs written in different languages.

2   Background and Related Work

n-**Version Programming/Execution.** Running several versions of the same program in parallel to improve software reliability dates back to the 1970s [8,9,14,18,20,30]. Chen and Avizienis [8,9] rely on the cooperation of the various versions of the program: part of the process of *n*-version programming is to specify interesting kinds of data, and points of synchronization where each version explicitly presents that data to a coordinator process, who then judges which versions have produced correct data (via some voting mechanism, for example) and which need to either be aborted or otherwise corrected. Once this coordination step is complete, the (correct) versions can resume their work.

Modern works on *n*-version execution [4,6,11,12,26,34,41] follow this model in the sense that system calls and their arguments are the synchronization points and interesting data, respectively. Thus, correct versions of the same program generate the same sequence of system calls with the same arguments, including not only outputs, but also any form of reads: only one process actually reads; the results are shared with the others. This naturally side-steps the main challenges of differential monitoring we discuss in Sect. 3. However, it requires the different versions to be very closely related, to a point where it is implausible for the versions to be developed independently, or in different programming languages.

Though limited in this way, *n*-version execution can be used to guard against memory-related safety and security problems by varying memory layouts of data structures, including the stack, between versions [4,12,26,41]. Another scenario in which two programs are related sufficiently closely are program updates: *n*-version execution can be used to have an oracle for regression testing, and also to update running programs in the middle of processing requests [6,34].

While the core idea of differential monitoring is the same as that of n-version programming, the technical and theoretical environment is vastly different today, and our proposed blueprint and the challenges we discuss in Sect. 3 reflect this. Like n-version execution, we focus on the interactions of programs with the environment rather than arbitrary program state in order to both provide a less intrusive interface and exploit modern hardware/operating system architecture, but unlike n-version execution, we seek to recover the idea of truly diverse implementations.

Differential Testing. Differential Testing [15,24,32] is a well-known technique to test programs for which multiple versions exist. A large number of automatically generated test inputs are fed to $n > 1$ supposedly equivalent programs. Any differences detected in their output indicate possible bugs that need to be investigated. This technique has been fruitfully applied to finding bugs in Javascript debuggers [31], C compilers [42], and SQL databases [37,38,40].

DiffStream [27] is a framework supporting differential testing of stream outputs, which is closely related to our implementation of differential monitoring. They key technical difference is that differential monitoring does not only track and compare a set of (potentially unbounded) streams, but also needs to help programs stay in sync (see Sect. 3). For system calls and other events, the atomicity of stream elements can itself be in need of specification, as one system call may be equivalent to a sequence of several other ones. Finally, DiffStream ignores the question of what to output for equivalent but unequal streams.

Knight and Leveson [28,29] took issue with the claim that independently produced programs contain independent errors. Their experiments showed that faults exhibited by programs written independently by different programmers to the same specification are not completely independent. As a result, n-version execution has dropped high-level correctness claims, instead focusing on targeted variations (which are thus not independent of each other) of a program, and thus finding errors related to those variations. On the other hand, differential testing shows that a large variety of bugs can be found (and eliminated) by simply comparing the outputs of different but supposedly equivalent programs.

Run-Time Verification/Monitoring. Run-time verification (RV) is the general area of monitoring and possibly enforcing that a given program satisfies some properties, typically related in some way to the program's overall correctness [2,25]. In RV, a program generates a trace of interesting events, and a specification of the program's behavior allows us to build a monitor that checks such a trace of interesting events for whether it (possibly or definitely) conforms to the specification. A considerable body of work exists on various specification languages based on linear temporal logic and similar logics [1,5,7,13,23,35], and there are specification languages specifically for properties of streams [39], but these languages are interpreted over individual traces, rather than tuples of traces produced by supposedly equivalent programs. Especially in the area

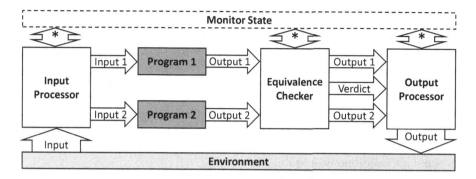

Fig. 1. The logical parts of differential monitoring

of security, languages like Hyper-LTL [10] are used on sets of traces (or, often-times, pairs of traces). However, similar to n-version execution, hyperlogics are usually interpreted over sets (or pairs) of traces that are generated by multiple executions of a single (often reactive or otherwise nondeterministic) program.

In process algebra, there has been much work on trace equivalence and other equivalence relations for comparing individual behaviors [19,21,22], but comparatively little attention to the online monitoring and enforcement of these equivalences. The definition of distinguishability in DiffStream [27] echoes some of our concerns. Interestingly, enforcement [17] has been a concern of n-version programming [8,9], which implements it by voting among the different versions.

3   Challenges

The goal of differential monitoring is to provide a low-cost, black-box, end-to-end run-time verification method, where the low cost relates to both the effort required in terms of specification and any run-time overhead caused by monitoring. There are two key challenges here: first, that an executable program may over-specify the desired behavior of the other program; second, how much "enforcement" a differential monitor may perform, say, by delaying or reordering inputs to the monitored programs, and by "merging" outputs of the monitored program (e.g., interpolation of different outputs, or voting for $n \geq 3$ programs). These challenges are two sides of the same coin, with the monitor trying to ensure that the monitored programs run independently as if they were running alone, yet are kept sufficiently in sync to produce equivalent results. A more advanced differential monitor may adjust scheduling decisions by the operating system, or try to synchronize the effects of some otherwise nondeterministic system calls.

Figure 1 shows the logical parts of a differential-monitoring setup: typically, a program would receive its inputs from and send its outputs to some environment, including the rest of the system it is running on as well as any network or other devices it has access to. The differential monitor inserts itself into this relationship on both ends, and additionally does this for two programs at once. The *input processor* is the part of the monitor that handles any input the monitored programs receive. By default, it simply duplicates any inputs it receives and forwards them to both programs. The *equivalence checker* receives the outputs of both programs and checks them for equivalence, which by default simply means equality. Finally, the *output processor* produces the output that is finally sent to the environment. If equivalence is defined as equality, its default behavior is to send the output of one of the programs to the environment as long as the equivalence checker's verdict is positive, and some error message aborting the programs when the verdict becomes negative. However, for more complex notions of input processing, output equivalence, output merging, and error handling can be specified. All three components may communicate with each other via some notion of monitor state.

Each program may expect to see the effects of its output in the environment. Thus the monitor may have to slow down the inputs and/or outputs of the faster program to let the slower program catch up. In general, a differential monitor should prevent either program from being confronted with an environment state it does not expect, keeping up the illusion that it is running alone. Beyond using additional memory to buffer input or output elements as in DiffStream [27], differential monitors may need additional power and resources to ensure that the different programs' interactions with their environment do not get too out-of-sync. Kallas et al. [27] already recognized that some parts of the output (for example, timings and random numbers) may have to be relaxed or ignored for equivalence checking, though deciding on the "merged" output may be harder.

In differential monitoring, the program specification is replaced by the monitor specification, which ought to be simpler. All three components of a differential monitor have to be accompanied by a specification defining exactly when and how to defer, transform, deem equivalent, and merge any inputs or outputs. The precise form and power of such specifications, and of the monitors implementing them (e.g., their memory needs), will be an interesting area of research, as will be the automatic synthesis of differential monitors from formal specifications.

4   Experimental Results

In this section, we report on experiments evaluating the feasibility of differential monitoring and the overheads it causes in practice based on a simple framework.

Experimental Setup. To test the basic overheads of running two programs side-by-side, duplicating inputs and comparing outputs, we modified a current version of the Linux kernel to support an additional system call that activates monitoring for a pair of processes and any of their children. In particular, we watch the basic file operations of these processes. When a file is opened, we determine whether its operations need to be monitored. For example, regular files opened in a read-only fashion can be ignored and any further interactions of the programs with them incur no overhead. On the other hand, non-seekable files (pipes, the user's terminal, etc.) need the monitor to provide the same data to both processes. Finally, files opened for writing are monitored to ensure that both programs write the same data to them.

In terms of our model from Sect. 3, the input processor duplicates all inputs (mostly reads from the standard input) by buffering the result of the faster reader to also provide it to the second process. The equivalence checker checks the bytes written out for equality; neither monitored writes nor reads need to match exactly in terms of how many bytes are read/written in a single system call—the monitor will proceed as far as possible. The input processor holds up the faster program by not returning from the write system call until all bytes a process wanted to write have been matched and sent to the environment. If the output of the two programs does not match, the monitor aborts both programs— this is of course the most extreme measure that could be taken, but suffices for our goal of measuring overheads in the case where both programs are correct. We did test that our monitor indeed stops programs that do not produce equivalent output, and does so before actually printing that output.

Our benchmarks often write a large number of small output lines in rapid succession. For this case, an optional, experimental optimization allows the faster program to continue execution until it gets too far ahead, buffering writes in the meantime. This is valid when programs do not need to see the effects of their outputs on the environment immediately and expect the writes to always succeed, as is the case for our test programs, or, for example, web servers. In general, a monitor specification would specify in what cases this optimization can be applied. By default, our benchmarks run without this optimization.

This simple prototype of course does not capture the full complexity of the specifications eventually needed to run more complex programs side-by-side, but it lets us explore the overheads of what we believe are the most common cases in differential monitoring. To this end, we wrote several small benchmark programs in C, Java, and Python, sometimes using different algorithms between the programs, and ran them in various pairings and alone to compare the slowdowns caused by our monitor. Due to space constraints, some data on our experiments is only contained in the technical report [33]. As the relevant metric we compare, for each pairing of programs, the wall-clock time of running the pairing against the wall-clock time of the slower program (which is a natural lower bound for the pairing). All benchmarks were run on a minimal Gentoo installation using our modified kernel on an Intel(R) Core(TM) i5-4690K processor with 16GiB RAM and a mid-level SSD.

Main Benchmark: Primes. Consider verifying programs that should answer queries about whether a given number n is prime or what the nth prime number is. Any black-box attempt to verify the outputs of such a program invariably needs to do a similar amount of work as the original program.

For this benchmark, we picked two algorithms to determine primality: the Sieve of Eratosthenes and the Baillie-PSW [36] primality test. We implemented the former in C and the latter in Java. The programs have two modes. In inter- active mode, they accept a stream of queries for either the n-th prime number or whether a given number n is prime, and produce a corresponding answer. In non- interactive mode, they simply enumerate all the primes up to a certain index,

		Program 1	Program 2	WT-1	WT-2	WT	Overhead	WT-O	Overhead-O
Interactive	Sml Qs	C	C	3.11s	3.11s	3.13s	0.56%	3.13s	0.69%
		C	Java	3.11s	3.82s	3.87s	1.31%	3.80s	-0.33%
		Java	Java	3.82s	3.82s	3.84s	0.69%	3.92s	2.74%
	Lrg Qs	C	C	1.83s	1.83s	1.87s	1.94%	1.84s	0.35%
		C	Java	1.83s	2.32s	2.36s	1.79%	2.33s	0.63%
		Java	Java	2.32s	2.32s	2.48s	7.17%	2.33s	0.56%
		Program 1	Program 2	WT-1	WT-2	WT	Overhead	WT-O	Overhead-O
Non-Interactive		C	C	0.40s	0.40s	0.43s	8.06%	0.42s	4.53%
		C	Java	0.40s	0.66s	0.69s	4.80%	0.67s	2.74%
		C	Java-E	0.40s	0.28s	0.56s	39.80%	0.47s	17.63%
		C	Python	0.40s	4.22s	4.25s	0.75%	4.32s	2.35%
		Java	Java	0.66s	0.66s	0.77s	17.75%	0.69s	5.10%
		Java	Java-E	0.66s	0.28s	0.77s	16.68%	0.68s	3.66%
		Java	Python	0.66s	4.22s	4.42s	4.72%	4.33s	2.70%
		Java-E	Java-E	0.28s	0.28s	0.38s	33.33%	0.31s	7.94%
		Java-E	Python	0.28s	4.22s	4.32s	2.31%	4.35s	3.20%
		Python	Python	4.22s	4.22s	4.49s	6.48%	4.33s	2.57%

Fig. 2. Benchmark results for primes

in our case up to the 10 000th prime. For that mode, we also included another Java ("Java-E") and a Python implementation of the Sieve of Eratosthenes.

Figure 2 shows the average running times (in seconds) of 20 runs for each language on its own (WT-1/WT-2) and in a paired monitored setting (WT), and the corresponding overhead. For the interactive mode, in one run we generated 300 queries with $n < 4\,000$, and in the other, we generated 10 000 such queries with $n < 500$, trading off internal computation time vs. interaction with the system. As we see, the overhead is negligible for the fewer requests where both programs spend more time simply computing the response, while it is still relatively low for programs where our monitoring code is invoked more often. The overheads for the non-interactive version are significantly higher—they are writing significantly more lines than the interactive version in less time; the write-buffering optimization mentioned above (results shown in the "-O" columns) drastically improves our results. Overall, Java seems to suffer the most from being run side-by side with another program; however, this is also true for just running the Java program twice at the same time without monitoring. We believe the cause to be the optimization behavior of the JVM, which spawns around 12 threads for these single threaded applications. In so far as the negative overhead of the C/Java pairing is not a measuring artifact, it is likely for similar reasons as the negative overheads for the Echo benchmark discussed below.

Sort. For this benchmark, we implemented Insertion-Sort in C, Merge-Sort in Java, and Quicksort in Python. In interactive mode, they accept three sorts of commands: one to add a number to a currently maintained list, one to print the list in sorted order, and one to clear the maintained list. The input we generate

	Program 1	Program 2	WT-1	WT-2	WT	Overhead	WT-O	Overhead-O
Interactive	C	C	1.47s	1.47s	1.56s	6.54%	1.49s	1.77%
	C	Java	1.47s	1.52s	2.62s	72.63%	1.57s	3.19%
	C	Python	1.47s	1.51s	2.05s	35.78%	1.55s	2.85%
	Java	Java	1.52s	1.52s	2.77s	81.91%	1.60s	5.13%
	Java	Python	1.52s	1.51s	3.81s	150.46%	1.64s	8.19%
	Python	Python	1.51s	1.51s	2.28s	50.81%	1.55s	2.55%
	Program 1	Program 2	WT-1	WT-2	WT	Overhead	WT-O	Overhead-O
Non-Interactive	C	C	5.55s	5.55s	5.84s	5.23%	5.74s	3.52%
	C	Java	5.55s	0.52s	6.22s	12.07%	5.84s	5.24%
	C	Python	5.55s	0.54s	5.88s	5.96%	5.67s	2.30%
	Java	Java	0.52s	0.52s	1.11s	114.45%	0.75s	44.70%
	Java	Python	0.52s	0.54s	1.26s	132.56%	0.70s	29.61%
	Python	Python	0.54s	0.54s	0.84s	54.80%	0.64s	17.34%

Fig. 3. Benchmark results for sort

for interactive mode sorts the list on roughly every 10th command, and clears it after roughly every 6 of those, which makes for relatively short lists, but still a high output-to-input ratio. In non-interactive mode, the programs read in a list of 100 000 numbers from a file, sort it, and print the result. As an interesting variation, we give each program a different permutation of the same list—as this does not affect the results of sorting those lists, the programs still produce the same out. In this way, this benchmark simulates different ways in which programs may keep private data. The net result of this setup is that the programs do a batch of reading first (except for the C program, whose insertion sort is running while reading the list), followed by a large burst of writes (this is also true for the C program). As we can see in Fig. 3, the high rates of writes for both modes can cause quite extreme overheads, which again can be brought down significantly with our write-buffering optimization.

Further Benchmarks. We only briefly describe our other two benchmark programs here. More details on them can be found in the technical report [33].

Echo. Echo was intended to be a worst-case benchmark for our framework: the programs written in C, Java, and Python simply read text from the standard input line by line and write it back to the standard output, thus maximally using both our input-splitting and output-comparing facilities. Overheads for Echo reached 67.50% for two Java programs (10.26% for two C programs), which fell to 10.05% (−1.24% for C-C) using our writer-buffering optimization. The same optimization made all other pairings produce negative overhead, as it turned out that the programs were now parallelizing the reading IO operations.

Mod-Squares. Mod-squares was designed to simulate single-threaded computational activity that is not parallelizable and works in constant memory, thus eliminating any sort of resource constraints other than the extra computation and coordination caused by the monitor. At its core, it simply squares a (hard-coded constant) number some number of times, always modulo some other number. The highest overhead, again in the Java-Java pairing, was 34.42% (the C-C pairing had 4.20%), which the write-buffering optimization reduced to 7.45% (or 0.22% for C-C).

Discussion. Our benchmarks tested a general framework to monitor the IO operations of programs written in different programming languages. Previous work would have been unable to do so, as works in multi-version execution [26, 41] depend on the programs making the exact same system calls, which would already be violated by the Java and Python virtual machines' startup activities, while DiffStream [27] works on a different level of abstraction and does not consider having to delay outputs. The overheads we saw for our main benchmark are relatively low, and naturally somewhat related to the ratio of work a program does to how often it interacts with its environment and thus the monitor. The other benchmarks we ran consider various worst-case scenarios with extremely heavy interaction with the monitor; overheads in these benchmarks go up to 150% in extreme cases. These extreme overheads go down to 45% with our write-buffering optimization, showing that there is much room for optimizations both in our basic implementation and in exploiting monitoring specifications to allow for more efficient processing of those particular cases.

5   Conclusion

Differential Monitoring has the potential to be a comparatively light-weight runtime-verification method that is able to check programs' end-to-end behavior in an efficient way, simply through redundancy and overengineering. Similar efforts have both a long history and recent activity, and the ubiquitousness of multi-core hardware suggests that the approach can be applied in many scenarios without too much of a performance penalty. For complicated programs, the lack of formal specification is not absolute, but turned upside down: a differential monitor may need a specification of two programs *potential differences*, which should be comparatively small in any case. The precise formalisms for such a specification will draw heavily on existing work on runtime monitoring but pose some interesting challenges on their own, including for their eventual implementation. However, we believe that these challenges can be overcome, thereby significantly adding to the toolbox that runtime verification offers its users to increase the quality of software.

Acknowledgement. The authors would like to thank Borzoo Bonakdarpour, Derek Dreyer, Adrian Francalanza, Owolabi Legunsen, Matthew Milano, Manuel Rigger, Cesar Sanchez, and the members of the IST Verification Seminar for their helpful comments and insights on various stages of this work, as well as the reviewers of RV'21 for their helpful suggestions on the actual paper.

References

1. Barringer, H., Falcone, Y., Havelund, K., Reger, G., Rydeheard, D.: Quantified event automata: towards expressive and efficient runtime monitors. In: Giannakopoulou, D., Méry, D. (eds.) FM 2012. LNCS, vol. 7436, pp. 68–84. Springer, Heidelberg (2012). https://doi.org/10.1007/978-3-642-32759-9_9
2. Bartocci, E., Falcone, Y. (eds.): Lectures on Runtime Verification - Introductory and Advanced Topics. Lecture Notes in Computer Science, vol. 10457. Springer, Heidelberg (2018). https://doi.org/10.1007/978-3-319-75632-5
3. Bauer, A., Leucker, M., Schallhart, C.: Runtime verification for LTL and TLTL. ACM Trans. Softw. Eng. Methodol. **20**(4) (2011). https://doi.org/10.1145/2000799.2000800
4. Berger, E.D., Zorn, B.G.: DieHard: probabilistic memory safety for unsafe languages. In: PLDI 2006, p. 158–168. Association for Computing Machinery, New York (2006). https://doi.org/10.1145/1133981.1134000
5. Bonakdarpour, B., Navabpour, S., Fischmeister, S.: Time-triggered runtime verification. Formal Methods Syst. Design **43**(1), 29–60 (2013). https://doi.org/10.1007/s10703-012-0182-0
6. Cadar, C., Hosek, P.: Multi-version software updates. In: HotSWUp 2012, pp. 36–40 (2012). https://doi.org/10.1109/HotSWUp.2012.6226615
7. Chen, F., Roşu, G.: Parametric trace slicing and monitoring. In: Kowalewski, S., Philippou, A. (eds.) TACAS 2009. LNCS, vol. 5505, pp. 246–261. Springer, Heidelberg (2009). https://doi.org/10.1007/978-3-642-00768-2_23
8. Chen, L., Avizienis, A.: N-version programming: a fault-tolerance approach to reliability of software operation. In: FTCS 1978, vol. 1, pp. 3–9 (1978)
9. Chen, L., Avizienis, A.: N-version programming: a fault-tolerance approach to reliability of software operation. In: FTCS 1995, 'Highlights from Twenty-Five Years', p. 113ff (1995). https://doi.org/10.1109/FTCSH.1995.532621
10. Clarkson, M.R., Finkbeiner, B., Koleini, M., Micinski, K.K., Rabe, M.N., Sánchez, C.: Temporal logics for hyperproperties. In: Abadi, M., Kremer, S. (eds.) POST 2014. LNCS, vol. 8414, pp. 265–284. Springer, Heidelberg (2014). https://doi.org/10.1007/978-3-642-54792-8_15
11. Coppens, B., Sutter, B.D., Volckaert, S.: Multi-variant execution environments. In: Larsen, P., Sadeghi, A. (eds.) The Continuing Arms Race: Code-Reuse Attacks and Defenses, pp. 211–258. ACM/Morgan & Claypool (2018). https://doi.org/10.1145/3129743.3129752
12. Cox, B., et al.: N-Variant systems: a secretless framework for security through diversity. In: USENIX-SS 2006. USENIX Association, USA (2006). https://www.usenix.org/conference/15th-usenix-security-symposium/n-variant-systems-secretless-framework-security-through
13. Demri, S., Lazic, R.: LTL with the freeze quantifier and register automata. ACM Trans. Comput. Log. **10**(3), 16:1–16:30 (2009). https://doi.org/10.1145/1507244.1507246
14. Elmendorf, W.: Fault-tolerant programming. In: FTCS 1972, pp. 79–83 (1972)
15. Evans, R.B., Savoia, A.: Differential testing: a new approach to change detection. In: ESEC-FSE companion 2007, pp. 549–552. Association for Computing Machinery, New York (2007). https://doi.org/10.1145/1295014.1295038
16. Falcone, Y., Fernandez, J., Mounier, L.: What can you verify and enforce at runtime? Int. J. Softw. Tools Technol. Transf. **14**(3), 349–382 (2012). https://doi.org/10.1007/s10009-011-0196-8

17. Falcone, Y., Mariani, L., Rollet, A., Saha, S.: Runtime failure prevention and reaction. In: Bartocci, E., Falcone, Y. (eds.) Lectures on Runtime Verification. LNCS, vol. 10457, pp. 103–134. Springer, Cham (2018). https://doi.org/10.1007/978-3-319-75632-5_4

18. Fischler, M.A. et al.: Distinct software: an approach to reliable computing. In: 2nd USA-Japan Computer Conference, pp. 1–7 (1975)

19. Fokkink, W.J.: Introduction to Process Algebra. Texts in Theoretical Computer Science. An EATCS Series. Springer, Heidelberg (2000). https://doi.org/10.1007/978-3-662-04293-9

20. Girard, E., Rault, J.: A programming technique for software reliability. In: IEEE Symposium on Computer Software Reliability, pp. 44–50 (1973)

21. Glabbeek, R.J.: The linear time - branching time spectrum. In: Baeten, J.C.M., Klop, J.W. (eds.) CONCUR 1990. LNCS, vol. 458, pp. 278–297. Springer, Heidelberg (1990). https://doi.org/10.1007/BFb0039066

22. van Glabbeek, R.J., et al.: The linear time—branching time spectrum II. In: Best, E. (ed.) CONCUR 1993. LNCS, vol. 715, pp. 66–81. Springer, Heidelberg (1993). https://doi.org/10.1007/3-540-57208-2_6

23. Grigore, R., Distefano, D., Petersen, R.L., Tzevelekos, N.: Runtime verification based on register automata. In: Piterman, N., Smolka, S.A. (eds.) TACAS 2013. LNCS, vol. 7795, pp. 260–276. Springer, Heidelberg (2013). https://doi.org/10.1007/978-3-642-36742-7_19

24. Groce, A., Holzmann, G., Joshi, R.: Randomized differential testing as a prelude to formal verification. In: ICSE 2007, pp. 621–631. IEEE Computer Society, USA (2007). https://doi.org/10.1109/ICSE.2007.68

25. Havelund, K., Reger, G., Roşu, G.: Runtime verification past experiences and future projections. In: Steffen, B., Woeginger, G. (eds.) Computing and Software Science. LNCS, vol. 10000, pp. 532–562. Springer, Cham (2019). https://doi.org/10.1007/978-3-319-91908-9_25

26. Hosek, P., Cadar, C.: VARAN the unbelievable: an efficient N-version execution framework. In: ASPLOS 2015, pp. 339–353. Association for Computing Machinery, New York (2015). https://doi.org/10.1145/2694344.2694390

27. Kallas, K., Niksic, F., Stanford, C., Alur, R.: DiffStream: differential output testing for stream processing programs. PACMPL 4(OOPSLA) (2020). https://doi.org/10.1145/3428221

28. Knight, J.C., Leveson, N.G.: An experimental evaluation of the assumption of independence in multiversion programming. IEEE Trans. Softw. Eng. 12(1), 96–109 (1986). https://doi.org/10.1109/TSE.1986.6312924

29. Knight, J.C., Leveson, N.G.: A reply to the criticisms of the Knight & Leveson experiment. ACM SIGSOFT Softw. Eng. Notes 15(1), 24–35 (1990). https://doi.org/10.1145/382294.382710

30. Kopetz, H.: Software redundancy in real time systems. In: IFIP Congress 1974, pp. 182–186. North-Holland (1974)

31. Lehmann, D., Pradel, M.: Feedback-directed differential testing of interactive debuggers. In: ESEC/FSE 2018, pp. 610–620. Association for Computing Machinery, New York (2018). https://doi.org/10.1145/3236024.3236037

32. McKeeman, W.M.: Differential testing for software. Digit. Tech. J. 10(1), 100–107 (1998). http://www.hpl.hp.com/hpjournal/dtj/vol10num1/vol10num1art9.pdf

33. Muehlboeck, F., Henzinger, T.A.: Differential monitoring. Technical report 9946, IST Austria (2021). https://research-explorer.app.ist.ac.at/librecat/record/9946

34. Pina, L., Andronidis, A., Hicks, M., Cadar, C.: MVEDSUA: higher availability dynamic software updates via multi-version execution. In: ASPLOS 2019, pp. 573–585. ACM (2019). https://doi.org/10.1145/3297858.3304063

35. Pnueli, A., Zaks, A.: PSL model checking and run-time verification via testers. In: Misra, J., Nipkow, T., Sekerinski, E. (eds.) FM 2006. LNCS, vol. 4085, pp. 573–586. Springer, Heidelberg (2006). https://doi.org/10.1007/11813040_38

36. Pomerance, C., Selfridge, J.L., Wagstaff, S.S.: The pseudoprimes to $25 \cdot 10^9$. Math. Comput. **35**(151), 1003–1026 (1980)

37. Rigger, M., Su, Z.: Detecting optimization bugs in database engines via non-optimizing reference engine construction. In: ESEC/FSE 2020, pp. 1140–1152. Association for Computing Machinery, New York (2020). https://doi.org/10.1145/3368089.3409710

38. Rigger, M., Su, Z.: Finding bugs in database systems via query partitioning. PACMPL **4**(OOPSLA) (2020). https://doi.org/10.1145/3428279

39. Sánchez, C.: Online and offline stream runtime verification of synchronous systems. In: Colombo, C., Leucker, M. (eds.) RV 2018. LNCS, vol. 11237, pp. 138–163. Springer, Cham (2018). https://doi.org/10.1007/978-3-030-03769-7_9

40. Slutz, D.R.: Massive stochastic testing of SQL. In: VLDB 1998, pp. 618–622. Morgan Kaufmann (1998). http://www.vldb.org/conf/1998/p618.pdf

41. Volckaert, S., De Sutter, B., De Baets, T., De Bosschere, K.: GHUMVEE: efficient, effective, and flexible replication. In: Garcia-Alfaro, J., Cuppens, F., Cuppens-Boulahia, N., Miri, A., Tawbi, N. (eds.) FPS 2012. LNCS, vol. 7743, pp. 261–277. Springer, Heidelberg (2013). https://doi.org/10.1007/978-3-642-37119-6_17

42. Yang, X., Chen, Y., Eide, E., Regehr, J.: Finding and understanding bugs in C compilers. In: PLDI 2011, pp. 283–294. Association for Computing Machinery, New York (2011). https://doi.org/10.1145/1993498.1993532

Ortac: Runtime Assertion Checking for OCaml (Tool Paper)

Jean-Christophe Filliâtre[1]([⊠]) and Clément Pascutto[1,2] [iD]

[1] Université Paris-Saclay, CNRS, ENS Paris-Saclay, Inria,
Laboratoire Méthodes Formelles, 91190 Gif-sur-Yvette, France
{jean-christophe.filliatre,clement.pascutto}@lri.fr
[2] Tarides, 75005 Paris, France

Abstract. Runtime assertion checking (RAC) is a convenient set of techniques that lets developers abstract away the process of verifying the correctness of their programs by writing formal specifications and automating their verification at runtime.

In this work, we present `ortac`, a runtime assertion checking tool for OCaml libraries and programs. OCaml is a functional programming language in which idioms rely on an expressive type system, modules, and interface abstractions. `ortac` consumes interfaces annotated with type invariants and function contracts and produces code wrappers with the same signature that check these specifications at runtime. It provides a flexible framework for traditional assertion checking, monitoring misbehaviors without interruptions, and automated fuzz testing for OCaml programs.

This paper presents an overview of `ortac` features and highlights its main design choices.

Keywords: Runtime assertion checking · OCaml · Software engineering

1 Introduction

OCaml is a general-purpose programming language featuring imperative, functional, and object-oriented paradigms. OCaml code is structured into modules. Each module comes with an interface, which exposes some of its contents (*e.g.* types, functions, or exceptions) and ensures a proper abstraction barrier. OCaml features an expressive type system that provides strong guarantees. An OCaml program will never try dereferencing a null pointer, for instance. Yet, it does not protect against programming errors such as accessing arrays out of their bounds, incorrectly implementing an algorithm, etc. Thus, good practices of software engineering apply to OCaml as well, including rigorous testing using technologies such as QuickCheck or fuzzing. We extend this toolset with `ortac`, a runtime assertion checking tool for OCaml. This tool is still under development. It is an open-source project available at https://github.com/ocaml-gospel/ortac.

© Springer Nature Switzerland AG 2021
L. Feng and D. Fisman (Eds.): RV 2021, LNCS 12974, pp. 244–253, 2021.
https://doi.org/10.1007/978-3-030-88494-9_13

We build upon Gospel, a behavioral specification language for OCaml [9]. Interfaces are annotated with formal specification, such as function contracts, type models and invariants, and logical definitions. Our tool consumes these interfaces and produces wrappers that check the Gospel function contracts and type invariants at runtime while maintaining the abstraction barrier. This paper presents an overview of `ortac` features and highlights its main design choices.

A critical feature of `ortac` is the identification of the executable subset of Gospel. Indeed, Gospel was not explicitly designed for runtime assertion checking—it is also used for deductive verification of OCaml code via the Why3 platform [13]—and annotations may contain unbounded quantifiers or uninterpreted logical symbols. In the process, `ortac` ignores anything that is not executable.

We address several features of OCaml that are challenging for runtime assertion checking. For instance, `ortac` suitably wraps OCaml functors (modules parameterized over modules) to ensure proper usage of their parameters. Interesting issues also arise in Gospel specification. For instance, contracts can express that a function is responsible for verifying a precondition, which coincides with a defensive programming idiom. In that case, the `ortac` wrapper checks that the function indeed performs this verification. Another convenient feature of Gospel is a structural, polymorphic equality. Consequently, `ortac` has to identify uses of this equality that can be implemented and checked at runtime.

We start with a motivating example (Sect. 2). Then we describe the tool architecture and discuss some technical aspects of `ortac` (Sect. 3). We conclude with related work (Sect. 4) and perspectives (Sect. 5).

2   Overview and Motivating Example

Let us illustrate the workflow of `ortac` on a simple OCaml module for modular arithmetic. Our interface is contained in a `modular.mli` file shown in Fig. 1. The corresponding implementation in `modular.ml` is omitted as its contents is not used by `ortac`. The `Modular` module is parameterized by a `Modulus` module, and exposes an abstract type `t` and three functions: a constructor `of_int`, an exponentiation `power`, and a division `div`.

Invoking the `ortac` executable on `modular.mli` produces a new module implementation in `modular_rtac.ml` containing a wrapper around the implementation, with the same interface as the unwrapped module. The generated code depends on the unwrapped module at runtime as it calls the original functions, but its implementation is not used nor altered during the generation. The generated code also depends on an external lightweight support library: `ortac-runtime`. We illustrate this procedure in Fig. 2. The client code can then freely call this wrapper, either in testing code or fuzzing code, or directly in production.

For instance `modular.mli` declares a function `power` that takes two arguments x and n. Its contract consists of two clauses. The `checks` clauses specifies a dynamic precondition n >= 0, meaning that the function must verify this

```
1    module type Modulus = sig
2      val m : int
3      (*@ ensures m > 0 *)
4    end
5
6    module Modular (M : Modulus) : sig
7      type t = private { v : int }
8      (*@ invariant 0 <= v < M.m *)
9
10     val of_int : int -> t
11     (*@ r = of_int x
12         requires x >= 0
13         ensures  r.v = x mod M.m *)
14
15     val power : t -> int -> t
16     (*@ r = power x n
17         checks  n >= 0
18         ensures r.v = (pow x.v n) mod M.m *)
19
20     val div : t -> t -> t
21     (*@ q = div x y
22         ensures x.v = (y.v * q.v) mod M.m
23         raises  Division_by_zero -> y.v = 0 *)
24   end
```

Fig. 1. Modular module interface (`modular.mli`).

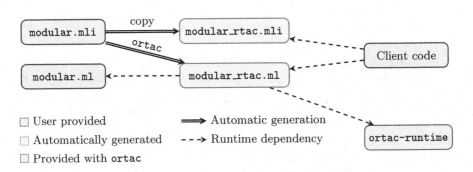

Fig. 2. Workflow using `ortac`.

property in its implementation and raise `Invalid_argument` if it is not met. The `ensures` clause is a postcondition, stating that `r.v = (pow x.v n) mod M.m` holds in the post-state, after calling the function. Therefore, `modular_rtac.ml` also contains a `power` function, with the same arguments, and verifies the contract with the following steps before returning the result:

- Call the original unwrapped `power` with arguments x and n, and keep the result in r.

- Check that if n is negative, the call raised the Invalid_argument exception, and that no exception was raised otherwise.
- Check that the postcondition r.v = (pow x.v n) mod M.m holds.

Note that Gospel's semantics is defined using mathematical integers. In the formula above, the functions pow and mod operate over arbitrary-precision integers and machine integers r.v, x.v, n, and M.m are implicitly promoted to arbitrary-precision integers by the Gospel type-ckecker.

If any of these verification steps fails during the execution of the client, the contract is violated, and the instrumented code reports the error precisely using the location of the contract and the clauses that failed:

```
$ ./client
File "modular.mli", lines 15-18, characters 2-43:
 Runtime error in function 'power':
 - the post-condition 'r.v = (pow x.v n) mod M.m' was violated.
```

3   Code Generation and Tool Architecture

In this section, we describe the translation of Gospel's formulas into Boolean OCaml expressions (Sect. 3.1). We then show how they are combined to generate function wrappers that check contracts and invariants (Sect. 3.2). Finally, we provide a few highlights on the modularity of ortac and how it helps developers customize its behavior (Sect. 3.3).

3.1   Translating Formulas

Gospel is a tool-agnostic specification language: one can use it for both Deductive Verification (DV) and Runtime Verification (RV). Because of this, most formulas are not executable. For instance, they may contain unbounded quantifiers or logical symbols that are axiomatized but not implemented. The first step of the generation consists of identifying the executable subset of these specifications and compiling them into Boolean OCaml expressions whenever possible. In this process, ortac ignores formulas that do not translate and emits a warning to the user.

Mathematical Integers. As mentioned in the previous section, integers in specifications use mathematical, arbitrary precision arithmetic. We use the zarith library to implement integers with these semantics with a marginal performance cost. It uses native integers whenever possible and GMP integers when needed. This implies that the instrumented code detects discrepancies between machine computations and their mathematical counterpart, and thus report overflows to the user.

Quantifiers. The use of exists and forall quantifiers in formulas generally makes them non-executable, because the quantifier domain may be unbounded. However, ortac identifies some bounded quantifiers patterns, such as forall i. <term> <= i < <term> -> ..., and properly translates them.

Equality. Gospel provides a logical equality that lets developers write easy to read formulas with the = operator. Although OCaml provides a polymorphic structural equality function, its use is limited. Its semantics may not coincide with the logical equality in the specification, and its execution may fail or diverge on functional or cyclic values. Instead, `ortac` leverages the type-checking information to generate safe monomorphic equality functions whenever the type permits.

Gospel Standard Library. Specifications can use functions from the Gospel standard library, an interface containing purely logical declarations for arithmetic operations and data containers such as arrays, bags, or maps. To execute them, `ortac-runtime` provides an implementation of this library using the most appropriate data structures. Some of these data structures require additional information to be implemented efficiently. For instance, an implementation of maps based on balanced trees requires a total order over the elements. In those cases, we use the same approach as for equality and derive them from the typing information when possible.

Undefineness and Runtime Exceptions. After `ortac` translates a formula into an OCaml expression, it is still possible that its execution raises an exception, *e.g.*, due to a division by zero or an array access out of bounds written in the specification. We catch any such failure in the wrapper and report it accordingly to the user.

3.2   Wrapping the Functions

After identifying and translating the executable subset of the specification formulas, `ortac` generates a wrapper around each function from the interface. Let us illustrate the translation schema on a generic example with two declarations, contained in a module `Original`. In the following, `<X>` denotes the translation of an executable formula X, and `<failure>` includes the code reporting the specification violations to the user.

```
1  type t = ...
2  (*@ invariant I *)
3
4  val f : t -> t
5  (*@ r = f x
6      checks   C
7      requires P
8      ensures  Q
9      raises   E -> R *)
```

The wrapper for `f` first verifies that the pre-state satisfies the preconditions and the invariants on input values. We also compute special `checks` preconditions at this point, but nothing is reported yet, since we expect the wrapped function itself to raise an exception in that case.

```
1  let f x =
2    if not <I x> then <failure>;
3    if not <P> then <failure>;
4    let c = <C> in
5    ...
```

The wrapper then calls the unwrapped function and examines any raised exception. In any exceptional function exit, the wrapper checks the invariants on the input values.

- If f raises an Invalid_argument exception, reporting the checks precondition C was not met, the wrapper indeed checks that property.
- If f raises an exception registered in a raises clause, the associated postcondition is checked along with checks clauses: in case of a violation, f should raise Invalid_argument instead.
- Finally, we consider any other exception a violation of the specification, since all possibly raised exceptions should appear in a raises clause.

```
4    ...
5    let r = try Original.f x with
6      | Invalid_argument _ ->
7        if c then <failure>;
8        if not <I x> then <failure>
9      | E ->
10       if not c then <failure>;
11       if not <R> then <failure>;
12       if not <I x> then <failure>
13     | e ->
14       if not c then <failure>;
15       <failure>
16   in
17   ...
```

If f exits normally, we check that c is verified—otherwise, f should have raised an exception—along with the postcondition Q, and invariants on both the inputs (when modified) and outputs. Finally, we return the value computed by f.

```
16   ...
17   if not c then <failure>;
18   if not <Q> then <failure>;
19   if not <I r> then <failure>;
20   r
```

Note that our wrappers only test function calls that go through this interface, because only the interface contains specifications; the wrappers never check internal calls, including for recursive functions. For instance, if the function f calls a function g internally, then the wrapper for f still calls the original g, and not its wrapper. However, when `ortac` wraps a functor `module F(A) = B`, both the argument module `A` and the output module `B` are wrapped, and thus internal calls from `B` to `A` are checked.

3.3 A Modular Architecture

On top of the wrapper generator, `ortac` provides a framework for using the generated code in multiple settings. Its modular architecture lets contributors write custom *frontends* that control various aspects of the generated code.

Failure Modes. By defining the exact contents of the `<failure>` code, frontends can set up various reporting strategies. For instance, effectively failing solely on preconditions enables `ortac` to only check the correct usage of the library by the client. One can also easily define a monitor-only mode, where errors are logged but do not interrupt the execution of the program.

Custom Code. Arbitrary code can come along with the wrapper. For instance, this allows frontend developers to integrate it into a test framework or expose it with a different interface. Frontends can also redefine or extend the runtime library used by the instrumented code.

The `ortac` framework comes with a default frontend that immediately fails when a failure occurs to report it as soon as possible, as shown in Sect. 2. We also provide a fuzzing frontend, which pipes the instrumented code into an `american fuzzy lop` [1] powered executable that feeds the library with random inputs to find specification violations without the presence of user-written client code.

4   Related Work

Runtime assertion checking techniques have been implemented for many languages, with various design choices. Eiffel [17] is the first introduction of behavioral contract-based specifications in a programming language, together with runtime checking. JML [7,10] is a behavioral specification language for Java, (mostly) executable by design and thus amenable to runtime assertion checking, e.g., OpenJML [11]. SPEC# [3] extends the C# programming language with support for function contracts. AsmL [4,5], then Code Contracts [2], implement similar yet less intrusive approaches for the .NET Framework. SPARK [16] also integrates program specifications into its host language, Ada. Frama-C [19] provides runtime assertion checking for C with its E-ACSL plugin [12,20], which identifies and translates an executable subset of ACSL [6].

JML initially enforced machine arithmetic [10] before adding support for mathematical integers [8], and now uses the latter by default. SPARK also supports both modes but uses machine arithmetic by default. E-ACSL only supports mathematical integers, with significant optimisations [15] to limit the performance overhead. `ortac` supports mathematical integers by default, although it enables frontends to override this behavior to use machine arithmetic instead.

A distinctive feature of `ortac` is that is implements a rather large logical library, namely the Gospel standard library. Other runtime assertion checking tools either come with a very small logical library (*e.g.*, SPARK) or only provide an annotated subset of the programming standard library (*e.g.*, `libc` for E-ACSL or the Java standard library for OpenJML).

When it comes to undefineness—undefined or exceptional behaviors arising in formulas—`ortac` is similar to E-ACSL and SPARK, and raises exceptions when the evaluation of a formula fails. JML, on the other hand, substitutes undefined values with an arbitrary value of the correct type.

Note that while some tools provide powerful instrumentations to detect pointer unsafety, the type system of OCaml provides such guarantees natively in the language. In particular, `ortac` does not need to support a `valid(p)` construct—like E-ACSL does [14]—for user code nor Gospel formulas and avoids the subsequent overhead on the assertion checking generated code.

5   Conclusion and Perspectives

We presented `ortac`, a non-invasive runtime assertion checking tool for OCaml, based on formal specifications of module interfaces.

The project is under active development, and we are adding many features that extend the expressiveness of the tool. In particular, we are currently focused on supporting type models, which let the developers abstract their types with logical projections. We also plan to leverage Gospel's `equivalent` clauses to verify program equivalence and extend the support for user-provided functions such as equality and comparison.

We are already using `ortac` on industrial quality code developed at Tarides, namely in some components of Irmin, a distributed database built on the same principles as Git. First, it provides an additional, more formal documentation of some OCaml functions. Second, it alleviates the writing of tests, since the properties to be checked are written only once and are attached to the interface instead of the test cases. Last, `ortac` generates code that is integrated into a model-based fuzzing framework based on `afl-fuzz` [1] and Monolith [18], which further simplifies the testing process by automatically generating relevant test cases.

Currently, our use of `ortac` is limited to pre-deployment testing. We still need to measure the overhead of the runtime verification to determine if `ortac`-instrumented code can be deployed in contexts where performance is important.

References

1. `afl-fuzz—American fuzzy lop`. https://lcamtuf.coredump.cx/afl/
2. Barnett, M.: Code contracts for .NET: runtime verification and so much more. In: Barringer, H., et al. (eds.) RV 2010. LNCS, vol. 6418, pp. 16–17. Springer, Heidelberg (2010). https://doi.org/10.1007/978-3-642-16612-9_2

3. Barnett, M., Leino, K.R.M., Schulte, W.: The Spec# programming system: an overview. In: Barthe, G., Burdy, L., Huisman, M., Lanet, J.-L., Muntean, T. (eds.) CASSIS 2004. LNCS, vol. 3362, pp. 49–69. Springer, Heidelberg (2005). https://doi.org/10.1007/978-3-540-30569-9_3

4. Barnett, M., Schulte, W.: Contracts, components, and their runtime verification on the.net platform. Technical report MSR-TR-2002-38, April 2002. https://www.microsoft.com/en-us/research/publication/contracts-components-and-their-runtime-verification-on-the-net-platform/

5. Barnett, M., Schulte, W.: Runtime verification of .NET contracts, vol. 65, pp. 199–208. Elsevier (2003). https://www.microsoft.com/en-us/research/publication/runtime-verification-of-net-contracts/

6. Baudin, P., Cuoq, P., Filliâtre, J.C., Marché, C., Monate, B., Moy, Y., Prevosto, V.: ACSL: ANSI/ISO C specification language (2008)

7. Burdy, L., et al.: An overview of JML tools and applications. Electron. Notes Theor. Comput. Sci. **80**, 75–91 (2003). https://doi.org/10.1016/S1571-0661(04)80810-7. https://www.sciencedirect.com/science/article/pii/S1571066104808107. www.jmlspecs.org Eighth International Workshop on Formal Methods for Industrial Critical Systems (FMICS 2003)

8. Chalin, P.: JML support for primitive arbitrary precision numeric types: definition and semantics. J. Object Technol. **3**, 57–79 (2004)

9. Charguéraud, A., Filliâtre, J.C., Lourenço, C., Pereira, M.: GOSPEL -providing OCaml with a formal specification language. In: FM 2019–23rd International Symposium on Formal Methods, Porto, Portugal, October 2019. https://hal.inria.fr/hal-02157484

10. Cheon, Y., Leavens, G.: A runtime assertion checker for the java modeling language (JML), January 2002

11. Cok, D.R.: OpenJML: JML for Java 7 by extending OpenJDK. In: Bobaru, M., Havelund, K., Holzmann, G.J., Joshi, R. (eds.) NFM 2011. LNCS, vol. 6617, pp. 472–479. Springer, Heidelberg (2011). https://doi.org/10.1007/978-3-642-20398-5_35

12. Delahaye, M., Kosmatov, N., Signoles, J.: Common specification language for static and dynamic analysis of C programs. In: Proceedings of the ACM Symposium on Applied Computing, pp. 1230–1235, March 2013. https://doi.org/10.1145/2480362.2480593

13. Filliâtre, J.-C., Paskevich, A.: Why3—where programs meet provers. In: Felleisen, M., Gardner, P. (eds.) ESOP 2013. LNCS, vol. 7792, pp. 125–128. Springer, Heidelberg (2013). https://doi.org/10.1007/978-3-642-37036-6_8

14. Kosmatov, N., Petiot, G., Signoles, J.: An optimized memory monitoring for runtime assertion checking of C programs. In: Legay, A., Bensalem, S. (eds.) RV 2013. LNCS, vol. 8174, pp. 167–182. Springer, Heidelberg (2013). https://doi.org/10.1007/978-3-642-40787-1_10. https://hal-cea.archives-ouvertes.fr/cea-01834990

15. Kosmatov, N., Maurica, F., Signoles, J.: Efficient runtime assertion checking for properties over mathematical numbers. In: Deshmukh, J., Ničković, D. (eds.) RV 2020. LNCS, vol. 12399, pp. 310–322. Springer, Cham (2020). https://doi.org/10.1007/978-3-030-60508-7_17

16. McCormick, J.W., Chapin, P.C.: Building High Integrity Applications with SPARK. Cambridge University Press, Cambridge (2015)

17. Meyer, B.: Applying "design by contract". Computer **25**(10), 40–51 (1992). https://doi.org/10.1109/2.161279

18. Pottier, F.: Strong automated testing of OCaml libraries. In: Journées Franco-phones des Langages Applicatifs (JFLA), February 2021. http://cambium.inria.fr/~fpottier/publis/pottier-monolith-2021.pdf
19. Signoles, J., Cuoq, P., Kirchner, F., Kosmatov, N., Prevosto, V., Yakobowski, B.: Frama-C: a software analysis perspective, vol. 27 (2012). https://doi.org/10.1007/s00165-014-0326-7
20. Signoles, J., Kosmatov, N., Vorobyov, K.: E-ACSL, a runtime verification tool for safety and security of C programs (tool paper). In: RV-CuBES (2017). https://doi.org/10.29007/fpdh

Gaussian-Based Runtime Detection of Out-of-distribution Inputs for Neural Networks

Vahid Hashemi[2] , Jan Křetínský[1] , Stefanie Mohr[1(✉)] ,
and Emmanouil Seferis[1,2]

[1] Technical University of Munich, Munich, Germany
mohr@in.tum.de
[2] AUDI AG, Ettingerstr. 60, 85057 Ingolstadt, Germany

Abstract. In this short paper, we introduce a simple approach for runtime monitoring of deep neural networks and show how to use it for out-of-distribution detection. The approach is based on inferring Gaussian models of some of the neurons and layers. Despite its simplicity, it performs better than recently introduced approaches based on interval abstractions which are traditionally used in verification.

1 Introduction

Learning deep neural networks (DNN) [2] has shown remarkable success in practically solving a large number of hard and previously intractable problems. However, direct applications in safety-critical domains, such as automated driving, are hindered by the lack of practical methods to *guarantee their safety*, e.g. [3,4]. This poses a serious problem for industrial adoption of DNN-based systems. Companies struggle to comply with safety regulations such as SOTIF [19], both due to lack of techniques to demonstrate safety in the presence of DNN as well as due to the actual lack of safety, e.g. accidents in automated cars due to errors in DNN-based perception system used [5].

One of the key requirements is the ability to detect novel inputs [20], for which the DNN has not been trained and thus the only responsible answer is "don't know". Such inputs are also called *out-of-distribution (OOD) examples* [10]. Whenever such inputs occur, an alarm should be raised announcing the unreliability of the current output of the DNN, so that rectifying actions can be taken. Various runtime monitors for this task have already been proposed recently. Cheng et al. [1] monitor which subsets of neurons in a given layer are activated for known inputs; whenever a very different subset is activated, an alarm is raised. Henzinger et al. [16] monitor activation values of neurons and envelop the tuples into hyper-boxes (multidimensional intervals) along the

This research was funded in part by the DFG research training group *CONVEY* (GRK 2428), the DFG project 383882557 - Statistical Unbounded Verification (KR 4890/2-1), the project *Audi Verifiable AI*, and the BMWi funded *KARLI* project (grant 19A21031C).

L. Feng and D. Fisman (Eds.): RV 2021, LNCS 12974, pp. 254–264, 2021.
https://doi.org/10.1007/978-3-030-88494-9_14

program analysis tradition; whenever a very different tuple is observed (outside of the boxes), an alarm is raised.

In this short paper, we propose a very light-weight and scalable approach. Similarly to [16], we monitor the activation values. However, instead of discrete and exact enveloping, we learn a more continuous and fuzzy representation of the recorded experienece, namely a Gaussian model of each monitored neuron. Whenever many neurons have sufficiently improbable activation values on the current input, we raise an alarm. Surprisingly, our simple monitor is equally or even more accurate than the similar state-of-the-art [16] even though we take no correlation of the activation values of different neurons into account and instead we monitor each of the neurons separately, in contrast to the multi-dimensional boxes of [16].

Our Contribution can be summarized as follows:

- We present a new and simple method for OOD detection based on Gaussian models of neuron activation values.
- We show that our method performs better than state-of-the-art techniques for out-of-distribution (OOD) detection.

Related Work. In our work, we focus on the detection of OOD-inputs, arguably [10] one of the major problems in AI safety.

State of the Art. A recent work by Henzinger et al. [16] is very similar to our approach. The authors consider the neuron activations of one layer for all samples of the training data. For each class in the dataset, they collect the activation vectors of the class samples, and cluster them using k-Means [17]. They increase the number of clusters successively, until the relative improvement drops below a given threshold τ. For each cluster, they construct a box abstraction that contains all samples of that cluster. In the end, each class in the data corresponds to a set of boxes. Finally, during testing, they check whether the activation vector of a new sample is contained in one of the boxes of its predicted class; if not, they raise an alarm. This approach can be extended to more layers, by taking the element-wise boolean AND of the layer "decisions". That is, an input is accepted if only if it is contained in the abstractions of all monitored layers. While the idea of looking at the activations of neurons in a layer is similar to our approach, the difference is in the detection of OOD samples. In contrast to using box-abstractions, we use Gaussian models. This reflects better the actual distribution of values of the neurons, as can be seen in Sect. 4.2.

OOD-Detection. Previous works have suggested, for example, using the maximum class probability or the entropy of the predicted class distribution as an OOD indicator [11], or training a classifier to distinguish clean and perturbed data, using ensembles of classifiers trained on random shuffles of the training data [12]. Besides, two popular approaches closely resemble the methods of runtime monitoring, namely ODIN [13] and the Mahalanobis-based detector [14]. ODIN first applies temperature scaling on the softmax outputs of a DNN to reduce the standard DNN overconfidence, and then applies a small adversarial–like perturbation of the input. If after that the maximum class score is below some threshold, the sample is considered to be OOD.

In contrast, the detector of [14] measures the probability density of a test sample by using a distance-based classifier. Another line of work involves generative models for OOD detection, attempting to model the distribution of the data, such as in [15]. By definition, OOD detection runs at test time, and thus many proposed approaches can be viewed under this setting. Other related approaches include using Bayesian learning methods [9], which can output prediction uncertainties, DNN testing [3], which are methods attempting to find problematic inputs, or building DNN architectures that are robust by construction, for example using interval bound propagation, abstract interpretation, or other methods [6–8].

2 Preliminaries

2.1 Deep Neural Networks

DNNs come in various architectures suitable for different tasks, however, at the core, they are composed of multiple *layers* of computation units called *neurons*. The task of a neuron is to read an input, calculate a weighted sum, apply a function called the *activation function* on it and output the result, called the *activation value*. We number the layers $1, 2, \ldots, L$ where layer 1 is called the input layer, layers $2, \ldots (L-1)$ are called the hidden layers and layer L is called the output layer.

More formally, given an input $\vec{x}$ to the DNN, we have:

$$\vec{h}^1 = \vec{x}$$
$$\vec{h}^{l+1} = \vec{\phi}^{l+1}(\vec{h}^l) \quad l = 2, \ldots, L$$

where $\phi_i^l(\vec{x})$ defines the element-wise computation of the neurons $i = 1, \ldots, N_l$ in layer l. The details of the computation are not necessary to understand the following work.

DNN can perform various tasks, the most usual being classification and regression. Whereas the first type labels its input with a category from a finite subset of classes, the second type outputs non discrete but real values. We consider only classification DNNs in this work. Neuron activations are vectors of activation values produced by neurons in some layer of a DNN. It is generally believed that layers closer to the output encode more complex features. This result has been supported by our results, which can be seen in Table 1. We refer to h_i^l $i = 1, \ldots, N_l$ as the activation of neuron i in layer l.

3 Our Solution Approach

In this section, we discuss our approach for synthesizing an OOD detector based on Gaussian models. In statistics, Gaussian models are used to model the behavior of data samples. We adapt this idea to model the behavior of a neuron by a Gaussian model.

Consider a DNN as a classifier that distinguishes between $\{c_1, ..., c_{N_L}\} = C$ classes. One layer l of this DNN contains N_l neurons. For each class $c_o \in C$ in the training data set, we feed samples $x_j^{c_o}$, $j = 1, ..., m$, into the network, and record the activations $n_i^{c_o}(x_j)$ of each neuron for $i = 1, ..., N_l$.

We collect those vectors $\vec{n}_i^{c_o}$, and calculate the mean and standard deviation, $\mu_i^{c_o}, \sigma_i^{c_o}$ of these values for each monitored neuron. We assume that the distribution of these values is approximately Gaussian. Thus, we expect the majority of samples to fall within the range $[\mu_i^{c_o} - k\sigma_i^{c_o}, \mu_i^{c_o} + k\sigma_i^{c_o}]$, where k is typically a value close to 2, containing 95% of the samples. During testing, we feed a new sample x to the DNN. We then do the following: we record the class c that our DNN predicts on x, and also retrieve the neuron activation values $n_i^c(x)$. We check if the activations of each neuron i falls within its range for the predicted class.

More formally, we check if

$$\forall i = 1, ..., N_l \;:\; n_i^c(x) \in [\mu_i^c - k\sigma_i^c, \mu_i^c + k\sigma_i^c] \tag{1}$$

For a better understanding, we have the intuition depicted in Fig. 1. The data in the plot is random but shall give an idea of how the approach works. There are two neurons that output different values, which are depicted as black dots. On the one hand, they are shown in a 2D-plane, which is used for the abstraction of Henzinger et al.; on the other hand, they are shown projected onto one dimension next to the axes, for our approach. The approach of Henzinger et al. fits interval boxes to the values that the neurons can take. The interval boxes are drawn in blue. Our approach calculates intervals based on fitted Gaussians. The mean of the Gaussian is depicted as a red cross next to the neuron activations. The red line marks the interval that we consider as good for the neuron.

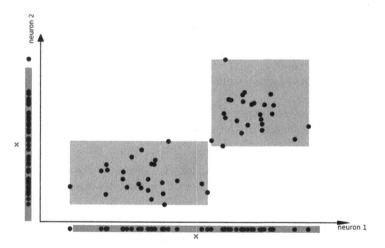

Fig. 1. This is an intuition of the Gaussian models on neuron activations. Black dots mark the values of the neurons. Once, in a 2D-plane together with the blue boxes that represent the abstraction of Henzinger et al., and once projected to one dimension only. The red lines mark the interval $[\mu_i^c - k\sigma_i^c, \mu_i^c + k\sigma_i^c]$ for the two neurons respectively. Those intervals are the basis for our approach of OOD-detection. (Color figure online)

Each neuron "votes" independently if the new sample is valid or not. Samples within the distribution are expected to obtain a large number of votes, while OOD samples should obtain less. Thus, we collect the votes of all neurons, and then we compare them to a threshold; if they are below it, we consider x as an OOD sample, otherwise we consider it as correct. In that way, we can detect OOD inputs at runtime.

Note that this approach can also be extended to use multiple layers. For this, we compute the votes for each of the monitored layers. If they are below the threshold in at least one of the layers, we flag the sample as OOD.

An issue here is finding appropriate voting thresholds. For that, we use a suitable validation set. Normally, we should not make assumptions for the OOD data, and assume that we do not have access to them. In this case, we can use a suitable surrogate validation set, containing another unrelated dataset, e.g. adversarial examples or noisy images. In case we monitor more than one layer, the voting thresholds are computed individually for each layer.

4 Experiments

In this section, we analyze the experimental results of our approach. We will apply our approach for OOD detection to some example datasets and DNNs. We use the setting of Henzinger et al. [16], and we compare our result with theirs.

4.1 Datasets and Training

There are 4 datasets on which we evaluate our approach: MNIST, F-MNIST, CIFAR-10 and GTSRB (German Traffic Sign Recognition Benchmark) [18].

- MNIST is a dataset that contains images of digits. They shall be classified into ten classes, i.e. 0, ..., 9.
- F-MNIST consists of images of clothes, which shall also be classified into ten categories.
- CIFAR-10 is made of images of ten distinct classes from different settings.
- GTSRB contains images of German traffic signs that can be categorized into 43 classes.

All of the four datasets are used for classification. We train two different architectures of DNNs, NN1 and NN2, with the architectures of [16]. Those are:

- **NN1:** Conv(40), Max Pool, Conv(20), Max Pool, FC(320), FC(160), FC(80), FC(40), FC(k)
- **NN2:** BN(Conv(40)), Max Pool, BN(Conv(20)), Max Pool, FC(240), FC(84), FC(k)

Here, FC is a fully connected layer, $Conv$ is a convolutional layer, $MaxPool$ is 2×2 max pooling, and BN is batch normalization. The activation function is always the RELU. NN1 was trained 10 epochs for MNIST, and 30 for F-MNIST, while NN2 was trained 200 epochs for CIFAR-10 and 10 for GTSRB. A learning rate of 10^{-3} and batch size 100 were used during training. NN1 is used for MNIST and F-MNIST, while NN2 is used for CIFAR-10 and GTSRB.

The evaluation is performed on two measures: the detection rate (DTERR) and the false alarm rate (FAR). The detection rate counts how many samples were correctly marked as OOD out of all OOD inputs. The false alarm rate (also known as Type-1-error) counts how many samples were marked as OOD but are not OOD, out of all marked inputs.

4.2   Gaussian Assumption

In this work, we used Gaussian distributions in order to approximate the output of each neuron. To verify that this is a valid assumption, we show in the following the distribution of values of the neurons.

We pick each dataset and select one random neuron from one of the monitored layers. Then, we plot the histogram of that neuron's output. We also show the Gaussian distribution we would expect to have, according to the measured μ and σ (Fig. 2).

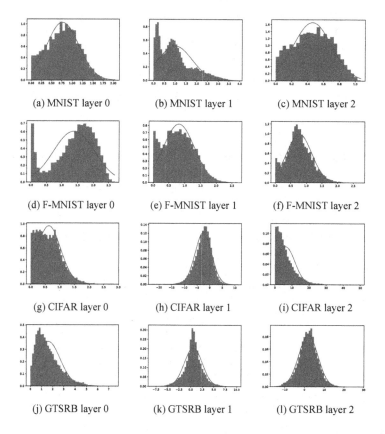

Fig. 2. Histogram of neuron outputs, along with the Gaussian distribution with the sample mean and variance.

We see that there are some small differences. For some neurons, the Gaussian assumption is very accurate, e.g. f, h, k, and l. For some other cases the histograms indicate a slightly different behavior, e.g. a, d, e, g, i. However, in general they show that the neuron's outputs follow more a Gaussian behavior than a uniformly distributed one. It seems especially that the problem is rather that the parameters μ and σ do not exactly fit the true underlying Gaussian. One could think of calculating the parameters differently, or even using other models in future. Overall, the assumption that the neuron's outputs are Gaussian-like seems to be true.

4.3   Evaluation Steps

Following the setting of Henzinger et al., we perform the following steps for each dataset: we train the DNN for the first k classes of the dataset, and consider the rest as OOD. This results, for example, in a DNN that was only trained on the digits from 0 to 5. Digits from 6 to 9 are considered as OOD. Having now constructed the networks and datasets in this way, we can apply our approach, and compare the results with the ones of Henzinger et al.. We monitor all linear hidden layers of the DNNs for both approaches. We use the interval $[\mu-2\sigma, \mu+2\sigma]$ for each neuron and class label, while for Henzinger's approach, we use the parameters mentioned in their paper. Note that the monitor of Henzinger et al. outputs boolean values (e.g. x is inside or outside of the boxes), while ours outputs numerical scores (e.g. number of "votes" for an input x). In order to be able to compare the two approaches, we have to select a threshold for our approach, in order to convert its output to a boolean value (e.g. $votes(x) < \tau \Rightarrow OOD$).

For this, we set the threshold at a quantile of the in-distribution data, so that the FAR is similar to the one of [16]. For example, for a quantile $q = 50\%$, we set the voting threshold in a way that 50% of the known in-distribution data pass through. Having set the FARs on a similar level, we can then compare the detected errors of the approaches.

In the case where we monitor more than one layer, we use the same quantile q in every one of them, and then combine votes as described before, i.e. x is accepted if the votes of each layer are above the corresponding threshold. Having a different quantile threshold for every layer improves performance, but might also be prone to overfitting. Note also that the threshold q is not the same across experiments: in each run, we modify it in order to match the FAR of [16] on that particular experiment. The results are shown in Fig. 3.

Each of the datasets has its own plot, where we have in red the values that the approach of [16] achieves, and in blue the values of our approach. For both of them, we measure the detection rate (DTERR) shown as a solid line in the left plot, and the false alarm rate (FAR) shown as a dashed line in the right plot. We see that the performance of our approach is mostly comparable or better than [16]. Especially, on CIFAR, our approach clearly outperforms the approach of Henzinger et al. in terms of the detection rate.

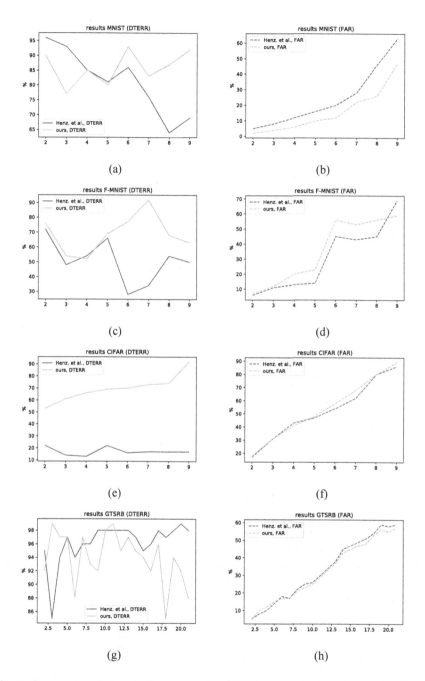

Fig. 3. Comparison between the approaches of Henzinger et al. and ours, for the cases of MNIST, F-MNIST, CIFAR, and GTSRB datasets. Here, $DTERR$ and FAR are shown in separate diagrams. The number of classes on which the network was trained is depicted on the x axis.

Overall, our approach seems promising and shows already good results. However, we also have to indicate some problems with both approaches, namely the occasional low detection rate or high false alarm rates. This is problematic for industrial applications, and shows us the difficulties involved, and the need for stronger approaches.

4.4   Parameter Study

In this section, we perform a study on the parameters of our approach. For simplicity, we focused on the MNIST dataset. The DNN in this case was thus NN1 with a total of eight layers. We want to particularly investigate the effects of the number of layers.

Table 1. Results on different layers, and different combination of layers. The evaluation is performed on the detection rate and the false alarm rate. Layers closer to the output layer show a higher detection rate than layers earlier in the DNN. The combination of several layers only results in a small improvement compared to the usage of only one layer.

Layers	$DTERR$ (%)	FAR (%)
5	44.6	8.7
6	69.2	5.3
7	73.0	5.4
8	73.5	6.4

Layers	$DTERR$ (%)	FAR (%)
(5,6)	70.3	8.3
(6,7)	77.0	6.5
(7,8)	76.4	6.8
(6,7,8)	79.5	7.5
(5,6,7,8)	80.0	9.8

At first, we look at different layers in the DNN. The fifth layer seems to contain less important information in comparison to layer six, seven, and eight. When we only monitor layer five, the DTERR is almost 20% lower as for the other layers, while the FAR does not change significantly. We can thus verify the intuition that the features of the later layers in a DNN are more meaningful. If we combine the voting of several layers, we can see that the detection rate is slightly increased. Especially, the bad DTERR of 44% by only using layer five can be drastically improved by adding the knowledge of layer six, namely to 70%; while the FAR even decreases slightly. The combination of other layers can still increase the DTERR up to 80.0%, however, it comes with a slightly higher false alarm rate. Thus, for a more light-weight approach, it could be recommended to stick with fewer layers. Additionally, there may also be another different voting system for several layers, e.g. incorporate a weighted voting system for the layers and granting later layers more influence on the result.

5   Outlook

A natural next step would be to use additional information given by the correlation between the neurons. So far, we only considered the Gaussians of each neuron independently.

Instead, we can consider a subset of neurons $n_k \in S$ and fit a joint Gaussian distribution $N(\mu_S, \Sigma_S)$ on them. This subset can be an entire layer, where we fit a Gaussian distribution on the entire vector of layer activations, but it can also be a smaller subset of neurons. This offers the advantage of reduced computations, and an easier estimation of the covariance matrix (which is hard in high dimensions). The approach is flexible, and allows us to consider arbitrary subsets of neurons with varying sizes. Predictions can then be combined again by voting. For multidimensional Gaussian distributions, a simple threshold with μ and σ is no longer possible. Instead, one can use the Mahanalobis distance, $M^2(x) = (x-\mu)^T \Sigma^{-1}(x-\mu)$, which is a notion of distance from the distribution center. A suitable threshold for $M(x)$ is then to be calculated.

Besides, for a subset of neurons, a more precise model that can be used is a mixture of Gaussians. This might be more accurate since the Gaussian distributions as above are only imprecise approximations of the true distribution, while in contrast, Gaussian mixture models can approximate any probability distribution to any precision.

6   Conclusion

In this work, we considered the problem of runtime monitoring of DNNs, which forms an important step towards applying deep learning to safety-critical systems. Specifically, we focused on the sub-problem of OOD detection, and developed a lightweight detection method based on Gaussian models of neuron activation values. This can be extended in various ways as described before, and gives more accurate results than the recent work of Henzinger et al. [16]. Interestingly, the results suggest that reflecting correlation of the activation values (as in [16]) is less important than handling outliers through voting on learnt models (as here). Actually, the rigid and complete coverage by the boxes does not seem as adequate as the learnt approximations.

While we showed already a good efficiency on OOD inputs, the industrial requirements suggest that further improvements are necessary to reach real-world applicability. Our preliminary results invite further investigation along these directions. In particular, runtime monitoring by more complex probabilistic models, such as Gaussian mixtures, or using DNN-based probability estimation methods such as Normalizing Flows seem very promising.

References

1. Cheng, C.-H., Nührenberg, G., Yasuoka, H.: Runtime monitoring neuron activation patterns. DATE (2019). https://arxiv.org/abs/1809.06573

2. Goodfellow, I., Bengio, Y., Courville, A.: Deep Learning. MIT Press (2016). https://www.deeplearningbook.org/
3. Huang, X., et al.: A survey of safety and trustworthiness of deep neural networks. CoRR (2018). https://arxiv.org/abs/1812.08342
4. Ortega, P., Maini, V.: Building safe artificial intelligence: specification, robustness, and assurance. Deep Mind blog (2018). https://medium.com/@deepmindsafetyresearch/building-safe-artificial-intelligence-52f5f75058f1
5. Wikipedia: List of self-driving car fatalities. Wikipedia article (2018). https://en.wikipedia.org/wiki/List-of-self-driving-car-fatalities
6. Wong, E., Kolter, Z.: Provable defenses against adversarial examples via the convex outer adversarial polytope. In: ICML (2018). https://arxiv.org/abs/1711.00851
7. Gowal, S., et al.: On the effectiveness of interval bound propagation for training verifiably robust models. In: NIPS (2018). https://arxiv.org/abs/1810.12715
8. Mirman, M., Gehr, T., Vechev, M.: Differentiable abstract interpretation for provably robust neural networks. In: ICML (2018). https://files.sri.inf.ethz.ch/website/papers/icml18-diffai.pdf
9. McAllister, R., et al.: Concrete problems for autonomous vehicle safety: advantages of bayesian deep learning. In: IJCAI (2017). https://www.ijcai.org/Proceedings/2017/661
10. Amodei, D., Olah, C., Steinhardt, J., Christiano, P., Schulman, J., Mané, D.: Concrete problems in AI safety. CoRR (2016). https://arxiv.org/abs/1606.06565
11. Hendrycks, D., Gimpel, K.: A baseline for detecting misclassified and out-of-distribution examples in neural networks. In: ICLR (2017). https://arxiv.org/abs/1610.02136
12. Lakshminarayanan, B., Pritzel, A., Blundell, C.: Simple and scalable predictive uncertainty estimation using deep ensembles. In: NIPS (2017). https://arxiv.org/abs/1612.01474
13. Liang, S., Li, Y., Srikant, R.: Enhancing the reliability of out-of-distribution image detection in neural networks. In: ICLR (2018). https://arxiv.org/abs/1706.02690
14. Lee, K., Lee, K., Lee, H., Shin, J.: A simple unified framework for detecting out-of-distribution samples and adversarial attacks. In: NIPS (2018). https://arxiv.org/abs/1807.03888
15. Ren, J., et al.: Likelihood ratios for out-of-distribution detection. In: NeurIPS (2019). https://arxiv.org/abs/1906.02845
16. Henzinger, T.A., Lukina, A., Schilling, C.: Outside the box: abstraction-based monitoring of neural networks. In: ECAI (2020). https://arxiv.org/abs/1911.09032
17. Bishop, C.M.: Pattern Recognition and Machine Learning. Springer, Heidelberg (2006)
18. Stallkamp, J., Schlipsing, M., Salmen, J., Igel, C.: The German traffic sign recognition benchmark: a multi-class classification competition. In: Proceedings of the IEEE International Joint Conference on Neural Networks, pp. 1453–1460 (2011)
19. ISO/PAS 21448. Road vehicles - Safety of the intended functionality. https://www.iso.org/obp/ui/#iso:std:70939:en
20. Pimentel, M.A.F., Clifton, D.A., Clifton, L.A., Tarassenko, L.: A review of novelty detection. Signal Process. **99**, 215–249 (2014)

Parallel and Multi-objective Falsification with SCENIC and VERIFAI

Kesav Viswanadha[1]([✉]), Edward Kim[1], Francis Indaheng[1], Daniel J. Fremont[2], and Sanjit A. Seshia[1]

[1] University of California, Berkeley, USA
kesav@berkeley.edu
[2] University of California, Santa Cruz, USA

Abstract. Falsification has emerged as an important tool for simulation-based verification of autonomous systems. In this paper, we present extensions to the SCENIC scenario specification language and VERIFAI toolkit that improve the scalability of sampling-based falsification methods by using parallelism and extend falsification to multi-objective specifications. We first present a parallelized framework that is interfaced with both the simulation and sampling capabilities of SCENIC and the falsification capabilities of VERIFAI, reducing the execution time bottleneck inherently present in simulation-based testing. We then present an extension of VERIFAI's falsification algorithms to support multi-objective optimization during sampling, using the concept of rule-books to specify a preference ordering over multiple metrics that can be used to guide the counterexample search process. Lastly, we evaluate the benefits of these extensions with a comprehensive set of benchmarks written in the SCENIC language.

Keywords: Runtime verification · Formal methods · Falsification · Cyber-physical systems · Autonomous systems · Parallelization

1 Introduction

The growing adoption of autonomous and semi-autonomous cyber-physical systems (CPS) such as self-driving vehicles brings with it pressing questions about ensuring their safety and reliability. In particular, the increasing use of artificial intelligence (AI) and machine learning (ML) components requires significant advances in formal methods, of which simulation-based formal analysis is a key ingredient [25].

Even with notable development in simulators and methods for simulation-based verification, there are four practical issues which require further advances in tools. First, simulation time can be a huge bottleneck, as falsification is typically done with high-quality, realistic simulators such as CARLA [13], which can be computation-intensive. Second, modeling interactive, multi-agent behaviors using general programming languages like Python can be very time-consuming.

L. Feng and D. Fisman (Eds.): RV 2021, LNCS 12974, pp. 265–276, 2021.
https://doi.org/10.1007/978-3-030-88494-9_15

Third, autonomous systems usually need to satisfy multiple properties and metrics, with differing priorities, and convenient notation is needed to formally specify these. Fourth, we need to develop specification and sampling methods for falsification that can support multiple objectives. These issues have all been addressed in this paper with a series of features aimed at improving the scalability of falsification methods, both in terms of execution time and the richness of objectives that can be specified and falsified.

There has been prior work that addresses these four issues separately. There have been several ideas for falsification or, conversely, optimization of CPS subject to multiple objectives [5,6,10,22,30]. There are other tools that address simulation-based testing of CPS, including in a parallel context [3,4,21]. There has also been some prior work on exploration methods for constrained falsification [29]. However, these methods tend to either focus on testing specific CPS components (as opposed to full closed-loop CPS) or require complex code to use in a practical setting. More importantly, to our knowledge, no prior work has *jointly* addressed all of these issues and demonstrated these in a single tool. In this paper, we do so by extending the open-source VERIFAI toolkit [14].[1] VERIFAI is reasonably mature, having been demonstrated in multiple industrial case studies [15,18]. Our contributions to the toolkit support:

1. *Parallelized falsification*, running multiple simulations in parallel;
2. Falsification using the latest version of the SCENIC *formal scenario specification language*, extending support to the "dynamic" features of SCENIC for modeling interactive behaviors [17];
3. The ability to specify for falsification *multiple objectives with priority orderings*;
4. A *multi-armed bandit* algorithm that supports multi-objective falsification, and
5. Evaluation of these extensions with a comprehensive set of self-driving scenarios.

These contributions have had a profound impact on the capabilities of VERIFAI. With parallel falsification, we were able to cut down drastically on execution time, achieving up to $5\times$ speedup over the current falsification methods in VERIFAI using 5 parallel simulation processes. Using the multi-objective multi-armed bandit sampler, we were able to find scenarios which falsify five objectives at the same time.

2   Background

SCENIC is a probabilistic programming language [7,16,17] that allows users to intuitively model *probabilistic scenarios* for multi-agent systems. A *concrete scenario* is a set of objects and agents, together with values for their static

---

[1] Documentation of the extensions covered in this paper is available at: https://verifai.readthedocs.io/en/kesav-v-multi-objective/.

attributes, initial state, and parameters of dynamic behavioral models describing how their attributes evolve over time. In other words, a concrete scenario defines a specific trace. The state of each object or agent, such as a car, includes its semantic properties such as its position, orientation, velocity, color, model, etc. We refer to the vector of such semantic properties as a *semantic feature vector*; the concatenation of the semantic feature vectors of all objects and agents at a given time instant defines the overall semantic feature vector at that time. Agents also have behaviors defining a (possibly stochastic) sequence of actions for them to take as a function of the state of the simulation at each time step. A SCENIC program defines a *distribution over concrete scenarios*: by sampling an initial state and then executing the behaviors in a simulator, many different simulations can be obtained from a single SCENIC program. SCENIC provides a general formalism to express probabilistic scenarios for multiple domains, including traffic and other scenarios for autonomous vehicles, which can then be executed in a number of simulators including CARLA [13]. In previous work on VERIFAI [14], the tool supported an earlier version of SCENIC without interactive, behavioral specifications. In this paper, we provide full support for SCENIC's newer dynamic features.

VERIFAI is a Python toolkit that provides capabilities for verification of AI-based systems [8]. A primary capability is *falsification*, the systematic search for inputs to a system that falsify a specification given in temporal logic or as a cost function. VERIFAI can use SCENIC as an environment modeling language, sampling from the distribution over semantic feature vectors defined by a SCENIC program to generate test cases. It then simulates these cases according to the dynamics specified in the SCENIC program, obtaining trajectories for each object. For a more detailed description of VERIFAI's falsification capabilities and interface with dynamic scenarios specified in the SCENIC language, please see [17].

After simulating a test case, VERIFAI evaluates the system's specification over the obtained trajectory, saving the results for offline analysis. These results are also used to guide further falsification, specifically by VERIFAI's *active samplers*, such as the cross-entropy sampler [24]. These samplers use the history of previously generated samples and their outcomes in simulation to drive the search process to find more counterexamples.

3   Parallel Falsification

In the typical pipeline used by a VERIFAI falsifier driven by a SCENIC program, semantic feature vectors (parameters) are generated using samplers in either SCENIC or VERIFAI These parameter values are then sent by the VERIFAI server to the client simulator to configure a simulation and generate a corresponding trajectory. This trajectory is then evaluated by the monitor, deemed either a safe example or a counterexample, and added to the corresponding table in the falsifier. Naturally, a bottleneck of this process is the generation of the trajectory in the simulator, as this is a rather compute-intensive task that can take a minute or more per sample, depending on the scenario description.

We present an improvement on this pipeline by parallelizing it using the Python library Ray [19], which encapsulates process-level parallelism optimized for distributed execution of computation-intensive tasks. Figure 1 illustrates the new setup: we instantiate multiple instances of the simulator and open multiple SCENIC server connections from VERIFAI to the simulator instances for performing simulations (the connections now being bidirectional so that the behavior models in the SCENIC program can respond to the current state of the simulation). We then aggregate the results of these simulations into a single error table documenting all the counterexamples found during falsification.

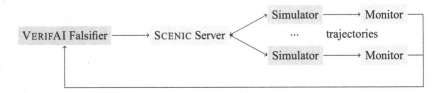

Fig. 1. Parallelized pipeline for falsification using VERIFAI.

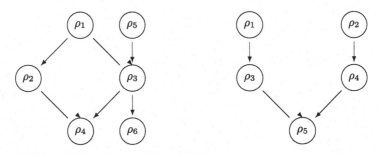

Fig. 2. Left: example rulebook over functions $\rho_1 \ldots \rho_6$ [11]. Right: graph G used in experiments.

4   Multi-objective Falsification

There are typically many different metrics of interest for evaluating autonomous systems. For example, there are many well-known metrics used in the autonomous driving community to measure safety: no collisions, obeying traffic laws, and maintaining a minimum safe distance from other objects, among others [28]. It is also natural to assert, for example, that it is more important to avoid collisions than to follow traffic laws. We now discuss how to specify these metrics and their relative *priorities*.

4.1   Specification of Multiple Objectives Using Rulebooks

Let $\rho(x)$ be a function mapping a simulation trajectory generated by SCENIC or VERIFAI to a vector-valued objective, where $\rho_j(x)$ is defined as the value of the j-th metric. Censi et al. [11] have developed a way to specify preferences over these metrics using a *rulebook* denoted by $\mathcal{R}$ – a directed acyclic graph (DAG) where the nodes are the metrics and a directed edge from node i to node j means $\rho_i(x)$ is more important than $\rho_j(x)$. We denote this using the $>_R$ operator, e.g. $\rho_i >_R \rho_j$.

Figure 2 shows an example of a rulebook over six metrics $\rho_1, \ldots, \rho_6$. In this example, we can make several inferences, such as ρ_1 is more important than ρ_3, ρ_3 is more important than ρ_4, and ρ_5 is more important than ρ_3. However, there are also many pairs of objective components that cannot be compared; for example ρ_1 and ρ_5. We would like to have a way to order objective vectors to know which values are maximally violating of the specification during active sampling. Because of these indeterminate incomparisons, the rulebook $\mathcal{R}$ only allows for a *partial ordering* $\succ$ over the objective vectors. Intuitively, we can think of this partial ordering as preferring examples that have lower values of higher priority objectives since we are trying to minimize the values of each objective for falsification. However, if there is any other indeterminate or higher priority objective that has a higher value, the $\succ$ relation does not hold. To satisfy these properties, we define our $\succ$ operator as follows:

$$\rho(x_1) \succ \rho(x_2) \triangleq \forall i \left(\rho_i(x_2) < \rho_i(x_1) \implies \exists j \neq i \left(\rho_j >_R \rho_i \wedge \rho_j(x_1) < \rho_j(x_2) \right) \right)$$

As an example, consider our rulebook from Fig. 2. Let $\rho(x_1) = \begin{bmatrix} 1 & 1 & 1 & 1 & 1 & 1 \end{bmatrix}^T$, and $\rho(x_2) = \begin{bmatrix} 1 & 1 & 2 & 1 & 0 & 1 \end{bmatrix}^T$. In this case we have $\rho(x_2) \succ \rho(x_1)$ because $\rho_5(x_2) < \rho_5(x_1)$, and even though $\rho_3(x_2) > \rho_3(x_1)$, $\rho_5 >_R \rho_3$ according to the rulebook, so the comparison of ρ_5 for the trajectories takes precedence. Since the rulebook defines a partial ordering over values of ρ, it is possible to have two trajectories x_1 and x_2 such that $\rho(x_1) \not\succ \rho(x_2)$ and $\rho(x_2) \not\succ \rho(x_1)$. In such cases, both values of ρ are maintained in the sampling algorithm; see below for more details.

4.2   Multi-objective Active Sampling

When performing active sampling to search for unsafe test inputs, we need a specialized sampler to support having multiple objectives to guide the search process. Most of the samplers previously available in VERIFAI focused either entirely on exploration of the search space or entirely on exploitation to find unsafe inputs; we present a sampler that balances these and builds up increasingly-violating counterexamples in the multi-objective case.

The Multi-armed Bandit Sampler. We present a more robust version of VERIFAI's cross-entropy sampler called the *multi-armed bandit sampler*; the idea of this sampler is to balance the trade-off between exploitation and exploration. To understand the motivation for the sampler, we first look at the formulation of the multi-armed bandit problem. Consider a bandit which has multiple lotteries, or "arms", to choose from, each being a random variable offering a probabilistic reward. The bandit does not know ahead of time which arm gives the highest expected reward, and must learn this information by efficiently sampling various arms, while also maximizing average earned reward during the sampling process.

Carpentier et al. [9] present the Upper Confidence Bound (UCB) Algorithm that effectively balances both of these goals, subject to a confidence parameter δ, by sampling the arm j that minimizes a quantity Q_j dependent on the number of timesteps t, the number of times the arm j was sampled $T_j(t-1)$, the observed reward of arm j given by $\hat{\mu}_j$, and the confidence parameter δ:

$$Q_j = \hat{\mu}_j + \sqrt{\frac{2}{T_j(t-1)} \ln\left(\frac{1}{\delta}\right)}$$

Qualitatively, this works as a balance between exploitation of the reward distribution learned so far (the first term), and exploration of seldom-sampled arms (the second term). We can easily see that this can be readily adapted to our cross-entropy sampler in VERIFAI, which splits the range of each sampled variable into N equally spaced *buckets*, which can be considered the "arms". We take $\hat{\mu}_j$ to be the proportion of counterexamples found in bucket j.

To compute μ_j for a vector-valued objective, we present the following incremental algorithm which builds up counterexamples that falsify more and more objectives (according to the priority order) over time. The steps of this algorithm are as follows. This assumes that the sampler is responsible for generating a d-dimensional feature vector.

Setup

1. Split the range of each component of the feature vector into N buckets, as in the cross-entropy sampler.
2. Initialize matrix T of size $d \times N$ where T_{ij} will keep track of the number of times that bucket j was visited for variable x_i.
3. Initialize a dictionary c mapping each maximal counterexample found so far to a matrix c_b of size $d \times N$ where $c_{b,ij}$ counts how many times sampling bucket j for variable x_i resulted in the specific counterexample b.
4. Sample from each bucket once initially, updating c and T according to the update algorithm described below. The purpose of this is to avoid division by zero when computing Q, as $T_j(t-1) = 0$ at initialization [2].

Sampling

1. Compute a matrix $\hat{\mu}$ where $\hat{\mu}_{ij}$ represents the observed reward from sampling bucket j for variable i by taking $\sum_b c_{b,ij}$.
2. Compute a matrix Q based on the upper confidence bound formula above. For the confidence parameter, we use a time-dependent value of $\frac{1}{\delta} = t$.
3. To sample x_i, take the bucket $j^* = \arg\max_j Q_{ij}$. *Break ties uniformly at random*. This is a key step in the sampling process as it is frequently the case initially that several buckets will have the exact same Q_j value, so we need

to avoid bias towards any specific bucket. Sample uniform randomly within the range represented by bucket j^*.

Updating Internal State

1. Given the objective vector value ρ, we compute our vector of booleans b as described above.
2. If b does not exist in the dictionary c and is among the set of maximal counterexamples found so far, i.e. $\forall b' \in c, b' \not\succ b$ as defined by the rulebook $\mathcal{R}$, add b as a key to the dictionary c and initialize its value as $0^{d \times N}$.
3. For any $b' \in c$ such that $b \succ b'$, remove b' from c.
4. Increment the count c_b at each position $c_{b,ij}$ for the bucket j sampled from x_i.

5   Evaluation

We present a set of experiments designed to evaluate (i) the speedup in simulation time that we expect to see from parallelization; (ii) the benefits of the multi-armed bandit sampler in balancing exploration and exploitation; and (iii) the improved capabilities of falsification to support multiple objectives. We have developed a library of SCENIC scripts[2] based on the list of pre-crash scenarios described by the National Highway Traffic Safety Administration (NHTSA) [20]. For a list of the scenarios, see [27]. These scripts cover a wide variety of common driving situations, such as driving through intersections, bypassing vehicles, and accounting for pedestrians.

We selected 7 of these scenarios, running the VERIFAI falsifier on each one in CARLA [13] for 30 min, with individual simulations limited to 300 timesteps ($\sim$30 s). For all of these scenarios, the monitor specifies that the centers of the ego vehicle and other vehicles must stay at least 5 m apart at all times. This specification means that counterexamples approximately correspond to collisions or near-collisions. All parallelized experiments were run using 5 worker processes to perform simulation.

Figure 3 shows the results of running these scenarios with a variety of configurations. First, across the scenarios, we observed a 3–5x speedup in the number of simulations using 5 parallel simulation processes. The variation in the number of samples generated can be attributed to *termination conditions* set in SCENIC, which terminate simulations early if specific conditions are met. For some of these scenarios, termination occurred much sooner on average than other scenarios, leading to more simulations finishing in 30 min. These values also serve as partial evidence of the effectiveness of the multi-armed bandit sampler compared to cross-entropy, as the proportion of counterexamples found is comparable for the two samplers despite the increased exploration component in the multi-armed bandit sampler.

---

[2] Full listing and source code of these SCENIC scripts is available at: https://github.com/BerkeleyLearnVerify/Scenic/tree/kesav-v/multi-objective/examples/carla/Behavior_Prediction.

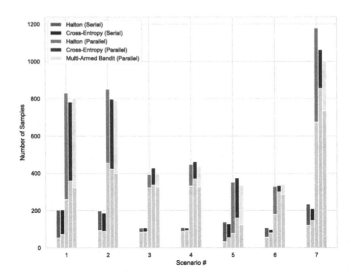

Fig. 3. Comparison of (i) the serial and parallel versions of the falsifier for cross-entropy and Halton sampling and (ii) the multi-armed bandit sampler with the cross-entropy and Halton samplers all in parallel. The orange part of the bars represent the number of counterexamples found out of the total number of samples. (Color figure online)

To validate the scalability and explorative aspect of parallelized falsification, we present two metrics in Table 1. The first metric is the *speedup factor*, which is the ratio of the number of sampled scenarios in parallel versus serial falsification, averaged across the Halton and cross-entropy samplers. We are also interested in a metric of coverage of the scenario search space, as this ensures that a wide range of scenarios are tested by falsification. To this end, we present the *confidence interval width ratio* metric. This metric is computed by generating a 95% confidence interval [12] which provides a lower and upper bound on the probability that a randomly generated scenario results in unsafe behavior. Since confidence intervals are generated with the assumption of uniform random sampling, we only compute them for the serial and parallel Halton samplers since they are an approximation of random sampling. We take the ratio of the widths of the intervals in the parallel versus serial case to compare how tight we are able to make the bound in each case with the same level of confidence. The width of the interval in the parallel case is significantly smaller - up to half the width of the serial case. Since the width of the interval is proportional to $1/\sqrt{n}$ for n samples, this makes intuitive sense and can be viewed as having double the coverage of the search space.

Figures 3 and 4 show the qualitative benefits of the multi-armed bandit sampler. The number of counterexamples generated by the multi-armed bandit sampler is higher than for the Halton sampler, but only slightly lower than cross-entropy. However, we can clearly see that multi-armed bandit sampling achieves

Table 1. The speedup factor and confidence interval width ratio metrics for the 7 scenarios.

Scenario #	1	2	3	4	5	6	7
Speedup factor	3.96	4.27	3.87	4.27	2.73	3.26	5.04
CI width ratio	0.51	0.48	0.48	0.53	0.61	0.56	0.44

a balance between number of counterexamples and their diversity that cross-entropy and Halton do not.

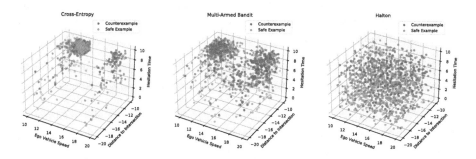

Fig. 4. Comparison of points sampled for cross-entropy, MAB, and Halton samplers.

To demonstrate the effectiveness of the multi-objective multi-armed bandit sampler in falsifying multiple objectives, we used a SCENIC program that instantiates the ego vehicle, along with m adversarial vehicles at random positions with respect to a 4-way intersection and has all of them drive towards the intersection and either go straight or make a turn. The monitor, similarly to before, specifies metric components ρ_j which say the ego vehicle must stay at least 5 m away from vehicle j. We use the following three rulebooks: a completely disconnected graph representing no preference ordering, a linked list structure $L \triangleq \rho_1 >_R \rho_2 >_R \dots >_R \rho_5$ representing a total ordering, and the graph G on the right in Fig. 2. We found that when using L or G, we were able to falsify 4 of the 5 objectives with serial falsification, and all 5 objectives in the parallel case. When having no preference ordering, we were able to falsify 3 of the 5 objectives with serial falsification and 4 of the 5 objectives in the parallel case. By contrast, when we combined all of these objectives in disjunction as one single objective (such that only falsifying all 5 objectives is considered unsafe), the cross-entropy sampler was unable to find any counterexamples.

We have also tested these methods in experiments with the LGSVL simulator [23]. Using a multi-objective specification with a variety of common driving situations, we were able to generate a wide range of test cases that cover much of the space of possible scenarios. These experiments were run with Apollo, an open-source autonomous driving software stack [1]. We discovered a number of bugs in Apollo using these new capabilities of VERIFAI and SCENIC, such as issues with stopping for pedestrians and properly avoiding encroaching vehicles [26].

6   Conclusion and Future Work

The extensions to SCENIC and VERIFAI we report in this paper address important problems in simulation-based falsification. First, we cut down significantly on execution time by supporting parallel simulations. Second, we allow the simple specification of high-level yet complex scenarios using the interface between dynamic SCENIC and VERIFAI. Third, we support multi-objective specification through the formalism of rulebooks. Lastly, we are able to falsify these multi-objective specifications in a way that is intuitive and scalable using the multi-armed bandit sampler. We hope these extensions prove useful to developers of autonomous systems.

There are a few directions for future work. For example, it might be interesting to see if generating random topological sorts of the rulebooks to create total ordering works well in practice. One could also run covariance analysis on the features to determine if they can be jointly optimized for better active sampling. Further comparison and analysis across other competing active and passive samplers is needed. Lastly, there has been some work in connecting these ideas to real-world testing [18], but especially with multi-objective falsification, this is an interesting future direction. In an industry setting, it may also be worthwhile to scale up parallel falsification even further to run on cloud instances for increased efficiency, which is technically possible but yet to be implemented.

Acknowledgments. This work is partially supported by NSF grants 1545126 (VeHI-CaL), 1646208 and 1837132, by the DARPA contracts FA8750-18-C-0101 (AA) and FA8750-20-C-0156 (SDCPS), by Berkeley Deep Drive, and by Toyota under the iCy-Phy center.

References

1. Apollo: Autonomous Driving Solution. http://apollo.auto/. Accessed 22 July 2021
2. The upper confidence bound algorithm, September 2016. https://banditalgs.com/2016/09/18/the-upper-confidence-bound-algorithm/
3. Abbas, H., Fainekos, G., Sankaranarayanan, S., Ivančić, F., Gupta, A.: Probabilistic temporal logic falsification of cyber-physical systems. ACM Trans. Embed. Comput. Syst. **12**(2s) (2013). https://doi.org/10.1145/2465787.2465797
4. Annpureddy, Y., Liu, C., Fainekos, G., Sankaranarayanan, S.: S-TaLiRo: a tool for temporal logic falsification for hybrid systems. In: Abdulla, P.A., Leino, K.R.M. (eds.) TACAS 2011. LNCS, vol. 6605, pp. 254–257. Springer, Heidelberg (2011). https://doi.org/10.1007/978-3-642-19835-9_21
5. Araujo, H., Carvalho, G., Mousavi, M.R., Sampaio, A.: Multi-objective search for effective testing of cyber-physical systems. In: Ölveczky, P.C., Salaün, G. (eds.) SEFM 2019. LNCS, vol. 11724, pp. 183–202. Springer, Cham (2019). https://doi.org/10.1007/978-3-030-30446-1_10

6. Arrieta, A., Wang, S., Markiegi, U., Sagardui, G., Etxeberria, L.: Employing multi-objective search to enhance reactive test case generation and prioritization for testing industrial cyber-physical systems. IEEE Trans. Industr. Inf. **14**(3), 1055–1066 (2018). https://doi.org/10.1109/TII.2017.2788019

7. BerkeleyLearnVerify: Berkeleylearnverify/scenic. https://github.com/BerkeleyLearnVerify/Scenic

8. BerkeleyLearnVerify: Berkeleylearnverify/verifai. https://github.com/BerkeleyLearnVerify/VerifAI

9. Carpentier, A., Lazaric, A., Ghavamzadeh, M., Munos, R., Auer, P.: Upper-confidence-bound algorithms for active learning in multi-armed bandits. In: Kivinen, J., Szepesvári, C., Ukkonen, E., Zeugmann, T. (eds.) ALT 2011. LNCS (LNAI), vol. 6925, pp. 189–203. Springer, Heidelberg (2011). https://doi.org/10.1007/978-3-642-24412-4_17

10. Castro, L.I.R., Chaudhari, P., Tumova, J., Karaman, S., Frazzoli, E., Rus, D.: Incremental sampling-based algorithm for minimum-violation motion planning. CoRR abs/1305.1102 (2013). http://arxiv.org/abs/1305.1102

11. Censi, A., et al.: Liability, ethics, and culture-aware behavior specification using rulebooks. CoRR abs/1902.09355 (2019). http://arxiv.org/abs/1902.09355

12. Clopper, C.J., Person, E.S.: The use of confidence or fiducial limits illustrated in the case of the binomial. Biometrika **26**(4), 404–413 (1934). https://doi.org/10.1093/biomet/26.4.404

13. Dosovitskiy, A., Ros, G., Codevilla, F., Lopez, A., Koltun, V.: CARLA: an open urban driving simulator. In: Proceedings of the 1st Annual Conference on Robot Learning, pp. 1–16 (2017)

14. Dreossi, T., et al.: VerifAI: a toolkit for the formal design and analysis of artificial intelligence-based systems. In: Dillig, I., Tasiran, S. (eds.) CAV 2019. LNCS, vol. 11561, pp. 432–442. Springer, Cham (2019). https://doi.org/10.1007/978-3-030-25540-4_25

15. Fremont, D.J., Chiu, J., Margineantu, D.D., Osipychev, D., Seshia, S.A.: Formal analysis and redesign of a neural network-based aircraft taxiing system with verifai. CoRR abs/2005.07173 (2020). https://arxiv.org/abs/2005.07173

16. Fremont, D.J., Dreossi, T., Ghosh, S., Yue, X., Sangiovanni-Vincentelli, A.L., Seshia, S.A.: Scenic: a language for scenario specification and scene generation. In: Proceedings of the 40th annual ACM SIGPLAN conference on Programming Language Design and Implementation (PLDI), June 2019

17. Fremont, D.J., et al.: Scenic: a language for scenario specification and data generation. CoRR abs/2010.06580 (2020). https://arxiv.org/abs/2010.06580

18. Fremont, D.J., et al.: Formal scenario-based testing of autonomous vehicles: from simulation to the real world. In: 23rd IEEE International Conference on Intelligent Transportation Systems (ITSC), September 2020

19. Moritz, P., et al.: Ray: a distributed framework for emerging AI applications. CoRR abs/1712.05889 (2017). http://arxiv.org/abs/1712.05889

20. Najm, W.G., Smith, J.D., Yanagisawa, M.: Pre-crash scenario typology for crash avoidance research, April 2007. https://www.nhtsa.gov/sites/nhtsa.gov/files/pre-crash_scenario_typology-final_pdf_version_5-2-07.pdf

21. Qin, X., Aréchiga, N., Best, A., Deshmukh, J.V.: Automatic testing and falsification with dynamically constrained reinforcement learning. CoRR abs/1910.13645 (2019). http://arxiv.org/abs/1910.13645

22. Ramezani, Z., Eddeland, J.L., Claessen, K., Fabian, M., Åkesson, K.: Multiple objective functions for falsification of cyber-physical systems. IFAC-PapersOnLine **53**(4), 417–422 (2020)

23. Rong, G., et al.: LGSVL simulator: a high fidelity simulator for autonomous driving. In: 2020 IEEE 23rd International Conference on Intelligent Transportation Systems (ITSC), pp. 1–6 (2020).https://doi.org/10.1109/ITSC45102.2020.9294422

24. Sankaranarayanan, S., Fainekos, G.: Falsification of temporal properties of hybrid systems using the cross-entropy method. In: Proceedings of the 15th ACM International Conference on Hybrid Systems: Computation and Control, HSCC 2012, pp. 125–134. Association for Computing Machinery, New York (2012). https://doi.org/10.1145/2185632.2185653

25. Seshia, S.A., Sadigh, D., Sastry, S.S.: Towards verified artificial intelligence. ArXiv e-prints, July 2016

26. Viswanadha, K., et al.: Addressing the IEEE AV test challenge with Scenic and VerifAI. In: The IEEE Third International Conference on Artificial Intelligence Testing (2021)

27. Viswanadha, K., Kim, E., Indaheng, F., Fremont, D.J., Seshia, S.A.: Parallel and multi-objective falsification with Scenic and VerifAI. CoRR abs/2107.04164 (2021). https://arxiv.org/abs/2107.04164

28. Wishart, J., et al.: Driving safety performance assessment metrics for ADS-equipped vehicles, April 2020. https://doi.org/10.4271/2020-01-1206

29. Zhang, Z., Arcaini, P., Hasuo, I.: Hybrid system falsification under (in) equality constraints via search space transformation. IEEE Trans. Comput. Aided Des. Integr. Circ. Syst. **39**(11), 3674–3685 (2020)

30. Zhou, X., Gou, X., Huang, T., Yang, S.: Review on testing of cyber physical systems: methods and testbeds. IEEE Access **6**, 52179–52194 (2018). https://doi.org/10.1109/ACCESS.2018.2869834

A Theoretical Framework for Understanding the Relationship Between Log Parsing and Anomaly Detection

Donghwan Shin[1]([✉])[iD], Zanis Ali Khan[1][iD], Domenico Bianculli[1][iD], and Lionel Briand[1,2][iD]

[1] University of Luxembourg, Luxembourg, Luxembourg
{donghwan.shin,zanis-ali.khan,domenico.bianculli,lionel.briand}@uni.lu
[2] University of Ottawa, Ottawa, Canada

Abstract. Log-based anomaly detection identifies systems' anomalous behaviors by analyzing system runtime information recorded in logs. While many approaches have been proposed, all of them have in common an essential pre-processing step called log parsing. This step is needed because automated log analysis requires structured input logs, whereas original logs contain semi-structured text printed by logging statements. Log parsing bridges this gap by converting the original logs into structured input logs fit for anomaly detection.

Despite the intrinsic dependency between log parsing and anomaly detection, no existing work has investigated the impact of the "quality" of log parsing results on anomaly detection. In particular, the concept of "ideal" log parsing results with respect to anomaly detection has not been formalized yet. This makes it difficult to determine, upon obtaining inaccurate results from anomaly detection, if (and why) the root cause for such results lies in the log parsing step.

In this short paper, we lay the theoretical foundations for defining the concept of "ideal" log parsing results for anomaly detection. Based on these foundations, we discuss practical implications regarding the identification and localization of root causes, when dealing with inaccurate anomaly detection, and the identification of irrelevant log messages.

Keywords: Log parsing · Log analysis · Anomaly detection

1 Introduction

Logs record the critical state and events of the system at runtime, providing valuable information for monitoring and troubleshooting. Further, logs are often the only data available that record the system's runtime behavior. Therefore, to

This work has received funding from the Celtic-Next project CRITISEC and NSERC of Canada under the Discovery and CRC programs. Donghwan Shin was partially supported by the Basic Science Research Programme through the National Research Foundation of Korea (NRF) funded by the Ministry of Education (2019R1A6A3A03033444).

© Springer Nature Switzerland AG 2021
L. Feng and D. Fisman (Eds.): RV 2021, LNCS 12974, pp. 277–287, 2021.
https://doi.org/10.1007/978-3-030-88494-9_16

ensure the reliability of a system, *log-based anomaly detection* has been widely studied with the aim of automatically deciding if the logs contain any anomalous patterns that do not conform to the expected behavior of the system [9].

While many approaches have been proposed for log-based anomaly detection, all of them have in common an essential pre-processing step called *log parsing*. This step is needed because automated log analysis requires structured input logs, whereas collected logs are usually free-formed or semi-structured text strings printed by logging statements (e.g., `printf()`, `logger.info()`) included in the source code. Log parsing essentially consists in converting collected logs into structured input logs (e.g., by identifying the message templates corresponding to the various log entries); it is an active research topic that has received considerable attention [6,9,25].

Despite advances in log parsing and log-based anomaly detection, to the best of our knowledge, no existing work has thoroughly investigated the impact of the "quality" of log parsing results on anomaly detection. In particular, the concept of "ideal" log parsing results with respect to anomaly detection has not been defined and formalized yet. The lack of such a conceptual framework makes it difficult, when performing empirical studies on anomaly detection techniques, to determine if the root causes of inaccuracies in anomaly detection are due to the limitations of log parsing techniques.

In this short paper, we propose a theoretical framework for defining and discussing what are ideal log parsing results for anomaly detection. In particular, we consider log parsing as an information abstraction process that converts collected logs into structured logs. Since automated anomaly detection relies on structured logs, its best operating conditions are when the minimum amount of information that is necessary to distinguish normal from abnormal behaviors is present in such logs. To this end, we formally define the concepts of *distinguishability* and *minimality*, which further lead to the definition of *ideal* log parsing results. We also discuss practical implications related to log parsing and anomaly detection and present future research directions derived from our theoretical framework.

The rest of the paper is organized as follows. Section 2 explains the notations and basic definitions that will be used throughout the paper. Section 3 formalizes the key concepts regarding ideal log parsing results for anomaly detection. Section 4 discusses practical implications of the proposed theoretical framework. Section 5 discusses related work. Section 6 concludes the paper and provides directions for future work.

2   Preliminaries

This section introduces basic notations and concepts that will be used throughout the paper.

We use uppercase letters to denote *collections* (i.e., sets and sequences) and lowercase letters to denote *elements* in a collection. Specifically, $\{\dots\}$ denotes a set and $\langle\dots\rangle$ denotes a sequence. For simplicity, we use the same notation $|S|$ to denote the *cardinality* of a set S and the *length* of a sequence S.

Index	Log Message
1	Receiving block blk_471078 src: /1.2.3.4:56 dest: /1.2.3.4:78
2	Receiving block blk_471078 src: /4.3.2.1:65 dest: /4.3.2.1:78
...	...
14	Verification succeeded for blk_471078

Fig. 1. Example from HDFS Logs [10]

Definition 1 (Log Messages and Logs). *A* log message *m is a string printed by a logging statement in the source code. A* log *l is a finite sequence of log messages, denoted by* $l = \langle m_1, m_2, \ldots, m_n \rangle$.

For instance, Fig. 1 shows a simplified[1] example from the actual log produced by running HDFS [10]. In this case, the example log can be denoted by $l_{ex} = \langle m_1, m_2, \ldots, m_{14} \rangle$ where m_{14} is the string "Verification succeeded for blk_471078".

Definition 2 (Normal and Abnormal Logs). *For a set of logs L, a log* $l \in L$ *is said to be* normal *if and only if it represents a normal behavior of the system. Otherwise, l is said to be* abnormal. *Normal and abnormal logs are denoted by* $L_n \subseteq L$ *and* $L_a \subseteq L$, *respectively; for a given L and the corresponding* L_n *and* L_a, *we have* $L_n \cap L_a = \emptyset$ *and* $L_n \cup L_a = L$.

Notice that Definition 2 is independent from the nature of anomalies (e.g., point and collective [3]). The definition only assumes that normal and abnormal behaviors of the system are known and distinguishable in logs. This assumption can be easily satisfied when the accuracy of anomaly detection techniques, including log parsing techniques, are evaluated in controlled experiments using known benchmarks; furthermore, enhancing the quality of logs to distinguish normal and abnormal behaviors has been actively studied [12,22–24]. In the rest of the paper we adopt this definition and make its underlying assumption.

3   Ideal Log Parsing Results for Anomaly Detection

3.1   Log Parsing as Abstraction

Intuitively, log parsing is a process that converts original logs composed of free-formed messages into structured logs, by extracting key information from individual log messages. For example, some log parsing approaches, such as Drain [8] and MoLFI [15], may extract key information from m_1 in Fig. 1 as an event template "Receiving block <*> src: <*> dest: <*>" characterizing the event of

---

[1] In general, logs may contain extra information, such as timestamps and logging levels (e.g., info, debug) for individual log messages. However, we omit such information since log parsing deals with log messages characterizing the states or events of the system.

receiving a block, where symbol `<*>` indicates the position of a parameter value determined at runtime. With respect to these approaches, all messages that match the template, such as m_2 in Fig. 1, represent the same event of receiving a block. In this sense, we can consider log parsing as an *abstraction* process that generates "abstract" key information that represents multiple "specific" messages. Notice that different log parsing approaches yield different abstraction results (not even necessarily in the form of templates). For example, a log parsing approach that simply counts the number of tokens would abstract m_1 as the integer 7 (as m_1 contains seven tokens). To keep our presentation general, we introduce an abstraction function τ that represents a log parsing approach.

Definition 3 (Log Parsing as an Abstraction Function). *Given a set of log messages M and a generic set of parsing results A, a log parsing approach can be represented as an abstraction function* $\tau \colon M \to A$.

Notice that the definition of A is left generic, to accommodate different types of results yielded by log parsing techniques.

Using the concept of τ, the results obtained by a parsing approach can be seen as an abstraction of the original log itself.

Definition 4 (Abstraction of Log). *Given an abstraction function τ representing a log parsing approach and a log* $l = \langle m_1, m_2, \ldots, m_n \rangle$, *the abstraction of l using τ, denoted by* $\tau^*(l)$, *is defined as* $\tau^*(l) = \langle \tau(m_1), \tau(m_2), \ldots, \tau(m_n) \rangle$.

In other words, τ^* can be considered as an abstraction function for a log, extended from τ. Similarly, we can further extend τ^* to consider a set of logs as follows.

Definition 5 (Abstraction of Set of Logs). *Given an abstraction function τ representing a log parsing approach and a set of logs L, the abstraction of L using τ, denoted by* $\tau^{**}(L)$, *is defined as* $\tau^{**}(L) = \{\tau^*(l) \mid l \in L\}$.

Based on these definitions, $\tau^{**}(L)$ represents the results of using a log parsing approach (abstracted by τ) on a set of logs L; in our context, it represents the structured input logs provided as input to an anomaly detection approach.

Running Example. To better understand the above definitions, let us consider a set of logs $L_{ex} = \{l_1, l_2, l_3\}$ where $l_1 = \langle m_a, m_b, m_c \rangle$, $l_2 = \langle m_b, m_a, m_c \rangle$, and $l_3 = \langle m_a, m_b, m_d \rangle$ and each message in $\{m_a, m_b, m_c, m_d\}$ is different from the others. Let us assume to use a log parsing approach that yields an integer value, such that both m_a and m_b are mapped to 1 while m_c and m_d are mapped to 2 and 3, respectively. We can represent the log parsing approach as the abstraction function τ_{ex} defined such that $\tau_{ex}(m_a) = \tau_{ex}(m_b) = 1$, $\tau_{ex}(m_c) = 2$, and $\tau_{ex}(m_d) = 3$. Using τ_{ex}, we can see that the abstraction of l_1 is $\tau_{ex}^*(l_1) = \langle \tau_{ex}(m_a), \tau_{ex}(m_b), \tau_{ex}(m_c) \rangle = \langle 1, 1, 2 \rangle$. Similarly, $\tau_{ex}^*(l_2) = \langle 1, 1, 2 \rangle$ and $\tau_{ex}^*(l_3) = \langle 1, 1, 3 \rangle$. As a result, the abstraction of L_{ex} is $\tau_{ex}^{**}(L_{ex}) = \{\tau_{ex}^*(l_1), \tau_{ex}^*(l_2), \tau_{ex}^*(l_3)\} = \{\langle 1, 1, 2 \rangle, \langle 1, 1, 3 \rangle\}$.

This example shows that different logs (e.g., l_1 and l_2) can be *indistinguishable* when abstracted using a certain log parsing approach. This is directly related to one of the key concepts for defining the ideal log parsing results for anomaly detection, which will be detailed in the next section.

3.2   Ideal Log Parsing Results

As described above, log parsing abstracts L to $\tau^{**}(L)$, possibly resulting in different logs indistinguishable from each other as a result of abstraction. For the main anomaly detection step that takes $\tau^{**}(L)$ as input, if normal and abnormal logs are indistinguishable in $\tau^{**}(L)$, then it is impossible to correctly identify abnormal behaviors from it. It is thus important to formalize the concept of *distinguishability* of log parsing results:

Definition 6 (Distinguishability of Log Parsing Results). *Given a non-empty set of normal logs $L_n \subset L$ and a non-empty set of abnormal logs $L_a \subset L$ (where $L_n \cup L_a = L$ and $L_n \cap L_a = \emptyset$), an abstraction function τ distinguishes L_n and L_a if and only if $\tau^{**}(L_n) \cap \tau^{**}(L_a) = \emptyset$. In this case, $\tau^{**}(L)$ is called* d-maintaining *(maintaining the distinguishability) between L_n and L_a.*

In other words, *d-maintaining* log parsing results maintain the distinction between L_n and L_a after the abstraction of log parsing. For our running example used in Sect. 3.1, let us additionally consider $L_n = \{l_1, l_2\}$ and $L_a = \{l_3\}$. Since $\tau_{ex}^{**}(L_n) = \{\langle 1, 1, 2\rangle\}$ and $\tau_{ex}^{**}(L_a) = \{\langle 1, 1, 3\rangle\}$, $\tau_{ex}^{**}(L_n) \cap \tau_{ex}^{**}(L_a) = \emptyset$, and therefore $\tau_{ex}^{**}(L_{ex})$ is *d-maintaining* between L_n and L_a.

However, distinguishability is only a necessary condition for log parsing results to be ideal. For example, if we consider an abstraction function $\tau_=$ such that $\tau_=(m) = m$ for every message m, $\tau_=^{**}(L)$ is *d-maintaining* between arbitrary L_n and L_a (since $\tau_=^{**}(L_n) = L_n$, $\tau_=^{**}(L_a) = L_a$, and $L_n \cap L_a = \emptyset$ by definition). However, $\tau_=^{**}(L)$ does not represent the ideal log parsing results because $\tau_=$ does not produce an actual abstraction (since it is just defined as the identity function). Indeed, as long as log parsing results maintain the distinguishability between L_n and L_a, a higher degree of abstraction (i.e., mapping more messages to the same parsing result) leads to better operating conditions for anomaly detection, as it minimizes the "information" contained in the structured input logs (i.e., the log parsing results) that must be analyzed by the main anomaly detection step. Furthermore, since anomaly detection is largely based on Machine Learning (ML) [9], including Clustering, Support Vector Machine (SVM), and Long Short-Term Memory (LSTM), the abstraction of log parsing can significantly improve the learning performance of anomaly detection by reducing dimensionality (i.e., the number of features)[2]. Therefore, we should additionally consider the concept of *minimality* of the information contained in log parsing results.

---

[2] This is because distinct $\tau(m)$ for each message m that appear in L can lead to one or more dimensions. In ML, dimensionality reduction is an essential topic to improve predictive power [1].

To formalize the minimality concept, we first need to define the information contained in log parsing results. Since the core of log parsing is to abstract individual messages, we consider the information contained in $\tau^{**}(L)$ in terms of its unique entities (i.e., abstracted messages) as follows.

Definition 7 (Information in Log Parsing Results). *Given a set of logs L and an abstraction function τ, the information contained in L as abstracted by τ, denoted by $I(L,\tau)$, is defined as $I(L,\tau) = \bigcup_{l \in L} \{\tau(m) \mid m \in l\}$.*

For our running example, the information contained in L_{ex} abstracted by τ_{ex} is $I(L_{ex}, \tau_{ex}) = \{\tau_{ex}(m_a), \tau_{ex}(m_b), \tau_{ex}(m_c), \tau_{ex}(m_d)\} = \{1, 2, 3\}$, meaning that τ_{ex} reduces the information from $\{m_a, m_b, m_c, m_d\}$ to $\{1, 2, 3\}$ through abstraction.

Using $I(L, \tau)$, we can define the concept of ideal log parsing results by considering both distinguishability and minimality as follows.

Definition 8 (Minimal Distinguishable Log Parsing Results). *Given a non-empty set of normal logs $L_n \subset L$ and a non-empty set of abnormal logs $L_a \subset L$ (where $L_n \cup L_a = L$ and $L_n \cap L_a = \emptyset$), we say that $\tau^{**}(L)$ is minimally d-maintaining between L_n and L_a if and only if (1) $\tau^{**}(L)$ is d-maintaining between L_n and L_a and (2) there is no abstraction function τ' such that $\tau'^{**}(L)$ is d-maintaining and $|I(L, \tau')| < |I(L, \tau)|$.*

Taking the running example again, $\tau_{ex}^{**}(L_{ex})$ is *d-maintaining* (but not minimally) because there exists τ_{new} such that (1) $\tau_{new}^{**}(L_{ex})$ is *d-maintaining* and (2) $|I(L_{ex}, \tau_{new})| < |I(L_{ex}, \tau_{ex})|$. Specifically, if $\tau_{new}(m_a) = \tau_{new}(m_b) = \tau_{new}(m_c) = 12$ and $\tau_{new}(m_d) = 3$, then $\tau_{new}^{**}(L_n) = \{\langle 12, 12, 12 \rangle\}$, $\tau_{new}^{**}(L_a) = \{\langle 12, 12, 3 \rangle\}$, $I(L_{ex}, \tau_{new}) = \{12, 3\}$; therefore $\tau_{new}^{**}(L_n) \cap \tau_{new}^{**}(L_a) = \emptyset$ and $|I(L_{ex}, \tau_{new})| = |\{12, 3\}| = 2$ is less than $|I(L_{ex}, \tau_{ex})| = |\{1, 2, 3\}| = 3$. However, $\tau_{new}^{**}(L_{ex})$ is *minimally d-maintaining* because there is no τ' such that $|I(L, \tau')| = 1$ and $\tau'^{**}(L)$ is *d-maintaining*. As a result, $\tau_{new}^{**}(L_{ex})$ represents the ideal log parsing results for anomaly detection.

4 Applications

4.1 Localization of the Causes of Inaccurate Anomaly Detection

When anomaly detection accuracy is not 100% (i.e., some abnormal behaviors are not correctly detected or some normal behaviors are incorrectly detected as abnormal), it is important to know exactly where the problem lies (in the log parsing step, in the main anomaly detection step, or in both), in order to improve the results. Using our theoretical framework, we can localize the cause of inaccurate anomaly detection results. Specifically, for a set of normal logs L_n and a set of abnormal logs L_a, we can distinguish the following three cases.

Case 1. If the log parsing results is minimally d-maintaining between L_n and L_a, the main anomaly detection step must be the cause of the inaccuracy, because the log parsing results are ideal for anomaly detection.

Case 2. If the log parsing results is d-maintaining between L_n and L_a but not minimally so, a perfect anomaly detection approach could achieve pinpoint accuracy. However, as discussed in Sect. 3.2, making the log parsing results minimally d-maintaining could significantly increase anomaly detection accuracy.

Case 3. Otherwise, inaccurate anomaly detection results are inevitable due to the low-quality log parsing results. We can further investigate the issue of log parsing results by focusing on exactly what prevents the log parsing results from being d-maintaining between L_n and L_a.

The above characterization has important implications for researchers who want to assess the accuracy of their anomaly detection approaches. As non-ideal log parsing results decrease anomaly detection accuracy, *it is recommended to use ideal log parsing results in controlled experiments* to properly assess the performance of a technique, independently of log parsing. Also, if possible, using various log parsing results including minimally d-maintaining, d-maintaining but not minimal, and non-d-maintaining ones, would provide a better picture on how anomaly detection would work in practice, depending on the quality of the log parsing results.

4.2 Removal of Unnecessary Log Messages for Anomaly Detection

As discussed in Sect. 3.1, some messages become indistinguishable through the abstraction of log parsing. One may wonder whether simply removing some of the messages could contribute to further reduce the amount of information contained in the log parsing results. Indeed, in our running example, $\tau_y^{**}(L_{ex})$ remains minimally d-maintaining even if we remove m_a and m_b from L_{ex}. However, this is not always true. For example, consider a normal log $l_n = \langle m_x, m_y \rangle$ and an abnormal log $l_a = \langle m_y \rangle$. While we can consider an abstraction function τ such that $\tau(m_x) = \tau(m_y)$ and $\tau^*(l_n) \neq \tau^*(l_a)$, removing m_x from the logs makes l_n and l_a indistinguishable. This example shows that, though there are messages that can be abstracted to the same entity, it does not necessarily mean that one of them can be removed without affecting anomaly detection accuracy.

Notice that existing log parsing techniques do not reduce the length of individual logs[3]. However, we know, as discussed above, that having minimal information necessary to distinguish normal and abnormal logs is the best operating condition for anomaly detection. In this sense, further research is needed to develop an automated approach for "greedy" log parsing techniques that not only abstract but also remove log messages to achieve minimality while maintaining the distinguishability of the results.

---

[3] Though the length of logs can be reduced in a pre-processing step by omitting certain messages or events based on domain knowledge, this is independent from log parsing, which just abstracts messages.

5   Related Work

To the best of our knowledge, there is no existing work that provides a framework to formalize the concept of ideal log parsing results for anomaly detection. This is mainly because most of the existing log parsing approaches, including AEL [11], Drain [8], IPLoM [14], LenMa [18], LFA [17], LogCluster [20], LogMine [7], LogSig [19], MoLFI [15], SHISO [16], SLCT [21], Spell [5], and Logram [4], have been proposed as general-purpose approaches rather than specialized for anomaly detection. The accuracy of all these approaches has been assessed with respect to the logging statements that produce individual messages. For example, the execution of the logging statement `printf("retry " + i)` in the source code, when the program variable i evaluates to 1, will generate the log message "`retry 1`". Then a log parsing approach is expected to reconstruct the form of the logging statement as a template "`retry <*>`" without accessing the source code, where symbol "`<*>`" indicates the position of the parameter value (i.e., "`1`"). In other words, the ground truth used to assess the accuracy of general-purpose log parsing is determined based on the logging statements that generated the input logs. On the other hand, there is no ground truth that guarantees the best operating conditions for anomaly detection. To address this challenge, we provide a theoretical foundation to precisely define key concepts, including the distinguishability and minimality of ideal log parsing results.

6   Conclusion and Future Research Directions

In this short paper, we proposed a theoretical framework that formalizes the concepts of distinguishability and minimality, showing that log parsing results that minimally maintain distinguishability between normal and abnormal logs provide the best operating conditions for anomaly detection. Using our theoretical framework, we also identified practical implications for researchers regarding the root causes for inaccuracy in anomaly detection and the removal of log messages that are unnecessary for anomaly detection.

Several future research directions can be derived from our theoretical framework.

Efficient Ideal Log Parsing for Experiments. We saw that having ideal log parsing results is important in controlled experiments to properly identify the cause of inaccurate anomaly detection results. However, getting ideal log parsing results for a given set of logs is not that simple since, for the logs containing n unique log messages, the number of all possible log parsing results (i.e., the number of all possible abstraction functions) is equal to the Bell number B_n (i.e., the number of all partitions of a set of size n) [2]. Indeed, the problem of identifying the ideal log parsing results can be regarded as an optimization problem to minimize the amount of information contained in the log parsing results while maintaining distinguishability between normal and abnormal logs. Also, there is additional information that is potentially relevant to address this problem, such as the similarity between messages. Therefore, developing an efficient approach is an appealing research direction. We plan to extend the theoretical framework to measure the degree of distinguishability and minimality of given log parsing results and use such measures as fitness functions in meta-heuristic search algorithms [13] to find optimal log parsing results for anomaly detection.

Log Parsing Approaches Tailored to Anomaly Detection. Since ideal log parsing results for anomaly detection require different properties than those sought by general-purpose log parsing approaches, solutions tailored to anomaly detection are called for. Notice that, to be used in practice, these approaches should be able to generate near-ideal log parsing results without being provided with normal and abnormal labels.

Empirical Studies. While we formalize the concepts of ideal log parsing results for anomaly detection, the impact of log parsing on anomaly detection in practice remains unclear. Therefore, to better understand such impact in real-world applications, more empirical studies investigating the relationship between log parsing and anomaly detection results are required.

Run-time Applications. The theoretical framework can also be used in an online setting where logs are produced at runtime (e.g., in the context of stream verification). For example, online log parsing techniques, such as Drain [8], dynamically update log parsing results given streaming logs. Therefore, as long as normal and abnormal behaviors are distinguished in logs, one could monitor the quality of log parsing results for anomaly detection at runtime by considering distinguishability and minimality. Opportunities for applications in such diverse settings are open.

References

1. Mohri, M., Rostamizadeh, A., Talwalkar, A.: Foundations of Machine Learning. The MIT Press (2012), https://dl.acm.org/doi/book/10.5555/3360093
2. Aigner, M.: A characterization of the bell numbers. Discret. Math. **205**(1), 207–210 (1999). https://doi.org/10.1016/S0012-365X(99)00108-9
3. Chandola, V., Banerjee, A., Kumar, V.: Anomaly detection: a survey. ACM Comput. Surv. **41**(3), 1-58 (2009). https://doi.org/10.1145/1541880.1541882
4. Dai, H., Li, H., Chen, C.S., Shang, W., Chen, T.: Logram: efficient log parsing using n-gram dictionaries. IEEE Trans. Softw. Eng. 1 (2020). https://doi.org/10.1109/TSE.2020.3007554
5. Du, M., Li, F.: Spell: streaming parsing of system event logs. In: 2016 IEEE 16th International Conference on Data Mining (ICDM), pp. 859–864. IEEE, Barcelona, Spain (2016)
6. El-Masri, D., Petrillo, F., Guéhéneuc, Y.G., Hamou-Lhadj, A., Bouziane, A.: A systematic literature review on automated log abstraction techniques. Inf. Softw. Technol. **122**, 106276 (2020). https://doi.org/10.1016/j.infsof.2020.106276

7. Hamooni, H., Debnath, B., Xu, J., Zhang, H., Jiang, G., Mueen, A.: Logmine: fast pattern recognition for log analytics. In: Proceedings of the 25th ACM International on Conference on Information and Knowledge Management, pp. 1573–1582. Association for Computing Machinery, Indianapolis, IN, USA (2016)

8. He, P., Zhu, J., Zheng, Z., Lyu, M.R.: Drain: an online log parsing approach with fixed depth tree. In: 2017 IEEE International Conference on Web Services (ICWS), pp. 33–40. IEEE, Honolulu, HI, USA (2017)

9. He, S., He, P., Chen, Z., Yang, T., Su, Y., Lyu, M.R.: A survey on automated log analysis for reliability engineering. CoRR abs/2009.07237 (2020). https://arxiv.org/abs/2009.07237

10. He, S., Zhu, J., He, P., Lyu, M.R.: Loghub: a large collection of system log datasets towards automated log analytics (2020)

11. Jiang, Z.M., Hassan, A.E., Flora, P., Hamann, G.: Abstracting execution logs to execution events for enterprise applications. In: 2008 The Eighth International Conference on Quality Software, pp. 181–186. IEEE, Oxford, UK (2008)

12. Liu, Z., Xia, X., Lo, D., Xing, Z., Hassan, A.E., Li, S.: Which variables should i log? IEEE Trans. Softw. Eng. **47**(9), 2012–2031 (2019). https://doi.org/10.1109/TSE.2019.2941943

13. Luke, S.: Essentials of Metaheuristics. Lulu, second edn. (2013), available for free at http://cs.gmu.edu/~sean/book/metaheuristics/

14. Makanju, A.A., Zincir-Heywood, A.N., Milios, E.E.: Clustering event logs using iterative partitioning. In: Proceedings of the 15th ACM SIGKDD International Conference on Knowledge Discovery and Data Mining, pp. 1255–1264. Association for Computing Machinery, New York, NY, USA (2009)

15. Messaoudi, S., Panichella, A., Bianculli, D., Briand, L., Sasnauskas, R.: A search-based approach for accurate identification of log message formats. In: 2018 IEEE/ACM 26th International Conference on Program Comprehension (ICPC), pp. 167–16710. ACM, Association for Computing Machinery, Gothenburg, Sweden (2018)

16. Mizutani, M.: Incremental mining of system log format. In: 2013 IEEE International Conference on Services Computing, pp. 595–602. IEEE, Santa Clara, CA, USA (2013)

17. Nagappan, M., Vouk, M.A.: Abstracting log lines to log event types for mining software system logs. In: 2010 7th IEEE Working Conference on Mining Software Repositories (MSR 2010), pp. 114–117. IEEE, IEEE, Cape Town, South Africa (2010)

18. Shima, K.: Length matters: clustering system log messages using length of words (2016)

19. Tang, L., Li, T., Perng, C.S.: Logsig: Generating system events from raw textual logs. In: Proceedings of the 20th ACM International Conference on Information and Knowledge Management, pp. 785–794. ACM, New York, NY, USA (2011)

20. Vaarandi, R., Pihelgas, M.: Logcluster - a data clustering and pattern mining algorithm for event logs. In: 2015 11th International Conference on Network and Service Management (CNSM), pp. 1–7. IEEE, Barcelona, Spain (2015). https://doi.org/10.1109/CNSM.2015.7367331

21. Vaarandi, R.: A data clustering algorithm for mining patterns from event logs. In: Proceedings of the 3rd IEEE Workshop on IP Operations & Management (IPOM 2003)(IEEE Cat. No. 03EX764), pp. 119–126. IEEE, Kansas City, MO, USA (2003)

22. Yuan, D., Park, S., Huang, P., Liu, Y., Lee, M.M., Tang, X., Zhou, Y., Savage, S.: Be conservative: enhancing failure diagnosis with proactive logging. In: 10th USENIX Symposium on Operating Systems Design and Implementation (OSDI 12), pp. 293–306. USENIX Association, Hollywood, CA (October 2012). https://www.usenix.org/conference/osdi12/technical-sessions/presentation/yuan

23. Yuan, D., Zheng, J., Park, S., Zhou, Y., Savage, S.: Improving software diagnosability via log enhancement. ACM Trans. Comput. Syst. **30**(1), 1-28 (2012). https://doi.org/10.1145/2110356.2110360

24. Zhao, X., Rodrigues, K., Luo, Y., Stumm, M., Yuan, D., Zhou, Y.: Log20: fully automated optimal placement of log printing statements under specified overhead threshold. In: Proceedings of the 26th Symposium on Operating Systems Principles, pp. 565–581. SOSP 2017, Association for Computing Machinery, New York, NY, USA (2017). https://doi.org/10.1145/3132747.3132778

25. Zhu, J., He, S., Liu, J., He, P., Xie, Q., Zheng, Z., Lyu, M.R.: Tools and benchmarks for automated log parsing. In: 2019 IEEE/ACM 41st International Conference on Software Engineering: Software Engineering in Practice (ICSE-SEIP), pp. 121–130. IEEE, Madrid, Spain (2019)

Specification and Runtime Verification of Temporal Assessments in Simulink

Akshay Rajhans$^{(\boxtimes)}$ ⓘ, Anastasia Mavrommati ⓘ, Pieter J. Mosterman, and Roberto G. Valenti ⓘ

MathWorks, Natick, MA 01760, USA
{arajhans,amavromm,pmosterm,rvalenti}@mathworks.com

Abstract. Formalization of specifications is a key step towards rigorous system design of complex engineered systems such as cyber-physical systems. Temporal logics are a suitable expressive formalism for capturing temporal specifications. However, since engineers and practitioners are often unfamiliar with the symbols and vocabulary of temporal logic, informal natural-language specifications still are used abundantly in practice. This tool paper presents the Temporal Assessments feature in Simulink® Test™ that strives to achieve the best of both worlds. It provides graphical user interfaces and visual examples for users to interactively create temporal specifications without the need to author logical formulae by hand, yet any user-authored temporal assessment is a valid logical formula in an internal representation. Iterative folding of clauses enables the specification to be presented to read like English language sentences. Key highlights of the feature along with examples of authoring and runtime verification of temporal logic specifications are presented.

Keywords: Formal specifications · Temporal logic · Runtime verification · Model-based design · Simulink · Simulink test

1 Introduction

Model-Based Design of complex engineered systems involves the creation of computational models and perfecting them as much as possible before building actual physical prototypes where design iterations and finding and fixing mistakes can be costly. Requirement specifications are useful for establishing correctness of design models. However, these specifications are often captured in natural-language sentences in enumerated lists (e.g., in a spreadsheet). Such informal specifications and can be incomplete, ambiguous, and inconsistent among each other.

Temporal logics such as the Signal Temporal Logic [9] are a formal alternative naturally suited for dense-time continuous or hybrid domain behavior evolutions seen in engineered systems, including cyber-physical systems. The research community has seen broad adoption of such logics for specification and runtime verification: a representative list of relevant work includes [3,4,6,8,11,12,14].

© Springer Nature Switzerland AG 2021
L. Feng and D. Fisman (Eds.): RV 2021, LNCS 12974, pp. 288–296, 2021.
https://doi.org/10.1007/978-3-030-88494-9_17

Yet, industrial adoption by practitioners has remained a challenge. One key barrier is the lack of familiarity with logical symbols and formulae. For example, in his HSCC 2015 Keynote, Deshmukh calls out formal requirements engineering as a "grand challenge" and mentions "[h]ow do [control designers] convey their intentions without using formalisms?" as a "[k]ey challenge for Toyota, Bosch, and others" towards that grand challenge [5]. As examples of additional barriers to adoption, Kapinski posits that "[o]ne reason why formal requirements have not yet been adopted by industry is that they can be difficult to create and debug" and that "[a] remaining challenge is in creating methods to visualize, or otherwise elucidate, the envelope (or complete set) of behaviors specified by the requirements." [2].

Starting with Release R2019a, Simulink® Test™ offers a new Logical and Temporal Assessments functionality[1] that aims to address some of these challenges and make formal specifications more accessible to engineers and practitioners. It provides a mechanism for authoring logical and temporal specifications via a graphical user interface (GUI) by simply filling out pre-existing template patterns, that is, without the need to write out a logical formula by hand. This interface provides visual representations of hypothetical passing and failing behaviors at authoring time as visual feedback to the user. Evaluation of specifications involves simulation of a Simulink® model specified as the system under test (SUT). Hierarchical subexpression tree evaluation provides a visual mechanism for the user to investigate assessment, and failing examples provide graphical and textual explanation of failures. The rest of this paper presents key details about authoring and evaluation of specifications using this functionality.

2   Authoring Temporal Specifications

We begin by covering some preliminaries.

2.1   Preliminaries

Simulink® is a graphical Model-Based Design environment for modeling, simulation, and automatic code generation of engineered systems, including cyber-physical systems. Simulink models are directed graphs with *blocks* forming nodes of the graph and *signal lines* forming the edges of the graph. Formal definitions of Simulink models and blocks can be found elsewhere [13] and are dropped from this paper for brevity.

Blocks may have internal continuous-time and/or discrete-time state(s) that are updated as per the corresponding differential and/or difference equations. As a software implementation, each block must define its *output* method, and may define *update* and/or *derivative* methods to realize the corresponding equations as applicable. Simulink's execution engine calls these methods in a predetermined order in a loop, called the *simulation loop*, until the simulation stop time is reached [7].

---

[1] https://www.mathworks.com/help/sltest/ug/temporal-assessments.html.

Signal lines are buffered values computed by the output ports of the driving blocks every time the *output* method gets called. In between such consecutive *output* method calls, the last computed value is held until a new value overwrites it. Note that for discrete-time blocks, this is a zero-order hold implementation, which is actually a continuous-time signal with possible discontinuities.

2.2   Authoring Temporal Assessments via a UI Element

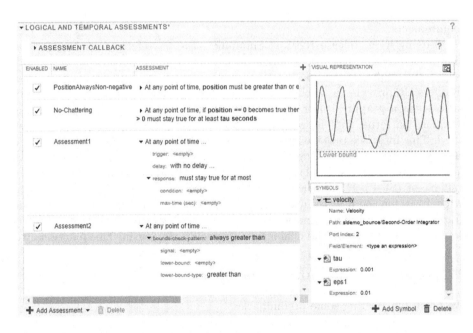

Fig. 1. UI Element for Authoring Logical and Temporal Assessments.

Logical and temporal specifications can be authored in structured English from pre-existing templates and patterns. Figure 1 shows a user interface (UI) element for authoring specifications. Clicking on 'Add Assessment' lets the user choose from pre-existing templates and patterns to construct a specification. The left half of the window in Fig. 1 depicts a mechanism for users to author specifications. Shown are a couple of new assessments with highlighted fields for the user to interactively select variations and/or enter expressions, as well as a couple of filled out and folded assessments that read like English language sentences.

Table 1 depicts the three classes of template patterns available for users to author. *Custom formula* captures if a given Boolean expression holds over all simulation time. *Bounds check* collection provides a set of frequently-used instances of *custom formula*, where the expression is whether a given signal value or a derived expression always stays *above*, *below*, *inside*, and *outside* bounds, with

Table 1. Template Pattern Classes

Template Pattern Class	Equivalent Logical Formula
Bounds Check	□ (signal satisfies bound constraint)
Custom Formula	□ φ
Trigger Response	□ $(\varphi_1 \rightarrow \Diamond \varphi_2)$

Table 2. Bounds check patterns and variations.

Pattern	Equivalent Logical Formula	Strict Variation(s)
Always less than	□ $(x < \mathtt{ub})$	□ $(x \leq \mathtt{ub})$
Always greater than	□ $(x > \mathtt{lb})$	□ $(x \geq \mathtt{lb})$
Always inside bounds	□ $((x < \mathtt{ub}) \wedge (x > \mathtt{lb}))$	□ $((x \leq \mathtt{ub}) \wedge (x > \mathtt{lb}))$
		□ $((x < \mathtt{ub}) \wedge (x \geq \mathtt{lb}))$
		□ $((x \leq \mathtt{ub}) \wedge (x \geq \mathtt{lb}))$
Always outside bounds	□ $((x > \mathtt{ub}) \vee (x < \mathtt{lb}))$	□ $((x \geq \mathtt{ub}) \vee (x < \mathtt{lb}))$
		□ $((x > \mathtt{ub}) \vee (x \leq \mathtt{lb}))$
		□ $((x \geq \mathtt{ub}) \vee (x \leq \mathtt{lb}))$

Boolean combination of strict and/or non-strict inequalities (indicated using corresponding check-boxes) tabulated in Table 2.

Trigger response is a class of frequently-used temporal formulas of the type □ $(\varphi_1 \rightarrow \Diamond_{[a,b]} \varphi_2)$. The various combinations of triggers, response delays, and responses are tabulated in Table 3. Note that a logical condition *becoming* true captures the rising edge of the evaluation of the expression from false to true. This is typically not supported out-of-the-box in as an atomic expression in logics, but is a shorthand, similar in spirit to rise and fall operators [10], provided to the user who would otherwise need to construct a compound clause themselves. Similarly, an expression *staying* true for a specified period is another shorthand that absorbs a temporal operator within it. The three flavors of response delay form the implications $\rightarrow$, $\rightarrow \Diamond_{[0,b]}$, and $\rightarrow \Diamond_{[a,b]}$ respectively.

The flavors for response conditions include when an expression evaluates to true at the point of evolution as well as those where it evaluates to true and stays true for a range of time intervals. Additionally, there is also an until operator where a condition evaluates to true and stays true until a different condition becomes true. This is a timed until, so there is a maximum timeout period that the user can specify.

2.3 Visual Representation

The top right corner of Fig. 1 shows a visual representation of a fictitious trace that would pass the selected lower bounds check. The user can regenerate additional passing and failing visuals including ones with a dynamic lower bound

Table 3. Trigger response pattern ($\varphi_1 \rightarrow \Diamond_{[a,b]} \varphi_2$) and its variations

Element	Variation
Trigger (φ_1)	whenever <condition1> is true
	<condition1> becomes true
	<condition1> becomes true and stays true for at least
	<condition1> becomes true and stays true for at most
	<condition1> becomes true and stays true for between
Response delay ($\rightarrow \Diamond_{[a,b]}$)	with no delay
	with a delay of at most
	with a delay of in between
Response (φ_2)	<condition2> must be true
	<condition2> must stay true for at least
	<condition2> must stay true for at most
	<condition2> must stay true for between
	<condition2> must stay true until <condition3> becomes true

in order to get a visual intuition about the kind of specification they are entering. Note that these fictitious traces are not the actual behaviors of the SUT model since at authoring time SUT simulation is not invoked. Appropriate visual examples are also available for other templates such as trigger-response.

2.4   Symbol Resolution

The bottom right corner of Fig. 1 shows the symbol mapping UI element, where the symbols appearing in authored assessments can be mapped to either a signal in the SUT model or to an expression. The named symbol `velocity` is shown to be mapped to a signal in the SUT model, whereas the symbols `tau` and `eps1` are mapped to simply their defined constant values. (In an alternative implementation, they could have instead been mapped to workspace variables).

2.5   Example

As a running example, let us consider a bouncing ball model in Simulink (example model `sldemo_bounce` that ships with the product) [1] as the SUT. We express a logical bounds-check condition `PositionAlwaysNon-negative`, which checks that the position of the ball always stays non-negative. This specification is intended to be a sanity check that the model has been constructed correctly. Additionally, we author a trigger-response specification `No-Chattering`, which checks whether after each bounce, within a small time period ϵ_1, whether the velocity remains positive for at least a specified finite time period of τ seconds. Figure 2 shows the two authored specifications folded to read as English sentences.

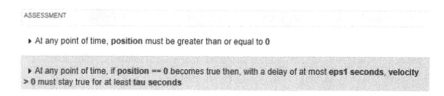

Fig. 2. Example specifications for a bouncing ball model.

3 Runtime Verification of Temporal Assessments

Runtime verification of the logical and temporal assessments invokes a simulation of the SUT and checks whether the simulation trace satisfies the specifications. Figure 3 depicts a passing evaluation of the sanity-check condition `PositionAlwaysNon-negative` defined in Sect. 2.5. The UI shows the assessments, the symbols used in the assessment (in this case only `position`), and a foldable subexpression evaluation tree.

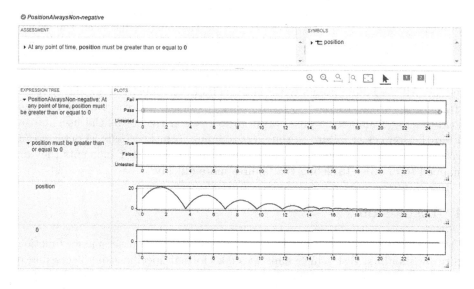

Fig. 3. Satisfaction of `PositionAlwaysNon-negative`.

The assessment `No-Chattering` from Sect. 2.5 turns out to be not satisfied by the SUT. Figure 4 shows a portion of the UI where we see a pictorial and textual explanation of the failure. There is at least one point in simulation time (at 20.35 s) where the response condition of (`velocity > 0`) does not stay true for at least τ s. The explanation provides the exact simulation time within less than τ s from the trigger plus a delay of ϵ_1 when it becomes false. It turns out there are 94 other simulation times when the assessment also evaluates to false, and the left and right arrows let the user navigate to other failure points in time and read the corresponding failure explanation.

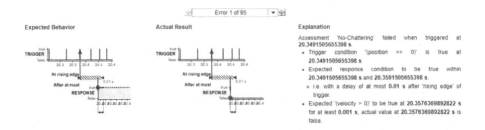

Fig. 4. Graphical and textual explanation of failure of No-Chattering.

Figure 5 shows another portion of the failing assessment UI which shows the foldable and expandable subexpression evaluation tree. The top trace shows the evaluation of the overall assessment resulting in fail, pass, and untested values over time. In case of trigger response formulas, since they take the form of an implication ($\varphi_1 \rightarrow \varphi_2$), the formula can be vacuously true when the trigger precondition φ_1 evaluates to false. All such points in time are shown in gray (untested value), whereas shown in green (pass value) are those where the trigger condition φ_1 evaluates to true and the response condition φ_2 evaluates to true. All the failing points towards the end of the simulation are shown in red (fail value) where the trigger condition φ_1 evaluates to true but the response condition φ_2 evaluates to false. Such an expression tree helps the user narrow down the sources of failure in time (by zooming into the x axis as depicted) as well as, in subexpressions and thereby in corresponding SUT elements they are mapped to in order to debug the failures more quickly.

4   Discussion

This tool paper presented the new logical and temporal assessments functionality in Simulink Test which aims to make formal specifications accessible to practitioners who may not be familiar with logic symbols and vocabulary. A graphical user interface enables users to enter formal specifications without the need to write out logical formulas by hand. Iterative folding of subexpressions enables the formulas to be read like English language sentences. Yet, because these are syntactically correct formulas by construction, they are formal and unambiguous. Symbols used in the formulas can be mapped to expressions or signals from a Simulink system-under-test model.

The design choices made in developing this functionality are based on the voice of our industry practitioner customers since the early days of development. For example, the supported classes of template patterns strive to achieve the balance between expressivity (capture most commonly used specifications) and

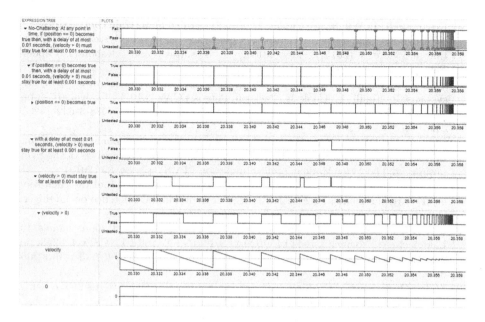

Fig. 5. Violation of non-chattering specification with a detailed expression tree of assessment evaluation.

simplicity (keep it intuitive for practitioners). Visualization examples provide additional feedback to the user about whether the specification they are authoring is the one they have in mind. Lastly, the deliberate use of the untested value is another such design choice because showing such vacuously true instances as pass is non-intuitive to practitioners.

Our hope is that this new functionality facilitates broader mainstream adoption of formal specifications by industry practitioners.

Acknowledgments. Contributions by Dr. Jean-François Kempf and Dr. Khoo Yit Phang to an earlier extended abstract on this topic are gratefully acknowledged.

References

1. Simulation of a bouncing ball. http://www.mathworks.com/help/simulink/examples/simulation-of-a-bouncing-ball.html
2. Allgöwer, F., et al.: Position paper on the challenges posed by modern applications to cyber-physical systems theory. Nonlinear Anal. Hybrid Syst **34**, 147–165 (2019)
3. Annpureddy, Y., Liu, C., Fainekos, G., Sankaranarayanan, S.: S-TaLiRo: a tool for temporal logic falsification for hybrid systems. In: Abdulla, P.A., Leino, K.R.M. (eds.) TACAS 2011. LNCS, vol. 6605, pp. 254–257. Springer, Heidelberg (2011). https://doi.org/10.1007/978-3-642-19835-9_21
4. Bartocci, E., Manjunath, N., Mariani, L., Mateis, C., Ničković, D.: CPSDebug: automatic failure explanation in CPS models. Int. J. Softw. Tools Technol. Transf. (2021). https://doi.org/10.1007/s10009-020-00599-4

5. Deskhmukh, J.: Will future cars have formally verified powertrain control software? In: Keynote Talk, 18th International Conference on Hybrid Systems: Computation and Control (2015). Slides: https://www.cs.utexas.edu/~deshmukh/Papers/Talks/hsccKeynote.pptx

6. Donzé, A.: Breach, a toolbox for verification and parameter synthesis of hybrid systems. In: Touili, T., Cook, B., Jackson, P. (eds.) CAV 2010. LNCS, vol. 6174, pp. 167–170. Springer, Heidelberg (2010). https://doi.org/10.1007/978-3-642-14295-6_17

7. Han, Z., Mosterman, P. J., Zander, J., Zhang, F.: Systematic management of simulation state for multi-branch simulations in Simulink. In: Proceedings of the Symposium on Theory of Modeling and Simulation (TMS), pp. 84–89 (2013)

8. Hoxha, B., Mavridis, N., Fainekos, G.: VISPEC: a graphical tool for elicitation of MTL requirements. In 2015 IEEE/RSJ International Conference on Intelligent Robots and Systems (IROS), pp. 3486–3492 (2015)

9. Maler, O., Nickovic, D.: Monitoring temporal properties of continuous signals. In: Lakhnech, Y., Yovine, S. (eds.) FORMATS/FTRTFT -2004. LNCS, vol. 3253, pp. 152–166. Springer, Heidelberg (2004). https://doi.org/10.1007/978-3-540-30206-3_12

10. Maler, O., Ničković, D.: Monitoring properties of analog and mixed-signal circuits. Int. J. Softw. Tools Technol. Transf. **15**, 247–268 (2013)

11. Ničković, D., Lebeltel, O., Maler, O., Ferrère, T., Ulus, D.: AMT 2.0: qualitative and quantitative trace analysis with extended signal temporal logic. In: Beyer, D., Huisman, M. (eds.) TACAS 2018. LNCS, vol. 10806, pp. 303–319. Springer, Cham (2018). https://doi.org/10.1007/978-3-319-89963-3_18

12. Ničković, D., Yamaguchi, T.: RTAMT: online robustness monitors from STL. In: Hung, D.V., Sokolsky, O. (eds.) ATVA 2020. LNCS, vol. 12302, pp. 564–571. Springer, Cham (2020). https://doi.org/10.1007/978-3-030-59152-6_34

13. Akshay Rajhans and Pieter J. Mosterman. Graphical modeling of hybrid dynamics with Simulink and Stateflow. In Proc. of the ACM International Conference on Hybrid Systems: Computation and Control (HSCC) 2018, p. 84–89

14. Ulus, D.: Online monitoring of metric temporal logic using sequential networks (2019). https://arxiv.org/abs/1901.00175

PerceMon: Online Monitoring for Perception Systems

Anand Balakrishnan[1]([✉]), Jyotirmoy Deshmukh[1], Bardh Hoxha[2], Tomoya Yamaguchi[2], and Georgios Fainekos[3]

[1] University of Southern California, Los Angeles, USA
{anandbal,jdeshmuk}@usc.edu
[2] TRINA, Toyota Motor NA R&D, Ann Arbor, USA
{bardh.hoxha,tomoya.yamaguchi}@toyota.com
[3] Arizona State University, Tempe, USA
fainekos@asu.edu

Abstract. Perception algorithms in autonomous vehicles are vital for the vehicle to understand the semantics of its surroundings, including detection and tracking of objects in the environment. The outputs of these algorithms are in turn used for decision-making in safety-critical scenarios like collision avoidance, and automated emergency braking. Thus, it is crucial to monitor such perception systems at runtime. However, due to the high-level, complex representations of the outputs of perception systems, it is a challenge to test and verify these systems, especially at runtime. In this paper, we present a runtime monitoring tool, PerceMon that can monitor arbitrary specifications in Timed Quality Temporal Logic (TQTL) and its extensions with spatial operators. We integrate the tool with the CARLA autonomous vehicle simulation environment and the ROS middleware platform while monitoring properties on state-of-the-art object detection and tracking algorithms.

Keywords: Perception monitoring · Autonomous driving · Temporal logic

1 Introduction

In recent years, the popularity of autonomous vehicles has increased greatly. With this popularity, there has also been increased attention drawn to the various fatalities caused by the autonomous components on-board the vehicles, especially the perception systems [16,24]. Perception modules on these vehicles use vision data from cameras to reason about the surrounding environment, including detecting objects and interpreting traffic signs, and in-turn used by controllers to perform safety-critical control decisions, including avoiding pedestrians. Due to the nature of these systems, it has become important that these systems be tested during design and monitored during deployment.

Signal temporal logic (STL) [17] and Metric Temporal Logic (MTL) [11] have been used extensively in verification, testing, and monitoring of safety-critical

© Springer Nature Switzerland AG 2021
L. Feng and D. Fisman (Eds.): RV 2021, LNCS 12974, pp. 297–308, 2021.
https://doi.org/10.1007/978-3-030-88494-9_18

systems. In these scenarios, typically there is a model of the system that is generating trajectories under various actions. These traces are the used to test if the system satisfies some specification. This is referred to as *offline monitoring*, and is the main setting for testing and falsification of safety-critical systems. On the other hand, STL and MTL have been used for *online monitoring* where some safety property is checked for compliance at runtime [6,19]. These are used to express rich specifications on low-level properties of signals outputted from systems.

The output of a perception algorithm consists of a sequence of frames, where each frame contains a variable number of objects over a fixed set of categories, in addition to object attributes that can range over larger data domains (e.g. bounding box coordinates, distances, confidence levels, etc.). STL and MTL can handle mixed-mode signals and there have been attempts to extend them to incorporate spatial data [3,13,18]. However, these logics lack the ability to compare objects in different frames, or model complex spatial relations between objects.

Timed Quality Temporal Logic (TQTL) [5], and Spatio-temporal Quality Logic (STQL) [14] are extensions to MTL that incorporate the semantics for reasoning about data from perception systems specifically. In STQL, which is in itself an extension of TQTL, the syntax defines operators to reason about discrete IDs and classes of objects, along with set operations on the spatial artifacts, like bounding boxes, outputted by perception systems.

In this project, we contribute the following:

1. We show how TQTL [5] and STQL [14] can be used to express correctness properties for perception algorithms.
2. An online monitoring tool, *PerceMon*[1], that efficiently monitors STQL specifications. We integrate this tool with the CARLA simulation environment [8] and the Robot Operating System (ROS) [20].

Fig. 1. The PerceMon online monitoring pipeline.

Related Work. S-TaLiRo [2,10], VerifAI [9] and Breach [7] are some examples of tools used for offline monitoring of MTL and STL specifications. The presented tool, *PerceMon*, models its architecture similar to the RTAMT [19] online monitoring tool for STL specifications: the core tool is written in C++ with an interface for use in different, application-specific platforms.

---

[1] https://github.com/CPS-VIDA/PerceMon.git.

2   Spatio-Temporal Quality Logic

Spatio-temporal quality logic (STQL) [14] is an extension of Timed Quality Temporal Logic (TQTL) [5] that incorporates reasoning about high-level topological structures present in perception data, like bounding boxes, and set operations over these structures.

STL has been used extensively in testing and monitoring of control systems mainly due to the ability to express rich specifications on low-level, real-valued signals generated from these systems. To make the logic more high-level, spatial extensions have been proposed that are able to reason about spatial relations between signals [3,12,13,18]. A key feature of data streams generated by perception algorithms is that they contain *frames* of spatial objects consisting of both, real-values and discrete-valued quantities: the discrete-valued signals are the IDs of the objects and their associated categories; while real-valued signals include bounding boxes describing the objects and confidence associated with their identities. While STL and MTL can be used to reason about properties of a fixed number of such objects in each frame by creating signal variables to encode each of these properties, it is not possible to design monitors that handle arbitrarily many objects per frame.

TQTL [5] is a logic that is specifically catered for spatial data from perception algorithms. Using Timed Propositional Temporal Logic [4] as a basis, TQTL allows one to *pin* or *freeze* the signal at a certain time point and use clock variables associated with the freeze operator to define time constraints. Moreover, TQTL introduces a quantifier over objects in a frame and the ability to refer to properties intrinsic to the object: tracking IDs, classes or categories, and detection confidence. STQL [14] further extends the logic to reason about the bounding boxes associated with these objects, along with predicate functions for these spatial sets, by incorporating topological semantics from the $S4_u$ spatio-temporal logic [12].

Definition 1 (STQL Syntax [14]). *Let V_t be a set of time variables, V_f be a set of frame variables, and V_o be a set of object ID variables. Then the syntax for STQL is recursively defined by the following grammar:*

$$
\begin{aligned}
\varphi ::=\ & \exists\{id_1, id_2, \ldots\}@\varphi \mid \{x, f\}.\varphi \\
& \mid \top \mid \neg\varphi \mid \varphi \vee \varphi \mid \bigcirc\varphi \mid \ominus\varphi \mid \varphi\, \mathbf{U}\, \varphi \mid \varphi\, \mathbf{S}\, \varphi \\
& \mid C\_TIME - x \sim t \mid C\_FRAME - f \sim n \\
& \mid \mathsf{C}(id_i) = c \mid \mathsf{C}(id_i) = \mathsf{C}(id_i) \mid \mathsf{P}(id_i) \geq r \mid \mathsf{P}(id_i) \geq r \times \mathsf{P}(id_j) \\
& \mid \{id_i = id_j\} \mid \{id_i \neq id_j\} \mid \boxed{\exists}\, \Omega \mid \Pi \\
\Omega ::=\ & \varnothing \mid \mathbb{U} \mid \mathfrak{BB}(id_1) \mid \overline{\Omega} \mid \Omega \sqcup \Omega \\
\Pi ::=\ & \mathsf{Area}(\Omega) \geq r \mid \mathsf{Area}(\Omega) \geq r \times \mathsf{Area}(\Omega) \\
& \mid \mathsf{ED}(id_i, \mathrm{CRT}, id_j, \mathrm{CRT}) \geq r \mid \Theta \geq r \mid \Theta \geq r \times \Theta \\
\Theta ::=\ & \mathsf{Lat}(id_i, \mathrm{CRT}) \mid \mathsf{Lon}(id_i, \mathrm{CRT}) \\
\mathrm{CRT} ::=\ & \mathsf{LM} \mid \mathsf{RM} \mid \mathsf{TM} \mid \mathsf{BM} \mid \mathsf{CT}
\end{aligned}
$$

Here, $id_i \in V_o$ (for all indices i), $x \in V_t$, and $f \in V_f$. In the above grammar r is a real-valued constant that allows for the comparison of ratios of object properties.

In the above grammar, $\neg\varphi$ and $\varphi \vee \varphi$ are, respectively, the negation and disjunction operators from propositional logic while $\bigcirc\varphi$, $\ominus\varphi$, $\varphi\,\mathbf{U}\,\varphi$, and $\varphi\,\mathbf{S}\,\varphi$ are the temporal operators *next, previous, until,* and *since* respectively. The above grammar can be further used to derive the other propositional operators, like conjunction $(\varphi \wedge \varphi)$, along with temporal operators like *always* $(\Box\,\varphi)$ and *eventually* $(\Diamond\,\varphi)$, and their past-time equivalents *holds* $(\boxminus\varphi)$ and *once* $(\Diamondminus\,\varphi)$. In addition to that, STQL extends these by introducing freeze quantifiers over clock variables and object variables. $\{x, f\}.\varphi$ freezes the time and frame that the formula φ is evaluated, and assigns them to the clock variables x and f, where x refers to pinned time variables and f refers to pinned frame variables. The constants, C_TIME, C_FRAME refer to the value of the time and frame number where the current formula is being evaluated. This allows for the expression $x - $ C_TIME and $f - $ C_FRAME to measure the duration and the number of frames elapsed, respectively, since the clock variables x and f were pinned. The expression $\exists\{id_1\}@\varphi$ searches over each object in a frame in the incoming data stream—assigning each object to the object variable id_1—if there exists an object that satisfies φ. The functions C(id) and P(id) refer to the *class* and *confidence* the detected object associated with the ID variable. In addition to these TQTL operations, bounding boxes around objects can be extracted using the expression $\mathfrak{BB}(id)$ and set topological operations can be defined over them. The *spatial exists* operator $\boxdot\,\Omega$ checks if the spatial expression Ω results in a non-empty space or not. Quantitative operations like Area$(\cdot)$ measure the area of spatial sets; ED computes the Euclidean distances between references points (CRT) of bounding boxes; and Lat and Lon measure the latitudinal and longitudinal offset of bounding boxes respectively. Here, CRT refers to the reference points—left, right, top, and bottom margins, and the centroid—for bounding boxes. Due to lack of space, we defer defining the formal semantics of STQL to Appendix A and also refer the readers to [14] for more extensive details.

3   PerceMon: An Online Monitoring Tool

PerceMon is an online monitoring tool for STQL specifications. It computes the quality of a formula φ at the current evaluation frame, if φ can be evaluated with some finite number of frames in the past (*history*) and delayed frames from the future (*horizon*).

The core of the tool consists of a C++ library, `libPerceMon`, which provides an interface to define an STQL abstract syntax tree efficiently, along with a general online monitor interface. The *PerceMon* tool works by initializing a monitor with a given STQL specification and can receive data in a frame-by-frame manner. It stores the frames in a first-in-first-out (FIFO) buffer with maximum size defined by the horizon and history requirement of the specification. This enables

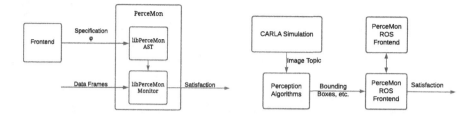

(a) General architecture for PerceMon. The *frontend* component is a generic wrapper around `libPerceMon`, the C++ library that provides the online monitoring functionality, for example, a wrapper for ROS, a parser from some specification language, or a Python library.

(b) Architecture of the integration of PerceMon with the CARLA autonomous vehicle simulator and ROS middleware platform.

Fig. 2. The design of the *PerceMon* tool allows us to define application-specific wrappers to interface with the core `libPerceMon`, thereby increasing portability of the tool for use in various environments.

fast and efficient computation of the quality of the formula for the bounded horizon. An overview of the architecture can be seen in Fig. 2a.

The library, `libPerceMon`, designed with the intention to be used with wrappers that convert application-specific data to data structures supported by the library (signified by the "Frontend" block in the architecture presented in Fig. 2a). In the subsequent section, we show an example of how such an integration can be performed by interfacing `libPerceMon` with the CARLA autonomous vehicle simulator [8] via the ROS middleware platform [20].

3.1 Integration with CARLA and ROS

In this section, we present an integration of the *PerceMon* tool with the CARLA autonomous vehicle simulator [8] using the ROS middleware platform [20]. This follows the example of [9] and [26] which interface with CARLA, and [19], where the tool interfaces with the ROS middleware platform for use in online monitoring applications.

The CARLA simulator is an autonomous vehicle simulation environment that uses high-quality graphics engines to render photo-realistic scenes for testing such vehicles. Pairing this with ROS allows us to abstract the data generated by the simulator, the PerceMon monitor, and various perception modules as streams of data or *topics* in a publisher-subscriber network model. Here, a *publisher* broadcasts data in a known binary format at an endpoint (called a *topic*) without knowing who listens to the data. Meanwhile, a *subscriber* registers to a specific topic and listens to the data published on that endpoint.

In our framework, we use the ROS wrapper for CARLA² to publish all the information from the simulator, including data from the cameras on the autonomous vehicle. The image data is used by perception modules—like the YOLO object detector [22] and the DeepSORT object tracker [25]—to publish processed data. The information published by these perception modules can in-turn be used by other perception modules (like using detected objects to track them), controllers (that may try to avoid collisions), and by PerceMon online monitors. The architectural overview can be seen in Fig. 2b.

The use of ROS allows us to reason about data streams independent of the programming languages that the perception modules are implemented in. For example, the main implementation of the YOLO object detector is written in C/C++ using a custom deep neural network framework called *Darknet* [21], while the DeepSORT object tracker is implemented in Python. The custom detection formats from each of these algorithms can be converted into standard messages that are published on predefined topics, which are then subscribed to from PerceMon. Moreover, this also paves the way to migrate and apply Perce-Mon to any other applications that use ROS for perception-based control, for example, in the software stack deployed on real-world autonomous vehicles [15].

4   Experiments

(a) In this scenario, the configuration is such that the sun has set. In a poorly lit road, a cyclist tries to cross the road.

(b) Here, a partially occluded pedestrian decides to suddenly cross the road as the vehicle cruises down the street.

Fig. 3. The presented scenarios simulated in CARLA aim to demonstrate some common failures associated with deep neural network-based perception modules. These include situations where partially occluded objects are not detected or tracked properly, and situations where different lighting conditions cause mislabeling of detected objects. In both the above scenarios, we also add some passive vehicles to increase the number of objects detected in any frame. This allows us to compute the time it takes to compute the satisfaction values from the monitor as the number of objects that need to be checked increases.

---

² https://github.com/carla-simulator/ros-bridge/.

In this section, we present a set of experiments using the integration of *PerceMon* with the CARLA autonomous car simulator [8] presented in Sect. 3.1. We build on the ROS-based architecture described in the previous section, and monitor the following perception algorithms:

- *Object Detection*: The YOLO object detector [22,23] is a deep convolutional neural networks (CNN) based model that takes as input raw images from the camera and outputs a list of bounding boxes for each object in the image.
- *Object Tracking*: The SORT object tracker [25] takes the set of detections from the object detector and associates an ID with each of them. It then tries to track each annotated object across frames using Kalman filters and cosine association metrics.

We use the OpenSCENARIO specification format [1] to define scenarios in the CARLA simulation that mimic some real-world, accident-prone scenarios, where there have been several instances where deep neural network based perception algorithms fail at detecting or tracking pedestrians, cyclists, and other vehicles. To detect some common failure cases, we initialize the *PerceMon* monitors with the following specifications:

Consistent Detections. φ_1 : For all objects in the current frame that have high confidence, if the object is far away from the margins, then the object must have existed in the previous frame too with sufficiently high confidence.

$$\varphi_1 := \forall\{id_1\}@\{f\}. \left(\left(\varphi_{\text{high prob}} \wedge \varphi_{\text{margins}}\right) \Rightarrow \ominus \varphi_{\text{exists}}\right)$$
$$\varphi_{\text{high prob}} := \mathsf{P}(id_1) > 0.8$$
$$\varphi_{\text{margins}} := \mathsf{Lon}(id_1, \mathsf{TM}) > c_1 \wedge \mathsf{Lon}(id_1, \mathsf{BM}) < c_2 \tag{1}$$
$$\wedge\, \mathsf{Lat}(id_1, \mathsf{LM}) > c_3 \wedge \mathsf{Lat}(id_1, \mathsf{RM}) < c_4$$
$$\varphi_{\text{exists}} := \exists\{id_2\}. \left(\{id_1 = id_2\} \wedge \mathsf{P}(id_2) > 0.7\right)$$

Object detection algorithms are known to frequently miss detecting objects in consecutive frames or detect them with low confidence after detecting them with high confidence in previous frames. This can cause issues with algorithms that rely on consistent detections, e.g., for obstacle tracking and avoidance. The above formula checks this for objects that we consider "relevant" (using φ_{margins}), i.e., the object is not too far away from the edges of the image. This allows us to filter false alarms from objects that naturally leave the field of view of the camera.

Smooth Object Trajectories. φ_2 : For every object in the current frame, its bounding box and the corresponding bounding box in the previous frame must overlap more than 30%.

$$\varphi_2 := \forall\{id_1\}@\{f_1\}. \left(\ominus\left(\exists\{id_2\}@\{f_2\}. \left(\{id_1 = id_2\} \Rightarrow \varphi_{\text{overlap}}\right)\right)\right)$$
$$\varphi_{\text{overlap}} := \frac{\mathsf{Area}(\mathcal{BB}(id_1) \sqcap \mathcal{BB}(id_2))}{\mathsf{Area}(\mathcal{BB}(id_1))} \geq 0.3 \tag{2}$$

In consecutive frames, if detected bounding boxes are sufficiently far apart, it is possible for tracking algorithms that rely on the detections to produce incorrect object associations, leading to poor information for decision-making.

We monitor the above properties for scenarios described in Fig. 3, and check for the time it takes to compute the satisfaction values of the above properties. As each scenario consists of some passive or non-adversarial vehicles, the number of objects detected by the object detector increases. Thus, since the runtime for the STQL monitor is exponential in the number of object IDs referenced in the existential quantifiers, this allows us to empirically measure the amount of time it takes to compute the satisfaction value in the monitor. The number of simulated non-adversarial objects are ranged from 1 to 10, and the time taken to compute the satisfaction value for each new frame is recorded. We present the results in Table 1, and refer the readers to [14] for theoretical results on monitoring complexity for STQL specifications.

Table 1. Compute time for different properties, with increasing number of objects.

Average Number of Objects	Average Compute Time (s)	
	φ_1	φ_2
2	7.0×10^{-6}	7.3×10^{-6}
5	1.4×10^{-5}	2.3×10^{-5}
10	5.4×10^{-4}	6.3×10^{-4}

5 Conclusion

In this paper, we presented *PerceMon*, an online monitoring library and tool for generating monitors for specifications given in Spatio-temporal Quality Logic (STQL). We also present a set of experiments that make use of *PerceMon*'s integration with the CARLA autonomous car simulator and the ROS middleware platform.

In future iterations of the tool, we hope to incorporate a more expressive version of the specification grammar that can reason about arbitrary spatial constructs, including oriented polygons and segmentation regions, and incorporate ways to formally reason about system-level properties (like system warnings and control inputs).

Acknowledgment. This work was partially supported by the National Science Foundation under grant no. CNS-2039087 and grant no. CNS-2038666, and the tool was developed with support from Toyota Research Institute North America.

A Semantics for STQL

Consider a data stream ξ consisting of *frames* containing objects and annotated with a time stamp. Let $i \in \mathbb{N}$ be the current frame of evaluation, and let ξ_i denote the ith frame. We let $\epsilon : V_t \cup V_f \to \mathbb{N} \cup \{\text{NaN}\}$ denote a mapping from a pinned time or frame variable to a frame index (if it exists), and let $\zeta : V_o \to \mathbb{N}$ be a mapping from an object variable to an actual object ID that was assigned by a quantifier. Finally, we let $\mathcal{O}(\xi_i)$ denote the set of object IDs available in the frame i, and let $t(\xi_i)$ output the timestamp of the given frame.

Let $\llbracket \varphi \rrbracket$ be the quality of the STQL formula, φ, at the current frame i, which can be recursively defined as follows:

- For the propositional and temporal operations, the semantics simply follows the Boolean semantics for LTL or MTL, i.e.,

$$\llbracket \top \rrbracket(\xi, i, \epsilon, \zeta) = \top$$
$$\llbracket \neg\varphi \rrbracket(\xi, i, \epsilon, \zeta) = \neg\llbracket \varphi \rrbracket(\xi, i, \epsilon, \zeta)$$
$$\llbracket \varphi_1 \vee \varphi_2 \rrbracket(\xi, i, \epsilon, \zeta) = \llbracket \varphi_i \rrbracket(\xi, i, \epsilon, \zeta) \vee \llbracket \varphi_2 \rrbracket(\xi, i, \epsilon, \zeta)$$
$$\llbracket \bigcirc \varphi \rrbracket(\xi, i, \epsilon, \zeta) = \llbracket \varphi \rrbracket(\xi, i+1, \epsilon, \zeta)$$
$$\llbracket \ominus \varphi \rrbracket(\xi, i, \epsilon, \zeta) = \llbracket \varphi \rrbracket(\xi, i-1, \epsilon, \zeta)$$

$$\llbracket \varphi_1 \mathbf{U} \varphi_2 \rrbracket(\xi, i, \epsilon, \zeta) = \bigvee_{i \leq j} \left(\llbracket \varphi_2 \rrbracket(\xi, j, \epsilon, \zeta) \wedge \bigwedge_{i \leq k \leq j} \llbracket \varphi_1 \rrbracket(\xi, k, \epsilon, \zeta) \right)$$

$$\llbracket \varphi_1 \mathbf{S} \varphi_2 \rrbracket(\xi, i, \epsilon, \zeta) = \bigvee_{j \leq i} \left(\llbracket \varphi_2 \rrbracket(\xi, j, \epsilon, \zeta) \wedge \bigwedge_{j \leq k \leq i} \llbracket \varphi_1 \rrbracket(\xi, k, \epsilon, \zeta) \right)$$

- For constraints on time and frame variables,

$$\llbracket x - \mathsf{C\_TIME} \sim c \rrbracket(\xi, i, \epsilon, \zeta) = \begin{cases} \top, & \text{if } \epsilon(x) - t(\xi_i) \sim c \\ \bot, & \text{otherwise.} \end{cases}$$

$$\llbracket f - \mathsf{C\_FRAME} \sim c \rrbracket(\xi, i, \epsilon, \zeta) = \begin{cases} \top, & \text{if } \epsilon(f) - i \sim c \\ \bot, & \text{otherwise.} \end{cases}$$

- For operations on object variables,

$$\llbracket \{id_j = id_j\} \rrbracket(\xi, i, \epsilon, \zeta) = \begin{cases} \top, & \text{if } \zeta(id_j) = \zeta(id_k) \\ \bot, & \text{otherwise.} \end{cases}$$

$$\llbracket \mathsf{C}(id_j) = c \rrbracket(\xi, i, \epsilon, \zeta) = \begin{cases} \top, & \text{if } \mathcal{O}(\xi_i)(\zeta(id_j)).\text{class} = c \\ \bot, & \text{otherwise.} \end{cases}$$

$$\llbracket \mathsf{C}(id_j) = \mathsf{C}(id_k) \rrbracket(\xi, i, \epsilon, \zeta) = \begin{cases} \top, & \text{if } \mathcal{O}(\xi_i)(\zeta(id_j)).\text{class} \\ & \quad = \mathcal{O}(\xi_i)(\zeta(id_k)).\text{class} \\ \bot, & \text{otherwise.} \end{cases}$$

$$\llbracket \mathsf{P}(id_j) \sim r \rrbracket(\xi, i, \epsilon, \zeta) = \begin{cases} \top, & \text{if } \mathcal{O}(\xi_i)(\zeta(id_j)).\text{prob} \sim r \\ \bot, & \text{otherwise.} \end{cases}$$

$$\llbracket \mathsf{P}(id_j) \sim r \times \mathsf{P}(id_k) \rrbracket(\xi, i, \epsilon, \zeta) = \begin{cases} \top, & \text{if } \mathcal{O}(\xi_i)(\zeta(id_j)).\text{prob} \sim r \\ & \quad \times \mathcal{O}(\xi_i)(\zeta(id_k)).\text{prob} \\ \bot, & \text{otherwise.} \end{cases}$$

- For the area, latitudinal offset, and longitudinal offset,

$$[\![\mathsf{Area}(\mathcal{T}_1) \sim r]\!] = \begin{cases} \top, & \text{if } \mathsf{Area}(\mathfrak{U}(\mathcal{T}_1, \xi, \zeta)) \sim r \\ \bot, & \text{otherwise.} \end{cases}$$

$$[\![\mathsf{Lat}(id_1, \mathrm{CRT}_1) \sim r]\!](\xi, i, \epsilon, \zeta) = \begin{cases} \top, & \text{if } f_{lat}(id_1, \mathrm{CRT}_1, \xi, i, \epsilon, \zeta) \sim r \\ \bot, & \text{otherwise.} \end{cases}$$

$$[\![\mathsf{Lon}(id_1, \mathrm{CRT}_1) \sim r]\!](\xi, i, \epsilon, \zeta) = \begin{cases} \top, & \text{if } f_{lon}(id_1, \mathrm{CRT}_1, \xi, i, \epsilon, \zeta) \sim r \\ \bot, & \text{otherwise.} \end{cases}$$

where, $\sim \in \{<, >, \leq, \geq\}$, and
- f_{lat} computes the *lateral distance* of the CRT point of an object identified by $\mathcal{O}(\zeta(id_1))$ from the *Longitudinal axis*;
- f_{lon} computes the *longitudinal distance* of the CRT point of an object identified by $\mathcal{O}(\zeta(id_1))$ from the *Lateral axis*; and
- $\mathfrak{U}(\mathcal{T}, \xi, \zeta)$ is the compound spatial object created after set operations on bounding boxes (defined below).
- And, finally, for the spatial existence operator,

$$[\![\boxdot \mathcal{T}]\!](\xi, i, \epsilon, \zeta) = \begin{cases} \top, & \text{if } \mathfrak{U}(\mathcal{T}, \xi, \zeta) \neq \emptyset \\ \bot, & \text{otherwise.} \end{cases}$$

Here, the compound spatial function, $\mathfrak{U}$ is defined as follows:

$$\mathfrak{U}(\varnothing, \xi, \zeta) = \emptyset$$
$$\mathfrak{U}(\mathbb{U}, \xi, \zeta) = \mathbb{U}$$
$$\mathfrak{U}(\mathfrak{B}\mathfrak{B}(id), \xi, \zeta) = \zeta(id).\mathrm{bbox}$$
$$\mathfrak{U}(\overline{\mathcal{T}}, \xi, \zeta) = \mathbb{U} \setminus \mathfrak{U}(\mathcal{T}, \xi, \zeta)$$
$$\mathfrak{U}(\mathcal{T}_1 \sqcup \mathcal{T}_2, \xi, \zeta) = \mathfrak{U}(\mathcal{T}_1, \xi, \zeta) \cup \mathfrak{U}(\mathcal{T}_2, \xi, \zeta)$$

References

1. ASAM OpenSCENARIO Specification. Technical report, ASAM e. V. (March 2021). https://www.asam.net/standards/detail/openscenario/
2. Annpureddy, Y., Liu, C., Fainekos, G., Sankaranarayanan, S.: S-TaLiRo: a tool for temporal logic falsification for hybrid systems. In: Abdulla, P.A., Leino, K.R.M. (eds.) TACAS 2011. LNCS, vol. 6605, pp. 254–257. Springer, Heidelberg (2011). https://doi.org/10.1007/978-3-642-19835-9_21
3. Bortolussi, L., Nenzi, L.: Specifying and monitoring properties of stochastic spatio-temporal systems in signal temporal logic. In: Proceedings of the 8th International Conference on Performance Evaluation Methodologies and Tools, pp. 66–73. VAL-UETOOLS 2014, ICST (Institute for Computer Sciences, Social-Informatics and Telecommunications Engineering) (December 2014). https://doi.org/10.4108/icst.Valuetools.2014.258183

4. Bouyer, P., Chevalier, F., Markey, N.: On the expressiveness of TPTL and MTL. In: Sarukkai, S., Sen, S. (eds.) FSTTCS 2005. LNCS, vol. 3821, pp. 432–443. Springer, Heidelberg (2005). https://doi.org/10.1007/11590156_35

5. Dokhanchi, A., Amor, H.B., Deshmukh, J.V., Fainekos, G.: Evaluating perception systems for autonomous vehicles using quality temporal logic. In: Colombo, C., Leucker, M. (eds.) RV 2018. LNCS, vol. 11237, pp. 409–416. Springer, Cham (2018). https://doi.org/10.1007/978-3-030-03769-7_23

6. Dokhanchi, A., Hoxha, B., Fainekos, G.: On-line monitoring for temporal logic robustness. In: Bonakdarpour, B., Smolka, S.A. (eds.) RV 2014. LNCS, vol. 8734, pp. 231–246. Springer, Cham (2014). https://doi.org/10.1007/978-3-319-11164-3_19

7. Donzé, A., Jin, X., Deshmukh, J.V., Seshia, S.A.: Automotive systems requirement mining using breach. In: 2015 American Control Conference (ACC), pp. 4097–4097 (July 2015). https://doi.org/10.1109/ACC.2015.7171970

8. Dosovitskiy, A., Ros, G., Codevilla, F., Lopez, A., Koltun, V.: CARLA: an open urban driving simulator. In: Conference on Robot Learning, pp. 1–16. PMLR (October 2017). http://proceedings.mlr.press/v78/dosovitskiy17a.html

9. Dreossi, T., et al.: VerifAI: a toolkit for the formal design and analysis of artificial intelligence-based systems. In: Dillig, I., Tasiran, S. (eds.) CAV 2019. LNCS, vol. 11561, pp. 432–442. Springer, Cham (2019). https://doi.org/10.1007/978-3-030-25540-4_25

10. Fainekos, G., Hoxha, B., Sankaranarayanan, S.: Robustness of specifications and its applications to falsification, parameter mining, and runtime monitoring with S-TaLiRo. In: Finkbeiner, B., Mariani, L. (eds.) RV 2019. LNCS, vol. 11757, pp. 27–47. Springer, Cham (2019). https://doi.org/10.1007/978-3-030-32079-9_3

11. Fainekos, G.E., Pappas, G.J.: Robustness of temporal logic specifications for continuous-time signals. Theor. Comput. Sci. **410**(42), 4262–4291 (2009). https://doi.org/10.1016/j.tcs.2009.06.021

12. Gabelaia, D., Kontchakov, R., Kurucz, A., Wolter, F., Zakharyaschev, M.: On the computational complexity of spatio-temporal logics. In: Proceedings of the 16th AAAI International FLAIRS Conference, pp. 460–464. AAAI Press (2003)

13. Haghighi, I., Jones, A., Kong, Z., Bartocci, E., Gros, R., Belta, C.: SpaTeL: a novel spatial-temporal logic and its applications to networked systems. In: Proceedings of the 18th International Conference on Hybrid Systems: Computation and Control, pp. 189–198. HSCC 2015, Association for Computing Machinery (2015). https://doi.org/10.1145/2728606.2728633

14. Hekmatnejad, M.: Formalizing Safety, Perception, and Mission Requirements for Testing and Planning in Autonomous Vehicles. Ph.D. thesis, Arizona State University (2021)

15. Kato, S., et al.: Autoware on board: enabling autonomous vehicles with embedded systems. In: 2018 ACM/IEEE 9th International Conference on Cyber -Physical Systems (ICCPS), pp. 287–296 (April 2018). https://doi.org/10.1109/ICCPS.2018.00035

16. Lee, T.B.: Report: Software bug led to death in Uber's self-driving crash (May 2018). https://arstechnica.com/tech-policy/2018/05/report-software-bug-led-to-death-in-ubers-self-driving-crash/

17. Maler, O., Nickovic, D.: Monitoring temporal properties of continuous signals. In: Lakhnech, Y., Yovine, S. (eds.) FORMATS/FTRTFT -2004. LNCS, vol. 3253, pp. 152–166. Springer, Heidelberg (2004). https://doi.org/10.1007/978-3-540-30206-3_12

18. Nenzi, L., Bortolussi, L., Ciancia, V., Loreti, M., Massink, M.: Qualitative and quantitative monitoring of spatio-temporal properties. In: Bartocci, E., Majumdar, R. (eds.) RV 2015. LNCS, vol. 9333, pp. 21–37. Springer, Cham (2015). https://doi.org/10.1007/978-3-319-23820-3_2

19. Nickovic, D., Yamaguchi, T.: RTAMT: Online Robustness Monitors from STL. arXiv:2005.11827 [cs] (May 2020). http://arxiv.org/abs/2005.11827

20. Quigley, M., et al.: ROS: an open-source robot operating system. In: ICRA Workshop on Open Source Software, vol. 3, p. 5. Kobe, Japan (2009)

21. Redmon, J.: Darknet: Open source neural networks in c (2013–2016). http://pjreddie.com/darknet/

22. Redmon, J., Divvala, S., Girshick, R., Farhadi, A.: You only look once: unified, real-time object detection . In: Proceedings of the IEEE Conference on Computer Vision and Pattern Recognition, pp. 779–788 (2016). https://www.cv-foundation.org/openaccess/content%5Fcvpr%5F2016/html/Redmon%5FYou%5FOnly%5FLook%5FCVPR%5F2016%5Fpaper.html

23. Redmon, J., Farhadi, A.: YOLOv3: An Incremental Improvement. arXiv:1804.02767 [cs] (April 2018). http://arxiv.org/abs/1804.02767

24. Templeton, B.: Tesla In Taiwan Crashes Directly Into Overturned Truck, Ignores Pedestrian, With Autopilot On (June 2020). https://www.forbes.com/sites/bradtempleton/2020/06/02/tesla-in-taiwan-crashes-directly-into-overturned-truck-ignores-pedestrian-with-autopilot-on/

25. Wojke, N., Bewley, A., Paulus, D.: Simple online and realtime tracking with a deep association metric. In: 2017 IEEE International Conference on Image Processing (ICIP), pp. 3645–3649 (September 2017). https://doi.org/10.1109/ICIP.2017.8296962

26. Zapridou, E., Bartocci, E., Katsaros, P.: Runtime verification of autonomous driving systems in CARLA. In: Deshmukh, J., Ničković, D. (eds.) RV 2020. LNCS, vol. 12399, pp. 172–183. Springer, Cham (2020). https://doi.org/10.1007/978-3-030-60508-7_9

Tutorial Paper

Formal Analysis of AI-Based Autonomy: From Modeling to Runtime Assurance

Hazem Torfah[1]([✉]), Sebastian Junges[1], Daniel J. Fremont[2], and Sanjit A. Seshia[1]

[1] University of California, Berkeley, USA
{torfah,sjunges,sseshia}@berkeley.edu
[2] University of California, Santa Cruz, USA
dfremont@ucsc.edu

Abstract. Autonomous systems are increasingly deployed in safety-critical applications and rely more on high-performance components based on artificial intelligence (AI) and machine learning (ML). Runtime monitors play an important role in raising the level of assurance in AI/ML-based autonomous systems by ensuring that the autonomous system stays safe within its operating environment. In this tutorial, we present VERIFAI, an open-source toolkit for the formal design and analysis of systems that include AI/ML components. VERIFAI provides features supporting a variety of use cases including formal modeling of the autonomous system and its environment, automatic falsification of system-level specifications as well as other simulation-based verification and testing methods, automated diagnosis of errors, and automatic specification-driven parameter and component synthesis. In particular, we describe the use of VERIFAI for generating runtime monitors that capture the safe operational environment of systems with AI/ML components. We illustrate the advantages and applicability of VERIFAI in real-life applications using a case study from the domain of autonomous aviation.

1 Introduction

In recent years, there has been an increase in autonomous and semi-autonomous systems operating in complex environments and relying on artificial intelligence (AI) and machine learning (ML) components to perform challenging tasks in perception, prediction, planning, and control. However, the unpredictability and opacity of AI/ML-based components has hindered the deployment and adoption of autonomous systems in safety-critical applications. To raise the level of assurance in autonomous systems, it is thus important to understand under which

This work is partially supported by NSF grants 1545126 (VeHICaL), 1646208 and 1837132, by the DARPA contracts FA8750-18-C-0101 (AA) and FA8750-20-C-0156 (SDCPS), by Berkeley Deep Drive, by the Toyota Research Institute, and by Toyota under the iCyPhy center.

L. Feng and D. Fisman (Eds.): RV 2021, LNCS 12974, pp. 311–330, 2021.
https://doi.org/10.1007/978-3-030-88494-9_19

environment conditions the behavior of an AI/ML-based component is trusted to keep the system in a safe state. Runtime monitors can help monitor environment conditions to maintain situational awareness, and are also useful for tasks such as hardware failure detection, sensor validation, performance evaluation, and system health management. Thus, runtime monitors are indispensable in the deployment of autonomy in cyber-physical systems (CPS).

Developing techniques to automatically construct runtime monitors that accurately capture the safe operating conditions of AI/ML-based components is a key challenge in the quest for safe and reliable autonomous systems [40]. It is particularly important to capture conditions that ensure that system-level safety specifications are met. Traditionally, monitors are constructed from formal specifications given in some logical formalism, which poses a problem in the setting of autonomous systems: while the requirements on the system are typically well-understood and easily formalized, the conditions on the *environment* under which the system will be correct are not (fully) known. Consider, for example, an ML-based perception module in an autonomous car used for tracking speed signs. The perception module is trained on a data set of labeled images of signs, but correct behavior of the module may depend on other factors such as the velocity of the car or the weather. Analyzing the module in isolation with this data set does not tell us anything about its behavior under such environment factors. One instead needs to construct a model of the system's environment and its other components, and analyze the behavior of the module in that context. There is an urgent need for a systematic approach for understanding at design time how AI/ML-based components behave in complex environments, and from this analysis, constructing reliable runtime monitors that ensure AI/ML-based components are only executed under their safe operation conditions.

In this tutorial, we present such an approach based on VERIFAI [11], an open-source toolkit for the formal design and analysis of systems that include AI or ML components. We explore the various features of VERIFAI through its capabilities of generating runtime monitors for capturing the safe operation environment of AI/ML-based components. VERIFAI provides multiple features including (i) formal modeling of autonomous systems and their environment; (ii) formal specification of AI-based autonomous systems; (iii) falsification, fuzz testing, and other simulation-based runtime verification methods; (iv) computational methods for diagnosing and explaining the success and failure of AI/ML-based autonomous systems; (v) specification-driven synthesis of parameters for AI-based autonomy, and (vi) techniques for runtime monitoring and assurance. We present the complete pipeline of VERIFAI, from modeling the environment of a system to generating the corresponding runtime assurance modules.

VERIFAI follows a data-driven approach to learning monitors. Data is generated using VERIFAI's simulation-based runtime verification techniques. VERIFAI allows us to analyze AI/ML-based components using system-level specifications. To scale to complex high-dimensional feature spaces, VERIFAI operates on an abstract semantic feature space. This space is typically represented using SCENIC, a probabilistic programming language for modeling environments [17].

Using SCENIC, we can define scenarios, distributions over spatial and temporal configurations of objects and agents, in which we want to deploy and analyze a system. By simulating the system in the different sampled scenes and applying the formal analytical backends of VERIFAI, we can create the training data sets needed for building the monitors.

Once the training data is created, specialized algorithms for learning different types of monitors can be applied. We discuss the different types of learning algorithms for learning monitors from data. These vary from exact algorithms to statistical approaches such as PAC-based learning algorithms with their passive and active variants. We discuss the advantages and disadvantages of the these algorithms with respect to our setting.

VERIFAI has been applied in several real case studies including with industrial partners (e.g., see [16,19]). We report on one case study from the domain of autonomous aviation, in collaboration with Boeing [16]. We analyzed TaxiNet, an experimental autonomous aircraft taxiing system developed by Boeing for the DARPA Assured Autonomy project. In a previous effort using VERIFAI [16], we falsified the system, diagnosed root causes for a variety of identified failure cases, and generated synthetic data to retrain the system, eliminating several of these failures and improving performance overall. In this paper, we build on this case study to describe the automated pipeline needed for the construction of runtime monitors for AI/ML-based systems and illustrate the advantages and applicability of VERIFAI in generating such monitors.

Outline. The rest of this paper is organized as follows. We start with a motivating example from the domain of autonomous aviation. In Sect. 3 we present the general architecture of VERIFAI and its ability to model environments using the SCENIC language. Section 4 introduces the process of generating data for learning runtime monitors. In Sect. 5 we discuss and compare the different types of data-driven monitor learning algorithms and discuss some of the monitors we learned with these algorithms. In Sect. 6 we integrate the monitors into an architecture for runtime assurance. We conclude with a discussion of important desiderata for runtime monitors and directions for future work.

2 Motivating Example: Autonomous Aircraft Taxiing

Consider the scenario of an airplane taxiing along a runway depicted in the images in Fig. 1. This scenario is based on a challenge problem provided by Boeing in the DARPA Assured Autonomy program. The plane is equipped with a perception module, a deep neural network called TaxiNet, that based on images captured by a camera mounted on the plane estimates the *cross-track error (CTE)*, i.e., the left-right offset of the plane from the centerline of the runway. The estimated values are forwarded to a controller that adjusts the steering angle of the plane in order to track the centerline.

The deep neural network is a black box, with no further information provided about what images were used to train the network nor any knowledge about

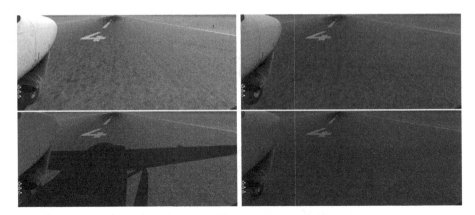

Fig. 1. Example input images to TaxiNet, rendered in X-Plane, showing a variety of lighting and weather conditions [16].

potential gaps in the training set and corresponding potential failure cases. Our goal is to construct and equip the system with a monitor that captures the conditions under which the deep neural network is expected to behave correctly and alert the system about any violation to switch in time to more trustworthy safe components (such as human control).

Many factors can influence the behavior of the deep neural network, and often are not considered in the training process. For example, while TaxiNet was trained on images, its behavior may depend on high-level parameters such as weather conditions (like overcast or rain), time of day, the initial airplane position and heading on the runway, the frequency of skid marks on the ground, or the velocity of the airplane. We refer to these factors as *semantic features* (discussed further in the next section). For our goal, these features must be measurable and monitorable at run time.

Once we fix the semantic features which we intend to use to monitor the neural network, the next step is to establish a connection between values of these semantic features and the value of a system-level specification. For example, the system-level specification could be one requiring that the CTE value should not be larger than 2.5 m over more than 10 time steps. A monitor for validating the performance of the deep neural network is one that based on the semantic features predicts whether the system-level specification will be violated. For example, under rainy weather conditions, the monitor might predict that the network will consistently yield poor CTE estimates and lead to the plane deviating too far from the centerline.

To establish such a connection, we need a systematic approach that allows us to find the environment conditions under which the aircraft significantly deviates from the centerline when using the deep neural network. We need to explore the diverse set of scenarios possible under different instantiations of the aforementioned semantic features. We need to analyze the executions of the system to identify distinct failure cases and diagnose potential root causes resulting in

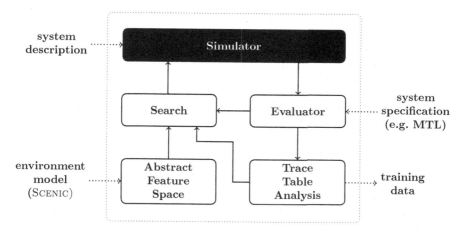

Fig. 2. The architecture of VERIFAI.

unsafe CTE values. Lastly, we need to deploy the right learning techniques that based on data generated by the exploration and analysis processes, learn a monitor that predicts a faulty behavior of the system. With VERIFAI we provide a toolkit that includes all the necessary features for learning such a monitor.

3   The VerifAI Framework

VERIFAI follows a paradigm of *formally-driven simulation*, using formal models of a system, its environment, and its requirements to guide the generation of testing and training data [11]. The high-level architecture of VERIFAI is shown in Fig. 2. To use VERIFAI, one first writes an environment model which defines the space of environments that the system should be tested or trained against. Simple models can be specified by manually defining a set of environment parameters and their corresponding ranges; more sophisticated models can be built using the SCENIC probabilistic modeling language, as we will describe below. In either case, the environment model defines an abstract *semantic feature space*, representing environments as vectors in a space of *semantic* features such as object positions and colors. Such a space can have much lower dimension than the "concrete feature space" of inputs to the system (e.g. the space of images for our aircraft taxiing scenario), and it ensures that any counterexamples we find are semantically meaningful, unlike traditional adversarial machine learning [12]. On the other hand, actually testing the system requires turning abstract features into low-level sensor data, for which we depend on a simulator. In order to support a variety of application domains, VERIFAI provides a generic simulator interface allowing it to make use of any simulator which supports the desired domain of systems and environments.

Once the abstract feature space has been defined, VERIFAI can search the space using a variety of algorithms suited to different applications. These include

```
1   # Time: from 6am to 6pm. (+8 to get GMT, as used by X-Plane)
2   param zulu_time = (Range(6, 18) + 8) * 60 * 60
3
4   # Rain: 1/3 of the time.
5   # Clouds: types 3-5 for rain; otherwise any type.
6   clouds_and_rain = Discrete({
7       (Uniform(0, 1, 2, 3, 4, 5), 0): 2,      # no rain
8       (Uniform(3, 4, 5), Range(0.25, 1)): 1.  # 25%-100% rain
9   })
10  param cloud_type = clouds_and_rain[0]
11  param rain_percent = clouds_and_rain[1]
12
13  # Plane: up to 8m to left/right of the centerline,
14  # 2000m down the runway, and 30 degrees to left/right.
15  ego = Plane at Range(-8, 8) @ Range(0, 2000),
16               facing Range(-30, 30) deg
```

Fig. 3. SCENIC runway taxiing scenario (updated slightly from [16]).

passive samplers which seek to evenly cover the space, such as low-discrepancy (Halton) sampling, as well as active samplers which use the history of past tests to identify parts of the space more likely to yield counterexamples. Each point sampled from the abstract feature space defines a concrete test case which we can execute in the simulator. During the simulation, VERIFAI monitors whether the system has satisfied or violated its specification, which can be provided as a black-box monitor function or in a more structured representation such as a formula of Metric Temporal Logic [27]. VERIFAI uses the quantitative semantics of MTL, allowing the search algorithms to distinguish between safe traces which are closer or farther from violating the specification. The results of each test can be used to guide future tests as mentioned above, and are also saved in a table for offline analysis, including monitor generation.

To enable modeling the complex, heterogeneous environments of cyber-physical systems, VERIFAI accepts environment models written in the SCENIC domain-specific probabilistic programming language [17]. A SCENIC program defines a distribution over configurations of physical objects and their behaviors over time. For example, Fig. 3 shows a SCENIC program for a runway taxiing scenario used in our previous case study [16]. This program specifies a variety of semantic features including time of day, weather, and the position and orientation of the airplane, giving distributions for all of them (with cloud type and rain percentage being correlated, for example). While this scenario only involves a single object, SCENIC's convenient syntax for geometry and support for declarative constraints make it possible to define much more complex scenarios in a concise and readable way (see [17] for examples). SCENIC also supports modeling dynamic behaviors of objects, with syntax for specifying temporal relationships between events and composing individual scenarios into more complex ones [18]. Finally, SCENIC is also simulator- and application-agnostic, being successfully

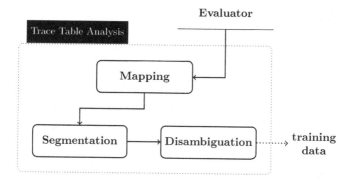

Fig. 4. Training data generation

used in a variety of CPS domains besides aviation including autonomous driving [19], robotics [17], and reinforcement learning agents for simulated sports [3]. In all these applications, the formal semantics of SCENIC programs allow them to serve as precise models of a system's environment.

4   Training Data Generation

In this section, we discuss the generation of training (and testing) data for the data-driven generation of monitors. The training data for a monitor M is provided as a table of labeled traces of the form (σ, ℓ), where σ is a sequence of events from the space of inputs over which the target monitor is defined, and ℓ is a truth value indicating whether σ should be accepted or rejected by M. Training data in this form is generated from the execution runs of several simulations through a process consisting of three phases, *mapping, segmentation*, and *disambiguation*, as depicted in Fig. 4.

4.1   Mapping

The role of the mapper is to establish the connection between the sequence of events collected during a simulation and the inputs to the monitor. In general, the mapper consists of:

– **Projections:** *mapping a sequence of simulation events to a (sub)set of events that can be reliably observed at runtime.* A monitor must be defined over inputs that are observable by the system during runtime. Properties of other entities in the environment may be known during simulation, but not during runtime. Thus, the data collected at runtime must be projected to a stream of observable data. We especially want to project the data onto *reliable* and *trustable* data. Some data may be observable, but should not be used by a monitor because it is not based on reliable hardware or because it typically is unreliable in the particular scenario at hand. For example, a monitor for validating the confidence in the TaxiNet camera-based neural network can be based on the data of the weather condition and the time of day, whereas it might be better to refrain from using the images captured by the camera or the output of the neural network perception module.

- **Filters:** *mapping traces to other traces using transformation functions that may have an internal state (based on the history of events).* Beyond project-ing, we may use the data available at runtime to estimate an unobservable system or environment state by means of filtering approaches and then use this system state (or statistics of this state) as an additional observable entity. For example, to validate the conditions for TaxiNet, we may want to use data computed based on an aggregate model that evaluates the change in the head-ing of the airplane. A filtering approach must (implicitly or explicitly) use a model that connects the observed traces with the notion of a system state based on the dynamics: in our example, the definition of the aggregate. The model does not need to be precise, although the quality of the monitor surely benefits from added precision. Furthermore, uncertainty in the model may be made explicit, be it nondeterministic [22], stochastic [44], or both [26]. These filters can also be based on neural networks [7].

At all times, mappers should preserve the order of events as received from the evaluator.

4.2   Segmentation

Once the sequence of events from the simulator have been transformed to traces over adequate input data, they are forwarded to a segmentation process. The result of the segmentation process is a table of pairs (σ, ℓ) where σ is an infix of a trace received from the mapper and ℓ defines the behavior of the ideal monitor M_{true} upon observing a sequence of input data σ.

Extracting Segments (Windowing). Rather than considering traces from the initial (simulation) state, a sliding window approach can be used to generate traces σ of fixed length starting in any state encountered during the simulation. This approach is important to avoid generating monitors that overly depend on the initial situation or monitors that (artificially) depend on outdated events. For example, the behavior of TaxiNet may depend on the size of skid mark patches along the runway. Small patches may not cause major errors in the CTE values or perhaps only for a short recoverable period of time. Larger regions of skid marks may however cause a series of errors that could lead the airplane to leave the runway. A monitor for TaxiNet should check for continuous regions of skid marks over a fixed period of time. Therefore, the monitor does not need the entire history of data, as the plane will recover from small patches, but the monitor should switch from TaxiNet to manual control when the plane drives over a long region of skid marks. In general, the length of segments needs to be tuned based on the application at hand and the frequency in which data is received. We remark that the loss of information due to ignoring events earlier in the history can be partially alleviated by adding a state estimate to the trace using an appropriate filter in the mapping phase.

Computing Labels. When determining the labels ℓ for each of the extracted segments σ, one needs to take into account the requirement that monitors for validating safe operation conditions must be predictive [8,9], i.e., after observing σ, the verdict of the monitor is one that predicts whether the safe operation conditions will hold in the future. In our TaxiNet scenario, we want the monitor to alert the system in advance, such that the airplane does not deviate much from the centerline in the (near) future. Segments should thus be associated with the behavior of the plane a few steps into the future. The latter can be characterized with respect to a prediction horizon, usually defined based on the time needed for executing certain contingency plans to ensure the system stays safe. Once a prediction horizon of length n is determined, a segment is labeled with the truth value corresponding to evaluating some property φ up to n steps into the future (along the original simulation run). The property φ is defined over the events of traces received from the evaluator, and may be different from the system-level property used by the evaluator. In particular, it could be an aggregation over the labels computed by the evaluator, e.g., defining a threshold for the allowable number of deviations from the centerline over a period of time.

4.3 Disambiguation

After the table of training data is created by the segmentation process it can be forwarded to any learning algorithm that generates a suitable artifact for the monitor. In the next section, we elaborate on this generation process and discuss what features one might need to consider in choosing the artifact. In general, the data resulting from the mapping and segmentation process may be ambiguous, i.e., the table may include pairs (σ, ℓ) and (σ', ℓ') where $\sigma = \sigma'$ but $\ell \neq \ell'$. In this way, learned monitors can fail to be completely consistent with the data; depending on the learning method used, such inconsistencies can lead to undefined behavior. To further guide the learning process, one may want to apply a preprocessing step, a disambiguation algorithm, that resolves ambiguity in the data set. Such preprocessing can be either conservative and always label a trace as violating a safety property if any pair labels it as violating, or take a more quantitative approach (e.g. if labels are MTL robustness values, averaging all such values for the trace).

5 Monitor Generation

In this section, we discuss different ways to translate the available data from a simulation interface and high-level system description into a monitor M_{syn}. In particular, we aim to construct an efficiently-computable function that for any trace σ yields whether the monitor should issue an alert, i.e., $M_{\mathrm{syn}}(\sigma) \in \mathbb{B}$.

We wish to construct this monitor from the training data (and the simulation interface) outlined in the previous section. Furthermore, the simulation-based environment described above allows us to compare against the ideal monitor M_{true} and define quality metrics in terms of false positives, false negatives, etc. with respect to a sampled set of traces.

5.1   Learning Methods

In general, we can distinguish between *exact* and *approximate* learning methods, on the one hand, and *passive* versus *active* learning on the other.

Exact and Approximate Learning. We start with a comparison between exact and approximate learning and explain why approximate learning is more suitable for our setting.

Exact Learning. In exact learning [23,48], the idea is to learn an artifact matching the labeled samples, i.e., $M_{\text{syn}} = M_{\text{true}}$. The guarantee that these approaches typically deliver is that they yield the simplest (and according to Ockham's razor, the best) explanation for the training data. If the training data were to be exhaustive, the monitor would be perfect. Using exact learning algorithms in our setting, however, comes with two main challenges. First, the training data is in most cases noisy, whereas many efficient exact learning algorithms require noise-free data. Such an assumption is unrealistic in our setting, even if the system is deterministic, due to quantization and nondeterminism in the simulator. While nondeterminism can be resolved by a disambiguation process (as outlined in the previous section) and using methods such as in [1], this will result in very conservative monitors that are not robust to noisy data. Second, the presence of multiple sensors may yield a large alphabet size, which poses a serious challenge even for state-of-the-art learning algorithms [1,30]. For example, looking at the training data generated for TaxiNet, even if we further discretize the data by splitting the time of day into 16 different hours (counting night times as one), 6 types of clouds, 4 rain levels, 8 intervals for the initial position of the plane, and a simple binary flag for the skid marks, we already obtain an alphabet size of 6144. Finer discretizations necessary for high-quality monitors would have even larger alphabets.

Approximate Learning. To construct monitors that are more robust to noisy data, we may rely on approximate learning methods that learn an optimal monitor for the training data with respect to a quantitative objective (e.g. the misclassification rate). The literature includes a plethora of techniques for learning optimal artifacts, including but not limited to, techniques for learning decision trees [6,34], decision lists [36], or neural networks [5]. The typical guarantee for a monitor generated using these methods is a statistical one, often in the form of a *probably approximately correct* (PAC) monitor [49]. That is, assuming a sufficient amount of training data from the simulator, the generated monitor will with high probability be (optimally) correct on most of the traces observed at runtime. While approximately correct monitors do admit false negatives and false positives, by adequately defining the weights of the quantitative objective we may bias the learning process towards false positives. In the TaxiNet example, we used an algorithm for learning decision trees and increased the weights corresponding to the false positives. This allowed for the learning of monitors that triggered more false alarms, but resulted in a fewer number of misclassifications of dangerous situations where the plane left the runway.

Active Versus Passive Learning. Both exact and approximate learning can be either active or passive. In our setting, passive learning is simpler to apply than active learning. We briefly mention some of the challenges.

Passive Learning. Passive learning starts from a data set collected *a priori*. This data would typically follow the distribution as specified in the environment model. However, the training set can be primed to include more negative examples (even if they rarely occur). In particular for passive learning, it is interesting to further prepare the data, e.g., by taking a windowed approach. The major downside of exact passive learning is its NP-hardness in the presence of a large alphabet (set of events) [33].

Active Learning. In active learning, the learner adaptively runs the simulations. Thus, the data is no longer pre-selected: rather, we give the learner direct access to the simulator. The challenge here is that we then must produce a simulation that after mapping and segmentation yields a particular requested trace. A naive workaround for this problem is to run the simulator until such a trace is found and heavily rely on caching. While generally, such an approach is not feasible, there are cases where the observation trace contains enough information to control the simulation accordingly: e.g., consider a car where the observation is throttle and steering, or a setting where we only vary the initial (static) part of the environment. Furthermore, most learners select traces that accelerate learning (possibly ignoring properties of the trace such as its relative likelihood). This selection scheme can pose a challenge for creating monitors for rare events. Finally, while (approximate) active learners are typically more data-efficient than passive learners, their statistical guarantees are weaker.

5.2   Learning Monitors for TaxiNet

We used VERIFAI in experiments implementing the aircraft taxiing example introduced in Sect. 2. For a given deep neural network implementing the perception module, we used VERIFAI to learn a monitor which decides, based on the initial configuration of the airplane, weather conditions, time of day, and skid marks, whether to use an autopilot dependent on the perception module or switch to manual control. In the following, we provide some details on the experimental setup and results.

Fig. 5. Example runs using TaxiNet without and with learned monitor. On the left: TaxiNet without learned monitors. On the top right: TaxiNet with monitor learned using mapper 1. On the bottom right: TaxiNet with monitor learned using mapper 2. Note that that the deviation from the centerline is greater on the left than on the right

Experimental Setup. Our setup uses VERIFAI's interface to the X-Plane flight simulator [35]. The perception module was executed as part of a closed-loop system whose computations were sent to a client running inside X-Plane. As a client, we used X-Plane Connect [45], an X-Plane plugin providing access to X-Plane's "datarefs". These are named values which represent simulator state, such as the positions of aircraft and weather conditions, etc.

The deep neural network was trained on images collected from several X-Plane simulations, where each image was labeled with the CTE value observed in that image. The images were taken from a camera mounted on the right wing facing forward, as shown in Fig. 1. The environment was modelled by the SCENIC program depicted in Fig. 3, originally used to falsify and retrain TaxiNet in [16]. The evaluator used the MTL specification $\varphi = \Diamond_{[0,10]} \Box(\text{CTE} < 2.5)$, requiring that the plane get within 2.5 m of the centerline within 10 s and maintain that maximum CTE for the entire simulation. We used the robust semantics for MTL, subsequently mapping positive robustness values (including 0) to true and negative values to false. To label the traces for monitor learning, we used a smoothed version of our specification designed to ignore short-term violations: specifically, we defined the label to be true when the property φ was true at least 8 out of 10 times in the 10 time steps following the prediction horizon of 5 time steps. Traces from 500 simulations were annotated with the truth value of the smoothed specification at each time step. We then applied a procedure for learning optimal decision trees over this training data.

Learned Monitors. We used two mappers for constructing two types of monitors. The first mapper used a segment length of 1 and filtered out all simulation data except for the weather conditions, the time of day, and the initial configuration, thereby covering all static factors. Using this mapper, our approach resulted in a monitor that mainly issued alerts in the afternoon, between 12 pm and 6 pm, in clear weather conditions. This matched our observation (also made in [16]) that the perception module did not behave well under these conditions, leading the airplane to exit the runway in most simulations (see the top row of Fig. 5 for an example). During these times we noticed that the shadow of the airplane confused the perception module, which was an indication that the neural network may have not been trained on data during these times and weather conditions. In fact, in very cloudy weather conditions during the afternoon, where no shadow can be observed, the number of alerts by the monitor decreased drastically. This result is in line with the manual analysis performed in [16]. There, the TaxiNet network was retrained on images during these times and weather conditions, which successfully eliminated the negative influence of shadows and yielded more robust performance.

Continuing our experiments, we further noticed that even after integration of the learned monitor, in many simulations the plane deviated from the centerline and left the runaway near markers indicating 1000 ft down the runway (shown in the bottom left image in Fig. 5). This showed that the static features filtered by the first mapper were not enough to characterize the safe operating conditions of the perception module. To overcome this problem, we implemented a second mapper that additionally includes information about the skid marks on the runway (using a segment length of 10). Indeed, close to the 1000 foot markers, the runway had a long region of black skid marks that covered the white centerline, resulting in images on which TaxiNet produced wrong values. Using data that included information about the skid marks, our approach was able to learn a monitor that after driving for a period of 10 time steps over a skid mark region, issued an alert forcing a switch to the safe controller (manual control), which maneuvered the airplane back to the center (as shown in the bottom right image in Fig. 5). As soon as the plane left this region, the monitor switched back to using TaxiNet.

6   Runtime Assurance

Runtime assurance (enforcement) techniques aim to ensure that a system meets its (safety) specification at runtime [9,13,38]. Abstractly speaking, a runtime assurance module modifies the behavior of the system when necessary so that the system remains in a safe state. The key ingredient of runtime assurance components is a monitor (also referred to as decision module, shield or mask) that triggers a modification in the system's outputs. Realizations of runtime assurance vary, and span from suppressing [2] to manipulating the system's executions [42].

In the setting where the goal is to evaluate the performance of a black-box component, as in the case of TaxiNet, runtime assurance is realized by switching to a provably-safe operating mode, i.e., switching to a verified controller that, although it may potentially be less performant than the black-box, is guaranteed to enforce the safety properties of the system. A prominent example of

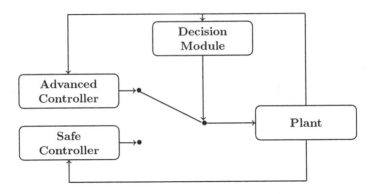

Fig. 6. The Simplex architecture

such a runtime assurance architecture is the *Simplex architecture* [42], which has been used in many domains, especially avionics [41] and robotics [31]. A runtime assurance module based on Simplex, depicted in Fig. 6, typically consists of two controllers, an advanced controller (AC) and a safe controller (SC), and a decision module that implements a switching logic between the AC and SC. The AC is used for operating the system under nominal circumstances. The SC is a certified backup controller that takes over operating the system when anomalies in the behavior of the AC or its safe operating conditions are detected. An SC for TaxiNet could stop the plane and/or ask for human intervention. The decision module decides whether it is necessary to switch from the AC to the SC to keep the system in a safe state and when to switch back to the AC to utilize the high performance of the AC to optimally achieve the objectives of the system. In our TaxiNet example, the decision module is realized by the learned monitor, the AC is a controller that is built on top of the TaxiNet neural network, and the safe controller is a simple mock controller mimicking human control.

When realizing a runtime assurance architecture like Simplex, we should keep the following aspects of the implementation of the decision module in mind:

- the decision module should execute asynchronously, i.e., it should be able to trigger a switch whenever necessary.
- the decision module should aim to use the AC as much as possible without violating safety, i.e., it should switch from SC to AC (AC to SC) as often (little) as possible.
- the decision module needs to be efficient, i.e., it needs to provide, as early as possible, a correct assessment to switch between the AC and SC.

To this end, programming frameworks are needed to implement runtime assurance modules that are guaranteed to satisfy these criteria. An example of such a framework is SOTER [9,43], a runtime assurance framework for building safe distributed mobile robots. A SOTER program is a collection of asynchronous processes that interact with each other using a publish-subscribe model of communication. A runtime assurance (RTA) module in SOTER consists of a safe controller, an advanced controller, and a decision module. SOTER allows programmers to construct RTA modules in a modular way with specified timing behavior, combining provably-safe operation with the feature of using AC whenever safe so as to achieve good performance. A key advantage of SOTER is that it also allows for straightforward integration of many monitoring frameworks.

The design and implementation of the decision module is critical to achieve principled switching between the AC and SC that keeps performance penalties to a minimum while retaining strong safety guarantees. Monitors can be defined and implemented using a variety of frameworks [10, 14, 15, 21, 28, 29, 32], ranging from automata and logics to very expressive programming languages with a trade-off between expressivity and efficiency guarantees. The choice of monitor language depends on the requirements of the application and constraints of the implementation platform.

7   Discussion

We have seen how to use VERIFAI and SCENIC to learn runtime monitors for autonomous systems, and how these monitors help to achieve runtime assurance. In this last section, we discuss a more general wish list for such monitors and prospects for additional learning methods to explore.

7.1   Desiderata for Effective Monitors

Runtime monitors for autonomous systems should satisfy several different criteria in order to be useful in practice. While our criteria align partially with those given in [37] for runtime monitors in general, we will see some differences. We also emphasize that our desiderata are not strict requirements: indeed, to the best of our knowledge, no current formalism or method achieves them fully.

Implementability. A monitor should be realizable on the target system and be executable during runtime. This requires that all data the monitor depends on is available and that the monitor can compute the resulting alerts with in a response time sufficient for the system to take corrective action.

Regarding the availability of the inputs, we remark that while we may evaluate monitor performance during simulation by taking into account the ground truth or unobservable data, the real monitor cannot. This concern necessitated the mapping and disambiguation phases in our discussion above.

On the real system, monitor performance is an additional factor. Promptness (i.e., the lag of the monitor) and memory-efficiency (are sufficient resources available) are well-known concerns [14]. In particular, complex numerical or iterative monitor definitions can be problematic, as are huge lookup tables. However, to put these concerns into perspective, we remark that many AI-based controllers are themselves more resource-consuming than traditional embedded controllers. To ensure performance, a first step is limiting the history-dependency through segmentation. A second step is to limit the size of the artifact, which most learning formalisms support (e.g., limiting the depth of the tree or the size of the network during learning). While we provide monitors in an executable format, compilation onto a real system is currently beyond the scope of our tool.

Quantitative Correctness. Achieving absolute correctness, i.e., ensuring that $M_{syn}(\sigma) = M_{true}(\sigma)$ for all possible traces σ, is unrealistic as it would require an exhaustive search through the joint behaviors of the system and its environment. Indeed, AI-based components are most helpful in settings such as perception where correct behavior is difficult to capture in a formal specification, so that there is little hope for fully-correct monitors. A popular approach in verification when full correctness is out of reach is to generate an over-approximate (sound) monitor that only admits a one-sided error. However, such monitors are generally too conservative. Conservative monitors yield many alarms, which typically leads to their outputs being disregarded, defeating their purpose. Rather, we advocate to allow two-sided errors, but to discount false positives over false negatives. Thus, while our monitors do tend to almost always raise an alarm when necessary, they may still err on the conservative side.

To reduce quantitative error, one possibility is to increase the amount of simulation data, thereby covering corner cases with a higher probability. This is not the only option: in order to avoid indistinguishability of various traces, it can also be helpful to increase the variety of data that may be used by the monitor, as we saw in Sect. 5.2. A third possibility is to increase the expressivity of the monitor formalism: relatively simple models such as decision lists, trees, and finite automata may not be able to adequately capture the underlying dynamics determining system safety in a compact monitor. More elaborate frameworks such as RTLOLA [4,14,46] deliver more flexibility in defining a monitor, while still ensuring a performant implementation as described above.

Trustworthiness. Monitors for autonomous systems which are quantitatively correct in the sense above do not come with the same hard guarantees that many specification-based monitors provide. However, in order to alleviate weaknesses of the system, they must be *more* trustworthy than the system itself. For validation and certification, monitors can be inspected either manually or by verification and other tools. A level of explainability or (machine-)interpretability is thus a central aspect that must be considered when constructing monitors that come with statistical or empirical correctness claims [47]. One approach that VERIFAI supports is to simulate the system including its monitor, generating concrete examples of monitor failures using falsification. However, we observe that to some extent, explainability trades off with increasing the quantitative correctness of the tool, as monitors based on a plethora of inputs can be harder to understand and analyze. To better understand the trade-offs, one can use techniques for exploring the Pareto-optimal space of monitors [47].

7.2   Monitor Refinement and Synthesis

Beyond classical learning approaches, an alternative is the use of (oracle-guided) inductive synthesis [24, 25], e.g., counterexample-guided inductive synthesis to learn a monitor by querying an oracle. Such an approach can be used as an extension of active or passive learning algorithms, or alone.

Inductive synthesis is heavily used in the context of programming languages but can also be used for perception modules and control [20]. Rather than learning a program, we learn a monitor. The main idea here is that rather than learning a complete monitor, we have a skeleton of the monitor that may be extracted from domain specific knowledge or learned. In our aviation example, we might search for a monitor that combines the forward speed and estimated CTE and compares this to some threshold. The question to find a monitor then is to find a function of forward speed, CTE and a threshold.

Rather than first collecting the training data offline, an inductive synthesis solver will typically assume some candidate monitor and then use an oracle (here, VERIFAI) to evaluate the system with and without the monitor to find false positives and false negatives. These samples are counterexamples that can be used to refine the candidate monitor into a more accurate monitor. We remark that the criteria for the synthesis loop to accept a monitor can either be as in the exact learning case, or PAC-based.

Another direction for monitor synthesis is the paradigm of *introspective environment modeling* (IEM) [39, 40]. In IEM, one considers the situation where the agents and objects in the environment are substantially unknown, and thus the environment variables are not all known. In such cases, we cannot easily define a SCENIC program for the environment. The only information one has is that the environment is sensed through a specified sensor interface. One seeks to synthesize an assumption on the environment, monitorable on this interface, under which the desired specification (e.g. safety property) is satisfied. While very preliminary steps on IEM have been taken [39], significant work remains to be done to make this practical, including efficient algorithms for monitor synthesis and the development of realistic sensor models that capture the monitorable interface.

Acknowledgments. The authors are grateful to Johnathan Chiu, Tommaso Dreossi, Shromona Ghosh, Francis Indaheng, Edward Kim, Hadi Ravanbakhsh, Marcell Vazquez-Chanlatte, and Kesav Viswanadha for their valuable contributions to the VERIFAI project. We also thank the team at Boeing helping to define the TaxiNet challenge problem including especially Dragos D. Margineantu and Denis Osipychev.

References

1. Aarts, F., Jonsson, B., Uijen, J., Vaandrager, F.: Generating models of infinite-state communication protocols using regular inference with abstraction. Formal Methods Syst. Des. **46**(1), 1–41 (2014). https://doi.org/10.1007/s10703-014-0216-x
2. Aceto, L., Cassar, I., Francalanza, A., Ingólfsdóttir, A.: On runtime enforcement via suppressions. In: CONCUR. LIPIcs, vol. 118, pp. 34:1–34:17 (2018)

3. Azad, A.S., et al.: Scenic4RL: programmatic modeling and generation of reinforcement learning environments. CoRR, abs/2106.10365 (2021)

4. Baumeister, J., Finkbeiner, B., Schwenger, M., Torfah, H.: FPGA stream-monitoring of real-time properties. ACM Trans. Embed. Comput. Syst. **18**(5s), 88:1–88:24 (2019)

5. Bortolussi, L., Cairoli, F., Paoletti, N., Smolka, S.A., Stoller, S.D.: Neural predictive monitoring. In: Finkbeiner, B., Mariani, L. (eds.) RV 2019. LNCS, vol. 11757, pp. 129–147. Springer, Cham (2019). https://doi.org/10.1007/978-3-030-32079-9_8

6. Breiman, L., Friedman, J.H., Olshen, R.A., Stone, C.J.: Classification and Regression Trees. Wadsworth (1984)

7. Cairoli, F., Bortolussi, L., Paoletti, N.: Neural predictive monitoring under partial observability. CoRR, abs/2108.07134 (2021)

8. Chou, Y., Yoon, H., Sankaranarayanan, S.: Predictive runtime monitoring of vehicle models using Bayesian estimation and reachability analysis. In: IROS, pp. 2111–2118. IEEE (2020)

9. Desai, A., Ghosh, S., Seshia, S.A., Shankar, N., Tiwari, A.: SOTER: a runtime assurance framework for programming safe robotics systems. In: IEEE/IFIP International Conference on Dependable Systems and Networks (DSN) (2019)

10. Deshmukh, J.V., Donzé, A., Ghosh, S., Jin, X., Juniwal, G., Seshia, S.A.: Robust online monitoring of signal temporal logic. Formal Methods Syst. Des. **51**(1), 5–30 (2017). https://doi.org/10.1007/s10703-017-0286-7

11. Dreossi, T., et al.: VERIFAI: a toolkit for the formal design and analysis of artificial intelligence-based systems. In: Dillig, I., Tasiran, S. (eds.) CAV 2019. LNCS, vol. 11561, pp. 432–442. Springer, Cham (2019). https://doi.org/10.1007/978-3-030-25540-4_25

12. Dreossi, T., Jha, S., Seshia, S.A.: Semantic adversarial deep learning. In: Chockler, H., Weissenbacher, G. (eds.) CAV 2018. LNCS, vol. 10981, pp. 3–26. Springer, Cham (2018). https://doi.org/10.1007/978-3-319-96145-3_1

13. Falcone, Y., Mounier, L., Fernandez, J.-C., Richier, J.-L.: Runtime enforcement monitors: composition, synthesis, and enforcement abilities. Formal Methods Syst. Des. **38**(3), 223–262 (2011)

14. Faymonville, P., et al.: StreamLAB: stream-based monitoring of cyber-physical systems. In: Dillig, I., Tasiran, S. (eds.) CAV 2019. LNCS, vol. 11561, pp. 421–431. Springer, Cham (2019). https://doi.org/10.1007/978-3-030-25540-4_24

15. Finkbeiner, B., Sipma, H.: Checking finite traces using alternating automata. Form. Methods Syst. Des. **24**(2), 101–127 (2004)

16. Fremont, D.J., Chiu, J., Margineantu, D.D., Osipychev, D., Seshia, S.A.: Formal analysis and redesign of a neural network-based aircraft taxiing system with VERIFAI. In: Lahiri, S.K., Wang, C. (eds.) CAV 2020. LNCS, vol. 12224, pp. 122–134. Springer, Cham (2020). https://doi.org/10.1007/978-3-030-53288-8_6

17. Fremont, D.J., Dreossi, T., Ghosh, S., Yue, X., Sangiovanni-Vincentelli, A.L., Seshia, S.A.: Scenic: a language for scenario specification and scene generation. In: PLDI (2019)

18. Fremont, D.J., et al.: Scenic: a language for scenario specification and data generation (2020)

19. Fremont, D.J., et al.: Formal scenario-based testing of autonomous vehicles: from simulation to the real world. In: ITSC (2020)

20. Ghosh, S., Pant, Y.V., Ravanbakhsh, H., Seshia, S.A.: Counterexample-guided synthesis of perception models and control. In: American Control Conference (ACC), pp. 3447–3454. IEEE (2021)

21. Havelund, K., Roşu, G.: Synthesizing monitors for safety properties. In: Katoen, J.-P., Stevens, P. (eds.) TACAS 2002. LNCS, vol. 2280, pp. 342–356. Springer, Heidelberg (2002). https://doi.org/10.1007/3-540-46002-0_24
22. Henzinger, T.A., Ho, P.-H., Wong-Toi, H.: Algorithmic analysis of nonlinear hybrid systems. IEEE Trans. Autom. Control **43**(4), 540–554 (1998)
23. Isberner, M., Steffen, B., Howar, F.: LearnLib tutorial - an open-source Java library for active automata learning. In: Bartocci, E., Majumdar, R. (eds.) RV 2015. LNCS, vol. 9333, pp. 358–377. Springer, Cham (2015). https://doi.org/10.1007/978-3-319-23820-3_25
24. Jha, S., Gulwani, S., Seshia, S.A., Tiwari, A.: Oracle-guided component-based program synthesis. In: ICSE (1), pp. 215–224. ACM (2010)
25. Jha, S., Seshia, S.A.: A theory of formal synthesis via inductive learning. Acta Informatica **54**(7), 693–726 (2017). https://doi.org/10.1007/s00236-017-0294-5
26. Junges, S., Torfah, H., Seshia, S.A.: Runtime Monitors for Markov Decision Processes. In: Silva, A., Leino, K.R.M. (eds.) CAV 2021. LNCS, vol. 12760, pp. 553–576. Springer, Cham (2021). https://doi.org/10.1007/978-3-030-81688-9_26
27. Koymans, R.: Specifying real-time properties with metric temporal logic. Real-Time Syst. **2**(4), 255–299 (1990)
28. Leucker, M., Sánchez, C., Scheffel, T., Schmitz, M., Schramm, A.: Tessla: runtime verification of non-synchronized real-time streams. In: SAC, pp. 1925–1933. ACM (2018)
29. Maler, O., Nickovic, D.: Monitoring temporal properties of continuous signals. In: Lakhnech, Y., Yovine, S. (eds.) FORMATS/FTRTFT -2004. LNCS, vol. 3253, pp. 152–166. Springer, Heidelberg (2004). https://doi.org/10.1007/978-3-540-30206-3_12
30. Mens, I.-E., Maler, O.: Learning regular languages over large ordered alphabets. Log. Methods Comput. Sci. **11**(3) (2015)
31. Phan, D., Yang, J., Grosu, R., Smolka, S.A., Stoller, S.D.: Collision avoidance for mobile robots with limited sensing and limited information about moving obstacles. Formal Methods Syst. Des. **51**(1), 62–86 (2017). https://doi.org/10.1007/s10703-016-0265-4
32. Pike, L., Goodloe, A., Morisset, R., Niller, S.: Copilot: a hard real-time runtime monitor. In: Barringer, H., et al. (eds.) RV 2010. LNCS, vol. 6418, pp. 345–359. Springer, Heidelberg (2010). https://doi.org/10.1007/978-3-642-16612-9_26
33. Pitt, L., Warmuth, M.K.: The minimum consistent DFA problem cannot be approximated within any polynomial. J. ACM **40**(1), 95–142 (1993)
34. Ross Quinlan, J.: Induction of decision trees. Mach. Learn. **1**(1), 81–106 (1986)
35. Laminar Research. X-Plane 11 (2019). https://www.x-plane.com/
36. Rivest, R.L.: Learning decision lists. Mach. Learn. **2**(3), 229–246 (1987)
37. Sánchez, C., et al.: A survey of challenges for runtime verification from advanced application domains (beyond software). Formal Methods Syst. Des. **54**(3), 279–335 (2019)
38. Schneider, F.B.: Enforceable security policies. ACM Trans. Inf. Syst. Secur. **3**(1), 30–50 (2000)
39. Seshia, S.A.: Introspective environment modeling. In: Finkbeiner, B., Mariani, L. (eds.) RV 2019. LNCS, vol. 11757, pp. 15–26. Springer, Cham (2019). https://doi.org/10.1007/978-3-030-32079-9_2
40. Seshia, S.A., Sadigh, D., Shankar Sastry, S.: Towards Verified Artificial Intelligence. arXiv e-prints (2016)

41. Seto, D., Ferriera, E., Marz, T.: Case study: development of a baseline controller for automatic landing of an F-16 aircraft using linear matrix inequalities (LMIs). Technical report CMU/SEI-99-TR-020, Software Engineering Institute, Carnegie Mellon University, Pittsburgh, PA (2000)

42. Sha, L.: Using simplicity to control complexity. IEEE Softw. **18**(4), 20–28 (2001)

43. Shivakumar, S., Torfah, H., Desai, A., Seshia, S.A.: SOTER on ROS: a run-time assurance framework on the robot operating system. In: Deshmukh, J., Ničković, D. (eds.) RV 2020. LNCS, vol. 12399, pp. 184–194. Springer, Cham (2020). https://doi.org/10.1007/978-3-030-60508-7_10

44. Stoller, S.D., et al.: Runtime verification with state estimation. In: Khurshid, S., Sen, K. (eds.) RV 2011. LNCS, vol. 7186, pp. 193–207. Springer, Heidelberg (2012). https://doi.org/10.1007/978-3-642-29860-8_15

45. Teubert, C., Watkins, J.: The X-Plane Connect Toolbox (2019). https://github.com/nasa/XPlaneConnect

46. Torfah, H.: Stream-based monitors for real-time properties. In: Finkbeiner, B., Mariani, L. (eds.) RV 2019. LNCS, vol. 11757, pp. 91–110. Springer, Cham (2019). https://doi.org/10.1007/978-3-030-32079-9_6

47. Torfah, H., Shah, S., Chakraborty, S., Akshay, S., Seshia, S.A.: Synthesizing pareto-optimal interpretations for black-box models. In: FMCAD. IEEE (2021)

48. Vaandrager, F.W.: Model learning. Commun. ACM **60**(2), 86–95 (2017)

49. Valiant, L.G.: A theory of the learnable. Commun. ACM **27**(11), 1134–1142 (1984)

Author Index

Printed in the United States
by Baker & Taylor Publisher Services